Akbar's Farewell

LETTERS FROM A FATHER

AF520567

Praise for *The Emperor's Writings*

'India looks different after reading *The Emperor's Writings*. Fascinating and moving!'

—**H.E. Herman Van Rompuy,** Honorary President, EU Council

'A must-read masterpiece: Exciting, interesting, well-researched, and full of timeless wisdom.'

—**Prof. Dr Abied Alsulaiman,** University of Leuven (Belgium)

'*Stilistisch en inhoudelijk magistraal.* A masterpiece, qua style and content.'

—**Prof. Idesbald Goddeeris,** KU Leuven

'*Een historische roman van wereldklasse.* A world class historical novel.'

—**Tertio (Frans Crols)**

'*Intellectueel entertainment, een verhaal vol drama en avontuur, dat tegelijk ook vragen opwerpt over het leven.* Intellectual entertainment, a story full of drama and adventure, which at the same time raises important questions about the human condition.'

—**Ondernemen**

Akbar's Farewell

LETTERS FROM A FATHER

A Novel

Dirk Collier

AMARYLLIS
An imprint of Manjul Publishing House Pvt. Ltd.
• C-16, Sector 3, Noida, Uttar Pradesh 201301, India
Website: www.manjulindia.com
Registered Office:
• 2nd Floor, Usha Preet Complex, 42 Malviya Nagar, Bhopal 462 003 – India
Distribution Centres
Ahmedabad, Bengaluru, Chennai, Hyderabad,
Kochi, Kolkata, Mumbai, Noida, Pune

Akbar's Farewell: Letters from a Father by Dirk Collier

Copyright © Dirk Collier, 2011, 2025
All Rights Reserved

Dirk Collier asserts the moral right to be
identified as the author of this work.

First published in India in 2011, under the title:
The Emperor's Writings: Memories of Akbar the Great

This edition first published in paperback in India in 2025

ISBN 978-93-5543-803-4

Cover Design: Ishan Khosla Design
Illustration: Ashraf Ansari

Printed and bound in India by Parksons Graphics Pvt. Ltd.

This edition is for sale in the Indian subcontinent,
Southeast Asia and the UAE only.

Some words are with diacritical marks when appearing for the first time; in subsequent appearances, the diacritical marks have been removed for easy readability.

The content of the book is the sole expression and opinion of its author, and not that of the publisher. No warranties or guarantees are expressed or implied by the publisher's choice to include any of the content in this volume. Neither the publisher nor the author shall be liable for any physical, psychological, emotional, financial, or commercial damages, including but not limited to, special, incidental, consequential or other damages.

All rights reserved. No portion from this book may be used or reproduced, stored in or introduced into a retrieval system, or transmitted, in any form, or by any means (electronic, mechanical, photocopying, recording or otherwise) without the prior written permission of the Author and Publisher. Any person who does any unauthorized act in relation to this publication may be liable to criminal prosecution and civil claims for damages.

To Anne, Bart & Ellen
Juliette, Alix & Jim

Since wars begin in the minds of men,
it is in the minds of men
that the defences of peace
must be constructed

(UNESCO Constitution, 16 November 1945)

Contents

PART II

PART III

List of Characters[1]

Abū-l Fazl
Shaykh Abū-l Fazl 'Allāmī (1551–1602); minister at Akbar's court.

Adham Khān
Mughal army officer; Māham Anaga's son.

Bābur '*The Tiger*'
Akbar's grandfather; founder of the Mughal Empire.

Bairām Khān
Akbar's guardian and regent of the empire.

(Rājā) Bhagwān Dās
Hindu general at Akbar's court; son of Rājā Bihārī Mal.

(Rājā) Bihārī Mal
King of Amber (Jaipūr) in Rājpūtānā; Akbar's faithful ally; father of Akbar's first Hindu wife.

(Rājā) Bīrbal
Hindu minister at Akbar's court.

(Prince) Dāniyāl
Akbar's third son.

Gulbadan
Akbar's aunt, half-sister of Emperor Humāyūn.

(Prince) Muhammad Hakīm
Akbar's half-brother; ruler of Kābul.

[1] Names not appearing in this list will be clear from the context.

Hakīm Alī Gilanī
Akbar's physician.

Hamīda Bānū Begam
Akbar's mother.

Humāyūn
Akbar's father, second of the Mughal emperors of India.

Ji Ji Anaga
One of Akbar's nurses; spouse of Shams-ud-dīn.

Kāmrān
Humāyūn's brother and bitter rival.

Māham Anaga
Akbar's favorite nurse and foster mother; mother of Adham Khān.

(Rājā Kūwar) Mān Singh
Hindu general at Akbar's court;
nephew, adopted son and heir of Rājā Bhagwān Dās.

Makhdūm-ul Mulk
Leading Muslim cleric.

Mīr Abdul Latīf
Akbar's personal teacher and trusted friend.

(Shaykh) Mubārak (of Nāgaur)
Abū-l Fazl's father.

Mun'im Khān
Prince Muhammad Hakīm's guardian and governor of Kābul;
later Akbar's prime minister.

(Prince) Murād
Akbar's second son.

Pīr Muhammad Khān
Mughal army officer; Bairām Khān's assistant and later, rival.

Salīmā Sultān Begam
Akbar's favorite cousin and wife; widow of Bairām Khān.

(Prince) Salīm

Emperor Jahāngīr, Akbar's eldest son and successor, fourth of the Mughal emperors (1569–1627).

Shams-ud-dīn

Husband of Akbar's nurse Jījī Anaga; later prime minister.

Sher Khān Sūr, Sher Shāh Sūr

Emperor Humāyūn's rival.

Sikandar Sūr

Successor of Sher Khān Sūr

Tardī Beg

Mughal army officer and governor of Delhi.

(Rājā) Todar Mal

Highly talented Hindu general and minister at Akbar's court.

Cover Illustration

The illustration on the front cover is that of Akbar, and has been created by carefully arranging words written in Arabic calligraphy. The word that forms the face under the turban is 'Abū'l Fath', and means 'Father of Victory'. Embodying the chest and back, 'Jalāl-ud-dīn' means 'Splendour of Religion'. The abdomen or lower arm of the figure is shaped by the word 'Muhammad'. 'Akbar' constitutes the back of the head and turban. 'Pādshāh', which means 'Emperor', forms the inside part of the left leg. The hand holding the flower has been shaped by 'Ghāzī', meaning 'Conqueror'. Lastly, the crossed legs at the bottom and the lower arm are formed by 'Akbar-e-Āzam', which means 'Akbar the Great'.

First Letter

جہانگیر

Jahangir

In the name of God, the Compassionate, the Merciful

From the King of Kings,
Shadow of God on Earth,
Bower of all Necks and Bender of all Knees,
Jalal-ud-Din Muhammad AKBAR Padshah,
By the Will of God, Supreme Ruler of all the lands
of the Hind and the Ganga from ocean to ocean,
To his beloved son,
Shahzada Sultan Muhammad Salim,
God willing, soon to be
Nur-ud-Din Muhammad JAHANGIR Padshah.

In this fiftieth and, most probably, last year of the Ilahi Era
This day of Doshanbeh, the eleventh day of Mehr
Yawm al-Ithnayn, 20 Jumada-l-Ula, 1014[1]
about three hours before dawn.

---

[1] The *Ilahi* Era was established in 1584, in Akbar's 29th regnal year, and was based on the Persian (solar) calendar. 20 Jumādā-l-Ūlā, 1014 A.H. refers to the Muslim (Hijri) lunar calendar and corresponds to Monday morning, 23 September 1605 of the Julian Calendar (which was in force in Europe at the time of Akbar's birth and remained applicable in Great Britain until 2 September 1752), or 3 October 1605 of the Gregorian Calendar, i.e. the current Common Era.

My dearest son, impatient heir and eager successor,
My dearest Shaykhu Baba[2],

You will probably be surprised to find out that I can write, after all.

I know everybody believes I am illiterate – that I can barely sign my own name. Until a few years ago, they were quite right. And to a large extent, they still are – much to my regret.

Although my mind is much quicker than most, and notwithstanding my interest in the fascinating world of learning and books, I have always had this strange ailment: not to be able to see a written text as other people apparently can. To me, reading has remained as difficult as it is for children in their first months at school. Countless hours of secret practising, under the patient and respectful guidance of Abu-l Fazl, have been of little avail; it has become painfully apparent, that further progress is not possible.

Abu-l Fazl, my trusted friend. Writing his name still brings tears to my eyes. When I think of how he was murdered and his body desecrated, how his head was cut off, thrown into the latrines and left to rot, I feel again the rage rising in me – I feel the hatred burning in my throat like filthy vomit.

Had Abu-l Fazl's murderer been anyone else, I would have persecuted him to the end of the world. I have never enjoyed the execution of an enemy, but I would have made him suffer days, if not weeks, of unspeakable, agonizing pain, before finally watching him choke to death on his own guts.

But revenge is impossible, for the murderer of my dearest friend happens to be you, Salim—you, my son, my heir, my only hope for the future.

I am the King of Kings, and although I should be careful not to pay too much attention to flatterers, I am indeed, most probably, the mightiest ruler on earth. Yet, for all my might and wealth, there is no one more utterly powerless than I am. For how could revenge appease my tormented mind? It would simply wreck my life. It would destroy all my hopes and dreams of true immortality – my life-long ambition for creating an everlasting, glorious dynasty of powerful, just rulers who will continue

---

[2] Shaykhu Bābā: *'Daddy Shaykh; dear little Shaykh'*: nickname for Akbar's son and successor Salīm, the later Emperor Jahāngīr (1569–1627).

my bloodline and forever honor my name in grateful remembrance.

Therefore, for my own sake, and even for the sake of poor Abu-l Fazl's memory, I must make sure that his life of tireless dedication has not been in vain. I must put aside my anger, and substitute it with fatherly kindness and understanding.

Maybe Abu-l Fazl's death has been a sign from God. Maybe He, who is the Lord of the Day of Judgement, but also the Acceptor of Repentance, the Pardoner and the All-Forgiving, maybe He wanted to show me that in order to achieve my worldly ambitions, I must follow the path of the Hindu saints whom I so fondly listened to for so many nights. At least this time, I must admit that only the path of ahimsa, the path of non-violence will lead me to real victory.

I believe I do understand you quite well, my son. You are not that much different from me, you know.

You definitely have the potential to become a great king, perhaps even greater than I; but I regret to say, there is also a very real danger that you might become an utter failure. A child of many prayers, you have been raised in a protected environment of unequalled luxury. But luxury breeds self-indulgence and laziness, it makes people weak—weak, like your unfortunate brothers Murad and Danyal, who drank themselves to death; weak, like the many opponents I encountered and defeated, despite their vast territories, their wealth and their much larger armies. What has become of all their might? Those among them who are not dead, now make haste to kiss my stirrup. So easy is it for power to slip away from the careless.

But you can be a great king, Salim. In your veins flow the strong blood of our glorious ancestors, the great Genghis Khan and Amir Timur the Iron, the Unconquered Ruler of the Seven Climates[3]. Like me, you combine the bold audacity and strength of Turk and Mongol warriors with the shrewd refinement of Persian kings. Moreover, it is clear from your pleasant appearance that you have also inherited many of your noble mother's Rajput traits. All this should amply suffice to make you a strong ruler.

But you will not become a truly great king, unless you also attain wisdom, my son; and wisdom is a precious gift that God only bestows

---

[3] Genghiz Khān (1162–1206) and Timur Leng (Tamerlane) (1336–1405).

on those who truly seek to acquire it, on those who are ready to listen to others with genuine respect and humility.

Never be afraid to listen to others, my son, no matter how different they are from you and no matter how alien their manners may seem to you. Wisdom, I have learned, can be found in conversations with black-robed Jesuits and white-robed shaykhs, with skeleton-like, ash-smeared Hindu renunciants and well-fed mullahs.

For the truth, my son, is like a beautiful diamond. It is one; yet it has thousands upon thousands of facets, colours, aspects, reflections. Every person who honestly seeks the truth will have something important to tell you. But remember that no one will ever possess it entirely. The whole truth is the privilege of God Himself; God, to Whom alone belongs the Beautiful Name *al-Haqq*, as the Holy Quran teaches us.

Therefore, put your trust in those who seek the truth in humility, but keep a safe distance from those who claim to have found it. And remember, a wise man, much more so a wise King, opens his mind to others, but never surrenders it.

As you know, the quest for wisdom and truth has haunted me, all my life. Fortunately, the Almighty has blessed me with ample opportunity to meet many wise and learned people from all faiths from all parts of the earth.

How to convey to you this little wisdom that I have managed to acquire, my son? This question has never left my mind, since I first sensed how your burning ambition to become king yourself was pushing you towards insurrection against me.

Mind you, I think I understand what may have been your motives, and I do not really want to blame you too harshly. I have been forced to succeed my father, may God grant him the eternal bliss of Paradise, at the much too early age of thirteen. But who knows what I would have done if I had still been a mere crown prince at the age of thirty? Most probably, like you, I would have wanted my own kingdom. Most probably, like you, I would have been courting the idea of insurrection.

What was I to do? I so badly wanted to talk to you, for days and nights, exchange views with you, offer you my advice. But I painfully realized that you would never really listen to me until I would cease to be a rival to you.

So, with the help of poor Abu-l Fazl, may God reward him in

abundance for his faithfulness and dedication, I acquired the skill of writing.

Fortunately, for a person with my ailment, writing is much easier than reading. You do not have to decipher someone else's writing and guess which vowels go with which consonants; you just have to put on paper the sounds of the words that enter your own mind.

Finding myself able to write down my thoughts with relative ease opened up a whole new world for me. Now, I would be able to speak to you at the only time you would really listen: after my death.

It took me countless hours and every free moment of my days and nights to compile all these writings and documents, which I thought would be of interest to you. For all the pain and effort it took, I thought it was well worth it. It was a good plan. Nobody but my faithful old friend Abu-l Fazl knew about this newfound skill and secret activity of mine; and after my death, he would have made haste to show you the hiding place of my writings in the Court archive. You would then read my letters, and through them, in a few hours' time, acquire what has taken me years of reflection.

But then, Abu-l Fazl was assassinated, and it turned out you were behind the murder. For all my grief and anger, I realized I needed to act quickly and take the matter into my own hands.

First, I had to reestablish full authority and bring you back into the fold. For weakness never breeds respect. The weak only get contempt. Maybe sometimes, when they are lucky, they are pitied. But I don't want anybody's pity. I want to be respected. Admired, revered and loved, if possible; hated and feared, if necessary; but always respected.

By the will of the Almighty, I succeeded. We are now officially reconciled; you, the respectful Crown Prince and obedient vassal, and I, the undisputed Monarch. What is even more important: You are back in control of yourself, no longer under way to drink yourself to death like Murad and Danyal did.

Now is the time for me to act, and take care of my succession. If I wait any longer, we will grow apart again. Worse still, if I wait any longer, there may even be a war of succession between you and young Khusrau, between my son and my grandson.

This, I must prevent at all costs.

As you know, yesterday afternoon, I arranged for an elephant fight on the banks of the Yamuna between your champion Giranbar and Khusrau's champion Abrup. To me, this was much more than just one of the many hundreds of elephant fights I have ordered for my amusement and distraction. Giranbar's victory was a reassuring sign to me: You and you alone should be my successor. As is taught by the age-old laws and customs of our great Chagatai[4] nation, it would be contrary to nature to bypass the father in favor of the son.

But the fight made it distressingly clear that I have no time to lose. The unseemly squabble between your supporters and Khusrau's was a clear warning. I must act immediately if I am to prevent a struggle between my blood and the blood of my blood, a struggle that could ruin everything I have worked for.

Be it so. I will not hesitate any longer. Tonight, I will start taking the poison, at irregular intervals and in varying doses. I guess it will take me a couple of weeks to die from the ensuing dysentery. I trust even good Hakim[5] Ali Gilani's potions and medicines will be quite powerless against it. Not a very glorious death, I admit, but an effective and not too painful one, and one that will not arouse too much suspicion.

And when I shall feel the end is near, when I approach the unfathomable, black abyss of death, and prepare to prostrate myself before the unspeakable majesty of the Giver of Life, I will have you called to my bedside. I will have you girded with my father's sword, and as a formal sign of the commencement of your reign, I will adorn your head with the Imperial turban. I trust it will not take you long to find this letter inside the turban, and I trust you will thereafter go to the archive and retrieve the remainder of my writings, underneath the fifth-floor slab in the outer right corner of the room, underneath the place where my revered grandfather Babur's memoirs are kept.

Take some time to read these writings, my son. Through them, you

---

[4] Chagatai: Turkish speaking Turko-Mongol tribes in Transoxania and adjacent territories in Central Asia, named after Chagatai Khān, second son of Genghis (Chingīz) Khān, who had inherited those regions after his father's death. Emperor Akbar's grandfather Bābur was a Chaghatai Turk who, after being driven from his homeland by Uzbek rivals, established himself in Kābul, and from there, invaded India and established the Mughal dynasty. The word 'Mughal' is Persian for 'Mongol'– a misnomer that stuck.

[5] Hakīm: doctor, physician.

will get to know me better. Keep them to yourself, and use them to your benefit. I hope they will help you to avoid some of the mistakes I have made.

Do not blame yourself for my death, my son. My time has come. The joys of life, the hunting parties, the nights of laughter and friendly conversation, the cups of wine, the soft-scented melons of Kabul and Kashmir's sweet grapes, the tender breasts and firm thighs of harem girls, even the wisdom of Sadhus and Sufis, they all seem to have lost their attraction to me.

I must now finish the task that I have been created to accomplish, and in good order, hand over my realm to my successor. I leave you my world; seize it, Jahangir[6] Padshah, and rule over it with justice and wisdom.

May you lead a good and glorious life, my dear son, and may you receive guidance and blessings in abundance from the Ultimate Ruler of this world and all worlds to come; the One of thousands upon thousands of most Beautiful Names; the First, the Last, the One, to Whom lead thousands upon thousands of paths.

May He, the Compassionate, the Merciful, the Acceptor of Repentance, the Pardoner, the All-Forgiving, graciously nullify my multitude of sins—the small and the great, the known and the hidden. May He repair what was wrong in my life, complete what I should have finished, and multiply in infinity what little good I have done or intended to do.

May He engulf me in the unfathomable and limitless ocean of His tender Mercy.

[6] Jahāngīr: Seizer of the World, World Conqueror – the official name chosen by Akbar's son and successor Salīm upon his accession to the throne.

PART I

[7] *Sahar*, Dawn.

Second Letter

کلانور

Kalanor

I was thirteen years of age, growing taller and stronger every day, and things were going well. As the young crown prince of the empire, I thoroughly enjoyed my first official assignment and felt immensely proud and important. My blessed father, Emperor Humayun[8], may God's gentle light forever shine upon him, had just appointed me as governor of the entire Panjab. I headed a strong force of elite horsemen, under the able guidance and watchful eye of Bairam Khan, my strong and competent new *ataliq*[9], a battle-hardened Turkoman warrior, sipahsalar of the imperial army[10]. He had been my father's iron right arm for years.

Our task was to deal with Sikandar Sur and his followers, who were still roving the Siwalik hills up north and were hoping for an opportunity to usurp my father's throne.

God was smiling upon us. Sikandar Sur was really no match for someone as deadly as Bairam Khan. Never wasting any time, he went about his task of eliminating the enemy forces, with the same effortless

---

[8] Humāyūn (6 March 1508, Kābul–*26 January 1556, Dillī), second of the Mughal emperors of Hindustān.

[9] *Atālīq*: Guardian

[10] *Sipahsālār*: Commander-in-Chief of the Army, Marshal.

efficiency as a tiger killing a herd of goats.

His tall, sinewy figure seemed to be everywhere in the camp. He talked to regular soldiers as well as army leaders, dealt with supply matters, listened intently to scouting reports, ordered hit-and-run attacks and all-out assaults. Our men blindly obeyed him. They would have followed him to the very gates of hell. They sensed that he would have never ordered them to do anything he would not be prepared to go through himself.

Although he would always dress plainly, not much different from the ordinary soldiers, he looked invincible in his mail armour and dark blue clothes. The black turban he wore when we were not engaged in battle, gave him an even darker appearance. His face was tanned and lined, with high cheekbones, a long hooknose and a thick, black beard. His piercing eyes under bushy eyebrows and his thin-lipped, disdainful mouth gave him a stern, haughty expression. He hardly ever smiled or laughed, but when he did, he showed a row of strong, white, pointed teeth.

While he painstakingly kept me safe, he did make sure I saw plenty of action and would always take the time to explain every move of ours and the reasons behind it. I was learning every day and never felt more excited in my life. Everything was going well, extremely well.

Late in the afternoon on Shanbeh, the 14th of Bahman[11], after yet another day of successful military operations, we were resting in the Imperial Army camp on the banks of the Ravi river near Kalanor, admiring the beauty of God's creation, as the setting sun was painting the land with colours of copper and gold. We had just finished washing and were getting ready to turn towards Mekkah and start our evening prayers when a messenger from Dilli came galloping into the camp.

It was clear immediately, from the disconcerted look on his face, from the way his horse had been driven to utter exhaustion that this was highly important and extremely bad news. Faulting, stammering, the messenger told us that my blessed father had been critically injured in an accident in his library. There was little hope for his recovery.

What had happened? It appeared that my revered father had been studying for a few hours in his cherished library in the Sher Mandal building, as he had always been so very fond of doing. At sunset, he

---

[11] Saturday, 27 January 1556 on the Julian Calendar.

had gone to the rooftop observatory with several of his astrologers and other learned men, to observe the first visible movements of the celestial bodies. In the west, Esfand[12] was vaguely discernible on the horizon. From the observer's perspective, the sun was setting three fingers' breadth away from it, towards the south. Half an hour later, Venus would be setting close to the same spot. Saturn, high up in the sky, and Mars, in the Bahman[13] constellation, would then form a straight line above it. My blessed father was deeply convinced that it was all of profound significance.

He was about to retire to his quarters for a moment, standing on top of the steep staircase when suddenly, the muezzin's call to prayer was heard. My unfortunate father hastened down the flight of steps, in order to properly face the qiblah [14] and start his prayers when his foot got caught in his robe, and he fell headlong down the stairs. He received a violent blow on his right temple, making blood seep out of his ear. The court physicians later said that his skull had been fractured.

Before losing consciousness, he found the strength to order a messenger to be sent to warn me and Bairam Khan about the accident. His last words, according to those present, were: 'I accept the Divine summons.' Three days later, he passed away.

My poor, unfortunate father. May God grant him the peace of the Gardens of Paradise, for the life he led on this earth brought him but little of it. So many grand ambitions, plans and dreams. So many interests and occupations. So few of them fulfilled.

He was born a mighty prince, heir to the throne of the vast dominions conquered by Babur the Tiger, my glorious grandfather.

Yet, despite this auspicious birth, he spent most of his adult life as a wandering exile, when Sher Khan Sur, his Afghan neighbor and erstwhile vassal, threw him out of his own kingdom.

Sher Khan Sur was a treacherous snake, no doubt about that. But much as I hate to admit it, he was an abler soldier and ruler than my father was, and he organized and defended his stolen empire well. My

---

[12] *Esfand*: Pisces.

[13] *Bahman*: Aquarius

[14] *Qiblah*: The direction of Mecca

poor father spent the following fifteen years of his life in bitter exile, at times little more than a common marauder, with a dwindling group of ragged followers, before God finally restored him to power, after Sher Khan's death.

Alas, he did not get much to enjoy the sweet taste of victory. A mere six months later, he lost his life in a silly accident on the stairs of a library.

My father and his library. I do not think there was a single place in the world he liked any better.

He really was a scholar at heart, my blessed father, a man with a mind even more restless than mine. Whenever he found the time, provided he was not wasting it in opium's false paradise, he would be working on some kind of contraption, feverishly drawing, calculating or he would sit in his library, reading voraciously, adding yet another insight to his vast knowledge about the movements of celestial bodies, the properties of metals and precious stones, flowers, herbs and plants, the four elements and their relationship to the letters of the sacred Arabic alphabet, and many other such lofty matters.

Unfortunately, he deluded himself into thinking that all these learned endeavours were vitally important in the task of government. Literally, everything and everybody in his court and army was referring in some way or other to the stars and the planets, and the colours, numbers, substances and attributes associated with them.

He would wear different colours each day of the week, each referring to a different planet. Similarly, all the nobles, officers, artisans and the like were divided into categories, each referring to the stars and the elements. He designed and built a vast array of complicated inventions and contraptions, of varying and often doubtful practical use, ranging from portable bridges to a floating palace, and a huge tent with twelve partitions, corresponding to the twelve signs of the Zodiac, with lattice openings at the exact spots where the light of the corresponding stars would fall through. He also had a large, perfectly round carpet made, with circles representing the orbits of the planets and colours symbolizing the elements. He used to play a strange game on it, whereby the courtiers had to take their places on the carpet near the planet corresponding to them. My father, seated on a throne, would occupy the circle of the Sun. A dice was used, which had on its sides, pictures of a person standing, sitting, reclining, crouching, etc. Every participant would throw the dice, and assume the position indicated, inviting, of course, laughs from the others. My father would then comment on the astrological significance of the constellations, and link them to events past, present and future. All members of the court pretended to be very fond of the game...

So many learned and intricate pastimes, inventions, rules, arrangements, divisions and subdivisions. Each and every one of them, the result of so many lofty thoughts. Yet, virtually none of them served any practical purpose whatsoever. Not one of his ingenious inventions managed to halt or even delay his enemy Sher Khan, who drove him out of his own kingdom. Not a single one of his learned observations and calculations warned him, that he would fall to his death from the stairs of his own library.

I do not mean any disrespect to my revered father in telling you all this, my son. I loved my father; I honor and cherish his memory; I owe him my life and my throne. He has given me love, protection, education and I do share his admiration for men of wisdom, learning and science.

However, there is no doubt in my mind that my blessed father's lot in life was a direct warning from God to me, and to you, and to all the Gurkaniyya[15] Padshahs following us: in this world, God only favors the people who act.

It may very well be, that the universe is One, that the eternal decisions of God (Who owns the past, the present and the future) can be revealed to us through the constellation of the stars, the properties of numbers and the like, but one thing has become very clear to me throughout my life. God only helps those who are willing to help themselves, my dear son. The world of study and knowledge, fascinating and enchanting as it is, may help us to understand Him better, but will in itself not bring us any nearer to Him. God favors people who *do*

---

[15] The Mughal emperors never referred to themselves as *Mughal* (i.e., Mongol) at all. They called themselves *Silsila-i-Gurkaniyya*, the Gurkanid Dynasty, in reference to Tamerlane's (Amīr Temür's) title of *Gurkan*, from the Mongolian *gürägän* or *kürägän*, son-in-law, a title accorded to all those who had married a princess of Genghīz Khān's blood, as did Amīr Temür, and as did Bābur's father (Akbar's great-grandfather), Umar-Shaykh Mirza. Timur/Temür considered himself the rightful heir to all the lands conquered by Genghīz Khān.

something. He wants us to take our destiny into our own hands, not to leave it to the stars and numbers. Wars are not won by astrologers, but by warriors who act boldly and swiftly.

When the news of my father's death was brought to us, I fell to the ground, weeping and lamenting, as a loving son of that young age would be expected to do on such a mournful occasion.

But to be honest, I found it very difficult at that time to feel any of the appropriate feelings. I should have felt overwhelming, gut-wrenching grief and sadness, but instead, my head felt numb, as if I had been drinking wine, and disgraceful thoughts were galloping through my mind.

However much I tried to picture my father as I had known him during his life, I could not stop myself from thinking about what would be happening now to his body. I thought of his imposing face, the black eyes under stern eyebrows, the stringy, pointed black beard, which would move up and down when he spoke, and which he always fondled absentmindedly, whenever he was reading something. How many days would have to go by, before this face disappeared, before this noble head turned into a fleshless skull, plucks of scalp and beard still sticking to it?

I also found myself questioning all the things I had earlier assumed to be true. How was it possible that my father, who was so well acquainted with celestial sciences and versed in the mysteries of the stars, had not been able to foresee this catastrophic event? Why had God allowed him to be fatally injured, precisely at the moment he was answering the call to prayer? Did God care at all about our hopes and plans? Would He protect me against my enemies, or was He just watching all our strife and wars, the way cruel young boys look at the desperate struggles of a termite on an anthill?

I do not recall feeling afraid, but I very clearly realized that my own future was far from certain. I was only thirteen, yet I knew more than enough about the world to realize that I would have to fight for my father's inheritance. And the stern look on Bairam Khan's face proved to me that he was thinking exactly the same.

Bairam Khan, who had been the driving force behind my father's restoration to power, once again proved himself the ablest of generals and the most loyal servant of the Empire.

Khan Baba, my strong Protector. When I think of him, I have this nagging feeling of guilt, this feeling that many people have when they remember their own parents, the painful awareness of having received much more than one deserves or could ever repay, the realization that one should have shown them much more gratitude, obedience, love and respect when there was still time to do so. May God reward him in eternity for his faithfulness, and may God forgive me for the ungratefulness with which I later treated him.

As always, he acted swiftly and without hesitation. My father's death was kept a secret for as long as possible. False messages about his recovery were sent to Lahore. Back in Dilli, a loyal cleric by the name of Mullah Bekasi, who happened to have my father's build and the same shape of beard, was dressed up in my father's robes, and made the usual daily appearance to the public from the balcony on the riverside of the fort.

Meanwhile, Bairam Khan moved on all fronts. First of all, he secured the loyalty of his personal rival, Tardi Beg, an influential Turkoman officer, appointing him as governor of Dilli.

He also very aptly persuaded me to resist the temptation of riding into Dilli ourselves.

'You see, Your Majesty,' he explained, 'we have to realize that our hold on Hindustan and the other dominions is not as strong as we would like it to be.'

He drew a map in the sand. 'Kabul and Qandahar, up here in the far west behind the Khyber Pass, are not our concern right now. As arranged by your father, they are under the government of Prince Muhammad Hakim, your younger brother, and his guardian Munim Khan. To be honest, I do not like Munim Khan very much, and I do think there is a very real danger, that he and your brother will sooner or later try to become independent from your throne; but as I said, they are not our immediate concern. At least for now, Kabul is secure; it could even become our refuge, if ever, God forbid, some kind of disaster would befall us.

The situation back here in Hindustan is far more dangerous, Your Majesty. Yes, our troops do hold Dilli, Lahore and the other main cities, but the fight is far from over. Sikandar Sur and the other would-be heirs of Sher Khan are waiting for an opportunity to strike again and drive us out of these lands, just like they did to your blessed father fifteen years ago. I know, we have defeated them twice; but as you know, they are still roving the Siwalik hills. We must continue to smoke them out, chase them and reduce their forces as much as possible before we head back to Dilli. Otherwise, before long, they will be back to challenge us.'

The following weeks were spent in preparation of my formal accession to the throne. A brick platform was built in a garden at Kalanor, while astrologers engaged themselves in complicated calculations and feverish disputes about the most auspicious moment for the enthronement ceremony.

In the meantime, we kept harassing Sikandar Sur's forces. Compared to my later conquests, it was of course but a small-scale war, and I was only a boy. But I am proud to say that with Bairam Khan's wise counsel, I fought it skilfully, not as a hard-hearted, ruthless conqueror, who leaves nothing but death and devastation, but as a prudent and wise king who desires the welfare of his subjects. Towards the enemy troops, we showed nothing but merciless, vengeful, stern determination. We killed anyone who dared to oppose us, pursuing them tirelessly, at all times of the day and night, attacking them when and where they least expected it, gradually wearing out their will to resist. On the other hand, however, we painstakingly avoided causing any harm to the peaceful inhabitants of the region, whether Muslim or Hindu. The strictest orders were given to pay, promptly and generously, for whatever supplies we obtained from them. We treated their village elders with respect and left their possessions, temples, homes and women untouched.

Thus, it should be, my son. The common people should know their king to be powerful and just. They should realize they have nothing to fear if they stay loyal to him; but nowhere to hide, if they do not.

When children came near our camps, we did not chase them away. On the contrary, we put some effort into teaching them to ride a horse, wield a sword and handle bows and arrows with some accuracy. It is good that the boys of the country aspire to fight for their king when he needs them. Small armies of motivated and skilful volunteers fight so much better than large hosts of mere conscripts.

A few more raids against the weakening followers of Sikandar Sur, and we would be making our triumphant entry into Dilli. That was our plan.

Little did we realize, it would take us nine more months, and a devastating battle against a formidable new adversary, before we would finally be in a position to enter my father's capital.

The astrologers had finally come to an agreement on a felicitous day and hour for my formal accession to the throne. It was to be exactly at noon, on Adineh, the second of Rabi ath-Thani of the Hijri year 963[16]. Three days before, the Khutbah[17] had been read in my name for the first time in the mosques of Dilli, Agra, Lahore and the other cities of the Empire.

I ascended the coronation platform, wearing a heavy golden robe and a dark blue turban, lavishly adorned with precious pearls. I was accompanied by the sound of blaring trumpets and thundering war drums. The long, golden fringes of the shiny red-and-gold Imperial canopy were gently swaying in the warm breeze.

The Amirs, Khans and other nobles all stood around the platform in a hexagon, symbolizing the six sides of the universe: north, south, east, west, up, and down. In the entrancing rhythm of the war drums, they chanted, over and over, the same two words: 'Padshah salamat, Padshah salamat!'[18].

Bairam Khan handed me my father's sword, brought in from Dilli, especially for the occasion. I accepted it like a reigning monarch would, without bowing my head, yet hoping no one would notice my shaking hands. I unsheathed the sword and pointed it high towards the sun. All those present followed my example. I slowly turned around, saluting the cheering nobles on all six sides of the platform, and finally sat down on the Throne.

My first official deed of government was to appoint Bairam Khan as Wakil of the Empire and bestow on him the lofty titles of Khan Khanan and Sipahsalar Itizad-i-Daulat Qahira.[19]

---

[16] Friday, 14 February 1556 of the Julian calendar.

[17] *Khutbah*: formal prayer for the reigning monarch.

[18] *Pādshāh Salāmāt*: Hail to the Emperor.

[19] *Wakīl:* Administrator of the Imperial Household. *Khān Khanān, Sipahsālār, I'tizād-i-Daulat Qāhira*: Lord of Lords, Commander-in-Chief of the Army, Stay of Victorious Dominion.

The astrologer had suggested I do this, probably following Bairam Khan's orders, but I would have taken the initiative of my own accord anyway. I sensed it was vitally important to strengthen Bairam Khan's position in relation to the other high officials of the Empire.

I made a sign, and two guards handed me a black and gold robe, made especially for the occasion. I took it in my hands, briefly touched my shoulders with it, and laid it on the shoulders of Bairam Khan, who knelt down on one knee in front of me, bowing his head. The Amirs, Khans and other nobles cheered to congratulate him, but to my satisfaction, they did so with audibly less enthusiasm than when they had been acclaiming me.

The astrologer proceeded to talk to the assembly about the future of my reign. Lengthy and learned, his sermon was. He did his very best to convince everybody about the invincibility of my stars, demonstrating at length how my horoscope predicted, without a shadow of a doubt, that God Himself had clearly and unequivocally decided that I would become one of the greatest Monarchs the world had ever seen, stronger, wiser, mightier than Genghis Khan, Temür, Sargon, or Iskandar.

I must confess that his pompous, extravagant flattery pleased me more than I cared to admit. I felt shivers going down my spine, when he solemnly, one by one, read out the names of all my ancestors, all the way up to Adam, all those glorious names, including Babur, Miran Shah, Temür Gürgan, Mughal Khan, Türk, Yafeth, Noah, Enoch, Seth and Adam himself. Peace be upon them, and may their graves be holy and filled with God's light.

Yet, what a heavy burden to hear all those glorious and important names, all of them mighty and glorious kings of kings, all of them dead and buried and no longer there to help me.

Here I was, a thirteen-year-old boy King, with no safe territory to call my own, surrounded by strong and experienced enemies. And the fate of this entire glorious and mighty dynasty was now on my shoulders.

When the astrologer had finished his allocution, all the Amirs, Khans and officers, all the supporters of our dynasty, one by one, came forward, took a solemn oath on the Holy Quran, and pledged their allegiance to me.

Gold, jewels and bags of coins, the first ones minted in my name, were distributed among the participants.

The rest of the day was spent eating and drinking and exchanging kind and pleasant conversation. Bairam Khan made sure I met with every one of the nobles and spent with each of them an amount of time proportionate to their rank and merit, recounting, in detail, every individual's accomplishments and the services they had rendered to my father and grandfather.

And in the night, as I lay wide awake and unable to sleep, I thought about my father. I saw before my mind's eye his gentle face, his charming smile, and that dark, pointed beard of his. It was as if I could feel his strong hands lovingly fondle my hair, as they used to do when I was just a little boy. I remembered how he had tried to explain to me the many things he knew, and I understood that even in anger, he had always wanted to show me how much he loved me.

Suddenly, with unbearable clarity, the bitter truth stood before me.

For the first time, I fully realized, not only with my head, but also deeply in my heart, that my father was dead and gone, that I would never see him smile again, that I would never have the opportunity to get his advice, never again enjoy a meal with him, or hear the sound of his pleasant voice.

And I wept bitterly.

Third Letter

جالندھر

Jalandhar

Later in life, I have been back to Kalanor a number of times. I never liked it very much. Those provincial surroundings, the plain brick coronation platform, the unimpressive, ill-kept gardens, none of them really convey the impression that this is the place where one of the greatest kings in history ascended the throne.

I have given orders for the garden to be embellished, and a few decorative constructions to be built around it, to add a bit of standing and dignity to it. It may be good and wise for a king to remember the humble circumstances of his own beginnings, but his subjects should not be reminded about them too often.

I really ought to have more fond and grateful memories of the place. After all, this is where my reign started, a relatively humble start for what became an unparalleled series of glorious victories and conquests, the foundation of one of the most powerful and prosperous empires the world has ever seen. If anything, the humility of my origins should increase my satisfaction and pride over the results I achieved.

Yet, as I stroll the peaceful garden, it seems I still sense the tension in the air, the doubts and fears of my army commanders, the ominous threat of defeat and disintegration. No matter how proud I was at the coronation, I knew very well, despite all the oaths of allegiance, how precarious my hold on my father Humayun's heritage was. Kalanor reminds me, all too clearly, how narrowly I escaped defeat and oblivion, and how much I owe my good fortune to sheer luck.

But that is not even the main reason why I dislike the place so much. Kalanor reminds me, more than I care to admit, of all the sad mistakes of my youth. It reminds me, how much I owe my success to the loyalty and dedication of other people, whom I later misjudged and paid back with arrogant ingratitude. No matter how good my excuses, no matter the amends I made, the forgiveness I asked and did obtain, those sins will stay with me until the day I die. The wrong we have done can be forgiven, its consequences mitigated, but no one can undo the fact that it has been done. No matter how much we would want it otherwise, our errors have become part of our lives. We can only hope, that when we are admitted in the gardens of Paradise, God, praise be upon Him, will somehow re-write the stories of our lives, and make them perfect. Will this not be the ultimate blessing of Paradise? That God will heal every wound, remove every scar, reunite us with those we have harmed, and allow us to see them again, without any trace of sadness, guilt or remorse? How I wish it would be like this! May I be reunited one day with my friend and teacher Bairam Khan, and may there be nothing but joyful laughter between us.

In the days following my accession to the throne, Bairam Khan had to intervene more than once to restore discipline among the troops. I knew, all too well that any mistake from our side, any setback in the fight against our enemies, and our host of followers would quickly disappear before our very eyes. The victorious and the powerful are never short of friends and supporters, but loneliness, bitter loneliness is the fate of the defeated.

Bairam Khan was acting in my best interest, of course. But could I be absolutely sure? Was he really acting to protect me? Or did he want to further his own ambitions? The first, tiny seeds of suspicion and jealousy had been sown in my heart. They would later become an overgrowing, tangled mass of poisonous bindweed.

We continued our operations in the Siwalik hills, until the torrential rains of the monsoon transformed the entire country into a swamp, making cavalry actions nearly impossible. Cavalry unable to move freely is always at risk, and it soon became evident that Sikandar Sur's forces were even more afraid than we were, at the risk of getting pinned down in a single spot. They withdrew to the north, whilst we moved south, towards Jalandhar, where we remained for some five months.

I spent the time horse riding, hunting, target shooting, wrestling, and practicing my fighting skills with sword, lance, mace and battle axe. It brought me great joy to feel how I was growing stronger and better every day.

Bairam Khan also saw to it that my education continued. By that time, my teachers had given up all attempts to teach me to read and write, but I very eagerly listened to all kinds of books being read to me by my new teacher, Mir Abdul-Latif, may God be well pleased with him. Under the old man's guidance, I willingly learned by heart many surahs of the Holy Quran, and hundreds of beautiful Persian and Arabic prayers, poems and stories, by Jalal-ud-Din Rumi, Sanai, Hafiz, and many other saintly teachers.

By far the fondest memories I have of the afternoons and evenings, when I was instructed in the history of the great empires of old.

Most of all, of course, I loved to hear about my own ancestors: Genghis Khan the Great, and Amir Temür the Iron. Needless to say, my favorite hero was my own grandfather, the conquering Tiger of Hindustan, the great Zahir-ud-Din Muhammad Babur Padshah, may his grave be holy. I enjoyed listening to his memoirs, the *Tuzuk-i Baburi*, or *Babur Nama*, as they call them in Persian these days. How I love these writings! So grand, yet so unassuming, so full of wisdom and down-to-earth practical advice; all those shrewd, astute insights, those honest, candid statements, all of them written in plain, crystal clear, down-to-earth Turki.

Many times, when Mir Abdul-Latif was talking to me about history, Bairam Khan himself would join us, listening intently to the teacher's reading, sipping fresh sugared water with lime and eating quite impressive amounts of almonds, figs and dates, ostensibly without being very much aware of it.

After a while, he would stop eating, dismiss the teacher, and start drawing battlefield maps on the ground with the point of his sword and teach me all there is to know about our strategies and tactics, our weaponry, and those of our opponents. In great depth and detail, he taught me the appropriate deployment and use of cannon, horsemen and foot soldiers on the battlefield, as well as the rules governing troop movements, encampments and fortifications, and many other related subjects, which are highly important for a king to master most thoroughly.

Bairam Khan did so much more than telling me a few fascinating stories. He did not even talk that much about bravery, glory or honor. He explained to me the art of warfare, like a physician demonstrating how to prepare a medicinal potion, like a carpenter or a mason showing how to build homes and furniture, or like a merchant explaining the tricks of the trade to his successor.

'War is not as messy as it looks, Your Majesty,' he used to say. 'Victory or defeat is not merely the result of fate or coincidence, not even of bravery. Warfare is an art, a science, just like astrology, or medicine. Like the movements of the sun and the moon and the other celestial bodies, warfare is governed by inescapable, iron laws. The task of an army leader is to thoroughly understand them and to put them to use to his own advantage.

The most important law of warfare, Your Majesty, the law that contains all others, is the following: 'All other things being equal, God favors the larger army!'

You see, Your Majesty, any major battle can be thought of as a series of encounters between two opposing armies, during which every soldier tries to kill as many enemies as possible. Suppose there are two such armies, one 30,000 strong, the other 10,000. Suppose one out of ten attempts on either side to kill enemy soldiers is successful. After the first encounter, the smaller army will have killed one thousand of its opponents, and the larger army will have killed three thousand, leaving 29,000 against 7,000. At the second encounter, the smaller army will only be able to kill 700 enemies, while losing 2,900 of its own troops, leaving 28,300 against 4,100 at the third encounter. At that time, supposing both armies continue to fight as valiantly as before, the large army will lose 410 men, leaving 27,890, but the smaller army will lose another 2,830 soldiers, leaving it with a mere 1,270 men for the last and final encounter, during which it will be completely annihilated, while the victorious army still retains a large fighting force of 27,763 men. Such is the simple arithmetic of a battle of attrition, Your Majesty. The larger army wins.

There are, however, many ways to influence the working and outcome of this fundamental law of war, and a good army commander knows how to put them to use in his own favor.

Superior weaponry will increase the army's effectiveness. Longer-ranging guns and bows will allow your soldiers to start killing their enemies before incurring any casualties themselves. Fortifications, entrenchments, bulwarks, shields and armour will reduce the effectiveness of enemy attacks.

Even more important than equipment is the fighting spirit of your men. Each army may have its number of heroes, but the vast majority of your soldiers will be just ordinary men, afraid to die, and naturally inclined to avoid the heat of the battle and flee from danger. An ordinary soldier, when left to himself, will feel the urge to run away, or in contrast, to attack prematurely, in an instinctive effort to get the battle over with as quickly as possible. He will discharge his bow or musket in the general direction of the enemy, without taking proper aim, thereby wasting his own army's killing power. When his army suffers a setback, he will flee in panic, allowing himself and his comrades to be slaughtered. And when his army is victorious, he will start plundering and fail to pursue the fleeing enemy, thereby wasting the opportunity to annihilate him, allowing him to come back to fight another day.

This is of course typical for an army of inexperienced conscripts, but even in an army of battle-hardened professional soldiers, it is always lurking beneath the surface. An able commander knows these weaknesses, and knows how to counteract them. He will at all times maintain order and discipline in his army. He will foster his men's courage, reminding them of the rewards of war: spoils, booty, security for their families, honor and glory for themselves. When fighting infidels, he will remind them of Allah's blessings awaiting those who die in Jihad.

He will keep his army exercising every day so that the proper behaviour in battle becomes routine to it. He will not only pay attention to the cavalry, but to the foot soldiers as well. He will teach them, for instance, that in the face of an enemy cavalry charge, by far the best thing they can do is to firmly hold their ground, in tightly closed ranks. It may take more than ordinary courage, not to move when thousands upon thousands of thundering hooves are rushing towards you, but it is by far the most effective defense. Horses, no matter how battle-hardened, no matter how obedient they may be to their master, will never run at full speed into a solid wall. When approaching well-closed ranks of disciplined and determined infantry, they will inevitably slow down, exposing themselves and their riders to arrows and musket fire.

Elephants, on the other hand, should if possible be fought behind deep trenches, or, if there is no time to dig them, they should be fought with flexible, fast-moving infantry battlelines, clouds upon clouds of arrows, volleys of cannon and musket fire, and swift hit-and-run cavalry charges. Elephants are very hard to kill and will slam through any fixed battle formation trying to oppose them, but when they are wounded and enraged, they are almost impossible to control and therefore quickly become as dangerous to their own army as to their opponent's. When commanding an elephant force, it is essential to keep them in the rear, out of reach of enemy cannon fire, and to bring them to bear only near the end of the battle, when the enemy formations have been driven together in a compact mass and the time has come to move in for the final kill.

The greatest emphasis needs to be put on speed. The commander will have his archers and musketeers train every day, over and over, how to replace each other in quick succession, so that the battle formation is able to deliver a constant flow of arrows and musket fire.

When all this is done diligently and put into practice on a regular basis, a king should always seek conquest and war, lest his army become lazy and ineffective[20]. Yours will be a battle-hardened fighting force, able to defeat armies, vastly superior in numbers.

Then comes maybe the most difficult part, the proper deployment of your fighting forces. No matter how good the soldiers and their equipment are, that in itself is not enough. Troops need to be deployed and sent into action in accordance with the requirements of the battlefield. This is perhaps the most important and also the most difficult skill of warfare.

Smaller armies fight much better on narrow, restricted battlefields, where mountains, hills, forests, rivers, lakes and the like are blocking the deployment of their adversary. This kind of terrain enables a smaller army, using its greater mobility and the element of surprise, to transform the war into a series of smaller hit-and-run battles, in which, when and where it strikes, it can effectively outnumber its opponent. The whole

---

[20] One of Akbar's famous quotes.

purpose of troop movements and manoeuvres in open battlefields is to create similar conditions. As demonstrated so ably by your glorious grandfather Babur Padshah, may Allah smile on him and make his grave holy, an enemy host of overwhelming strength can be turned into an ineffective, helpless mass of cannon fodder, when you succeed in blocking its ability to properly manoeuvre and deploy its fighting force.

Consider, Your Majesty, your grandfather's immortal victory at Panipat, on the 9th of Rajab, 932[21], the victory that won him the throne of Hindustan. He had less than twenty thousand men, against over one hundred thousand under Sultan Ibrahim Lodhi of Dilli.

Sultan Ibrahim also had about one thousand fighting elephants at his disposal. Our army mainly relied on horse archers but was ably supplemented by four thousand musketeers and about one hundred fifty cannons of various kinds. These new ways of fighting made the difference that day. Your grandfather had come to realize, long before his opponents in Hindustan, that cannons are not only essential when laying siege to a fortress, but can also be put to great use on the open battlefield.

Babur Padshah knew he wouldn't stand a chance unless he could force the enemy army to fight on a narrow front. He therefore positioned his forces to the east of Panipat, between the town walls and the Yamuna River.

The right wing had the town walls to its right, while the left flank was protected by ditches, felled trees, and artificial hedges made of thorny shrubbery, all the way to the riverbanks. This made sure that the army could not be bypassed and surrounded by the enemy. The centre stood behind mobile defenses made of gun carts, linked together with chains or ropes; behind and in between them were archers and musketeers, behind movable wooden mantlets. At regular intervals, he left openings in the front, a bit less than a bow shot wide, through which assaults of up to five thousand horses could be launched.

Babur Padshah's preparations were impeccable, but Sultan Ibrahim Lodhi refused to give battle, and quite rightfully so. Time was very much on his side. He had no difficulties of supply, whereas Babur Padshah would sooner or later be forced to withdraw or leave his entrenched position and attack.

---

[21] Saturday, 21 April 1526 (Julian Calendar).

For seven days, in the blazing heat of early summer, the armies faced each other.

With a series of cavalry raids, Babur tried to provoke the enemy into attacking him, but Sultan Ibrahim ignored all insults and would not move. As morale in our camp was deteriorating fast, Babur Padshah then decided to launch a night attack, on the 7th of Rajab. Five thousand men moved into Lodhi's camp, but they were in for a very unpleasant surprise. The Afghans were ready and waiting for them. Fortunately, our forces did not confuse bravery with foolishness. They were able to disengage and withdraw without too many losses. Had they continued their attack, they would most certainly have been annihilated.

Ironically, it was this defeat that won the war for us. After another day of waiting, shortly after dawn on the 9th of Rajab, encouraged by their easy victory, the Afghans moved in for what they thought was the final kill.

It went exactly as Babur Padshah had planned. The mighty Afghan cavalry charge, which had started on too broad a front, was slowed down considerably when it had to squeeze itself through the narrow funnel created by our entrenchments, their left flank pushing sideways into their centre formation.

Babur Padshah's forces waited in silence until the Afghan front was well within reach of our artillery. Then, the cannon opened up, their projectiles penetrating up to six lines deep into their formation, followed by devastating blasts of the multi-barrelled field guns. As the large guns reloaded, deadly volleys of our infantry muskets and rockets further decimated the enemy vanguard. One could see the bullets and missiles piercing enemy shields and armour. The Afghan front lines tried to turn around and move out of reach of our guns, but the attacking ranks behind slammed into them. Their entire fighting force had turned into a compacted, disorganized mass, unable to move, defenseless fodder for our mortar bombs and the clouds upon clouds of arrows that kept raining down on them.

Babur Padshah did not waste any time to seize the opportunity.

The best of our cavalry, fearless, battle-hardened Turkoman archers on the swiftest Iraqi horses, stormed through the openings in our defenses, wheeling around the Afghan flanks and effectively preventing them to manoeuvre.

The Afghans fought bravely and with honor, repeatedly charging our front lines at the centre in an effort to break out of the trap, but it was to no avail. Very few of them even reached our positions, and those who did were finished off quickly.

As your illustrious grandfather writes in the *Tuzuk-i Baburi,* 'The sun had mounted a spear high when the onset of battle began, and the combat lasted till mid-day when the enemy was completely broken and routed, and my friends victorious and exulting. By the grace and mercy of almighty God, this arduous undertaking was rendered easy for me, and this mighty army, in the space of half a day, laid in the dust.'

Ibrahim Lodhi's corpse was found amid sixteen thousand fallen Afghans. When his head was brought to Babur Padshah, he ordered the Sultan's remains to be washed and shrouded in the finest cloth, and buried with honor, at the spot where he and his men had fallen.

Your noble grandfather ordered his son, Shahzada[22] Sultan Humayun, your glorious father, to ride into Agra, Lodhi's capital, and sent another contingent of troops to occupy Dilli. The next day, he followed the army into Dilli, where for the first time, the *khutbah* was read in his name. Hindustan was his. Praise be to God!

This glorious battle, Your Majesty, contains in itself the entire art of warfare. For generations upon generations, army leaders of all nations will speak in awe and admiration about Babur Padshah's magnificent victory at Panipat.'

Bairam Khan was so right, my son. The study of this battle is indispensable for the education of all generations to come. It contains in itself almost the entire art of warfare. Moreover, it was with this battle that we established ourselves as the rulers of Hindustan. Promise me, my son, on my grave, that you will never allow any of the princes of our dynasty to forget where they came from.

The battle of Panipat. How many hours did we spend, talking about it, analysing it. Little did we imagine at that time, that only a few weeks later, we too would find ourselves fighting at Panipat, fighting desperately for our own survival.

[22] Shāhzāda: Prince (literally, offspring of the Shāh).

Fourth Letter

پانیپت

Panipat

Sikandar Sur was not the only one coveting the throne of Hindustan. There were, alas, quite a number of other would-be heirs to the throne of Sher Khan Suri, eager to revive their glorious ancestor's empire.

Sher Khan was a devious traitor; he stole my father's dominions. Because of him, my father spent more than fifteen years in miserable exile. As my father's son, I hate him for it. Yet, as my father's successor, much as I hate to admit it, I owe him a debt of gratitude.

For all his conniving treachery, Sher Khan was an insightful, wise ruler. He clearly understood that conquest alone is not sufficient to build an empire. In fact, victory in battle is only the beginning of the work. Conquests, my son, are only like castles of sand unless they are properly consolidated and strengthened. Consider Temür's victories, or Genghis Khan's; they were like grassland fire. Spectacular, awesome, but spent quickly, leaving nothing of any lasting value.

Building a throne is an art; keeping it is quite another, my son. Never assume that our Dynasty rules over Hindustan because it is our God-given right to do so. It will be your duty as Padshah, to maintain and increase the strength of our Empire. Every waking moment of your life should be devoted to it, expanding it through conquest, and consolidating it through wise government. Dominions and territories need to be administered; populations need to be integrated. Do not take this lightly. It is a never-ending task and a heavy burden, and it should always be on your mind, whether you are waging war, administering justice, securing revenue to the treasury, organizing commerce and agriculture, or favoring the arts.

Sher Khan understood this. He was a much better ruler than I care to admit in public. So much so, that I have thought it wise to take over many of his institutions and practices. Good ideas are good ideas, no matter where they come from, my son.

Fortunately for my father and for our dynasty, Sher Khan was not allowed to stay in this world for long. God, who is infinite justice, caused him to die in an explosion of one of his own rockets, only five years after he had stolen my father's throne. And after Sher Khan's death, the once so powerful Sur dynasty quickly went into decline.

Sher Khan's youngest son and successor, Jalal Khan, who ruled under the name Islam Shah, died of a painful disease eight years later. He and his father had been competent rulers, but their successors were weak and divided, and quickly squandered their strength in a fratricidal civil war.

Jalal Khan's twelve-year-old son was brutally murdered by his worthless uncle, Mubariz. The son of a bitch cut the poor boy's head off, right before his desperate mother's eyes. His own sister! Such can be the lust for power, stronger than the laws of God and men, more enchanting than the rapture of opium, sweeter than a woman's embrace.

Mubariz assumed the title of Adil Shah. But he was not only a treacherous murderer, he was also an indolent pig, who left all the affairs of the state to Hemu, his deceased predecessor's prime minister, a dwarfish Hindu of humble origins and frail stature, unimpressive but highly competent, clever, tenacious, and dangerous like a cobra.

While Hemu's power was on the rise, Mubariz (Adil Shah) wasted his days playing music, singing, dancing, drinking, and enjoying the pleasures of the harem. Meanwhile, his empire was crumbling around him. Let the emptiness of his worthless life be a warning to you, my son. The path of self-indulgence may be pleasant and easy, but it does not lead to success in this world.

As I said, Mubariz promptly lost control over his empire. His cousin Sikandar Sur seized the Panjab. Another cousin, Ibrahim Sur, took possession of Dilli and Agra, and Muhammad Shah set up an independent realm in Bengal, leaving only Bihar to the usurper. Every Sur was waging war against all others; no surprise that this ruinous infighting brought the proud reign of the Surs to an ignominious end.

Ibrahim Sur was chased out of Dilli by Sikandar Sur and later decisively defeated by Hemu. He fled to Orissa, where he died, forgotten.

As for the other Surs, God Almighty has chosen our dynasty to be His right arm in chastising them.

Indeed, the fighting between the Surs gave my blessed father Humayun the opportunity to take back what was rightfully his. He defeated Sikandar Sur, first time at Machhiwara, then again at Sirhind, forcing him to flee to the Panjab, where Bairam Khan and I were chasing him when my father died in that unfortunate accident on the library roof.

It has, thus, been God's will that I would be the one to reunite the lands of Hindustan.

We were still encamped at Jalandhar, preparing ourselves to resume the operations against Sikandar Sur, when the news was brought to us, that Hemu had crossed the border of Adil's dominions and was marching against us from the south.

The history of Hindustan would have been very different indeed, had the plans and ambitions of this conniving devil of a man met with God's approval. Hemu had been fighting Adil's battles against the other Surs in the west, proving himself a most able general and leader of men, winning no less than twenty-two battles for his master. Each time, he grew more powerful. Outwardly, he behaved like Adil's most loyal servant, but very soon he must have come to the conclusion that he could do much better for himself. He accumulated immense wealth, only to spend it with cunning generosity, gradually buying himself the loyalty of the Afghan Amirs. The conquest of Hindustan would be his final step towards absolute power.

Hemu's forces advanced via Gwalior to Agra, which they captured without a fight, as the commander of our garrison in that city, Iskandar Khan Uzbeg, withdrew towards Dilli to join forces with Tardi Beg, the newly appointed local governor. One would have expected them both to hold the city and keep Hemu's army occupied until we joined them with the main body of our army. Instead, Tardi Beg panicked. He allowed his vanguard to be slaughtered before his very eyes without intervening and fled to the northwest, abandoning 1,000 fine horses, 160 elephants and other valuable booty to the enemy. So precipitous was his flight, that Hemu, suspecting a ruse, did not dare to follow him.

Hemu entered Dilli in triumph. This was the opportunity he had been waiting for all his life. He distributed all the captured treasures among his Afghan nobles, keeping only the elephants for himself. He had coin struck in his own name, held his court under the imperial canopy, called himself Raja Vikramaditya and assumed the dress and style of the great Hindu kings of old. His Afghan commanders started calling him Hemu Shah, and I suspect his Hindu followers were dreaming of a whole new era. He was ready to claim the throne of Hindustan for himself.

Bairam Khan was livid when the news of Tardi Beg's shameful retreat was brought to us.

'I must have been out of my mind to entrust Dilli to this cowardly heap of dog vomit,' he hissed.

'Measures will have to be taken, Your Majesty,' he mumbled, talking more to himself than to me, 'but we have to be careful. Cowardice is contagious, like the plague! We need to convince the other Amirs first; we desperately need to stay united and bring everybody back in line.'

Preparations were made for a hasty march. Much to our regret, we were forced to leave a sizeable cavalry force behind in the Panjab, to make sure Sikandar Sur would not be able to attack us from the rear.

We quickly moved southeast with the rest of the army. A courier was sent to Tardi Beg, carrying a firman[23] ordering him to meet the imperial army at Sirhind.

Two days later, we met, about two hours before noon. I was pleasantly surprised to see how Bairam Khan warmly embraced Tardi Beg, affectionately calling him his *tuqan*[24]. He then proceeded to welcome the other commanders of the Dilli and Agra garrison, and the two groups of army commanders started greeting each other. As often happens when the situation is grave, the reunion was just a tad too joyful, the embraces over-friendly, the voices exaggeratedly loud, the

[23] *Firmān*: Imperial Order.

[24] *Tüqān:* elder brother.

conversations interspersed with just a bit too many jokes and laughs. Despite the conspicuous display of optimism and joy, the atmosphere felt distinctly awkward.

Fortunately, this uneasy exchange of courtesies, formalities and civilities did not last too long. Bairam Khan clapped his hands to get everybody's attention and the conversations stopped abruptly.

'We need to talk, my friends,' he said, with a tone of sadness in his voice. Instantly, as if they were performing a ceremony rehearsed many times over, the Amirs went into the main tent in the most orderly fashion, sitting themselves down in a circle, the highest in rank sitting in front, the others in the back.

'My brother Tardi Beg has, thus, chosen to regroup with the rest of the imperial forces before attacking the enemy,' he said, thus, offering Tardi Beg an elegant way to explain his cowardice as an astute strategic move.

Alas, the dumb fool failed to seize the hand extended to him. Arrogance, the mother of error, the hallmark of stupidity.

'My brother confuses his dreams with reality,' he snapped. 'It is utter folly to oppose this accursed infidel with our forces. He has over a thousand war elephants, of a kind never seen before! Terrifying, huge like mountains, mouths like the jaws of a dragon, sabres attached to their tusks and trunks. And despite their size, they are amazingly swift. The fastest Iraqi horse would not be able to outrun these mountains of death. Nothing in this world matches their strength. I saw them uprooting strong trees like blades of grass, just for the fun of it. I saw one of them grab a man and his horse, effortlessly fling them into the air and trample both of them to death. And unlike all other elephants, they seem to be impervious to pain when wounded. I saw two of them being hit by at least twenty arrows in their forelegs, trunks and ears. It did not seem to bother them at all. They just kept rushing forward, smashing into our lines, killing everything and everybody on their path. I am telling you, my brothers. This is no normal enemy we are facing. Not only does he outnumber us, ten to one at least. He has weapons he could not possibly have obtained by any normal means. I am telling you, he is protected by the most powerful magic, supported by Ash-

Shaytan himself[25]. There is only one sensible thing we can do. Go back across the Khyber Pass into Kabul, join forces with Prince Muhammad Hakim and Munim Khan, avail ourselves of the most powerful magic to break this infidel's black witchcraft, and then come back to reclaim what is rightfully ours.'

'If we run away now, without a fight,' Bairam Khan replied, ignoring the insult and trying to control his anger, 'we may never get a chance to take Hindustan again. Don't you see what this infidel is doing? He is trying to rebuild the great Hindu empires of old, and if we do not stop him, he might just get away with it. He is an astute general, an able leader of men. Before long, he will have armed and mobilized the Hindu masses. They have been used to foreign Muslim rulers for centuries, but this is their chance to rise again. Ours is a holy task, my brothers. If we don't stop Hemu, it's only a matter of time before he will drive Islam out of these lands. He may allow the Afghans to stay for a while as his vassals, but he will wipe them out as soon as he feels strong enough to do so. If we run away now, we will need ten times our current strength to come back. Moreover, if we run away now, we betray the cause of Islam, we betray our oath of loyalty to Emperor Humayun and his legitimate heir. Worse of all, we forever lose our honor. It will take generations for people to forget our scandalous cowardice. To possess a throne, to possess an army ready for battle, and then to run away without a fight, like a bunch of women. That is not how I wish to be remembered. Do not forget, my brothers, we all have to die someday. When we die is not so important, and it is in the hands of Allah anyway. Much more important is how we spend our lives. How much better is it, to die at the age of forty, sword in hand, fighting like a man, spitting death in the face, than to die a despicable coward twenty years later.'

'All of you Shia heretics seem to be obsessed with martyrdom,' Tardi Beg retorted, his face full of contempt. 'Sensible people understand that the cause of Islam is much better served by living men fighting tomorrow than by powerless martyrs dying today.'

Bairam Khan's hand moved towards the hilt of his sword.

At this time, Shams-ud-din Muhammad Atga Khan intervened. He

---

[25] *Ash-Shaytān*: (The) Satan, the Devil.

was a longstanding and faithful ally of my father, respected throughout the army for his bravery and wisdom. Moreover, as the husband of my foster mother Ji Anaga, one of the nurses who had taken care of me as a child, he was related to me as my *Atga*, my foster father, and thus, one of the most important nobles at the imperial court.

He stepped between the two men and thundered, 'Enough of this, my brothers! Is this a time for us to be divided? Tardi Beg Khan, with all due respect, let me warn you, here and now, that I will personally kill anybody who tries to incite one Muslim against the other in this time of danger and war. Do we not all worship Allah? Do we not all recognize the noble Prophet Muhammad as His Messenger, eternal blessings be upon him? We have to stand united against the threat of this infidel. And I agree with my Lord Khan Khanan. We simply cannot afford to run away. Who has forgotten the miserable years of exile before our beloved Emperor Humayun was able to recover the throne of Hindustan? I will not be chased out again without a fight. And let Hemu be helped by the devil. We will be the allies of Allah Himself. Let us prepare for battle, my brothers, let the astrologers help us choose the most auspicious time and place, and let us put our trust in the Almighty. After all, not a single leaf falls from a tree, if He does not want it. How would He then allow this infidel to defeat us, unless it is His divine will?'

The Amirs all nodded in consent. One of them shouted 'Allahu Akbar[26]!' and before long, everybody was proclaiming God's greatness.

Bairam Khan raised his hand and said, 'You have spoken well, my friend. Thus, it shall be done. Let the astrologers prepare their horoscopes, by all means. We will head south tomorrow.'

The Amirs retired to their own quarters. As soon as everybody had gone, Bairam Khan began pacing up and down the tent.

After a while, he mumbled, 'No, this has gone far enough.'

Then, turning to me, as if he had failed to notice me before, he said, 'The coming days will be difficult and demanding. Perhaps Your Majesty wishes to go hunting this afternoon? The plains around Sirhind are pleasant, games abound. Your Majesty will not have the opportunity

---

[26] *Allāhu Akbar*, 'God is greater', or 'God is the Greatest'. *Akbar*: comparative / superlative of the Arabic adjective *Kabīr*, great.

to distract Himself in the coming days.'

I, of course, suspected what Bairam Khan was up to, but chose to say nothing. I realized he was probably right, and to be honest, despite the gravity of the situation, the prospect of being on my own for a couple of hours was extremely tempting.

I rode back into the camp near sunset. My attendants handed the game we had killed to the kitchen servants. I proceeded to the imperial tent, where Maulana Pir Muhammad Shirwani helped me to dismount.

'I need to inform Your Majesty,' he stammered, 'that Tardi Beg is dead.'

'Tell me how this happened,' I replied, not in the least surprised, yet trying to hide my anger, that an important measure like this had been taken without consulting or even informing me.

'Bairam Khan sent me to Tardi Beg, to invite him for a meeting in his pavilion. At first, Tardi Beg refused to come, but I replied, truthfully, that the Khan Khanan had requested to see him to discuss the strength of Hemu's army and the strategy to be followed. Reluctantly, Tardi Beg then accompanied me to the Khan Khanan, where he received a cool but courteous welcome. The Khan Khanan asked a thousand questions about Hemu's forces, the number and weaponry of his troops, their battle tactics, and so on.

The conversation went well, as long as they were discussing cannon, cavalry and the like. But when Tardi Beg again started talking about Hemu's elephants, in an effort to explain why he had failed to defend Dilli, Bairam Khan burst into a torrent of abuse.'

'Spare me your imbecile ramblings about elephants raised by the devil!' he yelled. 'You are a despicable coward, and an idiot as well. If you had any honor in your miserable carcass, or even a bit of sense in your thick swine's head, you would have held Dilli, seizing every opportunity to weaken Hemu's forces and wear him out. A couple of days later, we would have had the opportunity to attack him from behind, cut off his supplies and fight him on two fronts. And now, thanks to your cowardice and stupidity, we will have to face him in the open field.'

He paused, and resumed, in a much friendlier tone of voice, 'In difficult times like these, Tardi Beg Khan, it is important to stay united. The best way to redeem yourself, and to have everybody forget this incident, is to lead your men into battle and fight bravely. If you can promise me that, I will never again mention this incident.'

'I don't need any favors from a Shia heretic,' Tardi Beg retorted angrily.

'Besides, I have not decided yet. But I will act as I damn well please,' he added defiantly.

The Khan Khanan did not reply at all. Not a muscle moved in his face. It was as if he had not heard the insult. Addressing himself to me, as if Tardi Beg was no longer present in the tent, he said softly, 'It is almost time for noon prayers. I need to wash and prepare for them.'

As soon as Bairam Khan left the tent, two of his guards stepped in. Before Tardi Beg had a chance to move, they drew their swords and plunged them into his chest. As he sank down, dying, they wiped off the blades on his clothes, courteously bowed to me, and went out again, without a word.

Tardi Beg still tried to say something, gasping for air, blood gushing out of his mouth, his fingers clasping his own clothes as if they could save him. But he died a few moments later.

Soon after, the Khan Khanan stepped back into the tent, his face and hands still wet from washing for prayers.

'There was no other way, my friend,' he said to me, without looking at Tardi Beg's body, 'Please join me for the noon prayer.'

We went out and worshiped with the others. After prayers, he ordered his guards to bury the corpse outside the camp, and went out to inspect the troops.'

'Where is Bairam Khan now?' I asked.

'He has requested me to read this letter to Your Majesty,' Pir Muhammad replied, taking out a folded piece of paper from his clothes.

To this day, I still remember how the letter went, almost word for word.

'Your most noble and gracious Imperial Majesty,' it started, 'I humbly, respectfully and desperately implore Your Majesty to remain firmly convinced that the only motives for my decisions and actions have been the strength of Your Majesty's Empire, the stability of Your Majesty's Throne, and the safety of Your Majesty's life.

Being wise for his age, and gifted with astute insight in worldly matters, Your Majesty will agree with me that the execution of Tardi Beg had become inevitable. He was quickly becoming a source of bitter division in our army. It was only a matter of time before he would have instilled his own treacherous cowardice in the hearts of many of Your Majesty's subjects.

Indeed, it is my honest belief that if this treacherous coward had been allowed to remain alive, Your Majesty would have been at great risk of losing his throne, and maybe even his life. It was therefore my sacred obligation, before Allah, and before the memory of Your Majesty's blessed father, who has entrusted Your Majesty's safety to my care, to get rid Your Majesty's Court from the presence of this treacherous element.

I have chosen not to fight and kill him myself, as I would have liked, but to have him summarily executed, as he deserved. Indeed, it should be clear to all, that Tardi Beg's death was not a personal issue between me and him, but a matter pertaining to Your Majesty's Throne.

I clearly understand that I have deserved Your Majesty's anger, not having requested Your Majesty's permission before inflicting capital punishment on one of Your Majesty's army leaders. However, knowing the kindness and compassion of Your Majesty's noble heart, and fearing that Your Majesty's youthful inexperience might cause him to underestimate the clear and immediate danger threatening him and his rightful throne, I have thought it advisable to take matters in my own hands. If Your Majesty, in His infinite goodness, had decided to spare Tardi Beg's life, I would have been faced with the most painful of dilemmas: to obey my Emperor, and in doing so, betray his best interests, or to serve him through disobedience. Desiring at all costs to avoid such a difficult choice, I have elected to do what I know was right.

I humbly beg Your Majesty to take pity on me and to continue to admit me in his noble Presence. However, should my insolence have displeased Your Majesty too much, I shall take my leave, depart from Your Majesty's dominions, and, if Allah wills it, retire to Mekkah.

I remain at all times Your Majesty's most humble, obedient and dedicated servant.

Bairam Khan Badakhshani, Wakil, Khan Khanan, *Sipahsalar Itizad-i-Daulat Qahira,*

Son of Sayf Ali Beg Badakhshani,
Son of Mahmud Ali Beg Badakhshani,

Son of Pir Ali Beg Kurdistani,
Son of Mir Ali Shukr Beg Baharlu, of the Nation of the Qaraquilu Turks

Without a word, I went inside the imperial tent, leaving Pir Muhammad standing outside, still holding the letter in his hands. I had the greatest difficulty not to start screaming and stamping my feet in anger. Such insolence! How did he dare to treat me like a child. How did he dare to take such important decisions on his own without even consulting me.

I forced myself to think as calmly as I could. The tone of his letter was obedient enough, but that did not fool me. Had he not sent Pir Muhammad as his messenger, rather than talking to me, face to face? Had he not clearly stated that he would leave the Empire and go into exile to Mekkah, rather than humbly submitting to my verdict? Did such an arrogant, headstrong attitude not clearly show the limits of his obedience and loyalty? Could I still trust him? Whom did he really serve? The seeds of doubt, already sown, grew their poisonous roots in my soul.

But what was I to do? I could not possibly afford to dismiss the most competent and respected leader of my army. Had he not offered me his loyalty? Had he not referred to his forefathers, who had been faithful supporters of my ancestors? Moreover, as far as Tardi Beg was concerned, had his decision not been the right one as always?

I stepped back outside the imperial tent, where Pir Muhammad was still standing, nervously crumpling up Bairam Khan's letter.

'Tell the Khan Khanan,' I said, 'that this is no time for us to be divided. Tell him I need him here to help me lead the army against the infidel Hemu and his followers. Tell him, he has done well in punishing Tardi Beg,' I added. 'Tell him...'

I wanted to say, 'Tell him I have forgiven him for taking this decision without asking my permission,' but I chose not to lie.

'That's all,' I said. 'Go now.'

The coming days were spent in preparation for the coming battle with Hemu.

At least for some time, Tardi Beg's execution had the desired effect. There was no more talk of fleeing to Kabul. Nevertheless, the morale of our troops left much to be desired. Hemu's generalship and the strength of his army was the subject of many a whispered conversation. As Abu-l Fazl described it, Perturbation found its way into the hearts of imperial servants, through the instrumentality of empty-headed babblers, from whom no army is ever free, or rather, there are armies of such.

Bairam Khan and the officers did their best to counter the growing defeatism. Through a judicial mixture of encouragement, promises, veiled and open threats, and emotional appeals to the men's sense of honor and religion, they at least managed to keep an outer semblance of order and discipline. The few deserters all got caught, and their severed heads, on spikes near the tents where they had been camping, dissuaded others from following their example. The astrologers, after having examined the shoulder blades of a freshly slaughtered sheep, again proclaimed the invincibility of my stars with such vehement authority and persuasion that I began to believe them myself.

Hemu, who must have been informed about our troubles through his spies, eagerly seized the opportunity. He marched north towards us, as fast as he could, which was wise. One should never hesitate to seize an opportunity as it presents itself. In the process, however, he got a little overconfident.

He sent his artillery (rockets, cannon, mortars and the like) ahead towards Panipat, escorted by a relatively weak vanguard of ordinary troops. Undoubtedly, his plan was to prepare a defensive artillery position for his army, similar to the one my grandfather Babur had used thirty years before. At Panipat, he would block our passage, forcing us to turn back and flee, or to risk a suicidal frontal attack. He was out to destroy us, exactly the same way my own grandfather had destroyed his rival.

Had he succeeded in his plan, we would indeed have had no alternative but to refuse battle and flee north. Ours was the smaller army. We would most certainly have been annihilated, had we dared to attack that defensive position.

Bairam Khan immediately sensed the danger when our scouts informed us about the arrival of Hemu's vanguard at Panipat.

'We absolutely must seize that artillery before the main body of Hemu's army arrives, Your Majesty,' he explained. 'If the enemy manages to deploy it in the narrow passage at Panipat, we have no alternative but to turn back as fast as possible and build up a defensive position of our own, further north. Let us send ahead a strong force of the best of our cavalry. God willing, they still may arrive in time. If they fail, they will still be able to extricate themselves and join us back here.'

Thus, it was done. Bairam Khan ordered a vanguard of the best and bravest to ride like the wind to Panipat, still about ten *kos* [27]further south, and to seize Hemu's cannons at all costs. We would follow them as fast as we could with the remainder of the army. According to Abu-l Fazl (writing many years later, about things he never witnessed and that happened when he was only six years old), I led the troops with a tranquil mind, an open brow, a prayerful heart, a just intent, a right principle, a wide capacity, a strong hand, a firm foot, a high spirit, a lofty soul, a right plan, a shining countenance, and smiling lips.

He always was a shameless flatterer.

The next day, scouts came with reassuring news. Hemu's artillery was ours. The enemy had fled in disarray without much resistance. There had been no losses from our side.

'This is of course excellent news, Your Majesty,' Bairam Khan said when the scouts had left, 'but the fight is far from over. Hemu can no longer use this artillery against us, but neither can we use it against him, unless we somehow manage to arrive there ahead of his army. This means that he would have to stay where he is right now, and I don't think he will make that kind of mistake.'

He was right. Hemu, much closer to Panipat than we were, drove his army as fast as he could. It was clear what he was up to, to get his artillery back and bring it into position, or at the very least, prevent us from using it against him.

The morning of Panjshanbeh, the 24th of Aban of the first year of my reign[28], when we were still about three kos removed from the town, scouts came in with the news we feared. Hemu's army had arrived and was launching a massive attack. Our vanguard troops, knowing their duty, were fighting back as hard as they could. They were, however, vastly outnumbered and in dire need of help.

Leaving the slow artillery carts and the supply train behind us under the protection of a small rearguard, we rushed towards Panipat,

---

[27] The Kos is a distance measure, roughly equivalent to 2.5 miles or 4 km.

[28] Thursday, 5 November 1556 (Julian Calendar).

with as many combat troops as possible—all of our horse archers and heavy cavalry, and a large number of musketeers and archers. The foot soldiers were riding, by two or three, on the backs of reserve horses, camels and elephants.

Bairam Khan, in full battledress, with glittering iron scale breast armour over a full body suit of mail, personally led the march, galloping back and forth alongside the column on a shiny, pitch-black stallion, his black mantle flying behind him. The mail neck and shoulder protection, hanging down from his spiked Turkish helmet, jumped up and down with each bound of his horse. The men cheered as he passed them by. He looked invincible; and, I hate to admit, I felt jealous of him.

By the time we arrived on the battlefield, the brave men of our vanguard were on the verge of defeat. The left and right wings of Hemu's army, war elephants and Afghan cavalry, were pushing forward, in an effort to outflank and encircle them. Our men were fighting desperately to prevent this, but it was too uneven a battle. Tears came to my eyes when I saw some of the best of our men killed by crossbows and musket marksmen before they even had the chance to fight back. God does indeed favor the larger army.

Bairam Khan left me in the rear, with close to three thousand of our best men on the fastest horses. They would be able to bring me into safety if things would turn out badly for us. He galloped to the front of the ranks, slid down the nose bar of his helmet, and made his horse prance, as he drew his curved Turkoman sabre. Keeping the horse balancing on its hind legs, its forehooves clawing in the air and iron scale armour glittering in the sun, he held his sword high, and shouted, 'Allahu Akbar! Yah Muin! Allahu Akbar![29]. The battle cry was taken over by all of our army, as the battle drums signalled the order to attack.

The army entered into battle as instructed. The main body of our cavalry stormed forward in a two-pronged attack along the left and right flanks, to relieve our vanguard. They were followed by as many musketeers and archers on foot as could be transported to the front line. The centre was formed by the remaining foot soldiers, about four thousand horsemen, backed up by our elephants, and the returning vanguard cavalry. We were visibly outnumbered. Hopefully, our

[29] Allāhu Akbar: God is greater / the greatest. Yah Mu'īn: Oh (Divine) Helper.

rearguard would arrive in time.

For some time, our cavalry onslaught halted Hemu's advance on the flanks. The Afghan enemy horsemen, their mounts already exhausted from the earlier battle, suffered heavy losses, and a considerable number of enemy marksmen were killed by a well-directed volley of musket fire. Many of our cavalry reached the enemy lines, and I saw untold acts of bravery when I witnessed groups of our horsemen picking out an individual enemy elephant and harassing it with arrows and distracting it, while one or two of them quickly dismounted to stab it deep in the belly with long lances.

Yet, despite those initial successes, the battle did not go well. There seemed to be an unlimited supply of fresh enemy troops, and, as Tardi Beg had warned us, most of the enemy elephants were remarkably well disciplined, obedient to their mahauts and pushing forward despite many wounds. Slowly but surely, our flanks were driven back to the centre, and our losses began exceeding theirs.

Suddenly, the ground started shaking, as we saw a grey wall of elephants rushing straight towards us. Hemu, who must have seen the weakness of our centre formation, and probably wanting to finish the battle before the arrival of our artillery, was moving in for the kill. Judging by the royal canopy in the rear of their formation, he was personally leading the charge. Thousands of Hindu soldiers were shouting, *Gopal! Gopal!*, and I remember wondering, despite the excitement of the moment, what their battle cry meant[30].

It was clear we were in desperate trouble, our centre vastly outnumbered, and the left and right wings, in dire straits themselves, unable to come to our rescue.

'You have not won yet, you stinking infidel pig,' I heard Bairam Khan hiss, as he rode forward to direct the defense of our centre.

Despite their small numbers and the desperate situation, our central cavalry performed admirably, charging the enemy front in well-timed, successive waves, each delivering a volley of arrows in quick succession, while our infantry archers and musketeers moved their mobile defenses forward to support them, killing most of the enemy troops riding the front line of elephants. Thousands upon thousands of arrows were shot

[30] Gopāl, Sanskrit Gopāla: cowherd, protector of cows; one of Lord Krsna's names.

slantwise in the air towards the enemy ranks behind the front line, in an attempt to bring disarray to the enemy onslaught.

Alas, it was of little avail. There were just too many of them. It would not be long before we would be forced to flee or be annihilated. Bairam Khan and the Amirs began organizing the retreat, creating openings in the rear formations for the front-line cavalry to fall back through. Maybe, we could still escape with a sizeable force and come back to fight another day.

Then, suddenly, for no apparent reason, the enemy onslaught faltered. Groups of two, four, ten elephants broke the ranks and abruptly turned around. Only moments later, the entire enemy host was fleeing in utter panic.

We had won! How could this be?

Fortunately, our commanders kept their calm, and our troops, despite the hardship of the battle and the heavy losses we had sustained, knew their duty. In circumstances like this, many armies have failed to take advantage of the situation. It is only natural for soldiers who have narrowly escaped death and are exhausted, to rejoice in victory and break off the fight. That, however, is a mistake. A fleeing host of enemies may come back to fight another day, and should therefore be hunted down, always.

Wave after wave of our cavalry, including most of the three thousand that had been guarding me, went after the enemy and slaughtered them by the hundreds.

'Spare the mahauts and the Afghans who surrender their weapons,' Bairam Khan ordered. Indeed, a wise conqueror thinks of the battles to come, knows how to combine firmness with magnanimity, and turns some of today's enemies into tomorrow's grateful allies.

The pursuit was still ongoing when it became clear what had caused the sudden collapse of the enemy host. An officer came to us with, strapped to horseback, what seemed to be the meagre corpse of a dwarfish, bony little man, the great Hemu himself. He had been turned over to us by his own mahaut.

Two men pulled him off the horse and held him by the arms to keep him from falling down. He was still alive, but barely so. An arrow was sticking out of the socket of his left eye. It had hit him from the right, probably glancing off the nose bar of his helmet, piercing his left eye, and entering the bone in the back of the socket towards his left temple, where it got stuck, ostensibly without entering the brain. It must have been a stray arrow, one of the many hundreds shot randomly in the air to harass the enemy troops in the back. It had been a lucky shot, or, as Abu-l Fazl preferred to put it in more flowery language, an arrow from the bent bow of Divine Wrath.

I know, my son. Were this an adventure book, I would be accused of bad writing. But this, alas, is how it actually happened. I would have much preferred our victory to have been more glorious, but I cannot help it. Our entire Empire has been founded on one lucky stray arrow, and God only knows what Hindustan would have looked like today if Hemu had stayed a few paces more to the rear.

I do not know whether Hemu was fully conscious when they brought him before me. He did not say a word and did not react to anything we said or did. He just hung there between our men, his left hand covering his injured eye, the arrow sticking out between his fingers, blood flowing over his face and hand. He was breathing heavily, obviously in a lot of pain, moaning slightly each time he exhaled.

I kept staring at this little man. He looked so harmless and pitiful, despite the gold thread loincloth and the shining armour and heavy jewellery covering his frail chest. His head, bald with only a few plucks of hair on the sides and the back looked like the skull of some heinous kind of bird. How could this pathetic, lowborn little Hindu have become so powerful?

Bairam Khan drew his sword and handed it to me. It was time for me to earn the title of Ghazi [31].

I know that Abu-l Fazl, as I said was but a small child at the time of the battle and never witnessed it, wrote that I magnanimously refused to kill Hemu, saying that there was no honor in slaying a defenseless wounded enemy. Like many other such stories, he probably heard this one from the mouths of flattering courtiers and repeated it, in a commendable attempt to demonstrate my nobility of character.

Alas and of course, it is not true. What would have been the point of arguing with my guardian, who had just saved my Throne, if not my life? How could I leave the death of so many of the best of my men

[31] *Ghāzī*: conquerer, victor, slayer (of the infidel).

unavenged? Why would I risk undermining my own authority and reputation with those who survived? Besides, in the state Hemu was in, killing him quickly seemed to be the most merciful thing I could do for him.

It is true, however, that I did hesitate for a moment, thinking to myself, as I stood there with Bairam Khan offering his sword to me, how regrettable it was, that a man of such outstanding ability could not be put to better use in my own service.

'Go on, Your Majesty', Bairam Khan insisted, interrupting my thoughts. I took the sword, and the men let go of Hemu's arms. He sank to his knees; I struck him in the back of the neck before he could fall to the ground. I felt the spine cracking under Bairam Khan's sabre, but the blow was not strong enough to sever the head completely. The other bystanders sank their swords into the twitching corpse, anxious to stain their swords with the blood of so powerful an enemy. Bairam Khan took back his sword, and severed Hemu's head from the trunk, cutting through the throat with an ostensibly effortless, routine movement of the wrist, like an experienced butcher.

'Iskandar Khan Uzbeg,' he instructed, 'take half of the cavalry, on the freshest horses, and hunt down as many survivors as you can find. Proceed to Dilli, and occupy the city. We will join you there as soon as possible. Shah Quli Mahram, have the rest of the troops build a tower of heads in front of the city's north gate; we will assemble there as soon as it is finished. Collect the spoils, and get the army ready to head further south, as soon as the rearguard and the artillery have arrived.'

About two hours later, the entire army had assembled in front of Panipat‘s northern wall in battle array, including over one thousand five hundred elephants, ten thousand horses, and all the artillery taken from Hemu's army. Mounds of spoils had been assembled and sorted: jewellery, gold, food supplies, muskets, gunpowder, swords, bows, arrows, spears, pikes and other arms and equipment. Towering above all the piles was a pyramid of over ten thousand severed heads.

In case you are wondering, Salim, the heap had the height of a tall man riding on the back of a camel; and at its foot, you needed about twelve camels to surround it. I saw then, why Genghis Khan and Amir Temur had so often done this during their conquests. Nothing sends a clearer message than a pile of enemy heads. I remember feeling horrified and fascinated at the same time. I could not stop staring at them. It seems my mind's eye still sees every detail. The heads still wearing helmets or turbans, and the bare ones; the necks cut off clean and straight, and the ones with frayed edges, as if the head had been torn rather than cut off; the eyes and mouths closed as if sound asleep, the ones staring and gaping in horror as if still alive, the ones with a careless, drunken look, with sleepy, half-open eyes and drooling mouths; most of them covered with blood and dust as could be expected, but a large number, surprisingly clean. Many of them, I would say at least one out of six, had ostensibly been killed while running away. In the back of their heads was a short, straight, clean cut, about the length of a middle finger, where the flange of a war hammer had entered their skull, or a broad, deep dent, with reddish, jagged edges, where the mace had slammed into the back of their helmet.

Under the thundering sound of the kettledrums, Bairam Khan and I rode towards the pile of heads. Our horses, at a restrained trot, proudly raised their forelegs high at each step. Bairam Khan, still in full battle armour, was guiding his horse with his knees, in the fashion of the great steppe warriors who had been his ancestors.

His left hand carried Hemu's head, holding its hair. The arrow had been pulled out of the eye socket, undoubtedly in order to avoid any misunderstandings as to the cause of death. In his right hand, he held a heavy cavalry lance with a long, straight, sword-like blade, without any barbs. Four yak tails were hanging from its shaft: it was clearly a lance brought into Hindustan from the frigid highlands of the faraway kingdom of Fergana by my grandfather Babur.

We halted, facing the troops, our backs to the pile of heads.

'Behold, the heads of those who wanted to oppose us!' Bairam Khan shouted, looking over his shoulder, his face and voice full of contempt.

'And behold, the head of the mighty infidel Hemu!' he added, holding the severed head high. 'Slain by the noble hand of our august young Emperor, his Imperial Majesty, Jalal-ud-Din Muhammad Akbar Padshah Ghazi! Hail to the Emperor!'

Accompanied by the drums, the troops chanted, 'Padshah Salamat, Padshah Salamat!', for what seemed an eternity.

'My friends, my brothers,' Bairam Khan shouted, stopping the clamour, 'our enemies call us Mughals, because we came from up north. Our enemies say we are but a bunch of savages. Well, let them. Let them. I, for one, consider it the greatest honor to be called a Mongol, when I think of our invincible forefathers. Today, my brothers, we have entered history and proven ourselves to be their worthy sons. We have wiped out an overwhelmingly powerful enemy army, vastly superior to us in numbers, animals, weapons and equipment. We have captured many spoils and rest assured, my brothers. All of you will be much richer tomorrow than you woke up this morning.

There is no doubt in my mind, that all this has only been possible with the support of Allah Himself, praise be upon Him!

My brothers, we have been victorious in today's battle with a small army. But now, we have the means to build one of the mightiest armies the world has even seen. Nothing, absolutely nothing or nobody will stop us now. Allah Himself will be our Guide to further conquest and glory!'

The crowd cheered enthusiastically.

'And let our enemies make no mistake,' Bairam Khan said, casually tossing Hemu's head in the sand. He paused for a moment, until it had almost stopped rolling. From the hip, he thrust the lance down the severed neck. He sure knew how to handle a lance: the pike had penetrated the base of Hemu's skull, and its tip was sticking out at the top of the head, like a bloody, malformed kind of horn. The face was ghastly, with the bleeding, empty left socket and the right eyeball, upturned and white, seemingly staring at the crowd. The mouth was hanging wide open, gaping like the jaws of a fish of prey; the long, bony teeth dirty dark red with the blood that had entered the mouth at the time of death. A few twines of sticky hair were dangling from the side and the back of the head. I do not think a devil in hell could look more hideous.

'Let our enemies make no mistake,' Bairam Khan repeated. 'They better get used to the idea: the Mughals are here to stay!'

Bairam Khan shook the head off the lance, and barked his orders.

'Khwaja Ambar Nazir, take three hundred good men and bring this head to Kabul. Inform the members of the court about our glorious victory. Tell them that it will not take long before all the lands of Padshah Humayun will be fully under control. They will be relieved to hear that the days of the glorious Padshah Babur are back. Request the high-born ladies of the court to kindly prepare themselves for the journey, and join us here in Hindustan in due course.

Abdullah Khan Uzbeg, take Hemu's trunk, and hang it from a gibbet, jewels and all, for everyone to see. Let it stay there until there's nothing but a few rotten bones.

The rest of you, army leaders, have your men bury the dead, and have the camp prepared for the night. You may tell your men to help themselves to extra rations of meat, and feast and celebrate, but not too late into the night. Tomorrow at dawn, we proceed to Dilli!'

Fifth Letter

دلّی

Dilli

Iskandar Khan Uzbeg had done his job well. There was not a single incident on our way to Dilli.

Along the road were mounds of severed heads, alternated with rows of heads on spikes, and here and there, a corpse that had been hanged or impaled. I guess defeat and annihilation had come much too close for our men to show mercy towards any surviving enemies. As Abu-l Fazl put it, 'Iskandar Khan Uzbeg delivered some of the malignant and useless from the prison of existence, and put the distracted inhabitants of the country in order.' He always did have a way with words.

Dilli itself, its inhabitants having remained as neutral as possible throughout the conflict, had remained unharmed, and the people had gathered to welcome us. Still, the Uzbeg had taken no chances. His archers could be seen on every rooftop along the way, and groups of horsemen were standing guard, ready to disperse the crowd at the slightest sign of trouble.

We entered the city in triumph at an hour chosen by the astrologers.

It must have been an overwhelmingly impressive sight for the people. To be honest, I was quite impressed myself.

I was riding the tallest elephant of them all, Hemu's preferred fighting champion Hawai, an absolutely huge, vicious mountain of muscles, now deceptively meek and docile under the hands of

Hemu's mahaut, one of the many Hindustani elephant drivers who had been spared after the battle.

I would have much preferred to ride Hawai myself, as I would do so many times later in life. You know I adore animals: horses, elephants, camels, dogs, hunting leopards, hawks. I don't know whether there is any truth in the Hindu belief of reincarnation, but if there is, I must have been an animal attendant in one of my previous lives. But of course, an Emperor does not drive his own elephant. I was sitting on Hemu's throne in the turret on Hawai's back, under the imperial canopy, wearing my coronation robe and turban, and many jewels of gold and pearls and precious stones, all of which had belonged to my father and his father before him.

For the first time, I really felt like the true Emperor, the focal point of the entire parade. The crowd cheered enthusiastically. I could not help being much impressed at the thought that all these people were now my subjects.

With the thunder of the drums pounding in my chest, and the interminable column in front and behind me, I felt the blessings and protection of God, and despite the excitement of the day, a warm, almost peaceful feeling came upon my soul. I made a solemn vow, to myself, to God, to my ancestors, and to the thousands who had died for me at Panipat, that I would make good use of all this military might. Never again would I allow myself to get into a position where I would need to fight for my life. On the contrary, I would make sure any opponents would be running for theirs. Somehow, I knew that my life, from that moment on, would be one of conquest and triumph. It was my destiny, and God's manifest will. He had given me victory against impossible odds. He wanted me to become one of the greatest kings the world had ever seen. I was determined not to disappoint Him.

The parade arrived at the imperial fortress near the Yamuna River[32].

There, in front of its gates, Bairam Khan and I supervised the distribution of the spoils of war. As Bairam Khan had promised, the men all became rich that day. We kept almost nothing for the Imperial treasure. There would be ample occasions in the future to replenish it.

32 Also called Jumna.

Right now, it was more important to secure the undivided loyalty of our men.

Honorary titles and positions were given to leaders who had distinguished themselves in the battle, Abdullah and Iskandar Khan Uzbeg, Ali Quli Khan Shaibani, and a number of others. All of them were rewarded with the governorship of a province. The border regions of our territories were, thus, entrusted to the care of experienced and competent commanders.

On Bairam Khan's explicit request, Pir Muhammad Shirwani was given the title of Khan, as well as the prestigious function of *Nasir ul-Mulk*, Helper of the Realm. He was, thus, to become the supervisor of my personal service and household and would assume his new duties a few days later. For the time being, he was sent with a strong group of cavalry to Alwar, west of Agra, to bring that area under control and deal with Hemu's family.

He came back three days later, with a train of carts laden with treasure, and the head of Hemu's elderly father. There had been a brief struggle with remaining enemy troops. Most had been killed, and a few survivors had fled southwest towards Ajmir, duly pursued by a force of our men.

It appeared that Hemu's father had been brought before Pir Muhammad. In a gesture of generosity and religious zeal, he had offered the old man his life, if he would convert to Islam. He refused with dignity.

'For eighty years I've worshiped my God according to my religion,' he said. 'Why should I change it at this time, and why should I, merely from fear of my life, and without understanding it, come into your way of worship?' Pir Muhammad had not wasted any time on religious debate, and answered him in the tongue of the sword, as the chroniclers put it.

I could not help feeling a bit sad when I heard the story. What glory is there in killing a grief-struck, elderly man? And I was very much intrigued by his last words. He had spoken about 'my Go', rather than 'the Gods', in plural; didn't these Hindus believe in many gods, rather than one?

And I wondered what God's verdict over him would be. Would this defenseless old man really be thrown in hell for having refused to accept the true religion of Islam? Somehow, I thought not. Clearly, the old man's intention had been to serve God, however misguided his superstitious idolatry might have been. Would that not suffice to obtain the blessings of God's mercy? If I would forgive him, would God not do the same?

For the first time in my life, the thought entered my mind, that religion, at least the way we understand it, is much less important to God than we think. He attaches more importance to what people do and what lives in their hearts than to their ways of worship, or the prophets they believe in.

Anyway, Hemu's father's death confirmed Pir Muhammad Shirwani's fast-growing reputation as a competent but ruthless army leader. The appointment of this humble mullah to the position of *Nasir ul-Mulk* was an important promotion indeed, but Bairam Khan clearly wanted to reward whom he thought was his loyal ally. It would, alas, prove to be one of his rare mistakes. As will be explained later, it did not take long before Pir Muhammad conveniently forgot the duty of gratitude he owed his benefactor.

I have had many similar experiences myself, my son. The promotion of a meritorious, commendable person is not always a good move. It may bring to the surface certain weaknesses, which had hitherto remained hidden. This is the case, in particular, for authority-related vices, such as pride, conceitedness and arrogance.

Make it a habit, my son, to observe the ones you have promoted. How are they treating their subordinates? How do they behave when they meet their former and current peers? And how about their attitude towards you? Any sign of arrogance? Any conspicuous, cowering servility, hiding other, more dangerous feelings? A wise monarch, my son, should make it his task to understand the human soul and fathom its hidden depths.

Our triumphant entry into Dilli culminated in sumptuous celebrations, designed to impress, even more than to entertain, with abundant and delicious food of all kinds, and valuable gifts for everyone in the city. The highlight of the evening was a display of fireworks (a Rose Garden of Fire, as my good old friend Abu-l Fazl called it in his chronicle), whereby a large puppet representing Hemu was burning amidst the dancing and cheering crowd.

The next day, for the first time in my life, I woke up as the chief resident of the Dilli palace. Finally, my life as Emperor had started. I must say, I have the fondest memories of the weeks that followed.

Bairam Khan did see to it that my education continued. I had grown quite fond of Mir Abdul-Latif's lessons, starting with readings from some book or other, followed by discussion, reflection, and comparison with other books, a pastime I have continued to appreciate throughout my entire life.

Other than that, there were few pressing affairs of the state. The military situation was stable. The new regional governors were getting organized. I had, thus, ample opportunity to get acquainted with the daily life at the Imperial Court.

To be honest, I must confess that the duties of kingship did not occupy my mind as much as they do now. I thought of little else but enjoying my newfound life of luxury. I walked around the palace and its gardens, delighted in the thought that it all belonged to me. I loved the reverence, and the constant attention surrounding me, with literally hundreds of people going out of their way to please and serve me, to fulfil and even anticipate my every wish.

I could not believe the variety and quality of food that suddenly became available to me, day and night: the most exquisite meats, fish, fowl, vegetables, fruits, nuts and sweets, imported from the most faraway places. What a world of difference from the frugal, hasty meals I had taken in the days before the battle of Panipat.

I particularly enjoyed the cold drinks they served me, deliciously chilled with real ice, shipped to the palace on large, flat-bottomed barks traveling the Yamuna. Fresh ice, harvested from the mountains far up north, still very much outside our dominions at that time, acquired at great expense, brought to the palace cellars after a journey of several days, just for my comfort and that of a handful of others who could afford to pay for it, and were fortunate enough to be associated with me.

I believe I can more or less guess what you are thinking as you are reading this, my son. I do realize you are accustomed to so much more than a bit of ice, brought to you from Kashmir. What seemed to me the luxuries of Paradise, would probably look rather frugal to the both of us now, accustomed as we are to all the opulence the world has to offer. The old palace in Dilli is nothing, compared to the lofty buildings and entire cities that have been built during my reign.

Nevertheless, do not take your wealth for granted, my son. It has taken a lot of hard work. And God does not mind His creatures taking pleasure in the beauty and the many delights of His creation, for He is Himself the source of all pleasure and enjoyment. But He does not like the self-indulgent, the lazy, the weaklings who forget their duties.

But as I said, those thoughts were not on my mind back then. I just wanted to explore and enjoy this wonderful, exciting new life that had been given to me.

I must say, Pir Muhammad, now proudly called Pir Muhammad Khan since his promotion, was doing an excellent job in his new assignment as *Nasir ul-Mulk*, the head of my household and personal assistant.

He entrusted most of the daily management of the palace, the food, the decoration and such things, to Maham Anaga, the dear woman who had been my chief nurse and foster mother throughout my youth. She was a great help to him, always busy, never leaving a detail unchecked.

But Pir Muhammad kept himself personally involved as well. He tried his very best to see to it that my every desire was fulfilled, before I expressed it. Sometimes, before I even thought about it myself. He proved himself to be knowledgeable and wise, in a practical, down-to-earth sort of way.

Knowing how fond I was of outdoor activities, he immediately organized a hunting party for me. It was a gazelle hunt with some of the best cheetahs, fast as lightning. In my early years, I was quite fond of all kinds of hunting; dangerous wild boar hunts on horseback with lances; drives with hundreds of beaters; tiger hunts, with muskets and bows on the back of an elephant; fowl hunting with hawks and falcons. But I've always had a particular weakness for cheetahs. They move with such majesty. They are such a fast and efficient killers, so wild and dangerous, yet so surprisingly meek and docile when tamed.

When I returned from that first hunt, he had arranged entertainment with acrobats, music and dancing, during dinner.

He must have been watching me looking at the dancing girls. The golden jewels adorning their hair, face, body, arms and legs; their beautiful silk and muslin dresses; the graceful curve and roundness of their hips; the elegant shape of their legs in the long transparent skirts or trousers; their breasts, delightfully visible through those gauze fabrics, so aptly called woven air[33]; the enchanting movements of their bejewelled arms and long-fingered hands; and the elegant, tip-toe steps of their shapely feet, delightfully adorned with golden ankle chains and toe rings.

'Would Your Majesty like a companion for tonight?' Pir Muhammad Khan inquired discreetly, without even a semblance of that vulgar tone of conspiracy, which people tend to use when they are alluding to the desires of the flesh. He had asked the question in the same innocent, self-evident way as if he had been inquiring when and what I wanted to have for dinner.

'Yes, why not,' I replied, trying to sound as casual and uninterested as possible.

'Unless Your Majesty instructs me otherwise, I will send him a different girl every night,' he replied, again sensing what was on my youthful mind.

Ah, my son, what can I tell you about those carefree, blissful first nights? They were sheer heaven. What a world of difference with my first clumsy amorous attempts with young serving-girls as a twelve-year-old in the palace of my father. Then, it had all been hasty and messy and disappointing. Now, it was absolute perfection, the opportunity created by royal birth, wealth and power. The excitement of newly discovered, untrodden paths of pleasure, and the lust and self-evident vigour of youth.

I hope and pray that after my death, God will not send me to hell. But even if He does, I will always remain grateful for the glimpse of paradise in those first nights in Dilli. The luxurious baths; the silk and satin sheets; the scented oils and sweet perfumes; entrancing dances; golden jewels on soft naked skin; the twisting of perfectly rounded hips; the delightful, gentle wiggling of proud, naked breasts; the sweet faces, all eyes and smiling teeth in the soft candle light; the taste of mango juice and honey, trickled on firm, dark nipples; the giggling chases in the rooms and corridors of the royal quarters; the soft veils playfully binding the wrists of sweet, smiling captives; the scent of soft, velvet

[33] The muslin worn by Mughal ladies had such romantic names as *daft hawa* (woven air), *ab-i-rawan* (running water, and *shabnam* (night dew) (Early 2007, 138).

skin; the tender kisses on moist and avid lips; the soft hands and mouths everywhere; the finger nails, clawing deep in the skin of my back at the moment of divine climax.

There were even times when, in the impetuous rashness of youth, I asked Pir Muhammad Khan to send me two or three girls at once, but after a few attempts, I gave up on that practice. Despite the promise it had seemed to offer in my young, lustful imagination, it came out disappointingly messy, much less pleasurable than I had hoped. More bodies, it appeared, do not necessarily lead to more passion. No, much sweeter are the memories of the times when there was kindness besides lust, friendly conversation besides passion, the nights when I peacefully fell asleep against the back of my companion, my hand on her breast.

Do not worry, my son. I will not go into any further detail. I know children find it distinctly awkward to hear about their parents' amorous relations. And even among friends, and after many cups of wine, only the coarse and the vulgar will go into sordid little details about their bedroom adventures.

Yet, it seems important to me that you should know the whole story of my life, and learn from it. I think I do have to tell you something about the weaknesses of my youth, for it is about time you learned to overcome yours.

I do not want to hurt your feelings, but until a few months ago, you were little more than a pathetic drunk, well under way to drink yourself to death. You may be learned, intelligent, and refined, but you are also lazy and self-indulgent. This is, of course, understandable given the opulence you are accustomed to, but that does not make it any less worrying.

Be aware, my son, that the first, and by far most important task of a King is to conquer his own self.

Look at me. Have you not always known me as a strong-willed ruler, very much in control of everything and everybody, in command of himself in the first place?

I am fond of good food, yet I eat only once a day. Most of the time, under the influence of the wise teachings of Hindu and Jain saints, I even abstain from the meat I liked so much when I was young.

You know how much I like wine and spirits, and I admit that I do get drunk every once in a while, mostly on gentle evenings when the moon is soft, and when I am enjoying good company. Yet, I will often go for days without drinking anything but water, for I believe this is necessary if I want to remain in control of myself; and for that very same reason, I rarely enter opium's false paradise.

I adore the pleasures of the harem, even at my advanced age, for God has graciously given me health and vigour. However, I will not allow the women who happen to be sharing my bed to interfere with the affairs of the state or run my life, unlike you. It is all right to love a woman, but that should not dominate your life, my son. Would you ever see me running after a woman, like a peacock in heat? Never! And neither should you, my son: an Emperor must always, above all things, remain Emperor.

It is important for you to realize, my son, that your father was not born this strong. I have the same desires and weaknesses as any other man. The only thing I have learned, much better than you have, is to allow pleasure into my life, without being ruled by it. I may give in to my passions, every once in a while, but I can usually keep them under the control of my will.

Learn to control yourself as well, for it is unwise and unworthy to allow one's desires to run one's life. There is so much more to life, my son, than the pursuit of vulgar pleasure.

Bairam Khan, at first, cheerfully approved of my amorous adventures. When he saw the smile on my face, my tiredness from the lack of sleep, he actually encouraged me.

'Great to be a man, isn't it, Your Majesty? Is there anything more delightful than the companionship of a willing, beautiful, naked woman? Every morning when I wake up, I thank Allah that I was not born a girl. I would really hate it, if I had to share my bed with something as ugly as a man.' He laughed heartily at his own joke. It was one of the rare occasions he was not dead serious.

The next day, after a particularly wild night with very little sleep, I was a bit late for my daily public appearance on the balcony. Bairam Khan looked at me intently but said nothing.

The day after that, I arrived much too late. He still did not say anything, but publicly reprimanded Pir Muhammad Khan instead.

'Nasir ul-Mulk,' he barked, knowing very well that I could hear him, loud and clear, 'next time, kindly see to it that His Majesty is able to attend our public ceremonies on time. You know how important it is to avoid rumours and gossip.' He was of course right, but I felt humiliated and angry.

The following day, in the afternoon, I deliberately did not show up for a private audience with a messenger who had just arrived from the Panjab.

Immediately after the audience, my guards announced Bairam Khan's arrival at the entrance of the royal quarters. I did not dare to deny him access, and had him shown in.

He looked at the jars of wine and spirits, the half-empty cups, the ruffled sheets and veils. He sat himself down opposite me, uncomfortably close, clearly smelling my breath reeking of drink, and noticing the dilated pupils of my eyes. I had indeed been drinking some of that opium-laced rose water my father enjoyed so often.

'Your Majesty, I need to talk to you, before the evening meal,' he said.

'Why don't you speak to me right now? I am afraid I have other plans in the afternoon,' I replied defiantly.

'I need to talk to you when you are sober,' he answered quietly, with a sad look on his face.

Seeing that I wanted to answer back, he continued, slightly raising his voice.

'With respect, Your Majesty, I am your *ataliq*, and I have requested an urgent meeting with you about important affairs of state. I will present myself two hours before evening prayers.'

He got up, and left, clearly not intending to take no for an answer.

I slept the better part of the afternoon and woke up with a terrible headache, in the foulest of moods. I wanted to drink some more wine, just to upset Bairam Khan, but I was feeling too sick and lousy.

When Bairam Khan arrived at the indicated hour, I was starting to feel a bit better. Some cool lime sherbet had just been brought in; I did not offer him any and started eating.

He ignored the insult.

'Your Majesty needs to be more careful about how he spends his time,' he stated, clearly not bothering to waste any time on civilities. 'There is nothing wrong with entertainment and amusement, but Your Majesty should remain mindful of his duties as Emperor. People need to be able to see him, young, bright, strong; they need to take guidance and leadership from him. That can only happen if he remains in control of himself.

Your Majesty should therefore be very careful with wine, and even more so with opium, for they dull and blunt the mind, and weaken the body. They should be taken sparingly if taken at all. They can be enjoyed with moderation in the evening when the day is over and it is time to relax, but not during the day, or when the affairs of state need to be managed.'

'I am the Emperor, and I will do as I please,' I said defiantly, looking him straight in the eye.

He stared back, not in the least intimidated. To my astonishment, his stern face suddenly became friendly, and he gave me a warm, almost encouraging smile.

'Of course, you will do as you please,' he agreed condescendingly, dropping the formal Your Majesty. 'The only real question is, which 'you' is it going to be?' He paused as if he wanted to allow some time for these rather strange words to take root in my soul.

'I am going to tell you two true stories which have greatly influenced the way I look at life. You will then better understand what I mean,' he explained.

'As you know, a few years ago, after he had been driven out of his dominions by Sher Khan Sur, your father was forced to spend a number of years in Persia. As you know, I was among your father's followers and travelled with him everywhere. During our stay, we visited many cities and met many people.

One evening, in the beautiful city of Herat, I had the good fortune of making the acquaintance of a learned, white-bearded Sufi teacher. He was trembling and weak with old age, but still had the brightest mind one can imagine.

Years before, he told me, when he was still a young man, he had been a merchant and had travelled to the most faraway places, even to far away ports in the lands of the Firanghis[34].

[34] Firanghī: 'Frank', i.e. European, Christian.

On one of those travels, he visited Rumiyah[35], a beautiful city, pleasantly located in the fourth climate. It is the residence of a man they call Papa, who is the spiritual head of the Nazariyya[36] sect. There, the Sufi had many conversations with local men of learning, who all tried to convince him to abandon Islam and convert to their strange religion.'

'What do these Nazariyyans believe?' I asked, finding myself interested in spite of myself. 'Which God do they worship?'

'They do worship the one and only true God, Allah, the God of Ibrahim, like us Muslims, and also like the Jews, although they call Him by many different names, such as *Dio, Dios, Deus,* and also *Ghott,* a word that sounds a bit like the Persian word *Khoda.* So, these Nazariyyans do worship Allah, but somehow, they have come to think that He consists of three persons, an idea as preposterous as it is blasphemous.

The first of these three Gods, they call the Father. The second, according to them, is the prophet Isa ibn Maryam[37], whom they call Yehsus or something like that in their languages. They also call him God the Son.

To be honest, I am not quite sure who the third divine person is, according to that strange faith of theirs. I think it may be Maryam, the saintly mother of the prophet Isa, may Allah receive her in His mercy. The Nazariyyans indeed call her Mother of God. And they, apparently, also worship a deity called the Holy Spirit, but I am not quite sure who that is supposed to be. So you see, it all seems very complicated, and in reality, while the Nazariyyans do claim they serve the one and only true God, they are really not much better than the idol-worshipping Hindus.

Mind you, it is, of course, true that the prophet Isa ibn Maryam, may the blessings of Allah be upon him, was an extraordinarily holy man. He holds a highly exalted rank among the prophets. Allah Himself saved him from death on the cross. His mother Maryam, together with Asiyah, the wife of Pharaoh, Khadija, the Prophet Muhammad's first wife, and Fatimah, his daughter, is one of the Four Perfect Women of

---

35 Rome.

36 Nazariyya: 'Nazarean', i.e. Christian.

37 'Īsā ibn Maryam: Jesus, Son of Mary.

Islam. But it is, of course, utter blasphemy to state that a mere man could, in fact, be Allah Himself, or that Allah had a son. Allah is One, there is nothing and no one like Him. He definitely has no mother, no father, and no son!

Anyway, coming back to this Sufi teacher, he told me about a long and inspiring conversation he had one night with a learned and kind man. This man had not been trying as hard as the others to convert him to the Nazariyyan sect but had seemed to be more genuinely interested in finding out what exactly we Muslims believe and comparing it to what the Yahudis, the Nazariyyans, and the ancient Greek philosophers have to say. They had stayed up practically all night, both of them quoting from books from each other's traditions. 'That night, I truly learned', the Sufi said, 'that God is greater than the differences between men.'

They talked about Allah's creations, the heaven and the earth; and about us, humans, our position in Allah's universe, and our duties in this life. The Nazariyyan sage quoted from a very interesting small book, written seventy years before, by a learned Nazariyyan priest who was also a nobleman. His name, if I remember well, was Mirandollah[38].

In that book, Allah Himself is described as talking to Adam, the first human being. And Allah says, 'I have created this universe with everything in it, the sun and moon, stars and planets, oceans, mountains, plants, animals, Everything in it has its own place and obeys its own laws, which I, Allah, have ordained in My infinite wisdom. Only you, Adam, you are an exception. I have created you in such a way, that you will have to choose your own place in the universe and make your own laws. It will be up to you, to sink deeper than the lowest animal, or to rise above the angels.'

Bairam Khan paused, looking at the ground.

'I know you love books, Your Majesty. For some strange reason, you are unable to read, but you like to listen to books and the stories they hold. Well, our lives are just like those storybooks. We have been thrown into life without asking for it, and we will have to leave it someday when it is Allah's will that we do. In between, we are writing our story. It consists of the things that happen to us, and how we react

---

[38] The Italian Renaissance philosopher Giovanni Pico della Mirandola (1463–1494). The text is *Oratio de Dignitate Hominis* (1486), Discourse on the Dignity of Man.

to them. Within limits, we can do whatever we want, but one thing is absolutely impossible for us. We cannot avoid writing our story.

When I leave here, there are many possibilities open to you, many things you can write in the book of your life. You can write, 'And then, he made up his mind to become a great Emperor' or 'And then, he got drunk again' or 'And then, he prayed to Allah to give him strength' or 'And then, he sat down, not knowing what to think' or 'And then, he inquired about the situation in the Panjab.'

There are thousands upon thousands of ways the story of your life can go, Your Majesty. They may lead up, or down. They may go in a straight line, or via all kinds of detours. You, and you alone, are the writer. You decide. However, there is one thing you cannot do, and that is not writing your story. Even if you decide to step out of this life and kill yourself, you would still be writing your story, 'And then, he killed himself.'

Much as I resented admitting it to myself, I knew Bairam Khan was right.

I offered him some of my lime sherbet. He accepted with polite gratitude, pretending he had not noticed it up to that moment.

'You spoke of two stories, Khan Baba. What is the second one?'

'This first story was a general one, applicable to every human being. The second one concerns you more directly and I have to warn you. You will not be pleased to hear it, but I have promised your revered father, may his grave be holy, that I would tell it to you when the time would come.

It was a little over one year ago. You had just been named governor of Panjab, and I had been appointed as your *ataliq*. As you know, this had been celebrated with impressive ceremonies. Towards sunset, I was informed that your father wished to see me. I wondered why, the audience had finished only two hours before. Two guards escorted me to your father's private chambers.

With all due respect, Your Majesty, I was truly shocked by your father's appearance, so completely different from the extravagantly attired demigod I had seen a couple of hours before.

It was truly dreadful to behold. The majestic attire, the jewels, they were all gone. He wore a simple cotton tunic and had even taken off his turban. I had never seen him without a turban before, not even when we were camping in the deserts of Sindh. The air in the room was comfortable. Yet, he was sweating profusely and shivering at the same time, as if in fever with cold sweat.

I entered the room and prostrated myself, touching the ground with my forehead. He made an impatient gesture to approach the platform where he was sitting.

'Sit next to me, Khan Khanan', he ordered and clapped in his hands.

'Bring me one-quarter of my usual portion for now,' he said to the servant who came in. They brought him a milky liquid, which I knew to be opium-laced rose water, which, unfortunately, you seem to be familiar with as well. He drank it immediately as if overcome with an unquenchable thirst.

'This will be enough to ease my discomfort without clouding my mind,' he explained apologetically. 'As you probably know, I would have taken my usual portion of opium about two hours ago. I will have some more when we are finished talking. We have had so little opportunity to really talk, my dear friend, and it is important that we do. You have just been appointed as my son's *ataliq* and protector, and it is essential that you know my hopes and fears for him. I do not expect to die any time soon, but one never knows. The stars do not always reveal everything, they can be misread.'

He closed his eyes and leaned back, allowing the opium to work. The trembling stopped, the agitation subsided, but his mind was clearly still not at ease.

'It is for the best that you have seen me sweating and trembling like this', he said, guessing what I was thinking. 'I am the Emperor and I do as I please, but if I am completely honest with myself, it is no longer me taking and enjoying opium. The opium is taking me, and it has been for years. Not that I would want to have it any other way. I simply cannot bear the thought of giving up this blissful feeling of total relaxation and well-being, the clear, gentle white light that melts away all my troubles and worries. But if I am honest with myself, as I intend to be tonight, my friend, I must confess. I am opium's powerless prisoner. I get very sick when I do not get it in time. I always have to plan the dose I will be taking. Too much of it will cloud my mind, but without it, I am unable to think of anything else until I do get it. I will often break off important activities or conversations with people of my Court, just to be able to indulge in my pleasure. When I take a large dose, when it starts to work and before I glide into a blissful sleep, I can see it all so clearly before my eyes. It seems I am filled with Divine knowledge and wisdom. Without reasoning, without words, I completely understand the universe, how it all hangs together, the elements, the spheres, the colours, the numbers, the letters, all of Allah's majestic creation and the symbols that stand for it.

At the same time, I then see the glorious calling of our Gurkaniyya Dynasty. We are chosen to conquer and rule. I see how we will follow the footsteps of our glorious ancestors, and go way beyond where they have ever trodden. I see how I and my descendants will regain control of Samarqand, Tashkent, Bukhara, and all the lands that rightfully belonged to our ancestors. And after that, who knows? If Allah wills it, absolutely nothing will stop us.

But when the opium has worn out, and before my body grows restless for a new dose, I see the world and my life as it really is.

I see how I have been given power and wealth, and how I squandered it. Let's face it. Most of my life, I have been a king only in name: a homeless warlord, a fugitive, wandering from one place to the other with a dwindling host of followers, often in great danger, and forced to leave my infant son and heir in the care of dubious allies and unfaithful relatives. Fifteen of the twenty-six years of my reign, including the first twelve and a half the years of my own son's life, I have spent on the edge of disaster, fleeing from my enemies, humiliating myself to find some shelter and help, hoping, against all odds, to recover the throne from which I had been driven by that dark-hearted Afghan traitor, may Allah's wrath duly punish him for his treachery.

Fifteen years, Bairam! Fifteen years of misery and despair, before it finally pleased Allah to grant my armies the sweet taste of victory.

Make sure Akbar learns from my mistakes, Bairam. Make sure he does not fall into the trap. The throne is the loneliest place in the realm. My revered father used to say, 'No bondage equals that of sovereignty.' How right he was. In the end, there is no one you can trust but yourself. Tell Akbar, that the better he is able to remain in control over his own self, the easier it will become for him to remain in control of others. I know that when you are the king, you can do as you please. You can eat and drink whatever you like, enjoy the pleasures of the harem, and have all kinds of entertainment organized just for you. Yet, the more you allow your cravings for these things to run your life, the weaker you will become.

When the time comes, Bairam, make sure my son knows all this, before it is too late. Tell him about these things. He will be smart enough to understand. After all, his grandfather Babur was his age when Allah put him on the throne.'

Bairam Khan paused and looked at me intently.

'With all due respect, Your Majesty, that time has come. I do not mean any disrespect to you, or to your father, whom I loved and revered, and supported at the peril of my own life. However, the truth must be told. Your father did have the tendency to indulge too much in his own pleasures and private interests. There is nothing wrong with recreation every once in a while, but a ruler should rise above his weaknesses. As your grandfather once wrote to your father. Retirement matches not with rule.

Your father, may Allah grant him peace, was aware of his weaknesses. He had high hopes for you, Your Majesty. He took pride in your strength and resilience, your sharp mind and broad knowledge. He believed in you and wanted you to become a strong Emperor, stronger than he himself had been. Do not disappoint him, Your Majesty. Become the great Emperor you know you can be.'

He paused again, probably waiting for me to react. I didn't. I couldn't. I knew he was right, but I felt hurt by the brutal way he had described my father.

Nevertheless, I must admit: that evening was a turning point in my life. It would still take me a few more years before I would really take my life into my own hands. Even after that, there have been too many instances where I had too much to drink or lost my self-control. But Bairam Khan's wise words have stayed with me and have been my guide for the rest of my life.

Let them be a lesson to you, too, Salim. Remember the fate of your brothers. Control yourself. You owe it to our Empire, and you owe it to yourself.

'I need to brief Your Majesty on the military situation', Bairam Khan said after a brief silence, returning to the affairs of state, as if nothing had been said or happened.

'I have excellent news but also some disturbing news, Your Majesty. Let me start with the former. Ajmir and the surrounding country are ours. Our men have done an excellent job. The last remnants of Hemu's followers have been hunted down. Ajmir, the sacred city of Ajmir! Your Majesty is now the guardian of Khwajah Muin ud Din's[39] grave, the peace of Allah be upon him. Never have the lands of Hindustan seen a holier Muslim saint; thousands of pilgrims, Hindus and Muslims alike, travel to Ajmir each year, to invoke his powerful intercession, and seek solace and wisdom near his sacred tomb. It is truly a sign from heaven that this holy place is now under our protection!'

'And the bad news?' I asked.

'The messenger from the Panjab told me that Sikandar Sur's men have come down from the Siwaliks. They are plundering the Panjabi countryside and threatening the Lahore garrison. Well, it's probably for the best. We have to deal with this vermin sooner or later. We may as well get it over with.'

[39] Khwājah Muīn ud Dīn Muhammad Chishti (1142–1236): one of the greatest Muslim saints in India. His tomb in the city of Ajmer still is a very important place of pilgrimage, for Muslims and Hindus alike.

Sixth Letter

مانکت

Mankot

There is not much to tell. Of course, we won. From then on, we would always win. With but a few exceptions, you being one of them, my son, I've never again felt under any real threat and victory has always been mine.

Our commander in Panjab, who as I told you had been left behind when we set out to confront Hemu, had done his best, considering the forces at his disposal. In his defense against Sikandar Sur, he dealt an important pre-emptive strike against a few local traitors who had been taking bribes from Sikandar Sur's spies. Regrettably, he then had to withdraw back into Lahore, when his vanguard was defeated by the enemy's main army.

Not to let things get out of hand, we quickly sent reinforcements to the Lahore garrison, a strong body of elite cavalry under Iskandar Khan Uzbeg, one of our best commanders, tough and utterly ruthless. Meanwhile, we prepared the main body of the army. On Doshanbeh the 26th of Azar[40], we set out to the Panjab.

It became a leisurely march, with lots of stops and hunting parties underway. The reports from the scouts were reassuring. Our people clearly had the situation under control.

We got more good news, from Bairam Khan's household back in Lahore. Ten days after we had left Dilli, he had become the father of a

---

[40] Corresponds to Monday, 7 December 1556 on the Julian Calendar.

son, Abdurrahim, whom of course you know very well, my son. Bairam Khan had sent his family to Lahore at the time we were marching against Hemu.

The child's mother came from the family of the Khans of Mewat and Bairam Khan's marriage to her dated back from the days of Humayun. When they recaptured Dilli, they had taken a wise measure to ensure political stability in the area. My father and Bairam Khan married the two beautiful daughters of one of the most powerful local zamindars [41]. The strength of an empire is not built on bulwarks and fortifications only.

Abdurrahim's birth was an excellent omen for our campaign and Bairam Khan organized a sumptuous celebration with superb food in abundance. The astrologers had calculated the child's horoscope and sent lengthy reports about the lines on its hands and forehead. The young Abdurrahim, they predicted, would have a splendid future and a position of major importance at the Imperial Court. At least this once, they have been proven right.

Even before our army had reached Jalandhar, Sikandar Sur, who realized he did not stand a chance against us in open country, fled back into the Siwalik hills. This time, however, there were no rains to protect him. We followed him deep into the hills and set up camps, first near the small town of Desuhah, next at Dahmiri. There, we celebrated the completion of the first year of my reign.

No doubt, Sikandar Sur's plan was to harass us with a number of hit-and-run attacks and to draw us into battle in difficult terrain crisscrossed with ravines, where our superior numbers would actually be a tactical disadvantage.

His hopes, however, were bitterly crushed as he never got a chance to put his plan to test. As he and his supporters would soon find out, we were using exactly the same strategy, and we were much better at it than them.

The main body of our army stayed encamped at Dahmiri, while Pir Muhammad Khan was sent out to roam the hills with a rather small but strong and mobile group of experienced horse archers, and some of our most warlike, not to say murderous, scouts. Villages that had provided

---

[41] Zāmīndārs: landowners.

support to Sikandar Sur were brutally punished, and the wealth of the local leaders, methodically destroyed.

It did not take more than a few days for the local zamindars to drop Sikandar Sur like a stone. They made haste to flock to our camp, throw themselves at our feet, and pledge allegiance to us.

Now without any local support, Sikandar Sur took refuge in the stronghold of Mankot. It is quite a strong fortress, consisting of four separate forts on adjoining hilltops, providing excellent cover, joined and enclosed by bulwarks, which are very difficult to approach, let alone assault. Inside its enclosure, it has an abundant supply of excellent fresh water, and the neighboring countryside is rich in all kinds of other provisions.

We, of course, decided to lay siege to the fort. Storming it would have cost us many lives, which we could ill afford to lose after the heavy casualties at Panipat.

In a few days, we had the fortress entirely surrounded by our entrenchments, and all its supply lines and escape routes completely sealed off. The only thing we needed now, was time and patience. Slowly but surely, Sikandar Sur's garrison would be choked to death.

Indeed, it became a leisurely, if somewhat boring, siege.

There was very little actual fighting. Slowly but surely, our trenches were moved closer and closer to the walls. Occasionally, marksmen on their ramparts tried to take shots at the men digging the entrenchments, but our superior numbers of archers and musketeers quickly forced them to take cover. Each time they dared to show themselves, their losses far exceeded ours.

They did make a few heroics, if futile, attempts to break through the encirclement. Each time they fought with honor, but never stood a chance. We were always on our guard; they never even managed to cross our front lines. Rather than a military threat, the Afghan sallies became a welcome distraction in the dreariness of those long, boring days, an ideal occasion for some of our young and warm-blooded officers to show their courage in close combat.

I was particularly impressed with the brave, not to say rash, behaviour of my hot-headed foster brother, Adham Khan.

He was the youngest and preferred son of my head nurse and foster mother, Maham Anaga, who had been with me and taken care of me throughout my youth. In the Chagatai tradition, he and I were, therefore, *koka* or *kukultash*, foster brothers united by a river of milk. He was six years older than me, strong and bold, and I liked him.

Ambitious, eager to rise to the highest positions in the army, and utterly fearless, he would throw himself in the middle of the fight, with no other protection than a simple coat of mail, a helmet and a shield, just like the ordinary soldiers. He was fast, and fought well. I saw him killing at least five enemies in a single encounter. Grateful and proud I felt, and resolved to promote him to the highest ranks as soon as an occasion would present itself. Little did I suspect what a mistake that would prove to be.

After those first few skirmishes, the Afghans made no further attempts to break out. Each time their losses had been much heavier than ours, and their numbers had been much smaller to begin with. Indeed, God does favor the larger army.

Still, they remained well entrenched in their fortress, stubbornly refusing to submit. Clearly, despite our promises to the contrary, they were convinced they would all be put to the sword as soon as they surrendered. Possibly, they were still hoping for some kind of miracle. Maybe some new enemy would attack us in the rear; maybe we would become reckless and make the mistake of storming the fortress.

But of course, nothing of the sort happened. There were no new enemies to attack us. On the contrary, the messages we received from the border provinces brought us nothing but encouraging news. Opponents were being subdued, new territories were being added to our dominions. Patiently, we continued the siege, undermining their morale, slowly starving them. We made sure they witnessed the daily arrival of abundant new supplies in our camp. We feasted in sight of their ramparts.

One evening towards the end of *Bahman* of that year[42], when I returned from a short hunting trip in the area, Bairam Khan came to greet me when I reached the camp.

'Your Majesty, today's messenger from Lahore has brought good news. The highborn ladies of the Imperial Court have arrived safely from Kabul, and are awaiting Your Majesty's instructions.'

---

[42] Early February of 1557.

'That is excellent news, indeed. Who is with the group?' I asked. 'I trust they have had a safe journey?'

'There is, of course, Your Majesty's revered mother, Her Majesty Maryam-Makani Qadasi-Arkani Hamida Banu Begam[43]. Accompanying her are several other highborn ladies, including Haji Begam, who as you know was one of your father's other spouses. There are also his half-sisters, Gulbadan Begam and Gulchihra Begam[44] and Your Majesty's charming cousin, Salima Sultan Begam.'

I smiled.

'She really is a nice girl, isn't she, Khan Baba? You still want to marry her, I gather? Don't worry, I haven't forgotten that my father promised you her hand in marriage as soon as Hindustan was ours again.

When we're done with Sikandar Sur, let's have the wedding. My father would not have wanted it any other way.'

Bairam Khan smiled gratefully.

'Your Majesty is most kind. It is truly a great honor for me to marry such a distinguished and honorable lady of the imperial family. I pledge I will honor and worship her.'

He kept silent for a while, clearly looking for words to say something unpleasant.

'Anything wrong, Khan Baba?'

'Your Majesty inquired whether the ladies have had a safe journey. Well, unfortunately, I have been informed that your two younger sisters passed away during the journey, peace be upon their chaste souls. Alas, it was Allah's will.'

I stared at my feet, not knowing what to say. It was hard to believe that those two playful, healthy children were dead.

I paused, picturing their pretty faces before my mind's eye.

'What a terrible, terrible loss for my poor mother. How exactly did they die? And how is my mother doing?'

'I don't know the circumstances of their passing, Your Majesty. I was told they had gotten ill during the journey. As for your mother, I

---

[43] Maryam-Makānī: Occupying the Place of (the Virgin) Mary; Who is of Equal Rank with (the Virgin) Mary. Qadasī-Arkānī: Pillar of Purity.

[44] Gul-Chihra: Rosy-Cheeked; Gul-Badan: Rose-Bodied.

was told, she has resigned herself to Allah's will. She is, so they say, much comforted by the prospect of seeing you again.'

'How about Muhammad Hakim and Munim Khan?'

'Your Majesty's half-brother and his *ataliq* have elected to stay back in Kabul. They have sent a message that they consider it their duty to keep that important city in secure hands.'

That typical, somewhat disdainful look was on Bairam Khan's face again.

'You don't seem too pleased, Khan Baba?'

'To be honest, Your Majesty, I neither like nor trust Munim Khan. I think he is one of those people who prefer to be number one in a small kingdom than number two or three in a large one. I suspect he plans to set up an independent kingdom back there in Kabul. I think it's only a matter of time before they declare their independence from the throne of Hindustan. Admittedly, I do not have any tangible proof; but I would advise Your Majesty to remain watchful. I am really not sure how far the ambition of Your Majesty's half-brother will go. He is still very young, but unhealthy ambitions are poisonous weeds that grow fast.'

Arrangements were made for the family reunion.

We met the cortege at one day's march from Mankot. Quite an impressive group, with a strong escort of about one thousand horses, guarding the small group of female elephants carrying the adorned palkis[45] in which the ladies were traveling.

There was, of course, an impressive pack train of camels and mules, carrying enough supplies to enable an extended stay, wherever it might be decided to pitch camp. Accompanying the train were soldiers' wives and children, who had come to visit their husbands and fathers.

Out of the first palki came, with some effort, my aunts Gulchihra and Gulbadan, the former, frail and shy, the latter, plump, merry, and talkative.

I could not help smiling, when I put my arms around her massive waist to embrace her, remembering that her name means rose-bodied.

The second palki was occupied by Haji Begam and Salima. I, of course, first paid my respects to my father's widow, knowing she had been very close to him. While I was talking to her, however, I found it

[45] Pālkī: palanquin.

difficult not to let my eyes wander off towards Salima. More than just my cousin, Salima has always been a dear companion to me. She is wise, kind-hearted, exceptionally bright and well-read. I have always been attracted to her. And there she was, my sweet cousin, exactly the way I remembered her, only, much prettier. She is a few years older than I am. Two years before, back in Kabul, she had been an overgrown, flat-chested, skinny adolescent, but now, she had turned into an attractive young woman, in the prime of her youth, neither too plump nor too skinny, precisely of the kind of girl I always fancied.

She must have guessed what I was thinking, because she gave me what I thought was a slightly mocking, yet friendly smile.

'I am happy to see my Emperor and noble cousin in good health,' she said, a bit stiffly, in contrast with her friendly smile. 'May Allah be your guide and protector, and grant you victory, in this war and all the others you will have to fight.'

'Thank you, my dear cousin. I am glad to see you are doing so well. It's been too long since we last met,' I said, and very much wanted to continue the conversation, but did not have the opportunity, for about thirty paces behind her, I saw my mother.

I reluctantly but hastily took my leave of Salima, and went towards my mother's elephant, to make sure she would not have to walk to meet me. A son should always behave like a son, even when he has become Emperor.

It had been quite a while since I had last seen my mother. In fact, I had spent most of my youth separated from my parents, in the care of relatives and foster parents.

But I always revered and respected my mother, and, I guess, feared her as much as I loved her. She was strong-willed, pious, and well-intentioned, no doubt, but opinionated, moody, extremely hard to please. The story goes she refused to consider my father's marriage proposal for forty days, despite her parents' insistence.

Our relationship has not always been easy. As you know, she lived on her own, residing in a palace in Dilli or Agra, with just a few of her close friends and confidantes. She clearly preferred her own quiet household to the busy life in the imperial *zanana*, with all those non-Muslims, the presence of whom she disapproved of, not to say abhorred.

But there has always been much tenderness and mutual respect between us, and despite our differences, she has done her utmost to further the interests of our family. But let me come back to all of that later.

My mother was visibly pleased to see her son, the Emperor, respectfully bowing down, kissing her hand and humbly touching her feet.

She made me stand up and hugged and kissed me. Taking me by the shoulders, she looked at me, smiling and crying at the same time.

In an effort to dispel the awkwardness of the moment, she began babbling enthusiastically in that melodious, elegant Persian of hers.

'My dear, dear boy! I am so happy to see you. You cannot imagine how much I have missed you. I have been so worried about you since your father passed away. Look how you have grown! How strong have you become! Your father would have been so proud of you!'

'Let's sit together and talk, Mother dear. It has been too long since we have seen each other,' I replied.

I courteously bowed to the other ladies, exchanged a few civilities with the army leaders, and accompanied my mother into her quarters.

Although she had not changed a great deal and there was still no grey in her black hair – after all, she was only fifteen years older than me – she somehow looked much older. The lines in her face had deepened, and her eyes looked dead-tired. I suspected she had spent many sleepless, tearful nights, mourning the loss of her two young daughters.

'Mother, I was very sad to hear that my dear little sisters have unexpectedly passed away. It must have been a devastating blow to you. May God grant you comfort and consolation,' I said softly.

She gave me a grateful smile.

'Praise be to Allah under all circumstances,' she said bravely, quoting the expression, which according to the tradition, the Prophet himself used when confronted with sad occurrences.

There was an awkward silence.

'Seeing you in good health takes away my sorrow, my son,' she lied, clearly trying to convince herself.

'One person can never replace another,' I answered. 'I know I cannot undo the sad loss of my sisters, but I will promise you the joy of a loving son.'

She hugged me, her lower lip trembling, her eyes turning red. She buried her face in my shoulder and started weeping, softly at first, then violently, sobbing like a child, her frail body shaking all over.

'My poor darlings! They were the light in my eyes,' she sobbed.

'Such good and gentle children. Why has Allah taken them away from me? Why, why did He bless me with these wonderful children, only to take them away from me? How will I ever get over their loss?'

She let go of me and sat down on the pillows on the floor, her face all red and wet with tears, her eyes staring at the carpets.

'Taminah[46] was only eight. Such a delightful, child. So full of life, always playing, laughing, singing, bringing a smile on everyone's face.

She was so excited about traveling to that strange and faraway country, Hindustan, to see her big brother, Akbar, who had become a mighty Emperor. She enjoyed the trip so much, a welcome distraction for a lively child like her. 'Traveling is so much more fun than sitting in that dull, grey palace in Kabul,' she would say almost every day. She was everywhere, always on the move, chatting with the soldiers, the cooks, the animal attendants. She adored being around the animals, feeding them, caring for them. More than once, I had to reprimand her, tell her it was about time she started behaving like a princess, rather than as a stable boy.

And then suddenly, when we were resting for a few days underway in Jalalabad, she got a fever. In a few hours, she became dangerously ill. The physicians gave her herbal tea to drink, the mullahs and astrologers used special prayers to Allah and magic to avert the evil eye, but nothing seemed to help even the slightest bit. Two days later, she was literally burning with fever, unable to eat or drink anything, her frail little body shaking all over. Every once in a while, she would speak, but what she said didn't make any sense. She was delirious, the physicians said. On the third day, she did not say anything anymore. She did not move at all, her breathing shallow and painful, her skin dry as sand. Her eyes were open, she hardly ever blinked. With every passing hour, her gentle, beautiful little face was shrinking.

I was desperate. I actually threatened the physicians, yelling and

---

[46] The actual names of Akbar's sisters are, as far as I have been able to ascertain, unknown.

screaming that I would have them executed if they did not quickly come up with a cure. The next moment I was begging them on my knees to save her. I am sure they did everything they could. But alas, nothing seemed to work. In the evening of that third day, without a word, without a sigh, my little darling stopped breathing.

Raushana and I howled like wild animals when it happened. We cried our lungs out. We implored Allah to help us, to perform a miracle, to bring her back to us. But it was, of course, all in vain.

When they carried her to her grave, in that distant city of Jalalabad, where she has no one to visit her, no one but strangers to light a lamp on her grave, I thought I would die too. Never in my life had I felt such grief and pain. May Allah forgive me, I even thought about killing myself, and go and lie next to her in that same grave, so she wouldn't be alone.'

Her voice faltered and she covered her face. Her shoulders were shaking violently. My poor mother. My poor little sisters. I felt so sad, so deeply sorry for her, but I could not find any words to say. I just held her tight and pressed my cheek against hers. Standing before such irreparable loss, what can we say? What can we do? The greatest comfort we can give to those we love is to hold them, and let our tears mix with theirs.

After a while, she let go of me. She smiled through her tears, touched my cheeks and patted my face with her shawl.

'I am very glad to see that you have a kind heart, my boy. It is a blessing for an empire and its people when their emperor is both strong and kind-hearted!'

She paused.

'The empire, that was one of the few things that kept me going. After all, was I not the widow of an emperor, and the mother of his successor? Everybody kept telling me, 'Your Majesty must be strong. Your Majesty has a task to fulfil!'

After three days of mourning, we continued our journey towards Hindustan. As we were leaving that wretched town of Jalalabad, I kept looking behind me, in the direction of Taminah's grave. Each time, Raushana would hug and kiss me, and cry with me, without a word.

My dearest Raushana. I owe her so much. She was only twelve, less than one year had passed since she had become a woman, but

I can tell you, very few adults ever grow to be so strong and wise. So gentle and sweet. Wherever she was, wherever she went, everything was good and beautiful.

Such a great support she was to me. She would cry with me when I was in despair; she made me smile when I tried to be strong; she comforted me with words of wisdom and compassion when thoughts and memories tortured my head. It seemed she had eyes only for me; never would she talk about herself or her own grief.

"Fortunately, I still have my Raushana," I often thought to myself. How I wish I had never done that. The worst things seem to happen to us when we think we are safe, don't you agree? It seems that Allah, or rather ash-Shaytan the devil, gets angry whenever we feel safe.

Our caravan arrived at Kotal Sitara near the Hind River. We camped there for a few days, enjoying the cool breeze and the majestic view of the water.

There, to my utter despair, my dearest Raushana fell ill as well. It started with some kind of mild indigestion, but very soon, she became violently ill, vomiting, her bowels indisposed, unable to eat or drink anything. Whatever the physicians tried, nothing seemed to help. She was growing weaker by the hour.

The poor girl never complained, not even once. She only seemed to be concerned about me. She told me not to worry, that everything would be for the best. Her last words, when she had hardly any strength left, were to the physician who was feeling her pulse, 'Please comfort my poor mother.'

For a week, I stayed at her bedside, watching her die before my eyes, powerless, desperate, praying night and day, feeling utterly guilty when I had dosed off for an hour, out of sheer exhaustion.

The eighth day, she quietly left this world. Fortunately, she did not suffer anymore. All her strength had left her and she was sound asleep, when her breathing became softer and shallower until it stopped completely.

The first few moments after her death, to my own surprise and shame, I did not cry. I did not seem to have any tears left. I was just sitting there next to her as I had been during those last days. Then, when I bent down to kiss her one last time, something in me seemed to break.

I started crying, covering her face with my tears, shaking her, telling her to wake up. Gently, the people around me tried to separate me from her and lead me out of the tent. I did not want to go, I threw myself on the ground, I howled and screamed.

I tore my clothes and yelled, 'Where are you now, Allah? Where is your compassion? Where is your love? Why do you torture me like this? How can you be so cruel? What have I done to you, to deserve a punishment like this?'

In my heart, I cursed Him, may He forgive me. In my thoughts, I called Him a bastard, a murderer of defenseless children. If it had been in my power, I would have cast Him in the deepest dungeons of His own hell.

Salima, Haji, Gulbadan and the others tried to calm me, taking hold of my wrists to restrain me, but the physician sent them away. 'Leave her alone, please. Her Majesty is ill with grief. Leave her.' Then, he turned to me, 'Let me help you, Your Majesty,' he said compassionately.

He handed me a beaker of milky fluid, of the kind your late father drank so often. 'Drink this, Your Majesty,' he said. 'It will help you in these hours of grief.'

I tried to push it away. I have always hated what that filthy brew did to your father. But the physician gently insisted: 'Trust me, Your Majesty. You must drink this, it will help you.'

I finally gave in and slowly drank the bitter potion. It had a faint, stale smell of roses gone bad and withering greenery. I did not feel a thing at first. Soon afterwards, however, I seemed to calm down a bit, and despite my sadness and despair, beautiful thoughts and visions found their way to my mind.

It was as if my soul was being filled with a kind, gentle light. I closed my eyes. I saw Taminah and Raushana, smiling in the gardens of Paradise. I saw myself reunited with them and your father, and with all other people, in happiness.

I sunk into a deep sleep. When I woke up, while realizing it had been nothing more than a dream, there was a glimmer of new hope in my heart. Someday, Allah would reunite me with my poor sweethearts, in a world where there will be no more tears.

Then I thought of my own blasphemous thoughts the day before. I had cursed Allah. I had insulted Him, rejected Him. I prayed for mercy and forgiveness, but my fears became worse and worse. What if He throws me in *Jahannam*[47]? What if He never allows me to see my daughters again?

After a few hours, I just could not stand it any longer. I desperately needed to talk to someone.

I asked to see the old mullah, who had been present at the time of Raushana's death.

'I am so scared, reverend master,' I cried. 'I am so afraid Allah will punish me for my blasphemous thoughts. When Raushana died, you know, I cursed Allah, in my thoughts, I even called Him...'

The Mullah raised his hand and looked at me earnestly.

'I don't need to know about any sins you may have committed, Your Majesty,' he interrupted. 'But I do understand that Your Majesty was overwhelmed with grief. This is why you refused to submit to Allah's will, and your mind harboured rebellious thoughts. This was indeed a sin, but then, none of us is without sins. Surely, Your Majesty, Allah understands and forgives. He is so much greater than any sin we could commit. The important thing is, Your Majesty has returned to Him and asked for His forgiveness and He will most surely grant it to you.'

'Are you sure about that, reverend master?' I asked.

'I am, Your Majesty. The Holy Quran itself confirms it unequivocally, in many places. Allah, may He be praised, is *at-Tawwab*, the Acceptor of Repentance. He is *al-Ghaffar*, The Forgiver; *al-Ghaffur*, the All-Forgiving; *al-Halim*, the Forbearing; *al-Afuw*, the Pardoner. From dawn to sunset, Allah is there to forgive us during the daytime, and from sunset to dawn, He is there to forgive us at night. The Holy Prophet Muhammad, eternal peace and blessings be upon him, described Allah's mercy as follows:

O son of Adam,
were your sins to reach the clouds of the sky
and were you then to ask forgiveness of Me,
I would forgive you.[48]

---

[47] Jahannam: Gehennah, Hell.

[48] From the Hadīth (traditions relating to the deeds and sayings of the Prophet Muhammad); this passage is from the *Hadīth Qudsī* collected by Abū Īsā Muhammad at-Tirmidhī, author of one of the six canonical collections of Hadīth.

'You see, Your Majesty, Allah does understand your grief and has gladly forgiven your sins, but He also wants you to be strong. He wants you to go on with your life, as the mother of the Emperor. He wants you to help your son, to guide and support him. Lead a pious and righteous life, Your Majesty, and you will see Allah will reward you abundantly.'

The mullah's kind words have been a source of comfort to me ever since. Now, each time I think about my daughters, I try to think about how I saw them in Paradise. I ask Allah to forgive my sins, and I do my best to imagine how He will give me my two little darlings back and reunite me with them in a world of total bliss where there are no more tears.

These thoughts do give me strength, but I must confess they do not take away the pain, my son. I hate to admit it to myself, but I feel best when I do not have to think and remember at all when my mind is occupied with other matters.'

She looked up at me, wiped away her tears, and put her hands on my shoulders.

'Now that I see you, my son, I know the good mullah was right. Allah wants me to go on living in this world. He wants me to be there to support you. You are still so young, my dear boy, and the world is fraught with danger. You need all the help you can get, even from a feeble woman like me.'

I kissed her, bowed and again touched her feet.

'I am most grateful for your help and guidance, Mother. May Allah grant you comfort and consolation. I promise I will be a respectful and loving son to you, and do whatever is in my power to bring you happiness.'

The next morning, we travelled back to Mankot. The ladies accompanied us, with their escorts and all their retinue. They would stay in the army camp for a few days before returning to the court at Lahore.

There were touching scenes of joyful reunions after so many months of hardship; old comrades, happy to see each other in good health. There was plenty of good food, and stories and presents to be exchanged. Everybody could now see with their own eyes. Hindustan was secure enough for the ladies of the imperial court to leave the safety of Kabul. It was even safe enough for them to come and feast in sight of the once so dreaded and powerful Sur family. There was magic in the air. This was only the beginning. We were witnessing the dawn of an extraordinary new era.

Celebrations were held every day well in sight of the enemy fort. We made very sure the defendants could see the ample supplies, the delicacies, the wealth, the luxury. Siege warfare is a war of minds, my son, more than of weapons.

To be sure, it did not miss its effect on Sikandar Sur and his Afghans. Soon, we received the visit of humble and submissive emissaries, bringing us proposals of peace. We treated them with courtesy but sent them back as soon as we heard they were trying to stipulate terms and conditions. We would accept nothing less than complete and unconditional surrender. We would promise nothing more than clemency and justice. Until they accepted these terms, the siege would have to continue.

After the Ladies and their cortege had left to go back to Lahore, the days again went by in dreary boredom.

I was desperate for ways to pass the time. I went hunting in the hills. I arranged for wrestling matches. I discussed books with my teacher. I received messengers and discussed their reports with Bairam Khan.

But elephant fights were my favorite. Hardly a day went by without one. I do not know how many hundreds I've organized in my life, but I have never grown bored of them. I just love the shouting, the dust, the smell, the mighty muscles and massive, ramming heads ...

Then one afternoon, things went terribly wrong.

Bairam Khan had been ill for a couple of days. He had developed some kind of fever, and a number of nasty, painful boils had appeared on his legs and the lower part of his body. The physician had given him herbal infusions, to bring down the fever, and regularly applied hot compresses to the boils, before opening them and washing the wounds with vinegar.

Bairam Khan, of course, had wanted to go about his duties as before, but the physician had ordered him in no uncertain terms to stay in bed: 'You will keep these wounds clean and you will rest, for at least a week, Khan Khanan! If you do not, you will surely contract blood poisoning, and then, you will have to rest forever!'

He had grudgingly given in and stayed in his tent, passing his time sleeping, listening to messenger reports, and reading – mostly Rumi and verses from the Qur'an and the Hadith[49]. Slowly, his condition was improving, but he was still very weak.

On the afternoon of the third day of Bairam Khan's illness, I had arranged yet another elephant fight, this time between Fatuha and Lagna, two of our finest, strongest, and most pugnacious elephant bulls.

It really promised to be a great spectacle. Both animals were massive and angry and vicious, eager to kill when given a chance. Right from the start, however, it all got out of hand. The mahauts had little control over the animals – they hardly managed to hold on to their necks! Soon, the fighting animals had left the arena, chasing each other all over the camp; spectators had to jump aside not to get trampled.

I thought it was great fun. I did see the mahauts' pleading looks; I knew they wanted me to give the sign to drop the canvasses over the elephants' eyes to calm them down. But I didn't. I was just too fascinated by the spectacle.

Suddenly, a deafening roar. Lagna's left tusk had lost its protective cover and had rapped across Fatuha's left flank, leaving a lacerated, profusely bleeding wound. The pain and anger seemed to double the victim's forces. He jumped up on his hind legs, kicking Lagna off balance, nearly throwing off its mahaut. He then rammed Lagna in the flank with such force that the other recoiled at least fifteen paces, hitting Bairam Khan's tent in the process.

The tent collapsed. For what seemed an eternity, the fighting animals were trampling all over it. Then, fortunately, the mahauts managed to drop the blindfolds. The animals, now unable to see each other, quickly calmed down, and were led away, each to a different corral.

We all stared at the fallen tent. Everybody cheered with relief, when we saw a curved dagger cutting through the canvass. Bairam Khan crawled out, dressed in his sleeping robe, his face grimacing from the pain in his legs, his hair sticky with feverish sweat.

'Khan Baba, are you all right?', I asked.

With visible effort, he restrained his anger. He bowed, or rather, nodded, stiffly.

'*Qorbanat*', he replied, in formal Persian, looking intently at my eyes.

---

[49] Hadīth: Traditions or Sayings of the Holy Prophet Muhammad.

There was an awkward silence.

'With Your Majesty's permission', Bairam Khan said slowly, 'I would like to retire and go lay down again. I am still feeling rather ill.'

Shams-ud-din, my *Atga*[50] reacted immediately. 'It would be a pleasure as well as a great honor for me, Khan Khanan, if you would care to accommodate yourself in my tent. Meanwhile, new quarters can be built for you.'

'You are most kind, my brother', Bairam Khan replied. 'With Your Majesty's permission...'

Without awaiting my reply, he bowed again, and walked, with some difficulty, to the Atga's tent.

I retired to my quarters, wondering what to think about Bairam Khan's reaction. '*Qorbanat*', he had said. Why *qorbanat*? Why not 'I am fine, Your Majesty, thank you for asking', in plain Turkish, or *alHamdu liLlah*, Praise be to God? Why this much less common Persian expression? He hardly ever talked Persian, most certainly not with me. In fact, as far as I could remember, this was the very first time... in reply to a question in Turkish! This was clearly no coincidence.

In itself, there was, of course, nothing wrong with *qorbanat*: it's a polite way to thank someone who has just inquired after one's health and well-being. But, as you know very well, the expression literally means 'thy sacrifice'. Why did he choose to call himself my sacrifice? Was it a covert reprimand for my reckless and irresponsible behaviour? Or did he actually mean to imply that I had done this on purpose, that I wanted to kill him? Could he really believe a terrible thing like that?

My suspicion was indeed correct. About three hours later, Shams-ud-din requested to be admitted to my quarters. With a grave, worried look on his face, he told me Bairam Khan had interrogated him – at length – about the incident; he wanted to know the exact sequence of events in every minute detail. He only calmed down somewhat, when Shams-ud-din had taken a solemn oath on the Holy Qur'an, swearing that to the best of his knowledge, the incident had been nothing more than an unfortunate accident.

---

[50] Atga: foster father. As related before, Shams-ud-dīn Muhammad Atga Khān was married to Jī Jī Anaga, one of Emperor Akbar's nurses.

I was profoundly upset. I felt insulted and angry that he held me in such low esteem. And to be honest, I also felt quite worried. What was I to do, if he were to turn against me?

The following days, I would often pay him a visit in his tent, politely inquiring about his health, asking his advice about the incoming reports from other regions of the empire, the military situation, and many other matters of state. He remained quite courteous, respectful and friendly. Neither of us mentioned the incident, but it was all too clear, neither one of us had forgotten about it.

Sure enough, it came to my ears that during the following weeks, he repeatedly interrogated a number of other people, much the same way as he had done in Shams-ud-din's tent. Clearly, the poisonous weeds of suspicion had been planted in his soul...

Fortunately, the siege offered some distraction. The situation in the enemy fort was now clearly growing desperate. The visits of Sikandar Sur's peace emissaries became more frequent. As a sign of good will, Sikandar invited ambassadors of the imperial army into the fort and even sent his own son as a hostage as a guarantee for their safety.

Shams-ud-din immediately volunteered to go as our ambassador.

'Even if they still refuse to surrender,' he argued, 'we will at least get some first-hand information about the situation inside.'

He returned with a number of exquisite gifts: gold, silk, carpets, and a couple of magnificent horses and elephants, surprisingly well fed at that. Most of these gifts were of course presented to me, but Sikandar Sur had also been shrewd enough, not to forget a few smaller, yet quite substantial individual gifts for Bairam Khan, Pir Muhammad Khan and Shams-ud-din himself, with personal and elaborately polite and friendly accompanying letters.

Shams-ud-din went back into Mankot with the same answer as before: the gifts were a hopeful sign that the beleaguered were willing to give up the rebellion and obey their rightful sovereign. Their lives would be spared, but the Emperor would not accept any other terms or conditions of any kind: their surrender was to be complete and unconditional.

For another two days, the fort remained closed and silent. Then, finally, after six months of siege, our patience was rewarded. On

Yeksanbeh, the 12th of Khordad of the second year of my reign[51], Sikandar Sur solemnly surrendered the keys of Mankot into my hands.

We granted him one request: he would be allowed to surrender with honor. His son would kneel and rub his forehead in the dust in his stead, thus asking forgiveness for the rebellion, but Sikandar Sur himself would be allowed to do obeisance according to the protocol observed by the senior members of my court.

At the agreed hour, the gates of Mankot finally opened up.

Riding their swift Afghan battle horses, Sikandar Sur and three of his officers came out. Crossing the narrow bridges that had been laid over the trenches, they entered the imperial camp, dismounted, and approached the platform on which I was sitting.

So, this was the great Sikandar Sur...

He looked disappointingly unimpressive – a middle-aged, weak, tired-looking man, visibly scared for his life. Unlike most Afghans, he did not wear a full beard, but only a long moustache, more customary with our men. Judging from his pale, sagging skin, he had until recently been rather chubby, but had lost a lot of weight during the siege. Likewise, his officers, though much younger and healthier than he, made a tired, weakened impression.

They all bowed and slowly approached the platform, until a slight movement of Bairam Khan's right hand indicated they had come close enough. There again, they bowed elaborately and repeatedly, like obedient and respectful vassals at my court were supposed to bow, touching, three times in a row, their foreheads, their chest and the dust of the ground with their right hand.

One of the Afghan officers handed Sikandar Sur a set of large iron keys on a small pillow made of red silk. He raised it in front of his chest and stretched his arms towards me.

'Your Majesty,' he mumbled slowly, as if chewing the words in his mouth, like a guest at a banquet, swallowing with great difficulty a dish he abhors, yet does not dare to refuse.

'Your Majesty,' he repeated, 'I surrender to you the keys of the fortress of Mankot.'

He paused again.

---

[51] Sunday, May 24, 1557 on the Julian calendar.

'I recognize Your Majesty as my lawful sovereign, to whom – and Allah is my witness! – I pledge my unwavering loyalty, and that of my men.'

I made a sign for Shams-ud-din to come forward and accept the keys on my behalf.

'Sikandar Khan,' I replied, 'eternal praise and thanksgiving be to Allah! In His infinite compassion and mercy, He has granted us the wisdom to avoid further unnecessary bloodshed. These lands of Hindustan need pious and competent men to administer them and ensure their prosperity. Let us leave behind the differences that separated us, and build a new future!'

He bowed, visibly relieved and grateful to see that we were keeping our promise to spare their lives.

I must confess, we had considered – at length – the option of killing him anyway. After all, there were many good reasons to do so: had he not caused us an inordinate amount of trouble? Was it not dangerous, if not outright foolish, to allow a Sur to stay alive? Hotheads like Pir Muhammad Khan and Adham Khan hadn't failed to make those points, convincingly and emphatically.

Yet, Shams-ud-din, Bairam Khan and I had, in the end, reached a consensus: living up to our promise, while more dangerous in the short term, could actually prove to be of greater benefit in the future.

'Treating him well sends a powerful signal to our other adversaries,' Shams-ud-din had argued. 'It will motivate them to surrender as well. Opposing Your Majesty means running like a hunted animal, risking one's life and possessions. Submitting to Your Majesty's rule and joining the Empire, in contrast, is the key to a life of peace, leisure and prosperity.'

'I very much agree,' Bairam Khan nodded.

'Besides, when you come to think if it, subduing a Sur and turning him into a vassal, is much greater a victory for us than killing him! If we execute him, he will remain a noble hero in the eyes of many Afghans, a noble warrior, dying honorably after an unequal, gallant fight. But if he submits, the whole era of the Surs becomes little more than a vulgar rebellion. Conversely, if you pardon him, Your Majesty, you show yourself to the world as a noble ruler, a king whose court is the refuge of the just and the lovers of peace, where it is good to live, *zire sayeye lotfe shoma*, as they say in Persian, in the shadow of your kindness...'

Yes, I would follow your Atga's advice, Your Majesty: we are taking a small risk, but we have so much more to gain!'

Thus, it was done. Sikandar Sur was not executed, nor maltreated. He was made to suffer the – arguably – worse fate of subtle humiliation.

I invited him to come closer and sit down on the carpet near the platform where I was seated. He and his men were offered various kinds of ice-cooled sherbets, freshly baked bread, fruits, nuts, and skewers of exquisitely roasted mutton, fowl and lamb.

For one brief moment, they did their best to hide how famished they were.

'Go ahead, enjoy', I said. 'There is more than enough!' They needed no further encouragement.

For a while, we engaged in pleasant conversation, about food, horses, hunting and similar subjects of common interest. When it comes to bringing people together, few things are as effective as food and friendly conversation.

Then, as we expected, Sikandar Sur made his final move.

'Your Majesty,' he said, trying to hide how tense he was, 'I speak on behalf of all of us in thanking Your Majesty for his most kind generosity. May Allah grant him a long, happy and healthy life! As I have told Your Majesty, I solemnly pledge to him my unwavering loyalty...'

He paused, trying to find the appropriate words.

'I am not a young man anymore, Your Majesty. While I am still in good health, thanks to Allah, much of my former strength has left me. I have no other desire than to live in peace and contribute to the prosperity of these lands. I would be most grateful if Your Majesty would allow me to remain here in the Panjab, as Your Majesty's governor. I solemnly swear, I will administer it diligently and honestly! The khutbah will be read in Your Majesty's name, every Friday, in all the mosques. I personally guarantee that a steady stream of revenue will flow into Your Majesty's coffers...'

Probably guessing from the expression on my face that I was about to say 'no', he rapidly added: 'Allah is my witness, may I die in agonizing pain and burn in hell if I am not speaking the truth! And I am willing to entrust my son, who is dearer to me than anything on this earth, to Your Majesty's protection, as a sign of my close alliance with Your

Majesty's Court and a guarantee of my unwavering loyalty!'

Maybe, under different circumstances, I would have yielded to these pleas and arguments. But Bairam Khan and I had talked this through: there was no way we were going to allow Sikandar Sur to remain in the Panjab. Even if he were speaking the truth – which I was inclined to believe – the Panjab was much too important a province, to leave it under the effective rule of someone else. My control over it had to be direct and absolute.

'Sikandar Khan,' I replied, 'there is much joy in my heart at the kindness of your words. Nothing is dearer to me than the prosperity of these lands and the friendship among all the people dwelling therein, especially between the brave and noble Afghans and ourselves. We will be most grateful, and our mind will be at ease, knowing that the beautiful province of Bihar prospers under your able governorship!'

'There is a subtle, yet important distinction to be made,' I continued, raising my voice, as he clearly wanted to say something in protest. 'There are, in fact, two kinds of governors, Sikandar Khan. There are local rulers, who have accepted, often reluctantly, to become the ally and vassal of another, mightier king. After their formal surrender, they continue to rule their dominions very much like before. Of course, they recognize the sovereignty of the king, which in practice means they allow the khutbah to be read and coin to be struck in his name, and they pay yearly taxes to him.

On the other hand, there are, what I would call, regular governors. These are trusted members of the king's Court, sent out to administer a province, in the name and on behalf of their lord and sovereign. Sikandar Khan, I trust you clearly appreciate the difference. We would like to avoid any confusion or misunderstanding in the minds of our subjects. Your predecessor, Sher Khan Sur, may Allah forgive his sins, has risen to power after a rebellion against my revered father. That rebellion has now come to a final end!'

It seemed he still wanted to say something in protest, but the expression on Bairam Khan's face quickly made him change his mind.

'As Your Majesty wishes,' he whispered, bowing his head, a tired man who had lost his final battle.

Bairam Khan smiled as he watched the Afghans go to their assigned tents.

'Your Majesty did very well,' he nodded. 'Spoken like a true King! I wish your father could have witnessed this!'

The next morning, Sikandar Sur, with a handful of followers and a strong escort of ours, left the Panjab, forever. As Abu'l Fazl would have phrased it, he never again removed the neck of submission from the collar of obedience. He administered his province with diligence and loyalty, until his death, barely two years later.

With him died the last of the remaining Surs.

The other Sur, Mubariz, had already met his well-deserved fate. Hemu's death had left him utterly helpless: without his iron right arm, his downfall was only a matter of time. Sure enough, around the time Mankot fell into our hands, the Sultan of Bengal attacked and crushed his remaining army. Barely three years had passed, since he had put himself on the throne after butchering his defenseless young nephew. The Bengalis killed him on the spot, like the scabby dog he was. I hear he was stabbed in the gut with a thin dagger and left to die, for hours, in excruciating pain. The filthy swine deserved every moment of it. I just wish I had been there to kill him myself.

Thus, ended the glorious Sur dynasty: with the execution of a fat, worthless pig, and the quiet passing of an obedient provincial administrator... It took a lifetime of hard work for one strong man to build a powerful kingdom; and just a few years for his successors to lose it... Let their downfall be a lesson to us, my son!

After the surrender of Mankot, we stayed a few more weeks in the Siwalik Hills. After all, it was the hottest time of the year; where could it be better to stay, than in a pleasant, mountainous country with plenty of fresh air and shade? Finally, on Shanbeh, the 19th of Mordad[52], when the monsoon rains were bringing refreshment to the parched lands, the army left the Siwaliks and marched to Lahore.

One week later, we made our triumphant entry into the city.

[52] Corresponds to Saturday, July 31, 1557 of the Julian Calendar.

Seventh Letter

لاہور

Lahore

We stayed in Lahore for four months and fourteen days. It was not a time I like to remember.

Not that there were that many problems – on the contrary, everything went for the best. The reports were quite reassuring. Each day, our hold on the newly acquired territories was getting stronger. The stream of revenues was growing every day. Law and order were reestablished, insurgents and marauders eliminated or forced to surrender.

The local chiefs made haste to pledge allegiance, bringing gifts, offering their daughters in marriage, requesting the favor to kiss the threshold of the Sublime Court and do homage, as Abu-l Fazl liked to put it. My Empire was growing more powerful by the day; Fortune was smiling on me.

Yet, it was not a pleasant time. More often than not, I found myself in a foul mood, bored, dissatisfied with everything and everybody, most of all myself. I guess this is not entirely surprising: after all, I was hardly fifteen years old, at an age where most youngsters are at odds with themselves; and unfortunately, I was no exception.

My problem was rather simple, and, in fact, not dissimilar to yours and my father's, Salim: I was lazy. As usual, Abu-l Fazl phrased it politely: 'in repose and pleasure, outwardly he wore the guise of one who did not attend to affairs...'

Truth is, I wanted to enjoy the pleasures of Kingship, but not shoulder its burdens; and that, alas, is not possible. Laziness is the soft pillow on which Satan sleeps. Being a monarch is not about following one's whims and interests, my son. It is about serving the Empire, supporting and guiding its subjects.

This may sound great, but in practice, it means listening to hundreds of reports, requests and complaints, oftentimes about trivial things you are not even remotely interested in. It means sitting in dreary ceremonies and boring discussions for hours on end. It means spending a whole lot of precious time exchanging civilities with people you do not even like very much.

Above all, it means working hard to remain in control. Do not be mistaken, Salim: staying in power is not as simple as it sounds. Of course, when you are around, everybody will be polite and obedient enough. Everybody will go out of their way to serve and please you, and to tell you the things you like to hear. Unfortunately, it is all too easy to be lulled asleep. Before long, you are the unwitting prisoner of your own courtiers, a misinformed, misguided buffoon in a golden cage.

A wise king will be careful, my son. He will check, re-check, and check again. He will never confide in just one single individual. A wise king, my son, is lonely, and works hard.

I of course knew all this, but somehow did not find the stamina to act upon it. I enjoyed myself with hunting, music and dancing girls, and left the day-to-day affairs to Bairam Khan.

When you leave a void, you should not be surprised to find that others fill it. When the elephant leaves, the tiger returns...

Indeed, Bairam Khan, hard-working as always, readily took charge of everything. Whenever I was around, he was courteous and obedient enough, but in my absence, he acted as the true head of the Empire.

This did not fail to raise serious concerns with the people who loved me (like my mother and Shams-ud-din), and arouse the bitter jealousy of others – above all, Maham Anaga and Adham Khan, her ambitious son. Soon, I found myself surrounded by rumours, intrigues...

My Court quickly turned into a hornets' nest.

In fact, the squabbling had already begun back in Mankot, when proposals were being made for me to marry my first wife, Ruqayyah, the daughter of Abdullah Khan Moghul. Bairam Khan was strongly opposed to the idea, because Abdullah Khan Moghul's sister had been married to Kamran, my father's brother and bitter enemy. Marrying this woman was a not only a risk, he argued, it was also disrespectful to my father's memory. But Maham Anaga, Pir Muhammad Khan and Shams-ud-din were very much in favor, as it was a sign of reconciliation and unity in the imperial family. In the end, much to Bairam's dismay, I followed the latter advice and married Ruqayyah.

I did not really mind the argument – in the end, there was a valid case to be made for both points of view. More disturbing was the outright hostility between the protagonists: not a day went by without reproaches and accusations.

All these incidents further complicated my relationship with Bairam Khan. Despite our mutual affection, we seemed to be constantly irritated at the other's attitude and behaviour; slowly but surely, we were drifting further apart.

A particularly disturbing incident happened three weeks after we had set up residence at Lahore. At the end of a long, boring day, where we had been listening to dozens of requests concerning petty local matters, I had enough of it all. There was still one more meeting scheduled, an audience with some local Panjabi zamindars who had come to pay homage. I did realize this was relatively important, but I just couldn't bear the thought of another two, three hours of sitting on a pillow, listening, nodding and exchanging civilities. I was really desperate to go out and do something else. And so I did: I told Bairam Khan to go ahead and receive the zamindars on my behalf.

He was visibly displeased, but to my surprise and relief, made no real attempt to talk me out of it.

'Your Majesty realizes this is a very important assembly?' he asked. 'Your Majesty allows me to take the necessary decisions?'

'Sure, sure, whatever,' I answered, and made haste to get out of the room.

I made my way to the stables, and spent the rest of the afternoon elephant riding, enjoying myself immensely. When I came back, I was in no mood to go back to the affairs of state, much less to listen to another one of Bairam Khan's sermons about the duties of kings.

I did not go to see him, did not send for him, and did not even bother to ask anybody else about the outcomes of the meeting. I went straight to my private quarters to have dinner. I enjoyed some cool wine, some music and a delightful dancing performance, and spent the rest of the night with one of the girls. She was extremely attractive, with long, black, curly hair, and truly understood how to please an eager young man; we enjoyed each other's company until deep into the night.

The next morning, much too early to my taste, I was informed that Shams-ud-din was requesting an urgent audience. I reluctantly got out of bed, and invited him to join me for my morning meal.

After the customary civilities, he began to talk about the situation in the Panjab and expressed his satisfaction that we now seemed to have this important region tightly under our control.

'The measures taken yesterday were harsh, but necessary, I think,' he added, probing the expression on my face.

I did not have the faintest idea what he was talking about.

'Yes, thanks for your help and support, Atga,' I answered vaguely.

He clearly was shocked, though he did his best not to show it. 'Your Majesty was informed about the execution of Takht Mal?' he asked.

'Of whom?' I asked, painfully conscious of how stupid that sounded.

'Takht Mal, the zamindar of Pathankot. I suppose Bairam Khan has asked Your Majesty's permission to have him killed?' he replied, visibly dismayed at my ignorance.

'We briefly talked about it, yes,' I lied. 'So, that was done yesterday, after the audience, Atga? Tell me how it went – I did not have the chance to talk to the Khan Khanan yet.'

Shams-ud-din hesitated, clearly worried by what he just heard. 'Well, Your Majesty: Bairam Khan had all the zamindars assembled in the hall of public audience. He was sitting where he would normally sit, on the right-hand side of the royal platform. One by one, they were called forward, paid homage, exchanged a few civilities, and received gold and other gifts in recognition of the renewed alliance.'

The fifth to be called forward was Takht Mal of Pathankot. Bairam Khan began the conversation quite amiably, as he had done with the others.

'My lord Takht Mal', he said, 'His Majesty is pleased indeed that henceforth, He will be able to count on the unwavering loyalty of the leader of Pathankot!'

'And I am of course very pleased to be able to be of service to His Majesty,' Takht Mal answered with a bow.

'Are you indeed?' inquired Bairam Khan. The smile on his face slowly disappeared. 'My Lord Takht Mal, I seem to recall, that Humayun Padshah, may Allah receive him in Paradise, used to pay you quite generously for your loyalty, did he not?'

Takht Mal was visibly getting worried.

'Yes, my Lord Khan Khanan, but...'

'I know,' Bairam Khan agreed, 'the forces of Humayun Padshah were driven out of Hindustan, and Sher Khan Sur came to power. There was very little you could do about that, was there? I agree, you needed to think about the welfare of your family and your people. Nobody will deny that you have acted prudently and wisely for yourself and your dominions! I suppose Sher Khan has paid you handsomely for your support as well, has he not?'

Takht Mal tried to smile apologetically and nodded, looking at the carpet at his feet. He was sweating profusely.

'When Humayun Padshah finally got back what was rightfully his, he understood and forgave you, did he not? He rewarded you for your renewed pledges of loyalty, did he not? And when he died, you did accept the gifts that were presented to you on behalf of his lawful successor, His Majesty Abu'l Fath Jalal-ud-Din Muhammad Akbar, did you not?'

Takht Mal nodded again. He tried to say something, his lips moved, but no sound came out.

'I know, I know, Sikandar Sur probably made you an offer you couldn't refuse,' Bairam Khan said with a sad, compassionate expression on his face. 'But from now on, we really want to make absolutely sure that we can count on Pathankot's unwavering loyalty! We will therefore pay you for your services, one last time.'

His eyes went towards the back of the hall. He made a slight, almost imperceptible gesture with his right hand. Before anybody realized what was going on, one of the guards, a Qazaqi raider who had been standing motionless at the back of the hall, dashed towards Takht Mal. In an instant, he threw a piece of thin hemp string over his head, looped it twice around his neck, and pulled it tight.

It was an impressive demonstration of fighting skills. Just one short, choking noise escaped from his victim's throat; then, there was absolute silence – his windpipe had been completely tied shut before he could blink an eye.

Takht Mal's face turned dark red, then purple. He was struggling violently, kicking his arms and legs, throwing his weight from left to right. It did not seem to bother the Qazaqi one bit. He passed the string one more time around Takht's neck, and skillfully knotted it tight. He let go of his victim, and calmly returned to the place where he had been standing, without even looking back.

Takht Mal desperately reached for the knot, tried to pull the string away, loosen it ... all in vain, of course. He fell to the floor, rolled and kicked a few more times, then lay still, on his back, his eyes and mouth wide open, his black tongue sticking out. It was a ghastly sight...

Bairam Khan looked each of the remaining zamindars in the eye, one by one. Then, his eyes singled out one of them. 'My Lord Bakht Mal, please come forward,' he said softly to the dead zamindar's brother.

The poor man obeyed, shaking like a leaf. For a while, Bairam Khan left him standing there, next to his brother's corpse.

'My Lord Bakht Mal,' he repeated, 'on behalf of His Majesty the Emperor and in my own personal name, I want to express our heartfelt regrets for the harsh measures that had to be taken. I trust you appreciate that there was no other way. At the same time, I would like to express our sincere hopes that the new zamindar of Pathankot will prove himself a loyal ally of the Empire of Hindustan. I trust we will be able to rely on you personally, will we not, my Lord Bakht Mal?'

He looked at him like a cobra looks at its prey.

'Yes, Your Majesty, I mean, my Lord Khan Khanan,' Bakht Mal stammered.

Bairam Khan kept looking at him, without blinking an eye.

'I can assure you, my Lord Khan Khanan, you can count on me! God is my witness, my Lord Khan Khanan...'

For what seemed an eternity, Bairam Khan said nothing. He just kept staring at him, his face inscrutable and expressionless. Finally, he nodded, smiling faintly.

'On your way out, my Lord Bakht Mal, you will receive a bag of gold coins and a pair of the finest horses, as a sign of His Majesty's appreciation of your pledge of loyalty!'

'You have our permission to retire, if you wish,' he added, looking at the stain between Bakht Mal's legs. The poor man had wet himself...'

Shams-ud-din paused. 'This is the story, Your Majesty. I am sure the Panjabi zamindars will not easily forget this lesson!'

I stared at the carpets, wondering what to say. 'The Panjab is vitally important to us,' I agreed after an uncomfortably long silence. 'It must be clear to everyone that insubordination can and will not be tolerated! Examples must be set!'

What else could I have answered? What else was there to say?

After Shams-ud-din had left, I kept pacing up and down, wondering what to do about Bairam Khan. Was I to reprimand him? Congratulate him? Ignore him?

I sent for him later that afternoon.

'Shams-ud-din told me what happened yesterday,' I said. 'I think you did the right thing, Khan Baba. I am just disappointed that you did not involve me in the decision, as you should have. This was not like with Tardi Beg's execution, when our survival was at stake. I was much younger, and less experienced back then. This time, you should have involved me!'

For a moment, I thought he was going to apologize, but he changed his mind.

'Your Majesty can be involved any time and to any extent He wants,' he snapped; 'meanwhile, I am trying to do my duty, the best I can.'

'I do not doubt that, Khan Baba, nobody does. But you should have involved me,' I insisted.

This time, he hesitated. 'Yes, Your Majesty is right. I do offer Your Majesty my sincere apologies. But I swear my only motive has been the security of the Empire,' he answered.

I just nodded, and said nothing. How could I be sure that he really meant it?

A few weeks later, there was yet another one of these incidents. Admittedly, this was a trivial matter, far less important, but still, a matter of principle, and it made me very angry.

We had received a messenger from Bahadur Khan, the newly appointed governor of Multan.

Many people had warned me against his appointment, because he was one of Bairam Khan's closest confidants, but a better man for the task could not have been picked: a brave and competent soldier, one of the heroes of our vanguard at Panipat, and a dedicated, strong-willed man. Unruly Multan was clearly in need of a strong governor like him. In only a few months' time, he succeeded in ridding the province from the Baluchi robbers who had been prowling the countryside. A sizeable number had been killed, the rest driven back into their rugged mountains. Peace and prosperity returned; revenues were flowing to our treasury.

This was, of course, reason enough to be satisfied. After hearing the messenger, I asked Bairam Khan to send Bahadur a congratulatory letter, and a suitable reward.

The next day, I was shocked to find out, that on top of a large sum of money and jewels, Bahadur had received two of the very finest elephants of the imperial stables! I kept calm, but inside, I was beyond myself with rage. Who did he think he was, giving away my property without my permission? And two of the finest animals of my stables? Such insolence!

To make things worse, on my way back to my quarters, I bumped into Maham Anaga, who did not fail to take advantage of the situation – she would rarely miss an opportunity to undermine Bairam Khan's position.

A phony smile on her face, she congratulated me:

'There is really no limit to the kindness of Your Majesty's noble heart! Such generosity! I just hope a rough soldier like Bahadur will duly appreciate it!'

'Yes, thank you,' I replied evasively.

She looked at me, with a hint of scorn. It was obvious she did not believe me. 'I assume these gifts have been sent on Your Majesty's orders?' she asked, clearly eager to make her point. 'Surely, the Khan Khanan would never have taken a decision like this without Your Majesty's permission?'

I did not answer. What could I say? Did I have to admit that I had not been informed?

She still did not let go of her prey.

'Your Majesty is far too good,' she sighed with an intensely sad, worried look on her face. 'Your Majesty should be more careful, think more of his own interests.'

'What do you mean, Mahamji?'

'I mean, Your Majesty has let this fellow become way too powerful,' she snapped.

In spite of everything, I was surprised at her bluntness.

'We should not forget, Mahamji,' I argued, 'that Bairam Khan has been appointed by my father! He was my father's strongest army leader; he defeated Hemu and the last of the Surs!'

'Nobody denies that he is competent and works hard,' she admitted. 'The only question is, Your Majesty: who does he work for? Do you not see, how power-hungry this man is? What's to happen in two, three years, when you will no longer require an *ataliq*? Will he gracefully step down? Are you confident he will obey, even if he does not agree with your decisions? Do not forget, Your Majesty: there are other candidates for the throne! There is your younger cousin, your uncle Kamran's son. And he may even nourish higher ambitions for himself! Sher Khan and Hemu are his shining examples: a competent minister may one day claim the throne for himself...'

'You are exaggerating, Mahamji, but I appreciate your concern,' I answered bravely. But her words had made a deeper impression on me than I cared to admit. She was right, I could not allow him to run the Empire on his own. I had to set things straight.

But that was much easier said than done. Surely, I could not afford to make a fool of myself and ask my presents back, like some kind of spoilt child? And what was I to do? Ignore it? Make a scene?

After a sleepless night, full of dark and angry thoughts, my mind was made up: I would summon him to my quarters.

I was just about to have him called, when the guards announced he requested a private audience with me.

To my surprise and relief, he looked nervous. There was a timid, subservient look on his face – very much unlike him.

'You wanted to see me, Khan Baba?' I asked, trying to sound as casual as possible.

'I wanted to obtain Your Majesty's permission to order the army to march back to Dilli.' He hesitated. It was blatantly obvious that he had not requested an audience to ask me this.

'As Your Majesty knows, the military situation in the Panjab and the other territories in western Hindustan appears to be sufficiently stable. I believe therefore, that our presence here in Lahore is no longer required. If Your Majesty agrees, we could head back east and take up residence in Dilli again, for the foreseeable future,' he added.

'That's fine with me, Khan Baba,' I replied. 'I have to admit, I was getting rather bored here in this drafty palace, anyway!'

Bairam Khan nodded. 'Very well, Your Majesty. I will make the arrangements for the march. I would also like to request...' He hesitated.

'Yes?' I asked.

'I would also like to request Your Majesty's permission to make the necessary preparations for my marriage to the honorable lady Salima Sultan Begam. As we have discussed before, Your Majesty's father promised me that I could marry her when Hindustan would be ours again, and Your Majesty confirmed that the arrangements could be made as soon as we had dealt with Sikandar Sur...'

'This has indeed been agreed,' I admitted. 'Well, go ahead with the arrangements! And tell me, when will be the *zifaf*?[53] Still over here in Lahore?'

He bowed.

'I am most grateful for this great honor! I promise Your Majesty, I will be a caring husband. If Your Majesty wishes, the ceremony can be organized on the way. We won't lose any time that way.'

'Very well, Khan Baba, so it shall be done. Congratulations!'

There was an awkward silence. Surely, this was not the moment to bring up the issue of the elephants. All things considered, a pair of top-class elephants was a small price to pay for peace in Multan...

'Tell me, Khan Baba, have you eaten yet? Come, sit down with me. It's been much too long since we had a chance to talk in private!'

We ordered food and sat down. We talked for hours, about all kinds of subjects, trivial as well as important: the affairs of state; the administration of the territory; and horses, hunting, food, women, poetry, religion... it was a delightful morning. Why could it not always be like that?

I watched him taking his leave, and for the rest of the day, I thought of little else than my relationship with this man, to whom I owed my life and my throne—this man, whom I loved, admired, envied, and feared. And I wondered how it all would end.

[53] Zifāf: bridal procession.

Eighth Letter

جلاندهر سرهند

Jalandhar, Sirhind

The army slowly made its way east. It was, again, more of a leisurely excursion, rather than a military manoeuvre. As usual in winter – it was the 26th of Azar of the Second Year[54] when we left Lahore – the weather was delightful: cool nights, full of stars, and sunny days with deep blue skies.

I was relieved to be in the open again at last; and I was not the only one. The fresh air seemed to have a beneficial influence on people's moods: there was much less gossiping, complaining and bickering.

Our first stop was at Jalandhar. Almost two years had passed since I had last set foot there. I was pleasantly surprised: under the monsoon rains, it had been a dull and dreary place, but under the clear blue winter skies, it had a festive look to it. Peace and order had been a blessing to the people: they seemed better off – their clothes newer and cleaner, their children livelier, their animals fatter.

Timid at first, the locals trooped together, eager to catch a glimpse of the cortege, with its power and wealth. They gladly accepted our gifts, and willingly supplied us with excellent fruits, vegetables, and clean drinking water. They were in for more impressive parades and celebrations.

There was, first of all, Bairam Khan's long-awaited marriage to my sweet cousin Salima.

---

[54] Tuesday, December 7, 1557 on the Julian calendar.

Not surprisingly, Maham Anaga, Pir Muhammad Khan and others had made more than a few attempts – not all of them very subtle – to convince me that this marriage was not in the Empire's best interest.

Bairam Khan would become much too powerful, they argued. Was he not wakil[55] and sipahsalar of the Empire? Was that not more than enough? Surely, it was ill-advised to grant him the honor of marrying the daughter of Humayun's sister, the granddaughter of the great Babur Padshah himself? It would all but elevate him to royal rank! It would make him even more arrogant and ambitious than he already was!

I must confess, the same thoughts had crossed my own mind; and truth be told, I would have much preferred to marry Salima myself; but I really couldn't go back on my father's promise. Besides, there were other sides to the argument.

I discussed the matter in private with Shams-ud-din, whom I appreciated for his level-headedness and honesty. Although he was by no means Bairam Khan's fan, he fully agreed: I simply had to honor my father's promise.

No single man had done more for the Empire than Bairam. Soldiers and officers revered him. I simply could not afford to go back on a solemn promise to such a deserving and important man. To do so, without clear and obvious reasons, would certainly undermine my reputation, not to mention my authority.

Moreover, Bairam Khan's marrying Salima was much more than a recognition and reward for services rendered: it was a renewed alliance between families. It would reconfirm and strengthen the ties of loyalty that united him and his household to my family. Indeed, Salima's father Nur-ud-Din Muhammad belonged to the respected Naqshbandi family, connected to the imperial dynasty for generations. Bairam Khan's mother being Naqshbandi as well, it was only becoming that he, in his position, should marry a girl from that family. Had not the Prophet Muhammad himself declared that matrimonial alliances are the way to secure friendship?

Thus, it was done. I do not remember the exact date of the marriage – it must have been about five weeks after we left Lahore,

[55] Representative; Prime Minister.

early in the month of Bahman[56].

Through my mother and other intermediaries, Salima had made it clear that she wished to give her consent in person, rather than through the office of a wakil[57], as was customary. In view of her high status and noble birth, nobody dared to argue with her. After all, it was permissible for an adult woman to give her consent herself – under both Shi'a law and our own. Even more importantly, thanks to Salima's decision, we didn't have to decide who would act as her wakil.

Nikah, the celebration of the marriage contract itself, took place in the courtyard of the small fortress, in the presence of only a few high-ranking witnesses, including myself. As you know, it is customary for the qazi and the partners to assemble in a convenient place, other than a mosque, which made the suitable locations at Jalandhar rather limited in number.

After the men had all gathered in the courtyard, Salima came in, together with my mother and the other ladies and their main servants. I was glad to see she had not followed the admonitions of the mullahs to veil her face with purdah; instead, she was wearing the classical dress of noble Turkish ladies, with muslin trousers under a long robe of gold-coloured silk, and a tall, jewel-studded headdress, strings of pearls hanging from it. Her bejewelled hands, and her feet, as far as they were visible in the open-heeled silk slippers, were adorned with intricate henna patterns, which according to the age-old custom had been applied the night before.

When everybody was seated, the qazi formally asked both spouses whether they consented to the marriage and the generous dowry. He proceeded with a rather boring sermon on marriage and the duties of spouses, after which the ceremony ended with the *Fatiha*[58].

Like any other Muslim, I had recited the first Surah of the Holy Qur'an countless times before. Yet, this time was special. As I stood there, together with my closest friends and family on that solemn

[56] Early February, 1558.

[57] In this context: legal representative, proxy holder: male attorney acting in the name and on behalf of the bride during the marriage contract proceedings.

[58] The opening chapter of the Holy Qur'ān.

occasion, it was as if I heard those words for the first time; I sensed God's majestic, humbling presence; shivers went down my spine, as I pronounced the solemn Arabic verses:

Bismi-Llahi ar-Rahmani ar-Rahim
Al-Hamdu li- Llahi, Rabbi-l-Alamin
Ar-Rahmani ar-Rahim
Maliki yawmi-d-Din
Iyyaka na'budu wa iyyaka nasta'in
Ihdina-s-sirata-l-mustaqim
Sirata-lladhina 'an 'amta 'alayhim
Ghayri-l-maghdubi 'alayhim
Wa la-d-dallin
Amin

In the Name of God, the Compassionate, the Merciful,
Praise be to God, Lord of the Worlds;
The Compassionate, the Merciful;
Lord of the Day of Judgement
You alone we worship, and Your aid we seek
Lead us in the Straight Path
The Path of those upon whom is Your Grace
Not of those upon whom is Your Wrath
Nor the astray
Amen.

The wedding ceremony having been concluded, Salima was carried in a closed palki to Bairam Khan's quarters, where, in accordance with our age-old customs, she would sit down to a repast with her old and new female friends and relatives, waiting for her husband to arrive after the night prayers.

Meanwhile, the proud bridegroom paraded through the streets on horseback, accompanied by his closest friends and allies, and a procession with music and torches. That evening, the army fraternized with the people of the town, feasting on all kinds of food in abundance.

I watched Bairam Khan, sitting at the banquet, happy, smiling, relaxed, and I must confess, I could not help feeling more than a bit jealous of him. Tonight, I thought, he would be sharing his bed with

Salima... It is true, she never was what one would call a ravishing beauty, even when she was still young, but as I told you, I have always found her extremely attractive.

It just shows on her face, the kind of person she is. She has that open, honest, engaging smile... everybody feels at ease with her, wants to be with her.

In those beautiful clothes, she looked just stunning. And again, it grieved me this sweet, attractive young woman would be marrying someone else.

Tonight, I thought, tonight he is going to undress her, he is going to see her naked... I imagined what blessing it would be, to lay down with her, to become one with her... Oh, how I envied him!

I could have had all the girls I wanted, but here I was, fantasizing about my cousin. For a number of days, in fact, I thought of little else than Salima, imagining what her naked body would look and feel like...

Such is the enchantment of women, is it not, my son? No matter how many have shared our bed, there will always be the others, tempting us...

We stayed at Jalandhar a few more weeks after the wedding. Four hours, twenty-eight minutes into Yawm al-Khamis, the 20th of Jumada 'l Ula of 965, the sun left Esfand and entered the sign of Farvardin, the new solar year[59]: the beginning of the third year of my reign. It seemed only months since I had ascended the throne! Such is the nature of time, my son: the months and years of our lives may seem long, but they slip through our fingers like desert sand. We must use them well, not waste them in idleness: they will never come back!

Three days and nights, we feasted. There was a drive hunt, with hundreds of beaters. And there was of course plenty of food and drink for everyone, with music, dancing and fireworks. For the first time, I had myself weighed on a large pair of scales, and to everybody's joy and amazement, my weight in coins of gold was distributed among the soldiers and the villagers: the Padshah is like God, the lord of the universe, Who gives without being asked.

After the celebrations, we left Jalandhar and headed further south

---

[59] Corresponds to the late evening of Thursday, March 10, 1558 of the Julian Calendar (Muslim days are counted from sunset to sunset). Esfand: Pisces; Farvardīn: Aries.

towards Dilli. When we had crossed the Sutlej near Ludhiana, messengers informed us about a minor uprising near Hissar – one of the many I have had to deal with in the course of my reign, and of no interest here. We ordered Pir Muhammad to head south through the countryside to crush the insurgents, whereas Bairam Khan and I continued along the main road towards Dilli with a smaller contingent. We would halt underway, at Sirhind, to pay our respects to my father's mortal remains.

Two and a half years before, when Hemu's army was marching towards Dilli, faithful servants had taken my father's coffin to a safer place. Not surprisingly, they chose Sirhind: an auspicious location, for it was there that my father had defeated Sikandar Sur's army.

The coffin had remained there, laid out in state in the central hall of the small fortress. Before entering, Bairam Khan and I knelt down and touched the doorstep with our foreheads. The room was dimly lit, with only a few candles; there were no guards or custodians of any kind.

The coffin had been placed on a small platform and covered with a large white shroud touching the floor. I looked at the oblong shape under the shroud, rounded at the corners; the head, slightly broader than the foot, and oriented north-south. Inside the coffin, I knew, my father's head was turned to the left, facing west, towards Mekkah.

I was relieved there was not even a hint of the stench of death in the room. The coffin must have been well sealed, I thought; or maybe there were two of them, one inside the other; or maybe, time had already completed its hideous work on my father's body, and reduced it to dry bones...

With difficulty, I managed to suppress these inappropriate musings about the corpse inside the coffin, and occupied my mind with prayer and pious reflections.

I prayed to God He would admit my father into Paradise, together with the rest of us, and that He would help me to protect my dominions, and rule over them justly.

I even prayed to my father in the coffin, though I knew very well it is an abomination for a true believer to pray to anybody or anything other than God Himself.

'My dear father', I implored, 'if you can, please help me, guide me, grant me wisdom and strength, grant I may be a worthy successor to you and our ancestors.'

After a few minutes, Bairam Khan took a small, hand-written prayer book from a leather purse attached to his belt. Speaking slowly, word for word, he recited:

'Peace be upon you, o dwellers of the grave!
May Allah grant you and us protection!
We pray to Allah for security, for ourselves and for you.
You are those who have gone before us, and we are following you.
We will meet you, if it pleases Allah.'

We stayed for a few more minutes and left the hall, walking backwards and bowing, as if taking our leave from a living king.

'As soon as feasible, I will have my father brought back to Dilli,' I said to Bairam Khan, looking back over my shoulder as we rode out of Sirhind. 'I will have a splendid mausoleum built for him! It will be the most magnificent building the world has ever seen, more beautiful and imposing than Temür's tomb at Samarqand! Thousands of years from now, people will say: "Surely, this must be the resting place of the greatest emperor of all time!'

Bairam Khan nodded approvingly.

'I am sure your revered father will appreciate this very much, Your Majesty. But there is one thing you can do, which will please him even more!'

'And what would that be?' I asked.

He paused, put his hand on my shoulder, and looked at me, like he had done that afternoon, back in Dilli, when he told me that living one's life is like writing a storybook.

'Make him proud, Your Majesty.'

Ninth Letter

دلّی، آگرا

Dilli, Agra

We proceeded towards Hissar, to check on the military operations. As expected, the rebellion had been crushed by the time we arrived. After a few days' rest, we headed towards Dilli; we reached the capital on the 4th of Ordibehesht [60].

The crowds were visibly more at ease than at the time of our first triumphant entry into the city. Clearly, after a period of understandable scepticism, people finally believed that Humayun's young successor was here to stay. After all, his armies had defeated the mighty Hemu, and Sikandar Sur; who was left to challenge him?

We stayed in the city throughout the summer and the rainy season. After six and a half months, we decided to move to Agra, fifty-two *kos*[61] southward, as we believed this would strengthen our hold on the southern border.

We travelled downstream on the Yamuna, in a fleet of flat-bottomed barks, beautifully adorned with precious silks; crowds gathered in awe, wherever we were passing by. People would, as it should be, spread the news about the unseen splendour of their ruler.

---

[60] Thursday, April 14, 1558 of the Julian calendar. Ordībehesht: Taurus.

[61] One *Kos* roughly equals 2.5 miles or 4 km.

We arrived in Agra on the 18th of Aban[62]. I was pleased to find the city lived up to its reputation, despite the heat of the season. It was clear why my grandfather had chosen to live there: the heat was not any less than in Dilli, but the breeze on the river brought refreshment, and many well-kept gardens added to the charm of the landscape. The arable land produced excellent fruits and vegetables. I would not go as far as the local poets and claim that the Yamuna River 'would make Baghdad ashamed of the Tigris and Egypt of the Nile', but I have to admit, it did have something distinctly majestic over it, and its water was indeed limpid and digestible.

I took up residence in the Badalgarha citadel, and witnessed how the matters of government were put into proper order. As the fort was rather dilapidated, we ordered repair and expansion works, which after a few years would impart to it the majestic, overpowering aspect it currently has. It is good the people see the greatness of their Emperor in the grandeur of His buildings.

Twice a week, we reviewed the affairs of state in the diwan-i-khas[63], with Bairam Khan and all the Officers and Pillars of the Empire, as they were called, in attendance.

Things went well for the Empire, our armies advancing on every front.

In the west, we captured the fort Jitaran in Rajputana[64], despite fierce resistance. As Abu-l Fazl put it, many of the stiff-necked Rajputs were conducted to the abyss of annihilation, and the country was cleared of the rubbish of stubborn rebels. Perhaps more importantly: in the south, we conquered the important city of Gwalior, which of course greatly contributed to the safety of our borders. And up north, the citadel of Jammu fell into our hands: an important first step towards the conquest of beautiful Kashmir.

Towards our enemies, our strategy remained unchanged. Those who dared to oppose us were levelled with the dust of annihilation, or hastened to the hell of extinction, as it is phrased in the chronicles.

---

[62] Sunday, October 30, 1558 of the Julian calendar.

[63] Hall of Private Audience.

[64] Near Jodhpur.

But those who were smart or chicken enough to surrender soon found out, to their own surprise and relief, that they had in fact opened the gates to their own wishes.

That is the way a wise emperor should operate, my son. Towards the obedient, he should be the strong and reliable guardian of peace and prosperity; to those who oppose him, he should be inescapable destruction.

Never forget, people are moved by mainly two things: their own self-interest, and fear; a wise ruler knows how to make use of both.

I once heard an anecdote about an Emperor, somewhere in Rum I believe, who compared the bond between a king and his subjects to a beautiful ring. It should be forged out of the gold of love, adorned with the gems of kindness and magnanimity, but also: hardened through an alloy of rigor and fear, for pure gold is too soft a material to create a durable jewel.

But I was sixteen, neither wise nor strong enough to put this into practice. What can I say, my son? What else can I do, but confess that my life was out of control? It pleases me not at all to think back on this period, but I have to, for your sake. Please understand: the uncertainty that has been tormenting you, I've had that, too! You will see: you will be facing the same problems as I have. You will find that outside enemies are usually not your greatest concern. Getting your own people to do what you want them to, is much more difficult! There is a lot of truth in Abu-l Fazl's mock despair, whenever a dispute at court annoyed him: My God, deliver me from my friends, and I will gladly deal with my enemies!

The atmosphere in Lahore had been bad enough, but now, it was becoming untenable. The animosity between Bairam Khan's followers and the camp of Maham Anaga and Pir Muhammad Khan had turned into outright hatred. Behind some outer semblance of unity during the audiences in the diwan-i-khass, there was nothing but spite and intrigue, everyone trying to discredit everyone else.

It is hard to believe, and even harder to admit, that a strong man like me was unable to call to order a bunch of squabbling, self-righteous courtiers, but what was I to do? After all, I was only sixteen at the time, still very inexperienced. And to make matters worse, I was alone: apart from my mother, far away in Dilli, who was there to turn to for support and impartial advice?

Not a month went by without some or other crisis or quarrel between Bairam Khan and the rest, where I would find myself standing by idly, powerless, as if I had nothing to say about it.

His Majesty was testing the men of the age, Abu-l Fazl wrote... The truth is, His Majesty did not know what to do! I just could not afford to take sides, without risking chaos, possibly even civil war.

And so, I did nothing at all.

Just like before, I seized every possible occasion to get away from the palace. As usual, Abu-l Fazl made brave attempts to describe my behaviour in polite euphemisms:

His Majesty was continually engaged in hunting deer with the cheetah, and in elephant fights, and such other external matters, which the superficial man regards as matters of insouciance, and left political and financial matters to the lovers thereof.

Indeed, I would spend days, if not weeks in a row, in the hunting grounds south and west of Agra. There, amidst the fields and the wilderness, in the awe-inspiring silence, far away from everything and everybody, I did not have to think about the palace and its quarrels. Nothing was more pleasing to my eyes than the graceful step of my cheetahs, and the sight of my hawks soaring above the land. In the excitement of the chase, I found peace of mind.

Back in the city, I spent as much time as I could with the soldiers, taking great pride in showing off my growing strength and martial skills. Indeed, I had become one of the very best marksmen in the army, with both musket and bow. I was an accomplished expert at loading and firing any type of cannon or rocket. All but the very strongest men, I wrestled to the ground, and there was absolutely no one who could handle animals the way I could. A worthy descendant of my Mongol and Turkish ancestors, I would ride the unruliest horses with the greatest of ease. The most vicious, murderous bull elephants, real man-killers like Dilsankar, Hawai, Faujbidar, Damudar, Jhalpa, Lakhna: I rode them all, better than any of the mahauts; meek like lambs, they became under my hand.

In the palace, I deliberately avoided private conversations, with Bairam Khan, Shams-ud-din, or anybody else. I was tired of all the quarrels, the accusations, the self-serving advice, the thinly veiled reproaches... When my presence in the diwan-i-khass was not required,

I would retire to my quarters, usually in the presence of one or the other sweet girl who was proud to comfort me with her firm, soft body.

Unfortunately, demons cannot be driven out by running away from them. The softness of women's breasts, the excitement found in hunting or sports: they provide but a fleeting moment of joy. He who tries to escape from the world, will soon discover that neglect of duty unsettles the mind and fills it with remorse and sadness.

The months went by. They became seasons, then years. I was now seventeen years of age, strong as a bull, in possession of all the wealth and luxury anybody could ever want; but happy, I was not. It was a time of insecurity, and darkness of thought. I felt like a prisoner, in my own palace, in my own life. It seemed to me, the animals in my stables were freer than I was. With each passing moon, I became less and less satisfied with my life, and hated myself for it...

It is not hard to understand why: all the elaborate rituals, the hands and foreheads touching the ground, the flowery titles and superlatives are of little help, when deep down, one knows one does not deserve them. Become the great Emperor you know you can be, Bairam Khan had told me, back in Dilli. But how? When? Would I ever be able to live up to that? Would I ever become as competent as he? He never seemed to get bored or tired, always asking the right questions, always making the right decisions...

His attitude, nevertheless, was a matter of great concern to me. Something about him had changed. The rivalry with Maham Anaga and Pir Muhammad Khan had made him irritable, suspicious, more stubborn even than before. At times, he behaved worse than a squabbling old harem hag. He could not stand anybody disagreeing with him, on anything. The slightest sign of divergence, the weakest opposition was taken as a personal insult, as an attempt to take away his privileges as regent of the Empire.

Despite my advancing adolescence, he kept on running the affairs of state, as if I was still a thirteen-year-old. In fact, rather than seeking my involvement and approval, as he should have done, it seemed he was taking more and more decisions on his own. Was he not supposed to inform me, discuss things with me? How long did he plan to hang on to power? Not once did he talk to me about handing over power and retiring to another function...

I did not fully realize it at the time, but Bairam Khan, for all his hard work and dedication, was less capable a leader than I would later become, at least in one important respect. He constantly made that fatal mistake that so many people in positions of power tend to make: being too preoccupied with his own thoughts and activities to take notice of the forces around.

This is not how power should be exercised, my son. A wise ruler is a keen observer of men and their motives; he knows how to be obeyed, respected, loved and feared at the same time. He will use gentle persuasion, or brutal violence, as required by the circumstances.

But Bairam Khan, unfortunately for him, was a soldier, not a court diplomat. He seemed to know only one way to get what he wanted: ordering people around, as if they were dogs, and brutal repression at the slightest sign of resistance. He cared little he was unpopular; his heavy-handedness made the ranks of his enemies grow larger by the day.

Maybe, I thought to myself, he was getting old: people approaching old age tend to confuse stubbornness with wisdom. But whatever the cause of his behaviour, it was becoming a major problem.

And so, day by day, he and I grew further apart...

I am really too tired to recount every incident that alienated me from him; that does not add much value to the story I want to tell you. Suffice it to say, not a month went by without one. Each time, I would find myself confronted with decisions that had been taken, things that had been done, that had been forced down my throat, and that I could do nothing about...

Despite the outrage of the Sunnis, I did nothing when Bairam Khan unilaterally appointed Shaykh Gada'i Kambu, a fellow Shi'a, to the important office of sadr, responsible for all the imperial lands and the administration of pensions and subsidies. After all, there was no reason for me to intervene. Shaykh Gada'i was a competent man, and did his work well. And I was wise and broad-minded enough to realize that God stands above the petty differences of men. Competence, decency, wisdom: they neither begin nor end at any man-made border...

Despite Maham Anaga's desperate pleadings, I did not intervene when Bairam Khan sent her son Adham Khan to the fortress of Hatkant near Gwalior, where the troublesome Bhadauriyah tribe was in revolt.

Bairam Khan's motives may have been self-serving, but he was probably right: Adham Khan, that hothead, would come of better use fighting the enemies of the Empire. And he did well. With God's help, he subdued the country, and the seditious received fitting punishment, the chronicles report...

But when Bairam Khan unilaterally dismissed Pir Muhammad Khan, ordering him to turn in his standard and kettledrums, and to go to Mekkah, I realized things could not go on like this. He may have had ample reason to be displeased with Pir Muhammad – it was certainly true that he had become annoyingly arrogant – but the dismissal of a senior official is no small matter. Was it not outrageous, that this had been decided without my permission?

And I was not the only one to be worried. Only a few days after the dismissal, I received a visit from my mother, who had travelled all the way from Dilli to see me. I did not have to guess what she wanted to talk to me about.

We exchanged a few civilities and went to my quarters.

'My son, we need to talk', she said, without any further introduction. 'What are you going to do about Bairam Khan?'

'What do you mean, Mother?' I asked.

'I think you know very well what I mean. Your father has been dead for three years now. You are becoming a grown man, my son. It is high time you took matters seriously.'

I wanted to answer something, but she impatiently put up her hand.

'I know what you are going to say, and I agree, Bairam Khan is a competent man. My question is, how much longer? Power is a dangerous thing, my son! It poisons even the purest of minds... What if this man gets inspired by Sher Khan's example? What if he claims the Throne for himself? What if he shifts allegiance to Kamran's son? And even if he does remain loyal: what kind of a king will you be, with that man next to you? I cannot believe You are prepared to settle for a life of indolence in the shade of your own wakil, like Mubariz, eclipsed by Hemu. Can't you see how he is eliminating his rivals, one by one? Can't you see, how he has been putting his Shi'a followers in the highest positions? What gave him the right to confiscate Pir Muhammad's property when he returned from Gujarat to Rajputana, instead of continuing towards Mekkah? Do you think your ancestors would have allowed that? A true King does not allow others to take important decisions like that in his stead! A true King does not beg, my son: he commands! A true King does not hope for things to happen: he makes sure they do!'

Noticing the growing anger on my face, she smiled, relieved to see her words had the intended effect.

'Nothing is lost yet, my son. You are still young; it is normal you rely on people who are more experienced. But time is running out! This is the fourth year of your reign; you are seventeen. It is time for you to assume full power!'

'What do you think I should do about Bairam Khan?' I asked. 'Surely, I cannot just dismiss him, after everything he has done for us?'

'He has done a lot to be grateful for,' she admitted. 'But I am confident there are ways to get rid of him without forgetting your debt of gratitude. There are many territories to be administered, new ones to be conquered...'

It took me a few more weeks before I finally decided to act.

Maybe, if Bairam Khan would have bothered to come and see me, if we would have had a chance to talk, I might still have changed my mind... I might have found a more graceful way out.

But it was not to be. A few days later, probably without being aware of it, he made what I decided were his two final mistakes.

In less than two weeks' time, two of my favorite mahauts, both of them low-caste Hindus, were executed on his direct order. One of them, a gray-haired, toothless, thin man of about fifty, had not been able to restrain an imperial elephant, when it suddenly attacked and killed one of Bairam Khan's animals. The poor fellow was beheaded on the spot.

The second one, a boy my age or perhaps a bit younger, lost his life when the elephant he was guiding along the banks of the Yamuna, suddenly dashed into the water and almost overturned the boat on which Bairam Khan happened to be resting. I was just on my way out, leaving for a short hunting trip, when I saw soldiers dragging the mahaut's corpse away. His head was still lying in the sand, staring at the sky with empty eyes, its mouth half open, as if it was about to ask, how this could have happened.

Only with great effort, I held back my tears. Bairam Khan had probably not given it a moment's thought when he had the boy killed:

after all, it was only a low caste servant, an infidel at that, who had endangered his life. An example had to be set. But I had shared so many fine hours with that simple mahaut. I had known him, liked him; I had made fun of the Hindustani mistakes he made in that clumsy Persian of his... And now, without my permission, because of this one silly incident, he was dead.

It is of course appropriate rulers have the right to life and death. After all, what would the world come to, if there were no punishment? As the ancient Hindu Laws of Manu put it, the whole world is kept in order by punishment, for a guiltless man is hard to find[65].

But kings should never forget that God alone is the source of all power, including our own. His will, and His will alone, should be guiding us, in all our decisions. Whether we let someone go free, or sentence him to die: our sole aim should be to serve God, and God alone.

We should never confuse the appeasement of our own anger with justice. This is why, already in the early years of my reign, I have given strict orders never to carry out any death sentence, unless and until I have repeated it three times during that same day – lest, in my anger, I do something irreparable. To err may be human, but in matters of justice, it is not. In matters of justice, error is inhuman.

There was one good thing about the poor mahaut's death: for the first time in my life, I had been given a good reason to hate Bairam Khan. And perhaps even more importantly: for the first time in my life, I knew my own judgement to be better than his. Suddenly, it had become much easier for me to remove him from office. I made up my mind: Bairam Khan had to go.

The die had been cast. I had taken the most painful decision of my life: I was about to dispose of the man to whom I owed everything. It gives me neither pride nor joy to think back on this, but what else was I to do? When one is born a King, there comes a time when one must take things in one's own hands, no matter how great the merits of your predecessor – is it not so, my son?

It took me several more weeks to work out my plan of action. If I say so myself: I handled it well.

I needed to tread carefully: Bairam Khan was not to be

[65] Quoted by Stanley Wolpert, page 201.

underestimated. Carefully, biding my time, I developed my plan.

As I expected, Maham Anaga and Adham Khan were more than eager to help, and I knew I could also count on Shams-ud-din's loyalty. Secret messages were sent to Pir Muhammad Khan, who was in Rajputana after having travelled as far as Gujarat, to keep himself ready to return as soon as possible.

When Bairam Khan was not around, we would meet in my private quarters and discuss the appropriate course of action.

'It's easy enough,' Adham Khan had stated with his usual impetuousness. 'There are plenty of opportunities to kill the bastard! If Your Majesty so wishes, I can do it myself! Bairam Khan does not like me, but he trusts me well enough to allow me in his presence. Yes, I could do it, one of the next few days, at a moment when his personal guards are not around: when we visit the mosque, or on our way to a meeting. Or I could invite him to my quarters for dinner, under some pretext or other, saying I need to discuss something with him in private, and have him assassinated, as soon as he comes in, just like he did with poor old Tardi Beg!'

Have Bairam Khan assassinated, after so many years of faithful service? No, I wanted nothing to do with it! And to this day, I am proud and grateful I did not take the easy way out: it would have haunted me for the rest of my life.

'There must be another way,' I said. 'A man like Bairam Khan does not deserve a fate like that.'

Adham Khan clearly did not share my scruples. 'Your Majesty is most kind and magnanimous. But he should keep in mind that this is for the higher good of His Throne! Your Majesty's kindness prevents him from seeing the clear and imminent danger this man represents. If I were in your position, Your Majesty, I would not be too sure about his loyalty! Just look at what this man has done over the last few years: there is simply no limit to his ambition and arrogance! Sooner or later, this Shi'a bastard will show his true colours! Sooner or later, ...'

I raised my hand to silence him.

'I am moved by my *koka's*[66] loyalty and devotion, and grateful for

[66] Koka: foster brother. Akbar and Adham Khān had both been suckled by Māham Anaga.

his courageous offer, but my mind is made up: I will not have Bairam Khan assassinated. Not only would it be unjust, it would be unwise! Bairam Khan has served my blessed father Humayun and me for so many years – his support has been invaluable to us! The officers and soldiers in the army all love and respect him, and for good reason – he is an excellent general! If I would have this man executed, after everything he has done for me, how could I expect the others to trust and respect me?'

Maham Anaga wanted to say something, but Shams-ud-din interrupted: 'Let us not discuss this any longer. His Majesty is right: killing Bairam Khan would be a grave sin in the eyes of Allah; moreover, it would probably do His Majesty's interests more harm than good!'

Adham Khan said nothing in reply. From the look on his face, it was clear he was not convinced at all. Knowing his violent temper, there was a real danger he would go ahead with his plan anyway.

'If Bairam Khan would be assassinated, without my direct order,' I added, looking Adham Khan straight in the eye, 'I would have no alternative but to have the murderer executed!'

Adham Khan bowed, visibly angered and insulted. 'As Your Majesty commands. I hope Your Majesty will never come to regret his kindness...'

There was an uncomfortable silence.

'How should we proceed?' Maham Anaga asked. 'Surely, it's dangerous to wait any longer! Your Majesty, in his kindness, may not believe it, but this Shi'a bastard is quickly taking control over the army! Over the last two years, he has given the rank of "commander of five thousand" to no less than twenty-five men, all of them his own personal supporters! Soon, all the army officers will be his vassals! If we wait any longer, it will be too late – there will be no army left to support us!'

'Who says we need to wait?' I said, trying to sound unperturbed. 'I can do exactly what he did to Pir Muhammad Khan: I can grant him leave to depart to Mekkah. He is a deeply religious man, and has not completed the Hajj – he may even welcome the idea! However, you are right – we must also be prepared to deal with the situation if he would refuse to go. It is never a good idea to leave matters of high importance to someone else's discretion! I think we better assemble a strong fighting force, somewhere outside Agra – up in Dilli, for instance. If Bairam Khan does rise against me, which I still do not believe he will, we will be in a good position to defend ourselves and crush the rebellion before he has had a chance to organize himself properly.'

And so it was done. On Sehsanbeh the 9th of Farvardin of the fifth year[67], we left Agra, with only a small escort, in order not to arouse suspicion, on the pretext of another hunting trip. I admit, it was not very glorious, nor courageous, but I do not think there was another way.

As prudence dictated, we took Abu-l Qasim, son of Kamran, with us. If Bairam Khan would rebel, he would at least not be able to use a grandson of Babur to legitimize his uprising. The Amirs were bound by an oath of loyalty to us, but it would be foolish to provide them with an excuse to join a rebellion...

We headed north and reached Sikandara. As the latest messages from Dilli had indicated that my mother was not feeling well, it did not arouse any suspicion that I ostensibly changed my mind about the hunting trip, and decided to travel to Dilli, to pay her a visit. A message was sent to Shihab ud Din Ahmad Khan, the governor of the city, to strengthen the defenses of the fort and prepare to receive us.

After a few days, we reached Dilli, without any noteworthy incident. As soon as we arrived, messages were sent to all the Amirs, informing them that now that I had reached adulthood, I had decided to relieve Bairam Khan of his command and take the matters of government in my own hands.

They say that Bairam Khan simply refused to believe the first rumours about his impending dismissal. When, after a few days, he realized that they were true, he sat still for hours, silent, his face wet with tears.

Yet, he flatly refused to take up arms against me, rejecting the advice of Shaykh Gada'i, Wali Beg and other supporters of his. When they insisted, he reportedly shouted:

'Leave me alone! I do not aspire to the throne. My aim was the conquest of Hindustan, and now, my work is done; I only want to serve the Empire...'

There was much unrest not to say panic among the courtiers in Dilli, when after a few days, reports came in that Bairam Khan

---

[67] Tuesday, March 19, 1560.

was advancing on the city. Preparations were made for war, but that failed to put any of them at ease; there were even a few cowards who suggested we retreat to Lahore, or even to Kabul... All of them were extremely relieved, when messengers delivered a letter, in which Bairam Khan 'respectfully requested to be granted the favor of being allowed a private audience with His Majesty'.

Of all the things I have done wrong in my life, this is probably the one I am most ashamed of: I refused to see him. Maham Anaga and the others had of course warned me against receiving him, arguing that it was a ruse, that I was endangering my life, but that was not the reason. I simply could not bear to see him face to face – I was too afraid of the shame, the guilt, the remorse...

In reply to his request, I sent him an official firman, ordering him to return to Agra, and giving him the permission 'to turn his attention to the bliss of pilgrimage'. Despite Maham Anaga's pleas to the contrary, I did add some friendly words, assuring him that he was like a father to me and dear to my heart, and that I would remit to him whatever extent of land he wished in Hindustan, so that his servants might remit him the proceeds, harvest by harvest and year by year.

Again, Bairam Khan complied with my request and prepared himself for travel. Quietly, he divested himself of his standard, kettledrums and insignia, and sent them to Court. To his supporters, who still tried to convince him to tread the path of rebellion, he reportedly answered:

'That's not what I want to write in the book of my life!'

He set out to the Panjab, and proceeded from there through Rajputana towards Gujarat, where he would take ship to Mekkah. The story would have ended then and there, had I not made a capital blunder: allowing Pir Muhammad Khan, who had returned to Dilli as soon as he heard about Bairam Khan's dismissal, to follow him into Rajputana. As he put it, he wanted to go there with a group of cavalry, to 'keep an eye on Bairam' and 'pack him off to Mekkah'.

I should have known much, much better. A man like Bairam Khan might accept injustice, but never an insult. Sure enough, when he became aware of Pir Muhammad's approach, he promptly turned around to fight. At the first sight of Bairam Khan's Turkoman horse archers, Pir Muhammad Khan ran like a rabbit...

Much more worried than I cared to admit, I tried to repair the mistake, sending Bairam another firman, in which I ordered him to continue on his pilgrimage, but it was too late. The matter would have to be settled on the battlefield.

Bairam Khan and his small army quickly turned east, into the Panjab. He left his family in the fort of Bathinda, then headed towards Jalandhar, clearly intent on taking Lahore.

Hasty preparations were made, and we left Dilli, sending Shams-ud-din ahead with a strong mobile force, to halt or at least slow down Bairam Khan's advance. I followed at the head of the main body of the army.

The unthinkable had happened. The imperial army was marching against Bairam Khan.

Tenth Letter

بیرام خان

Bairam Khan

Shams-ud-din did not waste any time. Driving his troops forward, he managed to block Bairam Khan's advance near the village of Gunacur near Jalandhar.

He sent emissaries, in a last attempt to convince him to submit, but it was too late: there comes a time, when a man like this will stand and fight.

Morale among the army was low. Bairam Khan's fighting force, though vastly outnumbered, was not to be underestimated: excellent soldiers, devoted to their leader, and commanded by the best general in Hindustan.

Bairam Khan attacked immediately, preventing us to deploy any artillery, and taking advantage of the fatigue of our soldiers and animals after their hasty advance. He had divided his fighting force into two wings: a cavalry vanguard, led by his main lieutenant Wali Beg; and the main group, which he commanded himself and consisted of about fifty excellent fighting elephants, supported by another cavalry force.

Shams-ud-din's vanguard cavalry, though clearly superior in numbers, was quickly routed by the fierce onslaught of Bairam's Turkomans. Many imperial cavalrymen turned around and fled without a fight, more out of fear than by enemy action.

Bairam Khan did not hesitate to seize the opportunity. He instantly attacked the main body of Shams-ud-din's army, which was standing on a small ridge behind a wide rice paddy. In an unorthodox but bold move, he sent his elephants up front, in a direct attack through the rice field, while he and his cavalry came out from behind on the left flank, leaving the rice field on his right.

If things would have worked out as he had planned them, he just might have pulled it off: Shams-ud-din's army would have been caught in a deadly pincer, its flank cut off and unable to move, while the centre was being swept away by the elephants.

Fortunately, however, with God's help, this plan failed. The paddy, planted with shali autumn rice, happened to be quite deep, and its bottom soil unusually soft; Bairam Khan's elephants, advancing very slowly, up to their bellies in the mud, got bogged down, harassed by clouds of arrows. A number of their leading mahauts died, and the attack faltered.

Shams-ud-din, an excellent soldier himself, was now free to launch a massive counterattack on his right flank, and block Bairam Khan's charge before it could reach his position.

Bairam Khan had gambled and lost – the battle was over for him. Unless he retreated immediately, his forces, much smaller in number than ours, would soon be encircled and annihilated. Only thanks to his generalship and the discipline of his men he managed to get away with most of his army, but at a heavy price. Wali Beg, badly wounded, and several leading officers were taken prisoner; and many excellent men fell, covering his retreat.

Shams-ud-din chased the fleeing enemy for about two kos. Then, he prudently abandoned pursuit and turned back, rejoining the rest of the imperial forces at Sirhind.

His victory was met with elation. A major battle, won against the great Bairam Khan! Who could still harbour any doubt about the invincibility of my stars? This victory was nothing less than a sign from Allah!

Our euphoria reached a new climax, when Mun'im Khan joined us from Kabul, at the head of a large and well-equipped army.

Sumptuous celebrations were held. Shams-ud-din was of course celebrated as a conquering hero and received lavish gifts, including the robes of honor, standards and kettledrums that once belonged to Bairam Khan, and the lofty title of Khan A'azim. The office of wakil and the title of Khan Khanan, however, I gave to Mun'im Khan: a ruler is wise to divide power, lest his servants become rivals...

The prisoners were dragged before me, chains around their necks and feet. I should have felt joy and pride, but could not help feeling deeply sad at the sight of these excellent, brave men who had somehow become my enemies. I refused to have them executed, in spite of pleas to the contrary: I sent them all to prison. With the exception of Wali Beg, who died of his wounds, all of them were later pardoned, and in time, reinstated as officers of the army. History proved me right: they all served me well.

After a few more days of leisure and celebration and a brief visit to the city of Lahore, we moved north towards the Siwaliks, to deal with Bairam Khan. Scouts had informed us he had fled to the stronghold of Talwara in the midst of the hills, and was forging an alliance with the local rajah. As we outnumbered him more than fifteen to one, morale in our camp was high – there could be no serious doubt about the final outcome.

Defeated enemies never fail to attract would-be heroes, eager to earn themselves a place in history. Sultan Husayn Jalair, the leader of our vanguard, was such a man. When our scouts first located Bairam Khan's whereabouts, he did not wait for reinforcements, but attacked him with only slightly superior forces.

It was a fatal mistake. The battle was a disaster: our vanguard was wiped out, with little or no losses to Bairam Khan; and Husayn Jalair paid with his life for his intrepidness.

All of a sudden, things were not so easy anymore. Our forces were still vastly superior to Bairam's, but this humiliating defeat changed everything. Who was to stop him from heading further west? What if he escaped into the hills? What if he recruited new allies? He only needed to win over one or two influential Amirs, and the tables could turn quite easily!

In the midst of heated discussions, guards announced the arrival of Jamal Khan, one of Bairam's trusted officers.

He knelt down, respectful, but unafraid.

'I have been instructed by Bairam Khan Badakhshani, to offer Your Imperial Majesty his total and unconditional surrender, and to hand over this letter.'

Mun'im Khan accepted the letter in my stead, and read it out aloud:

'Your Imperial Majesty,

Having reached the evening of my life, which I spent almost entirely in faithful service to Your Majesty and His august father, who is nested in the garden of Paradise, I now find myself Your Majesty's enemy. Never before has my heart been this heavy and filled with sorrow.

As Allah Himself and all His Angels are my witnesses, I would much rather die in agonizing pain than to continue war and strife between us! Too many good men have died in a fight which should never have taken place! If Allah, in His unending mercy, would grant me the bliss of Paradise, I would not dare to enter it, for fear of meeting Your Majesty's revered father, and having to explain that I had become Your Majesty's enemy.

I have therefore decided that I would much rather die as Your Majesty's prisoner and slave, than to go on living in freedom and in conflict with Him; I therefore offer Your Majesty my complete and unconditional surrender.

I humbly implore Your Majesty to find mercy in His heart, and pardon my loyal men and their officers. It would not only be an act of magnanimity, worthy of a noble King: it would further Your Majesty's interests. These men are experienced, outstanding soldiers, and each and every one on them has, under my personal supervision, taken a solemn oath on the Holy Qur'an and on the graves of their forefathers, that they will serve Your Majesty until death.

As for myself, I have no other wish but to undergo the sentence Your Majesty will pronounce against me, or to retire to places of holiness and wisdom, and prepare myself to meet my Maker.'

There was a long silence.

'Jamal Khan,' I finally asked, 'why is it, that Bairam Khan has decided to surrender, after having won an important victory against the imperial vanguard?'

'I do not know, Your Majesty. All I can say is that after the battle, we brought him the head of Sultan Husayn Jalair, who had fallen in battle. He held it in his hands, and looked at it, for what seemed like hours.

'Has it come to this,' he said, 'that I have to look at the severed head of a man who has been an officer in my own army, for years? How many battles has this man fought by my side, only to die as my enemy? This madness must end, here and now!'

Some of us tried to convince him, that he was now in a much stronger position, that he should move to the northwest, return with a stronger army... he just put up his hand and replied: 'I am sick of the world and its affairs!'

The next day, he arrived in person at the imperial army camp. I had him escorted to my tent immediately.

For a moment, he kept standing in the entrance – unafraid, but immensely tired and sad. He had lost a lot of weight; dark bags were showing under his eyes. He obviously had not had much sleep in many weeks.

The guards wanted to take his sword, but I ordered to leave him alone. He bowed stiffly, walked a few steps towards me, and knelt down. He took his sword by the sheath, and handed it to me.

'Your Majesty will do to me what is just,' he said calmly.

I took the sword in both hands, held it in front of me, pressed the hilt against my heart and forehead, and kissed it, as if I had just received a precious gift from a great king, rather than accepting a rebel's surrender.

'At the battle of Machhiwara[68], this sword has saved my father, may he enjoy eternal bliss in the gardens of Allah! It is this sword that has slain the mighty Hemu at Panipat! No one wears it better than you do, Khan Baba,' I said softly, handing him the sword back.

He accepted it as I had done, with both hands, holding it by the sheath, touching his chest and forehead with its hilt, and kissing it.

He wanted to say something, but remained silent. When I saw tears running down his face, I could no longer hold back my own. I rose from the pillows, took him by the shoulders, and made him stand up. I took the shawl I was wearing around my neck and used it to wipe his tears and mine.

'Sad and regrettable things have happened between us these past couple of weeks, Khan Baba. We must put them behind us. What are a few weeks of misunderstandings, compared to years of friendship?'

I had him sit down next to me, as an exceptional guest of honor, on my own pillows, at my right-hand side.

---

[68] Battle of Māchhīwāra: important battle in Emperor Humāyūn's ultimate recapture of India.

'You have not been taking proper care of yourself, Khan Baba. I want you to forget your worries, and dine with me!'

I ordered food and wine and told everyone to leave us alone.

We ate and drank, exchanged the usual civilities. I inquired about his health and that of his household, and was glad to hear that my lovely cousin Salima and his son Abdurrahim were doing well. Nevertheless, our conversation was interspersed with long, awkward silences.

'It is so sad that all this has happened between us, Khan Baba. I wish I could undo it all, and start anew.'

'Your Majesty does not need to apologize. It was more my fault than His. I should have asked Him how He wanted to run the affairs of government. I was a fool to have taken for granted that I could just carry on as if Your Majesty were still a young boy.

'I must confess, it has hurt me deeply to see that Your Majesty dismissed me without talking to me, but I do understand how this happened. There are more than enough people at Court who have planted the poisonous seeds of doubt in Your Majesty's heart about my true intentions. Then again, I am to blame for the wrong impression I created; I do understand why Your Majesty acted the way he did. It is Your Majesty's God-given right and obligation to occupy the Throne. In matters of such importance, one should never take any chances with people one does not trust.'

'I am truly sorry it had to go this way, Khan Baba', I repeated.

'It's probably for the best, Your Majesty. It was Allah's will. I am grateful I can leave Hindustan, at peace with myself, assured of Your Majesty's continued friendship and affection.'

'Do not leave, Khan Baba! Stay here with us! We desperately need honest and competent men like you! There are so many important tasks to assume, territories to administer, enemies to fight...'

'I am grateful for Your Majesty's offer, but would be obliged if He would allow me to continue on my journey to Mekkah. It has always been my wish to fulfil this sacred obligation. Is it not written that the recompense of Hajj is Paradise itself? I yearn to pray at the Ka'bah; I want to stone the pillars at Mina, I want to stand in the plain of Arafat, behold Jabal Rahmah, the Mountain of Mercy; I want to drink of the blessed waters of Zamzam. I want to travel to al-Madinah, pay my respects at the shrine of the Prophet, peace be upon Him and His household... I am fifty-five years old, Your Majesty. At this advanced age, one should not postpone any matters of importance...'

'Who am I, to stand between you and Allah, Khan Baba? But promise me one thing: come back to Hindustan, as soon as possible! I really need good men like you to advise me!'

'*In sha'a Llah*[69], Your Majesty, I promise. It is good to know that I will have a home back here.'

'Well, *Khuda Hafiz*[70], and come back soon, Khan Baba!'

'*Khuda Hafiz,* Your Majesty. May you live a good and glorious life!'

[69] *In shā'a Llāh* (Arabic): if God wills.

[70] *Khudā Hāfiz* or *Khodā Hāfez*: God Be your Protector/Guardian; one of many Persian expressions commonly used in Urdu.

Eleventh Letter

بیرام خان

Bairam Khan (2)

Five months had passed since Bairam Khan's surrender. I resided in Agra after a one-month sojourn in Dilli. Nothing of great importance happened in those first months. I took appropriate measures to put Kabul in order, when I learned that things were not going as they should, after Mun'im Khan's departure. And there was a first attempt from our side to take Kashmir. It was badly prepared, ill-executed, and failed miserably. A disappointment, but I vowed I would be back.

The atmosphere in Agra had changed. I was not the mighty Emperor I would be a few years later, but people clearly respected and feared me. It seemed the people were preparing themselves for a new, glorious, prosperous era. With my permission, Mun'im Khan took up residence in Bairam Khan's house, and many other nobles built pleasant dwellings near the Yamuna.

Then one afternoon in 968, it must have been towards the beginning of Esfand[71], the guards announced that Mun'im Khan requested a private audience. This did not bode well...

'I regret to have to inform Your Majesty,' he began, 'that my honorable predecessor, Bairam Khan Badakhshani, has passed away.'

'What? Is Bairam Khan dead? How can that be? He wasn't ill, was he?'

---

[71] Around the third week of February 1561, Julian calendar.

'No, Your Majesty. I am afraid he was assassinated.'

'Murdered? Who was it? I want to know who did this! I want the filthy son of a bitch executed – no, I want him tortured to death! I want to see him impaled! I want to see him strangled with his own guts! I want to feed his carcass to the dogs!'

'It happened in Pattan, down in Gujarat. After Your Majesty had graciously pardoned him, he was traveling leisurely towards the coast, where he intended to board a ship to Jeddah and move on to Mekkah. On the way, he visited shrines and mosques, giving alms to the poor, devoting his time to prayer, meditation, and edifying conversation with saintly hermits. People who were with him say he was at peace with Allah, with the world, with himself. In fact, no one had seen him so much at ease, in many years. He was looking forward to the Hajj and spending the evening of his life in peaceful retirement, amidst his loved ones.

'In Pattan, across the Gujarat border, the governor received him with courtesy and respect. The area being most pleasant, he decided to enjoy the gardens for a few days.

'The day of his death, the 14th of Jumada al Awwal[72], he had been enjoying a boat trip on Lake Sahansa Lang; it has a small island in the middle, with a charming pavilion. He and a few of his guards had spent the day on the lake and the islet; they came back in the late afternoon. They disembarked on the shore and walked to the spot where they had left their horses. The passable part of the shore is rather narrow and difficult, with boulders and pebble stones and bushes obstructing the view.

'There was a group of five or six Pashto-speaking Afghans sitting on the beach; one more was standing a few steps away from them. They seemed to be enjoying the view of the setting sun, engaged in what seemed to be pleasant conversation. As they were wearing the honorable white robes of pilgrims on the Hajj, Bairam Khan greeted them courteously, and did not pay much further attention to them.

'As he passed them by, the man who had been standing closest suddenly jumped towards him, and stabbed him in the back with a broad-bladed dagger that he had been hiding in his sleeve, yelling "That's for Machhiwara, you pig!"

---

[72] Friday, January 31st, 1561 (Julian calendar).

'The blade missed the heart, but pierced the left lung, the point of the weapon coming out at his chest. He must have realized instantly that his wound was fatal. He did not struggle or attempt to strike back, just calmly said "Allahu Akbar", and sank to the ground.

'The cowardly assassin dashed back to his comrades; instantly, many more of them came out of the bushes – there must have been about forty of them. They came towards Bairam Khan, who was lying on the ground, bleeding to death. Perhaps they wanted to finish him off, or take his head with them, as a trophy.

'One of his guards, a Qazaqi raider, jumped between them and his master. He killed one of the assailants with his throwing-knife and mortally wounded two more, before obtaining the bliss of martyrdom himself.

'His sacrifice gave Bairam Khan's other guards enough time to get their bows ready. Several Afghan pigs paid for it with their lives. The one standing closest to Bairam Khan was fortunate to die a merciful death, taking a direct hit in the middle of the chest, right through the heart. He staggered two more steps, an expression of disbelief on his face, and collapsed. He must have been dead before he hit the ground. The next two were less fortunate: both of them were shot through the throat. Your Majesty knows that our archers always try to hit their victims in such a way that they make a lot of noise before they die: nothing is more discouraging to an attacking enemy than the agony of fallen comrades! Sure enough, these two bastards fell to the ground, their hands clasped in vain around the shaft of the arrow, choking, gargling, their faces twisted in horror and pain.

'As if it had been rehearsed, the next three all got an arrow high in the stomach, right below the spot where the two halves of the rib cage meet, where even a minor blow causes the most excruciating pain. Provided the arrow has not penetrated too deeply, those who have been hit in that spot will die a long and horribly painful death, moaning as if they are vomiting their guts out, until they die of exhaustion.

'The pain of their fallen comrades clearly made the intended impression on the rest of the assailants: their onslaught faltered; they ran away for cover. The Turkoman guards pressed forward, intending to take their master into safety, but Bairam Khan, an outstanding soldier until death, stopped them.

"Leave me," he groaned – in Turki, so the Afghans would not understand. "Save my family! Make sure they do not hurt my family!"

'His head sank back on the pebbles of the beach. He looked at the sky and the lake, and lay still, trying not to cough, seemingly oblivious of his surroundings, resolved to die with dignity, in serene and complete submission to Allah's will. After a few more moments, he closed his eyes, and stopped breathing.

'The Turkomans arrived in the camp ahead of their assailants, just in time to bring everybody into safety, but could not prevent these unwashed, black-hearted pigs from ransacking and plundering the camp. The guards retreated south, taking four-year-old Abdurrahim and Bairam Khan's spouses and their retinue safely to Ahmedabad. They had to fight their way back, under constant threat of attack by gangs of Afghans who were following them. But those filthy pigs learned to keep their distance when a few mornings in a row, they found their guards dead, with purple-black faces, a thin string of hemp around their filthy necks – an unmistakable sign that our raiders had been paying them a nightly visit...'

'And what about the murderer?' I asked.

Mun'im Khan hesitated.

'That son of a bitch got what he deserved, Your Majesty! When he went for his horse, back on the shore of the lake, one of our men put one of these fishbone arrows into him – you know, those with a long, thin arrowhead and eight sharp little barbs, impossible to pull out. It went clean through the bastard's right kidney, and got stuck in the middle of his liver. It must have taken him days of horrible pain to die!'

'May his suffering continue in hell, for centuries upon centuries!,' I hissed.

'Tell me, Mun'im Khan...'

'Yes, Your Majesty?'

I wanted to have him take an oath on the Holy Qur'an – swear to me that the murderer was indeed dead, as he had described; but I did not dare to ask. Deep down, I knew he had been lying to me, making things up, to make me feel better. Probably, there had not been that many Afghan victims; probably, the murderer was alive and well. Justice is not always done in this world... as you well know, my son: assassins do not always get what they deserve.

'Tell me,' I said, calming myself down, 'who was this son of a bitch, anyway, and why did he murder Bairam Khan?'

'They say his name was Mubarak Lohani. His father was among the many thousands killed at the battle of Machhiwara – where, as Your Majesty knows, Bairam Khan led our troops to victory, when Humayun Padshah recaptured Hindustan. Apparently, he wanted to avenge his father.'

'What happened to Bairam Khan's body?'

'Your Majesty can rest assured – the Khan Khanan was given a decent burial. Some local faqirs, who had witnessed the incident from afar, took pity on him, and carried his body to the tomb of Shaykh Husam ud Din nearby.'

'I am glad to hear he was put to rest in a holy place. May Allah grant him the eternal bliss of Paradise! Maybe later, we should have his body brought to a place nearby: it would be good if I could visit him, light a lamp on his grave... And where is his family? I trust they are safe?'

'They are, Your Majesty. They are still in Ahmedabad. I hear they are doing well, under the circumstances. Many good people are helping them.'

'Have them come to Court as soon as possible. I wish to take all of them under my care.'

'With respect, Your Majesty, ...'

'Have it done now.'

'Yes, Your Majesty.'

For several weeks, I hardly slept, haunted by bitter, futile thoughts about what could and should have happened, if only I had done things differently; asking forgiveness, with nothing and nobody to answer me, but the silent, black void of the night.

Twelfth Letter

مخفی

Makhfi

From the Memoirs of Her Imperial Highness

Salima Sultana Begam Chaqaniani,

[73] 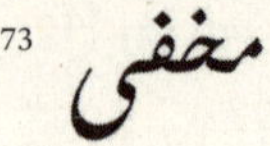

Widow of Bairam Khan

A small coffer of jewels and gold, and the clothes on our backs – that is all we managed to escape with, when Bairam's guards came galloping into the camp, shouting we had to leave immediately.

Looking outside the palki on the camel that was carrying me, I could see in the distance those filthy Afghan dogs plundering our camp, tearing down the tents, dragging off everything they got their dirty hands on. A group of about twenty of them chased us, probably thinking there were even greater spoils to be gained. They soon changed their minds. Our guards swiftly turned around in the saddle, riding backwards and shooting their arrows like the steppe warriors of old. The first three Afghans who came too close, paid for it with their

[73] Makhfī (the Hidden).

worthless lives, and the rest wisely returned to the much easier task of plundering our camp.

I cannot describe the storm of thoughts that rushed through my head. Just one moment before, I had been an important visitor, a high-born Gurkaniyya princess, granddaughter of Babur Padshah the Tiger, cousin of the powerful young Emperor of Hindustan, preferred spouse of the most wealthy and powerful nobleman of the Empire... And now, all at once, I was a nearly destitute widow, a fugitive, fearing for my life and that of my loved ones.

The king of Gujarat, while allowing us free passage, obviously did not dare to take sides; the emissaries we sent to his court, carrying urgent requests for troops to protect us, came back with polite but evasive promises and prayers. We were on our own, all alone in a foreign, hostile country.

Fortunately, I still had my husband's competent officers and true friends, Muhammad Amin Diwana and Baba Zambur, and their Turkoman and Uzbeg soldiers. I was really moved to see how these men, who could so easily have saved themselves, stayed with us, faithful to their fallen master, ready to lay down their lives for us if necessary.

The flight to Ahmedabad was a nightmare. The first few days, we lived in constant fear. But Bairam's men remained on their guard, and made the assailants pay dearly each time they tried to come near us. Our scouts even carried out a number of nightly raids themselves. Finding a few more of their men dead in the morning, the Afghans wisely chose to follow us from a much safer distance.

Down in Ahmedabad, we found a gated house in the northern part of town, which, our men reassured, was safe and easy to defend. There, we waited... hoping to get some kind of reply to the messages we had sent to faraway Hindustan. I thought I would never see it again.

In more than one way, those long months in the relative comfort and safety of the house in Ahmedabad were much worse than the days of hasty flight.

Now, I was alone with my sadness, grieving for the death of my strong, gentle husband.

I spent as much time as possible with little Abdurrahim. Such a sweet little fellow, and incredibly bright, too! It was truly amazing how easily he spoke both Persian and Turki with us, and Hindustani with the servants.

Despite his young age, it was clear that he would grow up to be a handsome man like his father: the same high cheekbones, the same long face and strong nose.

How often had I envied the child's mother! How often had I prayed to Allah that He would grant me the favor of bearing my husband another wonderful son, just like Abdurrahim! Alas, it was not to be...

His son's mother, I was not; but I clearly was Bairam's preferred wife, and I like to think, it was not just because I happened to occupy the highest rank in birth. No, Bairam Khan really loved me, not only as his wife, but also as his soul mate. It gave me much pride and satisfaction to find that, among all his wives and friends, I was the only person he would share his plans, hopes and fears with.

How I cherish the memories of our times together – the hours of pleasant conversation over dinner; the nights, when we were passionate lovers, his strong hands all over my body, his stern face suddenly full of tenderness...

How I loved watching him asleep in my bed – his lined, tan face; his hair and beard, with the grey hairs amidst the black ones. How I loved touching his chest, arms and hands – covered with so much hair, that I used to joke I had married a bear!

Bairam Khan... The kind of man I had always hoped I would marry some day: strong, competent, respected and feared by everybody, yet always considerate and gentle towards me. I had wanted to grow old with him and cared for our children and grandchildren, but it was not to be. He was gone forever... not even a grave for me to visit. There was nothing left for me to do but to remember him, pray for him, and cry for him.

At last, after months of waiting, encouraging news reached us from Agra: my cousin, young Emperor Akbar, wanted to take us under his care. He would personally take charge of Abdurrahim's education, and all of Bairam Khan's family would be residing at the Imperial Court, under his protection. Much as I resented Akbar for having dismissed my husband, I was grateful to return to a safer place.

And so, we finally left Ahmedabad behind us and travelled back to Hindustan, this time with a powerful force of three hundred elite cavalry escorting us all the way. We were safe – nothing but an all-out attack by a large army could pose any threat to us. Our assailants were nowhere to be seen, and we arrived safely in Agra, after an uneventful, if tiring, passage.

I rode into the daunting red sandstone fort, more or less resigned to my fate, with the prospect of a rather boring, but safe and comfortable life in the women's quarters of the imperial palace, where I would be treated with respect, as a widowed princess of royal blood. There, I would spend the long days, months and years of my life, attending to my toilette and attire, educating someone else's children, playing silly card games with the other women, gossiping, sowing, embroidering, reading, writing, and musing about what might have been...

The reunion was genuinely cordial. Akbar received us with every imaginable honor – a grandiose feast was organized, and grateful prayers offered to Allah. Our guards, who had protected us so bravely during those long months, the soldiers as well as the officers, received most generous rewards – enough gold, in fact, for them to live comfortably for the rest of their lives, and robes of honor, which they seemed to value even more. Akbar, I was happy to see, knew how to appreciate and reward loyalty.

We first assembled in the diwan-i-am[74], its courtyard lined with a guard of huge war elephants, rows of lancers and archers, and cavalrymen, all on pitch black, richly caparisoned horses.

As Akbar came in from the balcony and sat himself down on the throne, the elephants bent their front legs, the horses lowered their heads, and all the attendants bowed deep down from the waist, their right hands touching their heads.

It was the first time since my wedding that I saw my cousin. He had changed quite a bit, and for the better, I had to admit to myself. Despite his youth and the friendly expression on his face, he looked pretty imposing, with the natural authority of a true king. He was a grown man now, of medium height, but quite strongly built and broad-shouldered. In accordance with his status, he was richly attired in a robe of red silk, a long string of pearls around his neck, and a rather small, tightly rolled, bejewelled turban on his head. In accordance with the latest fashion,

[74] Diwān-i-ām: Hall of Public Audience.

his face was clean-shaven, apart from a moustache. Despite his Persian mother, his appearance was that of a full-blooded Turk. Judging from the portraits, in fact, he and our common grandfather Babur could have been brothers.

In response to the homage, Akbar nodded and raised his right hand a few times, and remained seated on the Throne for a few moments, until the official salutation was over. Then, in sharp contrast with the solemnity of the moment, he quickly came down from the platform, and personally embraced us all, one by one.

'My dear cousin!,' he said softly, as he took me by the shoulders and held me against him. It seemed to me that he was holding me just a bit longer than necessary. Was I imagining this, or was there more than just familial affection in the way he was looking at me?

There were tears in his eyes as he squatted down in front of little Abdurrahim.

'My dear little fellow,' he whispered, gently touching the boy's cheek. 'Don't you remember me? I am your uncle Akbar! My, you have grown! Let me look at you! You look just like your father, you know that? Would you like some sweets? What would you like to do? Would you like to take a ride on an elephant with me?'

Abdurrahim bit his upper lip and looked down.

'Go on, answer, His Majesty is asking you a question!' his mother said.

The child kept looking at the floor.

'Yes, Your Majesty,' it murmured.

'Did you hear?' Akbar asked triumphantly, addressing no one in particular. 'The way he speaks Turki – just like his father!'

He took the child in his arms and walked across the courtyard, pointing at various things, babbling all the way. They went to see the horses, and then the elephants; Akbar took some sweets out of his robe and had the child offer them to the animals. The little boy seemed fascinated.

'You see, Abdurrahim? You see the little finger they have at the tip of their trunk?'

He made a sign to the mahaut sitting on the largest elephant of them all. The man made the animal bend its front legs and sink down on its knees, and jumped off its back. Akbar, still holding Abdurrahim in one arm, put his foot on the elephant's left tusk, took hold of the rope around its broad neck, and sat himself down, digging in his knees behind the huge ears. He took the mahaut's spike, clacked his tongue, and made the animal stand again. He steered it out of the courtyard, disappearing for quite a while, and came back after what must have been an extensive tour of the premises. Little Abdurrahim looked proud as a peacock, his eyes big with excitement.

'You did great, Abdurrahim! You will become a great soldier! Well, did you like the elephant ride? Would you like to do that again some time?'

Abdurrahim nodded enthusiastically. All the attendants applauded as Akbar took the child by the hand and walked it back to its mother.

I looked around the courtyard, and my eye fell on Maham Anaga. The conniving bitch was watching the scene with a half-hearted smile, trying in vain to hide her jealousy. Several people had told me how she and that lap dog of hers, Mun'im Khan, had made more than one attempt to convince Akbar that it was unwise and dangerous to have the son of a rebel grow up at the imperial court. I was glad to hear that he had told them in no uncertain terms to shut up.

Fear and anger suddenly came over me. If anything happened to that little boy, I would, so help me Allah, personally scratch her eyes out!

She happened to look in my direction. She smiled faintly, but I felt her beady little crow's eyes probing into my soul, and I knew, she was guessing what I had been thinking. Just as well.

That same afternoon, about one hour before the evening prayers, one of my personal attendants came into my quarters and handed me a note from the chief eunuch:

His Imperial Majesty,
Abu'l Muzaffar Jalal-ud-Din Muhammad Akbar Padshah Ghazi,
King of Kings,
requests the honor of having dinner
with His dear Cousin,
the High-born Lady Salima Sultan Begam.

'Tell His Majesty, I will be honored,' I said wearily. It was not the answer I wanted to give, but a different one would have been quite unacceptable.

I went to dinner with reluctant resignation, with the prospect of a long, boring evening in the company of a spoilt, conceited young brat. I was pleasantly surprised, though, to see that dinner was served in a large, airy room overlooking the river. It had artfully sculpted stone lattice windows, which allowed the cool, healthy open air to mix with the heady perfumes of the palace. The room was lit by hundreds of candles and decorated with many flowers. Its white marble floor was almost entirely covered with beautiful Persian and Kashmiri carpets, all of them in the warmest shades of red. Contrary to what I had expected, Akbar was already in the room when I arrived. I made a slight bow to show him my respect, kicked off my slippers, and went to sit down on the pillows in front of him. Despite the awkwardness of the moment, the carpet felt soft and pleasant under my bare feet.

I had not planned to eat much, but I did anyway. There were at least fifty different dishes, all of them delicious: succulent mutton, lamb, fowl, and fish from the river, all skilfully grilled on skewers over a low charcoal flame, or simmered in rich, spicy gravy. Side dishes included several kinds of naan and roti[75], lentils, braised, boiled and steamed rice, eggs, cauliflower, peas with *panir*[76], and four or five other kinds of vegetables. Everything was presented on plates and saucers, kept warm with candles. On separate trays, there were also several kinds of sherbets, presented in beakers on crushed ice, and various kinds of fruit, all of which looked delicious.

Akbar made a gesture for the servants to put some of the food on our plates, and sent them off: 'Thanks. I'll call you if we need any help.'

He took two silver pitchers out of a large bowl, filled to the brim with crushed ice.

'Here, have some water,' he said, filling the largest of the two beakers on my tray.

'This is very special water, you know: from the Ganga! They bring it

---

[75] Flat, pancake-shaped kinds of bread.

[76] Fresh cottage cheese, somewhat similar to Italian *mozzarella*.

here every day, in large sealed earthen jars. It's supposed to be excellent for your health! I do not know whether that is actually true, but I have to say, no water I have ever drunk has a softer, purer taste! And have some wine, as well! This one here has been made from the best grapes from Kabul!'

He suddenly looked a bit worried.

'My blessed father always said, it is becoming for members of the royal family to drink wine,' he added apologetically.

I had a sip.

'I am not sure the mullahs would agree, but I really hope your father was right,' I said, 'it's really delicious!'

We both started eating. To my pleasant surprise, Akbar was courteous, attentive, and easily kept up a cheerful flow of pleasant conversation. Contrary to what I had feared, he did not try to make any amorous advances.

He kept asking dozens of questions, about Gujarat, about my accommodation in the palace, about Abdurrahim's education, about music and dance performances I had attended, books and poetry I had read...

I must admit, I was deeply impressed with his amazing knowledge of books. It was very hard to believe that I actually was talking to someone who had never learned how to read. There was not a book or writer he had not heard of, and hardly a poem he could not recite. The only slightly annoying thing about the conversation was his habit of constantly interrupting. In his eagerness to know and learn everything, he never seemed to have the patience to hear one explanation at a time: before I had a chance to finish the answer to one question, he had the next one ready. Not that I minded too much. At least it showed that he was not full of himself, but genuinely interested in what other people had to say. At times, though, I knew it did drive the mullahs crazy. Those who believe they possess the truth do not like to be interrupted...

Noticing that I had finished a few of the dishes on my tray, Akbar personally spooned out a second helping. The food was really delicious, and there certainly was more than enough of it.

'Is this all I get?' I inquired jokingly.

'I am sorry, would you like something else? I can order anything you want... some buffalo meat, maybe... even some beef, if you like!'

he apologized, clearly quite eager to please me.

'No, do not bother – I was just joking, the food here is more than enough to feed an army! But why would you worry about eating beef or not? You are not a Hindu, and you are the Emperor!'

'Yes, that's right, but you know, eating beef is extremely offensive to the Hindus, and I do not want to hurt their feelings if I can help it. You see, I don't want to be seen as just another foreign conqueror. Unlike our grandfather Babur, or my father Humayun, I was born here in Hindustan. This is my homeland, and I want all the people living on its soil to see me as their legitimate king, regardless of their religion! That's why I will try to avoid things that are offensive to the Hindus: perhaps they will learn to love and respect me, if they know that I will not willingly desecrate anything they consider as holy.' He paused. Seeing surprise and disbelief on my face, he insisted: 'Their customs may seem strange, but my teacher, Mir Abdul-Latif, agrees that contempt of any religion is contempt of God Himself!'

It was true what people said about Akbar: he had changed indeed. Much as I resented the way he had treated my husband, he was starting to intrigue me.

'I must confess I don't know much about the Hindus and their customs,' I said, 'but surely, their idols, their fires, their drums, their bells, their hundreds of gods and goddesses, all of this must be an abomination in the eyes of Allah?'

'I thought so too, but then I found, it's not that simple,' Akbar said.

'Despite the idols, they are really much closer to us than we think!'

He looked intently at me, I suppose to make sure I was still paying attention, or to guess my thoughts.

'You must have read the tales of the *Thousand and One Nights*, haven't you? You know the stories of Harun ar-Rashid, the wise Khalifah of Baghdad, don't you? I've always been fascinated by those episodes where he wanders around in disguise in the streets, observing the people, talking to them, finding out all kinds of things people try to hide from him. Well, since Bairam Khan left, I have been doing the same! Two or three times every month, I slip out of the fort, and spend the better part of a day or night on the streets of Agra! Only three of the guards know about it – I had them swear on the Holy Qur'an that they will keep this a secret.'

'But isn't that dangerous? What if something happens to you out there? Why do you want to risk your life like that?'

He gave me an amused look. 'Do not worry about me, Salima! I wear simple, dirty, shabby clothes: would-be robbers will take me for a poor, wandering traveller, with nothing worth stealing. Besides, I do not want to brag, but I'm really quite strong, you know – just like our grandfather was! Moreover, I am a well-trained, experienced soldier, and I'm always armed when I go out: I carry two throwing-knives, concealed in the sleeves of my tunic; I also have a large, broad dagger, hidden under my cloak in my belt behind my back, and even a sword, concealed in my walking stick! No, I can assure you, it will take more than a few robbers to get the better of me! Besides, are we not all in the hands of God? Not a speck of dust will move, unless He wills it.'

'You do not seem to agree?' he asked, noticing that I did not react much.

'I don't know,' I said. 'I have the impression many people use Allah's omnipotence to justify their own recklessness. Allah is almighty, but has He not created us as free beings, at liberty to do as we please? If that is true, then we should accept responsibility for our own acts. If we, for instance, decide to commit a sin, we should not blame Him for it; and neither should we when we get hurt because of our own recklessness!'

Akbar raised one eyebrow in surprise and amusement, and smiled approvingly, slightly nodding his head. 'I must confess, I had not looked at the matter from that perspective,' he admitted. He put his hand to his mouth and stared vaguely at one of the candle flames.

'Yes, you are quite right,' he admitted after a while, still gazing at the light, 'we should indeed not confuse trust in God with recklessness. But then, neither should we confuse prudence with cowardice!' He smiled, a bit self-righteously.

'You know, Mir Abdul-Latif once told me about the great Ibn Rushd[77] of Al-Andaluz, who used to say, that all good things are always in the middle of two extremes. A hero, for instance, stands midway between a coward and a reckless fool, don't you agree? Well, that is

[77] Averroes, (Abū-l Walīd Muhammad ibn Ahmad ibn Muhammad ibn Rushd, 1126–1198), Arabian *qādī* and philosopher, born in Cordoba, Spain. His works, translated in Latin, became the highest authority in the West on the philosophy of Aristotle.

where I want to be as well! Bairam Khan has always taught me, to do what I have to do, with prudence, but without fear! I do what I think I have to do, and if I have to die, so be it! If it happens, I can assure you, I will spit death in the face and die like a man, just like he did!'

'And what is so important about wandering around in the dirty alleys of Agra?'

'There, at least, I get to know what is going on in my country! A king is a very lonely person, you know. I live in a fortress, behind high walls; even when I'm traveling I'm protected by powerful armies and surrounded by all the wealth anybody could ever dream of. All of this is keeping me apart from the real life outside! I am completely dependent on other people to tell me what is going on! And now that Bairam Khan is gone, there are very few people I can really trust...'

I could not restrain myself.

'I am so relieved to hear that you realize, that old hag Maham Anaga and her entire clique are not to be trusted!'

He sighed.

'Salima, you know as well as I do, she has always been like a mother to me. She has fed me; she has risked her life for me when my father was still a homeless fugitive. I share your apprehension about Adham Khan – he has a foul and violent temper, and his ambitions are much greater than his abilities, but how can I blame a mother for loving her son, and wanting the best for him? I really do not want to hurt her feelings, if I can avoid it. But you do not have to worry about me, I've got it all under control!'

'I hope so, Your Majesty...'

'Salima, please do not call me Your Majesty! I am your cousin, and I want to be your friend... your best friend! I know, you must be sad, and you are probably angry with me, because of what happened to Bairam Khan, but I swear to you, I share your grief about what happened! I really didn't want to see Bairam Khan get hurt, you have to believe me! I really loved him, you know, like a father, and he loved me too!'

'I believe you did not intend these dreadful things to happen, but they have, and I would be lying if I said I haven't been angry with you for that. However, I have to admit that what you say is true: he did love you, he told me so, repeatedly. He even told me, that I shouldn't hold any grudge against you...'

'And, do you, Salima?'

'Let's not talk about it anymore.' I stared at my food, trying to evade his gaze.

'What was it you were trying to tell me about your wanderings in disguise in the streets of Agra?' I asked, trying to change the subject.

'O, yes, I wanted to tell you about the Hindus. One early morning, I walked past one of their temples. People came queuing in. In the morning, they have this ritual where the priests go into the sanctuary and wake up the god, as they say. They wash and dress up the idol inside, and make offerings of food and flowers to it; devotees come to the temple, to see the deity, pay their respects, and pray – they call it darshan, if I am not mistaken.

As I was standing there, in front of the entrance, there was this strange man looking at me.

'Looking for something, young Sahab?' he asked, in heavily accented but understandable Persian. His smile and the tone of his voice were perhaps a bit mocking, but not unfriendly. He looked weird: naked to the waist, with long, tangled locks of unkempt hair, ash smeared all over his arms, face and chest. On his forehead, there were three white stripes, and a lopsided, black-and-red eye in the middle.

'Am I allowed to go inside?' I asked. 'I am a Mussalman, you know.'

'So I see, young Sahab... Where are you from?'

'From Turan – I am a Turkoman. I am a cavalry officer in the emperor's army', I replied.

'So, why are you dressed the way you are, young Turkoman Sahab?'

I felt like a thief, caught red-handed.

'I just wanted to see how the Hindu people live,' I said. 'I dress inconspicuously so people do not take too much notice of me...'

'Eagerness to learn is the beginning of all wisdom, young Turkoman Sahab. Well, if you have come to this temple to learn and to worship God, you are most welcome to go in with me. Just take off your shoes and come in.'

I took off my shoes, and put them near the entrance, next to a whole row of other pairs. We came into the courtyard of the temple, where there were a number of smaller sanctuaries with images of deities inside. I saw people going from one sanctuary to the other, praying, paying their respects, offering a few flowers or grains of wheat. Some of them were walking around in circles around some or other deity.

'You spoke about worshipping God,' I said to my guide. 'How come you speak of God, as if there were only one? Don't you claim there are many gods?'

He smiled.

'Whether you worship one God, or many, young Sahab, that all depends on your personal development. There are many simple, uneducated people, for whom all the individual Hindu gods are as real and tangible as you and I. Most Hindus will tell you, however, that the individual gods are concrete manifestations of the One, the hidden, unknowable God, Who upholds this world and the countless billions of other worlds.

You see, we are all part of God, young Sahab. You and I, every person, animal and plant, everything that exists, is part of God, just like a spark is part of the fire, just like a tiny drop is part of the ocean. Eventually, we will all be reunited with Him. Through countless lives, we will eventually progress towards true knowledge, until we attain that divine moment when the soul attains perfect knowledge, truth and bliss, and is reunited with God.'

'If I wanted to convert to your religion, what would I have to do?' I asked.

'We do not try to convert anyone, young Sahab. We do not claim that there is only one way to God. Countless paths lead to God, and wisdom can be found everywhere – in fact, every path you follow, crooked or straight, will ultimately lead you to Him! You will attain union with God, because ultimately, that is your nature, young Sahab, for your soul is one with God. Think of yourself as a diamond, covered with dust and mud: you appear not to shine at all, but underneath the filth, you are as clean and pure as you have always been. Through thousands of lives, the dirt that covers you will be removed through the power of wisdom, until you attain your pure Self, which is identical with God. Indeed, each and every soul is created by God, is part of God, and is identical with God!'

Akbar paused, his eyes staring at the flame of a candle.

'Intriguing, isn't it? Well, maybe theirs is not the right religion. Maybe their way of worshipping is wrong. Still, I do not see why we could not live in peace with them: don't they want to serve the same

God as we do? Don't they want to live good and decent lives, as we do? As long as they do not harm anyone, as long as they recognize me as their king, they deserve my protection.'

He looked me straight in the eye, trying to guess what I was thinking.

'Mir Abdul-Latif, my teacher, always talks to me about *Sulh-i-kul*, Peace for All. That's what a king should accomplish, he says. I think he's right, Salima. I dream of a prosperous and mighty Hindustan, much larger than it is today, its many people worshipping the one true God in their manifold ways, united in peace, under the just rule of our dynasty.'

He paused, and mumbled, speaking more to himself than to me:

'I hope and pray almighty God will grant me the strength and wisdom to succeed.'

I had to admit, it was indeed true: Akbar really had changed. It would still take him a few more years, before he would become the world-renowned, mighty Emperor *Akbar-e-Azam*, Akbar the Great, but he clearly was no longer the unruly, spoilt brat of before. I would never have thought that pleasure-seeking youngster like him could be so preoccupied with religious truth, so eager to learn, so eager to do the right thing. I began to understand, why Bairam had liked him so much.

'I think you will be a wise ruler,' I said, and I really meant it. 'May Allah always be your guide and helper!'

'Thank you, this really means a lot to me,' he mumbled, shyly lowering his eyes and looking down at his food.

I looked through the lattice window. The moon, which had been barely visible near the horizon when we had started eating, was now high up in the sky, casting its silver light on the river. Many of the candles in the room were on the verge of going out.

'It is late, I should be getting back to my quarters,' I said. 'Thank you so much for the excellent food.'

'Stay a little longer,' he implored. 'You are not tired, are you?'

He poured us both some more wine.

'You know, Salima ...'

His face was turning a bit red. He cast his eyes down, staring at nothing in particular, somewhere in front of the pillows on which I was sitting.

'You know, it's been such a long time since I've had a conversation like this. I hope you did not find it too boring?'

'No, the food was excellent, and I feel privileged that you've shared your ideas with me. It's rather unusual for men to talk to women about serious matters like that.'

'Wisdom can be found everywhere, this much I have learned', he answered. 'You are a lady of royal blood, you've read many books, seen many things... I would be a fool if I did not value your opinion!'

He looked at me, and his face flushed up again.

'What would you say, Salima, if I were to ask you to be my wife?'

'It would make life much easier for you here in the fort,' he added, using the wrong arguments in his eagerness to please me, 'I am convinced, Bairam Khan would be happy to see that his wife is being taken care of!'

'I would be honored and flattered, but I would say no,' I said.

'Why, Salima? I swear, I would be a good and respectful husband to you!'

'I am a grown woman, and I can take care of myself! I do not want you to marry me out of pity, or to ease your guilty conscience about Bairam's death.'

'Salima, I swear, that is not the case! Bairam Khan and I have parted ways as the best of friends, you have to believe me! The bad blood that has been there between us was not only my fault, really – he must have told you! And I can assure you, I do not want to marry you out of pity! I really love you, you know; I always have! Ever since I was a small boy, I have always found you extremely attractive... I have to admit, I was a bit jealous of Bairam Khan, when he had the good fortune of becoming your husband...'

He paused.

'Besides, and perhaps more importantly, Salima, I really, really like you. I feel good when you are near me. Tonight, just looking at you, listening to you, I had this feeling of comfort and security – like being near a fountain under a shady tree, in the heat of summer, or near a nice charcoal fire on a cold winter night. No one else has ever made me feel like that... Not Ruqayyah, although she is a sweet girl and I do like her a lot, and not any of the other girls I've been with!'

He leaned across the trays and put his hand on mine.

'Salima, won't you at least consider my proposal? You would make me so happy,' he pleaded.

His hand felt dry and firm. The fingers might have been just a bit longer, but other than that, it looked exactly like a man's hand should, strong and sinewy, veins showing on the back.

I kept looking at his hand, avoiding his eyes, and heard myself answering:

'I will think about it.'

Five more weeks went by. Akbar made no further attempt to see me in private, but not a day went by without some precious gift delivered to my quarters. In that brief period, I amassed a fortune: earrings, necklaces, anklets, bracelets; diamonds, pearls, emeralds, rubies, textiles... all of the most exquisite quality. These were impressive gifts, even coming from a man as wealthy as Akbar...

Accompanying the gifts, there would always be something in writing: magnificent, hand-written books, illuminated with sublime miniatures, or individual poems on a single sheet of paper, about love, the beauty of nature, or the majesty of God. Most of the poems were from the best Persian masters, but there were also some of my own – I wondered, where he got them from – and there were a few other ones, which I had never read, usually quite short, only one or two concise, striking sentences, which I suppose were his own.

All of them were written in the beautiful, elegant Nasta'liq-style handwriting of the head eunuch, followed by a rather clumsy signature at the bottom of the page, just four simple letters, in plain Naskh[78] – probably one of the very few words he had ever learned to write:

اکبر[79]

I saw him every now and then. Most of the time, I would watch from behind the lattices, when he was attending to the affairs of state in the diwan-i-am, or when he was riding out for a hunting trip outside. Gradually I saw the kind of man he was becoming: relaxed and friendly

---

[78] Nasta'līq: cursive Arabic writing, with the letters slanting down from right to left. Almost all Urdu texts are written and printed in the Nasta'līq style.
Naskh: standard horizontal Arabic writing.

[79] Akbar.

with ordinary soldiers, servants and children; serious and eager to do what was right when he was asked to take a decision about matters of importance.

With each passing day, I found him a more likeable person, and I caught myself thinking about him, much more often than I cared to admit. How can a young widow remain indifferent to the idea of finding a strong and gentle new husband, who will care for her and protect her? How can a woman ignore the advances of a man of such incredible power and wealth, when he shows her such courteousness and respect? Besides, was it not becoming for a Padshah's granddaughter to occupy the highest possible rank? Why denying, that the life of an Empress is substantially more comfortable than that of a guest, even one of royal blood?

From time to time, I would meet him in the private quarters of the palace, in the presence of his household and attendants, when he was watching some dancers or other kinds of entertainment. We usually did not exchange more than a few friendly civilities, but it was obvious that much more was going on between us. How he could hardly keep his eyes off me; how he would always find a way to sit next to me, to accidentally touch my upper arm, or the bare skin of my hands or feet, allowing his fingers to linger just a bit longer than necessary; and my disappointment, on those rare occasions when he didn't succeed...

Then, one afternoon, when he was playing with little Abdurrahim, carrying him on his shoulders and galloping through the garden, he suddenly came running towards me.

'Salima, will you please be my wife?' he asked, still gasping for air, looking up a bit uncomfortably from underneath Abdurrahim's weight on his neck.

I smiled, and touched his face.

'I will,' I answered.

Thirteenth Letter

ماہم انگہ، ادھم خان

Maham Anaga, Adham Khan

Waking up next to Salima, in the soft, blue light of dawn... Just looking at her, the gentle rising and falling of her chest; her sweet face as the bluish light slowly turns golden; just looking, nothing else ...

Just looking, and knowing – not hoping, not thinking, but knowing – that everything is perfect. Never have I felt so truly blessed.

My fears, hopes, yearnings were gone – I no longer craved nor longed for anything. For some strange reason, I just knew, with tranquil certainty, that from then on, things would be going my way, and my way only.

Where did this blissful self-confidence come from? Salima was, of course, the main reason; but there was more than lover's rapture.

Marrying her was much more than the gratification of lust, more than love, more than the joy of finding a soul mate: it was my personal achievement. I had proven, to myself even more than to anybody else, that I had finally taken control over my own destiny.

People around me still failed to see it; but I was becoming the king whom the world would call *Akbar-e-Azam*, Akbar the Great.

Almighty God has given me many things to be grateful for – so many, that I feel unworthy and ashamed– but Salima has certainly been the most precious.

She is so much more to me than a wife of high birth, someone to share my bed and household with. It isn't difficult to find girls with fairer faces or slimmer thighs, but she is by far the best companion any man could ever want. Even later in life, when we had become rather infrequent lovers, she has always remained my dearest friend, my most trusted advisor. If, among the many women in the harem, I would have to choose one – as those Firanghi priests keep insisting I should – it would, without any doubt, be her.

Not that I would ever agree to even consider such a preposterous idea: men of position – emperors all the more – should be free to take any number of wives and concubines they please, for that is the way progeny is secured and alliances are forged. It is, moreover, by far the most agreeable and natural way to ease the yearning that God has put in the bodies and souls of men. Had He wanted it otherwise, would He not have made us different?

But while I never have been and never will be a one-wife-man, I admit: Salima has a special place in my heart. Everything about her is kindness, and balance. She is unassuming, yet full of authority. I love the way she walks; I love her voice, I feel good when she is around... and perhaps most importantly: I listen when she speaks.

As you will have gathered, it has not been easy to win her over, on the contrary – she does have a mind of her own! And in case you wonder where I got her diary: she herself read it to me, one evening. We had been married for a couple of years and were reminiscing about our life together, over a nice meal with some good wine. I found it endearing to hear her side of the story, and thought it might be of interest to you as well.

Yes, she does have a will of her own, and yet she is, among my many wives and concubines, the one I love the most. Relationships between men and women are at their best, in my view, when lust and companionship go together. I have never understood why so many men insist on marrying uneducated, subservient, ignorant girls. What good is a woman's body, when it is inhabited by the mind of an infant? What use is there for it, outside the bed and the kitchen? Beauty is like good food: when you have taken from it, it ceases to occupy your mind. When the urge of the loins has been satisfied, ignorant concubines quickly lose their charm. But a true soulmate is a treasure, inside and outside the bedroom!

The same goes for government: weaklings tend to attract other weaklings; the strong are not afraid to appoint the very best, who will help them rise above themselves. Remember this, my son: be extremely choosy about whom you admit to your service! Empires are not built, nor maintained, with nodding yes-men, like the worthless idiots you had, back in Allahabad! Compare them to the brilliant individuals at my Court: Abdurrahim, Man Singh, Todar Mal, Birbal, Abu'l Fazl...

But I am getting ahead of myself. Let me return to the months after Bairam Khan's death. As I said, marrying Salima was a tremendous achievement. I really had to push it through, against much opposition, covert and open.

You know I had given orders for Bairam Khan's family to be escorted back to Agra. I was vexed to see the preparations for the departure dragging on interminably. No less than three times, I had to ask Mun'im Khan about the state of affairs. Each time, he came up with some kind of lame excuse: the best troops needed to be selected; the supplies needed to be organized; permission needed to be obtained from the king of Gujarat for the escort to cross his territory... He clearly was dragging his feet.

Maham Anaga repeatedly tried to talk me out of my plan, with an insistence bordering on the insolent. 'Your Majesty, in His infinite goodness, chooses to forget, Bairam Khan was guilty of the heinous crime of rebellion! Surely, it is not becoming that the family of a rebel is invited to live with the Emperor!'

'Your Majesty's magnanimity is proverbial; would it not be more than sufficient, if He gave them permission to live in Bairam Khan's house in Lahore, rather than at Court in Agra? After all, he was not a member of the imperial family!'

'Your Majesty, in his kindness, is running a terrible risk in bringing Bairam Khan's son to court! He is only four years old, but time flies: in ten to twelve years' time, he may become extremely dangerous!'

I had more than enough. 'I appreciate your concern, Mahamji,' I snapped, 'but the decision is mine, and my mind is made up. I must ask you, not to bring this up again. And as far as Abdurrahim is concerned: Bairam Khan has been a father to me. It's my duty, *and* my wish, to see to this child's education, and I will.'

Noticing the bland, unimpressed look on her face, I added: 'It is very important, that everybody realizes this boy is under my protection. If anybody, no matter who it is, so much as thinks about hurting him, he will pay for it with his head, and that of his entire family!'

This time, the message had come across. Her face turned all red, she mumbled some kind of excuse, and retired to her quarters. I couldn't help feeling a bit guilty – little glory is there in threatening an old lady, even if she deserves it.

Then one day, after several months, I was informed Bairam Khan's family had arrived safely in Agra. I was overjoyed, and nervous at the same time.

When they had rested for a few hours, I officially invited them at Court, and received them with every possible honor.

I didn't forget to reward their guards took good care of the families of their fallen comrades. Such matters may seem trivial, are quite important. Justice and generosity should not be the exclusive privilege of the high-ranked. Ordinary soldiers, who are the backbone of any army, are keen observers – they feel, with unfailing certainty, whether their leader cares for them or not. And if you have those men on your side, you will be much stronger than if you settle for an army of mere conscripts. Victories will be won against impossible odds; rebellions will fail before they even start!

I was really moved to see little Abdurrahim: what a delightful little fellow! A bit bashful at first, he did not say too much; but I soon managed to win him over, taking him for a ride around the fort, on Dilsankar's neck...

I am so grateful God has entrusted him to my care. Now, forty years later, it brings me such joy to see how well he has done for himself. I see the courtiers stepping aside and bowing for the great Abdurrahim Khan Khanan, the most powerful man in the country, the Emperor's iron right arm, just like his father before him... and I smile, contented. It pleases me to see him go about his duties, with that self-evident confidence that is the fruit of competence and experience. I take pride in his wisdom, power and wealth. I really hope Bairam Khan is able to watch us from the hereafter. If he is, I know he is smiling.

The return of Bairam Khan's family to Court and my marriage to Salima marked a turning point in my life. As the clique around Maham Anaga was soon to find out, the era of the indolent and docile boy-king, with his all-powerful guardians and advisors, was over for good.

A peaceful transition, however, it was not. In the course of the following months, serious incidents occurred, which would ultimately lead to their downfall.

My first confrontation with them took place at the occasion of the conquest of Malwa, which I had ordered near the end of the fifth year of my reign[80]. Remembering Bairam Khan's sound advice, 'A king should always seek conquest and war, lest his army become lazy and ineffective,' I had sent Adham Khan and Pir Muhammad Khan south of our borders, to annex these fertile lands to our dominions.

At that time, Malwa was ruled by the so-called 'Shah' Baz Bahadur - if the word 'rule' can be used to describe a useless, wine-soaked life, dedicated to music and women. Baz Bahadur was the son of a Pashtun officer who had served under the Sur dynasty, and had governed the territory in practical independence. But his sole interest was to enjoy life – a very common trait, quite understandable and maybe even amiable, but extremely dangerous to those who wish to succeed in life, my son.

Our troops advanced, virtually unopposed, to the capital Sarangpur, where Baz Bahadur gave them battle. Deserted by his best officers, he was easily defeated, and put to flight. The news reached me a few days later. I was, however, much displeased to hear that Adham Khan and his crony had celebrated their victory with rivers of innocent blood. Dozens upon dozens of captives had been brought before them and slaughtered like cattle, while the two captains were cracking jokes. No one had been spared – not even women and children, or venerable old Shaikhs with copies of the Holy Qur'an in their trembling hands.

I do not mean to suggest, my son, that violence cannot be necessary. Harsh and brutal repression of the guilty will avenge the insulted Emperor, chastise the rebellious and, most importantly, keep other would-be offenders on the straight path of obedience. But arbitrary cruelty will achieve exactly the opposite: it will sow the seeds of new, more dangerous rebellions.

What infuriated me even more was the so-called booty that was sent to me: a few mediocre elephants, a bit of silk, that was all – whereas I

---

[80] March, 1561.

had been informed that Baz Bahadur possessed untold treasures of gold, jewels, elephants, horses, and a large harem, with hundreds of the most beautiful concubines and dancing girls! Adham Khan had kept them all to himself! Not only was this a breach of the rules: it was an insult, a sign of contempt, a direct challenge to my authority. I couldn't let him get away with this.

I saddled up an escort of a few dozen good men, and left for Malwa. Despite the blazing heat, we advanced rapidly – so rapidly, in fact, that we arrived way ahead of the messengers Maham Anaga had sent to forewarn her son.

Our sudden arrival took Adham Khan completely by surprise. He must have toyed with the idea of eliminating me, since I had only brought a few guards with me. If that was indeed his plan, he had to abandon it, when thousands upon thousands of his soldiers, recognizing the Imperial standards, dismounted and knelt in the dust to salute their Emperor.

I greeted the men, saying how glad and proud I was, and congratulated them on their glorious victory. But I didn't say a single word to Adham Khan, looking coldly past him, as he dismounted and reluctantly kissed my stirrup; I even refused to accept a change of clothes, and ostentatiously drank from my own water skin, ignoring the ice-cooled sherbet he offered me.

'I will retire into Sarangpur,' I said stiffly. 'Kindly have me informed about the spoils taken, so I may adequately recompense you and your men for your bravery.'

The demand clearly took him by surprise. 'Your Majesty... ,' he began, probably wanting to say something about the booty, but he obviously did not find the appropriate words. 'Certainly, Your Majesty,' he mumbled.

He offered me his own residence in town, but I said I preferred to sleep in Baz Bahadur's palace. I had no intention to spend the night anywhere near Adham Khan's harem, providing him with an occasion to avenge his honor. Excuses for treachery are not difficult to find, if one is looking for them.

I spent the night on the highest roof platform, choosing the coolest and least accessible spot, personally stationing my best men along the approaches. I slept like a baby. The next day, we were surprised to see Maham Anaga join us. The old woman had travelled all the way from Agra, ostensibly to congratulate her son and her Emperor on the conquest of Malwa. In reality, of course, she was desperate to patch things up between us. Despite my anger, I could not help feeling respect for her – such motherly devotion really deserved much worthier a son...

As ordered, the spoils of war were paraded. What I saw went beyond my wildest expectations. Scores of magnificent elephants, finest horses, cart loads of gold and precious stones, hundreds of magnificent girls...

To my dismay, I learned Baz Bahadur's harem had been much larger. Dozens of girls were dead, some killed by their own guardians! Regrettably, among them was Rupmati, Baz Bahadur's legendary queen, widely renowned for her radiant beauty. She was still alive when Baz Bahadur fled, but preferred poison to Adham Khan's greasy embrace.

Things went more or less back to normal, Maham Anaga and her son bending over backwards to please me. I divided the spoils, keeping, as is becoming, the lion's share for my treasury, and awarding smaller tokens of appreciation to Adham Khan and Pir Muhammad Khan, in recompense of their contribution.

The rewards I gave them were just enough not to be openly insulting, but far less generous than what would have been normal. Adham Khan's part consisted mainly of elephants – of the mediocre kind he had sent to me – plus a bit of gold, and a few girls, chosen from the plainest ones I could find. People should understand that loyalty is the fastest – and safest! – way to become wealthy.

I stayed in Sarangpur for one more day, then headed back to Agra, heading the train of spoils. We had barely left the city, when Abdullah Khan Uzbeg, the senior commanding officer of my escort, came riding next to me.

'Your Majesty,' he said, 'I am afraid some very disconcerting rumours have come to my ears.'

'Yes, what is it?'

'It is about Adham Khan...'

'Yes? Go ahead, tell me, I want to know!'

'They say Adham Khan kept two beautiful girls for himself.'

'Those two southern girls?'

'I believe so, Your Majesty.'

I knew right away which girls he was talking about. They had instantly caught my attention when Baz Bahadur's harem was paraded in front of me: two ravishing Hindu girls, tall and slender, dark-skinned, with splendid big eyes and magnificent, shiny white teeth. The gold of their jewellery and the saffron of their saris exquisitely matched the shiny colour of their skin. Observing the grace of their movements when they slowly walked past me, I had, in eager anticipation, been picturing in my mind how I would enjoy their company after a cool bath and a refreshing drink. I immediately halted the march, ordering a count of the spoils and an inspection of the Sarangpur garrison.

Outwardly, I kept composed and relaxed, but inside, I was boiling with rage.

What would I do if those girls were found in Adham Khan's possession?

Have him hanged? If it had not been for Maham Anaga, I would not have hesitated, but could I really do this to an old woman who had taken such care of me when I was a little boy?

Throw him in jail? Banish him? No, that was much too mild a punishment, and besides, it was dangerous: prisons and places of exile are cradles of rebellion... What else? Ignore the insult, bide my time, then take my revenge? However angry, I decided for the latter. Vengeance is oftentimes a dish best served cold...

My suspicions were confirmed: the girls were nowhere to be found – neither in the cortege, nor in the Sarangpur harem.

'Abdullah Khan,' I said, 'we have wasted enough time here. Let's head back to Agra – there are more important matters to be dealt with. But before we go, I want you to find out – discreetly – what exactly happened here!'

'Your Majesty can count on me; I will take a few of these palace servants aside, and ask them a few penetrating questions,' the Uzbeg answered ominously, caressing the hilt of his dagger.

It didn't take him long to find out the truth: Maham Anaga, in panic at what would happen to her son caught stealing from the Emperor again, had bribed one of the female harem guards to kill the two girls and bury them behind the palace walls. Severed heads do not talk, she was reported to have said...

'What are Your Majesty's orders?' the Uzbeg asked.

'As I said,' I answered, keeping icy calm, 'we have wasted more than enough time. We will go back to Agra – I'll deal with this later.'

I headed back as if nothing had happened. Surprisingly, I felt no hatred, no boiling rage, no fear. If anything, I felt relieved, free at last, free from whatever debts of gratitude I still had towards Maham Anaga or anyone else. From now on, I would take other people's advice because I wanted to, not because I owed them anything. My word, and my word only, would be law.

The journey gave me ample time to think. Upon arrival, I made my first move.

In a firman, full of pompous, hollow words of praise, which at times can be the most effective of insults, I relieved Adham Khan of his command and called him back to Agra. The seditious having been subdued, and the presence of two senior commanders no longer being required, I left the campaign in the able hands of my loyal and trusted helper, Pir Muhammad Khan.

It was, if I say so myself, a masterstroke. Not only was it a clear insult for an army leader to be called back in the middle of a campaign: it also deprived Adham Khan of any independent source of revenue; it reduced him to what he detested most: a life of idleness and boredom at Court, with lots of bowing and kneeling and nodding, completely dependent on me for his livelihood, and subject to the gloating, mockery and contempt of all the others. For, so much was clear: I would make him regret his disloyalty for the rest of his life.

As expected, Maham Anaga desperately tried to make me change my mind. She begged and pleaded. Her son, in his youthful impetuousness, might have done things displeasing to his Emperor, but had not meant any harm. He profoundly regretted his wrongdoings and would amend his ways. His abilities would be of much greater use to me, in fighting my enemies. He had no other desire but to serve me and expand my dominions.

Each time, I gave her the same reply, with a gentle and benevolent smile on my face as if I was doing her the greatest of favors: that her son's presence at the head of my troops was no longer required.

Maham Anaga's pleas were taken over, in thin disguise, by Mun'im Khan.

He had to inform His Majesty, with respect, that he was worried about the military situation in Malwa. It was his duty to warn His Majesty that it would be imprudent to assume that the major fighting was over. Of course, Baz Bahadur had been trounced, but there were disturbing rumours about him forging alliances to win back his lost kingdom. Rumour even had it: Malwa would soon be invaded by a major enemy coalition! It was to be feared that Pir Muhammad Khan on his own would not be up to the task.

From a military point of view, he was, of course, quite right: to lead a band of marauders is one thing, but to conduct a large-scale military campaign is quite another. The situation in Malwa, however, was the least of my concerns. If Pir Muhammad Khan managed to keep the enemy out, so much for the better. If not, I would be back soon!

What really worried me, was the lack of discipline in my own Court. Surely, I had not dismissed the great Bairam Khan, only to have someone else take his place? One way or the other, they would learn, there was only one man in charge: me, and nobody else.

Those loyal to me would have nothing to fear; I would be a just ruler, furthering the interests of the Empire and its inhabitants; I would seek wisdom wherever I could find it; I would eagerly listen to sound advice – but nobody, absolutely nobody, would exercise any power, unless and until and to the extent I had authorized.

My generals, governors, courtiers: willing or unwilling, they would come to understand that their only task, and the only way for them to gain any personal wealth and standing, was to obey me. Those who tried to serve themselves, would end up with nothing.

So I told Mun'im Khan I had the fullest confidence in Pir Muhammad Khan's prowess; and to make sure he clearly understood that I was lying, I added, with the sweetest smile on my face, that I did not want to deprive Maham Anaga of her son's companionship...

The next day, I made my second and final move: I dismissed Mun'im Khan as wakil, and appointed Shams-ud-din in his stead. The firman announcing the new appointment mentioned that 'the task of *wakil* being of utmost importance and a heavy burden on the shoulders of the incumbent, it was appropriate that it would, from time to time, be entrusted to someone else.' With a thinly veiled insult directed at Mun'im Khan, it added that, considering the threat in Malwa, it was becoming that the task was entrusted to Shams-ud-din Muhammad

Atga Khan, my devoted foster father, who had proven his valour and talent on the battlefield.

This time, Maham Anaga and her followers were wise enough not to try to make me change my mind, but did the only sensible thing under the circumstances: to comply with my orders, without discussion. Avoiding further confrontations with me, they made a brave effort to resume their lives at Court as if nothing had happened, waiting for an opportunity to regain the royal favor, once my anger would have subsided.

It was both amusing and sobering to see how everybody adapted their attitude towards the disfavored. The signs were subtle, but nonetheless clear: greetings became less cordial, polite bows of courtesy less deep, orders and requests less diligently executed. Indeed, as I already pointed out to you, my son, a group of people does not behave very differently from a herd of animals...

As I expected, Shams-ud-din – May God reward him! – proved himself an exemplary wakil: competent, efficient, loyal, and unobtrusive. Insensitive to flattery, abhorring gossip and intrigue, he went about his tasks, solely at the service and in the shadow of his Emperor. Maham Anaga's clique, my informants told me, was consumed with envy. It was exactly what I wanted to hear.

Fourteenth Letter

Ajmir

With Shams-ud-din's help, I seriously devoted myself to my duties. Following Bairam Khan's example, I made sure nothing escaped my attention: controlling, at random, even the smallest things; making sure everybody realized: the Emperor was watching.

Pleasantly surprising was it to find how easy it all came to me, and even more, how happy I felt. I still enjoyed hunting, cups of wine in the evening, the sweet companionship of women, but I no longer felt guilty, as I was doing my duty. Only those who are not lazy, truly enjoy the rewards of relaxation...

Indeed, as the *Firanghi*[81] padres would say: virtue is its own reward. Despite the frantic busyness of my life and the many uncertainties, my mind was at peace. I worked and I put my trust in God, devoting many hours to solitary prayer. Each time I worried, I would appeal to Him, asking Him to grant me the strength, endurance, and wisdom I needed.

Most probably under God's direct guidance, I started to inform myself firsthand about my subjects' living conditions, opinions, hopes and fears. As you will have read in the abstract of Salima's memoirs, I followed the great Harun ar-Rashid's example, and wandered in disguise through the streets and alleys of Agra. Gradually, and as I will explain

---

[81] 'Frank, Frankish', i.e. European.

in more detail later, those contacts helped me understand what God really wanted from me.

One Thursday evening at sundown, I joined a *mahfil-e-sam'a*[82] around a band of five excellent qawwali musicians. Together with the other listeners, I abandoned my soul to the entrancing rhythm of the tablas and the inspiring lyrics: *Kirpa karo Maharaj, Muin ud Din...*

The words of the hymn entered my soul like a direct message from God:

Master of all masters of truth, pride of all worlds, crown of the crowns, *Muin ud Din:*

With just a wink of your eye, success will be mine; Your door, the source of my fortune, is given to me by God.

Even before the song was over, my mind was made up: I would travel to Ajmir, to pray and meditate at the blessed dargah[83] of that saint of saints, Khwajah Muin ud Din Muhammad Chishti[84], the peace of God be upon him.

A few days later, early in the fourth month of the Hijri year 969[85], I left for Ajmir, accompanied by only a small military escort and a few attendants.

I of course made sure that Maham Anaga and her clique accompanied me: it wouldn't have been prudent to leave them out of my sight.

It was the first of many pilgrimages to Ajmir. I doubt tombs and shrines truly have the powers people ascribe to them, but there's no denying: the pilgrimage brought me all the blessings I had hoped for, and many more. Indeed, most of the good things in my life seem to have come to me through Muin ud Din and his offspring.

Crossing into Rajputana, it was disturbing to see the villagers fleeing in panic upon our approach. These lands were mine, they belonged to

[82] Assembly of Listeners.

[83] Tomb, shrine.

[84] See chapter 5, footnote 5. Khwājah Muīn ud Dīn Muhammad Chishti (1142–1236), founder of the Chishtiya Sūfī order in India, came to Ajmer from Persia in 1192. Still today, his tomb in the city of Ajmer is an important place of worship, for Muslims and Hindus alike.

[85] Mid January, 1562.

my Empire, and yet, it was painfully obvious that its inhabitants had learned to fear their Muslim rulers. I promised myself, the first thing I would do upon my return to Agra, would be to prohibit killing and enslavement of civilians in war.

For, as Abu'l Fazl phrased it: If the husbands have taken the path of insolence, how is it the fault of the wives, and if the fathers have chosen the road of opposition, what fault have the children committed?

Mind you, my son: the use of violence is of course necessary, for resistance must be crushed with firmness and determination, whenever and wherever it is encountered. But plunder is not the purpose of conquest. War must be followed by peace, harshness by magnanimity. Conquered lands must be blended into the Empire, through peace and prosperity. Their inhabitants must come to love and respect their new ruler. The Empire must be a source of pride, a safe home, worth fighting for.

Similar thoughts must have been on the mind of Raja Bihari Mal of Amber, who had submitted to us, but had in exchange been allowed to retain control over the region. Emissaries arrived, carrying gifts and flowery letters of praise, soon to be followed by the Raja himself, who came in person to kiss my stirrup.

The Raja was a remarkable man: imposing, daunting in spite of the humility of his gestures and attitude; and surprisingly gentle and peaceful, despite his warlike appearance. He was tall, broad-shouldered, remarkably strongly built for a man of his advancing age. By far the most salient feature of his appearance, however, was his dark, fleshy face under an orange turban. It was dominated, rather than adorned, by the most extravagant beard I had ever seen: a hand's-length long, parted in the middle of the chin, then brushed sideways and upward. His head looked at least four fingers wider on both sides, like the mane of a beast of prey.

Despite the singular extravagance of his appearance, he proved to be a rather simple, soft-spoken man, clearly anxious to do what was in the interest of his people. His black eyes under the brushy eyebrows looked a bit nervous, but not at all hostile.

He spoke slowly and used whatever Persian words he knew, making it rather easy for me to understand his Rajputana dialect.

He wished to reaffirm his unwavering loyalty to me – he had been a faithful supporter of my father, who had been a wise man and close to God; and he would continue to support his noble son. All he was asking for, was for him and the people of Rajputana to be allowed to live their lives undisturbed, according to their own traditions, and to serve God in the way their ancestors had taught them. In exchange, I could count on them and their swords to defend the Empire and expand its borders.

I assured him that this was exactly the way I saw things myself; that those who remained loyal to the Empire would be guaranteed *sulh-i-kul,* peace for all, even if they did not follow Islam; that it was reassuring for me to know that I could count on the valour and well-known military prowess of the noble Rajputs. If we, Hindus and Muslims, would allow ourselves to become enemies, we would severely weaken each other; and in the end, we would both lose. But together, we would be invincible.

He looked at me, inquisitively, his eyes slightly narrowed, clearly looking for some kind of evidence or confirmation that I really meant what I said. And I did: I was and remain firmly convinced that the lands of Hindustan are invincible, if only their inhabitants remain united.

Seeing the honesty in my eyes, he smiled, showing two of his upper front teeth: large and bright white and square, with a wide opening between them. Despite the wild beard and whiskers, he suddenly looked like an eight-year-old.

'I must congratulate His Majesty on his wisdom, despite his young age,' he said. 'It is a great relief for me and my people that we will be the allies of a man of God.'

He paused. The smile disappeared and a kind of sadness came into his eyes. He looked at me, pleadingly, as if asking for some kind of reassurance.

'Your Majesty, it would be an honor for me and my people,' he said, trying to read my reaction as he was speaking, 'if our Padshah would do me the honor of accepting my daughter in marriage.'

I bowed courteously.

'I am grateful and honored by your most kind and generous offer, noble Raja Bihari Mal. This marriage will be the symbol of our eternal friendship!'

'You and your family can rest assured that your noble daughter will be treated with the respect due to her high rank,' I added, trying to give him the reassurance he was looking for.

'Your Majesty is most kind. I will...'

He swallowed, with some difficulty, as if he was taking some kind of foul-tasting medicine, and then reluctantly finished his sentence.

'I will of course instruct my daughter to make herself fully acquainted with the rules applicable at Your Majesty's court, and to convert to Your Majesty's religion.'

'I am most grateful, but that will not be necessary,' I replied, ignoring the surprise on everybody's face. 'Your daughter will remain free to worship God in accordance with her own traditions, if she so prefers.'

He bowed deeply – this was clearly much more than he had ever expected or hoped for.

'Your Majesty is most wise and just. He can depend on me and my people under any circumstance!'

I took him by the shoulders in a friendly embrace, and he reciprocated the gesture. We agreed the wedding ceremony would take place on my way back to Agra, and that Man Singh, adopted son of Raja Bhagwan Das, the heir of Raja Bihari Mal, would accompany us to Court as well, and enter the imperial service.

Little did I know that this heir of his would become my greatest general, forging my Muslim and Hindu forces into one, invincible army; fighting and winning close to one hundred and twenty wars for me...

And little did I realize, that that bashful young Hindu girl, whom I did not know, whom I had yet to lay eyes on, of whom I did not even quite catch the name[86], was to become the great Qadasi-Arkani Maryam

---

[86] Surprising though it may be, the name of Akbar's first Rājpūt wife is a matter of some controversy. Apart from the title of honor, *Maryam uz-Zamānī* (i.e. 'Mary of the Age', a title that was bestowed upon her when she gave birth to Salīm), her maiden name is not known with absolute certainty. Popular tradition in India calls her by the name *Jodhā Bai* or *Jodh Bai* , which means 'Lady of Jodh(pur)'. This is clearly wrong: Akbar never did marry any princess from the Jodhpur area, and certainly never had a wife called Jodhā Bai: Jodhā Bai was, in fact, the name of one of Jahāngīr's wives. The leading opinion among scholars is that Maryam uz-Zamānī's maiden name was Rajkumari Hira Kunwari, alias Harkha Bai.

uz-Zamani[87], mother of the noble Prince Salim, heir to the Gurkaniyya throne, destined to become the great Emperor Jahangir...

Looking back on my life, it was then and there, with that friendly embrace of your maternal grandfather, that I founded my Empire.

Admittedly, it was my revered father – may he be received in the bliss of Paradise! – who gave me my inheritance: sovereignty over rich and important, if heavily disputed, dominions.

Admittedly, it was Bairam Khan – may he be rewarded in eternity! – who finished what my father had started. When he took on his task, many powerful enemies were threatening to wipe us out. By the time of his death, he had made us the dominant power in Hindustan – no neighbouring king could hope to challenge me and survive.

Yes, I owe my Empire to my father and to my *ataliq*; this much I have to admit. But it is I who made it three, four times larger, stronger and richer.

And not only is it so much larger, wealthier and more powerful: it is fundamentally different. The former sultans of Dilli, the Afghans in Bengal, Babur, Sher Khan Sur, Humayun – they were and remained foreign, Muslim rulers. The population of their dominions remained sharply divided between the ruling Muslim minority, and the subdued Hindu masses, sometimes persecuted, sometimes tolerated, but always despised as a bunch of pagan, blasphemous idol worshippers.

I have done my best to change that: I do not want to be the head of the Muslims alone, but of every man and woman in my Empire. I may not have been able to fully bridge the gap that exists between the many religions and traditions in our lands – probably nobody will ever succeed in doing that   I am proud to point out that my reign has truly brought *sulh-i-kul*, peace for all. Under my rule, everybody has enjoyed the freedom to serve and worship God according to his own traditions and beliefs; and many have come to understand, that all paths, no matter how diverse, will ultimately lead to Him, Who is compassionate and merciful to all. Many people have come to appreciate the other traditions, and friendships have developed across the boundaries of religion and origin.

---

87 Qadasī-Arkānī: Pillar of Purity; Maryam uz-Zamānī: Mary of the Age (see the previous note).

I have tried to weave together the many traditions of this land, just like strings of many colours are intertwined and knit together to form a beautiful carpet. I have been able to accomplish that, not only through showing respect for all faiths, but also and more importantly, through installing a different kind of government. Positions of responsibility in my Empire are no longer based on descent, origin, or inheritance, but on merit. The mansabdars govern their districts, not because they have inherited the territory from their fathers, but in my name and on my behalf, because I have appointed them, and until I choose to dismiss them. Hindustan no longer is a patchwork of fiefs and kingdoms that have surrendered to an invader: it is one Empire, under the rule of one Emperor, the sole and legitimate representative of God Himself.

The pilgrimage to Ajmir went as planned. I spent a few days in the city, praying near the shrines of Khwajah Muin ud Din and of his saintly daughter Bibi Hafez Jamal, visiting the various mosques, and seeking the blessings of learned and saintly men. Most of my time, I spent in solitary prayer and reflection, asking God to help me fulfil my destiny and to make me His worthy representative on earth.

On the return journey, my marriage to Raja Bihari Mal's daughter was celebrated at Sambhar. I was happy to find she was quite pretty, a bit frail perhaps, but graceful and noble-featured.

As could be expected from a princess of royal Rajput blood on her wedding day, she was richly attired, heavy golden jewellery adorning every visible part of her body. The parting of her beautiful black hair had been coloured deep red with henna, symbolizing her prayers for a long and healthy life for her husband.

But her face was expressionless, her eyes timid and downcast. It seemed she had been crying. I could not help feeling sorry for her – barely fifteen years old, and about to leave her home, her family, and everybody and everything she knew, to be married off to some stranger, and move to a land she had never laid eyes on... I asked Raja Bihari Mal to allow my new wife's personal cooks and servants to accompany her to Agra, as I wanted to make sure she would be attended to in the way she liked.

Throughout the ceremony and the following dinner, I tried to be as friendly and reassuring to her as possible. On our wedding night, I had the wisdom and restraint not to immediately impose myself, but spent the time getting to know her, talking to her the best I could, in Hindustani. When we were both dead tired, in the middle of the night, I invited her to come to sleep next to me, without touching her. My patience was rewarded. The next morning when I woke up, I was happy to find she had removed her clothes and cuddled up against me, ready this time to become my wife. I kissed her and gently called her Azizam[88]; and Azizam is what I have called her ever since, each time we met in private; and it is what I called her, when almost seven years later, God granted me the privilege to create you, my son.

[88] عزیزم My dear, my love (Persian).

Fifteenth Letter

ماہم انگہ، ادھم خان

Mâhâm Anâgâ, Adhâm Khân (2)

We headed back to Agra, arriving on the second of Esfand[89]. Twenty-six days later, grandiose festivities were organized to celebrate the beginning of the seventh year of my reign. Despite the exuberance of the feast, I could not help feeling a bit sad: six years already... six years had passed, never to come back again. Thus, life slips through our fingers, like sand ...

Shortly after the celebrations, reports came in: the situation in Malwa was getting out of hand.

Pir Muhammad Khan had done surprisingly well in the beginning, but then, as expected, had become the victim of his own daredevilry. After the conquest of Malwa, he had headed further south, capturing Bijagarh, again with much unnecessary bloodshed; he then invaded Khandesh, where Baz Bahadur had taken refuge. He captured the fort of Asirgarh and pushed forward all the way to Burhanpur, destroying and killing everything and everybody on his way.

But that is where his luck ran out on him. His advance was checked by a coalition of three local rulers: Baz Bahadur himself, aided by Mubarak Khan of Khandesh, and Tufal Khan of Berar.

He hastily retreated towards Malwa. Having reached the Narmada after dark, he insisted, against the good advice and repeated pleas of his

[89] Friday, February 13, 1562.

officers, on crossing it during the night. It proved to be a fatal mistake. In the middle of the river, he was thrown off his horse and drowned, 'the just retribution', as Shaykh Badaoni later phrased it, 'for the sighs of the orphans, the weak, and the captives.'

A minor setback for the imperial army, but a major step forward for me: a dangerous ally of Adham Khan's was out of the way.

Our army, having lost its commander, headed back to Agra, and Baz Bahadur even managed to temporarily recover his kingdom, but that didn't worry me. I would be back, whenever I wanted to: my army had not been lost; all it needed was a bit of rest, reinforcements, and a new and competent general to lead it back into battle.

This, Maham Anaga must have thought, was a chance to redeem herself and her son. She did her best to seize the opportunity and made more than one passing remark that her son would be overjoyed to avenge the death of his trusted friend Pir Muhammad Khan. I merely answered he could rest assured: justice would be done.

As I expected, Mun'im Khan had the same message. Adham Khan was itching to get back in the saddle. He would avenge his friend in rivers of blood. He would reestablish my authority in Malwa and the neighbouring territories. I assured him that I had no doubt whatsoever about the truth of his words, and that Malwa would indeed be restored to the Empire.

Whatever hopes they may have entertained, were shattered when I appointed Abdullah Khan Uzbeg to lead the invasion. The tough Uzbeg didn't disappoint me: in a few weeks' time, he crushed Baz Bahadur and drove him out of Malwa – this time for good. He wandered around for years as a landless fugitive, seeking refuge and support in the sultanates of the south – in vain, of course: none of the kings of the south wanted to give the mighty Mughal Emperor a pretext for war.

Eight years later, at Nagaur, he would finally surrender, rubbing his forehead in the dirt as a repentant sinner. I decided to pardon him. To execute an opponent, is to pay him tribute: it is to admit, that he was, to a certain extent at least, a true rival. To pardon: that is real supremacy.

I had him join my service – just like adding a wild elephant to a herd of tamed ones. Truth be told, he served me well: very few people had such thorough understanding of music and the arts. It would indeed have been a waste of talent, had he been executed.

But let me come back to my story. Abdullah Khan Uzbeg's appointment was, of course, the deathblow to Adham Khan's ambitions – a clear sign I had no intention of appointing him to a position of power ever again.

I knew it insulted and angered him beyond words. In fact, my informants kept warning me. But it was exactly what I wanted to hear – I wanted him to stew in his own juice, to resent me, to hate me, and not be able to do one thing about it. To take measures against him would have been an admission that he still mattered; to ignore him was to confront him with his own insignificance. In the end, he would endure the ultimate punishment, which is: to despise oneself.

With the wisdom of hindsight, I have to admit it was imprudent and reckless of me. He did constitute a real danger – I should have realized that, and acted accordingly. To underestimate an enemy is always a mistake!

Indeed, all this spite and hatred was like a festering abscess, waiting to burst - and so it did. In the hot afternoon of Shanbeh, the 5th of Khordad[90], I was resting in the zanana[91], while Shams-ud-din and other officials were meeting in the neighbouring courtyard, when suddenly, Adham Khan walked into the courtyard with his personal guards. They went straight to poor Shams-ud-din, who courteously rose to greet them. Without any warning, one of Adham Khan's henchmen drew a dagger and stabbed my loyal Atga in the chest. He tried to escape, staggering towards the gate, but the murderers easily caught up with him and struck him dead before he had taken five steps.

To this day, I do not know what exactly happened. Had the guards been bribed? Were they at loss as to what to do, as this was apparently some kind of reckoning between prominent courtiers? The fact is, they did not intervene, and Adham Khan ran up the steps to the terrace outside the harem unhindered.

I do not know what he was up to. Maybe he wanted to kill me, too, or maybe he just wanted to appease my anger with some kind of excuse; I guess I will never know. Fortunately, the eunuch on guard

---

[90] Saturday, May 16, 1562 of the Julian calendar.

[91] Women's quarters.

had the presence of mind to shut and bolt the terrace door, blocking the entrance to the zanana proper.

Meanwhile, I had been awakened by the noise, and came out of my quarters to see what was going on. Rafiq, the old family servant, in panic, pointed through one of the windows at poor Shams-ud-din's body in the courtyard.

Without another moment's thought, wearing nothing more than a loin cloth, I grabbed the sword one of the eunuch guards handed to me, and went out onto the terrace through the other door.

There he was.

'You *ozgal-i-kuni*[92] piece of shit, what have you done?,' I shouted, stepping in his direction.

He came towards me, bowing deeply, a phony grin on his face.

'Please wait a moment, your Majesty,' he said, and took hold of my right arm. Maybe this was a feeble attempt to overpower me, maybe he merely tried to prevent me from using my sword; but whatever his intentions, he clearly picked the wrong tactic, and the wrong opponent. I was only nineteen years old, but strong as a bull, and well-trained: few men could hope to defeat me in man-to-man combat. Indeed, God, who is just and merciful and gives in abundance without being asked, has graciously blessed the men of our family with strong limbs, and as you know, I have always found great pleasure in exercising my strength and fighting skills.

Maybe he should have tried to appease my anger; maybe he should have thrown himself at my feet, begging for forgiveness, inventing some kind of excuse for what had happened – I honestly do not know what I would have done. But this insolent attempt to restrain me made me beyond myself with rage. It did not take me much effort to pull my arm out of his grip, but I did not even bother to use the sword: in one swift move, I hit him straight in the face with my left fist – I could feel the bone in his nose break under my knuckles. He fell to the ground like a sack of flour, moaning, bleeding heavily – it looked as if he had been hit with a mace. I wanted to go on and kick him to death myself,

---

[92] Faggot's asshole (Persian). According to some historians, Akbar called him a *batchā i lada* (P): young of a dog, son of a bitch; or a *babesyā* (Hindustānī), i.e. a catamite, someone in the habit of getting sodomized.

but decided, in time, that he didn't deserve the honor. Regaining my composure, I coldly ordered the attendants to bind his arms and legs with their girdles, and to throw him off the terrace.

'He has violated my home and entered my harem, head first,' I hissed, 'so throw him out, head first!'

My command was executed, but rather clumsily – he landed on his legs, and though he probably did suffer a number of fractures, the fall did not kill him.

'Don't just stand there!' I yelled, still beyond myself with rage, and quite deaf to Adham Khan's desperate pleas. 'Drag that sack of shit up here, and throw him off the terrace, again, and again, and again if you must – I want him dead!'

They didn't have to do it a third time. He fell on his head; his neck snapped, and the brains dashed out of his fractured skull. For a few more moments, his arms and legs kept on twitching violently, like the wings and legs of a freshly slaughtered chicken. Then, he lay still, his eyes and mouth wide open. Not a pretty sight, but, all in all, a swift and merciful death.

I ordered the bodies of both victim and murderer to be brought to Dilli.

Shams-ud-din's sons, Yusuf and Aziz, began the construction of their father's tomb near the sacred dargahs of Khwajah Nizam ud Din and of the divine Amir Khusrau[93] – not too far from the spot where my own father has his final resting place. Adham Khan's body was to be committed to earth over two kos south of there, in a quiet area near the village of Mehrauli, about three hundred paces west from the beautiful Qutub Minar[94].

Poor Maham Anaga, who had been ill in her chambers since a couple of days, had heard some rumours that her son had gotten himself into trouble again; but nobody had found the courage to tell her what had happened.

---

[93] Nizam ud Dīn Auliya Chishti was a revered Sūfī sage; Amīr Khusrau, a famous Persian poet. The Nizamuddin area still is an important place of pilgrimage in Delhi.

[94] 'Axis of Islām', 73-meter high minaret-tower of victory, one of Delhi's main historical sights. Its construction started in 1193, under Qutub ud Dīn Aybak, first of the Muslim Sultāns of Delhi.

Brave and decisive as always, she asked for an audience, and despite her illness, came to beg my indulgence for whatever her son had done wrong this time. Upon her arrival, I reluctantly gave orders to admit her in my presence.

When I saw her, a tired, frightened old lady, I did no longer remember her devious intrigues. I just saw the woman who had taken care of me for so many years when I was a little boy, who had fed me, washed me, clothed me, kept me company and taught me so many things. All I saw was an old mother who had loved her own son above everything else, in spite of everything – what else is a parent to do? – and I pitied her.

I didn't have the heart to tell her that her son was dead in so many words; evading her glance, I said, softly, almost apologetically: 'Adham Khan killed my Atga – we had to punish him, Mahamji.'

Pale, her lower lip trembling, she found the strength to reply: 'Your Majesty did well,' and retired. She went straight to her quarters, never to leave them again. She ate and drank very little, and her illness, whatever it was, worsened quickly. Clearly, the will to live had left her. Forty days later, she expired.

I paid homage to her frail old body, and ordered it to be taken to Dilli, to be interred near her son – I even accompanied the bier for a short distance on its way.

I had a beautiful tomb erected above their graves, at my personal expense. If we are capable of showing mercy upon those who have wronged us, maybe God will find it easier to have mercy on us, on the day of resurrection...

The tomb is, if I say so myself, quite a graceful building, with its Afghan-style dome and the octagonal gallery of twenty-four arches, where people from the neighborhood gather in the evening for some cool shade and a quiet stroll. At dawn and at sunset, its yellow-ochre stone seems aglow with the peaceful, golden light of paradise... May it one day shine on us all, weak and pitiful human beings!

Sixteenth Letter

صلح كل

Sulh-i-kul[95]

You have read in Salima's diary how I would often leave the palace, in *tebdil*[96], strolling through the alleys of Agra, mingling with the ordinary people. A ruler should know what is on the mind of his subjects.

You have seen how I had my first real conversation with a Hindu devotee. If it is true that God directs our lives, there is no doubt in my mind, that this encounter was ordained by the Almighty Himself! But whatever its cause, it completely changed my outlook on the country I have been destined to rule.

Until that meeting, I had taken for granted that the Hindus are a bunch of idolaters - to be converted, if possible, to be repressed, if necessary. But in that memorable conversation, I came to understand that much wisdom is to be found in their writings, and much sanctity in their ways.

I still see him before my mind's eye: this frail, ash-smeared, skinny old man in his simple loincloth; his friendly, if slightly mocking smile, his patient, gentle eyes barely visible amidst his bushy wild hair and beard. I still hear his voice, explaining patiently and with great clarity,

---

[95] Peace for All.

[96] Disguise.

how, in spite of all the gods and goddesses, most Hindus believe there is only one God, of Whom we are all part, and to Whom we will all return.

'Most Hindus will tell you, young Sahab, that the many deities are avatars, manifestations of God under a certain aspect. There are others, for whom these individual deities are merely symbols, human attempts to describe certain aspects of the ultimate Reality in a more understandable language of images and stories. Some schools of Hindu philosophy altogether deny God's existence!'

'But how can that be?' I asked. 'Which one of these beliefs is true, according to the holy books of your religion?'

'All of them – and perhaps none of them, young sahab. As it is proclaimed in our sacred Vedas: There is One Truth; only men describe it in different ways.'

'And how would you describe God?'

'That depends, young Sahab. In my heart, I feel Him near me: a warm, benevolent Presence, a loving Father Who supports me throughout my existence, and calls me forward towards Him; Who knows me, far better than I do myself, and Who loves me, with a love deeper than anyone is capable of. It is the God from Whom I am separated, and to Whom I will return.

In my thinking mind, however, He is much more distant. There, I understand Him not as a person, but as Reality or Existence itself. He is the Force inside everything and everybody, without which nothing would exist at all; timeless, unborn, imperishable; but also: formless, blind, and I am afraid, without any feelings or awareness.'

'But that comes very close to saying that God and the world are one and the same thing – or that there is no God at all!'

'Perhaps, young Sahab. As I told you, there are schools of Hindu thought which flatly deny God's existence.'

Seeing the puzzled expression on my face, he continued:

'Young Sahab, I do not know much about your religion and the other Western religions. But it seems to me, they are all preoccupied with obedience, with punishment and reward; and they all follow a similar reasoning:

One: there is one almighty God, Lord and Creator of the Universe.

Two: God will reward the good and punish the evil.

Three: in order to obtain salvation, man must follow God's commands.

Four: there is only One True Faith, which God Himself has revealed to humankind, speaking through one or more Prophets and Holy Scriptures.

Five: he who fails to embrace this One True Faith and does not follow its precepts, will suffer the eternal torments of hell.

The Sanatana Dharma, or what you call the 'Hindu faith', young Sahab, is quite different. It is more preoccupied with the attainment of *wisdom*, and it readily acknowledges, that wisdom can be found everywhere. Consequently, it does not claim there is one single orthodox point of view leading to salvation. It has no central authority, it allows hundreds of contradictory opinions and practices to coexist. In fact, there is no such thing as the Hindu religion or philosophy – there are so many different beliefs and systems of thought in this country, that you could never study them all in depth in a single lifetime! Perhaps the only common feature of all these religions is their preoccupation with Moksha, Liberation, which can, and will be, achieved through wisdom or enlightenment.'

'And how do we attain that perfect knowledge?' I asked.

'In the course of many thousand lives, we create good or bad karma: the result of all our thoughts and actions. Everything we do or think has its inevitable consequences, and the lives we are born into, are the result of karma created in previous incarnations. That is why some of us are born as mighty kings, young Sahab...'

He paused, looking me straight in the eye. I tried to put on as disinterested an air as possible, but felt caught red-handed.

He smiled and continued:

'As I said, young Sahab: that is why some of us are born as kings, and others as latrine cleaners. Different as our lives may be, we are all on our way, back to God.'

'So, after death, we are born again, and God punishes or rewards us with a new life, worse or better than the one before?'

'Yes and no, young sahab. You see, God does not hate or punish anyone. What happens to us, is simply the inevitable result of our own thoughts and actions. Compare it to the fate of a man standing on top of a cliff, who decides to jump into the abyss below him. If, despite his hopes and prayers, he falls to his death, do you think it's God's punishment for his recklessness? No, young Sahab: the man will fall and perish, because such is the way things are – his death is nothing more than the natural and inevitable consequence of his own action. This is how the inexorable law of karma works, young Sahab: virtuous thoughts and actions produce good karma and lead to knowledge and liberation, whereas bad ones lead to bondage and suffering.

Another important thought to note here, young Sahab: does the man from our example fall to his death, because he is a sinner? No! He dies, because of his *ignorance*; he dies, because he holds the mistaken belief that prayer will save him from falling. This is another important teaching in Hindu religion: we create bad karma, out of ignorance.

There is a beautiful verse in one of the most important of our holy scriptures, the Srimad Bhagvadgita, where Lord Kṛiṣṇa Himself declares:

Even if thou art the worst of sinners
Thou shalt cross the ocean of sin
By the bark of Wisdom[97]

'So, in the end, will I, a Muslim, be saved?'

'Certainly, young Sahab! Lord Kṛṣṇa Himself proclaimed it in the Bhagvadgita:

Whatever and whichever way men approach Me,
Whatever paths they may choose
Finally lead to Me

Or, as one of my teachers once phrased it:

'As different streams having different sources all mingle their waters in the sea, so the different paths that men take, through different tendencies, various though they appear, crooked or straight, all lead to God.'[98]

---

[97] Bhagavat Gita, 4:36.

[98] Swami Vivekananda, quoted by Ed Viswanathan, page 9.

Live a good life, young Sahab, be a good Muslim – that will be amply sufficient! Serve Allah in humility, and never forget that in your religion, He is called the Compassionate and the Merciful. And maybe: try to learn something from us – learn to see and worship Him in everything and everybody you encounter!'

We walked up the stairs of the central sanctuary of the temple. He told me the names of the gods represented by the idols, what they stand for, the meaning of the objects they hold in their hands, and the strange animals they are riding: Ganeśa, the elephant-headed god, seated on a rat; Śiva, with his trident and his cobras; Durga, the invincible goddess with the many arms, mounted on a lion; Lakshmi, the goddess of wealth... and many more of them, but I was too busy watching the colourful crowd.

'I am afraid I will not be able to remember all this,' I said. 'I will have to come back some other time, and maybe learn some more about all these gods and what they stand for.'

'Any time, young Sahab! Eagerness to learn is always a good thing. And what is even more important: you are blessed with an open mind – preserve it well!'

He looked at me, still smiling, but dead-serious. It felt as if he was looking straight into the depths of my soul.

'Some of us, young Turkoman Sahab' – he spoke slowly, as if tasting every word before pronouncing it – 'some of us have the opportunity to touch many people's lives... Use your life well, young Sahab, and create good karma, for yourself and many others! Keep looking for your own true destiny! As it is said in our scriptures:

There is a Deity residing within you;
find It out,
and obey Its commands!'

Before I had a chance to ask him for some further explanation, he joined his hands and bowed his head.

'Namaste, I bow to thee, young Sahab – or rather, I bow to God, Who lives inside you! As they say in your own religion: *Khuda Hafiz*, may God be your Guide and Protector! If you will excuse me, I must go back and attend the temple ceremony.'

I touched my heart and forehead, as it is customary among Muslims, and then joined my hands and bowed my head, the Hindu way. '*Khuda Hafiz*, and Namaste, honorable sir! Thank you for your kindness and words of wisdom!'

I returned to the fort, and went straight to Mir Abdul-Latif, anxious to hear what he would have to say about all this.

He didn't hear me coming in at first, absorbed as he was in his reading.

I almost felt a bit jealous of him. As he was sitting there, the soft, golden light falling into his study, he looked the paragon of wisdom and peace.

Everything about him seemed holy, venerable: his eyes under the bushy grey eyebrows, studying the manuscript on the book-rest in front of him; the long, gray beard under the clean-shaven upper lip; the expression of peace on his pale, lined face; his plain, sallow woollen clothes and turban.

The Hindu sage in the temple had been right: there is wisdom to be found everywhere.

He suddenly became aware of my presence.

'Your Majesty! I am so sorry; I didn't hear you coming in! How can I be of service?'

'It is I who owe you an apology, Mir Abdul-Latif – I didn't mean to disturb you. But I would very much like your opinion about something I've just heard!'

I told him about my wanderings in disguise and about my visit to the Hindu temple. He listened intently, smiling approvingly throughout the story.

'I am so very happy to hear that Allah, praise be to Him, has blessed us with such a wise and noble Emperor,' he said.

He rose to his feet and went to a pile of documents in the corner of his study. Unerringly, he took out one paper from somewhere in the middle of the pile.

'Here is an important letter, Your Majesty – from the hand of Your Majesty's illustrious grandfather! I have been waiting for an opportunity to show it to you. It's a kind of will, in which Your Majesty's grandfather advises his high-born son, Your Majesty's father Humayun, on how to rule this country's diverse populations.'

He proceeded to read the letter to me. I found its message of such importance that I had it read to me in public, hundreds of times – not because I didn't remember its contents, for I had learned it by heart: I wanted all the mullahs and courtiers to hear I was governing Hindustan the way my revered forefathers had decreed it. Indeed, as you know all too well, my son, many are the times I have been accused of having abandoned Islam...

The letter reads as follows:

> All praise be to Allah.
> Secret Will of Zahir ud Din Muhammad Babur[99]
> To his son, Prince Nasir ud Din Muhammad Humayun, may God prolong his life.
> Written for the strengthening of the Empire.
> O my son, the Empire of Hindustan consists of various religions, domination and sovereignty whereof has been bestowed on you by the grace of the Almighty.
> It is appropriate that religious bigotries be wiped off the tablet of the heart, and justice meted out to each religion according to its own tenets.
> Specially, abstain from the sacrifice of cows, as this would tend to win the hearts of the people of Hindustan, and the populace of the country would be loyal to the Royal favors. The temples and places of worship of whatever religion under the royal authority may not be desecrated. Such justice may be adopted, that the king may be pleased with the rayyat[100], and the rayyat with the King.
> The advancement of Islam is better achieved with the weapon of obligation than with the sword of tyranny.
> Overlook the dispute between the Sunnis and Shi'as, since such weakness persists in Islam. Establish administration with the rayyat of various communities in accordance with the four principal elements so that the body of the empire may be free from different diseases.
> The model work done by his Late Majesty Temür Sahib Qiran

[99] Will of Bābur, quoted by Professor R. Nath, in *India as Seen by Bābur*, 21–22.

[100] Subjects.

should always be kept before the mind, so that you may become mature in the work of administration.

Written on the first of *Jamadi 'al-Awwal* 935[101].

Mir Abdul-Latif looked at me, making sure I had clearly understood.

'Your illustrious grandfather was right, Your Majesty: The most important, overriding principle that should guide any king of Hindustan, is *sulh-i-kul*, peace for all.

You see, Your Majesty: Hindustan is such a large country, its populations so diverse, that a way needs to be found to allow all these peoples to live together – if not in complete harmony, then at least in peace and mutual respect. A Muslim king who would try to impose Islam by the sword, would do himself, and Islam, a disservice. In the eyes of the Hindu masses, he would never be more than a foreign invader, a conqueror to be opposed or endured, but never a king to be loved and respected. Many more people might find the path towards the light of Islam under the guidance of a just, benevolent and tolerant sovereign, who is the true king of everybody – Muslims and non-Muslims alike.'

'Sor, reverend Master, you agree with that Hindu sage who said that all religions are the same, and will lead to salvation?'

'Yes and no, Your Majesty. Let there be no misunderstanding: in my opinion, Islam is the ultimate, most perfect of all religions, and the holy Prophet Muhammad – eternal peace and blessings of Allah be upon him and his household! – is the true Seal of the Prophets.

However, there should be no doubt: Divine revelation has been given to all humankind. The Holy Qur'an says so Itself, in various instances! It is written: 'Mankind is a single nation. So Allah raised prophets as bearers of good news and as warners, and He revealed with them the Book with Truth.'[102]

And it is written: For every nation, there is a Messenger[103], and: There is not a people, but a Warner has gone among them[104].

---

[101] January 11, 1529.

[102] Qur'ān, 2:213.

[103] Qur'ān, 10:47.

[104] Qur'ān, 35:24.

From time to time in history, the cool, limpid, soothing, life-bringing waters of the bottomless Ocean of Mercy that is Allah, have washed over the arid shores of humankind. The pools that have stayed behind, are the various religions revealed through the prophets. Through human error and sin, many of these pools have dried out or got polluted, and there is no doubt in my mind that among them, the religion of Islam is the deepest, the purest and the ultimate: indeed, it is the fulfilment and culmination of all other religions! However, we should never forget the Divine origin of those other religions. We should respect and revere the holiness in them, and compete with them in doing good deeds, without allowing them to lead us astray or confuse us with error.

Therefore, Your Majesty, while I remain profoundly convinced that Islam is superior to any other religion, I believe that where possible, we should be at peace with other religions, for they, too, have been inspired by the All-Merciful. Wherever one turns, there is the face of Allah!'

'So, is it your opinion that non-believers will be enter Paradise?'

'It is, Your Majesty. There is no doubt in my mind, that eventually, everybody will attain Paradise – Muslims and non-Muslims! Allah will reward the good and punish the evil, no matter where it comes from. The Holy Qur'an states that he who has done an atom's weight of good will see it; and he who has done an atom's weight of evil will see it[105]. But the purpose of Allah's chastisement, terrible as it may be, is not to torture us, but to purify our souls. Indeed, as it is written: Allah 'has ordained mercy on Himself[106]! Even the worst of sinners should not despair of the mercy of Allah![107] Yes, I am firmly convinced that hell, however long it will last, will cease to exist at some time. I do have to warn Your Majesty that many learned and respectable men will disagree with me. The highest-ranking Muslim scholar in Your Majesty's Empire, Makhdum ul Mulk, will probably tell you that hell is eternal, or that only Muslim sinners will ultimately be released from it, but I believe he is mistaken: Allah's mercy is limitless and extends to all humankind!

---

[105] Qur'ān, 99:7,8.

[106] Qur'ān, 6:12,54.

[107] Qur'ān, 39:53.

Allah does not punish in anger or revenge: the recompense He grants is but the natural consequence of our own actions; it will lead to salvation and unity with Him. There is no doubt in my mind: all souls, even those of the worst sinners, even those of non-Muslims, will ultimately be released from hell, when they are ready for their new and blissful existence in Paradise! That is clear from the Holy Qur'an, which states that those in Hell will abide there forever, illa ma sha'a Allah – except as Allah pleases. The gift of Paradise, in contrast, is truly eternal, a gift never to be cut off!

This reading of the Holy Qur'an is corroborated by the Sayings of the Prophet and other venerable traditions. For instance, 'Umar, the second Khalifah, may his grave be holy, has declared: 'Even if the dwellers in Hell may be numberless as the sands of the desert, a day will come when they will be taken out of it.' And the wise and learned Bukhari, the peace of Allah be upon him, has written: 'Surely, a day will come over Hell, when there shall not be a single human being in it!' So, you see, Your Majesty, I do not think that all religions are the same, but I do believe, that what that Hindu sage was saying, was in fact true: all paths, straight and crooked, will ultimately lead to Allah, because, in His endless mercy, He will forgive all sins and admit everyone in His presence.

Ours should therefore be a religion of peace, tolerance, and humility before Allah. While our faith is undoubtedly the best of all religions, we should be ready to acknowledge goodness and truth, wherever we find it, for Allah has given Truth and Wisdom to all peoples. We should remain humble, for our knowledge and insights, however brilliant, will always remain incomplete, imperfect. Human knowledge and wisdom, however sublime, compared to Divine wisdom, is like the flame of a candle to the light of a million suns. To Allah alone belongs the Beautiful Name *al-Haqq*[108]!'

'So, what you are actually saying, honorable Master, is that contempt of religion, any religion, is really contempt of God Himself?' I asked.

For a moment, Mir Abdul-Latif seemed to be hesitating.

'I have never phrased it so strongly, but yes, I suppose you are right, Your Majesty.'

---

[108] Al-Haqq: the Truth. One of the 99 Divine Names in Islamic tradition.

That afternoon, my son, I had, for the first time, a clear vision of the Hindustan I wanted to create. Not the Hindustan of the Lodhis and the Surs, not even that of Babur or Humayun. Not the Hindustan of Muslim conquerors ruling their Hindu vassals. In my mind's eye, I saw a prosperous and mighty Hindustan, its many people worshipping the one true God in their manifold ways, united in *sulh-i-kul*, under their Emperor, God's shadow on earth.

I hardly slept that night, praying that almighty God would grant me the strength and wisdom to succeed.

The next morning, before dawn – the colour of the sky in the east was barely starting to shift from black to dark blue – I ordered Hairan to be saddled, the finest and fastest Iraqi stallion in my stables, and rode out, strictly forbidding anybody to follow me. The guards and servants were not even surprised: I had done this before, one morning in the times of the long siege of Mankot, when, after a sleepless night, my mind was filled with darkness of thought, and I needed to get away from it all.

As Abu-l Fazl phrased it: 'His Majesty felt constrained by the presence of shortsighted men; he became averse to the servants of fortune's threshold and separated from them, and issued an order that no one in his retinue should be in attendance on him. He even sent away his grooms and suchlike persons, so that the solitude of his retirement might not be contaminated by the crowd.' Indeed, I wanted to be alone.

I left Agra behind me and headed east, towards the light of dawn, taking the direction of the hunting grounds, far away from any village. At first, I merely went at a brisk trot, but as soon as there was light enough, I made Hairan run as fast as he could, until his flanks were soaked with sweat, and flocks of foam were flying from his mouth.

I halted in the middle of the wilderness and jumped off Hairan's back. He immediately galloped away and disappeared from sight, but I made no attempt to stop him.

I looked around me. The sun was still behind the horizon, yet everything was turning copper-red with its first glow.

Suddenly realizing I was running late for *Salat as-Subh*[109], I hastily performed the ablutions – with clean sand, as is allowed for those who do not have any water at their disposal. I took off my upper tunic, spread it on the ground as a prayer mat, and began my prayers, facing west towards Mekkah, as is required.

When I had finished, I rose to my feet, slowly turned around and looked at the landscape and the sun, the rim of which was now above the horizon, setting everything aglow with its golden light.

Despite the balmy air, I suddenly shivered. In a way I can't describe, I felt overwhelmed with the unspeakable Majesty of God, the awesome, daunting Lord of all worlds, to Whom this giant, golden sun is but a tiny spark, and the mightiest empires of men but passing specks of dust in the winds of time.

It was as if I was standing before the divine throne, naked, powerless, yet comforted by God's loving, all-forgiving mercy, softer and gentler than moonlight. Tears rolled down my face, and I fell to my knees before the sun, touching the ground with my forehead, as in Salat prayer.

After a few moments of wordless prayer, my soul had become completely peaceful. I sat myself down, cross-legged, facing the sun, my arms stretched out and resting on my knees, the palms of my hands upwards – the way I had seen Hindu wise men meditating. In that position I stayed, thoughtless, motionless, I cannot say for how long, but when I opened my eyes again, the sun had reached the height of at least three men, and the air was starting to shimmer with its heat.

I again looked at the landscape. The magic was gone, but I felt rested and peaceful and strong as never before, my soul filled with tranquil happiness.

I suddenly noticed Hairan was back from his escapade; he was standing at about ten paces. I just held out my hand, and he readily came to me. I softly touched his muzzle, patted the flank of his neck, and jumped back in the saddle. At a leisurely pace, we headed back to Agra.

---

[109] First ritual prayer, to be prayed in principle before dawn, between the moment when *a thread* of light is visible at the horizon, and the actual rising of the sun. It is usually performed as a 'missed prayer', upon waking.

This was the first time I had ever prayed while facing the sun, and with my back turned towards Mekkah, but I didn't feel guilty at all. Clearly, I had felt the daunting but sweet presence of God, Who is everywhere: inside man's temples, mosques and churches, and maybe even more so, outside of them.

Countless times have I tried – and thankfully, often succeeded – to relive the blissful magic of that moment, meditating on a stone slab in the sun, or praying while looking at the light of a fire.

Light, fire, and the sun... Indeed, the Parsis are right: no man-made object better symbolizes God's gentle yet awesome power, or the ineffable mystery of His magnificent creation. Not the Hindu statues and temples; not the holy books of the Jews, Muslims and Sikhs; not the qibla in the mosques; not the Firanghi crosses and bells, or the golden halos of their icons.

Light, fire, and the sun: gentle and terrifying are they, like God Himself...

Without light, we cannot see, yet it can strike us with blindness; fire gives warmth to our homes and taste to our food, yet will reduce anything to ashes. The gentle, golden sun will call forward the crops from the earth, yet it is able to turn our fields into lifeless deserts and render fruitless the labour of our hands...

Evil tongues – including your own, my son – have held my prayers and meditations against me. 'The Emperor has abandoned Islam', they whispered behind my back, 'he has adopted the wicked ways of the pagans.'

Come on, you know better than that! Never, never have I worshipped anything or anybody but God! All my life, I have been, or tried to be, His faithful servant, in complete submission to His majesty – and what else is Islam, but submission to God?

One thing, however, I have come to realize: that all religions are but human attempts to understand God. Some may be better than others, but none of them is perfect, for no human being is perfect. Indeed, as Abu'l Fazl has quoted me saying: Each person, according to his personal condition, gives the Supreme Being a name, but in reality, to name the unknowable is vain.

God – eternal praise be upon Him – defies human explanations. He is *al-Awwal*, the first; *al-Akhir*, the last; *al-Ahad*, the one; *al-Wahid*, the unique; and always Akbar, greater. Greater is He, greater than any human mind could ever comprehend; and those who claim to know Him, are in error.

Seventeenth Letter

سلطنت

Saltanat[110]

Thus ended my youth, Salim my son: with the long overdue and well-deserved execution of a rebel, and the dawn of a great vision – that of a strong, prosperous and united Hindustan, ruled with firmness, generosity and justice by its rightful Emperor.

Merciful God, who gives in abundance to whom He has chosen, has made my dream come true, and given me much more than I could ever hope for. With His powerful help, I have removed all obstacles, and established what is probably the wealthiest and most powerful empire on the face of the earth – more than three times larger than Babur's!

Rarely, if ever, has the world seen an empire like the one you are about to inherit, my son. No enemy could ever hope to conquer it, if you maintain your vigilance. On the contrary, if you apply yourself to your task, and keep using your power in accordance with God's will, He may well allow you to expand our borders much further!

Soon, very soon, you will find yourself on the throne, my son. I beseech you: do not take your task lightly, for power is a precious treasure – much more easily lost than gained!

Remain on your guard, amidst and despite all the luxuries that surround you, for they will distract you from what is important.

Pleasure and repose, my son, are to be enjoyed like food: they are necessary to restore body and mind after work and exertion; but when

[110] Kingship, Empire.

taken in excess, they will bring nothing but sickness and ruin.

Just read the history books, and observe, how sloth and greed have been the ruin of so many a mighty king! Pleasure and wealth softened their spirit, made them hungry for compromise, when they should have prepared themselves for war. I implore you: never let this happen to you!

The throne is a lonely place, Salim my son. He who occupies it, needs to be strong, and watchful. He must realize he's locked in a golden cage – dependent on courtiers to tell him what is going on outside.

So true is it what the books have to say about this: rulers tend to get the advisors they deserve. The easiest way indeed to assess a ruler's ability, is to look at his courtiers: competent kings will always choose skilled assistants, and inept rulers inevitably pick the incapable ones. A true king has no use for flattering yes-men; what he needs, is a group of strong helpers, resourceful, hard-working, ambitious, and loyal – loyal enough to warn him, respectfully but unequivocally, if they believe he is making a mistake.

But no matter how competent your officials, and no matter how deep your affection and trust: you always need to keep a close watch over them, and make frequent and unexpected examinations into their conduct – for, as the saying goes, opportunity makes the thief!

A king must, above all, be an astute observer, an excellent judge of character. Ask yourself what people really think, my son; find out what it is that really drives them. Remember that pun Raja Birbal so fondly used: the difference between truth and lie is the distance between eye and ear, because what we see with our own eyes is true, but what we hear with our ears usually is not! So very true... Keep asking questions, a lot of them, all the time. And keep asking people for their advice, for 'Counsel is the Mirror of the Mind!'

But remain on your guard, my son. Resist the temptation to confide too much in people; be extremely careful what you say to whom. A king is wise not to reveal his inner thoughts – let him be a careful listener, rather than a smooth talker! As the saying goes, a secret is merely something divulged to only one person at a time...

Looking back on the long years of my reign, there have been – in my recollection at least – three periods, quite distinct from each other.

First, there were the eventful years of my now distant youth, which I have just finished describing to you: starting with the hasty enthronement of a young boy prematurely made Emperor, and ending with the execution of an unruly foster brother who turned out to be a murderous rebel.

Most people tend to look back on their own youth with a degree of wistfulness. They remember the vigour of their body when it was still young, free from diseases and infirmities; they remember the seemingly limitless promise of an unspoilt future. In the light of the evening sun, the road behind them seems to be paved with gold...

I, for one, do not share such rosy views of the past. No, my youth was not a period I am proud to remember. I do not have much liking for the spoilt young weakling I, or he, was at that time – torn as I, or he, was between jealousy and gratitude, between guilty laziness and burning but impotent ambition.

Should I write 'I', or can I write 'he'? A man is, of course, responsible for his own past actions, but if he manages to rise above his own self, and becomes an entirely different person, can he not take pride in that, and distance himself from those past mistakes? People can change if they want to, Salim, and so can you!

With God's help and guidance, I did change. I did manage to take control of myself and my surroundings, and came out much wiser and stronger, firmly resolved to fulfil my destiny: to become, with God's grace and blessings, His Shadow on earth.

It has not been easy. It has taken me many years of hard toil, many worries, and endless fighting against powerful enemies, outside and inside my realm. Many a strong man in my place would have been driven to despair; but with God's help, I succeeded.

The rewards for my hard work and trust in God have been rich and manifold, my son. Looking back, the second part of my reign can be summarized as four decades of conquest, triumph and ever-growing power and wealth – forty years the world will remember as the magnificent reign of *Akbar-e-Azam*[111], as people have come to call me – and rightfully so, for I have established one of the greatest empires

---

[111] *Akbar-e-Āzam*: Akbar the most Glorious, the Great(er). *Āzam* – greater, most important, magnificent, most glorious – is the comparative/superlative of *Azīm* – mighty, glorious, magnificent.

the world has ever seen; and I have ruled over it, supreme, and alone.

Alone, indeed. There is only one God in the universe, and likewise, there can only be one Padshah. So much I learned from Adham Khan's rebellion: a king should suffer no rivals! To be sure, I have continued to seek the advice and support of many good people and appointed them to positions of high power and responsibility, but never again have I allowed anyone to challenge my authority. Never anyone, except you, my son...

But now? My only son has become my rival, and I am a lonely, tired old man...

My invincible armies, the untold treasures, the sweet, soft-breasted girls in my zanana: they are at my disposal, but bring me no comfort. I tremble, when I think that what I have built over forty glorious years is now in grave danger.

Every night, I lie wide-awake, my heart full of grief, my face wet with tears, when I think of all the people who were part of my life and have passed away: two of my three beloved sons, and many an old friend, near and dear to my heart... Where are they, my friends and loved ones? Where have they gone, my years of glory? They have slipped through my fingers, like water, or desert sand...

In the pitiless dark of the night, I am worried sick about the future; and always, my thoughts and prayers return to you, my only surviving son and bitter rival...

Countless hours I've prayed to God, almighty and merciful, that He will enlighten your mind and bring you back to me. Countless times I've relived your insolent acts of rebellion – foaming with rage, weeping like a child, or both... I do not think you realize, how much you've hurt me, Salim. O, how I wish I could undo everything that has come between us!

But I shouldn't dwell upon those sad thoughts. I must finish what I have undertaken: I must tell you my story – is it not through stories that we learn best? I must tell you about my reign, make you reflect upon what it is to rule an empire, to determine the destiny of millions.

Here and there, you will have noticed, I've thought it appropriate to include a few court archives, or extracts from other people's private writings. Not only does this save me the trouble of writing everything myself: it's important you see that what I say and think is shared by people you respect.

Those who study the history of my reign will see an incessant series of wars and military campaigns, against numerous enemies, inside and outside the empire. Close to one hundred and twenty major battles have I fought during those long years, my son. I do not think it's necessary or useful for me to recount them all – you can read about them in the history chronicles. I will refer to some of them when I believe it is convenient for me to make my point. What is important for you to reflect upon, is the life I've led, so you may follow my example, learn from my mistakes, and more importantly, correct your own.

PART II

ظہر [112]

[112] Zohr, Noon.

Eighteenth Letter

Raf-e-Hejab[113]

In the Name of Allah, the Compassionate, the Merciful.
Private Notes
On the Youth, Coming of Age, and Rise to Absolute Power
of His Imperial Majesty, Jalal-ud-Din Muhammad Akbar-e-Azam114 –
May Allah may be well pleased with him;
May Allah grant him a long, healthy and prosperous life;
May Allah expand his borders, and put all his enemies to shame!

Written for the edification of posterity,
during these months of Muharram and Safar of 981115,
in this, the 18th Year of His Majesty's Glorious Reign,

by Mir Abdul-Latif, his humble teacher.

On the fourth day of the fourth month of the fourth year of young Prince Akbar's life[116], it pleased his august father, Emperor Jahanbani Jannat-Ashyani Nasir-ud-Din Muhammad

113 Removal of the Veil.

114 Akbar the Great.

115 May–June, 1573.

116 7th Shawwal 954 corresponds to November 20, 1547 (Julian Calendar).

Humayun, may Allah be well pleased with him, to ordain the start of his son's formal education.

The tutor, carefully selected for this most noble task, was Mullahzada Mullah Asam ud-Din Ibrahim, an experienced teacher and a man of profound knowledge, great wisdom, and irreproachable piety.

His Majesty the Emperor, eminently knowledgeable about the celestial sciences and well versed in the mysteries of the stars, had personally selected the auspicious hour on which his son was to meet his tutor for the first time, and receive his first scholarly introduction.

However, when that critical moment had arrived, the young prince was nowhere to be seen: he had gone out to play! Search parties were sent out in every direction, but he was nowhere to be found. Only hours later did he return, still in much too playful a mood to apply his mind to any learning.

Alas! To Emperor Humayun's bitter disappointment, this first day proved to be a bad omen for the entire remainder of his son's scholarly upbringing: Prince Akbar did not seem to care for education, and used every pretext to go horse riding or hunting, or engage in other outdoors amusements.

Truth be told, he did excel in all kinds of physical activities and martial arts, showing great agility and strength for his age, wrestling down boys two or three years older than him. Over the years, he developed impressive fighting skills and revealed himself an outstanding marksman.

The prince also showed a truly extraordinary aptitude with animals, domestic and wild, and in particular, with elephants, which he handled with amazing confidence and skill, as if he was one of the mahauts. Under his touch, the most vicious bull elephant would, as if by magic, turn into the meekest of lambs! The young prince would also spend many hours in his teacher's dovecot, growing almost as fond of pigeon-flying as his tutor was.

Not to say that Prince Akbar didn't show any interest in other, more serious matters. He would fondly listen to lessons about religion, poetry, or the art of counting; and he fondly listened to the stories of the great kings and warriors of old. But when it came to the all-important skills of reading and writing, he did not seem to be able to apply his mind to mastering them.

Despite all the desperate efforts of his tutor, he kept on confusing the various letters:

Ra ر with Za ز and Zha ژ ; Zal ذ with Dal د;

The loops in Hēh, in its four forms (ه ـهـ ـه هـ) with the loops in the middle forms of Fēh ـفـ, Qaf ـقـ, and Ayn ـعـ;

Fēh ف with Qaf ق and Vav و;

Ayn ع and Ghayn غ;

Hamza ء with Initial Ayn عـ ;

Sad ص and Zad ض; Za ظ and ط Ta ;

final Nun in its two forms ن ں, with Final Yēh ی;

the four letters derived from Jim: ح خ ج چ,

and those derived from Bēh: پ ث ب ت, and so on.

While this kind of confusion is of course perfectly normal for a beginner, it only seemed to grow worse over time, and so did Prince Akbar's diligence and zeal. At first, he had at least shown some willingness to cooperate, but after a few weeks, he lost all interest, and flatly refused to listen to any more reading lessons.

His father, himself a man of such eminent learning, was extremely displeased with his son's lack of progress, and dismissed Asam ud Din Ibrahim, reproaching him bitterly to have squandered his son's precious time with pigeon-flying and other trivial amusements, rather than with science and study.

Prince Akbar's second teacher was Maulana Hakim Bayazid, an eminent physician and descendant of one of the astronomers of the great Ulugh Beg. Hopes were high, but alas, this good man, too, utterly failed. He was dismissed by the time the prince reached his eighth birthday.

Emperor Humayun was bitterly disappointed, not to mention increasingly worried, about his son's future. He personally tried to persuade him of the importance of reading and writing. But Prince Akbar cleverly replied that the Prophet Muhammad – Allah's peace and eternal blessings be upon Him! – had been illiterate as well...

Emperor Humayun then put his trust in Allah and the stars: lots were drawn, to decide who of three scholars would become his son's next teacher.

Fate appointed Maulana Abdul-Qadir, whose efforts met with a bit more success. He didn't fare any better than his predecessors when it came to reading; but after a few days, he wisely chose to follow a completely different course. Giving up all further attempts to teach the prince how to read and write, he introduced him to a variety of books and scriptures, reading aloud some or other extract, and subsequently discussing with him the meaning of what had been read.

To everybody's amazement and relief, Prince Akbar turned out to be quite fond of these new lessons! With amazing ease, he learned by heart lengthy passages from the Holy Qur'an, the Hadith and many beautiful poems.

Even today, as an adult, he continues to do so. No matter how busy he is: whenever his duties allow him a moment of leisure, he will ask for books to be read to him. Over the years, he has achieved such high level of knowledge and understanding, that he is able to sustain a learned conversation about almost any subject of interest, quoting from the most varied sources of wisdom. Anyone who does not know him would readily swear that reading is his favorite pastime!

He has ordered the collection of a library of thousands upon thousands of books – in Persian, Arabic and Hindi, but also in Sanskrit, Turki, Kashmiri, and even Greek – about every imaginable subject, religious and profane.

Works he believes will be of particular interest to him are translated into Persian, so that he may personally acquaint himself with their content. He has, thus, recently asked Maulana Abdul-Qadir Badaoni to supervise the translation of the Mahabharata, which, as everybody knows, is one of the most important Hindu scriptures.

He also greatly appreciates the beauty of the books he commissions; many renowned illustrators and masters of calligraphy are permanently employed at the imperial court: men like Maulana Baqir, Mir Husayn-i-Kulanki, Muhammad Amin of Masshad, Maulana Abd ul-Hay, Maulana Dauri, Maulana Abdurrahim, Nizami of Qazwun, Ali Chamman of Kashmir, Nur ul-Lah Qasim Arsalah, and last but not least, of course, the incomparable Muhammad Husayn of Kashmir, deservedly honored with the title of Zarrin-qalam[117].

Despite his illiteracy, His Majesty greatly appreciates the beauty

---

[117] *Zarrīnqalam*: Golden Pen.

of writing and has no problem whatsoever in recognizing the various styles – Kufic, Ma'qali, Suls, Tanqi, Muhaqqaq, Naskh, Rayhan, Riqa, Gubar, Taliq and Nasta'liq; but still, he will angrily dismiss any attempt to teach him the skill of reading for himself...

When Prince Akbar was thirteen years of age, Emperor Humayun elevated him to the lofty rank of governor of the Panjab, and appointed Lord Bairam Khan, Sipahsalar of the imperial Army and Khan-i-Khanan, as his son's new Ataliq. His teacher Maulana Abdul Qadir, having expressed the pious and commendable wish to depart to Mekkah and dedicate his further life to study and prayer, was granted leave to retire.

To my great joy and surprise, the honor of teaching the young Prince then befell me, Abdul Latif of Qazwin, son of Mir Yahya, of the Sayfi Sayyids of Qazwin. Quite an unexpected honor for a poor and humble Mullah, just arrived at Court as a destitute fugitive from Persia...

Indeed, the enemies of my revered father having convinced the Esfahan authorities that our family was dangerous, because of our adherence to the Sunni tradition, we were sentenced to be imprisoned, pending an investigation into charges of treason. My aging father, too old and too infirm to flee, quietly awaited the Shah's soldiers, ready to die with dignity and in quiet resignation to the Divine Will. May it please Allah to reunite us in Paradise! As for me: obeying my father's command, and with Allah's help, I managed to bring my family into safety. We fled to Gilan, and from there, further east, into Hindustan. The Mughal governor at the frontier, aware of the Emperor's keen interest in matters of philosophy and religion, awarded me a letter of recommendation, and we travelled on to the Court in Dilli.

Like the Governor had predicted, we were well received. We were given comfortable, spacious living quarters, and almost every day, I had the honor of joining His Majesty and other learned men, in stimulating conversations on many an interesting subject.

I knew the Emperor was well pleased with me, but still, my appointment as his son's personal teacher came as a complete surprise. Honored and privileged as I felt, I was also terrified that I wouldn't be up to the task.

But Emperor Humayun was most kind and encouraging:

'Do not be too modest, Mir Abdul-Latif – I have full confidence in your abilities! Your family's reputation is well known. Your exquisite command of the Persian language, your acquaintance with both the Shi'a and the Sunni traditions, your vast knowledge of religion, literature and science, will make you the ideal teacher!'

Having thus been appointed to such lofty an office, I implored the support of Allah, and applied myself, to the best of my knowledge and abilities, to teach Prince Akbar what I thought a future emperor needs to know. I of course prudently continued the successful practice of my predecessor, reading to the prince about many a subject, discussing with him the content of what had been read, and comparing it with other sources of wisdom.

Most encouraging it was to see, how Lord Bairam Khan himself would also devote much of his time to the education of His Majesty, placing greater emphasis, of course, on matters of warfare and military governance of newly conquered dominions. He taught the prince about the battles fought by the Seal of the Prophets, Muhammad (Allah bless him and his household!), and the conquests of his able successors, the Right-Guided Khalifahs. He thoroughly instructed him in the history of the great empires and dynasties of the Umayyads, Abbasids, Mamluks, Buwayhids, Samanids, Ghaznavids, Hamdanids, Fatimids, and Seljuqs. Prince Akbar would listen fondly to all those stories about the great soldiers and kings, such as Iskandar the Conqueror; or Salah ud-Din Yusuf Ayyubi, Sword of Islam, Liberator of Jerusalem; or Sultan-i-Rum Mehmet the second, conqueror of Istanbul – and in particular, of course, to the famous deeds and accomplishments of his own glorious ancestors: Genghis Khan, Amir Temür, and Babur Padshah.

Then suddenly, wholly unexpectedly, Emperor Humayun, a strong and vigorous man in the prime of his life, received the Divine summons to leave this fleeting earthly life, and enter the realm of Eternity.

It was an irony of fate that he died, while obeying Allah's commandment: responding to the muezzin's call to evening prayers, he fell down from the stairs of his observatory, where he had been standing on the roof, talking to his astrologers. Fragile, so fragile is human life!

Soon after Emperor Humayun's unexpected demise, Bairam Khan, who had remained in charge of the affairs of state as His Majesty's ataliq, confirmed my appointment as the young new emperor's teacher. He and I would continue His Majesty's education, guided by the same principles as before.

A difficult but gratifying task it was. Despite His Majesty's often unruly behaviour, I clearly sensed that inside this restless youth, there was true greatness of soul, and majesty, waiting to emerge.

⁂

The first few years of His Majesty's reign were fraught with the gravest of dangers. Being myself a man of the pen rather than the sword, I must confess that in those days, I more than once despaired of the Empire's survival, surrounded as it was by such a multitude of mighty enemies.

Bairam Khan, however, acquitted himself admirably of his heavy responsibilities. Plying himself to his task – and aided, no doubt, by the almighty hand of Allah Himself – he managed to overcome the many challenges.

⁂

Nothing in this world stays the same; young boys become adults, and pupils become teachers: when His Majesty had reached the age of seventeen, he rather abruptly dismissed Lord Bairam Khan as his guardian and personally assumed the reins of government.

Bad and troubling times those were... times of mistrust, estrangement, rebellion and sin; but fortunately, also of forgiveness and reconciliation; and of true friendship, lost, but found again.

I do not want to dwell on these unfortunate events, as they bring back sad and painful memories. Besides, it is not necessary for me to recount them here, as they are still fresh in everybody's memory, and an extensive account of them can be read elsewhere. I do want to emphasize, however, that His Majesty and Lord Bairam Khan parted ways as the best of friends, with no bitterness left between them.

Bairam Khan was offered a new and high-ranking position, in accordance with his merits and abilities. But he chose to decline the offer and expressed the pious wish to first acquit himself of the sacred duty of the Hajj. Although reluctantly, His Majesty did grant him permission to leave his dominions, but not until after Lord Bairam Khan had promised, that upon his return from Mekkah, he would again join His Majesty's service.

With a warm embrace, he bade me farewell: 'In sha'a Llah[118], my learned friend, we will meet again, in a few years! Take good care of yourself – I look forward to many more nights of your learned and edifying conversation!'

Alas, it was not to be: Allah, Who is just and all-knowing, granted him the bliss of martyrdom, shortly after his departure.

Why did it have to end like this? Why was it ordained, that such a great and noble man had to lose his life at the hands of a filthy Afghan murderer?

I do not know... I have tried to resign myself to the thought, that nothing happens without good reason, and that it is futile for us, weak and ignorant creatures, to look for the reason behind the dispensations of Allah's omnipotence – praise be to Him under all circumstances!

But whatever motive Divine Providence may have had for allowing Lord Bairam Khan to leave this transitory world, one thing is certain: his death did help His Majesty to find the strength and courage to dedicate himself entirely to the task of government.

Within a remarkably short space of time, His Majesty's character appeared to have undergone the most profound change. Although still very much a seeker of pleasure, fond of hunting, sports and rough amusements, and indulging far too often in wine and other inebriating concoctions, he no longer ran away from his duties, but applied himself to his task with commendable zeal and diligence. It was, as the chroniclers have phrased it so aptly, as if he had emerged from behind the veil.

Alas, not everybody understood the sign of the times...

With Lord Bairam Khan out of the way, the clique around Maham Anaga, and that worthless son of hers, Adham Khan, thought they could control our young Emperor, and take advantage of his inborn kindness to serve their own selfish interests. Sadly mistaken were they, indeed!

(Follows an account of the events leading to Adham Khan's execution.)

~

With the death of Adham Khan – may Allah forgive his sins! – the atmosphere at Court changed markedly: everybody tried to keep as low

---

[118] God willing.

a profile as possible. So very true is it what the villagers say: When the tiger roars, the jungle keeps quiet...

It was of course widely expected that the Emperor, in furious and justified anger at Shams-ud-din's murder and the attempt on his own life, would wipe out the entire Maham Anaga clique, guilty or innocent. In any case, it seemed to be beyond any doubt that at least the main conspirators would be duly executed, as a stern but just warning to any other would-be rebels. The only question was: how far would the Emperor go?

In the same line of reasoning, everybody was expecting the atga khail, or 'foster-father horde', as Shams-ud-din's family was commonly called, to become all-powerful. It will be remembered that Shams-ud-din was the Emperor's foster father on account of his marriage to Jiji Anaga, and that his sons (among whom, the highly ambitious and rather unruly Aziz), therefore enjoyed a position of high prestige and influence at court as the Emperor's kokas, foster brothers – united with him, as the expression goes, by a river of milk.

Maybe, so people speculated, Shams-ud-din's elder brother, Mir Muhammad Khan Khalan, would be appointed as the new wakil? Or maybe the other brother, Sharif Khan? The elder son, Yusuf Muhammad, a hopeless drunkard, was an unlikely candidate, but Aziz, the younger one, was strong and dynamic, and the Emperor liked him – had they not played together when they were still young boys?

All these worldly-wise speculations proved to be sorely mistaken. All of Shams-ud-din's relatives, after having been judiciously placated with the sight of Adham Khan's bloodied corpse, were given lucrative and important, but far-away fiefs and military assignments in remote border regions. Rather than rising to absolute power as generally expected, the atga khail had thus, tactfully but effectively, been removed from Court!

As for Mun'im Khan: to be sure, he had been Maham Anaga's main supporter and trusted friend since many years, and was widely regarded as the real ringleader behind Shams-ud-din's murder – nobody believed there was even the remotest chance for him to escape death.

Similar thoughts must have crossed his own mind, for he attempted a hasty if futile escape – westward, to Kabul probably, or Persia perhaps. A detachment of the imperial guard tracked him down without too many difficulties, and arrested him in a small village not far from Agra.

The soldiers dragged him from a shabby peasant hut, crazy with fear, trembling, sweating, pleading, weeping...

But to his great relief and astonishment, the captain of the guard treated him with respect and courtesy. His Majesty urgently requested Mun'im Khan's presence in Agra, the soldier announced, stiffly but with consideration. It was His Majesty's wish to reinstate him as wakil, and bestow on him the lofty title of Khan Khanan, he explained.

Everybody – and I was no exception – stood amazed at such extraordinary generosity, and thought it was a serious mistake. It was a sign of weakness, people said, a dangerous error of judgement...

But it would soon become apparent, that His Majesty was neither weak nor confused – quite the contrary!

Mun'im Khan's fear quickly returned when he saw the cool reception that befell him upon arrival at the Agra fort. The guards treated him with cool politeness – more, so it seemed, like a high-ranking prisoner than like a guest of honor. Without even a private moment to freshen up or adjust his clothes and appearance, he was escorted to the Emperor's presence.

'That will not be necessary. His Majesty is quite anxious to see you,' the captain of the guard answered, when Mun'im Khan timidly asked for a moment's leave to retire to his private quarters. 'We have orders to escort you to the diwan-i-am[119].'

Mun'im Khan was terrified. No private interview with the Emperor, as one would expect would be the privilege of a high-ranking official? A public audience, in front of dozens of courtiers? This did not bode well...

'Mun'im Khan, I am so pleased to see you are in good health,' the young emperor said softly as Mun'im Khan bowed before the throne. There was, however, no smile on his face to match the kindness of his words.

A long and awkward silence followed. Mun'im Khan, who did not dare to open his mouth, kept staring timidly at the floor in front of him.

'I was grieved to hear you had left Agra so suddenly,' the Emperor resumed, a sad expression on his face.

---

[119] Diwān-i-khās: Hall of Private Audience; Diwān-i-ām: Hall of Public Audience.

Silence again. No one as much as blinked an eye.

'People are telling me, you were trying to run away, Mun'im Khan. I just couldn't believe them at first! Tell me, is this really true?'

There was amazement in his voice and facial expression, as if the very thought was unimaginable.

'No, Your Majesty.' Mun'im Khan's voice was barely audible.

'You were not? Well, what exactly were you up to?'

'Your Majesty,' Mun'im Khan stammered, sweating profusely, 'I wanted to visit my son in Kabul...' He hesitated.

'I am an old man, Your Majesty, and it's been such a long time since I have seen him,' he added, a bit more forcefully, as if on the verge of believing his own lies.

'You wanted to visit your son? And so, you left Agra, with little or no baggage, and without taking your leave of me? I somehow find that hard to believe, Mun'im Khan! I'll tell you more: I am actually starting to believe it is true what people are saying! Be honest now: you were fleeing, were you not?'

Mun'im Khan bowed his head, afraid to say anything.

'Well?'

'Yes, Your Majesty...'

'Go on.'

'I was scared, Your Majesty. I swear, Your Majesty, on the Holy Qur'an: my conscience is clear, I've done nothing wrong... but I was scared I would be blamed for Shams-ud-din's death.'

'And, should you not be?'

'As Allah is my witness: no, Your Majesty – I am innocent!'

'Are you going to tell me that you regretted Shams-ud-din's murder? That you opposed it, tried to prevent it? Do you seriously expect me to believe that?'

'I can assure Your Majesty, I swear...'

'How very convenient, was it not, to have a hothead like Adham Khan around, to do the dirty work for you?'

Mun'im Khan was now literally bathed in sweat and trembling with fear. It seemed the Emperor's eyes were wandering off, to the courtyard behind him, to the sinister line of rocks on which criminals and traitors are executed, their skulls cracked like walnuts under the front leg of a war elephant.

'I beg Your Majesty to have mercy on me, I swear I am innocent,' he yelled.

Again, a long and awkward silence. The Emperor looked at him, his face expressionless, inscrutable.

'Maybe you are... and maybe you are not. Maybe you did not actually tell Adham Khan, in so many words, to commit that murder, but I am pretty sure you haven't said or done anything to stop him either! Am I mistaken, Mun'im Khan?'

Mun'im Khan bit his upper lip. It was futile to deny the truth.

'On the contrary, you did everything you could to poison his soul, to make him jealous of my poor Atga, didn't you?'

Mun'im Khan bowed his head. Obviously, it was all over for him now.

A faint smile came over the Emperor's face.

'Thank you for being honest with me at last, Mun'im Khan. Would you mind passing me that beaker of sherbet,' he asked, after another long and awkward silence, pointing – with his foot – at the tray placed in front of the low, pillow-covered throne on which he was sitting. The sherbet was well within the Emperor's reach, and there were, of course, more than enough servants around to comply with any request he might have had. This was clearly a deliberate insult, and its message was equally obvious: in the presence of the Emperor, even the Khan Khanan is a servant.

'Go ahead, have some' he said, nodding at the bowl of sherbet with unexpected amiability. 'You must be thirsty from all that traveling around in this heat!'

Mun'im Khan scooped out a small portion, and took the beaker in both hands.

'Mm, quite delicious,' the Emperor said, smacking his lips, 'exactly the way it should be: the ice crushed, but not molten, the lime and mango juice well mixed and seasoned, not too sweet, not too sour, with just a pinch of salt...'

He paused, gazing dreamingly at the beautiful silk canopy above his head, seemingly absorbed in the contemplation of its beauty and the agreeable taste of his refreshment.

After a while, he again cast his eyes on Mun'im Khan and abruptly stopped smiling. For a few moments, he just stared at him, expressionless, unblinking, like a snake observing its prey. Then, his eyes seemed to relax again.

'The past, Mun'im Khan, we cannot change, but the present and the future are ours, don't you agree?'

'Yes, Your Majesty.' Mun'im Khan was still holding his beaker, clumsily, in both hands, too scared to take anything from it.

'I could of course keep myself occupied for a few weeks eliminating everybody who ever opposed Shams-ud-din. I guess, many people would expect me to do just that, don't you think so?'

He again looked at Mun'im Khan, his eyebrows raised, as if he expected an answer. 'The important question is, however: would that actually help the Empire? Would it make us stronger?'

He took another sip of his sherbet, and stared absentmindedly at the battlements of the outer walls.

'An empire should be fighting enemies outside its borders, not waste its good men and resources on internal strife, Mun'im Khan. So much remains to be done, so many battles are still ahead of us, and the Empire needs experienced and loyal men. The only question is: are you one of them, Mun'im Khan? Will I be able to count on you?'

'I swear on the Holy Qur'an, Your Majesty, I am your most loyal servant! Your Majesty can rely on me! Allah is my witness, may I die in agonizing pain if I should lie!'

'You will, if you do, Mun'im Khan – of that, you may rest assured!' The Emperor burst out laughing, followed by all those present, the soldiers in particular. He abruptly stopped and raised his hand, with a vague, tired gesture. The clamour stopped immediately.

'I have lost my wakil,' he said gravely, and paused. 'I have lost my wakil, and I need to appoint a successor for him – someone experienced and reliable, someone who will keep me well informed; a man who can represent me when my duty requires my presence elsewhere; who can lead a campaign for me, when I am involved in another.

You do have the right experience, Mun'im Khan, and you have sworn a solemn oath – an oath on the Holy Qur'an! – that I can count on your unwavering loyalty, have you not?'

'Yes, Your Majesty! Your Majesty can count on me! May Allah bless Your Majesty!'

'Go then, do your duty, remember your oath, and do not disappoint me again!'

Mun'im Khan wanted to say something else, but the Emperor cut him off with a friendly smile, accompanied, however, by a vague gesture of his hand, betraying impatience and irritation.

'You must be tired from all your travails, Khan Khanan. You have our permission to retire.'

Mun'im Khan clumsily put down the beaker he had been holding in his hands, its content molten and still untasted, and slowly made his way out of the diwan-i-am, stepping backwards all the way, bowing deeply with every step. The Emperor didn't even bother to watch him leave. He made a sign to the scribes to call forward the next visitor. For the rest of the afternoon, he went about his customary activities, as if nothing had happened, passing judgement in the disputes that were brought before him, and listening, with undivided attention, to reports from the provinces.

How much had we underestimated our young Emperor! In just a few months' time, he had managed to transform his Court beyond recognition – from a snake pit of intrigue, into the retinue of a supreme ruler.

Nineteenth Letter

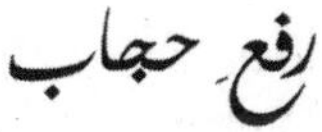

Raf-e-Hejāb[120] (2)

PART ONE

From the private notes of Mir Abdul-Latif

Rather than a mistake or a sign of weakness, Mun'im Khan's appointment was a true masterstroke. The highest office in the Empire was now in the hands of a mediocre yes-man, competent and experienced enough to be the Emperor's assistant and messenger, but much too weak and much too scared to harbour any dangerous ambitions.

It must be said, he learned his lesson well. Ever since that faithful day when he got pardoned, he has served His Majesty with unwavering, exemplary loyalty, in grateful obedience, and to the best of his abilities – limited though they may be.

'Yes, I know: he may not be the most brilliant of my generals, nor the most competent administrator,' His Majesty confided in me a few years later, on one of those rare occasions when he shared his private views with anyone, 'but it has been a real blessing that I wasn't able to find a better minister at the time! I think you will agree with me, my trusted old friend, that it would neither have been wise, nor safe, for me to appoint a strong and ambitious man in a position of that importance. Of course, I did need all the help and good advice I could get, but

[120] Raf-e-Hejāb (Removal of the Veil).

could I afford to leave my army in the hands of someone harbouring a burning ambition of his own? No, my friend – better a weak wakil than a dethroned emperor, wouldn't you agree?

Besides, even if I had managed to find a minister who was competent as well as loyal – someone like Bairam Khan, for instance: would that have been a good thing? To be honest, I don't think so! You see, my trusted old friend: now, the people have come to respect me. I like to think that most of my subjects love me, but even those who do not: at least they respect me. Suppose I had had a strong wakil at my side, someone like Bairam Khan: would they have respected me as much as they do now? Would they not have thought that everything I accomplished was really my wakil's work?'

I fully understood the reasoning behind His Majesty's decision, but I must confess I was quite worried at first, afraid he would slip back into his old bad habits, or that he would succumb to the obvious temptation of surrounding himself with nothing but flatterers devoid of any talent. But my fears have proven entirely unfounded. Rarely, if ever, has the world seen a king of such natural authority, or a Court of such magnificence!

We are now, as I am writing these lines, living in the 18th year of His Majesty's reign. He's thirty years of age, a strong, healthy man in the prime of his life. No king could be more impressive to behold, nor more worthy of praise and obedience: a paragon of majesty, wise, balanced, exuding confidence, benevolence, strength, and magnanimity! With advancing age, as he has become more self-assured and at ease about himself and his divine task in this world, his manner has become ever more refined, affable, and imposing alike.

The soldiers idolize him. They admire his courage and strength, and will fondly tell each other the well-known stories of his heroic deeds – like when, only eighteen years old, on foot and single-handedly, he killed an attacking tigress with just one blow of his sword; or when, one year later, during a hunting trip, he took on a gang of armed robbers, leading the charge, driving his elephant Dilshankar straight through the wall of the house where they had taken cover. He took no less than seven arrows in his shield, but he didn't care! Soldiers know bravery when they see it; they know their emperor would never ask them anything he would not dare to do himself! As he walks among their ranks, a bit bow-legged like most of them, from so many long hours on horseback, he truly is one of them. He touches their hearts when he inquires about their wellbeing and that of their families, addressing them, one by one, in their native Persian, Turki or Hindi.

And not only the soldiers adore him. He has a truly extraordinary ability to adapt himself to his audience. While always maintaining his dignity, he is, as it has so aptly been phrased in the chronicles, great with the great, and lowly with the lowly. Especially with the small and common people, his manner is particularly endearing: if ever there was a monarch deserving of the title *Gharib-Parwari*[121], it is indeed our beloved Emperor! Always will he show them kindness and indulgence, making time to hear their petty requests. He will smilingly accept the small gifts they offer him, raising them above his head, and holding them to his bosom with conspicuous gratitude – in stark contrast to the casual disdain with which he receives even the most lavish gifts, when he esteems the giver's pride exceeds his merit.

His conversation, in general, is reassuringly pleasant, polite and kindly; yet, he radiates awesome power and majesty, and his innermost thoughts will usually remain hidden, behind a faint, inscrutable smile. The way he moves, his demeanour; the power of his dreamy eyes, when they suddenly fix their gaze and peer right into your soul... As the chronicler phrased it so aptly, everything about him is in such perfect accord with royal dignity, that anybody would instantly recognize him as a great king.

At times, he does have a quick, not to say violent temper. Occasional outbursts of wrath can put him beside himself, as when he had his rebellious foster brother Adham Khan summarily executed. Such occasions, however, have become quite rare. As a rule, he will be forgiving and understanding, and he possesses such complete mastery of his emotions that he will seldom be seen otherwise than perfectly at ease.

In the administration of justice, he sincerely aspires to be fair to everyone, in accordance with what he believes is the true will of Allah. Unlike his father, who could ordain the harshest punishment for even

[121] Gharīb-Parwarī: Cherisher of the Poor; Persian expression, commonly used when addressing superiors.

the most trivial of offences, he strives to be magnanimous as well as equitable, and not to let his personal feelings interfere with his judgement.

It is true: there have been a few occurrences where, in anger and indignation, he has pronounced a harsh and brutal sentence, which he later came to regret. One time for instance, he found a guard asleep at his post, and in his anger, had him thrown off the ramparts. On another occasion, one of his senior palace servants had his feet cut off, for robbing the shoes of a poor man. In both instances, it can of course not be denied that the convicts had been guilty of grave offence. Indeed, is it not the essence of a sentry's duty to remain wakeful and protect those entrusted to his care? And what could be more hideous and despicable, than a well-paid courtier who misuses his position to rob a poor person of the last of his meagre possessions? Still, His Majesty felt much remorse at the severity of his verdict, and he decided to protect himself as well as his subjects from any such rash decisions in the future. He ordained that henceforth, whenever he sentences an offender to death or to the mutilation of a limb, he must be reminded three times before the sentence is carried out. Is this not the clearest evidence of exceptional wisdom and greatness of soul? How many other examples are there, of kings so desirous of justice that they have willingly restricted their own power? Thanks and eternal praise be to Allah, that He has blessed us with a King of such noble disposition!

But let me return to the events after Mun'im Khan's reinstatement. As it should be, life at Court was now revolving entirely around the Emperor. After what happened to Adham Khan, no one was reckless or foolish enough to push himself to the fore; not a single decision would be made without His Majesty's personal involvement and consent.

Not that he suddenly behaved like a tyrant: true power seldom needs to resort to brutality! On the contrary: I have the impression, that the mightier he has become, the more willing he is to listen to good advice. He is eager to attract to his service the very best people available. Over the years, many new faces have, thus, made their appearance at Court. It has become the most exquisite place in the whole world, home to a most impressive score of outstanding soldiers, administrators, scholars, poets, painters, architects, artisans and musicians.

Verily, is this not the hallmark of true greatness in a king: that he has the prudence to seek good advice, and the wisdom to put it to use?

Easy as this may sound, it is not – not at all! The self-absorbed and conceited will always be tempted to believe they can manage without any help, whereas the lazy and the weak will allow their courtiers to rule in their stead. Alas, both mistakes have been the ruin of many an empire; but our Emperor has the wisdom to avoid them both! His main courtiers are of such extraordinary ability that people have come to call them The Gems of Emperor Akbar's Court.

Mention should first be made of Raja Todar Mal, erstwhile an unknown, humble Hindu scribe from Laharpur, and now the most trusted and powerful of His Majesty's ministers. Despite the modesty of his manner, his presence is daunting. Conversations tend to fall silent wherever his tall, sinewy figure appears; the piercing black eyes in his stern, bony face constantly seem to be probing people's motives and honesty.

The story of Todar Mal's rise to power is as simple as it is remarkable. Immediately after Adham Khan's richly deserved execution, His Majesty, gravely concerned about the declining stream of revenues to the Treasury, decided to attract an expert. His eye fell on old Khwaja Phul Malik, the eunuch who had been working for several years at the court of Sher Khan Sur's son Islam Shah, earning himself the lofty title of I'timad Khan[122], on account of his well-deserved reputation as an outstanding and incorruptible administrator.

As usual, His Majesty's choice proved to be excellent. The old eunuch and his helpers worked day and night to put the Court's affairs in order: counting all the stocks, verifying every revenue account, sending inspectors to the farthest corners of His Majesty's dominions. Their efforts soon met with remarkable success: after only a few months, the stream of revenues to the treasure more than doubled! And as it was so aptly phrased in the Court chronicles, a stone fell on the glass of great men's reputations: quite a few local officials were found guilty of embezzlement. All of them were summarily dismissed and heavily fined; a few of them, guilty of the most flagrant outrages, had their

[122] I'timād: (Person in whom one has placed one's) reliance, dependence, confidence. Hence: support(er), help(er).

arms duly shortened, as a chronicler put it so eloquently – a warning that did not miss its effect on their successors!

Like all wise and capable men, old I'timad Khan had the good foresight to avail himself of the assistance of skilled helpers, regardless of their background. Among them was Todar Mal, a taciturn Hindu scribe who, on account of his outstanding competence and sense of duty, soon managed to attract His Majesty's attention. Exceptionally quick-witted, as will so often be observed in members of the Hindu race, he showed himself so amazingly proficient in the art of calculation, and gifted with such limitless capacity for hard work that very soon, the most difficult assignments were entrusted to him. After a few years, to the surprise and envy of many, he was appointed as I'timad Khan's replacement when the latter retired from office. The palace was rife with gossip: a low-born Hindu, appointed to one of the highest positions! Unbelievable as it sounded, it was but the first example of many.

Another extremely influential Hindu at Court and a remarkable, rather arrogant character, is a Brahmin from Kalpi originally called Mahesh Das. They say he came from an extremely poor family with few credentials, but thanks to his obvious literary talent, he managed to be admitted into the imperial service as a poet. Truth be told, the man is extremely bright, as good with words as Todar Mal is with numbers. But his mind is more playful: he is gifted with a special, rather irreverent wittiness, which His Majesty appears to appreciate very much. So much so, that this unknown, destitute Hindu vagrant can now call himself a raja – Raja Birbal, holder of the lucrative jagir of Nagarkot!

Two of His Majesty's most senior and powerful army commanders are Hindus as well – I am of course referring to Raja Bhagwan Das and Raja Kuwar Man Singh, the two Rajput leaders who accompanied the Princess of Amber after her marriage to His Majesty. Bhagwan Das is Raja Bihari Mal's son, and therefore, His Majesty's brother-in-law; and Man Singh, is Bhagwan Das' highly talented nephew, adopted son and heir. Both commanders are highly skilled warriors, strong, proud, and like most Rajputs, utterly fearless. In view of their obvious talent and valour, His Majesty has not only allowed them to lead their own Rajput soldiers, but has soon put them in command of large contingents of Muslim troops as well. This, in turn, alas and of course, has not failed to arouse the envy of many others.

Yes, His Majesty's tolerance and sympathy for the Hindus was – and still is – provoking many bitter comments, which undoubtedly he must have heard through his informers. Yet, he does not seem to care. On the contrary: he's determined to make his Court the true reflection of his Empire and its inhabitants, regardless of their religion, and will do whatever is in his power and seize every opportunity to further mutual understanding and appreciation between Hindustan's various traditions and religions.

Sometimes, I have the impression he does not merely want to promote peace among his subjects, but that he actually wants to unite them, to blend them together into a whole new people. Even his outward appearance and attire seem to symbolize this. Unlike his father and most Muslim noblemen, he does not wear a full beard; instead, he is clean-shaven, except for a moustache, in the fashion of his Turkish ancestors. In contrast, his hair is not close-cropped, as the Muslim custom dictates, but he has allowed it to grow long, like the Rajputs do, and has it tucked inside a tightly rolled turban, neither Muslim nor Hindu, but a kind of combination. That turban, by the way, is becoming quite fashionable nowadays.

Patronage of the arts is another case in point. In every kind of art or craft, he favors, promotes and rewards the blending of Muslim and Hindu styles – *sulh-i-kul* in stone and paint, as he likes to call it.

The buildings he commissions are of a novel, quite pleasant style, aptly called 'Hindustani', combining the shapes and ornaments of both traditions: Persian-style arches, domes and lattice work, with beams, pivots, niches, pillars, terraces and *chhatris*[123], as in Hindu palaces and temples.

Likewise, in music and painting, Muslim and Hindu traditions are happily joined together. The painters, musicians and artisans at Court come from literally everywhere and every background: Hindustanis, Bengalis, Gujaratis, Kashmiris, Persians, and Turanis[124]; Hindus, Jains, Parsis, Sunnis, Shi'as, and Sufis; all united in the Emperor's service.

---

[123] Umbrella shaped cupolas, usually resting on four pillars, used as ornaments on walls, terraces, minarets, etc.

[124] Turān: Central Asia, north of the Hindu Kush; more specifically, the territory called Transoxania, i.e. the land between the Syr and Amu Darya Rivers.

He requires them to live and work together, and encourages them to influence each other. 'The language of God is beauty,' he says.

This remarkably tolerant attitude – where does it come from? With all due modesty, I think I can state that our many conversations have greatly influenced him. Strange as it may sound: I, Mir Abdul-Latif, a trembling, feeble old man on the verge of death, I find myself among His Majesty's most intimate confidants! Many an ambitious courtier must have wondered why such honor should befall me, of all people: I am a man of the pen, not the sword; I know or care precious little about commerce, the administration of estates and dominions, and other such worldly matters. I am a man of books, a humble seeker of wisdom. Yet, it is not science or philosophy that brings him to my study: it's his remarkable interest in God and religion.

For a person of such young age in his lofty position, his interest in these matters is truly exceptional. Every day, he spends several hours in solitary prayer and meditation, his mind solely preoccupied with the adoration of the Almighty. Rarely has there been a king so eager to rule in complete obedience to the divine will.

Already around the age of fourteen or fifteen, he took interest, I am proud to say, in the humble insights I had to offer. I have indeed given these matters much thought and have come to the conclusion, that a king's primary duty towards Allah, and at the same time the greatest gift to his people, is to guarantee *sulh-i-kul,* security and peace for all, regardless of their religion. It is a principle that our young Emperor soon made this own, with commendable zeal and enthusiasm. With surprising, not to say disquieting speed, he developed in these matters a policy of his own, which, to my knowledge, makes him unique among Muslim rulers of any era.

Take his betrothal to the princess of Amber, for example. One could argue that down-to-earth political motives were behind this union; and of course, his decision to marry the noble Maryam uz-Zamani was inspired by his desire to secure the loyalty of the powerful Kachwaha Rajputs of Amber, without which there would have been little hope for him to subdue the rest of Rajputana and neighbouring Gujarat. And in itself, his marriage to a Hindu princess was not really a novelty: several other Muslim rulers before him had accepted in marriage the daughters of Hindu rajas. In all those cases, however, the new spouse, and usually all her relatives, immediately converted to Islam. Not the princess of Amber, however! Not only was she put under no pressure whatsoever to convert: the Emperor even had a Hindu shrine built especially for her inside the palace, so she would be able to worship according to her own religion! Similarly, His Majesty is extending to his new in-laws – Raja Bihari Mal, Bhagwan Das, Man Singh, and all the others – exactly the same honors, favors and distinction as he would convey to Muslim relatives by marriage, even though they quite openly remain devout Hindus.

Hindu noblemen, openly performing their rites inside a Muslim ruler's palace; a Muslim Sultan, treating Hindus like intimate friends and next of kin... It is unheard-of, and in the eyes of many, absolutely outrageous. I must confess: even among the moderate-minded, including myself, it is regarded with concern. Is he taking this too far? Why is he making things so hard on himself? Why all this effort to achieve an impossible friendship, when mere peace is sufficient? I am sure he realizes this, but he obviously does not care. He has a task to fulfil, a calling, a destiny: he's determined to create, slowly but surely, an entirely new Hindustan, in which the difference between Muslims and non-Muslims will be blotted out.

Already the days of Adham Khan, during Malwa campaign, he issued an explicit ban against enslaving the inhabitants of conquered territories, even of prisoners of war. 'We do not wish to lay waste to the lands that are added to our dominions,' the firman stated, 'we do not merely want to conquer them, we wish to rule over them in justice and in accordance with the will of Allah, so that they may prosper. From now on, it is therefore forbidden to deprive the dwellers of those lands of their freedom.'

Undoubtedly, this was a prudent and wise measure, intended to temper the army commanders' lust for plunder, and to stop them from depriving the land of its main source of wealth: the people who labour its soil.

While the regulation was a complete surprise to most courtiers, and consequently, much talked about, there seemed to be no disagreement about it. About one year later, however, the Emperor suddenly decided to abolish the pilgrim's tax, which since time immemorial had been levied on the visitors of Hindu shrines. He had witnessed the tax being collected during one of his hunting trips; and in the spur of the moment, without paying any heed to the objections of his courtiers, he decreed that it was abolished.

'It is contrary to the will of Allah to impose taxes on people whose sole intention is to worship Him,' he stated.

This time, there was much less understanding among the courtiers. What in Allah's name could have possessed the Emperor to show such indulgence towards idol-worshipping infidels? How did he think he would compensate the loss of revenue? Yes, it might help him to strengthen his alliance with the Rajputs; but surely, he must realize: this kind of behaviour is not at all helpful in showing the Hindus the error of their ways!

Incomprehension turned into profound indignation when in the year 971 – it must have been around the month of Rajab[125] – he took the ultimate step: abolishing the *jizya*.

As every educated person will know, the Holy Qur'an stipulates that *Ahl al-Kitab*, or People of the Book – that is to say, people who worship God, but do not recognize the Holy Prophet Muhammad to be His Messenger – are entitled to protection and will remain free to worship according to their own ways, provided they pay the tax called *jizya*. In the days of the Prophet, Peace be upon Him, this term *Ahl al-Kitab* referred to the Jews and to the adherents of the Nazariyah sect, who call themselves Christians.

After the conquest of Hindustan by the armies of Islam, however, it was the consensus among the ulama, that the Hindus, provided they submit to their Muslim rulers, can be considered as *Ahl al-Kitab* as well, since their scriptures, full of error though they may be, profess that ultimately – above and beyond the countless multitude of gods they worship in their temples – there is only one God. Similarly, also the Parsis can be considered as People of the Book, rather than mere pagans or disbelievers.

This is in perfect accordance with the Holy Qur'an, which clearly states that there are several divine revelations that haven't been mentioned explicitly it Its text. In Surah 10:47, for instance, it is stated that 'Every nation has its Messenger,' whereas Surah 10:78 proclaims:

[125] Early 1564.

'We sent Messengers before you; of some, we have related to you, and some we have not related to you.'

The Hindus were, thus, to be considered as People of the Book, and the *jizya* had been levied on them right from the advent of Islam into their lands.

And now, this tax was simply abolished, as if it were the most trivial of matters! Was it any wonder that it raised so much controversy and resentment among the Muslims?

Although a strong proponent of *sulh-i-kul*, I must confess that I feared that this time, His Majesty had driven things too far: rather than promoting peace among his subjects, was he not creating a dangerous rift between himself and all the ulama? Several times I tried to discuss the matter, but he refused to listen, stating, kindly but firmly, that his mind was made up.

But the debate could not be avoided. Only a few days after the firman had been issued, Abdullah of Sultanpur, better known under the lofty title of Makhdum ul Mulk[126], the highest-ranking of all the *ulama*, requested a private audience. To refuse to see him would have been quite unthinkable, and so, an audience was granted in the *Diwan-i-khas*, with no one present but His Majesty, Makhdum ul Mulk, and myself.

For those not familiar with His Majesty's Court, I should maybe explain that Makhdum ul Mulk, rightly or wrongly, has earned himself the reputation of being the most learned legal specialist in the Empire.

In the days of Sher Khan Sur, he had been appointed as his legal advisor, with the titles of Makhdum ul Mulk and Shaykh ul-Islam, position and titles he kept after Emperor Humayun's return to power.

Humayun held him in high esteem, and entrusted him with the instruction of his son in Islamic law. Prince Akbar, deeply devout and God-fearing himself, would even hand him his slippers, as a sign of respect.

It would be wrong for me to deny or belittle Makhdum ul Mulk's vast legal knowledge. I must confess, however, that I do not like him. He is, may Allah forgive me for saying so, a bigoted, greedy man, who frequently misused his position, persecuting people he had a personal grudge against, under the pretext of defending orthodoxy,

---

[126] Guide of the Kingdom.

and accumulating fabulous personal wealth in exchange for sometimes dubious legal opinions.

The audience started in a tense atmosphere. Waiting for the guards to escort Makhdum ul Mulk into the Diwan-i-khas, the Emperor seemed nervous, but did his best not to show it. He sipped absentmindedly from his lime sherbet, and stared at the ceiling. We waited in silence.

When Makhdum ul Mulk came in, the Emperor put his beaker down and courteously rose to greet him – a great honor. However, he did not step down from the low platform on which he had been seated: instead, he bowed down to give his guest a distant embrace, barely touching his shoulders.

'Honorable and learned Shaykh ul-Islam! It is, as always, a pleasure to see you! I trust you and your family are doing well?' the Emperor smiled. His gaze seemed to fix itself on his well-fed paunch.

'Subhan Allah[127], Your Majesty, we are all in good health,' replied Makhdum ul Mulk, his fingers nervously playing with the *tasbih*[128] he usually carries with him.

'And what brings you here, Shaykh ul-Islam?' inquired the Emperor, wasting no further time on formalities. 'Judging by the worried look on your face, it must be bad news! Is there a legal dispute that requires my urgent attention?'

Makhdum ul Mulk took a deep breath to summon up his courage.

'May Your Majesty forgive my impertinence, but I think it is my duty to convey the grave concern Your Majesty's recent firman has caused.'

'So? And what firman might that be?' The Emperor's face remained inscrutable, his voice perfectly calm.

'The abolishment of the *jizya*, Your Majesty. With all due respect, I must urge Your Majesty to reconsider, and to repeal this measure.'

The Emperor's face remained expressionless, showing neither anger nor sympathy.

'I'm afraid you'll have to explain this, Shaykh ul-Islam. What is the motive behind your request?'

---

[127] God be praised.

[128] Persian name for the *Subhah*, i.e. the 100-bead Muslim rosary.

'We are very much afraid that Your Majesty's generosity is against Your Majesty's best interest!'

'And why is that? And who is "we"? Who says so? Is it your opinion, or someone else's?'

'Begging your pardon, Your Majesty, but everybody says so: the Amirs, the ulama... We are all extremely worried this measure will reduce the Treasury's revenues, and hence, weaken the Empire!

And what is even worse, it will weaken the position of Islam! Those Hindu idolaters need to know their place! If we start treating them the same way as the true believers, they will never learn to see the wickedness of their ways! We should not forget: their numbers are much higher than ours! There will be no limit to their arrogance!'

'Are you implying it's my religious obligation to impose the *jizya*?'

'Well, yes, Your Majesty... the Holy Qur'an says so explicitly:

'Make war upon such of those to whom the Scriptures have been given, as believe not in Allah or in the last day, and forbid not that which Allah and his Apostles have forbidden, and who profess not the profession of truth, until they pay *jizya* out of their hand, and they be humbled.'

The Emperor appeared unimpressed.

'I am aware of this surah, but thank you for reminding me, Makhdum ul Mulk. Answer my question, if you please: is it your legal opinion that I have an obligation, under Shari'ah law, to impose the *jizya*?'

Makhdum ul Mulk was starting to feel uneasy.

'Well, Your Majesty, ...'

'As far as I am aware, honorable Shaykh ul-Islam, the *jizya* is not really a religious tax, is it?'

'Begging Your Majesty's pardon, but I'm afraid I have to say it is: the *jizya* is to be imposed on non-Muslims, never on Muslims, and it is explicitly mentioned in the Holy Qur'an, as Your Majesty knows. Therefore, it is most certainly a religious tax...'

'I'm afraid I must insist, Shaykh ul-Islam. I do not think it is... Honorable Mir Abdul-Latif, what's your opinion?'

I understood what the Emperor was aiming at, and couldn't help admiring his cleverness.

'Yes, I see what Your Majesty means: the *jizya* is a religious tax, but indeed, it is not really a tax on religion: it is a compensation for the protection offered to non-Muslims, and for their being exempt from compulsory service in the armies of the Muslim rulers.'

Makhdum ul Mulk wanted to say something, but I didn't let him interrupt me.

'That is precisely why non-Muslims who pay the *jizya* are referred to as *Ahl al-Dhimmah*, 'people under protection', and that is precisely why whole categories of non-Muslims are actually exempt from *jizya*, including all the females, the males who have not attained majority, the elderly, the crippled, the blind, the slaves, the monks, and so on – am I right, Shaykh ul-Islam?'

'Yes, but...'

'It is a tax, to be levied on any able-bodied non-Muslim man, who is able to fight, but exempt from serving in the Muslim army and allowed to live under its protection. You will recall that well-known story about Khalifah 'Umar, may Allah be well pleased with him, who once saw a blind *dhimmi*[129] begging, and finding that the poor man had to pay the *jizya*, not only exempted him from it, but ordered a stipend to be paid to him, from the Khalifah's treasury, for the rest of his life ... And I do not need to remind you, honorable Shaykh ul-Islam: there are several examples in Muslim history, where non-Muslims assisted their Muslim king in his battles, and in exchange, were exempted from the *jizya*!'

Makhdum ul Mulk tried to hide his anger, and said nothing. The Emperor nodded approvingly. 'I think you are quite right, Mir Abdul-Latif. So, we all seem to agree, that if I require the Hindus to fight in my armies, they in turn can ask me to exempt them from *jizya*. Am I right?'

We nodded in agreement, both of us equally astonished to hear our Emperor engaging in a legal dispute with such depth of knowledge.

A long silence followed, the Emperor looking pensively into his beaker of sherbet. He took a long sip, put the goblet down, rose to his feet, came down from the platform, and put his hands on Makhdum ul Mulk's shoulders.

'This is why I am in such dire need of learned and wise men like yourself, to help and support me, Shaykh ul-Islam! Your wisdom and learning are respected throughout this Empire and beyond! When you speak, everybody listens! You know the subtleties of the law, you know

---

129 Protected person (non-Muslim).

error when you see it – I need you to help me explain all this to our men! The Amirs are not learned like yourself, Shaykh ul-Islam – they're easily misled in matters of law, *falsafah*[130] and religion. Learned men like you must help them see the truth, and the wisdom behind their Emperor's policies!'

He kept looking Makhdum ul Mulk straight into the eye, his hands still on his shoulders. Finally, he let go of him, and went back to sit on the platform.

'Explain to them, Shaykh ul-Islam,' the Emperor continued, the expression on his face again composed and impassible, 'that I've exempted the Hindus from the *jizya*, because I do not want to exempt them from serving in my armies! Explain to them, how important it is for the Empire, to secure the loyalty of the Hindus, the powerful rulers of Amber in particular!'

'Surely,' the emperor continued, 'everybody knows how tough the Rajputs are: not at all peaceful and docile like most other Hindus, but a strong and proud warrior race, never conquered before by any Muslim invader!

Just suppose – Allah forbid! – that all of Rajastan, that is to say, Amber in the east, Jaisalmer in the west and Mewar in the south, would unite against us: it could take us maybe ten years or more to defeat them, and even if we were victorious, it would deplete our forces! And what would we have gained? We would have nothing more than what we currently have, and in addition, we would have become vulnerable to an invasion from other enemies, the rulers of Bengal for example, or the sultanates of the Deccan. If, however, we convince the Rajputs to fight on our side, no power on earth will be able to stop us! We can turn Hindustan into the mightiest and wealthiest Empire the world has ever seen!'

The Emperor again paused for an uncomfortably long time, as if to allow his words to sink in.

'But if we do want the Hindus to fight for us,' he continued, 'they must see us as their allies, and even better, as their brothers. They must see me as their legitimate Emperor – not as their conqueror, not as a foreign ruler to whom they reluctantly pay tribute. Yes, the noble

130 Philosophy.

princess of Amber is now married to me, and that is an important first step, but only the first step! It's essential that I make them feel part of the Empire, not just at peace with it! They must feel at home in my dominions, they must feel as safe in Agra, as in Amber!'

'I know, Shaykh ul-Islam, their way of worshipping is abhorrent to many devout Muslims. But is it not for Allah to judge them? Who else but He is the Lord of the Day of Judgement? Does not the Holy Qur'an itself speak of many religions? Is it not written:

'To every one of you, we have appointed a right way and an open road. If Allah had willed, He would have made you one nation; but that He may try you in what has come to you. So be you forward in good works; unto Allah shall you return, all together; and He will tell you of that whereon you were at variance'[131]? Besides, I am profoundly convinced that, Allah willing, the Hindus will find the way toward Islam much easier, if we are their friends. They are a God-fearing people, and open to other ways of worshipping than their own. I am convinced many of them will be attracted by the austere beauty of Islam. Help me explain this to the people, Shaykh ul-Islam!' The Emperor intently scrutinized his guest's face, trying to ascertain the effect of his words.

'I will, Your Majesty!' Makhdum ul Mulk hastened to declare.

The Emperor nodded in appreciation, and again remained silent for a few moments. Gradually, an expression of sadness came over his face, and he resumed, in a soft, but distinctly ominous tone of voice:

'It is never pleasant for a king to hear that his policies are the subject of discussion and criticism, Makhdum ul Mulk. I am grateful to you for your honesty, but people should realize, it has hurt my feelings, and caused me great pain, to hear they've been questioning my devotion to Allah. You may reassure them that, I am willing to consider this as the empty-headed babble of courtiers with too much time on their hands, the idle gossip that will always go around wherever human beings are gathered together... But let them take care, not to give me any cause to question their loyalty!

'Lest they forget, remind them of their oath! Remind them, that Allah Himself has put me on the Throne! Make sure they understand: disobedience against the Emperor is rebellion against the will of Allah!'

---

[131] Qur'ān, 5:51

'Can I count on you, Shaykh ul-Islam?' The Emperor's voice was barely audible, but somehow, ominously threatening.

Makhdum ul Mulk nodded hastily. Beads of sweat covered his forehead.

'Of course, Your Majesty! Your Majesty can count on me!'

'Thank you in advance for your help, Shaykh ul-Islam,' the Emperor nodded.

As in an afterthought, he added:

'And by the way, Shaykh ul-Islam, I am deeply touched by your concern for the imperial coffers. Let me put your mind at ease: there are other ways to fill the Treasury than extorting a meagre *jizya* from a score of poor peasants; besides, half of it probably gets embezzled before it has reached the Treasury! No, if I want to increase the Empire's wealth, I probably need to add a few new dominions to it; I need to convince neighbouring kingdoms to join me, or at least, pay tribute to me – not to extort more money from the common people! Besides, as the excellent work of I'timad Khan and Todar Mal shows, many dignitaries of the Empire have been rewarding themselves, more than handsomely I would say, with monies that actually may be due to the Treasury. It seems to me that if revenue is lacking, I should perhaps look into that matter first...'

He looked his guest straight into the eye for a few moments, then allowed his gaze to wander off.

'You have our permission to retire, Shaykh ul-Islam. Thank you again for your support.'

Makhdum ul Mulk was now soaked with sweat. He mumbled something about being grateful, and made haste to get out of the Diwan-i-khas, stepping backward, stooping as low as his fat belly would allow him.

For a while, the Emperor kept staring at the door, his face turning more and more angry, until he lost his composure, throwing his goblet on the floor, suddenly foaming with rage, and looking at me in great anger, as if I were responsible for Makhdum ul Mulk's behaviour.

'Who does this pompous, insolent bastard think he is, anyway? What is keeping me from having him hanged? Can you tell me that?'

'Your Majesty knows that this is not possible! I must urge Your Majesty to remain calm!'

'And why would that not be possible? Am I not the Emperor?'

'Your Majesty knows as well as I do: a Muslim king is required to rule in accordance with the law of Islam. A conflict with the ulama would undermine Your Majesty's authority: enemies of the Empire would find in it an ideal excuse to legitimize rebellion!'

My words were clearly not to the Emperor's liking, but thankfully, he realized I was right.

'Besides, I fully understand Your Majesty's displeasure, but I have to say: Your Majesty has handled this incident impeccably! The great Harun ar-Rashid couldn't have done it any better! And I admire Your Majesty's profound knowledge and insight in matters of law and government!'

In spite of himself, the Emperor smiled.

'I had a few good teachers, my old friend ... Besides, it's my duty to think about these things!'

He paused.

'We did set him straight, didn't we?'

'You did, Your Majesty, indeed you did!'

'Well, let's hope that will be the end of this discussion!'

'Let's hope so indeed, Your Majesty,' I said, smiling sheepishly, and realized how feeble it sounded. But I didn't know what else to say – for the very simple reason that in my heart, I knew the problems weren't over ...

The Emperor clearly sensed my embarrassment.

'It's getting late, and you must be tired, Mir Abdul-Latif! Thank you again for your much appreciated help and guidance! I wish you a restful night. *Khuda Hafiz*, my old friend!'

'*Khuda Hafiz*, Your Majesty! May Allah be Your Majesty's guide, guardian and protector!'

I returned to my quarters, took a sleeping potion, and went straight to bed. Despite my ardent prayers, my night was distressful, and sleepless.

PART TWO

هندوستان

Hindustan

Alas, Mir Abdul-Latif's anxious foreboding proved to be quite justified, my son. As I reread his comments, it is as if I see myself in that distant mirror, ingenuous, naïve amidst evident, looming danger. How could I be so blind? It was as clear as day: sooner or later, my tolerant attitude was bound to lead to dissidence and conflict. I guess I knew it all along, but refused to see it. Whatever the consequences, I would have it my way.

There were, as Mir Abdul-Latif observed, practical as well as religious considerations behind my policies. I genuinely desired to know the Divine will and to lead my life in submission to it; and at the same time, I was profoundly convinced that *sulh-i-kul* was the best – if not the only – way to guarantee the prosperity and stability of my dominions.

I already pointed out to you that with that policy of tolerance, I was following in the footsteps of my august father and grandfather, both devout but broad-minded Muslim rulers, who had little interest in or tolerance for religious strife. In fact, as far as the Sunni-Shi'a divide is concerned, my father Humayun, although a Sunni himself, had every reason to be favorably disposed towards the Shi'a. As you know, his favorite spouse, my mother and your grandmother, is a Shi'a, like most Persians; his iron right arm, my faithful *ataliq* Bairam Khan was a devout Shi'a as well; and last but not least: had it not been for the Shi'a troops which the Shah of Persia had so graciously put at my father's disposal, he could never have regained his throne.

Consequently, whenever confronted with strife between his Sunni and Shi'a followers, my father would say: 'We all worship the one true God, and we all recognize the Holy Prophet Muhammad as His messenger; let each man worship Allah according to his own tradition and to the best of his abilities, and leave the judgement of his brethren to the Almighty!'

My father and grandfather consciously strove to live in peace with the Hindus, too, leaving them free to live according to their own traditions, without trying to forcibly convert them to Islam. They understood the cause of Islam is much better served through peaceful coexistence, than through the wanton destruction of temples and shrines.

Thus, as I said: with *sulh-i-kul*, I was following the example of my ancestors. But as Mir Abdul-Latif astutely observed: I wanted much more than that. My dream was–and still is–to bridge the religious divide, to create an entirely new Hindustan, a truly united land that rises above the differences between its inhabitants. The more I thought about it, the more convinced I became: it was my destiny and my duty to unite Muslims and non-Muslims, to forge them into one nation! How exactly I would go about it, was not yet fully clear to me, but I had every hope that dialogue and reason would bind together what tradition and ignorance had separated.

I know, my son: it was hopelessly naïve, and it nearly cost me my throne. But make no mistake: no ruler of Hindustan can afford to ignore this issue! Unless his subjects live together as brothers, or at least as friends, they will continue to waste their strength in attempts to subdue or to break free from one another. But just imagine, my son, what it will be like, when Hindus and Muslims realize they are hairs on the same head, eyes in the same face! No power on earth will be able to resist their might!

Well then, my son: read; observe, how your father built his Empire; how he almost lost it, and how he won it back. Read and think, my son: reflect on what I did right, and where I went wrong. Above all, think about how you will preserve and expand what your father left you.

Twentieth Letter

فتح ، شورش ، ملک

Fath, Shuresh, Molk[132]

Consider this map of Hindustan, my son.

When my father died, there was not even a territory I could really call my own: I had no more than a claim on a long stretch of land along the Yamuna and Ganga, supported by a few garrisons; surrounded, however, by many powerful enemies.

Little more did I have, than a disputed title; my hold on the country was at best precarious. When Hemu's army chased Tardi Beg's troops out of Agra and Dilli, most people, including the majority of our own leaders, believed we would be driven back to Kabul, back to where my grandfather had started his conquest.

Seven years later, at the time of Adham Khan's death, that map looked very different indeed. The Panjab was mine, all the way down to the city of Multan and the territory between the Sindh[133] and the Sutlej Rivers. I firmly held the fertile basin of the Yamuna and the Ganga, from high up in the Himalayas, all the way east to Allahabad. Towards the south, my borders were secure, for I held Gwalior and Malwa. Moreover, my alliance with your mother's family had assured me of the loyal support of the strongest and bravest of the Rajput kings. Thanks in part to that alliance, I controlled a vitally important

[132] Conquest, Rebellion, Kingship.

[133] Indus.

part of Rajputana, from the left bank of the Chambal River, up to and including the sacred city of Ajmir.

In seven years' time, I had become the most powerful ruler in Hindustan. Kabul also belonged to me, though I must admit that in reality, it was ruled in practical independence by my younger half-brother Muhammad Hakim and his conniving but competent mother.

Qandahar, unfortunately, had been re-occupied by the Persians, around the time we took Mankot from Sikandar Sur. Not much we could do about it, as we had more than our hands full with our many rivals in Hindustan; but I swore that in time, Qandahar would be mine again.

All in all, I could be quite satisfied with what I had achieved: Babur's vast and wealthy dominions were mine again, and with a minimum of vigilance, no one could ever hope to dethrone me. I could look forward to a life of leisure and luxury.

But that was neither my hope, nor my ambition. Would I have been a worthy son of Genghis and Temür if I had decided, at barely twenty years of age, to spend the rest of my life sitting in a palace, getting fat? No, my son: a king worthy of that name should always be intent on conquest when he has the chance.

Besides, just look at the map, my son: Hindustan is inherently vulnerable, as it lacks strong natural borders and is completely land-locked. In order to make it truly powerful, Hindustan needs full control of Kashmir to the north, to the west: Kabul and Qandahar (the two entrance gates into Persia), plus at least the easternmost mountain ranges of Baluchistan, the entire course of the Sindh, including the territories of both Multan and Thatta, and, last but not least: access to the ocean, via Gujarat in the west and Bengal in the east.

But he who wishes to conquer Gujarat, first needs to control the fortresses of Rajputana...

Those were my thoughts when, at age twenty, I found myself in charge of my grandfather's Empire. I wanted it to be powerful, prosperous and independent, but realized that I would sooner or later need to bring Rajputana to heel, and annex the neighbouring sultanates of Gujarat and Bengal. Once those two goals would be achieved, it would only be a matter of time before the sultanates of the Deccan, the Firanghi coastal establishments, and the south of the continent, would eventually become ours.

At the beginning of the ninth year of my reign, near the end of the month of Esfand[134], I made my first move, against the kingdom of Garha-Katanga or Gondwana[135].

That territory was governed by Rani Durgavati, a descendant of the Hindu dynasty of Mahoba, on behalf of her young son Bir Narayan. As she and her n had repeatedly refused to submit to my authority, I sent Asaf Khan with an army to subdue them. Against overwhelming numbers, many of Rani Durgavati's twenty thousand men deserted her before the first shot was fired. But despite the hopelessness of her situation, she refused to yield and made a gallant stand with the remainder of her forces, near the town of Narhi.

Gallantry and foolishness are sometimes hard to distinguish. Her army was no match for ours, but she kept on leading her men with remarkable bravery, seated on a mighty war elephant, until she was herself disabled by two arrow wounds. Choosing death rather than disgrace, she stabbed herself to the heart and died nobly on the battlefield. Two months later, Asaf Khan marched on to her capital Chauragarh, where, pointlessly courageous like his mother, Bir Narayan chose to offer battle, and was slain as well.

It is truly sad that two people of such outstanding nobility and valour should have died–I would have gladly appointed them as governors over vast and rich territories, made them powerful and wealthy, married them into my family... but they did not want to listen to reason. They failed to see the sign of the times: those who oppose me, have only one of three choices: submit, flee, or die.

Rich spoils of gold, pearls, jewels and over a thousand elephants fell into Asaf Khan's greedy hands; despite what had happened to Adham Khan, he couldn't resist the temptation, and kept a large part of the booty for himself. I knew about it through my informants, but chose to ignore the insult. I had, so I thought to myself, more urgent and important things to do, and didn't want to waste any time before attacking the formidable strongholds of Chittor and Ranthambhore, control of which was indispensable if I ever wanted to annex Gujarat.

---

[134] Mid February 1564.

[135] In the current State of Madhya Pradesh.

But to my surprise and dismay, things didn't work out as planned. For the better part of three years, I suddenly found myself fighting in every part of the Empire – against my own Uzbeg army leaders.

Looking back, I think I've finally understood what moved these former friends and allies to suddenly rise in arms against me.

First, it should be remembered that the Uzbegs who helped my father and me to recover the throne of Hindustan, were not looking for a place to settle down. They were adventurers, looking for a war to join, thirsting for excitement and easy spoils. Their alliance with us was temporary, and their loyalty to my family, lukewarm at best. In fact, their ancestors and fellow countrymen in Turan were and are our family's hereditary enemies: let's not forget that the Uzbegs drove my grandfather Babur from his ancestral lands! And history is a convenient source of inspiration for those looking for excuses...

Second, the Uzbegs – bigoted Sunnis all of them – had always resented the appointment of Persian Shi'as and Hindu infidels to positions of high authority. Religious fervour, even more than history, is quite convenient an excuse for the pursuit of selfish interests...

As long as I kept the Uzbegs near me, as long as we were fighting the same battles, it was easy to keep them under control; but sending them off to remote regions, far away from my Court, was a big mistake: distance breeds estrangement, and estrangement breeds rebellion! It was a mistake, and one that could have been avoided. If I had recalled them earlier, assigned them to other tasks, maybe none of this would have happened.

But it did happen. With the wisdom of hindsight, it is easy to see how an excellent officer like Abdullah Khan Uzbeg became a rebel. You will remember that back in the days of Adham Khan, I had sent him to recapture Malwa after that region had been lost. Sure enough, he led a brilliant campaign, and recaptured Malwa in no time. But once the victory is won, distance and greed do their poisonous work: the soldier becomes a governor, the governor sets up a sumptuous court, and suddenly, the Emperor seems far away.

How easy, to keep part of the revenues for oneself; and when that first embezzlement goes undiscovered, how tempting it is, to keep on stealing, more and more... How far away is the Emperor, when his messengers take several days to reach you; how easy it is, to keep them waiting for days, before sending them back, with polite but evasive, noncommittal replies...

But Abdullah Khan Uzbeg grossly underestimated both the resolve of his Emperor and the competence of the Emperor's Ministers.

As usual, Todar Mal was quick to draw my attention to the growing irregularities in the revenues coming from Malwa, and the evasiveness of its governor's letters. And as usual, I had been quick to react: on Yeksanbeh, the 21st of Tir of the Ninth Year[136], I left Agra at the head of a powerful expeditionary force, and swiftly headed south, to Malwa.

Speed breeds victory! The rebels were taken by complete surprise by our rapid advance, and we overtook their main force near Mandu before they had the time to organize their defense.

A rather disappointingly small number of them were killed; the rest fled in disarray into Gujarat, from where, after a short while, they were thrown out by the local king – to whom I had sent a letter, demanding their immediate expulsion. Their small remaining fighting force completely disintegrated, while Abdullah Khan Uzbeg himself seemingly vanished from the face of the earth. It later appeared that he had made his way to Jaunpur, where he placed himself in the service of the local Uzbeg officers, who, as I will now relate, had ventured onto the ruinous path of rebellion themselves. But God spared me the grief of having to punish my old comrade: he died of natural causes, before the Uzbeg rebellion was finally – and quite literally – crushed.

Having thus defeated Abdullah Khan Uzbeg, I headed back to Agra by the middle of the month of Mehr[137], looking forward to a period of repose and leisure.

I thoroughly enjoyed the taming of a large herd of magnificent wild elephants, which I had managed to capture along the march, and ordered the building of a beautiful hunting palace–aptly called Nagarchain, or Amanabad[138]–about two and one half kos south of Agra. The repairs on the Red Fort were making excellent progress as well.

It was, so I thought, an outstandingly auspicious time. Indeed, how

---

[136] Sunday, July 17, 1564 (Julian Calendar).

[137] Early October, 1564.

[138] Abode of Peace.

to describe my elation, when I learned that one of the slave girls in the zanana, a pretty Persian with whom, three months back, I had spent a few pleasant afternoons, was expected to give birth in a few months!

I was overjoyed: not one of my many consorts had ever borne me a child, and I was getting scared, that maybe God had decided I was to remain childless... And now, three months before the beginning of the tenth year of my reign[139], twin sons were born unto me!

I of course ordered grandiose festivities, and announced that the children would be called Hasan and Husain. By choosing the names of the sons of the Prophet's daughter Fatimah and her husband Ali, names that are respected throughout Islam and popular with the Shi'a even more than with the Sunni, I again made it clear to everyone that I did not wish to make any distinction among the various denominations.

Alas! Soon after the festivities, the court physicians came to warn me that the two children were not in good health. Their mother's constitution had clearly not been strong enough to bear two children at once; as a result of that, neither of them had received sufficient nourishment from their mother's womb; their weight was far below what was considered healthy for a newborn.

The best and strongest nurses in the Empire were brought to Court; every three hours, the children were given drops of strengthening elixirs, prepared by preeminent physicians, from the most exquisite ingredients; continuous prayer services were held; the best astrologers were called upon to make powerful charms and incantations–but it was to no avail. In less than one month, my two sons were dead–one had lived barely one day longer than his brother.

I still see their pitiful little bodies, smaller than the length of my forearm; their tiny faces, which had been bright red at birth, pale as candle wax; their innocent little eyes and mouths slightly opened, as in silent protest against their fate...

I tried to console myself. I told myself, it was a good sign that at last, sons had been born unto me; that I was still young; that I would, with God's help, father many more children; that what had happened was just the way this world is, that many children die at a tender age; that maybe God had wanted to spare me the grief of seeing two sons,

---

[139] Late 1564.

born on the same day, grow up to be each other's bitter rivals, and see my life's work ruined...

But no matter how hard I tried to convince myself: this was a terrible disaster, and a very bad omen. What I had thought to be an auspicious period, now suddenly was full of pain, darkness and menace.

Unfortunately, my misgivings proved to be correct: misfortunes, indeed, rarely come alone... Soon after the loss of my sons, I found myself confronted with a second and far more dangerous rebellion of the Uzbeg officers.

This time, the main instigator was Ali Quli Khan, the general who, at the battle of Panipat, had earned himself the title of Khan Zaman. Supporting him were his brother, Bahadur Khan; their uncle Ibrahim Khan, governor of Surhurpur; and Iskandar Khan, governor of Awadh.

Having grown suspicious about the Uzbegs after Abdullah Khan's earlier misconduct in Malwa, I had summoned Iskandar Khan Uzbeg to Agra – I wanted to probe their intentions and assure myself of their continued loyalty and support. My suspicions proved to be justified. Iskandar blatantly disobeyed my orders and fled to Jaunpur, taking Ibrahim Khan of Surhurpur with him. Under Khan Zaman's leadership, the three now broke out in open rebellion, defeated our local troops at Nimkhar, and besieged the fortress of Manikpur.

I immediately sent Mun'im Khan to block any further rebel advance to the west, and crossed the Yamuna myself at the head of a large army three months later, on Panjshanbeh the 13th of Mordad of the Tenth Year[140].

The situation was grave and I couldn't afford to take any risk. It gives me no pleasure to recall this, but after many sleepless nights, I saw no alternative but to order the private execution of my cousin Abu-l Qasim, the son of Kamran, my father's treacherous brother and bitter rival.

Three months before, the evening before he left Agra at the head of our vanguard, Mun'im Khan had asked whether he could see me in private.

Wasting no time on further introductions, he said: 'I regret that I must advise Your Majesty to urgently rid himself from his cousin Abu-l Qasim!'

---

[140] May 24, 1565.

'What makes you say that, Khan Khanan? Abu-l Qasim has done nothing to hurt me; as far as I am informed, he keeps himself occupied with hunting and reading and similar innocent pastimes!'

'Possibly... But failing to eliminate Abu-l Qasim, leaving him behind in the palace while Your Majesty is far away, is to provide the insurgents with an ideal opportunity!

Your Majesty shouldn't forget that Emperor Humayun and his brother Kamran were bitter rivals! Who knows, one day, Abu-l Qasim might be tempted to claim the throne for himself! Moreover, as long as he lives, he's a godsend to those who wish Your Majesty ill: he's just what they need to give their rebellion an appearance of respectability! In him, they have found an alternative king to whom they can pledge their allegiance. I must insist, Your Majesty: it is too much of a risk to let him live!'

He paused and added, timidly:

'I know Your Majesty is honest and righteous, it's difficult for him to do what he believes to be unjust. And indeed, for all we know, Abu-l Qasim is still innocent. Sometimes, however, innocent blood needs to flow, to prevent even greater bloodshed; sometimes, an injustice is the only way to serve the greater good! Sometimes, we cannot choose between good and evil; sometimes, alas, we have to choose the lesser evil... Abu-l Qasim, in Your Majesty's place, would do the same! Such is the burden of kingship, Your Majesty: it sometimes requires hard sacrifices.'

I glanced at his innocent eyes and thought to myself, how much I had been underestimating the old fox. Much as I disliked what he had been saying, I appreciated his frankness and loyalty. I nodded, thanked him for his wise and honest advice, and expressed the wish that Allah might be his protector during the forthcoming campaign.

The rest of the day and night, and all the following weeks, I could think of nothing else. Much as I hated it, I knew Mun'im Khan was right. I considered and re-considered the alternatives, looking for a way out. But no matter how I tried, I didn't find one. The Empire was in grave danger; could I allow myself to squander my forefathers' inheritance, for the sake of one innocent man?

Abu-l Qasim's execution, I am relieved to say, was swift and painless; he was dead before he realized what was happening. But no matter how much I tried to console myself that it had been the only way out, that he in my place would have done exactly the same, I could not help feeling deeply sad and guilty. There was no way I could argue or explain it away: Abu-l Qasim's death was a sin, a sin for which, on the Day of Judgement, I will need God's mercy and forgiveness.

Ever since Abu-l Qasim's death, I have often wondered: does power necessarily lead to sin? Is it possible to be a king and to live a life of absolute righteousness? To be honest, my son: I do not know. All I know is that it's extremely difficult, and that I, although I did try, have not succeeded. May God, Who is the ultimate justice and mercy and Who knows the weaknesses of His creatures, forgive me!

We were ready for the campaign. I headed east, joined up with Mun'im Khan at Kanauj, and immediately marched on to Lakhnau. Iskandar Khan hastily fled the city, whereupon Khan Zaman, alarmed at my rapid advance, abandoned the siege of Manikpur and fled eastward.

After a few further skirmishes of little importance, I cornered him near Allahabad, and prepared myself for battle.

Having seen the might of my army and clearly fearing, rightly so, that he was no match for me, Khan Zaman sent a messenger to Mun'im Khan, asking for clemency and offering submission.

His letter talked about unfortunate misunderstandings, recalling the unwavering loyalty with which he had served my revered father and me, he appealed to the unbreakable bonds of brotherhood that had united us on the battlefield, and similar words to that effect.

What was I to do? Could I forget the major role the valiant Uzbegs had played at Panipat? Was I going to waste so many good soldiers in a fratricidal struggle, when so many cities and fortresses still remained to be conquered?

I decided to forgive and forget, and extended a general amnesty to the Uzbegs, leaving it to Munim Khan to work out the terms and conditions. Among others, it was agreed that all Uzbeg forces would remain north of the Gogra River, until I had returned to Agra.

Being so far east, I took the opportunity of visiting the Hindu holy city of Benares or Varanasi, on the Ganga. I spent a few leisurely days there, fascinated by the sight of the colourful crowd of pilgrims, priests and Hindu Sadhus, many of them stark naked, smeared with cremation ashes, with no other possessions on this earth than a begging bowl and a small trident, symbolizing Lord Shiva I was captivated and horrified at the same time, at the sight of the funeral pyres on the ghats[141], and the omnipresent smell of scorching human flesh.

Alas, my rest was short-lived. No sooner had I reached Varanasi, than Khan Zaman violated the terms of the truce, again crossing the Gogra and menacing Ghazipur and Jaunpur.

I immediately turned back and attacked them on several fronts, easily routing them wherever I found them. It was clear, they had grossly underestimated both my prowess at using mobile field guns, and the impeccable discipline and fighting skills of the Rajputs.

Again, impressed at the speed and overwhelming force I was capable of, Khan Zaman re-opened negotiations for peace, slavishly promising submission and unwavering loyalty. It clearly was a mistake, but I again allowed myself to be persuaded. My troops were weary of the long and exhausting campaign and the many forced marches, and I longed for the tranquillity of Agra and Salima's companionship. Once more, I forgave the rebels and reinstated them in their positions. On the 25th of Esfand[142], I headed back to the capital.

Things appeared to go well at first: no more reports of any disturbances, and the stream of revenues from Jaunpur showed no irregularity.

Alas, it proved to be the quiet before the storm. Eight months later, I received the perplexing notice that my half-brother Muhammad Hakim had left Kabul and was crossing the Khyber Pass at the head of a large invasion army!

Almost simultaneously, I learned that in Jaunpur, the *khutba* was now being read in Muhammad Hakim's name: the Uzbegs had encouraged him to invade Hindustan! It was, so they said, every good Muslim's duty to fight the emperor: he had turned Shi'a, or maybe even Hindu...

Beside myself with rage, I immediately marched into the Panjab, to repel Muhammad Hakim's invasion. Before long, I had the incompetent weakling on the run: after a few minor skirmishes, all of them disastrous

---

[141] Staircase-shaped river banks.

[142] March 6, 1566.

for his forces, he meekly headed back across the Khyber Pass, without offering battle.

I would have pursued him, all the way to Kabul if necessary, and finished him off; but unfortunately, that was quite impossible, for I realized all too well I could not afford to leave Hindustan, as long as the treacherous Uzbegs had not been dealt with.

To make things worse: while still in the Panjab, I received an alarming message from Mun'im Khan, that back in Agra, the Mirzas had broken out in open rebellion as well.

As you will probably know, my son, the Mirzas are distant cousins of ours: they are descendants of Temür's second son 'Umar Shaykh Mirza, whereas we descend from Temür through his third son, Miran Shah. Their ancestors had joined my grandfather Babur's service, but that apparently didn't prevent them from harbouring their own ambitions.

The whole family had joined the uprising: Muhammad Sultan Mirza, Ibrahim Husain Mirza, Muhammad Husain Mirza, Mas'ud Husain Mirza, Aqil Husain Mirza, Ulugh Mirza, and Shah Mirza. They roamed plundering through the countryside, at one moment even threatening Dilli.

Alas, the sparks of rebellion had set off a devastating forest fire, threatening to engulf my entire Empire...

I immediately headed back to Agra. Upon my arrival, I was relieved to find that Mun'im Khan had done excellent work: he had attacked the rebels head on, captured Muhammad Sultan, and chased the others into Malwa.

This allowed me to focus my attention to the Uzbegs. On the 25th of Ordibehesht of the Twelfth Year[143], I left Agra at the head of my troops, and marched east.

Finding upon arrival that the enemy had crossed over to the south bank of the Ganga, intending to proceed west towards Kalpi, I, as a chronicler put it, displayed my customary zeal and contempt of personal danger: I swam my elephant right across the swollen Ganga. About fifteen hundred brave men crossed the river with me, while the main body, under Raja Bhagwan Das and Khwaja Jahan, proceeded further west.

---

[143] May 6, 1567.

For the last time, the Uzbegs had made the mistake of underestimating me. Nearly all of them had been spending the better part of the night carousing, getting dead-drunk, and they had posted far too few sentries. At dawn on the 28th of Khordad[144], despite the weakness of my forces, I carried out a surprise attack on their camp.

I had placed musketeers and ban rockets at three carefully chosen locations, and ordered them to fire no less than half of all their ammunition in the first attack. It went as I expected: the Uzbegs, bewildered by the devastating fire from all sides, and seeing the Imperial standards, assumed that the entire army had fallen upon them, and fled without offering battle. A few kos further west, as planned, they ran into the main body of our troops. There was nowhere to run; all they could do, was to surrender, or fight.

As I expected them to do, they attempted to break out of the encirclement, concentrating their entire fighting force on the point where they thought our formation was the weakest, away from the Imperial standards: the Rajput foot soldiers. It was their last and fatal mistake. The Rajputs' discipline was impeccable; they held their ground, and our well-aimed rocket and mortar fire caused deadly carnage in the enemy ranks. A final, beautifully executed charge of Iranis and Turkomans on the right flank and Rajput elephant drivers on the left finished them off, with very few losses on our side.

Khan Zaman had fallen in battle, while Bahadur Khan, who had been captured alive, had been beheaded immediately after the fight. I was a bit disappointed when my soldiers brought me the two severed heads – after all their lies and treachery, I would have gladly watched their skulls cracking under Dilshankar's front legs.

No, this time, I was no longer in any mood for clemency. A few of the surviving younger officers, who could still be of use to the army, had their lives spared; the rest were herded together and trampled by my war elephants – killed, as Abu-l Fazl aptly put it, under the feet of the elephants, or rather, under the weight of their sins and ingratitude. The great Uzbeg rebellion, the gravest menace I had to face since Panipat, had been – quite literally, indeed – crushed.

In triumph, I headed back to Agra, where I sent Shihab ud Din

---

[144] June 9, 1567.

Ahmad Khan to Malwa, to deal with the Mirzas. They fled in disarray into Gujarat, where, for some time at least, they would find refuge. There were no more rebels left to fight. At last, I was free to fulfil my destiny: to build a united, powerful, invincible Hindustan.

Twenty-first Letter

راجستان

Rajastan

I guess most people in my situation would have been more than glad to take a few months rest, after so many hundreds of kos of marching and fighting in the blazing sun.

Not I. I felt elated and restless, eager to make up for the lost time. So much to be done, so little accomplished... Never had I felt so alive, so proud of myself, and so impatient.

Panipat and the early battles had been other people's work. But this major campaign had been led by me alone, and I had proven – to myself even more than to others – to be a worthy son of Temür and Genghis Khan. I had decided when to march, when to strike camp, where to deploy which troops and weaponry, how to secure supply, and when and where to attack. I had known how to motivate the men, when hardship was making them battle-weary. And maybe most important of all: I had forged all those separate and rivalling groups into one united army; through my personal courage and prowess, I had forever earned the men's respect. For the first time, Hindus and Muslims truly had a common leader. I could hardly wait to move on and start the work in earnest.

I have already pointed out, that for Hindustan to be powerful and prosperous, it needs to be in possession of Gujarat, and that in order to achieve this, it must control at least the major roads and fortresses of Rajastan.

Through my marriage to your beloved mother, through my prowess in battle, and thanks to my fairness in matters of religion, I had earned myself the loyalty and friendship of the powerful rajas of Amber; they were my closest friends and allies; they had become the backbone of my army. It was high time the other Rajput leaders followed suit.

But it soon became clear that this would not be achievable without war.

The ranas of Mewar prided themselves as the greatest kings of Rajastan; they were said to have taken a solemn vow, never to 'sully their blood' by giving a princess of their family in marriage to a Muslim.

That in itself didn't bother me all that much – I had more than enough wives and could easily do without a Mewari bride. What I did want to secure, was loyalty – an unconditional recognition of my sovereignty. And here, their attitude had at best been half-hearted.

It is true that Rana Uday Singh did send his son Sakat to Court as a conciliatory gesture, but it is equally true that he refused to attend on me in person – he even refused to pay me a simple visit to show his friendship and respect! Even worse, there was clear evidence that he had helped the Mirzas in their uprising!

This was an attitude I could and would not tolerate. I wasted no further time on parleys and negotiations: the treachery of the Uzbegs had made me weary of talks and treaties with unreliable opponents. It was high time my neighbor learned that those who refuse to be my allies, are my enemies, and must suffer the consequences.

I stayed in Agra no longer than strictly necessary to prepare for this major new campaign. Allowing myself but little leisure, I did take a few hours to inspect the work of the court painters and sculptors, and meet with a few artists recently admitted to Court. Among them, a talented young poet, named Abu-l Faizi, son of one Shaykh Mubarak; little did I realize that I had just made the acquaintance of the elder brother of the man who, some years later, would become my most influential courtier: Abu-l Fazl.

The preparations made good progress, and barely two months[145] after the suppression of the Uzbeg rebellion, I marched south into Mewar, heading straight for its capital, the formidable fortress of Chittor.

[145] September 9, 1567.

Our advance was unopposed. Rana Uday Singh, a spineless weakling, the unworthy son of a worthy father, as chroniclers have described him, cowardly left his capital under the command of his army leader Jai Mal, and ran to hide himself, deep in the Aravalli hills.

On the tenth of Aban[146], we pitched our camp – three kos long! – in sight of the western cliffs of Chittor, and prepared ourselves for a long siege. Heavy mortars (needed to hammer breaches in the massive walls) were cast on the spot: it would have been too cumbersome and time-consuming to take them along with us.

It was not going to be easy. Even today, so many years after its demise, Chittor remains dauntingly impressive. It is really a heavily fortified, steep cliff, rising abruptly from the surrounding plain, about one tenth of a kos high. Its length from north to south is a daunting one and one third kos; at its broadest point, it is over a quarter kos wide; at its base, it is no less than three and a quarter kos in circumference!

Upon arrival, I ordered an immediate frontal assault from the north-east and north-west, to test their defenses – hoping that maybe, if we managed to surprise and overrun them at the point of attack, we could avoid the loss of time and effort of a protracted siege.

Unfortunately, the defenders were well prepared, and well led. Two attack waves were repulsed with heavy losses; I had no alternative but to withdraw my troops beyond the range of the enemy guns and to begin the encirclement.

It took us more than a month of hard work before we finally had Chittor completely sealed off. As of then, no one could approach, enter or leave it without our permission. The noose was around their neck; now came the long struggle to pull it tight.

Direct assaults having proven costly as well as pointless, we began the cumbersome travail of digging *sabats*, which, as you know, are large ditches, protected by heavy logs of wood covered with rawhide. The works were executed under the competent direction of Raja Todar Mal and Qasim Khan, the master builder of the Agra fort.

I ordered the sabats to be built wide enough for horses to advance through them in rows of ten, and deep enough to be ridden through by a man, spear in hand, seated on the back of the largest elephant bull.

---

[146] October 23, 1567.

While this was quite time-consuming, it would make the final assault much easier and less costly.

Again it was painfully apparent that our enemies were determined, well-led, and amply stocked with gunpowder and projectiles. As soon as the sabats came within reach of their fire, they did whatever they could to hinder them, pounding them with nearly incessant musket and cannon fire. Despite the movable ramparts we used to protect our workers, heavy casualties were inflicted upon their ranks – sometimes as many as one hundred in a single day!

In spite of stiff resistance, we made progress, albeit annoyingly slowly. Every day, the sabats wormed themselves a bit closer towards the foot of the hill, like fat, giant snakes crawling towards their victims, waiting for an opportunity to strike.

As we edged closer to the foot of the cliff, we managed to inflict more and more losses on the defenders. Through loopholes in the *sabat* roof and the movable bulwarks, our musketeers fired incessantly at the defenders on the ramparts, forcing them to take cover more and more. I personally spent several hours every day in the *sabats* myself, firing one musket after the other while my attendants busied themselves reloading. It will be no surprise to you that I did more than my fair share of the killing: I have been shooting muskets since the age of five, and countless hunting parties have made me an excellent marksman: when I get a clear shot, I rarely miss, and I seem to have that innate hunter's talent, to be able to guess where the game – or in this case, the opponent – is going to show himself.

Despite the cover provided by the bulwarks, it was quite dangerous. One time, I was nearly hit by a cannon ball that went smashing through the sabat roof and killed several of my men. But I refused to move into safety, despite the pleas of my officers to do so. If you want your men to respect and admire you, my son, if you want them to go to the gates of hell for you, show them that you are not afraid of risking your own life. If God wishes to keep you alive, He will.

At long last, the time had come – or so it seemed: one of our sabats had reached the foot of the hill. Under Qasim Khan's direction, workers began digging a deep shaft, in which gunpowder charges would be set off to bring down Chittor's wall.

Everything seemed to go as planned. The charges were placed, the fuse was lit – there was a massive explosion, causing a landslide which took part of the wall with it. The breach was only ten paces wide – not as wide as I had hoped, but enough for the storm troops to force their way through. On Todar Mal's orders, they launched the assault.

Alas! What we didn't realize, was that two charges of gunpowder had been placed, which, unfortunately, had not gone off simultaneously. As our assault troops were rushing towards the breach, the second charge exploded. A few dozen defenders standing on top off the crumbling ramparts were killed as well, but by far the majority of the victims fell in our camp. Over two hundred of my men, some of the best and bravest, perished in the blast. I was forced to call off the attack and witness how the defenders repaired the breach and erected new defenses. Hearing their laughter and insults, I swore to myself I would make them pay dearly.

The next few weeks were spent in building new sabats and further weakening their defenses. But despite our hard work and the daily losses we inflicted, the defenders still showed no sign of weakness. Still no sign of their ammunition running low, no sign of shortage of food or manpower...

I managed to resist the urge to order another frontal assault, but I must admit, I was getting extremely impatient – a state of mind besiegers need to avoid, for impatience leads to impetuousness, and impetuousness to costly mistakes.

The time I did not spend fighting in the sabats or consulting with the army leaders, I spent in prayer, asking God to help me.

The days passed by without any real progress, and losses on both sides continued to be heavy. Much as I hate to admit it, there were times when I feared God was on my enemies' side... But I didn't give up praying, pledging myself to visit Ajmir as soon as God would grant me victory, and perhaps more importantly, promising Him that I would use my power only to serve Him.

Then, in the afternoon of the thirteenth of *Esfand*[147], the tide finally turned. As usual, I was standing in the sabat, when I saw a tall man

---

[147] February 23, 1568.

in heavy *hazar mikhi*[148] armour on the ramparts, directing the enemy troops.

I didn't know who he was, but shivers went down my spine. I felt like a hunter who has finally managed to track down his prey.

I asked for my favorite gun *Sangram* and patiently waited for the man to appear again. I do not know how long I waited, without a single move, hardly blinking an eye. Then at last, my patience was rewarded: there he was, exactly where I had been expecting him, right in front of my gun.

It was no more than a fleeting moment, but I still see it in my mind's eye, as if frozen in time: the sunrays on the man's shining armour, the blue sky, and Sangram's black barrel.

I squeezed the trigger and felt the butt slamming into my shoulder, my ears deafened by its thunder. Amidst the rising gunpowder smoke, I saw the man being knocked backwards as if he had been struck by lightning – I must have hit him full in the chest. The chaos on the ramparts and the yelling and screaming confirmed my suspicion: this must have been a very important man.

Less than an hour later, reports came in that most defenses had been deserted, and that large fires were burning inside the fortress.

'These must be *jauhar* pyres,' Raja Bhagwan Das explained. 'Your Majesty must have killed the enemy commander, Jai Mal Rathor. When the leader has fallen, the battle is lost, and the men prepare to die. The leading families will burn their own women and children, lest they should fall into enemy hands.'

His words were soon confirmed. The man I had killed was indeed Jai Mal Rathor, the leader of the garrison, and the death of the leader had sealed the fate of his army.

I seized the opportunity and ordered coordinated attacks on several points throughout the night. Musket fire kept the ramparts clear, while heavy mortars hammered the walls and new gunpowder charges were brought forward. Just before the break of dawn, we had again breached the wall, and the assault troops stormed in, thirsting for booty and revenge. I followed right after the first wave, amidst a group of battle elephants.

---

[148] *Hazār Mīkhī*: *Thousand Nails.*

A few thousand enemy soldiers still staged a few valorous but futile attacks. It seemed as if they were more eager to fall in battle than to win it, and we, of course, obliged them. After about an hour, the resistance broke down. A few dozen survivors made their last stand around Patta, Chittor's second-in-command; they were all trampled to death under my elephants.

At last, the fortress was mine. Contrary to my usual practice, I ordered all adult male prisoners to be killed on the spot. No soft-heartedness this time! Not only had they angered and insulted me by their stubborn resistance and the loss of so many of my best men; not only did I want to teach their coward king a lesson. After this long and costly siege, killing the able-bodied men was absolutely necessary, if I wanted to break Mewar's fighting capability. What would have happened if I had let them live? Their king was still around, hiding in the Aravallis like a coward, but probably waiting for an opportunity to raise a new army and come back to fight me. Most of Chittor's regular soldiers had perished in the battle, but much of the fighting had been done by farmers who had taken refuge in the fortress. If I had spared their lives, I probably would have had to fight them again someday!

No, I do not apologize for the 'slaughter of Chittor', as some have chosen to call it: it was the only way to avoid future bloodshed among my own troops!

No, I do not regret the massacre; the only thing I do regret is that I failed to kill them all: a few hundred of them managed to escape, passing themselves off as my own troops, driving their women and children bound in front of them, as if they were their prisoners.

I ordered Chittor vacated, its massive gates unhinged and transported to Agra as war trophies, and strictly forbade any repairs to the ramparts and defenses. Until the end of time, the fortress will remain there like I left it, daunting but powerless, emasculated, a tribute to the power of its conqueror.

Harsh as my verdict may have seemed to some, history has proven me right. As you know all too well, my son, this wouldn't be the last time that the Ranas of Mewar would be making trouble for us. Uday Singh, that spineless coward, kept hiding in the hills until his death; but his son and successor Pratap clearly inherited more of the fighting spirit of his forefathers; he would give us more than one headache.

But without Chittor and the other fortresses, he never posed any serious threat; without Chittor, the Rana of Mewar is nothing more than a nuisance, a gadfly, a small stone in our boot, annoying enough to make itself felt from time to time, but not enough to bother to stop and get rid of it.

I entrusted the government of the conquered territories to Asaf Khan and left Chittor on the eighteenth of Esfand[149], heading straight to Ajmir, as I had promised God I would.

Eager to show my gratitude and humility before His all-powerful majesty, I covered most of the forty-eight *kos*[150] on foot, and spent several hours on my knees before Khwajah Muin ud Din's sacred tomb, thanking Almighty God for the many favors He had bestowed on me throughout my life, and asking Him for His continuing guidance and protection.

Back in Agra on the third of Ordibehesht[151], I went to work immediately: despite the upcoming summer heat, I was eager to start the final campaign against the remaining Rajputana fortresses.

Much to my regret, I found myself forced to postpone these plans, when I learned that the Mirzas had again been carrying out raids into Malwa. I sent Ashraf Khan at the head of a strong cavalry force to chase them out, and stayed behind in Agra, using the hot summer months to supervise the ongoing construction works and reflect on matters of government.

The three Uzbeg rebellions, the invasion of Muhammad Hakim and the troubles with the Mirzas – it had made me think.

It seemed that the larger an empire gets, the stronger it becomes in comparison to its neighbours, but also, the more vulnerable to internal strife and disintegration. Is this really inevitable? And if not, what can be done to avoid it?

In complicated matters like this, it is always useful to hear the opinion of people of different backgrounds. I therefore met with Mun'im Khan, Raja Man Singh, Todar Mal, Birbal, and Mir Abdul-Latif.

---

[149] Saturday, February 28, 1568.

[150] 120 miles, or 192 km.

[151] April 13, 1568.

Knowing how sensitive some people are – Hindus in particular – about eating with people of another caste or creed, I invited them to join me after the evening meal.

We met in an open room on the eastern ramparts of Agra's Red Fort, overlooking the Yamuna River. The breeze from the river felt delightfully refreshing and comfortable after another hot summer day.

I ordered trays of ice and cooled drinks to be brought in, and told the servants to leave us alone.

As I expected, Todar Mal and Mir Abdul-Latif drank nothing but water, and Birbal and Man Singh had some sherbet, while Mun'im Khan and I were indulging in a few beakers of wine.

'I should probably not be drinking any sharab,' Mun'im Khan admitted, more to himself than to us, 'but it does taste great on a summer evening...'

'Indeed it does, Khan Khanan! And I would not worry too much: Allah, eternal praise be upon Him only, is prepared to forgive much worse sins than that,' I agreed, taking a sip. It tasted, as I expected, delicious.

'Mm – great, absolutely great,' I said, smacking my lips.

'Nice and cool, crisp, not too sweet... Ah, my friends, evenings like these are the raisins of life, don't you agree? A nice little breeze, a cool drink, and pleasant conversation – is this not what life is all about? Remember the great Hafiz's verse:

Hermits the flowing spring approve;
But poets the sparkling bowl enjoy:
And, till he's judged by Powers above,
Hafiz will drink, and sing, and toy!'[152]

Mun'im Khan applauded; Mir Abdul-Latif and the Hindus smiled and nodded courteously, although it was not clear from the expression on their faces what they were really thinking.

'Anyway,' I said, forcing myself to get down to business, 'much as I am tempted to start a conversation about the merits of wine and the meaning of life, this is not why I have invited you here tonight. Tell me, my trusted friends, what do you think of what has happened these last few months? Do you think we can rest assured that we have overcome all dangers?'

---

[152] Quoted by James Morier (1824), page 126.

Mun'im Khan was the first to break the ensuing silence.

'I believe we do, Your Majesty,' he said pensively; 'indeed, we have been attacked on many fronts; the situation has been quite perilous, and many a mighty empire might have collapsed under similar circumstances , but under Your Majesty's able leadership, we have overcome all adversities, and actually, we have come out much stronger! Your Majesty's army is without a shadow of a doubt the mightiest fighting force I have ever seen; not only is it large and well-equipped; it is cohesive, loyal, battle-hardened, and extremely effective!'

He stole a passing glance at Todar Mal and Man Singh, and continued:

'One would never expect an army consisting of so many different factions to hang together the way it does, but it does! All the men – Turks, Persians, Rajputs – they're devoted to you!'

He paused, and took a good mouthful of wine.

'And what is perhaps even more important,' he added, smacking his lips, 'I do not want to flatter, but Your Majesty is the most able army leader of his time! The speed with which Your Majesty moves his troops, the way he ensures their supply, the way he deploys them, the judicious use of rockets, musket fire, mortars – I have never seen such soldiership, not even in the days of the great Bairam Khan, may Allah be well pleased with him! Your Majesty is the Iskandar of his age!'

Much as I appreciated Mun'im Khan's words – after all, as Abu-l Fazl cleverly observed: Of all lies, flattery is the most effective! – it was not quite the advice I was looking for.

'I have to thank you for your kindness, Khan-i-Khanan! It is most encouraging to hear such words of appreciation from an experienced soldier like yourself! But my mind is not at ease: what pains me, is the treachery we have experienced. The Mewari resistance, I can understand – these people were misguided, they didn't know me, they considered me as a foreign invader! But the Uzbegs, the Mirzas – they have been my comrades in arms for so many years! Am I such a weakling, or such an animal, that people rise up against me, as soon as I've turned my back?'

'No, on the contrary!' Mir Abdul-Latif exclaimed. 'I am convinced that this is not Your Majesty's fault!'

He paused, looking for words to express his thoughts.

'It is clearly not a matter of how Your Majesty reigns over his subjects; on the contrary, Your Majesty is a promoter of peace, prosperity and justice; and the people are well aware of that!'

'That is very true,' Man Singh agreed. 'Look at the support we got from the villagers around Allahabad! After the battle, they actually helped us hunting down the remaining Uzbeg stragglers – they even brought us their heads! Would they have done that, if they liked the Uzbegs better than us?'

'That's exactly what I mean,' Mir Abdul-Latif said. 'These uprisings have nothing to do with government – only with greed, pride, arrogance of local governors!'

'It may be a matter of greed and pride and arrogance,' Birbal admitted, smiling faintly, 'but precisely for that reason, it is a matter of government!'

'With all due respect, honorable Mir Abdul-Latif,' he added, raising his hand as the old teacher wanted to interrupt him, 'government is not only a matter of righteousness and living in accordance with God's will; it is the art of achieving a perfectly organized empire, using less-than-perfect people!'

'You are so right, master Birbal,' Todar Mal concurred, with unusual enthusiasm. 'Human nature cannot be changed, but human behaviour certainly can! Opportunity makes the thief; indeed, it is my experience, that people who know they will be subject to thorough control, will think twice before they start stealing, no matter how selfish and greedy they are!'

'Precisely,' said Birbal. 'Human greed is like a fast-growing weed; it needs to be trimmed and cut back constantly, lest it overgrows everything – and even better is, not to allow it to take root! More often than not, local governors are left in possession of their jagirs for decades; no wonder they start behaving like they own the land! With each passing year, they feel more and more like kings, who by coincidence happen to have pledged allegiance to a faraway Emperor!'

'And how would you propose to change that, master Birbal?,' I asked, smiling, in spite of the insolent frankness of his tone, rather amused to hear how much his reasoning was similar to my own.

'Governors need to be Your Majesty's representatives; nothing less, nothing more!' Birbal answered without hesitation. 'They should be transferred to other stations on a regular basis, so that they do not start behaving like the owners of the land they have been assigned to!'

'And perhaps even more importantly, Your Majesty,' Todar Mal added, 'they should not be allowed to pay themselves from the revenues of their jagirs!

Governors should be dependent upon the Emperor for their personal wealth; they should receive salaries in accordance with their merit!'

'I think this is very sound advice,' I agreed. 'You are right: if I would have called back the Uzbegs to Agra much earlier, if I would have divided the Mirzas and moved them to different jagirs in time, maybe none of this would have happened!'

'Tell me something, my friends,' I added, as in an afterthought, 'in your opinion, are there any other governors in the Empire whom I should be calling back right now?'

I looked at them, one by one, and noticed how Mun'im Khan was evading my glance.

'Well, any ideas?'

Man Singh answered in Mun'im Khan's stead:

'It probably is rather delicate for the Khan-i-Khanan to say this, Your Majesty, but the family of his honorable predecessor, Shams-ud-din, may God receive him in his mercy: I fear they may one day pose a risk. Not that I have any reason at all to doubt their loyalty, but one should not forget that they all hold important jagirs in the Panjab, that they have very strong family ties, that they live only a few days traveling distance from each other... Again, I have no reason whatsoever to doubt their loyalty, but having heard Birbal's and Todar Mal's words: if I were in Your Majesty's position, I would consider assigning them to different jagirs...'

'Thank you for your wise and honest advice, Raja Man Singh. I will most certainly give it due consideration,' I answered, nodding in appreciation.

My trusted advisors had said exactly what I had been thinking and planning myself, but – and remember this, my son – when difficult decisions have to be taken, it is always preferable that the people around you have reached the same conclusion by themselves: this will avoid much idle gossip afterwards.

As it was past midnight, I thanked them again for their advice, bade them all a good and restful night, and retired to my quarters; but it took me several hours before I finally fell asleep.

As I lay awake in the night, I pondered over our conversation, and in particular, on the cleverness and perspicacity of Man Singh, Todar Mal and Birbal. I could not help wondering – it was not the first time, nor would it be the last – how it had been possible, that so smart and competent a race like the Hindus had been overrun so easily by a handful of Muslim invaders.

The only plausible answer I could and can come up with – other than divine intervention, of course – is that the Hindus were defeated because they had allowed themselves to be divided. Had there been a Hindu Akbar at the time, the invaders would never have stood a chance – the few survivors would have brought back tales of such horror, that no foreigner would ever again have dared to invade Hindustan!

It is our task, my son, to see to it that such an invasion will, indeed, never happen again.

⁂

Things went entirely as planned during the remainder of the year.

The Mirzas and their band of marauders were easily driven back into Gujarat; and Shams-ud-din's family members were called to Agra, where, as Abu-l Fazl would phrase it, they 'obtained the favor of kissing the threshold of the sublime court', and were all assigned to different jagirs elsewhere in the Empire, far away from each other. Only my foster brother Aziz Koka, who resided most of the time at Court anyway, was allowed to keep his fief in the Panjab.

I do not know, nor care, whether they guessed the reason behind their reassignment, and whether or not it suited their convenience. I did see to it, though, that they were more than handsomely rewarded for their loyal service, and showered with honors. Loyalty, my son, is a matter of mutual benefit...

With my borders secure and the affairs of the Empire in good order, I could at last direct my efforts towards the further conquest of Rajastan.

On the 29th of Bahman[153], I pitched camp before Ranthambhore, the great stronghold of the Hara clan, vassals of the Ranas of Mewar.

Ranthambhore is hardly smaller than Chittor, so I had resigned myself to another protracted siege. Sabats were dug, and fifteen huge mortars were dragged all the way to the top of the steep hill facing the stronghold.

After several weeks of siege, my mortars had been causing such destruction, that Rai Surjan Hara, the chief of Bundi and commander of Ranthambhore, sent us two of his sons as emissaries, asking for a truce. Raja Bhagwan Das and Man Singh were allowed to enter the fortress to negotiate on my behalf. At first, I didn't want to let them go – it would have been a disaster to lose my two most important allies over a single fortress, but they assured me they would be quite safe, since courtesy among Rajput chiefs is never laid aside, even in times of war.

It didn't take them long to reach an agreement. Barely six weeks after the start of the siege[154], I made my triumphant entry into the fortress.

Harsh as I had been towards Chittor, I treated Ranthambhore with clemency. In exchange for his pledge of loyalty, Rai Surjan Hara was offered lucrative and prestigious jagirs: first, an important command in Gondwana and then, governor of the holy city of Varanasi – a great honor and privilege for any Hindu. In addition, he and his family were offered exceptionally favorable terms and conditions: they would forever be allowed to keep their capital; they were exempted from sending me a bride, their wives and female relatives were under no obligation to participate in the bazars organized in the imperial zanana; their temples would not be touched; they could beat their kettledrums in the streets of Agra as far as the gate of the imperial fortress; they would be allowed to enter the diwan-i-am completely armed, and were under no obligation to prostrate themselves before the throne; their horses would not be branded with the imperial *dagh*[155]; their troops would never be placed under a Hindu commander other than a Rai of

---

[153] February 8, 1569.

[154] March 21, 1569.

[155] A flower branded on the forehead.

Bundi, and they would never be asked to cross the Hind[156].

I had ample reasons to be lenient. Ranthambhore in itself was worth a high price, but even more important was the message it sent to the other Rajput chiefs: I was the most generous and grateful of friends, but ruthless and lethal to those who chose to be my enemies.

The message did not fail to come across. Four months later, the fortress of Kalinjar, the siege of which, years before, had cost the life of the formidable Sher Khan Sur, surrendered to my troops without offering any serious resistance. Its leader, Raja Ram Chand Baghela, who had already demonstrated his obedience by sending the wonderful musician Tansen to the Imperial Court, was granted an important jagir near Allahabad.

Without a single additional shot being fired, the powerful Rajas of Jodhpur, Bikaner and Jaisalmer made their submission in the year that followed. Rajastan was finally mine, my troops able to move about freely, from Amber to the Thar Desert, and from the Panjab to the borders of Gujarat.

Even more importantly, its inhabitants no longer saw me as a Muslim invader, but as a loyal ally, a benevolent, equitable protector, with whom they gladly associated themselves. What had been a hostile and dangerous wilderness, had turned into my power base.

Only the Mewaris remained in the Aravalli hills. I let them. Of what use would it have been to waste more blood, treasure, and above all, time, on the conquest of an isolated hill range of little or no value, when my troops could go unhindered wherever I wished to send them?

No, I had more ambitious plans, and could hardly wait to carry them out.

❧

Thus, began the happiest period of my life, my son. A golden time, with a past to be proud of, and a future to look forward to. God had blessed me in such abundance that at times, it made me feel guilty. Everything, absolutely everything I ever wanted or hoped for, was given to me. I was twenty-five years old, healthy and strong, and well under way to become one of the mightiest kings the world had ever seen; but above

---

156 Indus.

all, my son, God had finally blessed me with what I feared would never happen: the birth of a strong and healthy little boy, of whom the astrologers predicted that he would become a learned, wise, just and powerful king – you, my dear son.

Twenty-second Letter

سیکری

Ṣikri (J)

PART ONE
From the private notes of Mulazim Hakim[157] Ali Gilani,
Jalinus-uz-Zamani,[158]
Personal physician of His Majesty the Emperor

The day after the mortal remains of the unfortunate newborn Princes Hasan and Husain had been committed to their final resting place, I received a summons to present myself at His Majesty's private quarters.

With grave concern, I obeyed. I knew His Majesty to be just and kind; yet, it would not have been the first time that an unfortunate occurrence, while solely due to the Divine will, is blamed on a hakim's alleged incompetence...

I was escorted to the spacious open room on top of the ramparts, overlooking His Majesty's beloved Yamuna River. As I entered and performed the taslim[159], I was surprised to see that there were no guards

[157] Mulāzim: personal attendant. Hakīm: physician.

[158] Jālīnūs-uz-Zamānī: 'Galen of the Age'; honorary title referring to the famous physician and philosopher Claudius Galenus of Pergamum (c. 130–c.200), whose teachings have dominated medical science in the Muslim and Western world for centuries.

[159] Formal bow, the back of the right hand touching the ground.

in attendance. Clearly, His Majesty wanted the conversation to remain strictly private.

'Thank you for joining me, Hakim Ali,' he said, pointing at a pillow at the foot of the low platform on which he was sitting. Although courteous, he was less friendly than usual – he seemed sad and preoccupied, if not irritated.

'Pray sit down. I wish to talk to you about the death of my unfortunate sons, may Allah smile upon them.'

It was as I feared, I thought to myself – the Emperor was blaming me for what had happened. I tried to swallow, but my throat felt dry and painful, as if an invisible hand was slowly choking me.

'I can assure Your Majesty...' I stammered, but he stopped me with an irritated gesture.

'Yes, I know, you have done your very best to save them, and I appreciate all your efforts,' he said impatiently.

I bowed, staring at my feet, afraid to look up.

'I know that what has happened cannot be undone, Hakim Ali,' he added, in a softer tone of voice. 'What I want to hear from you, is: what, in your opinion, has been the exact cause of their death?'

Again, I bowed, trying to hide my relief.

'The two little boys – Allah bless their immaculate souls! – were twins, Your Majesty. Twins will always be more at risk than single children, especially if their mother is not strongly built. You see, Your Majesty: the blood in a frail woman's womb is often insufficiently abundant to nourish two children full-term. When all the nourishment has been consumed, the womb will expel the children, causing them to be born with immature organs. Quite often, the lungs will be too small to properly air the body, causing it to overheat; also, in many cases, the stomach is unable to hold and digest sufficient quantities of food...'

'So, other than the will of Allah – praised be He under all circumstances – it was their mother's frailty that has caused the children's death?'

'Other than the will of Allah: yes, Your Majesty.'

'Tell me, could sickness or death of newborn children also be due to the constitution of the father?'

'On rare occasions: yes, Your Majesty... although I have to emphasize, this is quite rare.'

'And such was not the case here?'

'Most certainly not, on the contrary, Your Majesty!'

'What makes you so sure about that, Hakim Ali?'

'The fact that twins have been conceived, is in itself clear evidence of the presence of abundant and strong, well-formed sperm, Your Majesty.'

The Emperor looked pleased, but remained clearly unconvinced.

'May God give that you are right, Hakim Ali. But still, I cannot help feeling worried. I have bedded hundreds of women in my life; do you realize that up to now, not a single one of them has given me any children? Do you realize, that Hasan and Husain were the first sons ever to be born to me? How is this to be explained? If my sperm is, as you say, strong and well-formed, why has it failed so far to engender any offspring?'

'This can still be a coincidence, Your Majesty. I really do not think there is anything wrong with Your Majesty's constitution – the elements are clearly well in balance, as is apparent from Your Majesty's complexion, pulse, and all other vital signs. There is little advice that I could give Your Majesty to improve his current good health – other than what Your Majesty already does: eating and drinking in moderation, sleeping well, and exercising his body sufficiently for it to remain vigorous, without exhausting its strength.

There is, maybe, one additional advice that may be wise for Your Majesty to follow, and that is: moderation. For the gestation of children, it is of course advisable to have intercourse, but it may be recommended not to maintain too high a frequency. Especially in vigorous young men like Your Majesty, where abundance of red blood causes great appetite for all things which provoke the senses, all too frequent visits to the women's quarters will cause the sperm to overheat, and diminish in quantity. A pause of a few days will allow it to properly mature and absorb the right balance of the four elements, so that it attains both the right quantity and quality.

But I should again emphasize: no matter how strong and healthy a man is, and even if his sperm is of optimal strength, intercourse will not always lead to pregnancy – in fact, I would say that pregnancy is the exception, rather than the rule!'

'Is that so, indeed? And why is that, Hakim Ali?'

'I am afraid we do not know for sure, Your Majesty; but I should point out, that the natural order of things has clearly been ordained by Allah, who, in His endless wisdom, compassion and mercy, provides us with what we need – even if we do not always realize it. Indeed, intercourse and the delicate pleasure it provides, is certainly among Allah's most generous blessings. When performed with reasonable frequency, it is, without any doubt, quite wholesome, and clearly contributes to a healthy balance in both body and mind. Moreover, it will generally increase the affection between husband and wife, thus strengthening the bonds of marriage and the harmony of family life.

But it would not at all be desirable that all intercourse would always lead to pregnancy. Many families would have many more children than they are able to raise and afford; moreover, it might endanger the health and life of many women, for without doubt: pregnancy and labour are a heavy burden on a woman's body! So, it is very well possible for a healthy man like Your Majesty to have intercourse with many women, without pregnancy occurring. It's a matter of coincidence!'

'Coincidence, and the will of Allah, I suppose?'

'The will of Allah, indeed, Your Majesty. The best Your Majesty can do, in my humble opinion, is to pray to Allah, and to ask for His protection and guidance.'

PART TWO
From the private notes of Mir Abdul-Latif

With the conquest of the great Rajput fortress of Chittor, His Majesty's power had reached a new high point in his life. Yet, he seemed more restless and ill at ease than ever before.

'If I may be forgiven for saying so,' I ventured to observe, after he had been listening quite absentmindedly to a few Hadith[160] I had been reading to him, 'Your Majesty seems preoccupied. Is there anything I could be of assistance with?'

The Emperor smiled wearily.

'Thank you for your concern, Mir Abdul-Latif, but there's little or nothing you can do about it, I suppose.'

He looked at me, as if asking for confirmation.

'You know,' he explained, 'when it comes to the Empire, everything has been going my way, and the future looks bright. *In sha'a Llah*, it will not be long before Rajputana will be mine entirely, and I am taking a number of important new measures to strengthen my hold over the lands that belong to me. But I have to tell you, Mir Abdul-Latif, I have been saddened, deeply saddened, by the death of my two sons,' he said, suddenly looking intently at me, as if I had anything to do with it.

'Tell me, my honorable teacher and friend: what will become of this great Empire I have been building, if there is no one to leave it to?'

'It seems to me, Your Majesty should not worry too much – after all, Your Majesty is still very young!'

'You know as well as I do, Mir Abdul-Latif, that life is fleeting, like the waters of a mountain river – a man cannot hold on to it, it passes him by as it pleases! One day, he is strong and healthy; the next, they carry him to his grave, killed by a sudden onslaught of fever, or a hunting accident... Only Allah is the giver of life and death, we should not assume to be ours what belongs to Him only! What kind of king would I be, if I would not worry about the future?'

'I stand corrected,' I admitted. 'Still, Your Majesty should not give up hope! When the time is ripe, our prayers will be answered!'

---

[160] Hadīth: Traditions or Sayings of the Holy Prophet Muhammad.

'I do hope you are right, but I cannot help feeling worried. I do not know how many women I've had over the last few years, but I still do not have any children! Poor little Hasan and Husain – may Allah's light shine upon them! – were the first children born to me! How is this to be explained? How many times haven't I seen simple farmers, poor devils who can barely afford to marry one wife, blessed with five, six and more children, whereas I, with hundreds of wives and concubines, have none! No, I fear, that for reasons known only to Him, Allah has ordained that I should remain childless...'

'I can only say that Your Majesty should put his trust in Allah. Even if we do not always understand His reasons: what He ordains, is for the best, for He alone is the All-knowing, and His compassion and mercy are limitless. Those who put their trust in Him, will never be disappointed!'

'And do you believe that He has ordained, for some or other strange reason, that I should remain without offspring?'

'I do not know, but I am inclined to believe it's only because the time has not yet been auspicious. In due time, Allah will answer Your Majesty's prayers, this I strongly believe!'

'I pray you are right, venerable Master... I wouldn't mind waiting, for years if need be, if only I knew that all would work out for the best – but nobody seems to be able to give me a straight answer! I have of course asked the astrologers, many times, but as usual, their answers have been vague and inconclusive. Also back in Ajmir, at Khwajah Muin ud Din Muhammad Chishti's sacred tomb, nobody has been able to help me!'

'Now that Your Majesty mentions Khwajah Muin ud Din: not so far from here, in the town of Sikri, lives one of his descendants – Shaykh Salim Chishti. People say that he has inherited the wisdom and holiness of his saintly forefather; they say that Allah answers each and every one of his prayers, and that he's able to foresee the future!'

'Then I will visit this holy man as soon as possible, and ask him for his blessings! Will you accompany me, Mir Abdul-Latif, or do you think it will be too strenuous a journey for you? After all, you are an old man, and I would not want you to fall ill!'

'It's not that far, Your Majesty. It will be an honor and a privilege to accompany you!'

The messengers we had sent ahead had done their work: by the time we arrived in Sikri, the whole town had trooped together. The village elders knelt in the dust before the Emperor, pointing at the humble but well-intended offerings the inhabitants had prepared: food, carvings in wood and stone, carpets, woven fabrics, simple jewellery, and the like.

As always, the Emperor went out of his way to put the people at ease, eating some of their food and accepting their meagre gifts with conspicuous enthusiasm and gratitude, as if they were the most precious treasures on earth. And he more than returned the favor, for he ordered his soldiers to distribute gold coins – each one worth more than anything the villagers had ever laid their hands on.

After this friendly exchange of civilities, for which His Majesty took ample time – no less than an hour, without in any way showing his eagerness to see the Shaykh – he was finally escorted to the holy man's dwelling by the village elders.

Any person familiar with today's glorious city of Fatehpur Sikri would barely have recognized the town as it was in those days. It was no more than a few hovels at the foot of the hill, next to the Khari Nadi, the seasonal river which now has been dammed to form the beautiful lake that ensures the city's water supply.

The small hut in which the saint spent his days in hallowed silence and seclusion was outside the town, on the slope of the rocky hill which runs lengthwise along the river bank, and on which the current imperial city has been built. In those days, however, it was barren wilderness, and – apart from the occasional visit he got from his next of kin and from pilgrims asking for his blessings – the old Shaykh lived there, alone and secluded, far away from the noise of the town.

At the foot of the hill, the Emperor dismissed his escort; he and I ascended, on foot, the narrow rocky path leading to the hut.

Upon our approach, the Shaykh came out of his hut – a tall, sinewy man, surprisingly strong and healthy despite his nearly ninety years. There were still many black hairs in his wiry beard and eyebrows, and the surprising swiftness of his movements revealed that in his youth, he must have been a man of considerable strength and agility.

He walked a few steps in our direction, bowing woodenly, rather ill at ease as it would seem.

'*As-salamu aleikum*, honorable Shaykh Salim Chishti,' the Emperor said, bowing his head and touching his heart, ill at ease himself as well – indeed, how does an Emperor greet a saint, and how should a holy man salute his Emperor?

'*Wa aleikum salam*[161], Your Majesty,' the Shaykh answered, again bowing as deeply as he could. 'It is indeed an unexpected, undeserved honor for me, to meet so great and powerful a king, but I am afraid my scanty dwelling is quite unworthy to receive such noble visitor,' he proceeded, pointing apologetically at the hut.

'It is I who has to thank you for receiving me, honorable Murshid[162],' the Emperor answered, 'for I am in dire need of your wise counsel, your blessings, and your prayers.'

'I am entirely at Your Majesty's disposal,' the Shaykh answered, touching his heart.

'Allow me to present my teacher, the honorable Mir Abdul-Latif,' the Emperor proceeded, 'it is he who gave me the good advice to consult you.'

'It is a privilege to meet you, Sahab,' the Shaykh said, bowing again, and looking at me inquisitively from beneath his bushy eyebrows.

We arrived at the hut. The Shaykh went in and came back with his prayer mat, offering it to the Emperor to sit on. To me, he offered his winter mantle, but I politely declined, and sat myself down in the dust, as he did.

A small *tandur*[163], a water pot, a few pieces of crude earthenware, and a few books on two small wooden standards – that was, apparently, all he possessed in this world...

'This is really all I need,' he said, guessing my thoughts. 'In gratitude for my blessings and prayers, the simple people who come to visit me bring me some vegetables, some flour, *ghi*[164], dal, or *panir*[165] – those

[161] As-salāmu aleikum: (The) Peace (be) with you; Wa aleikum salām: and with you, peace; formal Arabic greeting, also used in Persian and Urdū.

[162] Guide, Master.

[163] Clay oven.

[164] Ghee, clarified butter.

[165] Firm cottage cheese, similar to Italian *mozzarella*.

are the only gifts I will accept. Indeed, what would I need gold, silver or jewels for? What more could I want than the things I already have? I enjoy peace and quiet, I eat the honest and wholesome foods of the people of the land; and if for a day or two, I have nothing to eat, I just go without, like they do. Since long I have given up eating meat, and I do not miss it at all. The Hindus are right, you know: one does not need to make one's body a grave of animals in order to remain healthy. On the contrary: I find vegetable food brings calmness, wisdom, and peace of mind.'

'How do you spend your days, reverend Master?,' I asked.

'I pray, and I read,' he answered. 'I have the Holy Qur'an, the Hadith, and a few poems of Rumi and Hafiz at my disposal – there is more than enough in those writings to fill a thousand lifetimes!'

'I do not see any qalam[166], ink, or paper, reverend Master? Surely, mankind would benefit from your wisdom, if you would commit your thoughts to writing?' I asked.

'I must admit, I have often thought about it,' the Shaykh said, smiling faintly, 'but if I'm honest, I must admit there is little, if anything, that I could write, that hasn't yet been written before – more eloquently than I ever could! To what use would it be, to add yet another volume of paraphrases to the vast libraries that have already been written? No, I am content, Sahab, just to sit here, and to give, to whoever comes to ask me for it, whatever little wisdom I have to offer. Verily, this is what I believe Allah has destined me to do.'

'I suppose it is mainly Muslims who come to see you?' the Emperor inquired.

'On the contrary, I would say, Your Majesty: I think I am even more popular among the Hindus!'

He paused and smiled.

'You know, that's the way the Hindus are: they see Allah as a huge, immeasurable mountain, and all the world's many religions as different paths leading up that same mountain. Different though all these beliefs may be, they are all equal, in a sense, since all of them will ultimately lead to the same Summit. The individual path a person is destined to

---

166 Qalam: wooden writing pen, usually made of reed, used in Arabic and Persian calligraphy. .

follow, is determined by birth; and birth, in turn, is determined by previous lives; ultimately, however, every person, nay, every living being, is destined to be reunited with Allah, that's what they believe.

Erroneous though their rituals may be, Your Majesty, I have often been favorably impressed by their God-fearing attitude. Each time, I am moved to see the respect and devotion with which they kneel before the Holy Qur'an, even if they do not know Its sacred message.'

'Do you try to convert them to Islam, venerable Shaykh?'

'In the beginning, yes, I did. I tried to convince them that their beliefs were wrong and displeasing in the eyes of Allah. But now... I've given up on that. I confine myself to answering any questions they may have, and offering them my blessings and prayers whenever they ask me for them. It is my experience that the frugal life I lead greatly appeals to them, much more than any learned reasoning.

I do not condemn them, I do not argue with them; I leave it to Allah's limitless wisdom and mercy to judge their hearts and minds, and to guide them unto the right Path, if He so chooses. Indeed, some of them do come back to me, asking for my help to become true Muslims; but even if they keep on worshipping the many gods of their forefathers, I do not mind. They show such deep respect and devotion, that I believe this is what Allah wants me to do: to lead a simple life, to offer prayers and blessings, and through my example, to incite all those who visit me, to worship the one and only true God.

Your Majesty may be familiar with the saying: The Mosque and the Temple Divide, but the Sufi Shrine Unites. How very true! As long as we preach and condemn and divide, we are creating fear, resistance, strife. But as soon as we bow and kneel down, together, in silence before Allah's unspeakable Majesty, we are united in our smallness before Him.'

The Emperor, visibly moved, nodded enthusiastically.

'This is exactly how I see things as well, honorable Shaykh! I strongly believe it is my duty to provide sulh-i-kul, peace and security to all, and thus, to unite all people in peace and security under God. That, I believe, is ultimately the best way to promote the sacred cause of Islam!'

'Indeed, Your Majesty. One just needs to think about the example of Ajmir, where thousands upon thousands of Hindus and Muslims pray together before the tomb of my illustrious forefather Khwajah Muin ud Din, may Allah be well pleased with him! How many Hindus have not found the path to Islam, standing before that sacred shrine? Indeed, if one looks at the history of Hindustan, Islam has invariably made the greatest and most lasting progress when it succeeded in uniting the people in peaceful prayer, without trying to forcibly convert them!'

The Shaykh paused, looking at the Emperor with a fatherly smile.

'Hindustan is blessed with so noble-minded and wise an Emperor! Clearly, Your Majesty has been chosen by Allah to achieve great things!'

'I pray to Him you are right,' the Emperor said.

'Your Majesty shouldn't worry – Allah is with him! I know Your Majesty is concerned about his succession, because he does not yet have a son to whom he will leave the Empire. But let me put Your Majesty's mind at ease: not one, but three strong and healthy sons will be born unto him, and all three will reach the age of adulthood!'

'You make me very happy, honorable Shaykh Salim Chishti – may Allah fulfil your wonderful prophecy! I hope you will forgive me for asking, but are you really sure that I have nothing to worry about – that indeed, three healthy sons will be born unto me?'

'This is my strong belief, yes, Your Majesty.'

'Is it your strong belief, or is it what you have actually seen in the future?'

'I do not really see the future, Your Majesty. Every morning, I pray to Allah, that He may be my guide; I ask Him to steer my tongue and make it an instrument of righteousness and truth.

When people then come and ask me about their future, I merely say what I think, what comes through my mind – that is all. I do not pretend to have any power of my own: I merely ask Allah that He may use me, and that is my only ambition – to be Allah's humble instrument. Just like the chisel and the hammer have no merit or ability of their own, but shape great things of beauty in the hands of the artisan, I merely wish for Allah to use me as He deems fit to do.'

'I must confess, I have never thought about it this way, but indeed, this should be every man's ambition: to be nothing but a willing tool in God's hands,' the Emperor agreed pensively. 'If you would allow me to come back on what you just said, honorable Shaykh Salim, about the sons you say will be born unto me: is there any other advice you can give me in this respect?'

'What does Your Majesty mean?'

'I mean, do you know which one of my many spouses and concubines will become the mother of my firstborn? Often have I prayed, that my son would be born out of Princess Salima, for I appreciate her wisdom, and like me, she is a descendant of the glorious House of Temür!'

After a few moments hesitation, Shaykh Salim replied:

'Make your firstborn a son of Hindustan, Your Majesty.'

∽

PART THREE
From the Memoirs of Her Imperial Highness
Salima Sultana Begam Chaqaniani,

مخفی[167]

Barely three months after Akbar had returned from his visit to Shaykh Salim Chishti of Sikri, the Court was buzzing with rumours, that the Princess of Amber was with child: she had not had her period, she was feeling sick every morning, and it was a well-known fact that the Emperor had been visiting her quite frequently, ever since his return from Sikri.

After a few more weeks, the slight but visible swelling of the Princess' belly proved that for once, the rumours had been right.

I have to confess that at first, I felt quite jealous of her. How ardently had I prayed that I would become the next Emperor's mother! Was I not Akbar's favorite? Was I not a descendant of Temür?

Knowing, however, that nothing in this world happens unless Allah wills it, I forced myself to banish these unworthy thoughts, and to resign myself to the divine will.

Having given the matter more ample thought, I came to understand and appreciate Allah's reasons: it was actually a very good thing, for the Empire and for our family, that the mother of Akbar's successor was not a Gurkaniyya princess, but a Hindu of noble Rajput blood.

Indeed, Akbar's extraordinary military power had been, to a large extent, the result of his ability to unite Muslim and Hindu forces under his victorious banners. And now, his son and successor was also Raja Bihari Mal's own grandson, and Raja Bhagwan Das' nephew! Indeed, this young Gurkaniyya prince would have royal Rajput blood flowing through his veins – not a foreign ruler, but a true son of Hindustan!

Yes, this was a good thing. And besides, I knew my duty as a Gurkaniyya princess. I would do what I had promised Akbar: I would be a loving mother and teacher to his son and heir.

Akbar's initial joy at his spouse's pregnancy was soon overshadowed by understandable worries. Was this indeed the first of the three sons

---

[167] Makhfī , 'The Hidden', artist name used by Salīmā as a poetess.

the Shaykh had promised would be born unto him? What if it was a girl? And if it was a son: how to make sure that what had happened to poor little Hasan and Husain would not happen again? The princess of Amber was a frail woman – how to keep her and her child in good health? Should he postpone the planned campaign against the fortress of Ranthambhore and stay behind with her?

After much deliberation and consultation of every teacher, physician and astrologer he could find, Akbar decided his pregnant spouse was to go to Sikri, where she and her servants and midwives were to reside until after the delivery. This, so he reasoned, 'would avail her of the utmost benefit of the saint's orisons'.

With great dispatch, a nice house was built for her, spacious and comfortable, on the flank of the hill overlooking the riverbank. As soon as the construction works had progressed sufficiently, she and her retinue moved to Sikri, where I went to visit her a few times during her pregnancy. Each time I saw her, doing so well, enjoying the tranquillity of the village and the frequent visits of her friends and relatives, far away from the crowded zanana and its gossip, it was difficult not to feel jealous again. But I did my best to hide my feelings – from her, and from myself.

Under the protection of the Shaykh's prayers, everything went well. At noon on the 18th of Shahrivar of the Fourteenth Year[168], in the middle of the season when the gentle rains bring life in abundance to the countryside, Raja Bhagwan Das' frail daughter gave birth to a remarkably strong and healthy boy, of whom the astrologers immediately predicted that he would grow up to be a just, mighty, world-adorning King of Kings, who would walk in his illustrious father's footsteps.

The fortunate mother received the lofty title of *Maryam uz-Zamani*[169], whereas the newborn prince himself was given the name Salim – Shahzada[170] Sultan Muhammad Salim, to be complete –, in grateful recognition of the holy man's prayers, and in an effort to ensure his life-long protection and blessings.

[168] Tuesday, August 30, 1569 of the Julian Calendar.

[169] *Mary of the Age*; see chapter 14, footnote 5.

[170] Son of a Shāh, Prince.

Akbar, however, rarely if ever called his son by his official name: even when he had grown much taller than his own father, he would always affectionately call him 'Shaykhu Baba'[171].

A healthy son and successor! Akbar was truly overwhelmed with joy. He came to visit the baby in the zanana as often as he could, holding, kissing and cuddling him all the time.

Akbar was, for that matter, not the only one to be so fond of the little boy: the Prince grew up as everybody's darling, mine in particular; a good-humoured, funny and bright little boy, who made the dull zanana suddenly seem full of life.

It's always amazing to see how quickly a child changes in its first three years, but Salim was truly remarkable. He seemed to literally soak up everything he saw and heard. By the time he was three, he spoke not only fluent Persian, the common language at Court, but also quite passable Turki, which we used among family members, and excellent Hindi, which he picked up from his mother and the servants.

Salim's remarkable sense of beauty, for which he is so renowned, manifested itself at a very early age. He could hardly speak, when he would already be pointing at every painting and drawing he saw, crowing 'Look, pretty, pretty!' Hours on end, he would he spend in the artisans' workshops, amusing himself with paper, paint, brushes, ink and qalams – drawing flowers and animals, and 'writing' pages upon pages of letters, many of them remarkably harmonious and shapely, coming from the hand of such a small child.

It was a surprise to no one that when, at the age of four years, four months and four days, he received his first formal instruction in the art of reading and writing, he proved to be a bright and diligent student, and it must be said that Akbar, despite his own inability to read and write, never failed to encourage him. Quite often, he would ask him to read him some poetry; and knowing most of these poems by heart, he actually proved himself quite able to help him with his reading practice!

Apart from his son's scholarly education, Akbar of course took a lively interest in his development as a soldier, personally teaching him how to handle guns and swords. He would enjoy himself for hours, wrestling with his little son and in the end, allowing himself to be

---

171 'Daddy Shaykh'; dear little Shaykh.

vanquished. He was also extremely satisfied to see, that Salim, although more prudent and considerate than most children, proved to be utterly fearless, just like his father.

Akbar's joy and pride were equalled by the immense gratitude he felt towards the holy saint to whose blessings and prayers he owed this good fortune. Salim was barely two months old when Akbar decided that Sikri was going to be the seat of the new imperial residence. Indeed, so he reasoned, was it not clear that Sikri was a most auspicious place? Was it not there that Babur had inflicted a crushing defeat on the Rana of Mewar? Did not Babur name it Shukri[172], because of that victory? Was it not clear, that the good Shaykh Salim Chishti's presence had brought God's further blessings on this place? Was it not there that Prince Salim had been born?

I tactfully tried to point out to him that it would take considerable time and treasure to turn that sleepy little farmers' town into the grand city he was envisaging. Was that kind of money not much better spent on Agra?

Akbar wanted nothing of the kind. Great kings before him had built grandiose new cities, and so would he. His capital would be Sikri – or Fatehabad, the City of Victory, or Fatehpur Sikri, as it would soon be called, the magnificent capital of Akbar the Great.

[172] Thanks.

Twenty-third Letter

سیکری

Ṣikri (2)

Blessed, I was truly blessed. The successor I had so ardently prayed for – you, my dearest son – had been born unto me at last; and the mighty fortresses of Rajastan, which for centuries had defied so many a powerful invader, were mine.

And it seemed there would be no end to my good fortune, for barely two months and twenty days after your birth[173], my son, the zanana was gladdened by the birth of your lovely sister, Shahzadi Sultan Khanam; and barely had we celebrated her birth, when it became apparent that yet another concubine was with child.

Verily, one blessing after the other was befalling me. The common people started calling me Akbar the Fortunate; and 'as lucky as Emperor Akbar' quickly became a commonplace expression. Could I deny it? Had I not been given more than any human being could ever deserve or reasonably hope for? I could only pray to God, offer Him my gratitude and devotion, implore His continued blessings, and pledge, from the bottom of my heart, that I would fulfil, to the best of my ability, the lofty tasks He would choose to put upon my shoulders.

In pursuance of the vow I had taken before you were born, my son, I set out as soon as possible to the sacred city of Ajmir, eager to place my

---

[173] Sunday, November 20, 1569 of the Julian Calendar – the 10th of Jumādā ul-Ukhra 977 A.H.

forehead on the cool white marble of Khwajah Muin ud Din's holy shrine.

Although escorted, as usual, by an impressive cortege with hundreds of horse archers and richly adorned, mighty war elephants, I covered the entire distance on foot, the whole ninety-one kos[174], every single step of the way, showing everyone the kind of man I was: the invincible Emperor and sovereign ruler of men; yet, a humble pilgrim before God.

I arrived in Ajmir on Panjshanbeh, the 21st of Esfand[175], and stayed there until shortly before the celebration of the fifteenth anniversary of my enthronement, spending my time in prayer and administering justice and charity.

As usual around that time of year, my thoughts went out to my unfortunate father, dead and gone, fifteen years already... I decided not to return directly to Agra, but to travel via Dilli instead, and pay my respects at his tomb, which, according to the reports I had received, was now completely finished.

I had visited the site before and had seen several drawings after its completion; yet, when I arrived, I was overwhelmed by its beauty and magnificence. The tranquillity of the gardens, the grandeur of the tomb, its perfect proportions – it was, as I had promised it would be, one of the most magnificent buildings the world had ever seen; a sublime resting place, worthy of a King of Kings; more beautiful, more harmonious, more imposing, I am sure, than Temür's tomb at Samarqand.

To be laid to rest in the perfect harmony and tranquillity of a building of such exquisite proportions... it somehow made death less intimidating. In due time, I thought to myself, I would concern myself with the construction of the mausoleum where, one day, my own body would find its last resting place.

But there would be plenty of time to worry about that later. Now, I wanted to live – live my life to the fullest, rise to true greatness: God's benevolent smile was upon me. I felt His strength in every part of my body; and my head was teeming with plans and ambitions.

The cortege unhurriedly made its way back to Agra. As usual, I

---

174 365 kilometers, 228 miles.

175 Thursday, March 2, 1570 (Julian Calendar).

amused myself with grandiose hunting parties – many of them in the middle of the night. I had come to enjoy the excitement of nightly hunting parties: the confused shouting of the drivers in the darkness, the breakneck cavalcades in pursuit of the fleeing deer, with nothing but the pale moon and flickering of torches to light the way.

Back in Agra, I celebrated the birth of the second of the three healthy sons the good Shaykh had promised would be born unto me: your dearly beloved and now so deeply regretted brother Murad had beheld the first light of day at Sikri, on Chaharshanbeh the 27th of Khordad of the Fifteenth Year[176].

Another healthy boy, born in the good town of Sikri, under the protection of the Shaykh's prayers! This could hardly be a coincidence; it strengthened my resolve to take up residence in that most blessed place, so that its auspiciousness might continue to protect me and my family.

I ordered grandiose festivities, and large amounts of treasure to be distributed among the people: I wanted everyone to share in my joy.

From the farthest corners of the Empire, governors and nobles travelled to Agra to offer me their congratulations. I gladly took this opportunity to strengthen the ties of loyalty and friendship that united them to me, making sure they became equally impressed by my power, as by my kindness and generosity. As I pointed out to you before, my son, a subject's faithfulness is like a delicate jewel: the precious but tender gold of his affection needs to be strengthened by the alloy of harder metal. The people should love their Emperor for his righteousness and generosity – but never should they stop fearing his power.

~

Two carefree, leisurely years slipped by, nearly unnoticed.

I spent the better part of those years traveling about the Empire. Indeed, it is not wise for an Emperor to always stay in the same place, my son: his moves and whereabouts should remain unpredictable; his subjects should realize, that in a few weeks or months' time, he might personally investigate their dealings.

To render thanks to God for Murad's birth and to beseech His continued guidance and blessings, I of course travelled to Ajmir first.

---

[176] Wednesday, June 7, 1570 (Julian Calendar).

About two months later, I headed northwest, to Nagaur, halfway between Amber and Bikaner. As I had done in back in Ajmir, I commissioned several important building works, including the embellishment of its famous seventeen-mouthed fountain.

It was there that I tasted the intense satisfaction of receiving the formal submission of the powerful Rajas of Bikaner and Jaisalmer, who had sent high-ranking ambassadors to pay deference to me and to offer me their princesses in marriage as a sign of their loyalty and friendship: Rajastan was mine.

It was also at Nagaur, that Baz Bahadur, the former king of Malwa, came to kneel before me, rubbing his forehead in the dust like a repentant sinner. For eight years he had been wandering around as a fugitive, vainly seeking support, avoided like the plague by everyone: nobody dared to provoke the wrath of the mighty great Mughal.

I of course graciously pardoned him and gave him an appointment at my Court. As I told you before, my son: to kill an opponent, in a way, is to honor him – it is to acknowledge, that to a certain extent at least, he was a true rival. To pardon him is to demonstrate one's supremacy, to emphasize his insignificance. And thus, it happened that the once so proud and recalcitrant king of Malwa ended up eating the bread of charity from his former enemy. He would spend the rest of his life at Court, entertaining me with his poetry and music – for which, I have to say, he was quite talented.

Shortly before the sixteenth anniversary of my enthronement, I traveled further north, crossing the Sutlej River into the Panjab. I visited the shrine at Pakpattan, and from there went to Dibalpur, the jagir of my foster brother Mirza Aziz Koka.

I have to say, I didn't quite like what I saw. Aziz did receive us with what appeared to be unfeigned enthusiasm, but there was something rather arrogant in the lavish open-handedness and the conspicuous display of brotherly love with which he received me. Not that I had any doubts about his loyalty – a new Adham Khan, he was certainly not. Conceitedness, however, is never a good quality, in any man – much less in a courtier.

But one must make do with what one has... And after all, Aziz was my foster brother, united to me by a river of milk; moreover, he was a brave and competent soldier.

I forced myself not to pay too much attention to his familiarities, and concentrated instead on strengthening our friendship, spending as much time with him as possible. I invited him to join me on my hunting trips, and we spent many hours eating and drinking together, sometimes all through the night.

It was reassuring to hear how enthusiastically he supported my plans for further expansion of the Empire. When I informed him of my desire to add Gujarat to my dominions, he could hardly wait to gird himself to battle.

'Gujarat is a real quagmire', I said, chewing on a succulent piece of lamb his cooks had prepared for us, 'there are currently no less than seven would-be kings fighting with each other over its throne!'

'That land and its people indeed deserve much better, Your Majesty,' Aziz nodded in agreement, 'they need order and justice, which only Your Majesty can give them!'

'Are you saying, my brother, that it is actually my duty to intervene, and to annex these lands to my dominions?'

In his excitement, he forgot all formalities.

'If not your duty, then certainly your right! Remember, your father once ruled over Gujarat – that alone makes your claim on it as good as anybody else's! Besides, don't forget: at this time, the Gujaratis are weak, they're busy fighting each other; but just imagine what would happen, if one day, the whole territory would fall into the hands of one strong king? You simply cannot afford to have such a wealthy and powerful neighbor at your doorstep!'

Despite the impertinence of his tone, I very much liked what he was saying – those were exactly my own views.

'Thank you for your advice, my brother,' I said. 'I knew I could count on you.'

'You just say the word, and my men and I are on our way,' he exclaimed, jumping up excitedly – and knocking over, in the process, his beakers of water, sherbet and wine – 'When do we attack?'

'Your zeal is commendable, my brother, but I think we should be patient: let us wait a bit longer for the opportune moment!'

'Wait? What on earth do we have to wait for? Surely, You are not afraid that we won't be able to deal with them?'

I choked back my growing vexation, and replied, in the friendliest tone of voice I could force myself to:

'Haste is the enemy of wisdom, my brother. I think we should allow them a bit more time to wear each other out. Why exhaust ourselves, if they're doing the job for us?'

'As Your Majesty commands. I do beg Your Majesty's pardon.'

It finally seemed to have dawned on him that his tone had been out of line. Seeing his embarrassment, my anger melted away, as quickly as it had risen. 'A few months from now, we will attack, my brother. Let's spend that time well! Your troops appear to be in good condition; keep them well occupied, make sure you've got ample supplies of gunpowder, rockets and cannons. And we need to spend some time on our battle plan. Gujarat is vast, and the great number of rivalling fiefdoms complicates the situation. We will need to split up our forces, but make sure they remain well coordinated.'

'As Your Majesty commands. Your Majesty can count on me.'

Satisfied with what I had seen and heard, I continued my journey, and travelled further north, to Lahore, where I administered justice and disposed of the affairs of the country under the guise of hunting, as Abu-l Fazl would politely phrase it. From there, I returned to Agra, again passing through Ajmir, and sojourning at Sikri for a few weeks.

I was happy to see the buildings I had ordered were making excellent progress. The sleepy little town of yore had changed beyond recognition: on the rocky ridge, where there had been nothing but wilderness: palaces, mosques, courtyards, towers and gates were rising up everywhere, like young greens in the monsoon season. The Khari Nadi had been dammed, as I had ordered; the ensuing lake was starting to form, and looked wonderfully inviting.

The venerable old Shaykh was the first among the town elders to come out to greet me, although I noticed he was walking with difficulty, and seemed to be in pain. He bowed, bid me welcome and thanked me, politely and profusely – a bit too politely and too profusely, I thought – for the undeserved honor I had bestowed on their undeserving and insignificant humble little hamlet.

I could not help smiling. The old man, so my informants told me, had been wandering around the construction site, shaking his head, and sighing that he wished the Emperor had been a little less grateful to him.

I took his hands in mine, dismayed to feel how frail they had become since the last time we met.

'Do not worry, revered Master,' I said, 'you will see: I will make this a place of splendour, and piousness!'

He gave me a long, scrutinizing look. After what seemed to be an eternity, he seemed to be reassured. He smiled and raised both his hands in blessing.

'Verily, Your Majesty is the greatest of kings. May Allah bless and protect him! I will pray for Your Majesty – both here, and from beyond my grave!'

'*Khuda nakhasta*, reverend Master![177] I pray to Allah, that He may grant you many, many more years among us – we are in such dire need of your guidance and wisdom!'

'Your Majesty is most kind to say this, and I am touched by his friendship, but he knows as well as I do, that it is neither possible, nor desirable for me to go on living much longer. I am a weak, old man; my time has come to leave this transient world. More than nine decades have I lived on this earth, Your Majesty – twice or thrice the life span of most people! Would it not be ungrateful, nay, unworthy, if I were to ask Allah for even more?'

His eyes wandered off and looked at the village of Sikri.

'It gives me great comfort to know that I have spent a long and happy life in this village, in the service of Allah and the many people who have sought my help; it fills me with joy and pride to know that my name will be remembered by the generations to come, when the silsilah[178] is recited after the Friday evening prayers. But I have lived enough. I am old and tired, and I yearn for the sacred silence of the grave, where, in the comforting presence of Allah's blessed Angels Munkar and Nakir , I will prepare myself for the Last Day. From there, if it pleases Allah, I will pray for those who will come after me, and blissfully await the sound of the Angel Israfil's trumpet[179].'

[177] God forbid (Persian).

[178] Unbroken chain of Sūfī masters, reaching back all the way to the Holy Prophet Muhammad. All Sūfī orders trace their spiritual lineage to Muhammad through his son-in-law Alī, except for the *Naqshbandi* order, which traces its lineage through Abū Bakr, the Prophet's father-in-law and first Khalīfah of Islām.

[179] According to the Muslim tradition, Israfīl is the angel who will announce Judgement Day, whereas Munkar and Nakīr are the angels who interrogate the deceased and

Barely a few months later, the old man passed away. They found him one morning, lying on his prayer mat, his eyes half open, still staring at the Holy Qur'an that he had been reading. The holy book was opened – it can hardly be a coincidence – in the middle of Sura Yunus. The last thing the Shaykh's eyes saw in this world, must have been Aya 56[180]:

It is He Who gives life, and causes death,
and to Him you shall return.

I ordered his body to be laid to rest in the middle of the sahn-i-ibadat[181] opposite the Jama Mashid. Within a matter of days, his sacred tomb became a place of refuge for seekers of wisdom, help and consolation from all over the country; for indeed, the good Shaykh is praying for us, from yonder side of the grave.

prepare them for the final resurrection.

180 Qur'ān 10:56. *Yūnus,* the title of Sūra 10, is the Arabic name of the Biblical prophet Jonah.

181 Sahn-i-Ibādat: Sacred Complex. *Jami Mashid*: Friday Mosque.

Twenty-fourth Letter

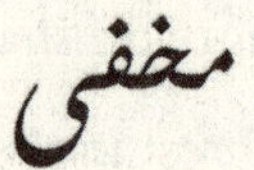

Makhfi[182]

From the Memoirs of Her Imperial Highness
Salima Sultana Begam[183] Chaqaniani

I have always enjoyed traveling: a change of air, a different landscape, the busyness of the encampments – welcome distractions, after long months at Court, where every day is drearily similar to the previous and the next.

Not that I have any reason to complain, and I really do not want to sound ungrateful – after all, who wouldn't want to live in a palace, safe and well protected, warm and comfortable in winter, cool in summer, with every imaginable convenience and luxury: beautiful gardens, water basins and fountains, exquisite food, beautiful clothes and jewellery, and scores of servants to attend to one's every wish?

Still, for all its comfort and luxury, and despite the many distractions and amusements, life does tend to get boring, when it is confined to the same buildings and the same faces, day in and day out.

I enjoy looking through the curtains of the palki[184], watching the changing landscape, and even more so, the people in the villages. I like

[182] 'The Hidden', artist name used by Salīmā as a poetess.

[183] Bēgam: Lady (Turkish).

[184] Palanquin.

to watch them leading their simple lives, tilling the land, tending their animals, preparing their food... They have little or no possessions, and very few moments of leisure, apart from the time they spend praying at their shrines and eating their frugal meals. Yet, it always strikes me, how, despite the poverty, the squalor and the dirt, they do not seem to be unhappy. I guess, they have all they need to be happy, provided their crops do not fail and they and their animals remain free from disease – indeed, what else does one really need, but freedom from hunger and disease, and the companionship of loved ones?

I've always been fascinated by the women, caring for their children, chatting with their mothers, sisters and friends; I've often wondered what my life would have been like, if I had been born among them, if I had been a simple farmer's wife, rather than one of the Emperor's many consorts.

One of many wives, indeed... Akbar's favorite, no doubt; the only one who has his ear, most certainly; but still, just one of many...

Again, I do not want to complain, and I would certainly not want to trade places with anyone. And after all, is that not the only relevant answer to the question of whether one is happy or not: whether one would like to be someone else? Still, it will not come as a surprise to anybody, that life in a powerful Emperor's zanana[185] is far from simple... How could it be, with over five thousand women living together inside a heavily guarded, walled city?

About three hundred of these five thousand women have ever shared Akbar's bed: his nikah and mut'ah[186] wives and concubines, plus the occasional pretty dancing girl that has managed to catch his attention. The rest of them are employed in the service of the zanana: from the well-dressed personal maidservants of the Begams, to the ragged cleaning women scavenging the sewers and latrines.

Every aspect of life is taken care of by females: cooking, cleaning, lighting, gardening, maintenance... everything. Even the guards inside the zanana walls are women: tough, strong, heavily armed female warriors from Turan and Afghanistan, recruited and trained especially

---

[185] Women's quarters, harem.

[186] Nikāh: official marriage. Mut'ah: temporary marriage, in principle allowed under Shī'a law only.

for this purpose. They will take orders from no one but the Emperor himself, and in his absence, from their officers who answer to the khwajasara[187]. There's but one gate connecting the zanana to the rest of the palace, and that is strictly guarded, every hour of the day and night. No male – not even the mukhanni[188] soldiers – will ever venture inside its enclosure, unless by the Emperor's express authorization.

Even among Akbar's officially wedded wives, there are many who will hardly ever get to see him in private. This should be no surprise either: most marriages have been concluded to seal an alliance with the new bride's family. If she has the misfortune of being rather plain-looking or otherwise uninteresting to him, she will not often meet him face to face after the marriage has been consummated! Most women inside the zanana thus, lead their lives without any male companionship; and this, in turn, will sometimes lead to friendships that – how shall I put it? – transgress the boundaries of sisterly affection...

Be this as it may: I do not mean to imply that Akbar treats any of his wives with neglect or disrespect. Indeed, he is most generous, to all of us: the highest-ranking women are paid staggeringly high salaries, of over one thousand rupees per month! In fact, Akbar's three most important spouses – Salim's mother, his first-wedded wife Ruqayyah, and I – receive no less than 1,610 rupees every month! Taking into account that many people survive on less than one rupee per month, that an average family in Agra (husband, wife and four children) can live quite comfortably off a mere five rupees per month, and that an entire tola[189] of pure gold will cost no more than ten rupees, it will be clear that we enjoy what the common people would call fabulous wealth.

And Akbar's generosity does not end there: at the occasion of both our solar and our lunar birthdays, on other festive occasions, and even for no particular reason at all, he will surprise us with lavish, not to say extravagant gifts of jewellery, clothes, perfumes, works of art, and the like. From time to time, he organizes a bazar inside the zanana, where the women sell their embroideries and handicrafts. On those occasions,

---

[187] The highest officer of the harem administration.

[188] Eunuchs.

[189] 1 *tola* = 11.66 grams.

he will always be in an excellent mood – kind and courteous to every single one of his wives, his favorites as well as the others – and will smilingly allow himself to be seduced into paying inordinate sums of money for the smallest trifles.

His open-handedness enables us to pursue whatever interest we have, and he allows us every freedom to do so.

Many highborn ladies, including his mother Hamida Banu Begam and our good-natured aunt Gulbadan, are spending fortunes on the construction of mosques, schools and other charitable projects. Humayun's other widow and first-wedded wife, Haji Begam, has busied herself deservingly with the construction of her late husband's magnificent mausoleum back in Dilli.

Salim's mother, on her part, appears to have inherited a singular talent for trade – all the more surprising, since this kind of activity, to my knowledge, has never been a tradition in her Rajput family, certainly not among the women! Anyway: as a pastime, she buys and equips scores of sea-going ships, has them laden with spices, silk and other goods, without ever leaving the zanana! Using a network of correspondents in various cities and seaports, she sells her merchandise to local and foreign traders from all over the world – Gujaratis, Sindhis, Persians, Arabs, and Firanghis[190] – often at twenty times the price she paid for it herself! Over the years, she has amassed a fortune of such immensity, that it would dwarf the treasury of many a king! Akbar strongly encourages her in her endeavours and will never fail to ask her about her undertakings. He is of course aware that she does not need the money, but all the same, he keeps paying her the same salary and buying her the same extravagant gifts he gives to the other wives.

I have to say, despite her being a Hindu and coming from an entirely different background, I have grown quite fond of her. I enjoy her conversation – an incessant stream of good-humoured babble (in quite faulty, but incredibly fast Persian, interspersed with lots of Hindi), about the most diverse subjects, ranging from bath oil and shoulder massage, to the equipment and crewing of ships!

Many times she has offered me the opportunity to join in with her in her undertakings, but I've always politely declined. Even though my

[190] 'Franks', i.e. Western Europeans.

personal wealth is much smaller than hers, I have more money than I could ever reasonably spend in ten lifetimes; and I have to say, I am not at all attracted to the tension and excitement that apparently is involved in trading activities. Every so often, she complains about ships lost at sea, or merchandise spoilt or stolen, but it never seems to put her off for more than a few hours. Every day, she prays and makes offerings to her elephant-headed god Ganeśa – to remove all the obstacles, she says – and to goddess Lakshmi, for wealth and prosperity. Nothing but superstitious nonsense, of course, but so far, it seems to have worked quite well for her! Akbar may be right after all: apparently, Allah does not really mind under which form we worship Him... Anyway, this much I know: trading is not for me, and it never will be. I am really a book person: I just love reading, and writing, the rustling of a well-cut qalam on paper. When the interests of our family do not require my attention elsewhere, I prefer to spend most of my time in the well-stocked library I have been able to build for myself over the years. As far as poetry is concerned, I am proud to say it rivals the imperial book collection!

Akbar likes to join me there, and often asks me to read to him from my collection. I must admit: I do enjoy these conversations very much.

Even after all these years, he keeps amazing me with his wit and knowledge – it's hardly imaginable that a man of such erudition is unable to read! Without a single mistake or hesitation, he will recite entire pages of Jalal-ud-Din Rumi, Sana'i, and Hafiz – and never fails to flatter me with extensive quotes from my own work as well...

What flatters me even more: he will always consult me about the affairs of state: new conquests; appointments he intends to make; firmans he wants to issue; disputes he needs to settle; roads, bridges, mosques and fortresses he wants to have built.... he will always carefully consider my opinion.

There are, to my knowledge, only three women Akbar will share his plans and concerns with. First and foremost, I am proud to say, there is me: if I am to believe his often-repeated assurances, I am his favorite, and without a doubt, his closest confidante. When he senses there is something I do not agree with, he will go to surprisingly great lengths to win me over. He sees me as a co-heiress of Babur's legacy, and appreciates what he calls my sound judgement.

Second, though not nearly as close to Akbar as I am, comes Salim's mother. Akbar highly respects and reveres her, as the mother of his first-born son and heir, but also appreciates her experience and quick wit. He's extremely interested in her trading activities, and even more so, in the information she has about the foreign traders she deals with. He will often ask her opinion in matters pertaining to the Hindus: religious sensitivities, relationships and rivalries among the innumerable castes and clans, and the like.

And then, of course, there's Akbar's own mother. Each time they meet, he will show her the highest respect: he will go out of his way to make sure she does not have to walk to meet him; he will help her dismount from her palki; he will even perform the taslim[191] and bend down to touch her feet as a sign of respect, before putting his arms around her shoulders to embrace her. On her part, she's visibly pleased with these lofty marks of honor – bestowed on nobody else in the Empire! – and she's justifiably proud of the incredible power and wealth her son has been able to amass in such a short period of time.

Yet, their relationship is not the easiest. Truth be told, she is not the easiest person to get along with either: hard to please, moody, used to getting her way in everything. They say that when she was only fifteen years old, it took her parents over forty days to convince her to take Humayun's marriage proposal into consideration!

Despite her admiration for Akbar's success, Hamida does not at all approve of her son's tolerance in religious matters. While she understands his reasons for an alliance with the Rajputs, she abhors the presence of Hindu shrines and priests in the imperial residence; she loathes the idea of her son joining his Hindu wife while she is worshipping the idols in her temple; she does not at all approve of her son participating in Holi, Diwali and the other Hindu festivals, and much less of him wearing a Hindu tikka on his forehead on those occasions!

And while she still appreciates to some extent the reasons behind his friendly attitude towards the Hindus, the presence of Firanghi priests at Court is a real thorn in her flesh. That he has invited them to find out more about the plans and ambitions of their rulers, is one

[191] Formal bow, whereby the back of the right hand touches the ground.

thing; but it's quite another, to make them permanent residents in the palace; to allow them the freedom to try and convert Muslims to their blasphemous errors; and not to silence them, when their foul-reeking mouths are hurling the worst insults at the Holy Prophet Muhammad, the blessings of Allah be upon him – how on earth is it possible that he allows this to happen?

'I really do not know what has possessed Akbar,' she often grumbles, 'to entertain those self-righteous, conniving, infidel bastards at his Court! How is it possible, that my son, a Muslim king, tolerates these outrageous insults of the Holy Prophet in his presence? If I had my way, I would have these slithering snakes beheaded, and all the other Nasraniyah[192] infidels thrown back in the sea, where they came from!'

She's tried several times to make him change his mind, and he in turn has tried to explain his reasons – but neither of them has been very successful.

Indeed, pious and God-fearing though he may be, Akbar is highly unorthodox. He knows all too well that many take offense; he knows that behind his back, people say he's betraying Islam; but he does not seem to care.

I remember one afternoon – we were having sherbet. Akbar's mother told him to his face that 'many good Muslims' at Court were scandalized he was praying with his back turned to Mekkah.

He merely smiled:

'I think I know who those 'good Muslims' are, mother... Please tell Makhdum ul Mulk, and all the other gossips, their comments remind me of that Sufi pilgrim who was found sleeping by the roadside in the Arabian desert, with his feet pointing in the direction of Mekkah. A mullah who happened to pass by, outraged at what he saw, rudely kicked him, shouting: 'You dirty pig! Are you not ashamed, your filthy feet pointing to Mekkah?'

Upon which the Sufi replied:

'I am so sorry I've offended you, honorable Sahab; I do beg your pardon, most humbly. If you kindly could point out, where in this world Allah is not present, I will gladly point my feet in that direction!'

---

[192] Nasrānīyah: 'Nazarean', i.e. worshipper of Jesus of Nazareth; Arabic term for Christian.

Akbar smiled, visibly pleased with his argument. Then, his face hardened.

'Revered mother, next time you see the right honorable Shaykh ul-Islam, tell him I do not, have never, and will never worship the sun, the moon, fire, or anything or anybody but Allah Himself! Tell him, I fully realize that the sun is but an insignificant spark compared to Allah's unspeakable majesty. But when I see the awesome, mysterious power Allah has put in fire and sunlight, I cannot but kneel humbly before Him Who has created all these wonders, next to Whom all the treasures of kings pale into insignificance! Rest assured, revered mother: I am a devout servant of Allah. But it seems I can hear His voice much more clearly in the silence of the desert, than amidst the noisy rituals of men. I feel His presence much more intensely when I see the sun, the mountains, the moon and the stars, than when I sit in the grandest man-made mosque – much more than when I have to listen to the pompous talk of Makhdum ul Mulk and the likes of him!'

The thorny subject of religion is now avoided altogether between Akbar and his mother, and whenever they meet, he will make sure to invite aunt Gulbadan, Ruqayyah and me to join them, so that he doesn't need to keep the conversation going all by himself. Hamida, in turn, rather than living at her son's Court, where she's constantly disturbed by things she does not approve of, prefers to live by herself. She usually resides in a beautiful palace in Dilli, where she runs her own household, with just a few confidantes to keep her company.

But in spite of all their differences: there is much tenderness and mutual respect between them; whenever the need arises, they will stand shoulder to shoulder to further the interests of our family.

Akbar clearly trusts and values his mother's wisdom and capabilities: for instance, at the time when he was leading his army to Kabul, to crush the rebellion up there, he has not hesitated to appoint her – her, not one of his generals – as the governor of Dilli; a task she performed admirably, by the way.

Women do play an important role in Akbar's life: he loves and reveres his mother; he's a gentle, caring, attentive husband; he respects us, much more than most other men respect their wives and mothers.

But sooner or later, we have to resign ourselves to the facts: he's not a one-woman man. He will never be the obedient son his mother would have liked him to be, and I fear he has never felt, for me or for anyone else, the burning passion the poets write about ...

I may as well face facts: I am not the love of his life; I am merely one of his best friends, who happens to be a woman he's attracted to. And that in itself makes me special, for real friends, people he will share his inner feelings with, he has but very few.

Now that Akbar is getting older and so much more predictable than before, things have settled down in the zanana. We all know where we stand, and over the years, we have become one family – with its fair share of gossip and petty quarrels, no doubt; but, thank God, with plenty of warm-hearted friendship as well.

It hasn't always been like that – not at all! When I married Akbar, the zanana was a cesspool of strife and jealousy of the worst possible kind! The breast of men has no milk, people say in Arabic – implying that men have no mercy, whereas women do. I do not know who invented this nonsense, but nonsense it is: there is nothing nastier on the face of this earth than the mind of a jealous woman. Gossiping, spying, intriguing... what could be more interesting to women who have little else to keep them busy? To make things worse: the maids and servants join in with their mistresses' quarrels, and will do whatever to stoke up the fire. Most of them run a secret but flourishing trade in charms, spells, amulets, potions, salves and the like – magic charms and perfumes to awaken the Emperor's desire; spells to secure his continuing love and devotion; potions to promote the buyer's pregnancy and to make sure her child will be male and healthy; amulets to avert the evil eye; curses to destroy their rivals, to make them unattractive and their wombs barren, to make their babies stillborn – or at the very least, female.

I remember as if it was only yesterday: a few days after my wedding, I had hardly taken up residence in the palace, when I had a short but laden conversation with Ruqayyah – normally the nicest person one could imagine, and actually one of my very best friends.

'So sweet of the Emperor that he has taken pity on you, after everything that happened to your husband, 'she said, in a compassionate tone of voice, and feigned sadness on her face.

'Yes, my cousin and I have always been very close,' I replied, with an equally friendly smile, which I hoped would look as condescending as possible. Better to be envied than pitied, the saying goes; and there is much truth in that.

Whether Ruqayyah and the others liked it or not: it was evident Akbar hadn't married me out of pity. The first few months, hardly a night went by without him sharing my bed, his passion awakened by a new body to explore – a body, as he smilingly confessed, about which he had often fantasized. He's a vigorous, passionate, attentive lover, and it would be a lie to pretend I am insensitive to this kind of attention: a woman who claims not to care whether or not she's attractive, is either dishonest, or abnormal.

I do not think I ever fooled myself into believing that I would remain the only woman in his life; but I have to admit, that the first time he went with another girl, I had my share of the feelings Ruqayyah must have had.

It was one late afternoon in the courtyard. Akbar had ordered a dancing performance of a new group of artists, recently brought to Court and trained by Tansen. All of Akbar's spouses had been invited, and as usual, I sat next to him. He had indicated that after the performance, he would join me in my quarters, if I wanted to receive him.

It was a truly festive occasion. We received gifts, exquisite clothes and jewellery; succulent food and drinks were served, and the performance, which went on until well after dark, was spectacular. The dancers and musicians were talented; the performance was outstanding. Akbar enjoyed it tremendously, and it soon became obvious that he was taking a lively and more than musical interest in the leading dancing girl, who, much as I hate to admit it, was quite pretty.

I watched him throughout the performance, clapping his hands, laughing, staring shamelessly at the girl's plump, wiggling breasts and shaking hips. She, in turn, clearly aware of his attention, openly smiled at him.

I could have slapped her, have her flogged, but what could I do? What indeed, but smile, and pretend to be amused? I spent the rest of the afternoon keeping up appearances, smiling, chatting, hoping no one would notice my anger and disappointment, knowing all too well that that hope was in vain: tomorrow morning, the entire zanana would know, that Akbar had spent the night with that vulgar slut, and not with me.

I managed to remain outwardly calm and relaxed, but retired to my quarters as early as I decently could, making some vague excuse about being tired and having had too much to eat. Contrary to my habit – much as I like wine at dinner with friends, I hardly ever drink on my own – I ordered an ice-cooled pitcher of wine. I drank, goblet after goblet, almost the entire pitcher; but rather than giving me the light-heartedness I was looking for, it made my mood even more sombre.

I did fall asleep, but not for long. I woke up in the middle of the night, with a pounding headache and a sour, burning stomach. I called the servant to bring me some lightly salted lassi[193], which quickly eased the heartburn, but I did not manage to go to sleep again. The rest of the night, I lay wide awake, angrier by the hour – angry with that arrogant dancing whore; angry with Akbar, angry with all men: insensitive, selfish pleasure-seekers, every one of them; dogs, eager to jump every bitch crossing their path...

I must have finally dozed off around dawn, for it was late in the morning when a servant came in to wake me, handing me an invitation from Akbar's mother to join her for the noon meal.

I bathed and dressed hurriedly and went to Hamida's quarters. She received me as usual, courteously but rather formally, conscious of her rank.

We chatted for quite a while, about the summer heat, the deplorable quality of the newly arrived fruit, Hamida's building projects, and similar harmless but hardly relevant subjects. But it was quite obvious that she had not just invited me to talk about the fruit and the weather. Throughout the conversation, she kept looking at me, askance, scrutinizing every expression on my face, keenly observing how much – or how little – I was eating.

'You do not seem to be hungry, my dear, 'she said, 'are you feeling unwell?'

'I've had too much to eat yesterday, and didn't sleep very well', I confessed.

'It must be all that wine, 'she said, making no attempt to hide her disapproval.

'I know what you are going to say, Salima. Akbar, Humayun, Babur,

[193] Yoghurt drink.

the entire Gurkaniyya dynasty, and all those other Chagatai savages: they think rather casually about drinking wine and spirits; but true believers shouldn't forget Allah has warned us against the dangers of drinking sharab[194]! Who are we, to think His commandments do not apply to us? Yes, I know what you are going to say, Allah is compassionate, merciful, all-forgiving; He knows our weaknesses, better than we know them ourselves! And no, I do not believe people who drink will be punished in hell... not for long, anyway. But do you believe that Allah would warn us against all these things, just for the sake of forbidding them? No! He forbids them for our own good, He knows what is best for us; and those who submit to His will, will never be disappointed!'

She made an impatient, dismissive gesture, as if annoyed with her own nagging.

'Anyway, I didn't invite you here to talk about drinking. I want to talk about you, and Akbar, and our family.'

She smiled and put her hand on mine.

'You did very well, last night, my child! I've carefully observed you: you didn't show how much Akbar's interest in that dancing girl upset you. You acted as if you didn't care, and indeed, that's exactly the way you should feel!'

She looked at me inquisitively, trying to guess what I was thinking.

'Listen to me, Salima! Do not let a trivial incident like this get to you, for that's all it is: a trivial incident! Yes, Akbar slept with a dancing girl, so what? That's the way he is, and for reasons known to Allah alone, that's the way most men are! Do not make yourself unhappy, fretting about things that are of no importance and that you cannot change! Believe me, we all have been through this. Sooner or later, we all have! Do you think my late husband Humayun – may Allah receive him in paradise! – ever stopped sleeping with dancing girls after he married me? Of course not!

Still, as you know and everybody knows, he always held me in the highest respect! Always have I been his favorite – he would go out of his way to please me, and hardly ever has he done anything that I didn't approve of!

And that's exactly the kind of influence you have on Akbar, Salima

194 Wine, alcoholic beverage.

– perhaps even more than I had on Humayun! He listens when you speak, he values your opinion, more than that of his most prominent advisors, more than that of his own mother!'

She stared pensively at the lamps in the back of the room, a bitter smile on her face.

'Men are like greedy little children, Salima! An attractive woman is a plaything to them, a toy they've got to have, as soon as they cast their eyes upon her; but once they have it, they very quickly lose their interest!

That a man wants to sleep with you, does not make you special, my child: what does make you special, is that you are his companion, that he listens to you!'

She suddenly leaned over to me, and took me by the shoulders. I was surprised to see tears in her eyes.

'Think about it, Salima, 'she insisted, 'think about who you are! you are not some vulgar concubine, whose livelihood depends on her prowess in bed! You are a queen, a queen of imperial blood, a Gurkaniyya princess!'

She let go of me and leaned back on her pillow.

'There's many ways to be an Emperor's wife, my child, 'she proceeded, with resignation in her voice, and a feeble, scornful smile on her face. 'Admittedly, there is only one woman who can lay claim to the title of first-wedded spouse. But what is that, other than an empty title? Does it not make her solitude even harder to bear, when willingly or unwillingly, she has to make room for other, younger, prettier women?

More enviable it is, to be his favorite, the one who ensnares him with her charms, and makes him drunk and foolish with lust. But more often than not, that triumph will be short-lived; for what is more common than a woman's body? And what body is more attractive than the one yet to be possessed?

No, my child: by far the strongest is she, who has managed to gain her husband's friendship and confidence: those are lasting sentiments, they do not depend on base attractiveness. Even when old age will have extinguished the fires of carnal lust in him, he will still be capable of affection!'

She again leaned over to me, gently touching my face.

'The most powerful and enviable is she who combines it all: the high-ranking spouse, who also is his favorite lover, his best friend, and the mother of his successor! Every day, I pray for you, my child! I pray, that this may happen to you; that you may become the mother of Akbar's first-born son. There's no other woman in the entire Empire who would be a more suitable Queen Mother! You are cultivated, wise; noble blood flows through your veins, and you have your husband's ear! Think about the influence you have! Do not let your mind be distracted by trivial things! Suppose, just for the sake of the argument, that Allah, in His wisdom, should decree that some other woman is to become the mother of Akbar's successor. Just imagine, that the child would be born from the womb of one of the Hindu wives, *Khuda nakhasta*![195] It would be even more important that you remain Akbar's favorite! The child's education would depend on it!'

It took me several days to regain my peace of mind. She was right, but that wasn't much of a consolation: Allah may have created us as reasonable creatures, but it takes more than reason to convince the heart. Jealousy is like black, bitter ink, its stains much easier made than washed out...

Fortunately, Akbar made it easy to forgive him.

The day after my meeting with Hamida, he sent me a message, asking me whether I would allow him to join me for the evening meal.

While friendly and courteous as always, he seemed rather tense. Clearly determined to avoid any awkward silence in the conversation, he talked incessantly, about every imaginable subject – except women. He spent some time discussing the affairs of state: his courtiers, measures he intended to take, and the like. Knowing my interest in the arts, he also talked about paintings he had ordered, buildings he had commissioned, poetry, and music – painstakingly avoiding any reference to the music performance two days earlier... and the plump-breasted dancing girl that had ruined my evening.

Near the end of the meal – it was deep in the night already and we were both getting tired – he suddenly asked:

'Salima, would you like to come with me on a hunting trip tomorrow?

[195] God forbid (Persian).

'I need to get out of the palace for a few days,' he explained, before I was able to answer.

'I desperately need some air, some peace and quiet, and a bit of exercise: horseback riding, walking, swimming in the river, eating in the open air... Would you like to come with me?'

I again wanted to answer, but he quickly went on, as if to prevent me from saying no.

'Besides, I would really like to spend some time alone with you, Salima! I need someone to talk to, a friendly face, someone who understands me, someone to give me some honest advice... There are so many important things I want to talk to you about, and we never seem to have enough time on our own in the palace!'

As usual, Akbar had made it virtually impossible for me to refuse. He has a way of getting what he wants, without actually giving direct orders. But I have to confess, I really loved the prospect of getting out of the palace for a few days.

We left at dawn on the next morning – that would allow us to travel to the hunting grounds in the wilderness, while it was still cool. At my explicit request, I did not travel in a palki, but spent the entire day riding next to Akbar, on an exquisite Iraqi white mare, one of the finest horses in the imperial stables, strong and fast as the wind, but very good-natured and docile. Before mounting her, I fed her a few greens and some sweets, talking to her, patting her neck and gently caressing her soft muzzle, to allow her to get used to my scent and the sound of my voice. The animal seemed to develop an instant liking for me, and I was very much looking forward to riding her for a few days.

We left Agra, accompanied by a strong escort of about two hundred horse archers, who would act as game drivers if Akbar wished to hunt, and protect us against any conceivable danger – human or animal – along the way.

Following us was a small train of not more than five pack animals and about twenty servants. Clearly, Akbar wanted this to be a simple excursion, not one of those grandiose expeditions his hunting parties usually turn into; he wanted to camp in the open, not in the luxurious city-like camps that are built wherever he travels.

I was appropriately dressed for the occasion, in a white hunting costume, quite similar to the clothing of the Arab nomads. As long as we travelled in sight of the escort, I covered my face with the long trailing piece of my turban, but as soon as we were riding through the open country, Akbar ordered the escorts to distance themselves about one hundred and fifty paces from us, so that we could enjoy some privacy, and I could unveil my face.

It felt a bit odd at first to be back in the saddle: I hadn't been on horseback since my youth in Kabul. Fortunately, riding is one of those skills that are never lost, once acquired. Before long, I found myself racing against Akbar – extremely satisfied to find that my mare was as fast as his stallion.

'Well, that was real Turkish blood at work,' he panted admiringly, after a long gallop at breakneck speed, where despite a few attempts, he had not managed to shake me off. 'I very much doubt if there is any woman in all of Hindustan who rides like this! Clearly, my dear wife and cousin, the blood of Genghis Khan and Temür the Iron is flowing in your veins, as it is in mine!'

'This is a magnificent horse you've given me,' I said, not knowing how else to react to the compliment. 'It is truly a pleasure to ride her!'

'She's a beauty, indeed, and she seems to like you a lot – as if you had worked with her for years! Well, she's yours, Salima – I would know of no better mistress for her!'

I thanked him, quite pleased with such a precious gift, but thought to myself, I would have little opportunity to really enjoy her – a quiet trot in a courtyard is really not the same as galloping in the middle of the wilderness...

Akbar must have sensed what I was thinking.

'We should do this much more often, Salima – then you will have more opportunity to really enjoy her! Life in a palace can get boring after a while, don't you agree?'

'Indeed it can be, 'I snapped, maybe a bit harshly, 'I must say, I often envy you men – your lives may be more dangerous than ours, but also, so much more exciting!'

'Well, yes, but...'

'Anyway, I can't tell you how much I am enjoying this trip – I really have to thank you!'

'There's hardly any need for that. It is I who am obliged to you, that you agreed to come with me!'

He turned astride in the saddle, looking intently at me.

'You know, I really like being with you, Salima! Of all the people in the world, you are the one I feel closest to... you know that, don't you?'

Before I could answer, he continued:

'You know, it's really true what they say: no lonelier place than the Throne! Power creates distance; there is hardly anybody I can really talk to, the way normal people can. You, Salima, you are the one closest to me! We share the same blood, you are not afraid of me as most other people are, and I know of no other woman as learned and wise as you are!'

I smiled faintly and looked down, not knowing how else to react.

'I also want to tell you, Salima, how impressed I am, and how much I appreciate you looking after little Abdurrahim the way you do! I really like that little fellow, you know, and I want the very best for him! He's so polite, so smart – it's unbelievable for a small boy his age! He's perfectly fluent in Turki, Persian and Hindi; he knows all the classics; he quotes from his father's writings – and all that, thanks to you, because you have taught him! And not only will he, thanks to you, most certainly grow up to be a wise and learned man; I believe he will be a great soldier as well, just like his father! I've watched him wrestling other boys: he is fast and strong, and brave, not at all afraid to hurt himself! And have you noticed how well he handles that wooden sword I've given him? I'm telling you, Salima, if he continues like this, I will make him as rich and powerful as his glorious father, may the peace of Allah be upon him!

'You know I really mean what I say, Salima. I know there have been regrettable misunderstandings between Bairam Khan and me, but I will forever be grateful for what he has done for me, and I will take care of his son, as long as I live!'

'You are a good man, Akbar, 'I murmured, fighting back my tears. 'I am grateful you are honoring my late husband's memory, and I really appreciate how much you are taking Abdurrahim's future at heart! May it please Allah, to send His angels to comfort Bairam Khan in his grave, and tell him, how well his little boy is doing!'

'Allah kare[196],' Akbar nodded in assent, piously raising his hands upward.

---

[196] May it please Allāh, may Allāh do so.

He steered his horse next to mine and leaned over to me, putting his hand on my arm and gently touching my cheek with the back of his middle and forefinger.

'Every day, I pray, Salima, that Allah may give me a strong and healthy son, one just like Abdurrahim, a son who will one day be my successor... and each time, I pray, that he may be born from you, for there is no one in the entire Empire who would be a more suitable mother to my son! But if, Khuda nakhasta, he's not: if he's to be born from another woman, you must promise me you will help me to raise him as your own! Regardless of the womb that has carried him: you have to be his mother, Salima! There's so many things only you can teach him: you can tell him about his ancestors, you can teach him to speak perfect Turki as well as Persian and Hindi, you alone can see to it that he grows up as a real Gurkaniyya prince and a worthy Emperor of Hindustan!'

In spite of the gravity of the moment, I could not help but smile, wondering whether perhaps Hamida had spoken to him.

'Well, will you, Salima?'

'Of course, I will be honored to do so, 'I said, putting my hand on his, and leaning over to kiss him on the lips – something he was clearly not expecting, and highly pleased by.

'When the time is there, 'I continued, 'it will, *In sha'a Llah*, be my privilege and sacred duty to help your son to grow up to be a great king! You may rest assured that I will teach, help and protect him to the best of my ability!'

'Thank you so much, Salima. You have no idea how much this means to me,' Akbar said softly, putting his arm around my shoulders and kissing me tenderly on the lips.

'You know, if we stick together and help each other, there's absolutely nothing in this world we cannot achieve!'

We travelled for the better part of the day, deeper and deeper into the imperial hunting grounds, taking only a few hours rest at high noon. We must have been at least nine or ten kos from any inhabited area, when, in the late afternoon, Akbar ordered the camp to be set up, on a beautiful, broad stretch of sandy shore, next to a wide river bend.

The soldiers secured the area, posting guards all around the encampment on both sides of the river, at a distance of about two hundred paces from us. Again, we were perfectly safe, yet far enough from the soldiers to be on our own.

A comfortable tent had been set up for us, but we decided to have our food outside, on the sand, enjoying the balmy evening and the changing colours of the sky and the water. When the sun was almost down, the servants lit maybe a hundred oil lamps, scattered all over the sand. We sat down in front of a simmering charcoal fire, similar to the one, a bit further, on which the servants were preparing our food for the evening: bread, vegetables and meat in gravy, prepared in tandoor clay ovens, and other pieces of meat, deliciously seasoned and carefully roasted on skewers above the glowing embers.

All of the meat we were eating had been hunted during our trip. Contrary to his habit, Akbar had left most of the hunting to his soldiers. The whole day, he had ridden next to me, pleasantly chatting, or whistling some or other popular song.

On two occasions, though, he showed us his remarkable riding and hunting prowess. First, chasing a large deer that had been driven towards us by the soldiers, he killed his prey with a single spear thrust between the shoulder blades. The next time, he shot a small antelope with his bow, at a distance of at least thirty paces, while riding at a full gallop. He hit the animal behind the left shoulder, right through the heart, killing it before it even hit the ground. The arrow shaft had gone in all the way up to the quills. I knew, he was showing off his prowess – do men not often feel the need to behave like that in public? Still, I was extremely impressed, and proud to be married to so strong a man. It was no coincidence that Akbar was held in such high respect by his soldiers.

When we had almost finished eating, Akbar ordered the servants to bring us two more pitchers of wine and two of Ganga water, in buckets of crushed ice – a luxury he would rarely do without – and we spent another hour or so in pleasant conversation, indulging in the deliciously cool drinks.

When I assumed a different sitting position, I must have inadvertently twisted my face into a painful grimace.

'Anything wrong?' Akbar inquired.

'My legs are a bit stiff, from that day on horseback – it's much more than what I'm used to,' I confessed.

'Let's take a walk by the river. Nothing like a leisurely walk to get rid of cramps and stiffness!'

He took me by the hand and helped me up. We walked towards the river, and he put his arm around my waist. We strolled for a while, looking in silence at the star-lit sky and the moon's silver reflection on the water. I thoroughly enjoyed the feeling of the cool wavelets and the soft river sand under my bare feet.

Behind a small bush, where he was sure the guards could not see us, Akbar stopped, gently pulled me towards him, and kissed me, softly at first, then, full of passion, caressing my back and neck, and softly running his fingers through my hair. Suddenly, he picked me up and carried me, as easily as if I were a small child, to our tent.

There, in the soft light of the oil lamps, we spent a nearly sleepless, wonderful night – one I will never forget, for the rest of my life.

My strong, dear husband! So formidable and awe-inspiring to the mightiest of the mighty, so kind and just towards the weak, so warm and gentle towards me! How often have I observed him through the stone lattice windows of the zanana, and admired him for the natural, self-evident ease with which he carries the heavy burden of his divine office!

They say that as a young boy, he was lazy, moody and unpredictable.

If that is indeed the case, he has clearly mended his ways: nothing in the Empire escapes his attention. And never once will he forget God: he may be king of kings, builder of empires, conqueror of lands, subduer of nations; but deep down, he has the soul of a faqir, a saintly errant, desiring nothing else but to plunge his soul in the silent depths of the Divine.

And like most of this kind of people, he cares very little about the generally accepted practices – hence his highly unorthodox way of praying, and his remarkably tolerant attitude towards non-Muslim religions, despite the offence it gives to his own mother and so many other good Muslims.

I've always been astounded at the calm resolve with which Akbar has been able to impose his will in these thorny matters. The first years of his reign, he was still relatively careful in his utterances and practices. But now, with every rebellion crushed and all the neighbouring kingdoms conquered, he makes no scruples whatsoever about doing exactly as he pleases: praying according to strange rituals of his own; organizing nightly debates about religion; allowing infidels to worship according to their beliefs – even at Court! – and granting them the same rights and privileges as Muslims.

I suspect there is more than one reason why he is doing this: he wants to promote peace and understanding among his subjects, no doubt; but he also wants to make clear that on this earth, the ultimate authority is his, and his alone. Regardless of their religious beliefs, whether they worship God in a mosque, a temple or a church: his subjects cannot be loyal servants of God, if they do not serve their lawful Emperor.

This is Akbar's ultimate message to everyone: his Court is the axis of the world; he is the centre, the middle point around which everything revolves; he, and only he is the authorized exponent of the divine will; he stands above all ulama and priests, of whatever belief or denomination; he, and no one else, is the bridge between God and men, the source of all power and majesty; he wants his Throne to be like the sun: radiating with justice, benevolence and kindness, but also, with awesome power and unattainable Majesty.

In every respect, he's the embodiment of Kingship itself – benevolent, charming, endearing, lovable; but imposing, unattainable, daunting.

Everything about him commands respect and awe: the way he dresses, walks and sits; his square-shouldered, strong and muscular build; the ease with which he controls the unruliest animals; his loud, thundering voice, which at times can be so enchantingly soft and warm.

I really admire the way he handles visitors and supplicants of all kinds and castes, listening intently to what they have to say, his head dropping slightly towards the right shoulder, his face either expressionless, or smiling faintly. Whatever the subject, whatever the time of day, and no matter how long he has been sitting in the audience hall, he will always respond with lucidity and wisdom.

As a rule, he will be remarkably kind and forgiving towards even the worst transgressors. It would be foolish, however, to mistake his generosity for weakness: warm-hearted though he may be, he can be quite ruthless and lethal when crossed.

No matter how friendly his smile, how kind his manners, there is a deep moat between him and the people around him – a moat, or some kind of glass wall, behind which everyone can see him, but no one can come near him.

His innermost thoughts will usually remain hidden, behind an inscrutable mask of courtesy and majesty. He may be the most open, friendly and accessible king and husband one could imagine; yet, he remains a mystery, even to his closest friends and family. Rarely, if ever, will he reveal his true feelings to anyone... except, from time to time, to me, and to Abu-l Fazl, when he was still alive.

'No lonelier place than the Throne, 'he often complains. I believe he honestly means it... and I think it explains the sombreness that so often befalls him, despite the incredible power he wields. With the Throne comes the daunting, God-given task to put it to good use; and also, utter loneliness, because in the end, the decision – and the responsibility before Allah – is his, and his alone.

It's not always easy to be married to a man of this stature. It's a privilege to be able to counsel and assist him, to know him more intimately than anybody else does. But I have to share the burden of an Empire with him.

Despite the wealth and comfort in which we both live, we're never at ease. We have a duty to fulfil: to preserve and protect the heritage of our ancestors, and to provide a future for our posterity.

In more than one respect, I share Akbar's solitude. If we would have been born as common people – simple farmers, maybe, or city merchants, or countryside nobles in a remote region, we would certainly have had a different marriage altogether. A tighter bond would have united us; I think we would have been inseparable companions.

Now, alas, I am merely an occasional visitor in his life – as he is in mine.

He is and remains the great King and Conqueror *Akbar-e-Azam*; and I am and will always be *Makhfi*, the Hidden.

Such is life: we were born alone, and we will die alone... Our family and friends, our spouse, our children: they are but fellow travellers, whom we meet along the way; and the higher and mightier we are, the more we walk alone.

Twenty-fifth Letter

گجرات

Gujarat (I)

Gujarat ... Its unfettered independence had been a thorn in my flesh for quite a long time, but now, I finally saw my way clear to add it to my dominions.

The road to it lay wide open, now that Rajastan and Malwa were mine; and the country was in dire need of a just ruler, one who could give it order, peace, and justice.

As I said earlier, the kingdom had fallen prey to utter chaos and anarchy. The rebellious Mirzas, driven out of Hindustan, had made themselves masters of the south, whereas in the north, Muzaffar Shah III, the nominal king – of doubtful legitimacy, as one chronicler aptly put it – had become a mere puppet in the hands of rivalling nobles who had divided the country among themselves.

One of them, I'timad Khan, cornered by an alliance between Muzaffar and one Sher Khan Fuladi, sent me a urgent message, begging me to intervene, and to reclaim the rightful inheritance of my most noble and august Father, and thus, bring to the country of Gujarat the justice, peace and prosperity enjoyed by the lands fortunate enough to live under the protection of the Commander of the Faithful, His Majesty Jalal-ud-Din Muhammad Akbar Padshah Ghazi, Emperor of Hindustan, Shadow of God on this earth.

This was all the encouragement I needed. To conquer Gujarat was my legal right, and it was my manifest destiny. Thus, on the 21st of Tir of the Seventeenth Year[197], the army left Sikri and headed east.

Underway, in Ajmir, it was my pleasure to supervise the arrangements for yet another imperial birth: one of the concubines in the zanana, a young Afghan, whose blue eyes, fair complexion and slender waist had caught my attention nine months earlier, was with child, and would, so the physicians informed me, not be able to continue on the journey with the cortege.

She and her retinue were installed in the house of the venerable old Shaykh Danyal, himself one of Khwajah Muin ud Din's successors and the most prominent attendant of the sacred shrine. I decided that if, in sha'a Llah, she would give birth to a boy, I would call him Danyal, in honor of his esteemed protector.

Day after day, I went to the shrine to pray, asking God for the safe and successful birth of another healthy and strong son, and invoking His almighty help and guidance in the war I was about to fight.

The remainder of my time, I used to my advantage surveying the final preparations for the invasion and discussing marching routes and battle plans with my army commanders.

Out of precaution – lest Muhammad Hakim or anyone else would try to take advantage of my absence – I also sent a sizeable fighting force up north, to the Panjab. Under the command of Birbal and Yusuf Khan, they were to reinforce the Lahore garrison and beat back any would-be invader.

For the attack on Gujarat itself, a powerful vanguard of ten thousand horse was to ride ahead, while I would follow two weeks later with the rest of the army. The strength and mobility of this advance guard and the distance between my two fighting forces would allow me to keep fully abreast of the strength and whereabouts of the enemy forces, and adapt my battle plans accordingly.

Thus, we proceeded. On the 31st of Mordad[198], the vanguard rode out of Ajmir; among them, a good number of my best officers. I marched forth on the 20th of Shahrivar[199], at the head of the other troops.

---

[197] Wednesday, July 2, 1572 (Julian Calendar).

[198] August 12, 1572 (Julian Calendar).

[199] September 1.

Apart from a disturbing but altogether insignificant incident in southern Rajastan, where I had to exterminate a band of rebels – loyalists of the rana of Mewar, no doubt – who had made the fatal mistake of trying to hinder my vanguard, the advance was uneventful – more a leisurely excursion than an arduous campaign.

One day, while we were hunting on the way to replenish the supply of meat , Citr Najan, my best cheetah, was chasing a deer, when suddenly a ravine appeared in front of them. The deer leapt into the air, a spear and a half high, and made itself across. To our astonishment, the cheetah, in its eagerness to catch its prey, didn't even slow down. With a lightning jump, it cleared the ravine, and going on at the same breathtaking speed, caught and killed the deer. All praised Allah, for this was, as everybody acknowledged, a very good omen.

A good omen it was, indeed: only a few days later, I received the news that my beloved third son Danyal had been born, on the 28th of Shahrivar[200], and was in excellent health. Shaykh Salim Chishti's prophecy had been fulfilled.

When the messenger brought me these good tidings, I dismounted from the elephant I was riding, knelt down in the direction of Mekkah, and pressing my forehead in the dust of the road, rendered thanks to the Almighty.

I did not return to Ajmir to pray at Khwajah Muin ud Din's shrine – there was a war to be fought and the advance guard counted on my support – but did decide to strike camp for a few days, spending many hours in prayer at the local mosques, and organizing, as is customary, splendid feasts in celebration of the birth of the new prince. Generous gifts were distributed to the people in the area; as Abu-l Fazl phrased it so elegantly, the coin of liberality was poured into the lap of the world.

I ordered that as soon as Danyal would be one month old, he was to be sent to Amber, to be entrusted to the care of Raja Bhagwan Das' spouse – another sign of the bonds of friendship and loyalty that united us.

After the festivities, I hurriedly proceeded further south. It was time to reclaim the throne my father had once occupied.

As we neared the border, the reports were most encouraging.

[200] September 9.

Muzaffar Shah, the Gujarati king, struck with panic on hearing about the approach of the mighty imperial army, had head over heels deserted his capital Ahmedabad, leaving his former ally Sher Khan Fuladi in charge of its defense. The latter, however, had himself deserted the city immediately thereafter. He was now heading south, to the region of Surat, where, no doubt, he was hoping to find new allies.

I ordered the army to proceed straight on to Ahmedabad, but first sent Raja Man Singh with a body of troops in pursuit of Sher Khan Fuladi's two sons: according to our informants, their father had sent them to the area of Pattan to bring their family and goods to places of safety; they were now heading south again to rejoin their father. As I expected, Man Singh routed their force without too much trouble. The two brothers managed to escape in the wilderness, but their valuable baggage fell into our hands.

On the 26th of Aban [201], I finally crossed the Gujarat border, and marched triumphantly into the city of Pattan, hailed and cheered by the local people as their liberator. I was showered with flowers and gifts, and the town elders, who had come to pay their respects, thanked Divine Providence that they could now peacefully eat their bread in the comforting shadow of His Majesty's kindness.

For a few days, we struck camp before the gates of Pattan.

Not without apprehension, I invited young Abdurrahim to join me for a short trip to Lake Sahansa Lang, on the shores of which, thirteen years before, his father Bairam Khan had met his untimely death, at the filthy hands of a stinking, coward assassin.

The delightful breeze and peaceful atmosphere around the blue waters of the lake seemed unreal. This was a place of repose, a place to make one's peace with God and the world – not a place for a good man to die!

I looked at Abdurrahim, strolling up and down the shore, squinting against the sun. He said nothing.

In silence, both of us absorbed in our own thoughts, we proceeded to the shrine of Shaykh Husam ud Din, where Bairam Khan's body had been laid to rest.

The shrine was in the immediate vicinity of the main mosque, and

---

[201] November 7.

was, as usual, surrounded by a tranquil courtyard where pilgrims gather before and after prayers. In its sacred shadow were a few simple graves, and our guide pointed to the most modest of them all. There, under a small nameless headstone, the great Khan Khanan of the Mughal Empire had been laid to rest.

We stood in silence before the grave. How terrible is death, I thought, how unjust: to reduce a life, so filled with greatness and nobility, to the impotent, numb silence of a nameless stone!

I bowed respectfully and started praying aloud in Arabic, as once Bairam Khan himself had done at the foot of my father's casket in Sirhind:

'Peace be upon you, O dwellers of the grave!
May Allah grant you and us protection!
We pray to Allah for security, for ourselves and for you.
You are those who have gone before us, and we are following you.
We will meet you, if it pleases Allah.'

The words sank into my soul. O, God, I thought, may it please You that one day, Bairam Khan and I may be reunited! What kind of Paradise can it be, o God, if we are to be deprived of the company of our friends and loved ones?

I knelt down, put my hands and forehead on the grave for a few moments, and remained there, in silence. When I rose to my feet again, I went to stand next to Abdurrahim, and whispered softly, in Turki, my eyes full of tears:

'God's peace be upon you, forever and ever, my faithful friend, my strong *ataliq*, my trusted guide, my beloved second father! Look: your son and I have come from afar to pay our respects, and to tell you, we have been taking good care of what you have left behind. Standing on your shoulders, noble Khan Khanan, we have seen far, and our arms have been victorious: Chittor, Ranthambhore, Kalinjar: they have all fallen, they are ours, and we promise you, it's only the beginning!'

I paused, and put my hand on Abdurrahim's shoulder.

'Behold your son, my friend – see what a strong and handsome young man he has become! You would be proud of him, my friend – a full-blooded Turkoman warrior, just like his father! You should see him on a horse – he rides like the devil, spears an apple at full gallop! He will go far, this son of yours: he's only seventeen, but already one of the best commanders in the army! And this I promise you, my friend, on your grave and on my own life, I will take care of him!'

All the time, Abdurrahim had said nothing, his head bowed deeply, staring at the headstone, his eyes glistening with tears.

When it was time for us to leave, he knelt down, kissed his father's grave and put his hands and forehead on it, as I had done; he then came back to me, fell to his knees, and kissed the edge of my cloak.

I made him rise to his feet again, and patted him on the shoulder.

'Henceforth, you will be the protector of your father's grave, Abdurrahim: from now on, the city of Pattan and its surroundings are your personal jagir!'

'Your Majesty is most kind,' he answered, 'and I swear to God that I will be worthy of Your Majesty's confidence!'

He hesitated for a moment and said, apologetically:

'With Your Majesty's permission, I would at some time in the future wish to move my father's remains to a resting place nearer to Your Majesty's capital. You see, Your Majesty, ...'

'Of course, my young friend! Nothing would please me more than to build for your father the tomb a man of his stature deserves! You decide when and where, I will see to it that it gets done!

Let me tell you, though what your father said to me, when I was your age, standing in front of my own father's casket: to take care of your father's grave is highly commendable; but by far the most important thing , is to make him proud!'

He bowed deeply and wanted to sink to his knees again, but I took him by the arm.

'Let's go back, Abdurrahim, we have work to do before Gujarat is ours!'

The next day at dawn, we broke up camp and headed further to Ahmedabad.

On the march, I tasted the satisfaction of accepting the submission of the fugitive king, Muzaffar Shah – my scouts had found him, hiding in a field, scared to death.

He fell to his knees, his face streaming from every pore, mumbling flowery phrases of abject flattery – about daring to approach the sacred dust of Your Majesty's feet, and being granted the privilege of making it the salve of his weary eyes, and of placing his entire submission and complete devotion at the foot of Your Majesty's Throne. After some time, I managed to interrupt his rambling and put him more or less at ease, stating that if he remained faithful to his promise, I would, in turn, not be unmindful of his loyalty. To demonstrate my friendship, I immediately set an example of justice: since his camp-followers had insolently plundered their sovereign's personal belongings, I had them rounded up and brought before me; those found in possession of plunder were forthwith crushed to death under the feet of my elephants, and the goods restored to its rightful owner. The times of lawlessness were over.

A few days later, I'timad Khan and his allies came to make their submission. It seemed there was nobody left to oppose us in the north of Gujarat. On the ninth of Azar[202], we marched in triumph through the gates of Ahmedabad, without a single shot being fired.

Arrangements were made for the government of my new province: I appointed my foster brother Aziz Koka as governor of the country north-west of the Mahi River, whereas I'timad Khan, whom I gave the benefit of the doubt, was made responsible for the southern part.

After a few days, on the 27th of Azar[203] to be precise, I left Ahmedabad and headed south towards the coast, to the port of Khambhat[204], where, for the first time in my life, I beheld the ocean.

I can't say how deeply impressed I was by its vastness and awesome beauty. I'd heard descriptions of the sea, so I knew what to expect: a vast body of water, stretching as far as the eye can see, waves glistening in the sun ... Yet, the sight of it well-nigh moved me to tears. It was as if God Himself showed me a glimpse of His unfathomable Mystery: all-powerful, daunting; yet gentle, inviting, unspeakably beautiful.

I wanted to feel what it is like to travel on those mighty waves. With a few of my officers and the local garrison commander, I boarded a ship, which, according to the commander's repeated assurances, was the fastest in the entire port. As I wished to go far out, and the wind was blowing straight from the sea onto the shore, we had to sail

---

[202] November 20.

[203] December 8.

[204] Cambay.

close to the wind, as the sailor at the helm called it. Crisscrossing into the sea at a sharp angle, sails pulled taut, ropes and planks creaking under the pressure of the wind, the ship took us deeper and deeper, until the shoreline was nothing more than a vague yellowish stripe at the horizon. Around us, there was nothing – nothing but deep-blue, glistening water, more beautiful in colour than the most precious emerald or sapphire any amount of money could buy; nothing but the pounding of the waves against the hull, salty droplets on my face, and the piercing, angry shrieks of dozens of white, long-beaked birds, sailing in the blue sky above us.

Not without regret, I ordered the boat to return to the port. With the wind and the waves now right behind us, we suddenly went at breathtaking speed, faster, it seemed to me, than the fastest horse.

Back on shore, I asked the local commander, a tall, thin man in his late fifties, with a lined, tired, worried-looking face, to show me around town. He was, he said, born in Sind, from a family of Arab merchants who had taken up residence there. Being, as he described himself, more a man of the sword than a man of learning or commerce, he had, when still a boy, obtained his father's permission to join the army of the king of Gujarat, and risen from the ranks, until his appointment as head the local garrison. He seemed a simple, honest man, and I very much appreciated the orderly state in which he kept the city entrusted to his care.

Despite the wars that had scourged the land, the port was bustling with activity. Merchants from nations and lands near and far – Gujaratis, Marathis, Rajputs, Hindustanis, Sindhis, Baluchis, Farsis, Arabs, Turanis, Syrians, Turks, even Firanghis[205] – were trading wares of all kinds, shouting, negotiating and bargaining frantically, with no other interpreter at their disposal than the gestures of their hands.

It was the first time I ever laid eyes on Firanghi merchants. To my surprise, most of them didn't look strange at all. They all had brown eyes, and not a single one of them had the red or yellow hair I had so often heard about; their skin, though fair, looked quite tan. They rather looked like Turks, I thought, if it wasn't for their strange attire: black trousers, sleeveless vests, and wide shirts, all of very poor quality, and

[205] Firanghī: 'Frank', European, Caucasian.

weird-looking hats of various, ridiculous-looking shapes.

'A lot of people here, from all around the world, it seems,' I said, pointing at the multitude of merchants amidst their wares. 'I see there's even Firanghis visiting your port; do you see many of them here?'

He grimaced with contempt. For a moment, I thought he was going to spit on the ground.

'Much more often than I care to, Your Majesty. These infidel dogs are everywhere these days!'

'You do not seem to like them very much, commander ...'

'I hate them, Your Majesty. Which decent person would not?'

'Surely, you are not afraid of them, commander? They come from far away, their numbers are small; how could they ever constitute a threat?'

He looked down and mumbled:

'Your Majesty is right – I should not presume to talk about things about which I know nothing. I beg Your Majesty's forgiveness.'

'Speak freely, Commander. I want to hear what you really think, not what you think I wish to hear; a wise king should avail himself of the experience of the people he meets – how else can his wisdom increase?'

He put his hand on his heart and bowed deeply.

'Allah be praised, it's true what they say about Your Majesty: we are blessed with a truly great king, wise and just! May Allah grant Your Majesty a long life, and may all Your Majesty's steps be fortunate!'

He paused, looking for the appropriate words to express his concerns.

'Your Majesty is wiser than I am, and despite his young age, much more experienced. I have no other desire in my heart but to serve my Emperor to the best of my abilities, and if necessary, lay down my life for him. But since Your Majesty has expressly commanded me to voice my opinion, I feel it's my duty to warn Your Majesty against those accursed Firanghis, for I am convinced they're extremely dangerous. Someday, they may even pose a threat to Hindustan itself!'

'You are exaggerating, old man,' I thought to myself. How could a handful of foreign adventurers ever pose a threat to a kingdom as vast and mighty as mine?

Probably guessing what I was thinking, he insisted:

'Perhaps I'm just getting old, Your Majesty; maybe the sombreness of old age is impairing my judgement. In fact, I hope from the bottom of my heart that I am mistaken. But I've been living on these shores for many years, and I have seen these Firanghis – *Purtugesh*, they call themselves, for there are many separate nations of them… I've seen them increase in numbers and arrogance, year after year; and what I've seen, worries me exceedingly.

When they set up their colonies and trading posts, they will sometimes ask the local king's permission, but as soon as that is granted, they behave like they own the place. Where local authority is weak, they will just steal the land, or as they say, take possession of it in the name of His Christian Majesty the King of Purtugal – as if that accursed infidel had any rights here!

Once they've established themselves, they're like lice, flees, warts: almost impossible to get rid of! Only a few days sailing south of here, on the Konkani coast beyond the lands of the Marathas, they've managed to carve out an entire kingdom – Goa, they call it. Sultan Adil Shah of Bijapur in the Deccan has repeatedly tried to chase them off, but his forces have been repulsed, time and again; the only thing he's been able to achieve with the help of Allah, is to keep them confined to the coastal area.

It's well-known how these Purtugesh have wreaked havoc among the innocent people of that peaceful region. They have exterminated every Muslim in the area – man, woman and child. Not a single believer is left alive in the entire country; only very, very few have managed to escape with their lives into neighbouring regions. The infidels even enlisted Hindu mobs to do their dirty work for them, offering a reward for every Muslim's head.

But the Hindus' treachery didn't do them much good. No sooner had the Muslims been eliminated, then the Hindus found themselves reduced to abject slavery, and all of their temples and shrines razed to the ground. Forcefully converted to the Firanghi religion, if they're found or merely suspected of having remained loyal to their old faith, they're forthwith imprisoned, tortured for weeks on end, and forced, under unspeakable pains, to betray all their friends and relatives. Then, they are roasted to death, on slow-burning pyres!

You see, Your Majesty, that is what makes these Firanghis so dangerous: they're fanatics. In spite of their utter lack of civilization, they seem to be convinced they and their blasphemous religion are destined to rule the entire world, and other people and religions are only there to be converted or eliminated. For us Muslims, they feel only hatred; for the Hindus, nothing but contempt!

Your Majesty has pointed out that their numbers are few and that they therefore do not pose a threat to us. Of course, that's right: not a single one of their ports and fortresses could withstand an all-out attack by Your Majesty's forces. Still, I fear that that wouldn't solve the problem. The Firanghis are like flies on a lion's head, vultures on a carcass, crows on a freshly seeded field: they can be chased away... only to come back a few moments later. Unless, by the mercy of Allah, we could kill them all, those who escape will always find an easy retreat into the sea, from whence they came. And here, I'm sad to say, lies our greatest weakness. Their ships are faster than that of any Muslim nation, be it Gujarati, Persian, Arab or Turkish, and the guns mounted on them carry much farther. Because of this, they control with impunity the traffic on the high seas between here and the port of Jeddah. Muslim pilgrims on the sacred Hajj are now compelled to avail themselves of Firanghi passports, full of Nazariyya[206] crosses and blasphemous drawings of the prophet Isa and his saintly mother, upon both of whom be the peace of Allah. Those who refuse to pay these scandalous ransom monies, are sure to be attacked and sunk by Purtugesh warships. Is it not an outrage that for the fulfilment of one of the most sacred obligations of Islam, Muslims need permission and assistance of infidel pirates?'

I thanked him for his advice, weary of the sombre tidings he had brought me. This was all grossly exaggerated, I thought. What did I care about a handful of infidel sea-rovers and petty merchants? Deserted regions – the sea included – will always be infested with robbers and hoodlums of all kinds: a nuisance, but hardly worthy of a king's attention! Surely, I had better things to do than to go equip a fleet – there were more dangerous enemies to be dealt with on land!

But with the wisdom of hindsight, I have to admit that the Gujarati commander was probably right: sooner or later, we'll have to deal with these Firanghis. Do not trust them, my son! Ask yourself the question:

[206] Nazariyya: 'Nazarean', i.e. Christian.

when the sultanates of the Deccan will have been brought to heel, what should be our next objective? The answer will of course depend on the situation at that time, including our relationship with the rulers of Persia and Turan, and the strength of their armies.

But shouldn't we seriously consider to build ourselves a strong fleet, to at least command the seas around us? He who rules the waves, rules more than a wasteland: he rules the highway connecting the whole world! He who dominates the seas, has unlimited access to knowledge and wealth, and thus, to power.

There is still time, of course: the Firanghis' numbers are low, we could crush them like bugs if we chose to do so; but we must keep an eye on them, and not let them become too strong, nor too rich.

Nothing would have pleased me more than a long, leisurely sojourn at the seaside, enjoying the cool breeze; the reports, however, were too alarming to ignore.

Ahmedabad and the north seemed to be under control, but further down south, the Mirzas – Ibrahim Husain in particular – persisted in their rebellious ways.

Ibrahim Husain was marauding around Baroda, barely two days marching from Ahmedabad, practically under my nose; Muhammad Husain still held the important port of Surat; and Champaner, east of Baroda, was occupied by Shah Mirza. Not one of these arrogant bastards had the decency to have the khutba read in my name; not one of them bothered to send any gifts to the imperial treasure; conciliatory letters remained unanswered. It was high time these dogs were taught a lesson. If they chose to refuse my hand in friendship, I would, as a chronicler aptly put it, show them my mailed fist!

But in my youthful impetuousness, I nearly made a fatal mistake. I should have taken my time and crushed them one by one, as I could have done quite easily; but I insisted on dealing with all three of them at once. Reaching the outskirts of Baroda, I dispatched Sayyid Mahmud Khan Barha with about half of my army towards the Mirzas' main stronghold Surat, near the mouth of the Tapti River. Another strong force under Shabaz Khan, was to head west and take Champaner.

I stayed behind near Baroda with the other army leaders, with little more than a personal guard – two hundred horse, all in all – to protect us.

But when I learned Ibrahim Husain's gang had been spotted nearby, moving north, no doubt attempting to evade the advance of the imperial army, I headed as fast as I could to the Mahi River, to cut off his escape.

My forces were of course much too small to give battle to any opponent worthy of that title, but I stubbornly refused to hear my officers' desperate pleas: I didn't want to be sensible; I did not want to be prudent; I refused to wait for reinforcements from Champaner; I would deal with that band of rabble myself.

Reaching the banks of the Mahi, we found that the enemy, over one thousand strong, had already crossed the river, and was camping in the small town of Sarnal, about two kos east of Thasra.

Against better judgement, I attacked immediately. Without scouting or preparation, I drove my mount through the ford in the river, and scrambled up the steep bank on the other side, forcing Man Singh, Bhagwan Das, Todar Mal and the others to do the same.

Ibrahim Husain, seeing this wild bunch crossing the river, hurried out of the town, looking for space to deploy his superior force. We, of course, pursued him as fast as we could, in an effort to prevent him from doing so.

Like so many other Gujarati towns, Sarnal was surrounded by a maze of narrow roads and tiny fields, fenced with thorn bushes and prickly-pear cactus – more unsuitable terrain for a cavalry battle was hardly imaginable.

This had two consequences. The most important and advantageous was that the enemy was unable to exploit his superior numbers. But the fight amidst this maze of bushes and thorns bore no resemblance to an orderly battle; it was little more than a vulgar, man-to man street fight between two rivalling gangs.

Man-to-man, indeed. Behind the front – or so I thought – I was looking for higher ground from where to direct the battle, when suddenly, I found myself face to face with three enemy troopers.

I don't know whether they realized whom they had in front of them, but from my shining armour and the magnificent caparison of my horse, they must have guessed I was quite an important man. Keen on plunder and reward, they fell on me. The two swordsmen riding in front attacked me left and right, while the third, carrying a long lance, came out from behind them to wheel around me.

I pranced my horse and threw myself upon the two swordsmen. I had to disable at least one of them, or they would have me completely surrounded in no time. Both my opponents, however, were experienced warriors. One parried my sword-thrust with his shield, and the other skilfully avoided my horse's flashing forehoofs; they had been thrown back, but not defeated. From the corner of my eye, I saw the lancer closing in on me from the right. I was about to turn around to face him and fend off his attack, when he was suddenly struck in the middle of the stomach by a Rajput javelin. He dropped his lance, grabbing, in vain, the shaft of the spear, and fell to the ground. I heard the thunder of hoofs behind me and saw a tall, bearded Rajput in hazar mikhi[207] armour galloping towards us: Bhagwan Das had come to my aid.

With remarkable agility for a man of his stature, the Raja tore his spear out of his dying victim at full gallop, and stormed forward, shouting his Lord Krsna's name 'Gopal!' from the top of his lungs.

I turned around to fight the two remaining enemies, but they seemed to have realized they now stood two against two. They made haste to save their skin; we, from our side, were prudent enough not to take any further risk, and returned to the troops.

The battle, meanwhile, had taken a favorable turn. The enemy's front lines had been scattered by the sheer ferocity of our attack, and in the fighting that followed, their bunch of marauders, man for man, proved to be much inferior to our own elite troops. When their front men had been cut down like grass, the next were seized with such panic they started to flee, hindering the others in their advance. That, in turn, led to more panic and confusion, which our men did not fail to exploit, chasing them wherever they went, cutting them down by the dozen. Ibrahim Husain himself, regrettably, managed to escape under the cloak of darkness.

The next morning, we returned to our camp and reunited with the reinforcements arriving from Champaner. The two hundred men who had fought so valiantly were covered with rewards, and Raja Bhagwan Das was honored with an Amir's banner and his personal kettledrums,

207 *Thousand Nails.*

an honor never before bestowed on a Hindu.

The battle of Sarnal has been hailed as one of my most glorious victories; and I have to say, my son, I was quite proud of it myself in those days.

Looking back on it, however, I've come to realize it was maybe the worst mistake I ever made, a wholly unnecessary act of foolish recklessness, which could easily have cost me my Throne and my life. My whole Empire could have ended then and there, in that insignificant skirmish, because of my stubbornness and daredevilry; and a number of excellent men, including Raja Bhagwan Das' own brother Bhupat, paid for my vainglory with their lives.

It pleases me not to admit this to you, my son, but I feel I have to. It's my duty to warn you against such dangerous and foolish mistakes.

Chance does favor the reckless sometimes, but a wise King owes it to himself and to the thousands depending on him, to keep cool at all times. Chroniclers and poets may love pitched battles and great deeds of valour, but a wise king knows that what counts is not battle, but victory.

Twenty-sixth Letter

گجرات

Gujarat (2)

With most of the Mirza rabble gone – or so I thought – only Surat remained to be conquered; it was time we got this over with. At dawn on the last day of the solar year – a uniquely auspicious moment, according to the astrologers' calculations – we left Baroda and leisurely travelled south, hunting and administering justice under way.

Eleven days later, we reached the outskirts of Surat, where we joined the men of our vanguard, who, I was pleased to find, hadn't been idling away their time: the area had been pacified, the city surrounded, and its supplies cut off. The only thing left to do, was to smoke them out.

Sure enough, after barely six weeks, the defenders were forced to capitulate. Much to their surprise and relief, I spared their lives. Only the garrison commander – a former officer in my father's army – had his tongue cut out, in just retribution for his faithlessness.

The whole incident wouldn't even be worthy of further mention, were it not for the encounter I had on that occasion with the famous Purtugesh.

We had just started the siege against Surat, when Todar Mal came to see me, a worried look on his face.

'Your Majesty,' he said, 'our informants tell me that a huge war fleet has arrived in the port of Daman, the Firanghi stronghold on the southern border of Gujarat. They say there are over twenty large battle ships and dozens of smaller boats, packed with soldiers!'

'Do we know what their intentions are?'

'No, Your Majesty. The Firanghi army has gone ashore, but it has not moved from the port.'

'I suppose they will be sending us an emissary soon. If not, we will send them one, and find out what they are up to. Make sure we have plenty of scouts everywhere, that we're not taken by surprise, in case they attack us!'

Indeed, the next day arrived an emissary, carrying a letter written in surprisingly fluent Persian, in which the humble servants of His Christian Majesty the King of Portugal presented the mighty King of Hindustan their respectful greetings and sincere wishes of good health, peace and prosperity.

As the country of Cambay – apparently the name they gave to Gujarat – had now been annexed to Hindustan's dominions, there were urgent matters of high importance that needed to be discussed, and they would therefore be extremely grateful, if His Majesty would kindly send them an Ambassador, who would be received with all the respect due to his lofty rank, and to whose personal safety they pledged their souls.

'Whom shall we send?,' I asked, casually looking at Todar Mal.

'With Your Majesty's permission, I will go,' he answered without hesitation.

'I was hoping you'd say that, my friend. No one in the entire army is smarter than you. Keep your eyes and ears wide open, and be sure to tell me everything! May God protect you.'

In the company of the Firanghi messenger and a small retinue, Todar Mal rode out. Two weeks later, he was back, in good health, accompanied by a small Firanghi delegation. I immediately invited him in my private quarters.

'I was quite impressed, Your Majesty! I counted twenty-two large war ships, many of them bigger than any ship I've ever seen, with scores of powerful cannons – these Firanghis are a force to be reckoned with! But they've received me with full honors, with flags raised and cannon shots fired to salute me upon my arrival, and everybody going out of their way to make my stay as comfortable as possible.

I've met several times with their Viceroy, the highest representative of their king in these lands. He was extremely courteous, and did his utmost to convince me of his people's friendly intentions. They truly seem quite eager to avoid any conflict with us, Your Majesty.'

'Why then this war fleet?'

'It appears they've been misled by the Mirzas, Your Majesty. The Mirzas had sent them a message, begging for their help and urging them to come, in their own interest – under the pretence that Your Majesty's armies were marching on Daman. But the Purtugesh quickly found out that the Mirzas were a spent force, as their Viceroy phrased it. They clearly do not want to get caught up in a war that is not theirs; in fact, the Viceroy told me the Purtugesh welcome the return of law and order to Gujarat, and expressed the hope that we would live together in peace and prosperity.'

'And what was your reply?'

'I told him that our Emperor is a just and peace-loving monarch, who favors mutually beneficial commerce and trade between the people on this earth, and does not object against the Firanghis establishing a few trading posts on the coast, provided they do not try to expand their dominions inland. I also told him it had greatly pleased our Emperor to hear about the valuable role the Purtugesh fleet is playing in the protection of peaceful merchants and pilgrims against pirates at sea. In short, I assured them they would have nothing to fear from our Emperor, as long as they remained a factor of peace, stability and prosperity.'

'Well said, Raja Todar Mal! What was their reaction?'

'They seemed to be quite relieved, Your Majesty. They reassured me that they fully recognize Your Majesty as the lawful sovereign of Gujarat and that they wish to live in peace with Your Majesty. As a sign of their good faith, they've pledged to withdraw their fleet back to Goa, and have sent one of their senior officers to accompany me. He wishes to offer Your Majesty a few gifts, as a token of their respect and friendship.'

'Excellent. I will receive him at once.'

António Cabral – that was his name – was a tall, strong man in his late thirties, with a trim, well-kempt, manly beard, long black curly hair, and honest eyes; calm, composed and unafraid, neither friendly nor hostile.

Apart from a plain white shirt and an elaborate kind of lace shawl around his neck, he was dressed in stern black clothes of rather mediocre quality. On his head, he wore a strange but jaunty hat, with a curly, waving feather. Upon approaching me, he took it off, bowed, and repeatedly brushed the ground with it – to all appearance, the way the Firanghis pay their respects.

An excellent soldier, that I saw at a single glance: self-confident without arrogance; fearless, yet composed and courteous; a man in control of himself and open to others, ready to make peace if possible, and war if necessary. I would have engaged him in my own army without a moment's hesitation.

It soon became apparent where the surprisingly elegant Persian letter had come from: the interpreter for the Firanghi delegation, a puny little man of distinctly unfavorable appearance, with a moth-eaten, thready beard, and a pockmarked, oily, quite unsavoury-looking skin, was a native Iranian!

His suit of clothes, though entirely black and made of the same inferior cloth, was different from those worn by the other members of the delegation: a long, ankle-length robe with a high collar and a short black shoulder mantle, and a strange-looking, wide-brimmed black hat; his only ornament was a simple necklace with a large wooden cross, on which was affixed a brass figure, representing the crucified, agonizing body of Isa ibn Maryam, or Jesùs, as the Firanghi call him. Not only was this man a convert to the Nazariyya sect; he was actually a Christian priest – a member, so I found out later, of the most influential and learned elite among the Firanghi priests: the Society of Jesùs , or the Jesuitas as they commonly call themselves.

Had I been aware of all this, I would probably have spent much more time with him, to learn more about the Firanghis and their religion, but I had other pressing obligations and no time to waste: there was a war to be fought, and I wanted to get it on with it as fast as possible.

Fortunately, Todar Mal's assessment proved to be correct: the Purtugesh, although clearly intent on conquest and expansion, as any ambitious nation should be, clearly understood that peace with the 'Great Mughal', as they apparently called me, was in their own best interest.

Cabral explained at length that the Purtugesh were a seafaring, merchant nation; that their home country was much smaller and less populous than Hindustan; that their main interest in this part of the world was to find spices and other wares to trade, which would increase their wealth and power, which in turn would help them hold their own with the rival nations of Firanghistan, primarily the *Shpanyol*, the *Ingresh*, the *Olandesh*, and *Fransesh*.

I of course wanted to learn more. Cabral readily answered all my questions, but I soon found myself completely lost in an intricate maze of countries, regions, warring Christian sects, rivalling kings, high priests and noblemen, all with barbarous, unpronounceable names no one in Hindustan or Persia had ever heard of. Firanghistan, so much was clear, was not a unified region, and – fortunately for us – neither were its inhabitants.

The peace treaty with the Purtugesh was quickly signed: we would not attack their coastal settlements, they would not interfere in the ongoing hostilities, nor try to expand any of their settlements inland; and their warships would continue to protect the Muslim pilgrims on their way to Mekkah.

As a token of their friendship and respect, they offered me a number of valuable and interesting presents, among which a painting, representing the exotic landscape of their home country, as well as a Purtugesh sword and musket, which highly evoked my interest.

The sword was straight-bladed, long and narrow – a weapon clearly designed primarily for thrusting from a certain distance. It was obviously not very suitable to hack or hew with, and too long, in my judgement, to be effective in close combat. However, the steel it was made of was of the finest quality, and its intricate and elegant knuckle guard looked both ingenious and effective. The musket, though oddly shaped and rather unhandy, had the most perfect steel barrel I had ever laid my eyes on. These Firanghis, unsophisticated though they looked, proved to be real masters in the art of metal foundry. As Todar Mal said: a force to be reckoned with...

As I wrote in the beginning of this letter, the further conquest of Gujarat posed no real problems. Surat capitulated in a matter of weeks, and up north, Aziz Koka inflicted a crushing defeat on the last remaining enemy army. Muhammad Husain Mirza, Shah Mirza and a few survivors fled into the Deccan. Peace and calm had returned to the region – or so I thought.

On the 23rd of Farvardin of the Eighteenth Year[208], I began the long journey back to Sikri, which, so I decreed, would henceforth be named Fathabad, City of Victory. About a month later, however, while I was inspecting the construction works, I overheard two Hindu masons calling it Fatehpur or Fathpur. I immediately thought to myself: this is the true name for my city! Places in Hindustan with names ending in -bad have been founded by Muslim rulers, and names ending in *-pur* refer to Hindu origins – everybody knows that. My capital, however, would be special: this would be a truly Hindustani city, uniting Hindu and Muslim building styles and combining, in its name, a Muslim concept with a Hindu ending.

I no longer used the name Fathabad; from then on, I called it Fatehpur Sikri; and the people duly followed suit.

But let me return to the events following the victory. On the way back, a messenger from Multan brought me the happy tiding that Ibrahim Husain Mirza was dead at last.

After the battle of Sarnal, that arch-rebel had made his way up north and had managed to rake together another bunch of thieves and robbers of the worst kind, with which he plundered the defenseless villages in the Panjab.

Fortunately, the local governor reacted swiftly; he surprised the rabble near Multan. In the ensuing battle, the rebels were all but wiped out, and Ibrahim Husain's younger brother Mas'aud and many other ringleaders taken prisoner.

Ibrahim Husain himself once again managed to escape, but got severely wounded a few days later in a skirmish with a gang of Baluchis. He was tracked down and marched off to the capital with the rest of the survivors. Alas, I didn't get the satisfaction of having him executed: his wounds proved to be so severe, that the bond between his perverse spirit and his vile body was dissolved, as Abu-l Fazl phrased it so elegantly. Upon my arrival, the troops presented me with his severed head.

The surviving rebels were paraded in front of me, sewn up in the rotting hides of asses, hogs and other unclean or ridiculous animals. Most of the prisoners – worthless hoodlums, anyway – were executed

---

208 Thursday, April 2, 1573 (Julian Calendar).

on the spot. A few of them, however – the ones who seemed innocent or useful – I chose to pardon.

Among those few was young Mas'aud, who, in an excess of zeal, had been brought before me in a truly pitiable state, more dead than alive, and – horrible detail – with his eyes sewn up. The boy's face was a ghastly sight, black and blue from the beatings he had taken, his cheeks full of gore, his eyelids swollen around the nasty black thread that held them shut...

'Is it not becoming and appropriate, that a traitor's eyes be downcast with shame?' the governor joked, a triumphant grin on his face. The troops seemed to appreciate the pun, but I didn't. What joy, merit, or glory is there in the suffering of a barely seventeen or eighteen year old kid, whose only crime it is to be a rebel's brother?

I ordered his eyes to be opened and his wounds to be dressed by my personal Hakim; after his recovery, the boy was to be enlisted in the army. The unfortunate lad, who, no doubt, had expected to die a horrible death, fell to his knees, sobbing barely intelligible words of gratitude.

Looking at him, I knew I had done the right thing. I felt peaceful, good about myself. Mercy is not an easy virtue, my son, a delicate plant, hard to cultivate, but its fruits taste much sweeter than the grapes of wrath...

∽

Were it not for the unpleasant surprise fate had in store for me a few weeks later, I would have had the fondest memories of my return to Fatehpur Sikri.

After those strenuous months of war, I enjoyed the leisurely life at court: cool, umbrageous buildings, splashing fountains, exquisite food, ice-cooled wine, sweet companionship of beautiful women and all those other luxuries; but this went much deeper. I was elated; it felt as if God's light was shining straight into my heart, for in everything and every detail, I knew myself to be blessed. I was strong and healthy; I was the happy father of three healthy sons; I was the mightiest and wealthiest king Hindustan had seen in many centuries, and with God's help, this was only the beginning!

Surely, this was no coincidence – it couldn't be. After all, not even a leaf will fall from a tree, unless God wills it! No, even though I was just an ordinary mortal like the rest, even if I had little personal merit, it was obvious, beyond a shadow of a doubt: I was – I am – God's chosen instrument on earth, entrusted with a special mission.

God Himself had given me a sign, when on the day of my triumphant return, amidst the interminable series of congratulatory speeches by enthusiast courtiers and flattering sycophants of all sorts, He caused my attention to be caught by the remarkable words of a humble Shaykh I had barely heard of.

The whole afternoon, I had been sitting in the diwan-i-am[209], receiving gifts and listening, with a mixture of pride and boredom, to the flowery words of praise of dozens of visitors, who had come from far and wide to congratulate me on the conquest of Gujarat. In overblown metaphors, one more lofty and far-fetched than the other, I was told that all the treasures, glory and power of this world pale into insignificance, when compared with the all-gracious and refulgent Presence of the Pearl of Royalty, the Gem of Magnificence, the Fountain of Justice and Benevolence, Quintessence of all earthly Perfection, His Majesty, the great King of Kings Abu-l Muzaffar Jalal-ud-Din Muhammad Akbar Padshah Ghazi, Commander of the Faithful, Double-bladed Sword of Islam, Terror of infidels, Lion of Lions, Tower of Strength, Refuge of the Sinners, Cherisher of the Poor, and many more of such niceties.

And then came this humble Shaykh, who had been allowed to present himself at Court, through a letter of recommendation from my foster brother Aziz.

Mubarak of Nagaur was his name, a poorly dressed, tired-looking man in his late sixties. Time, worry and deprivation had worn deep wrinkles down his cheeks, which his scanty beard was unable to hide; but his eyes were unusually lively, quick, and piercing.

He was accompanied by his two eldest sons: Abu-l Faizi, whom I knew as a talented poet, since he had been employed at Court since the days of Chittor, and a rather chubby young man, not much older than twenty, with a clean-shaven, round face, and the same keen, smart eyes as his father. In his hands, he was nervously fingering a bundle of closely written pages.

---

[209] Hall of Public Audience.

From the corner of my eye, I noticed Shaykh Mubarak's presence was clearly not to the liking of Abdullah of Sultanpur, the highest ranking of the ulama, better known under the lofty titles of Makhdum ul Mulk[210] and Shaykh ul-Islam; the greedy fat pig who, years before, had tried to oppose me when I abolished the *jizya* on the Hindus.

'Most learned and honorable Shaykh Mubarak, it is indeed a pleasure to see you! We have heard so many good things about you,' I lied, noticing with glee my words didn't miss their intended effect on Makhdum ul Mulk's conceitedness.

The Shaykh bowed deeply; hiding his trembling hands in his sleeves, he composed his features, and proceeded:

'Words fail me, Your Majesty, to express my and my sons' joy and gratitude, to be granted the undeserved honor and privilege to stand before Your Majesty's august presence. I probably do not need to introduce my elder son, Abu-l Faizi, whose verses have met with Your Majesty's favor, and who, Alhamdulillah, is enjoying the privilege of living at the imperial court, in the comforting shadow of Your Majesty's kindness.

This here is my younger son Abu-l Fazl, who has chosen to lead a life of study like his father; despite his young age, he has achieved a depth of knowledge and learning, which, if I say so myself, ranks him among the wisest philosophers in Your Majesty's dominions.'

This was quite a bold statement to make, and it didn't fail to catch my attention. Shaykh Mubarak proceeded:

'We possess but few earthly goods, Your Majesty, none of which are worthy to be presented to a mighty king. Knowing, however, Your Majesty's lively interest in matters of religion and science, we venture to place at the foot of Your Majesty's Throne these few writings by my son Abu-l Fazl, which perhaps Your Majesty will deign to have examined at a more suitable moment: it is a treatise, which Your Majesty may find of interest, on the most noble and holy Ayat 'l Kursi [211].'

Just as I expected, I thought to myself, a bit disappointed: the man merely seeks employment for this other son of his! Still, my interest

---

[210] Guide of the Kingdom.

[211] The *Verse of the Throne*, the 256th verse of the second chapter of the Holy Qur'ān.

had been awakened: if this young man was half as good as his father claimed he was, it would indeed be interesting to meet him some time.

'Thank you, Shaykh Mubarak,' I answered. 'We have indeed a great interest in the limitless world of books and the furthering of knowledge, and shall be interested to acquaint ourselves with your son's insights.'

'Your Majesty's kindness and wisdom are boundless,' the Shaykh mumbled, his forehead almost touching his knees.

I now expected to see the three of them bowing their way out, but to my surprise, Mubarak resumed his talk:

'I am aware that Your Majesty's time is precious and limited – that he has more pressing and important matters to attend to, than to listen to the inept stammer of a poor old man. Nevertheless, I would be most grateful if Your Majesty would allow me to express my profound gratitude and joy, that it has pleased Allah to send to Hindustan the true Khalifah, next to whom the reign of the great Harun ar-Rashid, of happy memory, will pale into insignificance!

In less than twenty years, this world will witness the advent of the thousandth lunar year since the Holy Prophet Muhammad – eternal blessings of Allah be upon him and his household! – led his followers to al-Madinah. Yes, the thousandth year of the Hijri Era draws nigh, and we have every reason to believe, that what has been foretold about the End of Time, is now about to manifest itself!

Eternal praise and gratitude be to Allah! In the noble person of Your Majesty, He has given us the noble Khalifah we are yearning for, not only to rule over us, but to be our spiritual guide in the critical times ahead. May Allah's blessings rain down on Your Majesty in abundance!'

The true *Khalifah*? The end of time? The spiritual guide of the people? Maybe the old man was just a sycophant like all the others, but I have to admit: his cryptic statements had roused my interest, and I was quite anxious to learn more about them.

But it would have to wait: these were no matters to be discussed in public. I thanked the Shaykh for his good wishes, and told him that I would soon require his and his son's presence in private audience.

I spent the night in ardent prayer, that God would grant me wisdom, and guide my steps.

∞

My worldly duties, however, left me but little time. There were building works to be supervised, revenues to be secured, justice to be administered – and on top of all that, as I will relate more extensively in another letter, the situation in Bihar and Bengal suddenly required my urgent attention. The days flew by in frantic busyness.

Just when things seemed to calm down a bit, alarming reports came in from Gujarat: the country was again aflame with an unexpectedly violent and dangerous new insurrection. In the south, Muhammad Husain Mirza had come back from the Deccan with a large army – how he had been able to raise one so fast, I will never know. His hordes invaded the area of Surat and occupied Khambhat[212], chasing out the imperial garrisons. Together with Sher Khan Fuladi's sons and a local Gujarati warlord named Ikhtyar ul Mulk, he was threatening Ahmedabad itself!

What was I to do? The invasion army had been disbanded, most troops had returned to their jagirs or had been sent east to Bihar. To call them back, to equip a new army would take several weeks; and the march back down to Gujarat, at least, another month or so: Ahmedabad was over two hundred kos[213] away – trading caravans needed two full months to cover that distance!

There clearly was no time for this. If these reports were accurate, we stood to lose the entire Ahmedabad garrison, and Aziz' life was in danger! The best I could do, was to head back immediately, as fast as I could, with whatever troops I had available: I would be able to join forces with Aziz, and I would at least have the advantage of surprise.

In two days, I hastily assembled a striking force – barely three thousand cavalry; not nearly enough, but hand-picked, battle-hardened, excellent men, and generously equipped at the Treasury's expense.

Well-meaning friends and advisors implored me to wait:

'They say, the enemy has over twenty thousand men, Your Majesty! If, Allah forbid, the Ahmedabad garrison would be defeated before Your Majesty's arrival, or if they fail to break through the encirclement, Your Majesty's forces will be outnumbered, seven to one! Shouldn't we build

[212] Cambay.

[213] 500 mles, 800 km.

a larger force before attacking, even if this would mean the temporary loss of Ahmedabad? At the very least, Your Majesty should think of his own safety! Let these three thousand be the vanguard, Your Majesty can follow later, with a larger force!'

They meant well, but I wanted nothing of it. This was something I would take care of myself: the Mirzas had defied me one time too many.

'The hoofs of my own horse will be the first to cross the Gujarati border,' I swore, making sure to repeat this oath several times in front of the troops: in times of trouble, there is no substitute for personal example.

Thus, it was done. We left Fatehpur on Yekshanbeh, the 11th of Sharivar[214], speeding through the country despite the blazing heat, covering over twenty kos[215] per day. Barely nine days later, we were standing on Gujarati soil.

I sent scouts to Ahmedabad, to warn Aziz: we would press on as fast as possible and attack the enemy's rear; this would allow him to break through the encirclement, and crush the rebels between hammer and anvil.

But it didn't quite work out that way.

Aziz, suspecting an enemy ruse to lure him into the open, stayed safely behind Ahmedabad's ramparts. The enemy, on the other hand, didn't take any chances. Hearing the rumours about the advent of an imperial army, Muhammad Husain Mirza left his ally Ikhtyar ul Mulk behind to block the gates of Ahmedabad with five thousand men, while he rode out, at the head of fifteen thousand, determined to check our advance at the Sabarmati River.

I have to say, it was quite an unpleasant surprise to descry in the distance on the other side of the river, not the imperial standards, but the detested red banners of the Mirzas, and a strong enemy host, complete with dozens of war elephants.

Impetuous and stubborn as I was, however, I refused to listen to prudence or reason, drove my horse through the river, and ordered the attack, even though there was no sign of Aziz and his men, and even

---

[214] Sunday, August 23, 1573 (Julian Calender).

[215] 50 miles, 80 km.

though the enemy clearly outnumbered us, five to one at least.

The rest, as you know, my son, is history: it was quite a pitched battle, but against all odds, we won – collecting over two thousand enemy heads on the battlefield, against a loss of barely one hundred of our own men.

How was this possible? Was it sheer luck, as some of my critics are whispering behind my back? No, definitely not! Was it divine assistance, as eager courtiers claim it was? It is quite tempting to believe so, but the truth, I'm afraid, is far less spectacular or miraculous.

I won the battle against vastly superior numbers, because, if I say so myself, I understand the iron laws of warfare, and know how to make them work for me. You will remember Bairam Khan's wise lessons: since, all other things being equal, God favors the larger army, the entire art of warfare is to influence and change the battlefield; it is to understand the advantages and disadvantages of your own and the enemy's situation, and then, to use overwhelming force where it matters.

Contrary to what people may think, my decision to attack was not merely a matter of impetuousness or daredevilry. I simply had to attack before the enemy had the chance to fully draw out his troops. Even more importantly, I had to lure him into a fight on the narrow stretch of flat land near the river. Remember Bairam Khan's wise lesson: when a large army is forced to fight on a narrow, restricted battlefield, its numbers are an impediment rather than an advantage, because they will slow it down and hinder its movements. A small army, on the contrary, should try to use its greater mobility and the element of surprise, so that, when and where it strikes, it is stronger than its opponent.

Perhaps even more decisive in this case, was the difference in the fighting spirit and ability of the men. I had myself a small but effective force of hand-picked, battle-hardened soldiers, devoted to their Emperor, ready to follow him to the gates of hell. The Mirza army, by contrast, impressive though it looked, was nothing but a bunch of hoodlums out for plunder: adventurers, robbers, mercenaries – worthless cannon fodder, nothing more.

The most important battle, my son, is that of the mind: a commander needs to overcome the natural weakness of his own men, and exploit that of the enemy. If I say so myself: that's exactly what I did.

I divided my troops into four fighting forces: Turkoman horse archers on both flanks; heavily armed, unflinching Rajput shock troops in the centre. Behind the front line on both flanks, I positioned my best marksmen, ordering them not to fire at random into the enemy host, but to carefully target the enemy leaders and their bravest soldiers. Around my person, I only kept a bodyguard of two hundred of the best men on the fastest horses, enough to escape unharmed if things would turn against us.

As I said, it was a pitched battle. Our men, though far better and braver than the enemy, were initially pushed back and nearly overwhelmed by the enemy's superior numbers. To make things worse, my horse got hit by a musket bullet and collapsed under me. It very nearly cost us the battle: for a moment, the men thought I had been killed. Fortunately, I was back in the saddle on another horse, just in time to prevent a complete rout. Seeing me alive and well, the men took heart and attacked with renewed courage.

After some time, my strategy finally started bearing fruit. With deadly effectiveness, my archers and musketeers had been picking out the enemy leaders; and the Rajputs were now making deep, bloody inroads in their ranks.

Muhammad Husain Mirza, realizing that his army was on the verge of collapse, pushed forward to encourage his men, when suddenly one of his elephants, seized with panic by an exploding rocket, wreaked havoc in his own rearguard. The ensuing panic was the end for him: his battle lines collapsed completely; everywhere, his men fled in disarray, slaughtered by the hundreds by our victorious troops. Muhammad Husain himself, wounded in the melee, was captured alive.

The battle was over. Our men were resting by the river bank, apart from a few who had been assigned the task of collecting the enemy heads, and digging graves and building funeral pyres for our fallen heroes.

Suddenly, a few of our scouts (a prudent commander always keeps a number of those on the lookout – don't you ever forget that, my son!) rode in the camp to warn me, that another army was advancing against us.

I first thought it was Aziz and his garrison, but for the second time that day, we were in for a most unpleasant surprise: this was the other enemy army under Ikhtyar ul Mulk, who, probably alerted by an emissary, had come to his ally's aid. I quickly had Muhammad Husain beheaded, and ordered the battle lines to be formed.

Our men, thank God, remained calm: disciplined and orderly, they took their positions, and advanced towards the enemy.

The enemy soldiers, from their side, were seized with panic, horrified at the sight of Muhammad Husain's bleeding head on a Rajput lance, and the tower of heads in the making in the background.

They didn't even try to put up a decent fight: before our men had reached their front lines, the entire enemy host had been transformed into a panic-stricken herd of sheep. Our men butchered them with virtual impunity – I don't think we lost a single soldier in the entire engagement.

Ikhtyar ul Mulk desperately tried to save his vile carcass, but Sohrab Turkman, one of my best scouts, spotted him, hunted him down like a falcon catches a rabbit, and as Abu-l Fazl phrased it so elegantly, relieved his shoulders of the burden of his head.

Thus, after barely a few hours of fighting, the rebellion was utterly crushed. There was a brief moment of panic when, to the men's bewilderment, a third army arrived at the scene, but this time, thank God, it was our own Ahmedabad garrison under my foster brother Aziz.

We joyfully reunited with our brethren and had ourselves a great feast on the river bank. As for the enemy: this time, the Mirzas had tried my patience once too many. Contrary to my habit, I decided to set an example. I personally ran my spear through the piece of scum that had slain Raja Bhagwan Das' brother in the battle of Sarnal, and ordered the summary execution of all the others.

I stayed in Gujarat no longer than strictly necessary. Leaving the governorship of the province in the hands of Aziz, I gave Todar Mal the special assignment to busy himself with the organization of revenue and tax collecting – a task of which, as usual, he would acquit himself admirably: only a few weeks later, the incoming revenue from Gujarat would swell, from the disappointing trickle it had been before, into an impressive, incessant stream of wealth, with which I could fund my further plans and ambitions. The province was finally mine.

We finished our tower of heads – one of the highest I ever built, a stern warning to the rebellious and the seditious – and marched back north.

Barely three weeks later, on the 23rd of Mehr[216], I rode, spear in hand, through the gates of Fatehpur Sikri, amidst the cheering crowd. I had been absent from the capital for forty-three days, all told.

It was, so the historians keep telling me, the fastest and most impressive campaign in history. No one, not even Iskandar or Genghis Khan, had ever won so complete and decisive a victory in so little time, against so distant and powerful an opponent.

Thus, my son, ended the rebellion of the proud Mirzas... As Abu-l Fazl wrote in his chronicles: from the height of presumption, they cast themselves into the abyss of ruin. They could have had so much, but they wanted it all. They could have lived carefree lives of ease and luxury; I would have allowed them to share in my power, wealth and glory; as kinsmen of the Emperor, the entire world would have held them in the highest esteem; but they threw it all away.

Who remembers them now? Who is there to pray for their souls? Who will light a lamp on their graves? Their fortunes, their names: gone and lost forever, in the dust of time.

[216] Monday 5 October, 1573 (Julian calendar).

Twenty-seventh Letter

ابو الفضل

Abu-l Fazl

From the private notes
of Mir Abdul-Latif

High noon, this day of Chaharshanbeh, the 2nd of Aban of the 18th year of His Majesty's glorious reign[217].

Unbearably hot it is, and though I can't sleep, I feel tired, dead tired; tired, like I never felt before in my life. Judging by the alarming decrepitude of this old, aching body, this eighteenth year of His Majesty's glorious reign will also be the last one of my life on this earth[218]...

My eyes are blurred by a grayish, milky haze, a kind of dirty mist, which seems to be growing denser by the day, and which not even the midday sun is able to dissipate. A few more months, weeks maybe, and I will have gone completely blind. Each time I move, my wrist is tortured by a nagging, crippling pain, and my fingers feel so

---

217 October 6, 1573.

218 Chāhārshanbeh: Wednesday. Ābān: the Persian solar month of Scorpio (October 23–November 22). The date corresponds to October 14, 1573 on the Julian calendar (October 24 on the present-day Gregorian calendar).

Mīr Abdul-Latīf died about two weeks later, on Saturday, October 31 (Rajab 5th, 981).

cramped and wooden, that I barely manage not to drop the qalam. I, who have written thousands upon thousands of pages of fleeting, harmonious, flawless Nasta'liq script, I find myself clumsily scratching the paper, smudging it with shaky, barely legible scrawls and scribbles, so disgracefully awkward and square, I feel deeply ashamed. Only a few years ago, if I would have caught a beginner bungling like this, I would have reprimanded him severely...

Allah is wise and compassionate, even when the fate He sends us seems harsh. Confronting us with the impotent feebleness of old age, He leads us onto the path of humility, which every man must tread, before he can enter Paradise.

It is, indeed, not hard for me to feel humble: my body is almost literally falling apart, like a decaying cart under its heavy burden. I realize, with calm, ice-cold certitude: these are the last pages I will ever write, for the day of my return to the Ultimate Reality behind the veil of this transient world is near.

Am I afraid to die, now that I feel death's black shadow over me? I really wish I could answer that question with a simple, unequivocal 'no': an old and supposedly wise man like me should be prepared to leave this world, not merely resigned to his fate, but actually looking forward to it! With shame, however, I have to admit, to myself if to no one else: I am not.

I do realize I have little reason to complain: I've had a good, fulfilling life, longer and much more comfortable than most could ever dream of. I have provided amply for myself and my family, I have been able to pursue all of my interests, and I enjoy the respect and esteem of the greatest men on earth. And surely, I will be man enough to face the pain and discomfort of death with courage and dignity. Exhaustion, nausea, shortness of breath: whatever the final hour will bring, I pledge I will bear it with supreme equanimity.

But my mind is not at ease. Day and night, I keep wondering: are they really true, all those things I learned and taught? Will Munkar and Nakir[219] really come to visit me in my grave, to prepare my soul

---

[219] 'The Unknown', and 'The Repudiating': the two Angels who are said to visit the dead in their graves, 'to interrogate them as to their belief in the Prophet and the true religion preached by him.'

for eternity? Will I be worthy of Allah's clemency, will He spare me the horrible tortures of hell? Will I be allowed to behold His unspeakable majesty and the everlasting bliss of paradise?

No matter how hard I try to chase them away, those nagging words of Khayyam's irreverent verse keep coming back to haunt my brain:

می برکف من نه که دلم در تاب است
وین عمر گریزپای چون سیماب است
دجیاب که آتش جونی آب است
هشدار که بیداری دواب خواب است

Come with old Khayyam, and leave the wise
to talk – One thing is certain: life flies;
One thing is certain, and the rest is lies:
The flower that once has blown, forever dies.[220]

No matter how hard I try to ban it from my mind, I simply cannot repress this blasphemous thought: when I'm dead, I'm gone. I will simply cease to exist; my mind will descend into the abyss of annihilation, it will disappear into the motionless, pitch-black darkness, where there is no light, no sound and no movement; it will sink into the void, where there is neither joy nor sadness; where there are no hopes, no prospects, no plans, no memories, not even regrets.

It's not the first time my mind is plagued by doubts of this kind, but never before have they been so compelling. Never have they drawn so nigh to absolute certainty, bitter and pitiless: soon, Mir Abdul-Latif will be no more; the only thing that will remain of him are these words. A few awkwardly scribbled pages, and my name: that is the only immortality I can aspire to.

---

[220] Abū-l Fath 'Umar al Khayyam (1047–1123): Iranian mathematician, astronomer, philosopher, and one of the most famous Farsi poets of all time. The verse and its poetic English translation by Edward Fitzgerald is quoted by Yavar Dehgahni in the Lonely Planet *Farsi (Persian) Phrasebook*, page 99.

A more literal (albeit, arguably, much less catching) translation is:

Mey bar kaf e man neh ke delam dar tāb ast	*Bring me Wine, for restless my Mind is,*
Vin omr e gorizpāy chon simāb ast	*and like Mercury this fleeting Life is;*
Daryāb ke ātash e javāni āb ast	*Youth's Fire: behold, mere Water it is;*
Hoshdār ke bidāri ye dolat khāb ast	*Beware, Fortune's Watchfulness: Sleep it is.*

I must admit, in spite of everything, it's a flattering and even somewhat comforting thought that some of the things I've said, done and written, may live on in the minds of people who will come after me – just like the words of so many writers and philosophers are alive in my own mind. Thoughts, indeed, are like contagious diseases: they keep on spreading, even when their first victim is long dead and buried. Thoughts may live forever, even if their thinkers do not.

But alas, I won't be around to take pride in them: nothing will be known to me, for there will no longer be a knower. Like a splashing drop of water that has fallen back into the ocean, I will no longer be separate: I will be one with the blind and deaf Force we call God, or Nature. I will become an unknowing part of that silent, mindless Power, that Power that creates and destroys, inexorably, majestically, awesomely, terribly, without knowing or caring, without love or hatred or any other feeling. I will be one with the all-encompassing, inescapable cycle of life and death, the Vortex that was, is, and will be, the great Happening, the ultimate union of everything and nothing, fullness and void, motion and stillness, the eye of the storm where nothing is moving.

This is not so terrifying – after all, have I not been dead or non-existent before I was born, for countless thousands of centuries? Why would the non-existence that follows life be more terrible than the one that precedes it? And what is the difference between non-existence and dreamless sleep?

But then again, there are these other moments, terrible and agonizing, when I fear the consequences of my own thoughts: what if I am mistaken? What if everything that has been written is true? Does my lack of faith make me a *murtadd*, worse even than a *kafir*[221], doomed to eternal hellfire? Is it not written that *kufr* is the only sin that Allah cannot and will not forgive, because it refuses Him and His mercy? Is it not said that every sinner will sooner or later be released from hell – every sinner, except the *kafirun*, who will be punished in all eternity? Have we not been warned, by generations upon generations of learned and pious men, that salvation depends entirely on the inscrutable will of Allah, Who guides aright the good and leads astray the wicked? Is

---

[221] *Kāfir*: infidel, person in a state of *kufr* (unbelief in God, blasphemy). *Murtadd*: apostate, person who has abandoned Islām.

this not corroborated in the Holy Qur'an itself? Have I indeed been led astray? Has my doom been inscribed on the eternal tables of Divine Wrath? Am I to be damned for all time?

Alas, if I were to ask the opinion of the sour, bigoted men of the Law – Makhdum ul Mulk and the likes of him – they would, no doubt, leave me little hope...

But could Allah's Divine Justice really be that harsh? Is it possible, that a compassionate and merciful God could destine some of His own creatures for eternal suffering?

Surely, if He's all-knowing, if not a speck of dust moves in the entire universe without Him being aware of it; if not even the most fleeting or hidden thought escapes His attention – surely then He must know, that I would never reject Him? Surely, He must know, that my poor, feeble mind never intended nor wanted to rebel against Him, that it was merely the helpless victim of questions – haunting, nagging questions that kept coming back, questions it found itself incapable of answering, yet unable to avoid? Surely, if Allah knows all my sins, will He not understand my weaknesses, and will He not appreciate my good intentions, however inept they may be?

If my wise and trusted friend Hakim Ali Gilani were here with me today, he would surely tell me, that I worry too much. In fact, he would probably smile, shake his head, and say something like: ' Don't you think, my learned friend, that Allah is greater than all the worries and cares of a compunctious old scholar like you? Have some wine, my old friend, and get some rest, you will feel much better!'

Maybe I should follow that advice, and order myself some wine, and maybe a bit of opium-laced rosewater as well. For a while at least, it will ease the pain in my bones. And who knows, it may give my poor, tormented head a few moments of peace.

Ali Gilani – Allah bless his soul! – is quite right: medicine, taken in moderation to treat an illness or ailment, is hardly haram[222] – a harmless, minor transgression at most. Why else would Allah have put them at our disposal? Just a few beakers, an hour or two of pain-free

[222] Forbidden, unclean.

repose – what a world of difference they make to a weak old man! I truly feel a bit stronger, and my wrist and fingers, thank God, are much less cramped and painful. I may yet be able to take advantage of the cool of the night, and get some more of this writing done.

Some more of this writing... Sometimes I wonder: why am I so eager to get this finished? For whom and why am I writing this?

First and foremost, I guess, I am doing it for my own comfort: it helps me to compose my fleeting thoughts, to discipline my wandering mind, to come to terms somehow with my ending life and my impending death...

And pretentious though it may sound: I also hope that these scribbles of mine may be of some significance to posterity.

Admittedly, they won't be of much interest to my family. My sons, I'm afraid, have little use for the anxious musings and speculations of an old man. They're doing quite well, they have their families, their means of sustenance, their occupation and position in life. They have come to know their father as a wise, learned, irreproachable man, a paragon of decency and respectability. Let them keep the pious image they have of me, and by all means, let them keep their unquestioning faith in God, if they still have it, for it is a source of great comfort and stability in life. Let them light a lamp on my grave as custom requires and pray for my salvation, but let them not be troubled by my doubts and weaknesses – that would neither be necessary, nor desirable.

I do hope, however, that my musings may be of some interest – maybe even of some practical use – to other people. Blasphemous though my thoughts may sound to some, they may actually be of some comfort to people whose mind is plagued by doubts akin to my own.

His Majesty, for one, may find my notes of particular interest. They will be my personal legacy to him – our last *falsafah*[223] conversation, so to speak.

He has a restless, inquisitive, free-thinking – some would say, 'irreverent' – mind; and never have I known a man of the world so eager to explore the mysteries of existence and the intricacies of religious doctrine.

'Discourses on philosophy have such a charm for me, that they

[223] Philosophy.

distract me from all else,' he once confessed in public; 'I sometimes have to forcibly restrain myself from listening to them, lest I should neglect the necessary duties of the hour!'

Who will take my place in those debates when I am dead? I do not know, but it's a comforting thought, that thanks to my writings, His Majesty will, from time to time, remember his old teacher.

I will not present these notes to His Majesty myself – he would, bless his soul, insist on sending me hordes of healers with potions and salves and incantations, and I wish to be left in peace during these last months of my life. No, I think I will entrust them to Hakim Ali Gilani, a good friend and a man of confidence, who has seen much and spoken little, a real physician if there ever was one. I will wait no longer. Tomorrow, I will ask him to come and pay me a visit. It would be foolish for a sick old man to postpone a meeting with his Hakim.

Such courteous, amiable man! I only sent him a small scribbled note, requesting a meeting with him in the course of the following week, but considerate as always, he presented himself at my quarters within the hour.

We exchanged a few civilities, whereupon he proceeded, with that mixture of sympathy and firmness so typical of physicians, to take my pulse, examine my eyes, palpate my stomach and the like. His ear to my chest, he listened, at length and with badly dissimulated concern, to the impotent shallowness of my breathing and the feeble, irregular beating of my weak old heart, but said nothing.

'What ailments exactly are you suffering from, honorable Master?' he inquired, trying to sound as casual as possible. I gave him a brief description of the most relevant of my complaints: my fading eyesight, my general feeling of weakness and exhaustion, and the at times excruciating pain in my wrist and fingers. Visibly relieved to retreat to more familiar terrain, he eagerly began commenting on the latter:

'Inside your wrist,' he explained, 'there is a kind of sheath, a fine tunnel so to speak, through which the tendons lead from your forearm to your hand.

In many elderly people, those tendons tend to swell, especially when performing repetitive tasks, for instance when writing a lengthy letter. And those aching fingers: you clearly suffer from an inflammation of the joints, also quite common in the elderly: that is causing those painful knobbles. I'm afraid there is no real cure for these ailments, my honorable Master and friend... The best you can do, is to take plenty of rest. I would advise you to do a little less writing, or better still, to call in a good scribe who can take dictation, rather than trying to write down everything yourself. Another advice: keep your hands warm, and soak them in hot water whenever you can.'

He went through the leather bag he had brought with him, and took out a small box filled with dark brown granules.

'If the pain becomes too severe, you can take some of these. One or two will alleviate the pain, three or four will help you go to sleep. Be careful, though: never take more than four grains at a time, and do not use them too often. Make sure you drink plenty of water when you take them, for they may cause constipation. If you do get problems with your bowel movements, do tell me: I can give you some medicine for that as well.'

He paused, looking for the right words.

'As far as your eyesight is concerned... it is rather hard to predict how that will evolve, reverend Master. You may experience increasing difficulties in recognizing details, faces and expressions. I will not lie to you: without adequate help, this may eventually lead to blindness. However, it is still possible to remove the clouded lens from the eye and restore much of the eyesight, but let's hope it won't have to come to that. Oftentimes, and may Allah grant this will be your case, the disorder progresses very slowly; you may be able to keep the eyesight you currently have. If you have difficulties reading, I can give you a specially polished magnifying glass – when you put it on the text you are reading, it will make the letters appear much larger and more legible.'

I put my hand on his arm.

'Allah be praised, that He has granted me the privilege of making your acquaintance, my learned friend! I am truly grateful for your help. Now tell me: how much longer do I have?'

'I do not know what you mean, honorable master...'

'I don't have much longer to live, do I?'

'I've found nothing abnormal for a man your age,' he answered evasively.

'I know you mean well, my friend, but I need to know the truth,' I insisted. 'Be honest now: how much longer do I have?'

'If there's one thing you have to avoid as a physician, unless you absolutely want to make a fool of yourself, it is to predict how much longer someone has got to live,' he retorted with a nervous chuckle.

'The hour of our death, reverend Master, is known to Allah alone. But you have asked me to tell the truth. Well, I won't lie to you: as you will have experienced yourself, your heart is what can be expected in a man of your venerable age: its beat is a bit irregular and weak. I will give you a tonic to strengthen it. In a few days, you should feel better. Let me reassure you: your condition is not at all uncommon in elderly people. I've seen people live for many years, with a heart much weaker than yours!'

'But you've seen many others dying from a condition less severe than mine, haven't you?'

He hesitated. With a faint, wistful smile, he nodded, acknowledging defeat.

'I must admit, I have, reverend Master.'

'Thanks for being honest with me, my friend. Do not worry, you have merely confirmed what I've known for quite some time now. Rest assured, I have not called upon you to find a cure that I know does not exist – I have lived a long and happy life, and have every reason to be grateful. No, my health is not the main reason I've asked to see you. I would, if you would be willing to accept, like to ask you to take care of a few practical matters for me when I'm gone.'

'Of course, you can always count on me, reverend Master! But I pray to Allah that many more years will come to pass before I am called upon to fulfil my promise!'

'May it please Allah, indeed, my good friend. Thank you so much for your appreciated help! Well, let me explain a few things to you.'

I conveyed to him a few practical matters regarding my estate – mainly instructions on how to divide it in equal parts, what to give to which child, and the like. Hakim Ali took due note of them. I went on to talk about my life, about the modest yet significant role I played in the development of His Majesty's thinking, and about my desire to leave him my memoirs.

He appeared quite interested and eager to cooperate.

'Could I have the honor of reading a few pages, reverend Master?'

I handed him a few pages about the Emperor's early youth and my appointment as his teacher. He read them intently, his eyes never once leaving the paper.

'This is really fascinating!', he exclaimed after a while. 'I am convinced His Majesty will be most pleased, not to say deeply moved, to hear the voice of his revered teacher reaching his ear through these writings! It will be an honor and privilege for me to be of assistance in so important an endeavour, reverend Master!'

He paused.

'But why and how, may I ask, did you decide to entrust your writings to me, reverend Master? Surely, there are many men at Court, well-versed in matters of philosophy and government, much more than I am?'

'Whom better to trust than one's own physician?,' I answered. On impulse, gave him the papers I had been writing the night before.

No sooner had I handed them over, I wished I hadn't. Why add those private musings to my memoirs? Had I not better destroy them?

But what was done could not be undone. I nervously looked at Hakim Ali's smart eyes flying over the lines, halting here and there to decipher a clumsily written word. When he had finished reading, he looked at me, with what seemed a mixture of compassion and admiration.

'Reverend Master, I am profoundly convinced the Emperor would be elated if you would be prepared to share these notes with him,' he said softly. 'As you so rightly point out, he does have an inquisitive mind, and his interest in matters of religion and philosophy is, indeed, truly remarkable!'

His smile broadened.

'And I have to say, I am most honored to read, that you think me worthy of your trust, venerable Master! However, as you say yourself: I really do think you worry too much – way too much! Your scrupulosity is of course to your credit, but I am sure you are taking it too far!'

He paused, looking for an argument that would convince me.

'Suppose, for the sake of the argument, reverend Master, that a man like me would suddenly find himself sitting on Allah's Throne of Judgement, and that a learned and wise old man like yourself would be brought before me by the angels of death. Suppose these angels would testify against you:

'We have questioned this wretched man's soul, and have found, beyond doubt, that he's an infidel. His faith weighs less than a grain of desert sand! There is nothing he does not doubt – absolutely nothing, not even Your very existence, o Lord of all worlds! Outwardly, he may have observed the fast of Ramadan and given alms to the poor, he may have prostrated himself five times per day, but the only prayer he is capable of without lying, is nothing more than two blasphemous lines: 'My God, if there is one: save my soul, if I have one.'

What do you think would be my answer, reverend Master?

Do you really think I would be so pitiless to say:

'I gave this man a long life among the true believers, yet he failed to serve Me. In doubting My existence and the truth of the glorious Qur'an, he has gravely sinned, and I am deaf to his supplications. Throw him in the flames of hell – eternal suffering will be his fate!'

Do you really think I would condemn my own creature to eternal suffering, on account of a mere mistake? Of course not! To eternal suffering, I would not even condemn the vilest murderer! Punish him, probably, for centuries if necessary; but in the end, after a certain amount of time, he would have expiated his sins and my wrath would subside!

And as far as you are concerned, reverend Master, my answer would be:

'I know of this man's doubts and errors, and I know he made them out of ignorance, not out of ill will. Throughout his life, he has honestly tried to be true, good and kind. And behold, those who serve Truth and Justice, are true servants of Mine. Go, and show this righteous man his well-earned place in Paradise!'

Consider, reverend Master: if this would be my mindset, if this would be the attitude of a sinful, limited man like me, how much more will it not be the position of Him Who is perfect, without a single blemish, the source of all holiness, compassion and mercy? How could Allah, who is nothing but goodness, ever desire the suffering of a pious, holy, gentle old man like yourself?'

I wanted to answer I was neither pious nor holy, but he quietly raised his hand.

I'm not a learned philosopher like you, venerable Master, but let me tell you something, as your physician: in my opinion, most, if not all, of those scruples and concerns of yours have to do with your melancholic temperament, more than with anything else!'

'What do you mean?'

'People like you, venerable Master, people whose temperament tends to be dominated by an excess of black bile, are studious and pensive in nature. They are sensitive, kind and considerate, creative in poetry and arts, but they also tend to be overly worried and preoccupied. Their character is noble and humble – humbler, in fact, than is good for their own health. They are often highly critical of themselves, dissatisfied about their own abilities and achievements. In some cases, they may suffer from such oppressive sorrow about themselves and the world, that it will render them completely listless.'

He paused and smiled reassuringly.

'What you need to do, is to go out more, reverend Master! Try to go for a brief walk every day, preferably in the cool of the morning: movement of the limbs promotes the formation of new red blood, the natural antidote to black bile; and sunlight helps to brighten the mind. And have a pitcher of sharab from time to time – if possible, in the company of friends. Friendly company is one of the best medicines against excessive bile – both black bile, which causes sombreness, and yellow bile, which induces anger. Above all, never be ashamed to laugh: laughter promotes the flow of wholesome juices; it opens the mind, makes it free from the prejudices that imprison it. What better remedy against sombreness and solitude, than pleasant conversation between kindred souls?

Speaking of kindred souls, reverend Master: there are two learned men I would like you to meet. With your permission, I would like to invite you to an evening meal, where they could make your acquaintance – I am sure it will be an interesting evening!'

'Well, I always enjoy meeting new people and learning new things,' I said.

'My entire life has been devoted to study, and the more I've learned, the more I realize how precious little I know. I will therefore accept with both hands whatever new wisdom I can find! A Yahudi[224] scholar from Tehran once told me, that their main book of learning – a compilation of thousands upon thousands of pages of commentaries called *Talmud* – has the first page missing; only to remind the scholars, that no matter how much knowledge they claim to have acquired, they have yet to arrive at page one! How true, how very true ...'

'Words of great wisdom, reverend Master!'

'Indeed... The older I get, the more I find that wisdom is everywhere – if only one cares to look! Now tell me, who are these two men you want me to meet?'

'Shaykh Mubarak of Nagaur, and his younger son, Abu-l Fazl.'

'Mubarak, the father of Abu-l Faizi the poet? The man who was presented at Court, through intercession of His Majesty's foster brother Aziz Koka?'

'Indeed, reverend Master. He seems to have made an excellent impression on the Emperor. Do you know him, by any chance?'

'We have never spoken, but by reputation, I know him quite well. I hear he's a man of great learning. However, he got himself into serious trouble with Makhdum ul Mulk!'

'So? How did that happen?'

'Around the year 960, twenty years ago already, during the Afghan rule still, Shaykh Mubarak, like so many others at that time, became convinced that with the approach of the thousandth year of the Hijri Era, the advent of the glorious Lord of the Latter Days, Sahab i Zaman[225] Imam Mahdi, was, or is, imminent.'

'What is your opinion about that prophecy, reverend Master?'

'What shall I say? Only Allah knows the truth. According to an oft-quoted prophecy, the latter days of Islam will be marked by a general decadence in faith and morals, until the advent of the Imam Mahdi, who will restore the true faith in its pristine glory. Through his teachings, every living human being will be led to true Islam, and an empire of righteousness will be established, after which the Day of Judgement will dawn. I have to say, it is not altogether implausible to believe so.

[224] Jewish.

[225] Lord of the Age.

Leading collectors of the Hadith, including Nisa'i, Abu Da'ud, Muslim, and Bayhaqi, have confirmed that the Prophet once said:

'Muhammad Mahdi shall be of my family, and of the descendants of Fatima[226].'

And Ahmad, Abu Da'ud, Tirmizi, and Ibn Majah, state that the Prophet at some other time said:

'When of time one day shall be left, Allah shall raise up a man from among my descendants, who shall fill the world with justice, just as before him the world was full of oppression'; and again, 'The world shall not come to an end till the king of the earth shall appear, who is a man of my family, and whose name is the same as mine.'

Since a few decades, many people have started to believe that the coming of the Mahdi is near. There are others who claim that he has already come into the world, as the Twelfth Imam of the Shi'a, who mysteriously disappeared and is believed to lead a hidden existence. To be honest, I do not know what to think about all this. I only know that since time immemorial, there have always been self-declared prophets from all creeds, claiming that the end of the world is near, and there have always been scores of people to follow them. Anyway, Shaykh Mubarak was among them: he became a follower of the infamous Shaykh Ala'i.'

'Who was that, reverend Master?'

'Surely, you must have heard of him? He was one of the many Mahdi preachers that appeared in Hindustan around that time. The son of a Bengali teacher, a saintly man who had settled near Agra after his return from Mekkah, leading a life of teaching and prayer, Ala'i himself clearly took after his father. Right from the early years of his youth, he appeared to combine the learning of a lawyer with the rigor of a saint. After his father's death, numerous pupils started gathering around him.

'Then, a few years later, under the influence of Mahdi teachings, he suddenly forsook all worldly goods, distributing all his possessions – even his books! – among the poor, turned faqir, and joined a wandering group of fanatics. The members of that fraternity gave up all work, as it is said in the Holy Qur'an: "Let not men be allured by trade or selling to give up meditating on Allah." They roamed the countryside, praying,

[226] The Prophet's daughter; wife of Alī.

preaching, and eking out their frugal meals in exchange for blessings.

'Every day, after each of the five obligatory prayers, they would be preaching in the villages, warning people about the end of time and the advent of the promised Mahdi, urging them to repent and devote their lives to God. Their ranks swelled by the day; soon, they found themselves strong enough to interfere with municipal matters, inspecting the bazaars, armed to the teeth, removing by force all articles which they considered forbidden, in defiance of the local magistrates if necessary.

Shaykh Ala'i's dubious fame soon reached the ear of the Afghan king Islam Shah, who summoned him to Agra. Although the king was resolved to put him to death as a dangerous hothead and ringleader, he became so charmed and impressed by Ala'i's saintly words about the vanities of this world and the ignorance of those who call themselves learned, that he let him live. To the amusement of the nobles and generals at Court, Ala'i effortlessly defeated and put to shame the Court ulama who tried to challenge him. Among his victims was the great Makhdum ul Mulk himself! Ala'i's reputation spread like wildfire, and day after day, new converts were joining him – among them, Shaykh Mubarak.

However, Makhdum ul Mulk and the ulama, who felt their positions threatened, refused to give up. After some time, they convinced the king that all these Mahdi teachings were nothing but dangerous and sinful Shi'a heresy, incompatible with established Sunni doctrine.

Before long, Ala'i and his followers found themselves banished from Court, a command they made haste to obey, for the great king Islam Shah was notorious for his severity, not to say cruelty, towards the enemies of the True Faith.

A few years passed by, when, rather unexpectedly, Islam Shah needed to quell some disturbances in the Panjab, and marched north. Up there, he again came across Shaykh Ala'i. When the king saw him, he said: 'Say that you recant, and I will not trouble you.'

But Ala'i did not want to listen to reason and started arguing against his sovereign, who, to keep up the appearance of authority, ordered him whipped. Rather unexpectedly, this mild punishment proved fatal to Ala'i, who was recovering from an attack of the plague. The whip ripped open one of the sores on his back. Only a few hours later, he died, burning with fever.

The downfall of the troublemaker Ala'i was a great victory for the court ulama, and persecution of all Mahdi preachers and disciples was the result. The troubles abated after the return of Emperor Humayun's, who always had much sympathy towards Shi'a doctrines. After Lord Bairam Khan's downfall, however, the persecutions started again: Emperor Akbar was still young and inexperienced at the time, and in matters of law, he would unquestioningly defer to the opinion of the ulama.

Thus, it came to pass that Makhdum ul Mulk one afternoon, taking advantage of His Majesty's youthful inexperience, obtained from him an order to prosecute one Shaykh Mubarak – whom His Majesty did not know – as one of the worst Mahdi heretics, an infidel who was not only damned himself, but led others into damnation.

As I said, this is something the Emperor would never allow today. Ever since Makhdum ul Mulk tried to oppose him on the abolition of the *jizya* tax on Hindus, he profoundly distrusts the ulama, and has taken the administration of justice firmly into his own hands. He will never condemn anybody, unless he has personally been convinced by the evidence!

Anyway, to continue my story: when Shaykh Mubarak heard about the new persecutions, he wisely decided to flee from Agra, leaving only a few humble belongings for his enemies to wreak their revenge on. In despair, he applied to Shaykh Salim Chishti of Sikri for protection, but the good Shaykh, knowing the wickedness of men, wisely advised him to head further west and to leave His Majesty's dominions, for a while at least.

Thus, he did. He fled to Gujarat, where he lived a simple and frugal, but satisfying life in the company of the pious, earning a modest living as a teacher. After the conquest of Gujarat, however, Mubarak found himself again living within the borders of His Majesty's dominions. He decided not to flee, but approached the newly appointed governor, His Majesty's foster-brother Mirza Aziz Koka. He told him the story of his life and implored his good offices. The generous-minded governor, convinced of Mubarak's innocence, provided him with a letter of introduction to Court.

That is when I saw Mubarak and his younger son for the first time in the flesh: during the audience in the diwan-i-am. I must say, although His Majesty did not have much time, he seemed to be quite pleased and impressed with Mubarak's speech and with young Abu-l Fazl's scholarship; and the fact that Makhdum ul Mulk hates them, is, I suspect, all the more reason for the Emperor to be interested in them!'

'That is what I suspect as well, reverend Master. I've met them a couple of times, and they seem to be exactly the kind of people whose company the Emperor enjoys: learned, intelligent, and free-thinking. I am convinced we haven't seen the last of them at Court!'

'It would be interesting to make their acquaintance,' I said.

'I will be my pleasure to have this arranged,' he answered.

That very same evening, he invited us to his residence.

The conversation started a bit stiffly, as can be expected when people meet each other for the first time, although Shaykh Mubarak went out of his way to please me and show his respect. In phrases most flowery, he rendered thanks to Allah that He had preserved him to that day; that it was an honor, a pleasure, as well as a privilege to be allowed to pay his most humble respects to the man, nay, the Mastermind, who had personally educated and formed the greatest monarch of all time; that I was the North Star of the Wise; the Aristatalis of the Iskandar of the Age[227]; the Beacon of Wisdom guiding the Ships of Power, and many more words to that effect – all vastly exaggerated and quite undeserved, but they pleased me more than I care to admit. Alas, even a supposedly wise old man cannot remain indifferent when his vanity is, thus, gratified.

Under the influence of the late hour, the pleasant conversation between learned men of obviously kindred spirits, and a truly exquisite repast, washed down with many a beaker of ice-cooled wine – which, as Hakim Ali Gilani kept assuring us, was medicine for elderly people and therefore not really haram – we soon found ourselves chatting like old acquaintances. Although slightly inebriated, having drunk much more than I am accustomed to, I did not fail to notice how cleverly Hakim Ali was steering the conversation towards the subject he knew I would find of great interest.

227 Aristatalis: Arabic for Aristoteles (Aristotle); Iskandar: Alexander.

'I had an interesting discussion the other day, with an acquaintance of mine,' he said, 'about our Emperor's remarkable – some would say, disturbing, if not outrageous – tolerance towards the non-believers. Abolishing the *jizya*, building Hindu shrines for his Rajput wives, and so on: people say he worships the sun, like a pagan! It would seem he actually favors the Hindus above the true believers! No one dares to speak out openly of course, but many of the ulama are whispering that the Emperor has gone much, much too far – in fact, that he has forsaken his duty as a Muslim ruler! Tolerance is one thing, they say, but should a true Muslim not be promoting Islam? Should a true Muslim not lead his fellow man to the one True Path? Is it not every Muslim's task to encourage virtue and forbid the wrong? And is that not the very essence of a Muslim king's task?'

'This is nonsense! Of course, the Emperor is right to be so tolerant,' young Abu-l Fazl exclaimed with unexpected vehemence. 'In matters of religion, there should be no compulsion – the Holy Qur'an says so explicitly[228]! And besides, the cause of Islam is much better served by tolerance and kindness than by repression! Where possible, and unless we are forced to fight in self-defense, we Muslims should be at peace with the others; we should compete with them in holiness, justice and good deeds. It's by far the best way to win over new converts: according to the sixteenth Surah of the Holy Qur'an, those who seek to please Allah will be guided by Him to *Paths of Peace*! And let us not forget that *as-Salam*, peace, is one of God's Most Beautiful Names!'

'I wholeheartedly agree with you, my young friend,' I said, 'but what would be your answer to those who state that good Muslims should shun the company of infidels, lest they be led astray or confused with error?'

'There is no doubt in my mind,' answered Abu-l Fazl imperturbably, 'that the religion of Islam is the best and purest of all religions. In fact, it is the essence, the fulfillment and culmination of all religion! Nevertheless, we should remind ourselves that Allah has allowed the other religions to exist, and that He has sent Messengers to all the peoples of the earth. While all other religions are less pure than our own, we should not forget that divine revelation is at their origin; and

228 Qur'ān, 2:256.

we shouldn't be surprised to find people among them, who, by divine mercy, have attained the highest degrees of wisdom and holiness!'

'Is it your opinion that there are infidels who will be allowed to enter Paradise?'

'It is, reverend Master. In fact, I am convinced that ultimately, everybody will attain paradise – Muslims and non-Muslims alike!'

'Even idolaters, guilty of shirk[229]? Even atheists, who have denied Allah's existence?'

'Even they.'

'And what would you say to those who disagree with you, quoting the words of the Holy Qur'an itself: 'Verily! Allah forgives not the sin of setting up partners in worship with Him, but He forgives whom He pleases, sins other than that; and whoever sets up partners in worship with Allah, has indeed strayed far away[230]'? And what to think of the stern warning in Ayat 91 of the third Surah: 'Verily, as for those who are bent on denying the truth – not all the gold in the world could ever be their ransom! It is they for whom grievous suffering is in store; and they shall have none to succour them[231]'? Is it not written, that shirk is the gravest of all sins, that no sin surpasses it in terms of gravity, severity and enormity? Is it not written, that to lead a virtuous life is of no avail to those who commit shirk? Is it not written that Allah may pardon all His servants' transgressions, but their refusal to submit to Him and Him alone, never?'

Abu-l Fazl's expression remained unperturbed.

'Exactly! All this is of course true, but it really concerns those who consciously, knowingly and willingly reject Allah, not those who have merely erred in good faith, nor those who repent. And sooner or later, even for the greatest sinner, there comes a time when he will see the error of his ways, repent his sins, and attain salvation!'

I was growing more and more fond of this bright young man. Still, I wanted to put him further to the test.

'And how, my young friend, do you reconcile what you just said

---

[229] Polytheism; the act of worshipping other gods.

[230] Qur'ān, 4:116.

[231] Qur'ān, 3:91.

with the fourth Surah, *Ayat* four and fourteen? Is it not written that Allah leads astray whom He pleases and guides whom He pleases; He is the Mighty, the Wise[232], and that He leads the wrongdoers astray; Allah does whatever He pleases[233]'? Does this not indicate, that for reasons known unto Him alone, Allah foresees and ordains who will transgress His commands and who will not? Does this not indicate, that Allah leads astray whom – again, for reasons known unto Him – He wishes to punish?'

Young Abu-l Fazl was still not in the least impressed. He merely smiled and said:

'Reverend Master, you touch upon a much-debated, thorny question: how to reconcile Allah's Omnipotence, his Omniscience, His Providence, His Justice, and His Mercy? Learned men of all generations – including the four of us present here tonight – have agonized over this problem: on the one hand, Allah is omniscient, He knows the past, the present, and the future; He therefore knows in advance whether a person will sin or not. He is also omnipotent, and therefore, nothing comes to pass, unless He wills it. But if He knows everything beforehand, and if nothing in this world happens unless He wills it, does not that imply that He actually *causes* evil? That He actually wants people to sin? That He has created a number of people, merely for the purpose of punishing them in all eternity? On the other hand, however: how can that be compatible with His Divine Justice and Mercy? How can it be called just, to punish an impotent, helpless creature, that has done nothing else than what it was predestined to do?'

He paused and looked at me.

'Go on, my learned young friend – I'm very interested to hear what you have to say about this!'

'A Paragon of wisdom and learning like yourself, reverend Master, is of course well-acquainted, much more than an inexperienced student like myself could ever be, with all the subtleties, complexities and intricacies of the debates between the various schools of *falsafah*: the Murjites, who set faith above works and emphasize the divine love

---

232 Qur'ān, 4:4.

233 Qur'ān, 4:27.

and goodness; the Qadarites, who affirm, and the Jabarites who deny, that men are responsible for their actions; the Mu'tazilites, who build their theology on the basis of reason, rejecting the qualities of Allah as incompatible with His unity, and predestination as contrary to His justice; and finally the Ash'arites, the classical scholars of what many consider to be orthodox Islam, who have formulated the doctrinal system that underlies the creed of most men of the Law like Makhdum ul Mulk.[234]

However subtle all their lines of reasoning, all these schools have, in the end, managed to come up with only two answers to the seemingly unsolvable problem of evil in a world created by an almighty and good God: either that we have an inadequate understanding of divine justice; or that we underestimate God's compassion and mercy. Either we believe that God exercises *jabr*, absolute compulsion; or we accept that He has given us *tafwid*, delegation of power and responsibility. Personally, I vastly prefer the latter solution!'

He paused. I noticed how his father was smiling and nodding in approval.

'As far as the first group is concerned,' he continued, 'there are, indeed, many scholars who emphasize the inescapability of God's inscrutable Will. Their reasoning is clear enough: Allah can do what He pleases, and everything He wills, comes to pass. Therefore, everything in this world, good and evil, must exist by His will: the faith of the believer, and the irreligion of the wicked. When He chose to create the sinners and unbelievers, willing that they would remain in that state to undergo the pains of eternal punishment, He did as when He created the serpents, the pigs, the scorpions and other vile and evil things. Wise ends of His own He had in view; and we, mortal creatures, have no right to inquire about them. As it is said in the *Mishkatu 'l Masabi*[235], with bone-chilling clarity: When Allah resolved to create the human race, He took into His hands a mass of earth, the same whence all mankind were to be formed, and in which they after a matter pre-existed; and having then divided the clod into two equal portions, He threw the one half

[234] Reynold A. Nicholson, *The Mystics of Islam*, page 5–6.

[235] The Niche for Lamps, a well-known compilation of Sunnī tradition, based on the work (AH 737) of Shaykh Walīyu ud-Dīn and Imām Husain al Baghawī.

into Hell, saying, 'These to Eternal fire; and I care not'; and projecting the other half into Heaven, adding, 'And these to Paradise; I care not.'

He paused again, slowly shaking his head.

'But what kind of Paradise would that be? What kind of Justice? What kind of Divine Compassion and Mercy? There would be no virtue, no wickedness, no acts good or reprehensible, no true punishment or reward. Only the arbitrary, inescapable Will of a stern, inscrutable God, who takes pleasure in burning one individual for all eternity, amidst red-hot chains and seas of molten iron, and granting another the bliss of eternal Paradise, just because He wills it? No, that is impossible! That is not the infinitely good God Who has spoken to us in the Holy Qur'an!'

He stopped speaking, apparently awaiting my reaction. I nodded encouragingly.

'Go on, my young friend; what is the solution to this problem, according to you?'

'I've given this much thought, reverend Master, and I have come to the conclusion that the key to understanding this transient world and the Qur'anic message, lies with the concepts of Divine Mercy, and human freedom!'

'What do you mean?'

'Allah is the Compassionate and Merciful Lord of the Worlds; every creature enjoys His Divine *rububiyat*[236] in accordance with its own nature. The ants crawl on the earth, the worms push their way in mud and dirt, the fish swim in water, the birds fly in the air, the flowers blossom in gardens, the elephants wander in the jungle and the stars revolve in the heavens. On every single one of them rests the protective eye of Allah's Providence, and there is none who is denied His blessings[237]!

Us, human beings, Allah has graciously put at the head of His magnificent creation; moreover, He has blessed us with the most precious of gifts: reason and freedom! Beasts are what they are, all individuals are the same: tigers are killers, antelopes skittish and shy, vultures eat carcasses. But we, human beings, we can (and have to!)

---

[236] Providence (literally: tender and caring nourishment).

237 Quote from Mawlana Abul Kazam Azad's Opening Chapter of the Qur'ān, (transl. Syed Abdul-Latīf), ed. Islamic Book Trust, Kuala Lumpur, 2001, pp. 20–21.

decide for ourselves what kind of person we will be! Of course, the talents we have are but weak reflections of the infinite Attributes of the Divine Being. Of course, circumstances determine the extent of our responsibility, negligible in some cases, and extremely grave in others, but anyhow, we've been given a choice; we are free agents, and to the extent we're free, we are responsible for what we do. If we go astray, that is the consequence of our own decisions – not the result of some arbitrary 'predestination'! No, Allah does not *cause* us to sin, He merely *allows* us to do so. All the Qur'anic references to God's 'letting man go astray', in my opinion, have to be understood against the background of what is written in the second Surah, Ayat 26 and 27: 'None does He cause to go astray save the iniquitous, who break their bond with God.' Is it not written, in Ayat 44 of the tenth Surah, that Allah does not wrong mankind at all, but mankind wrong themselves? Is it not written, in Ayat 182 of the third Surah, that Allah is not in the least unjust to the servants? No, God does not forsake anyone, except those who actually choose to be forsaken; that is to say, those who consciously, knowingly and willingly decide to reject Him.'

I could not help smiling and nodding approvingly. This wise young man had come to exactly the same conclusion as I had, so many years ago.

'But what do you have to say about Hell, my young friend? Does it not exist? Does not the Holy Qur'an warn us against its horrible tortures?'

'Hell does exist, but it has two quite distinct meanings', Abu-l Fazl answered, again without a moment's hesitation. 'On the one hand, it is the necessary loitering or purification almost every human soul will have to undergo before it can be reunited with its Maker. On the other hand, as a place or a state of eternal suffering, it is nothing more, nor less, than the logical consequence of freedom.'

'What do you mean by the logical consequence of freedom?,' I asked.

'If we are truly free,' Abu-l Fazl answered, 'then Hell is the theoretical possibility we have, to reject God – the possibility, in principle, to refuse the priceless gift that He's offering, for free. If we were unable to refuse, we would not really be free, would we? Therefore, if we truly are created free, then it must be possible for us – at least in principle – to keep refusing the mercy and salvation that God is offering us.

To put it another way: since we are truly free, it is logically inevitable that eternal Hell does exist as a *possibility*, but not that in fact, there are any creatures wicked and stubborn enough to dwell in it for all eternity. In other words: Hell exists, but it is, most probably, empty.'

'I see,' I said. 'That is why you claim that even the worst infidels will be saved?'

'That's right, reverend Master. I am and remain convinced that whoever worships God and does good deeds will attain salvation, whether or not he believes in the prophethood of Muhammad, whether or not he worships the Muslim way, and whether or not he lives in accordance with Shari'ah law. People born into other religious traditions – Yahudi, Nazariyya, Hindu, whatever – who have honestly attempted to serve God, will be accepted as true Muslims by Him, for He is compassionate and merciful!'

'And those who refused to worship Him? Those who adored idols? Those who have denied God's existence?'

'As soon as they see their errors and regret them, they will be forgiven,' Abu-l Fazl answered without hesitation.

He looked at me, verifying the effect of his words. His quick, beady, black little eyes seemed to be piercing right into the depths of my soul.

'Allah will accept everyone,' he continued, 'even those who have nothing to offer Him but their desire to be saved. And sooner or later, even the most obstinate, unrepentant sinner will see the light and will, thus, be saved!

Yes, it is inevitable: Hell, however long it may have to last, will at some time cease to exist. That is the only way I am able to make any sense of this world, the teachings of the Holy Qur'an and the moral laws that God has put inside my soul. Indeed, in the words of the Holy Qur'an Itself, Allah has ordained Mercy on Himself[238]! Even the worst of sinners should not despair of the mercy of Allah![239] The wise and learned Bukhari, may Allah be well pleased with him, gives us a similar description of Allah's indescribable mercy in the Hadith. He speaks of

---

[238] Qur'ān, 6:12,54.

[239] Qur'ān, 39:53.

how the Prophet, seeing a mother pressing her child to her bosom, asked his companions: 'Do you think that this mother could throw her child into the fire?' When his companions replied in the negative, he answered: 'Allah is much more merciful to His creatures than this woman is to her child!' In the same Hadith, God is described as having divided His mercy into one hundred parts. To the world, He sent one part, which is expressed in all the love His created beings are capable of, including the self-effacing love of a mother for her child. The remaining ninety-nine parts, He has kept for the Day of Resurrection...

I know, it is written that Allah is able forgive any sin, except *kufr* or *shirk*. But is it not also written that even for these sins, there is the remedy of *tawbah*, turning to the Truth of God? To me, it is crystal clear: merely *longing* for atonement will constitute sufficient *tawbah* in the eyes of Allah, even if you have nothing else to offer Him. Those who desire to be saved, will be. If Hell is eternal, then the only way to remain in it, is to consciously choose to do so, to willfully refuse and keep refusing the gift of Heaven. The Holy Prophet Muhammad himself has so testified: Allah, in His endless mercy, says to us: Should your sins reach the horizon of the heavens, and then you asked My pardon, I would pardon you![240]' No one should despair of Allah's mercy: the purpose of His chastisement, painful as it may be, is not our suffering, but our purification. He leads the submissive on smooth and pleasant paths, and firmly drives forward the reluctant, until, stumbling and murmuring, they finally obey Him. In the end, all creatures endowed with reason, even the worst of sinners, even unbelievers, even the devil himself, shall ultimately be released from Hell, when they are ready for their new and blissful existence in Paradise! As Umar, the second Khalifah, may his grave be holy, has declared: Even if the dwellers in Hell may be numberless as the sands of the desert, a day will come when they will be taken out of it. And in Bukhari, we read: Surely, a day will come over Hell, when there shall not be a single human being in it!

'You are indeed a man of great wisdom and wide reading, my young friend,' I said. 'However, one thing keeps puzzling me about the problem of *taqdir* or predestination. Does not God have perfect foreknowledge? If He knows what we will do in the future, does that not indicate that

[240] Cfr. Chapter 6.

He has pre-ordained our deeds? If He knows beforehand that we will sin, why has He created us the way we are?'

'I must admit, that will always remain a difficult problem,' Abu-l Fazl conceded. 'Still, God's foreknowledge does not necessarily imply that He has also pre-ordained everything. First of all, we should not forget that the limitations of time and space are nothing to God. To His infinite Being, unlimited space is as if it were a single point; and the past, the future and the present are the same to Him. He is the eternal Now; He immediately sees and knows every occurrence at every moment of time, in the same way as a mortal man knows what is passing before his very eyes. God's knowledge of the future therefore is like our own knowledge of the present. However, His knowledge of His creatures' deeds and decisions does not mean that He interferes with their free choices. In giving us the gift of freedom, He deliberately suspends His own omnipotence. The only thing that is pre-ordained, necessary and inevitable, is that everybody and everything that is in and of God will return to Him; and that anything false and imperfect is bound to disappear, just as surely and inevitably as a drop of water is bound to evaporate in the midday sun.'

'Predestination, after all?'

'Yes, predestination – in the sense that God is the only ultimate Reality and that nothing has any real existence outside Him: the entire universe and all its creatures and phenomena are but imperfect and transient reflections of His eternal Being and Attributes. To many scholars, ibn 'Arabi's doctrine of *wahdat al wujud*, the Unity of Being, and the principle of *tawhid*, the Oneness of Allah, is also the logical solution of that difficult problem of predestination against free will: in Allah's realm, the realm of *haqiqah*, the ultimate and only truth and reality, there of course is predestination, for all that belongs to Him will return to Him, and all that is estranged from Him, is but an illusion and sinks into nothingness. By contrast: in the exterior, transient world of *Majaz*, the world of multiplicity, the created world, there is free will: the freedom to return to the ground of all being, or to remain separated from It. That is what will make the loitering of Hell so painful: the further we have allowed ourselves to become estranged from God, the more of our haughty selves we will need to let go before we are ready for salvation.'

'I once heard a Sufi preaching,' Abu-l Fazl continued, 'in a way of reasoning quite similar to that of the Hindus: he said that since Allah is the one and only ultimate Reality, the human soul is necessarily an integral part of that divine Reality. Human souls are part of God, but have become separated from it at birth – in the same way that a splashing drop of water is, for a brief moment, separated from the ocean it came from. The drop is still essentially the same as the ocean, it still consists of the same water; yet, it utterly lacks the ocean's awesome power and majesty, because it has become separated from it. 'Seventy Thousand Veils,' said the Sufi, 'are separating Allah, the one Reality, from the world of matter and sense. And every soul passes, before its birth, through these seventy thousand. The inner half of them are veils of light; the outer half, veils of darkness. For every one of the veils of light passed through, in this journey towards birth, the soul puts off a Divine quality; and for every one of the dark veils, it puts on an earthly quality. Thus, the child is born weeping, for its soul remembers its separation from Allah, the One Reality. And when the child cries in its sleep, it is because its soul remembers something of what it has lost. Otherwise, the passage through the veils has brought with it forgetfulness (nisyan); and for this reason man is called insan. He is, so to speak, imprisoned in his own body, separated from Allah by these thick curtains.' [241]

Such is our human condition. Our soul is like a mirror covered with dust, a piece of metal in need of refinement. It needs cleaning, purification, transmutation by the force of fire. Man, to redeem himself, has to abandon his soul to the fire of spiritual passion. That is what dervishes and yogis try to accomplish: they try to pierce the seventy thousand veils, to recover the original unity of their soul with the One, and to get rid of all the falseness, the delusions and the passions that keep them separate from It. It may take us a long time, it may require the purification of Hellfire... but ultimately, all that is good in us will be reunited with its origin, and all that is bad will be washed away. And I might add that this image of the veils is quite consistent with what

241 After a quote from a Rifā'ī dervish cited by W.H.T. Gairdner, 'The Way' of a Mohammedan Mystic, (Leipzig, 1912); quoted by Reynold A. Nicholson, The Mystics of Islam, (London, 1914, republished by Arkana, London 1989, pp. 15–16).

the Holy Qur'an and the scholars have to say about the human soul.[242]'

'What exactly do you mean by that?'

'As you know, reverend Master, the Holy Qur'an teaches us that the human soul consists of an-nafs and *al-ruh*; *nafs* being the lower, individual soul, whereas *ruh* is non-individual Spirit, continuous with Being itself.

Ruh is alluded to in the Holy Qur'an: for instance, in Ayat 29 of Surah 15: 'I have made him and breathed into him of My spirit.' It's the gift of God's Spirit, the dignity which exalts man above the animals – even above the Angels. Because of its origin, *ruh*'s main characteristic is unselfish, self-effacing love for Allah. By its very essence, it is continuously longing for closeness and communion with God. It is the sense of utter dependence and humility before God. It is the desire to please Him, and resignation to His will. It is yearning to achieve union with God, to abandon all imperfection, to become a mirror of His divine light.

Nafs, in contrast, is the force that binds us to our bodily existence. It instills in us the desires and urges necessary to preserve and perpetuate ourselves, and to make us stronger. *Nafs* causes the basic urges and feelings we share with animals: hunger, thirst, the desire to lay with women and raise children, the need to rest, sleep and feel comfortable. *Nafs* is also what causes the impulses derived from those basic urges: the drive to further one's own interests and those of one's own kin; the lust after wealth, possessions, power, fame and influence.

It should be pointed out that *Nafs*, in and of itself, is not evil: without self-love, without the desire to increase our possessions, to dominate others, it would be extremely difficult to survive. *Nafs* is like the mount we have to ride during our journey through this earthly life – and that comparison is quite an appropriate one: a horse is a wild, dangerous animal, ready to throw and even kill its rider. Duly tamed, however, it becomes a faithful friend and ally who carries us to our destination. This is our task in life: to tame the forces of *nafs*, to use the free will with which we've been endowed, so that we may lead our

---

[242] Based on Shāh Shāhīdullāh ud Farīdī's essay *The spiritual Psychology of Islām*, quoted by Wahīd BAKSH RABBANI (Capt.), *Islāmic Sufism*, Lahore, 1984, fifth revised edition, Aligarh, India, 2001, pages 167 ff.

lives the way Allah has ordained us to do.'

'Verily, Allah has blessed you with a brilliant mind and much wisdom, my young friend,' I said to the young man I now knew would soon become my successor as the Emperor's closest confidant. 'I will put in a good word for you with the Emperor.'

It is hot and sticky in the room; that wretched pain in my wrist and fingers is back, and it's almost unbearable. Breathing is painful, tiresome; it feels as if someone had put a heavy stone on my chest.

It will not be long now – not more than a few days. The time has come to put down the qalam and await what is to come, in prayerful resignation.

May the Lord of all worlds have mercy on this poor old man, and may He grant wisdom to those who remain behind.

Soon, old Mir Abdul-Latif will be no more. His soul will effortlessly glide through the seventy thousand Veils, and beatifically succumb to the Ultimate Reality behind them. Gone will be the delusions that have kept it prisoner in this transient world; gone will be, in the first place, its own self. Nothing of him will remain behind in the world of the living – nothing, but a few words, and a name.

The flower of yore, withered in the sands:
As a mere name only it stands;
A naked name is what remains the bereft,
Naked names are all we have left.[243]

[243] Stat rosa pristina nomine; nomina nuda tenemus: the closing words of Eco's *Nome della Rosa*.

Twenty-eighth Letter

بنگال، موار

Mewar, Bengal

As I told you in the twenty-sixth letter, my son, Gujarat was not fully mine yet, when the situation in the east, in Bengal and Bihar more in particular, suddenly demanded my urgent attention.

Up to that moment, those territories had never been a primary concern of mine. Traditionally, they had always been more or less dependent on the sultans of Dilli, and that didn't change when I came to power: the Surs who ruled over Bengal made haste to swear allegiance to me.

In the ninth year of my reign, power in Bengal was seized by the Afghan Taj Khan Karanani, a former army leader of Sher Khan Sur; but he and his successor and younger brother Sulaiman, were wise enough not to provoke me, and fully recognized my authority. The khutba was read and coin was struck in my name, and sumptuous gifts were sent to Court regularly.

But when Sulaiman died – much regretted by his subjects – the problems started. His elder son Bayazid who had succeeded him, was murdered a few months later by Afghan army leaders, who raised his treacherous younger brother Da'ud to the throne.

Da'ud, a dissolute scamp who knew nothing of kingship, as one chronicler fittingly described him, thus inherited his father's vast treasure and powerful army, but alas, not his wisdom. Taking advantage of my absence, he forsook the prudence of his predecessors, and shamelessly assumed all the dignities of independent royalty, ordering coin to be stamped and the khutba to be read in his own name. Soon, he pushed the insolence even further, attacking and destroying the imperial frontier fort of Zamaniya in the Ghazipur district.

When I heard about these intolerable disturbances, I ordered Mun'im Khan, who'd stayed behind in Agra during my absence, to chastise the rebels forthwith.

Mun'im Khan hastily assembled a striking force and marched east, towards Patna. But after the first skirmishes, he was approached by Da'ud's chief minister Lodi Khan, who, with lavish gifts, flowery compliments and solemn oaths of friendship and submission, sought to placate him. Old Mun'im Khan, well in his seventies and weary of the hardships of travel, was more than glad to end hostilities, and granted peace on exceedingly lenient terms.

When I heard the news, I sent the much more level-headed Todar Mal with reinforcements. I imagine Mun'im Khan didn't appreciate the covert reproach I, thus, made him, but I thought it necessary, and alas, I was soon proven right: Da'ud, showing the viciousness of his nature, rewarded his faithful minister by confiscating his goods and having him executed, then entrenched himself in the fortress of Patna. We had to start all over again.

Mun'im Khan, ashamed and angered, laid siege to the city. Soon thereafter, fearing he would provoke my anger if the siege dragged out, and realizing that his force was not up to the task, he sent a messenger, imploring me to take personal charge of the campaign.

So I did. On the fourth of Tir of the Nineteenth Year[244], I left Agra at the head of a powerful army, accompanied by excellent generals including Raja Bhagwan Das and Raja Man Singh. The monsoon at its height, the rivers were dangerously swollen. But I insisted on traveling by boat: this would enable us to speedily transport the cannons and other heavy material, which otherwise would have gotten stuck in the mud on the rain-soaked roads.

Twenty-six days later, I reached Varanasi, where I stayed for three days, deeply fascinated, once more, by this ultimate fusion of sublimity and horror.

---

[244] Tuesday, June 15, 1574 on the Julian Calendar.

I proceeded on the Ganga, anchoring near Sayyidpur, where the Gumti flows into the Ganga. On the same day, we were joined by the rest of the army, which had traveled by land. The ladies and children were escorted to Jaunpur, while I advanced at the head of the army to the infamous ferry at Chausa, where, thirty-five years before, my father had been defeated by Sher Khan Sur. But this time, the omens were better, for upon arrival, I received a dispatch, announcing that the fortress of Bhakkar in Sind had just been added to my dominions.

Apart from the sad loss of one of my most exquisite prize elephants, we managed to bring the army safely across to the southern bank of the river, and proceeded to Patna, where we arrived on the twenty-second of Tir[245].

It must have been a painful surprise to Da'ud, to suddenly see the imperial army, complete with heavy cannons and war elephants, setting up camp near his gates. Never before in the history of Hindustan had a major battle been fought in the middle of the monsoon: it was thought impossible for a large army to cover any large distances before the beginning of the month of Aban[246]. And yet, there I was... God favors those who act, my son!

After careful scouting of the surroundings, I decided to first reduce the small fortress of Hajipur on the other side of the river, important for the enemy's supplies. The detachment I sent did an outstanding job despite the wild and dangerous river – over one kos wide in that season! – and the tough resistance of the Afghans. The heads of the enemy leaders were thrown in a boat and brought back to me, and I of course didn't fail to forward them to Da'ud, as a hint of the fate that awaited and in due course befell him, as a chronicler so aptly put it. Along with the heads, I sent Da'ud a message, challenging him to meet me in man-to-man combat.

As I expected, the coward didn't have the guts. That same night, he and his garrison sneaked out of the city and fled, as fast as they could, back to Bengal. I pursued the fugitives all the way up to Daryapur. Regrettably, they managed to escape, but we did return with a fabulous

---

245 Saturday, July 3.

246 Ābān: the Persian solar month of Scorpio (October 23–November 22).

amount of booty, including 265 prize elephants.

With Patna and Bihar now firmly under control, I decided to return to Dilli, leaving an army of 20,000 under Mun'im Khan and Todar Mal to complete the annexation of Bengal. The towns of Surajgarh, Monghyr, Bhagalpur and Kahalgam fell in quick succession, and after our scouts had taken out the enemy defenses, Mun'im Khan marched triumphantly through the fortified Teliyagarhi Pass, right into the Bengali capital Tanda, which he took, with little enemy resistance, on the thirteenth of Mehr[247]. Da'ud now fled into Odisha, while our forces continued their advance, easily establishing imperial authority in Satgaon, Ghoraghat and Burdwan.

After some months, however, there were growing tensions in our camp. The soldiers, exhausted after such a long and strenuous campaign in the heat and humidity of the Bengal marshes, were dying to get back home, and morale among the army leaders was not much better. Todar Mal had the greatest difficulties to convince the aged and weary Mun'im Khan to leave the relative comfort of the Bengali capital and pursue the campaign into Odisha.

Through his informants, Da'ud must have heard about the battle-weariness and discord in his opponent's army: he saw his chance and marched against our slowly advancing troops, his army clashing with ours near the village of Tukaroi, three and a half kos south-east of Dantan in the Midnapur district.

Unfortunately, Mun'im Khan was forced to engage before he was fully ready. The result was that his fighting force, consisting almost entirely of cavalry, had far too few cannons to support it. Da'ud's general Gujar Khan cleverly exploited this, and opened the battle with a massive elephant charge. His strategy very nearly worked: our vanguard and center were scattered by the irresistible mass of elephants; one of our senior commanders was killed, and Mun'im Khan himself, severely wounded, barely escaped with his life.

Defeat would have been inevitable, had it not been for Todar Mal's tenacity and skill. Leading our left wing, he wheeled around the flanks of the attacking elephants, killing several enemy mahauts and wounding many elephants. He then fell on the enemy with such vehemence that

[247] September 25.

their right wing was routed and driven off. The rest of our troops now took heart, regrouped and launched an all-out attack on the Afghan center and right flank.

The death of the enemy general, Gujar Khan, decided the battle. The Afghans fled in disarray, and our men, eager to avenge the losses they had sustained at the onset, pursued and slaughtered them by the hundreds. In Abu-l Fazl's words, Mun'im Khan's wounds and lacerations were healed by the balm of conquest. He ordered all the prisoners to be brought before him, and had their bodies separated from their souls; the collected heads served to build eight sky-high minarets on the battlefield.

Da'ud and the surviving Afghans fled to the fort of Katak[248], where, on the first of Ordibehesht of the Twentieth Year, coinciding with the first of Muharram of 983,[249] he made his submission to Mun'im Khan, handing over his nephew as a hostage.

Once again, Mun'im Khan, eager to put an end to the campaign, was talked around: Da'ud again got away with overly generous peace terms, including the governorship over much of Odisha.

Todar Mal, smelling deceit and foul play, openly opposed the treaty and refused to sign it. He would, alas, soon be proven right.

A few weeks later, Mun'im Khan headed north, to quell some disturbances in the Ghoraghat region. Ignoring the advice of his officers, he insisted on moving his capital from Tanda to the ancient capital Gaur, which, so he had heard, abounded with the finest buildings. Unfortunately, rumors about pestilence in that region proved to be true. Hundreds perished – so many, that the living no longer bothered to bury the dead, and just threw their comrades' corpses in the river.

Mun'im Khan, gravely ill himself, retreated back to Tanda, only to die upon arrival. May God receive him in His mercy!

Pending the arrival of new instructions, the officers appointed a new leader among themselves. But the new commander wasn't strong enough to maintain discipline. Everybody only thought of getting his booty out of pestilent Bengal as soon as possible. In utter indiscipline,

---

[248] Cuttack.

[249] April 12, 1575.

the army retreated to Bhagalpur in Bihar.

Treacherous Da'ud, still in command of substantial forces, owing to Mun'im Khan's ill-considered leniency, didn't scruple to again take advantage of the situation and reoccupied the whole of Bengal, including Tanda and the Teliyagarhi pass. But this was his last and fatal mistake. When I got word of this vexing news, I sent Khan Jahan, governor of the Panjab, to deal with the situation. At Bhagalpur, he intercepted the retreating Bengali army. With the able help of Raja Todar Mal, who had arrived from Fatehpur Sikri carrying my personal instructions, he managed to bring the men back to their duty.

Khan Jahan invaded Bengal, and to Da'ud's surprise and dismay, quickly recovered the important Teliyagarhi pass. Joining forces with Muzaffar Khan, governor of Bihar, he attacked Da'ud near Rajmahal, and after a pitched battle, defeated and captured him.

This time, Da'ud's promises and pleadings were to no avail. When I was barely one day's march outside of Fatehpur – I had decided to travel to Bengal and take personal charge of the campaign – I had the great pleasure of receiving my enemy's severed head. I had it put on a stake, and returned in triumph to the capital, where great feasts were organized, and to put it in Abu-l Fazl's words, waves of largesse quenched the thirst of the needy.

Bengal was finally mine – but I confess: imperial authority remained mainly confined to the cities. On the countryside, local landlords would keep much power for many more years. Indeed, it would be in those accursed, bug-infested marshes, that only a few years later, the most dangerous rebellion against my authority would break out.

Before Da'ud finally met his doom at Rajmahal, I also had to deal again with my old enemy, the Rana of Mewar.

As you know, when I attacked Chittor, Uday Singh had fled to the Aravalli hills, where he set up a new capital. I let him be: the conquest of wealthy Gujarat was of much greater importance and urgency. Of what use would it have been, to waste more blood, treasure, and above all, time, on the conquest of an isolated hill range of little or no value, when my troops could go unhindered wherever I wished to send them? Thus, I had allowed Uday Singh to live undisturbed in his hills, and he meekly stayed there until his death.

Regrettably, his son and successor Pratap had inherited more of the pride and fighting spirit of his forefathers. As a chronicler phrased it, race feeling taught him to hate the foreigners, ancestral pride to despise them, and high martial spirit, his grandfather's legacy, to resist them. Slowly but surely, he recovered some of his ancestral lands. It is true that without Chittor and the other fortresses, he was nothing more than a local nuisance; nevertheless, I thought it prudent to deal with him before he could pose any serious threat.

Towards the end of Farvardin of the Twenty-First Year[250], I sent Raja Man Singh with an army. Three months later, on the tenth of Tir[251], their advance was opposed by Pratap's forces at the entry of the Haldighat pass.

Truth be told: Pratap and his men fought with remarkable valor. Wave upon wave, clan upon clan charged the imperial lines with utter contempt of death. But despite their bravery and the few hundred casualties they managed to inflict on us, they were no match for our firepower, with our many field cannons and gun swivels, mounted on the backs of camels and elephants. Pratap, though seriously wounded, managed to escape to the hills, saved by his swift and faithful steed Chetak, and the exhausted imperial cavalry was unable to catch him.

Despite the victory, I was much vexed to hear Pratap had escaped. He had to flee deep in the wilderness, and one by one, his strong places fell into our hands; but later, when I transferred my capital up north to the Panjab, he again recovered much of his lost territory.

Even today – due to your culpable laziness and disobedience, as you well know, Salim! – his son Amar Singh has yet to be brought to heel. It's about time you took care of this, my son. The Rana of Mewar is nothing more than a nuisance; but his insolence is a stain on our armor. It's about time we dealt with them, my son. Promise me, that in due time, you will.

[250] April, 1576.

[251] June 21, 1576.

Twenty-ninth Letter

إبادت خانہ

Ibadat-Khana (I)

Master of a mighty empire, with no one left to challenge me, and no need to busy myself with my armies' smaller campaigns, I enjoyed a period of relative calm. Alongside the many hours devoted to the affairs of state, I finally found the leisure to occupy myself with my favorite pastime – religion, *falsafah*, and *kalam*[252]. I ordered the construction, on the palace grounds, of the *Ibadat-Khana* or House of Worship, a sacred meeting place dedicated solely to the study of God, where the most learned scholars of Hindustan and beyond would be invited to join me in learned reflection on the Divine Mysteries.

What was I hoping for? That every religious divide would be bridged by respectful dialogue? That the light of reason would erase all differences? If I ever did, it didn't take me long to awaken from that dream. As Hakim Ali Gilani put it so perspicaciously in the notes you are about to read, my son, I could and maybe should have known that his entire effort, however praiseworthy the motives behind it, was doomed to failure: far from uniting people's views, the debates seemed

---

[252] *Falsafah*: philosophy, i.e. the use of human reason in order to attain fundamental knowledge about the universe. *Kalām*: 'theology', the study of God and the Divine Attributes. Literally, Kalām means 'Speech', hence *ilm al-Kalām,* the *study of Divine Speech,* i.e. the science of the knowledge of God, His eternal Attributes, His Word, His Power, etc.

to merely exacerbate the existing differences. In the end, the open-minded did become more enlightened, the tolerant more tolerant; but the bigots, even more hostile and fanatic.

In spite of their sad failure, however, the debates in the Ibadat-Khana were of paramount importance in the history of the Empire, and you would be wise, my son, to study them carefully! Observe, my son, how an innocent quest for religious truth quickly turns into a row over the very foundation of our kingship; observe how my and your Throne is built, to no small extent, on the labor of those two people you respect so little: old Shaykh Mubarak and his brilliant son, Abu'l Fazl.

From the private notes of Mulazim Hakim Ali Gilani,
Jalinus-uz-Zamani,
Personal physician of His Majesty the Emperor

Much has been said, and no doubt, will be said about our beloved Emperor's religious convictions and policies. A man's inner beliefs remain a matter between him and Allah, unless and until, through his own words and deeds, he makes them a public issue. All the more so, when the man in question is the Emperor!

Whatever people may have to say about His Majesty's orthodoxy, no one can deny that he is, and always has been, an honest, God-fearing seeker of the Truth; and since he is an honest seeker of the truth, rather than one who claims to have found it, he is tolerant of and interested in all creeds and opinions, fond of the wise, be they Muslim faqirs, Hindu yogis, or whatever other kind of sage or priest. A king, yet the slave of dervishes...

From his father Humayun, who profoundly disliked the strife between Sunni and Shi'a, he inherited a profound distrust of bigotry and fanaticism. His pragmatism has strongly been encouraged and developed by his wise teacher, the greatly lamented Mir Abdul-Latif. He taught His Majesty, that a King's primary duty is to ensure *sulh-i-kul*, peace and prosperity for all his subjects, and that the cause of Islam is usually better served through peace and tolerance.

It was no great surprise to me, when in the month of Ramadan of

982[253], His Majesty suddenly issued orders for the construction of the *Ibadat-Khana*. The best and brightest would be invited to that sacred place, to join their Emperor in pious and learned discussions on the divine mysteries and man's duties towards the Creator.

The new building was to be erected in the palace gardens, near the former abode of Shaykh Salim Chishti; more precisely, at the spot that had been the dwelling of one of the Shaykh's most prominent disciples, the renowned ascetic Abdullah Niyazi of Sirhind. The Emperor ordered the ruined hermitage to be rebuilt, and a domed hall, of considerable dimensions and graced by appropriate ornaments, to be built around it.

At the outset, only Muslims were invited to the debates. There were four groups of them: the Amirs or leading nobles of the Empire; the ulama, learned specialists of Shari'ah law; the sayyids, descendants of the Holy Prophet Muhammad through his daughter Fatimah and Ali, may Allah be well pleased with them; and finally, to phrase it in the words of Abu-l Fazl: Sufis of clear heart, absorbed in beatific visions: a diverse group of shaykhs, faqirs and other holy men, who by virtue of their ascetic and pious life, their prayers and studies, were reputed to have attained a special communion with God.

At first, everybody was allowed to go and sit wherever he pleased in the building. But this led to such acrimonious, not to say ignoble, quarrels over who should take precedence over whom, that quite soon, the Emperor found himself obliged to assign separate quarters to each group: the shaykhs were to sit in the northern section; the southern side was reserved for the ulama; the sayyids sat west, and the Amirs east.

Evil tongues say that it was then and there, in the course of those heated debates, that the Emperor lost his faith and ceased to be a Muslim. That is blatant nonsense. His Majesty never renounced Islam, neither publicly nor privately. His devotion to God is undeniable. The truth of the matter is, that throughout his life, he has become convinced, that in the eyes of Allah, all religions lead to Him. As a result, he's a generous supporter of religious devotion in all its expressions – Islam in the first place. How else is it to be explained that he allowed his favorite spouse, her Highness Salima Sultana Begam, his aunt Gulbadan and several other highborn ladies of the imperial family, to leave the safety of the

[253] January 1575.

imperial Court for several years and undertake the hazardous voyage to Mekkah? That he revered with such deep respect the Prophet's petrified footprint, which the ladies brought back to Court upon their return? That he desperately yearned to become a Hajji[254] himself, and could only with great difficulty be persuaded that God required him to stay with his subjects? That he donated such large sums of money, to pay for the pilgrimage of poor Muslims who lacked the means to pay for the voyage themselves? No, the Emperor never abandoned Islam, never ceased to be an exceptionally pious devotee to the Almighty.

It is true, though, that the debates in the Ibadat-Khana did change him profoundly, in more than one way. It was there that his personal outlook on religion took its final shape: tolerant and freethinking, bordering on the heretical. These personal views and insights estranged him completely from religious authority in general, and from the Court ulama in particular.

As a privileged witness of – and at times an active participant in – these discussions, I believe I have an unbiased view of His Majesty's convictions. Following the example of Mir Abdul-Latif, I've decided to describe them as accurately as possible: the testimony of an honest eyewitness may be of importance to posterity, and in fact, I believe it is actually what His Majesty expects from me.

I remember that late afternoon, a few days after the demise of my old friend Mir Abdul-Latif, may Allah make his grave holy. Having obtained a private interview with the Emperor, I had presented him with his old teacher's private diaries. Even more enthused than I had expected, he immediately cancelled all other activities scheduled for that day, and urged me to start reading.

He listened with undivided attention, at times amused and visibly flattered by his teacher's praise, at times moved to tears.

'How good it is to be able to listen to him, once more!,' he sighed, wiping the tears from his eyes. 'It is as if he's reaching out to us from yonder side of the grave, to endow us with his wisdom!'

He took the papers in both hands, kissed them, and held them to his forehead, as the most sacred of writings.

'Never in my life have I regretted this much, that I never learned

254 Person who has completed the *Hajj* or sacred pilgrimage to Mecca.

to read myself,' he continued after a pause, wiping his eyes and looking at the closely written pages. 'How fascinating is the world of writing! It's like a sort of heaven, where the thoughts of the dead are preserved, even if their authors are long gone; where their wisdom is held in safekeeping, in hallowed silence, at the disposal of the living for guidance and inspiration!'

He paused, staring at the papers with glazed eyes.

'I only wish there was someone to continue Mir Abdul-Latif's memoirs,' he said, without looking at me or even raising his eyes from the papers.

'I know,' he continued, still talking more to himself than to anyone else, 'the Court has its own scribes, but official chronicles are not the same than the candid observations of an honest and astute observer...'

'Forgive me, honorable Hakim Ali, 'he said, suddenly raising his head after another long silence, as if awakening from a dream, 'we will need to continue this conversation some other time. There are a few urgent matters I need to attend to with Raja Todar Mal. Treasury matters and all that, you know...'

He thanked me again for my visit and bade me a good and restful night – the audience was over. Mumbling words of gratitude and respect, I bowed myself out of the room and retired to my quarters, not daring to ask whether I had to take his final observation as an order, a personal request, or a casual remark.

That same night, I began writing these notes, with the intention of presenting them to His Majesty at an appropriate occasion. That occasion, I believe, has arrived. Two days from now, we will be celebrating His Majesty's fortieth solar birthday[255], an age when it is appropriate to take stock of one's life, to look back at what is in the past, and to make plans for the remaining years ahead.

So many things have happened in those nine years since Mir Abdul-Latif's passing! The arrival at Court of two insolent Firanghi priests; acrimonious squabbles between lawyers, priests, sages and hermits of all sorts; the covert but growing opposition of the ulama, and the masterstroke with which the Emperor managed to rein in their power; the Bengali uprising and Muhammad Hakim's invasion, when suddenly,

255 Sunday, November 11, 1582.

the mighty throne of Hindustan seemed to be shaking to its foundations; His Majesty's brilliant campaign and easy triumph, followed by a series of bewildering innovations: a new calendar, far-reaching new laws; and the creation of a new religious society – some people say, an entirely new religion, a religion aspiring to replace or unite all others...

What to think this? It is good to pause for a while, and examine these remarkable occurrences in their proper perspective.

~

Where to begin? I've always had a lively interest in *falsafah* and religion, I've read extensively on the subject, I pride myself to be one of the few of my classmates who learned the entire Qur'an by heart by the time we were fifteen, but I by no means pretend to be an expert on either law or tradition: I've chosen the path of science. From a tender age, it has been my calling to study the wonders of God's creation, and to put to use whatever modest knowledge and skill I managed to acquire, in the fight against disease and human suffering. I neither have the ambition, nor the ability, to recount and discuss in exhaustive detail all the matters that were discussed; but it would be wrong to underestimate their significance, and I will try to summarize them to the best of my abilities.

I of course do not know what His Majesty's expectations were when he organized those wretched debates. To a certain extent, it was a pastime. It amused him to invite learned men, just like he could have ordered a performance of dancing girls, musicians or acrobats.

But it was more than intellectual entertainment. It was, on the one hand, a pious God-seeker's honest attempt to attain a deeper understanding of the Object of his veneration; and it was, on the other hand, an Emperor's attempt to strengthen his Empire. For indeed, I believe His Majesty harbored the secret hope, that under his mediation, all religions would be united or at least reconciled.

In the latter ambition, he was bound to be sadly disappointed. Far from uniting people's views, the debates seemed to merely exacerbate the existing differences. In the end, the open-minded did become more enlightened, the tolerant more tolerant; but the bigots, even more hostile and fanatic.

In hindsight, His Majesty could and maybe should have known that his entire effort, however praiseworthy the motives behind it, was doomed to failure. Debates between parties who claim to own the truth will, alas, never lead to any solution. Experience shows that everyone who attempts to unite or reconcile hostile religions, ends up creating yet another sect. He's bound to fail, for one simple reason, namely that the worst enemy of truth is not error, not even falsehood; but conviction itself. Nothing is more resistant to new insights than a convinced mind. Deaf and blind to anything outside itself, it is like a clenched fist, unable to grasp anything, unless and until it finally resigns itself to opening up.

Although he never publicly said so, at least not to my knowledge, the debates in the Ibadat-Khana must, thus, have been, right from the start, a bitter disappointment to our beloved Emperor.

I have already described the shameful bickering between the four groups of attendants, but that was only a foretaste of the strife to come.

As was to be expected, the fighting started in real earnest, with bitter arguments and accusations back and forth between Sunni and Shi'a. The latter, of course, accused the Sunni of having betrayed the Prophet and his family, and martyred the Prophet's own grandsons. The Sunni retorted that the Prophet had never ordained that his successors should be chosen among his own descendants, and that the Shi'a devotion to Ali and his would-be successors, the Shi'a Imams, was nothing but *ilhad*, heresy[256]. Indeed, argued the Sunni: the Shi'a tenet that their Imams are sinless 'channels of the divine light of the Prophet' (Nur Muhammadi), puts these Imams on practically the same level as Muhammad himself; it gives them a status of prophethood, in blatant contradiction with divine revelation, which clearly states that Muhammad, and Muhammad alone, is the Seal of the Prophets.

The argument soon became so heated that the Emperor ordered them to speak in turns, without interrupting. Alas, this hardly helped to soothe the tempers. The Sunnis, who were given the floor first, started arguing among themselves, on the question whether Shi'as are still to be considered Muslims. Only a minority was ready to concede that the Shi'a are Muslims, albeit guilty of *ilhad*. The majority maintained that the Shi'a have placed themselves outside Islam, and that they are, at best, entitled to the status of *Ahl al-Kitab*, People of the Book, like the Yahudis and the Isawis.

---

[256] Ilhād: heresy (literally, 'deviation'); heretics are called *malāhidah* in Arabic.

When the Emperor then gave the floor to the Shi'a representatives, they (after establishing the legitimacy of the claims of Ali and his party) maintained, on the contrary, that it was the Sunni who had placed themselves outside Islam, for, so they claimed, he who dies without knowing the Imam of his age, dies an unbeliever. Soon after that, they, too, lost themselves in endless quarrels amongst their own factions and sects: the majority Ithna'asshariyyah, or Twelve-Imam Shi'a, the Zaydi, or Five-Imam Shi'a, the Isma'ili Seveners, the Kharijites, and so on.

After a while, the Emperor grew tired of all this. He asked the participants to refrain, for the time being, from further debates on the Sunni-Shi'a divide and invited them to instruct him in what he hoped would be a less controversial subject: Shari'ah law and jurisprudence. Soon, we found ourselves entangled in a cobweb of rules, regulations, principles and precedents, which, as the Emperor did not fail to remark, seemed to be mainly preoccupied with rather trivial formalities.

How should *Namaz*[257] be said? Should one lean on one knee or both? Should the word *Amin* be pronounced softly, or audibly? Is it permissible to say Namaz for the dead? What is the validity and merit of a prayer for which the prescribed formalities have not been followed? What if those formalities have been omitted by mistake? What kind of prayer is one allowed to say before having performed the necessary ablutions? Is it permissible to pray, if one has neglected to shave one's armpits and pubic hair within the prescribed time? What is the validity of a prayer said while standing up or walking?

Can one eat a fowl, properly killed by a Muslim, when the feathers and entrails have been removed by an infidel? Can a chicken which has been retrieved from the mouth of a dog or a cat, still be eaten? What if it had been properly slaughtered before the dog or the cat stole it? What if its feathers had already been plucked: has the meat irrevocably turned *napak*[258], now that it has been touched by the dog's or cat's saliva? Is it possible to render it *pak* again, by washing it with pure water? What if the fowl was alive at the time it was snatched, and has died as a result

[257] Nāmāz: Persian for prayer.

[258] Pāk: pure; napāk: unclean.

of the dog's bite? What if it is still alive, but mortally wounded? Does it make any difference whether it has bled or not?

In the beginning, the Emperor seemed amused, rather than bored or irritated, by the unexpected complexity of these matters. Then, however, the inevitable incident occurred.

One evening, the ulama had debated at length among themselves about the necessary ablutions before prayer. There is no question that a bath is necessary when an emission of semen has occurred, but what if there has only been arousal? What if a few drops of slime have leaked from the penis and stained the clothes, although no effusion of semen has occurred? What if a man – or a woman – experiences arousal in the bath? Will that turn the washing water *napak*?'

'It seems to me,' the Emperor casually remarked after a while, an amused smile on his face, 'that a man and a woman who want to make love, better take their bath before they lie together – they will find each other's body so much more enjoyable! And I have to say, I fail to see how and why the emission of so tender a fluid would suddenly render a man unfit to pray to his Creator!'

No one dared to react, and the debate went on as planned. The next day, however, the Emperor's informants warned him that the palace was rife with gossip and controversy. Certain ulama – no doubt, Makhdum ul Mulk and his clique were behind this – were spreading the rumor that the Emperor had been mocking the precepts of religion; that he wanted to abolish the Law, or at least introduce *bid'ah*[259]; and many other reproaches to the same effect.

Fortunately, Shaykh Mubarak managed to put the issue to rest.

'It has come to His Majesty's attention,' he stated at the next assembly, 'that the recent debates in this very Ibadat-Khana have given rise to misunderstandings and confusion – not among the wise like ourselves, of course, but among the uneducated, the simple-minded, and those of malicious intent!'

There was a long, uncomfortable pause. Mubarak was keeping his eyes averted, but it did not escape anyone's attention, how the Emperor's inscrutable gaze rested, one by one, on each of the ulama – gauging, as it were, the very depths of their conscience.

[259] Bid'ah: unauthorized innovation in religious matters.

'As men of wisdom, my brethren,' Mubarak continued, suddenly in a much gentler, amicable tone, 'as men of learning, who have dedicated their lives to the study of Allah's message, it is our task to light the torches of wisdom in the darkness of error; we, my brethren, have to be beacons of light in the tortuous caves of confusion.

Now, the question before us is simple: is there a contradiction between the recommendation to bathe before the act of mating, and the precept to do so afterwards? Of course not! We all know, that to bathe after semen has been emitted, is to comply with a religious rule. But what is the purpose of that rule? Evidently, it has little, if anything, to do with bodily cleanliness: its main purpose is to remind us, that in prayer, our full and undivided attention, our entire mind and soul, should be with God, and God alone. On the other hand, the recommendation to wash before making love is of another kind: it's a practical piece of advice, based on reason, on considerations of personal hygiene and bodily comfort; it is a conclusion to which every right-minded person will arrive, when reflecting on the act of mating.'

'The obligation to wash after lying with a woman,' Mubarak summarized, 'is thus, a religious guideline, pertaining, not to intercourse, nor to hygiene, but to prayer; whereas the recommendation to wash before sleeping with her, is practical guidance pertaining to human life, a simple conclusion of factual experience, common sense, and reason. Is one recommendation right, the other one wrong? Of course not. Both are true and both are respectable, for both have their origin in God, Who has given us both reason and revelation, and Who is the source of all truth. And God being the foundation and essence of all truth, how could one truth ever contradict another? Impossible! God is merciful, and He is One – inside Him is no contradiction, and to state the contrary would be blasphemous!'

After this allocution, the gossip died down quickly. Whether it was thanks to Mubarak's persuasiveness, or out of fear for the Emperor's spies, I leave that aside. The important thing was that an open conflict had been averted, I thought to myself.

Alas, how could I be so naïve? Did I not sense the brooding hatred, behind the slick, courtly manners? How could I fail to recognize the insidious disease, the slowly festering abscesses under seemingly healthy skin? Clearly, it was only a matter of time, before the next one would erupt...

After his failed attempt to initiate a dialogue between Sunni and Shi'a, and after those frustrating discussions on the intricacies of the Law, the Emperor made another attempt at making the debates more productive and interesting. He longed, so he told the participants, to be initiated in all the knowledge and insights man had acquired into the eternal Attributes of the Divine and the mysteries of creation. A deeper understanding of God's greatness, he argued, can only help to increase our devotion.

The first mystery he invited us to reflect upon, was the purpose of creation.

'I've often wondered,' he said, 'why did God decide to create the world, what were His reasons ? Surely, He does not need us, or anything or anybody else? So, why does the world exist at all?'

'Human intellect, unfortunately, will never be able to penetrate the unfathomable depths of Allah's thinking,' Makhdum ul Mulk replied.

'It is quite true that He does not need us. We have to assume, therefore, that the purpose of creation is to honor and worship Him!'

'It is, without any doubt, our duty to worship the Creator, with all our heart,' Mubarak agreed. 'But as you rightly point out: that does not make creation less of a mystery. Is it not written, that if all the world would turn against its Creator, it would not in the least diminish His unspeakable majesty? And that if on the contrary, all people would suddenly become perfectly virtuous and devout, they couldn't add a single grain to God's glory, not the smallest pinch of salt, not the tiniest speck of dust? Allah is perfect, He possesses all and everything; nothing can be given to Him, and nothing can be taken away from Him. So, why has He decided to create the world? Out of a desire to be worshipped? I find that hard to believe, since He needs no reverence and stands above all flattery. No, I am rather inclined to think that creation is the necessary consequence of God's love, compassion and mercy. Since He is the all-Compassionate, the all-Merciful, His desire, nay, His nature is to share His Being with the created world.

I tend to follow what learned philosophers like Ibn Sina[260] and Al-Farabi had to say about this matter. God is one, eternal, completely self-sufficient. His acts are therefore caused with necessity by nothing else than His eternal Being. In God's eternal realm, understanding, will, decision and act are one. Everything coincides: what He thinks comes to pass, or more correctly: what He thinks, is. He stands above all time and space; the present, past and future stand together before Him.

Thus, the entire universe arises constantly and with necessity from God's eternal being. In the beautiful words of the so-called Brethren of Purity, the Ikhwan al-Safa: The generosity and virtues in God emanate from Him by the necessity of wisdom (bi-Wajib al-Hikmah), in the same fashion that light and brightness emanate from the sun. God's nature resembles a boundless, limitless sun. The blessed light of His divine Being radiates in eternity, constantly creating and recreating the world.'

'I very much like that image,' the Emperor said. 'But why and how is the world the way it actually is? How does God's eternal light give rise to such small and humble things, like a grain of salt, or an ant crawling in the sand?'

'To be quite honest, Your Majesty: I do not have the answer to that, and I fear no one really does. But in summary, the philosophers state that the whole of creation arises as the necessary consequence of God's Thought. Indeed, God's essential property and activity is thinking, the contemplation of His own eternal Being. From that contemplation arises everything else.

As a result of God's eternal self-contemplation, God's understanding of His own Self – the thinking of thinking, so to speak –, a second Intellect emanates from Him, which is characterized by the activity of self-understanding, the contemplation of God by God. By virtue of this contemplation, a third Intellect and the heavenly sphere corresponding to it is generated, and so on. Active intellect generates passive intellect, from which emanates prime matter and all the rest of creation: the celestial intellects, followed by the celestial souls, the celestial bodies, and finally, the terrestrial beings. Thus, the entire universe arises as a consecutive series of spheres and intellects – ten in total – emanating

---

260 Avicenna.

from God, but distinct from Him, and obviously, lower than Him. The lowest of these spheres is our own sublunary world, and its corresponding Intellect is the creating spirit that permeates all living things. All of this arises from God with necessity, for it is the consequence of His eternal essence, and not linked to anything external to Him.'

'I have to admit, this all sounds very complicated to me, and I'm not sure I understand it,' the Emperor said. 'But as I said: I very much like that image: that the created world is like the warmth and the light that flow from the sun.'

'Human words will never be able to adequately describe the Divine Reality,' Mubarak admitted, but the quest for ultimate truth – through *falsafah* and kalam – is without any doubt, the noblest possible endeavor of human intellect. And difficult though it sometimes may be, the insights it yields are more than worth the effort!'

'I think we need to be a bit more cautious, my learned friend,' Makhdum ul Mulk sneered. 'Have we not been warned against talking, and not keeping silent, about things about which the Companions of the Prophet have kept silence? What is the use of lofty human theories, when Allah Himself has blessed us with His own Divine tuition? Is Allah's truth not vastly superior to whatever 'lofty insight' we might ever come up with by ourselves?'

'Why would it be so wrong, my learned brother, to use the faculty of reason? Is reason not a gift of the Creator Himself?'

'Nonsense! The only legitimate use of reason is to seek to determine what God's commandments are! The aim of religious thought is not knowledge for knowledge's sake, but to find favor in the eyes of the Creator!'

'Are you saying, my learned brother, that it is wrong to practice kalam, to further our knowledge of the Divine mysteries?'

'Kalam may be acceptable and appropriate when it deals with practical human actions. But about the sacred mysteries of the Divine, silence is much better! Everything mankind knows or needs to know has been revealed by God Himself. Does not the word of Allah contain sufficient guidance and education for the faithful? Besides, who are we to judge the word of Allah? He judges us; we are not at liberty to judge Him or His Message!'

'Who says anything about judging the Creator or His message, honorable Shaykh ul-Islam? We are discussing the furthering of knowledge! Are we not human beings? Have we not been created with an independent mind? Is it not our right – nay, our duty! – to ascertain the validity of our beliefs? The Holy Qur'an Itself holds human intellect, 'aql, in high esteem! Does It not urge us to observe and think clearly, so that we may believe? Does It not invite us to ponder creation, to study the universe, the heavens and the earth, to reach insight and understanding in the eternal wisdom of the Almighty? Do the Hadith not say that the ink of a scholar is more sacred than the blood of a martyr? Did the Prophet himself not say that it is every Muslim's obligation to seek knowledge, even if he has to go to China for it?'

'What's the point of searching for the truth, if one already has it? All this fancy kalam of yours, my friend, is inherently dangerous! At best, it is redundant, confirming what has been revealed. But more often than not, it will lead to vain conjectures, confusion, unnecessary doubts, and even to heresy or outright disbelief! The Holy Qur'an, the Hadith, the acknowledged Tradition of the elders, they are all we need! In matters pertaining to the Divine, like in legal matters, the doors of ijtihad[261] have been closed, a long time ago!'

'Where is it written that the doors of ijtihad have been closed, my learned friend? Not one of the founders of the legal schools has ever claimed this, the Prophet never said so...'

'Noble and honorable Masters,' the Emperor suddenly interrupted, 'I am inclined to think that both of you are making a valid point: you, Shaykh ul-Islam, are quite right to warn us that we should avoid shallow thinking, and that we should not take it lightly when an apparent contradiction between faith and reason arises. However, I do believe that it is our right – and even our duty – to reconcile reason with revelation. As Shaykh Mubarak points out: since both are divine gifts to humankind, both should lead to the truth! The sacred path of faith, it seems to me, is much better trodden when it is lighted by the torch of reason!'

He paused and rubbed his eyes and forehead. No one dared to react to what he had just said.

'It is getting late, venerable masters,' he continued, suddenly looking dead tired. 'Tasks of high importance await us in the morrow. We better

[261] Ijtihād: interpretation.

adjourn for now and continue this most interesting debate the next time. Thank you all for your appreciated contribution.'

⁂

Barely had I retired to my quarters, when I received a summons to betake myself immediately to the diwan-i-khas. For some reason, I was not at all surprised. Shaykh Mubarak and Abu-l Fazl arrived at about the same time – no surprise either. Servants installed us on comfortable carpets and cushions, and brought us wine, water, sherbets, nuts, fruits, sweetmeats and other refreshments, while we waited for the Emperor.

We didn't have to wait for long. Impatiently beckoning us to remain seated when we wanted to jump to our feet to pay our respects, he sat himself down, and showered us with questions:

'Tell me, gentlemen, what do you think happened here tonight? I have the impression Makhdum ul Mulk truly means what he says, don't you? I can hardly blame him for that, can I? After all, that's what the ibadat-Khana is all about! But what to say about these claims he makes? Is it true that *falsafah* is actually forbidden under Islam? What does he mean, when he says that the doors of *ijtihad* are closed?'

'Makhdum ul Mulk is talking nonsense, Your Majesty,' Abu-l Fazl exclaimed. 'He's only out to protect his own position!'

'I wholeheartedly agree with your second statement, my son,' Mubarak said, 'but not entirely with the first. To be honest, I fear there is a deep and dangerous rift between Makhdum ul Mulk's position and our own, one which reason, unfortunately, is unable to bridge!'

'What do you mean, a gap *"unbridgeable by reason"*?' the Emperor asked.

'Alas, Your Majesty... whether we are aware of it or not, we have to choose between two basically different basic attitudes: primacy of faith, or primacy of reason. And in the end those two attitudes are, indeed, irreconcilable.

Those who want to place faith above reason will claim that the truth has already been revealed, and that all human reasoning contrary to revelation should be rejected forthwith. Or – worse still – that independent reasoning is to be avoided, or downright prohibited.

Those committed to reason, on the other hand, are willing, at least implicitly, to suspend their religious beliefs. Indeed, whenever we engage in *falsafah*, we start from two implicit but important premises. First, that human reason is able to ascertain the truth by following the laws of logic. And second, that truth is the highest good, something to strive for, regardless of the consequences. When we truly engage ourselves in *falsafah*, we accept to consider religious statements and issues exclusively in the light of human reason, without reference to the authority of revealed scriptures or tradition... and if necessary, to readjust our beliefs in the light of our new insights.'

'Of course,' the Emperor exclaimed. 'How could a dialogue between people of different traditions ever be possible, if they both refuse to listen to anything outside their own accepted religion? It would be like two deaf men shouting at each other!'

'I wholeheartedly agree, Your Majesty. And I am happy to say that many of the most brilliant minds in the history of Islam have taken that very same position. I would however be remiss in my duty towards Your Majesty, if I would try to hide from him that this very same attitude has been severely condemned by other scholars, precisely in the way Makhdum ul Mulk has done an hour ago. Indeed: *ilm al-kalam*, the logical study of God, His eternal attributes, His word, His power and so on, is a highly controversial subject, and many arguments have been brought forward against it. Some scholars have claimed that logic – the formal art of reasoning – is nothing but word-spinning, a product of the Greek language which has no place in Islam. Their reasoning is quite simple: '*Falsafah* often leads to disbelief. Therefore, those who use it are practicing heresy; or at the very least, they are introducing *bid'ah*, forbidden innovation.'

'Forbidden innovation?'

'Well, Your Majesty, this has to do the question to what extent the words of the Holy Qur'an can and should be interpreted. You see, there are two kinds of revelation in the Qur'anic text: on the one hand, there are a number of clear precepts which need no further explanation, and on the other hand, a number of more obscure or symbolic passages, which the believers have to accept without questioning.'

'And what would those be?'

'For example, the strangely 'human' descriptions of God, Who is said to have sight, and hearing, and a body; the assurance that the blessed will see the face of God in Paradise 'like a moon in a bright night'. No one knows the correct interpretation of these passages, 'save Allah, and those firmly rooted in knowledge', says the Holy Qur'an. Those who do attempt to come up with an interpretation of their own, have deviation in their hearts and desire controversy, the conservative scholars say, for they attempt to pass judgement over matters where it is impossible to know Allah's intentions; they are guilty of attributing to Allah what He has not attributed to Himself. Even if the allegorical language used does admit a certain interpretation, it is not necessarily limited to that specific meaning, and the interpreter might choose a reading that was not intended by Allah. The Prophet and his companions have always painstakingly avoided this, and it is mere arrogance of us to think that we would be able to achieve what the Prophet apparently thought himself incapable of.

Speculating about God from a position of ignorance and adding new interpretations that are not mentioned in the established tradition, is nothing more than arrogant word-spinning. It is *bid'ah*, sinful innovation. It is ijtihad – personal interpretation and private opinion – in matters that are not revealed in the Qur'an or the Sunnah, and that is never allowable, even if the conclusion would happen to be right, for – so they say – the doors of *ijtihad* have been closed.

The great al-Ghazzali – who was so wise, that people called him *Hujjat al-Islam*, the Proof of Islam – used to say that all speculation about the nature of God is like asking how many layers an onion has, or how many seeds a pomegranate. What difference does it make, anyway? The only really important thing to know is that they are acts of God! Only submission to God, not vain speculation about Him, can lead to certainty and peace of mind. Human reason is much too weak to grasp the sublime realities of the Divine; but, says al-Ghazzali, when God takes care of the heart, the breast lightens and the mystery of the spiritual realm is revealed, the veil of error vanishes and the reality of Divine things shines in the heart. Once the heart becomes owner of truth, the mind obtains certainty.'

Mubarak kept silent for a moment, as if reflecting on his own words.

'To be honest, Your Majesty,' he continued, 'there is much wisdom in these warnings. Indeed, Islam is not some kind of spectacle, merely to be observed and investigated from the outside. No one understands Islam, unless he submits, with all his heart and mind, to God's will.

And submission implies and presupposes submission of the intellect. In the final analysis, faith must have priority over reason. Faith has no need for rational justification; on the contrary, faith is the final arbiter of reason and its pretensions, and intellect unenlightened by faith is of no use. Even if individual philosophers cannot in general be charged with infidelity, their doctrines may lead many people to refuse the teachings of religion, and to believe these are merely human constructs and artifices.'

'So Makhdum ul Mulk is right, after all?'

'I emphatically believe he's not, Your Majesty! But there is no rational way I can prove or disprove my point of view. I will always look for a way to reconcile reason and revelation, if need be by reinterpreting the revealed sacred texts until there is no contradiction left. Based on reason, I have come to a concept of religion which is peaceful, tolerant, coherent and – in my interpretation at least – entirely in agreement with the Holy Qur'an and the teachings of the Prophet. Makhdum ul Mulk, from his side, will reject reason if he thinks its conclusions are contrary to the narrow-minded bigotry he confuses with faith.'

'With all due respect, my revered father,' Abu-l Fal interrupted, 'I think you are doing that self-righteous profiteer way too much honor! Who is he, anyway? Abdullah of Sultanpur, a shrewd lawyer, who – through flattery, deceit and sheer luck – managed to persuade the late Sher Khan Sur to admit him to Court, and got appointed Shaykh ul-Islam and Makhdum ul Mulk. And what has he been doing with those lofty titles, all those years? Nothing more than lining his own pockets, selling fatwas to the highest bidder! Do you really believe he cares one bit about Islam or the Prophet? The only thing he cares about is his own privileged, lucrative position and the cushy life he leads! The doors of *ijtihad* are closed – why do you think he keeps on saying that?

Because he and the likes of him are supposed to be the only ones to know the intricacies of the Law! Because that allows them to live on the backs of the simple people who depend on them, put their trust in them, and are too humble, too naïve or too scared to doubt the integrity of these profiteers!'

'I agree, Your Majesty,' I ventured to say. 'I am by no means an expert in religious matters, but I meet people from all walks of life, and I can testify that the vast majority has nothing but praise for

Your Majesty's wisdom and tolerance! Your Majesty should not be too concerned about the ulama – the only thing they care about is their own privileges!'

'I am touched by your loyalty, my friends,' the Emperor said, nodding approvingly. 'And I fear that what you are saying is true, alas ... but let's talk about this some other time, if you will. I would first like to come back on our previous subject of discussion. Shaykh Mubarak, you told us a few moments ago that some of the greatest minds in Muslim history have practiced Kalam and *Falsafah*, did you not?'

'Indeed, Your Majesty! Men of irreproachable morals and great learning – including the great scholar and physician Ibn Sina of Esfahan, or the lesser-known but brilliant[262] Abu-l Walid ibn Rusd of al-Andalus. Both of them have written magnificent treatises, in which they clearly show how the conclusions of *Falsafah*, far from being contrary to Divine revelation, can actually help us to better understand its richness.'

'And what exactly do these treatises say?' the Emperor inquired.

'Essential in Ibn Rushd's teachings is that reason cannot lead to conclusions that are incompatible with divine revelation, for truth cannot contradict truth! When reasoning leads us to a certain conclusion, there are two possibilities: revealed religion speaks about the subject, or it does not. When it does not, there's no problem: we are allowed to follow our conclusions without any further hesitation. When, on the other hand, religion does talk about the issue at hand, there are again two possibilities: either its message is in agreement with our conclusion, or it is not. If it is not, we have to re-examine our reasoning, but if it is not faulty, if we are not mistaken in our reasoning, we have to reassess our understanding of the divine revelation. We may have misconstrued the scripture's message, we may have failed to read it in combination with other passages, we may have overlooked its hidden meaning, the Hadith we have based our interpretation on may not have been authentic. One thing, however, is and remains absolutely certain: truth does not contradict truth! Therefore, if reason comes to a conclusion that is in apparent contradiction with revelation or tradition,

[262] Ibn Rushd (Averroes) has been of paramount importance in the development of scholastic philosophy in Europe; his influence on Islamic thought, however, has been rather modest.

the question arises whether the words of that revelation or tradition need to be understood in a figurative, rather than a literal sense. If I say: I am so hungry, I could eat an entire sheep, so thirsty I could drink the whole lake, is that a lie? No, it is merely an evocative way of describing my hunger or thirst. The statement could be misleading if taken literally; but when understood correctly, it is actually closer to the truth than if I would merely say that I feel 'very hungry' or 'very thirsty'! In other words: the use of an image may help to clarify the meaning of a text.

The Holy Qur'an is no different: it is, of course, the message of God to humankind – word for word, letter for letter – but It uses human language to convey that divine message. And in conveying Its message, It uses – with incomparable eloquence and beauty – all the available registers of human language: from calm, factual statements to the most inspired and refined poetry or the most vehement exhortations.

Another, related insight of Ibn Rushd is that the Holy Qur'an thus has several layers of meaning, each adapted to the intellect and education of the reader. The same passage may contain a simple, straightforward message to the uneducated and simple-minded; and deeper, hidden meanings for the benefit of the wise, deep insights which can only be discovered by profound research and reflection. It is, in fact, quite probable that the Holy Qur'an, as part of God's eternal Speech, possesses uncountable levels of meaning, including levels of knowledge unattainable to the human mind, containing all the secrets of the universe!'

'Uncountable levels of meaning...' the Emperor mused.

'Uncountable, yes, Your Majesty. The human mind could never encompass the totality of the divine mysteries. As the great al-Ghazzali said, God does not have a body with a shape, a size or a measure. He is not a substance, nor can substances define Him; He is not an accident, nor can accidents define Him. Nothing looks like Him. Quantity cannot limit nor define Him, either regarding measurability or regarding divisibility in parts. No region can enclose Him; no side can surround Him. No being – present, past or future – looks like Him, and nothing can be compared with Him.

He is seated upon the Throne of Heaven, beside which all the thrones of this earth vanish. And yet, has it not been revealed that

He is closer to us than our own jugular vein? A thousand universes cannot contain Him, and yet, He lives inside the heart of the humblest believer! In fact, nothing and nobody is deprived of His blessings and benevolence, and it is His desire to reveal Himself, to make Himself known to His creatures. In that sense, each creature thus, has an intimate knowledge of God, in accordance with its own nature and capabilities. To the plants and beasts, devoid of reason, He is the life force that drives and sustains them. We, human beings, have been endowed by the Creator with reason and emotion, and He invites us to understand Him with our mind, and love Him with our heart.'

'So, contrary to the conservatives, you are saying it's perfectly legitimate to strive to attain a deeper understanding of the divine mysteries?'

'It most certainly is, Your Majesty. It's a fallacy to believe – as unfortunately many people seem to do nowadays – that the doors of *ijtihad* are closed. Why would they be? The very depth of the sacred Truths contained in the Holy Qur'an and the ever-changing conditions of human life, both incite us to use reason, to find new solutions in new situations, to slake our thirst for knowledge from both the Holy Qur'an and the faculty of reason, which Allah has put in the minds of all people... Did the Prophet ever despise reason? Did he ever exclude the possibility of further ijtihad or kalam? Never! Did any of the founders of the great Islamic law schools ever claim their interpretation of the Law to be final? Never! And it's not difficult to see why: while the Law is eternal, the jurists are mere human beings; and no man is allowed to claim finality. So, those who believe the doors of *Ijtihad* to be closed are in fact turning the early teachers into prophets or idols, something these teachers themselves would have utterly rejected!'

He paused, looking for the appropriate words.

'However, we always need to remain honest and cautious: the search for Truth is far from easy; the path of kalam is steep, rocky, strewn with thorns and obstacles... and dangerous! For, as the conservatives never fail to point out: it easily leads to outright disbelief!

For instance, there was a certain Abu'l Ala al Ma'ari, who lived in Iran about four hundred years after the death of the Prophet: he went as far as to claim that religion was the enemy of reason! Two kinds of people are there in this world, he used to say: those endowed with reason, who have no religion, and those who do have religion, but are deprived of reason.'

'Quite a statement to make!'

'Indeed. But he was not the only one, although nobody went quite as far as he did. Take Ar-Razi for instance: considered by many as the most irreverent of all Muslim thinkers. He, too, utterly rejected any authority other than reason. For example: he utterly refused to take any position on death and the afterlife. He followed the old Greek philosophers, emphasizing the need to overcome one's fear: to those who believe in immortality, death should hold no dread; and those who believe that death is the end of our existence and that the soul perishes with the body, should find consolation in the thought that in death, there is no pain, whereas in life, pain is the inevitable companion of pleasure.

Ar-Razi maintained that as a good practitioner of true *falsafah*, one should never adhere to any school or sect – where one's thoughts and actions are bound to be curtailed, modeled on those of some master. One should of course be learning from one's predecessors, but one should aspire to surpass them – to come to new and higher insights. To those who object that without spiritual authority, man would rapidly succumb to hopeless confusion, contradiction, strife and error, ar-Razi answered that independent thinking is to be valued above consensus. Independent thinking, he stated, is the key to the liberation of the soul: people have been created with the ability to think for themselves – they do not need a leader to tell them what to do or think.

He flatly rejected the concept of prophets and revealed religions: 'How can anyone think clearly, while committed to old wives' tales, founded on ignorance, contradiction and bigoted dogmatism? How can one believe that God would prefer one people as the standard-bearers of humankind, making all the rest dependent on them? Why would the All-wise God do that, setting one nation at the other's throat, fomenting conflict, war and bloodshed?'

What God's goodness demands, says ar-Razi, is guidance for all. And this guidance, He has graciously provided through the gift of intelligence and reason.'

'Interesting... very interesting!' the Emperor exclaimed. 'What do you think about all this, Hakim Ali?'

'I am by no means an expert in religious matters, Your Majesty. But I have to admit: this man may have been a *murtadd*, but much of what he wrote, makes eminent sense to me. I agree with him that reason is a gift from the Creator and that therefore, we are allowed – if not required – to use it. In the end, what matters in the eyes of God is righteousness and honesty; and these traits can be found in decent people everywhere. I also believe that the religions of this world are merely human attempts at describing the unknowable Creator. All of them, in their own way, are valuable and respectable.'

'I see. Do you agree, Shaykh Mubarak?'

'I certainly do, Your Majesty. Religiousness is an essential human trait, common to Muslims and non-Muslims. Now, as the Holy Qur'an teaches us, religion has a twofold character. There is *salah*, which are the prescribed rituals and prayers – which tend to be very different from one creed to the other. On the other hand, there's *Din*, the true spirit of religion, the actual devotion to the Deity – which lives in the souls of all people of good will. Those who carefully read the message of the Holy Qur'an will understand that the ritual differences between the various religions aren't that important – they're discrepancies in the outward form, not the essence. For instance: it's a well-known fact the Prophet used to turn towards Jerusalem to pray. Later in life, he started turning towards Mekkah. Does that imply that his earlier prayers were of no value? Of course not! The Prophet did this to demonstrate that with the Holy Qur'an, God had given an entirely new revelation. But he didn't mean to imply that righteousness means one has to turn east or west. Ritual is not religion, not the measure of truth: it's merely the outward appearance of devotion. The only thing that really matters in the eyes of God, is righteous living and devotion to Him – which is: devotion to goodness, truth and justice. Devotion to God through righteous living – that's the essence of any true religion! All those who try to live righteously, will find favor in the eyes of Allah – of that I am firmly convinced!'

He paused, the expression on his face suddenly turning painful.

'But what do the ulama have to say about this? Exactly the opposite! What is it they keep whispering, behind Your Majesty's back? That tolerance towards the Hindus and other infidels is *talfiq* – mixing of religion! *Talfiq*, they say, leads to an unworkable, incoherent set of beliefs, which not only will never lead to God, but will lead good people into confusion! With the advent of the Qur'anic message, the Divine revelation has been completed, and all the other traditions have been superseded. Other religions may have found mercy in God's eyes in the past, but they no longer do – not since the Holy Qur'an has been revealed. Other religions are deviant from the truth; and if one's idea of God is deviant, union with Him becomes impossible. Denial of one link in the chain is denial of the whole; worshipping God without recognizing His Prophet is impossible.

Many ulama criticize the ban on the slaughter of cows: 'To refrain from slaughtering cows out of respect for the sentiments of *kafirs* is itself *kufr*,' so they say. 'It's aimed at demolishing Islam, for it encourages the infidels in their *kufr*!'

'What?' the Emperor thundered, suddenly seething with rage. 'Who said that?'

'I do not know, Your Majesty, it's only a rumor I heard...'

'From whom? I demand to know! These traitors must be brought to justice!'

'With all due respect, Your Majesty,' Abu-l Fazl intervened, seemingly calm despite the Emperor's anger, 'I believe there's a more effective way to solve this!'

'What do you mean? Are you suggesting I should just let this go by? You must be out of your mind!' the Emperor shouted, beyond himself. For a moment, I thought he was about to hit him, or worse.

'Your Majesty may have one or two ringleaders executed, as they deserve; Abu-l Fazl proceeded calmly. 'This will restore law and order, at least for a while, but it won't resolve the tension between Your Majesty and the ulama. The misled and the ignorant may believe there's a conflict between allegiance to their Emperor and loyalty to Islam!'

With what seemed to be a superhuman effort, the Emperor managed to control his rage. His eyes seemed to smolder with anger.

'Proceed,' he muttered, barely audibly.

'I beg Your Majesty to forgive me, but I believe it's my duty towards Him to speak my mind, to offer him my point of view, so that he may take the decisions he deems appropriate!'

The Emperor's features softened a little.

'Pray, speak, Shaykh Abu-l Fazl. I promise I'll never hurt you for being honest with me, even if I dislike what you are saying. After all, I shouldn't be asking for your advice, if I do not want to hear it!'

'Your Majesty is just and kind,' Abu-l Fazl mumbled, bowing his head. 'Well, I believe this conflict between Your Majesty and the ulama can never be resolved, unless we manage to establish, once and for all, the primacy of one above the other.'

'And how do you propose to do that, my learned young friend?' the Emperor asked, clearly amused in spite of the circumstances.

'We have to fight them with their own weapons, Your Majesty. We have to make them acknowledge – in an official fatwah! – that Your Majesty has the final word in legal matters; that, in case of any disagreement, Your Majesty's opinion will prevail!'

'And how would you persuade them to agree to sign a document like that?'

'Anyone familiar with the history of Hindustan, Your Majesty, has witnessed how in just a few years' time, Your Majesty has made it the most powerful Empire on this earth. No one can deny, that by the will of the Almighty, Your Majesty is the one and only true Khalifah, the Imam-i-Adil[263] of this age, the legitimate successor and representative of the Prophet, the ultimate authority in all matters of import in this world!'

'I see what you mean, my son,' Mubarak said, glowing with pride. 'Leave this one to me – I will start drafting the document right away!'

༄

And so it came to pass, that on the 21st of Shahrivar of the twenty-fourth year of His Majesty's Reign[264], a solemn declaration was issued, bearing the signatures and seals of the highest-ranking jurists and scholars of the Empire: Abdullah of Sultanpur, Makhdum ul Mulk; Shaykh Abd-un Nabi, Sadr us-Sudur[265]; Qadi Jalal-ud-Din Multani, Qadi ul Quzat[266],

---

[263] *Imām-i-Ādil*: Just Leader, i.e. the Sovereign.

[264] Wednesday, September 2, 1579.

[265] *Sadr us-Sudūr*: high official under the Wazir (Minister of Finance, Treasurer) presiding over the *Diwān-i-Rishālat*, a lucrative office dealing with religious foundations and stipends to scholars.

[266] Supreme Judge.

Sadr-i-Jahan, Mufti General[267]; Ghazi Khan Badakhshi, who had no rival in the science of falsafah and kalam; and Shaykh Mubarak of Nagaur, 'the most learned man of the Age', who was in fact, as we have seen, the real author of the text.

In one masterstroke, thanks to young Abu-l Fazl's ingenuity, the power of the ulama was broken: this *Fatwah* officially established the Emperor's position as final arbiter in all issues, religious as well as governmental. It formally acknowledged that the rank of Just Ruler (Imam-i-'Adil) is superior to that of any mujtahid[268] or interpreter of Muslim law, thus, recognizing the Emperor as the highest authority, and in fact, giving him the ultimate and virtually unlimited authority in all matters.

The text of this declaration, which evil tongues have ventured to call the 'Infallibility Decree', goes as follows:

'Whereas Hindustan is now become the center of security and peace, and the land of justice and beneficence, a large number of people, especially learned men and men of the Law, have immigrated and chosen this country for their home.

Now we, the principal ulama, who are not only well-versed in the several departments of the Law and in the principles of jurisprudence, and well acquainted with the edicts which rest on reason or testimony, but are also known for our piety and honest intentions, have duly considered the deep meaning, first, of the following Ayat of the Holy Qur'an:

'Obey Allah, and obey the Prophet, and those who have authority among you'; and secondly, of the genuine Hadith: 'Surely the man who is dearest to Allah on the Day of Judgement is the Imam-i-Adil; whosoever obeys the Amir, obeys Thee; and whosoever rebels against him, rebels against Thee; and thirdly, of several other proofs based on reasoning or testimony: and we have agreed that the rank of Sultan-i-Adil is higher in the eyes of Allah than the rank of a Mujtahid. Further, we declare that the Sultan of Islam, Amir of the Faithful, Shadow of God in the world, Abu-l Fath Jalal-ud-Din Muhammad Akbar, Padshah

---

[267] Legal functionary entitled to issue legal opinion (Fatwā).

[268] *Mujtahid*: highest legal authority, entitled to make original decisions of canon law (rather than merely applying precedents already established).

Ghazi (whose kingdom God may perpetuate!) is a most just, a most wise, and a most God-fearing king.

Should, therefore, in future, a religious question come up, regarding which the opinions of the mujtahids are at variance, and His Majesty, in his penetrating understanding and clear wisdom be inclined to adopt, for the benefit of the nation and as a political expedient, any of the conflicting opinions which exist on that point, and should issue a Decree to that effect, we do hereby agree that such a Decree will be binding on us and on the whole nation.

Further, we declare that should His Majesty think fit to issue a new order, we and the nation shall likewise be bound by it – provided always that such order be not only in accordance with some Ayat of the Holy Qur'an, but also of real benefit to the nation –; and further, that any opposition on the part of his subjects to such an order passed by His Majesty shall involve damnation in the world to come, and loss of property and privileges in this.

This document has been written with honest intentions, for the glory of God and the propagation of Islam, and is signed by us, the principal ulama and lawyers, in the month of Rajab in the year nine hundred and eighty-seven.'

Few weeks later, Abdullah of Sultanpur (Makhdum ul Mulk) and Shaykh Abd-un Nabi (Sadr us-Sudur) received the license to leave His Majesty's dominions, in order to obtain, as had been their ardent and pious desire, the sacred blessings of the Hajj. Escorted by armed guards, they were hastily marched off to the Gujarati coast and put on the first available ship headed for Arabia.

Not a living soul was left in the entire Empire to challenge our Emperor's supremacy. At least, so it seemed.

Thirtieth Letter

إبادت خانه

Ibadat-Khana (2)

From the private notes of Mulazim Hakim Ali Gilani

With Makhdum ul Mulk and Abd-un Nabi out of the way, and the remaining ulama reduced to respectful obedience, there was – so it seemed – nothing or nobody left to prevent His Majesty from pursuing his intellectual curiosity. Not surprisingly, he ordered the religious debates to be reopened; and equally unsurprisingly, be it to the utter dismay of many, the meetings were no longer restricted to Muslim scholars – and indeed, no longer focused on Islam. 'My object, o wise mullahs,' the Emperor declared to the assembly, 'is to find out and disclose the principles of genuine religion, trace them to their Divine origin, and thus, ascertain veritable truth!' More ambitious a goal is hard to imagine, but he seemed confident it was achievable.

In a few months' time, Fatehpur Sikri became a unique meeting place for dozens of scholars and holy men of all kinds – the more eccentric, the better, it seemed. Half-mad, rambling, 'illuminated' Sufis; daunting Parsi fire priests; Hindus – Sadhus and savants of all kinds and denominations, their bodies and faces smeared with cremation ashes, or painted with patterns and colours of ominous extravagance; austere, white-clad and even stark-naked Jains, mouths and noses covered with cloth, sweeping the ground in front of their feet, in a commendably scrupulous if futile attempt to avoid killing even the smallest, vilest, most insignificant of insects.

All these extraordinary characters found themselves invited to the palace, covered with gifts and honors, as if they'd been emissaries of the mightiest kings. In the Emperor's presence and under his protection, they rubbed shoulders with the ulama and their mortal enemies, the black-robed Firanghi fanatics. Verily, for all their mutual hatred, the latter two so strongly resembled each other in their contempt of all the others, that more than once, they seemed to be one and the same.

For hours in a row, His Majesty would converse with these men, questioning them about their practices and convictions, and inviting the others to comment on what they just heard. Strangely enough, although not one of these conversations ever led to any conclusion; although each one seemed to raise more questions than it answered, His Majesty never seemed to tire of them.

I neither have the ability, nor the intention, to try and compile a learned treatise on all the strange teachings and doctrines thus expounded to our Emperor during these long months – my mistakes would be manifold, and my readers needlessly distracted. It is, however, of the utmost importance that I at least try to recount a few of them, for it is quite impossible to understand the history and present condition of His Majesty's Empire, if one does not at least have some knowledge of the influence these remarkable debates have had on him.

Before pursuing this matter, I should say a few words about His Majesty's remarkable interest in the Firanghis.

Ever since he first met with their emissaries, he's been favorably impressed with them: the quality of their firearms, their self-assured – not to say annoyingly arrogant! – manner, their soldiery discipline. Fascinated by these people and the far-away places they came from, he absolutely wanted to find out everything there was to know about them.

Early in the year 986[269], he sent a well-traveled army officer – a Yemenite by the name of Habibullah – on a fact-finding mission to the Firanghi settlements down in Goa. The envoy was entrusted with ample funds, and accompanied by a group of craftsmen, ordered to carefully study and copy any paintings and artifacts they could lay their hands on.

---

[269] 1578.

The mission returned later that year, laden with a wealth of exotic objects. Worthy of particular notice was a man-sized wooden box, containing a series of metal pipes, which, when air is pumped through them, make the sound of many flutes playing together. And works of art: sculptures and paintings, admittedly of a different style than those made by Persians or Hindus, but skillfully crafted and quite beautiful. Most of the paintings represented Isa[270] and his mother Maryam (upon both of whom be peace), or some other Firanghi saint. They also carried several suits of clothes in the Firanghi fashion, both male and female; and a set of strange utensils, including small iron claws, which Firanghis use to eat their food, and tiny, hard-wooden pots, burnt and charred on the inside, mounted on a hollow reed. The inside of these little pots, about the width of a man's thumb, is filled with smoldering herbs, the smoke of which is inhaled, reportedly to improve digestion and overall health.

The Emperor was visibly pleased.

'You've done well, Habibullah!' He made a sign, upon which generous amounts of gold and silver were distributed among the emissaries. 'Kindly betake yourself to the Diwan-i-khas in one hour,' he added. 'I wish to hear in private what you have to say!'

An hour later, as ordered, Habibullah presented himself at the diwan-i-khas, where also Raja Man Singh, Raja Todar Mal, Raja Birbal, Abu-l Fazl, and I had been invited.

'So, my dear Habibullah,' His Majesty said, 'quite remarkable objects you've brought back! Tell me more about these Purtugesh: I gather you are quite impressed with what you've seen? What are these people like? Speak freely; tell me everything – the good as well as the bad!'

'To be quite honest, Your Majesty, the impression they gave me is mixed, at best. They indeed appear to be quite skilful in a few areas: their ships are enormous, their weapons are made of excellent steel, and their paintings are quite beautiful; but overall, they're nothing but arrogant, barbarian infidels!'

'Are they, really? And what makes you say that? What is it about them you dislike so much?'

'Everything, Your Majesty!'

---

[270] Jesus Christ.

'Indeed? I must confess, you are arousing my curiosity! What is it about them that is so barbarous?'

'To start with the simplest example, Your Majesty: they do not write from right to left like the believers do, but from left to right, in strange, rounded scribbles, more like symbols of witchcraft than normal, decent writing. Just like the letters of the Noble Qur'an have been given to mankind by Allah Himself, this kind of writing could only have come from the Evil One!'

'Their writing may be different, but does that necessarily mean it is so much inferior to ours?', the Emperor inquired, a gently mocking smile around his lips. 'Do not the Hindus write from left to right? Their script is different from ours, but I hear from those who've cared to study it, it's actually quite sophisticated, and easier to read than ours, because all the sounds one hears in speech are represented in it, whereas in ours, only the most important sounds are written!'

'Your Majesty is right, of course,' he admitted reluctantly, though clearly unconvinced. 'But I just wanted to point out, how different these people are. Their writing may or may not be equally legible as that of the Hindus, it is most certainly less orderly, and devoid of any grace or beauty. And everything else about these people leads one to believe, it must be much inferior.'

'Again, Habibullah: what makes you say that?'

'Just look their abominable costume, Your Majesty! We take pride in ample, graceful clothes, made of precious fabrics; theirs are usually plain black, made of cheap, coarse cloth, tightly fitted around their bodies – textile must be a scarce commodity in those barbarous lands! They're not ashamed to show themselves in public with their heads uncovered, their hair often long, like that of women, and more often than not, uncombed, unwashed, disgustingly greasy. They're not ashamed of wearing trousers, so tightly fitted around their legs, that one sees the shape of their private parts! Their homes, too, are devoid of any charm. They seem to be ignorant about the art of making carpets and cushions – although, one would think, these are indispensable to make one's dwelling a place of comfort. The ground in their homes is so bare, they're compelled to sit on wooden stools, rather than on regular carpets and cushions, like normal people. And their manners! On those rare occasions where one of them is invited to enter the dwelling of a believer, he will not even have the elementary decency of taking his boots off: he will actually defile his host's carpets with the dirt of the street!

And that's only one example. Their lack of morals and civilization is even more apparent from the way they treat their women. They're scarcely better than mindless animals! Female beasts do not hide their faces; neither do Firanghi women. Male and female beasts herd together, sharing the same stables; so do the Firanghis. Not only do the women show their faces to whoever chooses to look at them, they freely meet and converse with men who do not belong to their own family! It's not hard to imagine, their cities must be little else than giant brothels!

The list of abominations goes on and on, Your Majesty. Without any shame or apprehension, these savages eat the most unclean animals, of all shapes and kinds, no matter how repulsive: everything, from swine to turtles! When they kill an animal they're about to eat, they do not care to pray or return thanks to Allah, nor do they observe whatsoever rule of cleanliness or piety. Is it not true, that any Muslim worthy of that name will pray at least five times a day, and will at that occasion carefully wash his head, hands and feet? Is it not self-evident for him to wash before a meal; and to bathe or at least wash after every call of nature? Even the Hindus, ignorant idolaters though they may be, meticulously observe rules of cleanliness and decency; but they do nothing of the kind. More shameless and filthier a race is scarcely imaginable! Even when they pray, they do not bother to wash, and neither do they when they eat. To eat, they use small iron claws – maybe just as well: if they would use their dirty hands, they might poison themselves!'

He stopped, seemed to hesitate.

'Go on, Habibullah. You wanted to say something else?'

'I beg Your Majesty's indulgence for talking about such sordid things in His presence, but even after these barbarians have relieved their bowels of the stinking remnants of all the filth they ingest, they do not think it necessary to take a bath – they merely rub themselves with some or other leaf, or dirty rag, and that's it! And if that in itself isn't disgusting enough: they use their right hand! Their manners are repulsive, worse than the most backward desert tribes! Everything about them is weird, wrong, crooked!'

'I see... And what have you learned about their religion?'

'They claim to be God-fearing, but one hardly ever sees them praying. A few times a week, they go to their churches and worship images of Isa ibn Maryam[271] and other prophets – most of them false, of course. As Your Majesty knows, they claim that the prophet Isa – upon whom be peace – is in fact God himself! When they feel safe enough, they will never miss an occasion to curse the blessed Prophet Muhammad, calling him an impostor, a fraud, or worse! Towards the Hindus, they feel nothing but contempt, and towards us Muslims, nothing but hate and fear. I am sure they would kill every last one of us, if they had the chance!'

'Like we would probably do to them, if we had the chance,' the Emperor mused, clearly unimpressed. 'Speaking of killing: tell me more about the strength of their army, the way they're organized...'

The next two hours or so, poor Habibullah found himself under an intense bombardment of questions, about the dimensions and strength of the Firanghi battlements and fortifications, the make and caliber of their guns, the number of warships, horses and men at their disposal, their equipment, and so on. The good man did his best, but there's only so much one can find out in a few weeks...

When it had become clear – painfully clear – that no further information would be coming forward, the Emperor thanked him again and gave him leave to retire, with another purse of gold as an additional reward for his efforts and loyalty. Habibullah, visibly relieved, bowed himself out.

Despite the courtesy of the Emperor's manner, it was obvious that his curiosity had not been fully satisfied.

'It may well be,' he mused, talking more to himself than to us, 'that these Firanghis are barbarian infidels. But if I look at those things Habibullah brought with him, if I look at the quality of their steel, the make of their ships and their guns, it seems to me these Firanghis, ill-mannered though they sometimes may behave, are in possession of a wealth of knowledge well worth acquiring!'

A few days later, as coincidence would have it, a remarkable story was brought to His Majesty's attention. A report came in from the governor of Bengal that two Firanghi priests had been traveling through

[271] 'Īsā ibn Maryam: Jesus, Son of Mary.

the country, preaching and trying to win converts. Apparently, they had been saying quite remarkable things. Isa, or Jesùs as they called him, teaches us that it is our duty, not only to forgive, but to love our enemies, as much as we love ourselves; justice and honesty is due to everyone, whether friend or foe. A few Purtugesh merchants, who had been embezzling tax monies, had been publicly and severely reprimanded by the priests. They said: 'Give to the Emperor, what is due to the Emperor, says the Lord! To steal from the King, even if it's a foreign King, is to break God's Law!'

True or not, this story greatly impressed His Majesty. More than once, he mused that 'a religion which so unreservedly condemns dishonesty, even against an alien government, must have exceptional values and morals!'

The Firanghis never seemed to leave his mind. Day in, day out, he would talk and speculate about them. And as nobody at Court was able to satisfy his insatiable curiosity, queries for more information were sent to every corner of the Empire. When it was reported that there were two Purtugesh in Bengal, a sailor named Pedro Tavares, who had found employ in the Bengali ports, and an aging priest called Juliano Perreira, both men were summoned to render themselves to Fatehpur Sikri without delay.

They were received with courtesy and generosity. Hardly a day went by without one or more private audiences, during which His Majesty inundated them with questions. Every day, he found new reasons to invite them, more questions to ask, but the more information he got, the less satisfied he was. Especially the explanations about the Nazariyya religion fell disappointingly short of his expectations. Surely, with surprising vehemence for such a meek and amiable man, the old priest kept fulminating against the Holy Prophet Muhammad, calling him a fraud and an imposter, and the Holy Qur'an a heap of lies, but the information the old man was able to convey about the doctrines of his own faith was rather scanty, and quite confusing.

One God, consisting of three distinct Persons? The Father, causing the Son to be born as a mortal man, from the womb of the blessed Virgin Maryam? God the Father requiring His own son to be tortured to death, in remission of the sins of mankind? Isa, or Jesùs, one person with two natures: entirely man and entirely God?

None of this seemed to make much sense. And yet, entire nations believed this! The old priest, by his own admission a man of greater piety than learning, was unable to answer the Emperor's many questions. But down in Goa, he said, there was a famous school, the College of Saint Paul; it had been founded by a special order of very wise and learned priests, the Padres Jesuitas. All these padres had acquired a vast amount of knowledge during many years of hard study; they would most certainly be able to answer any remaining questions His Majesty might have, and God willing, would lead him to salvation.

Thus, it came to pass, late in the month of Azar of the twenty-third year[272], that yet another emissary was sent to Goa, carrying a highly unusual letter: one requesting the leaders of the Order of Saint Paul to send a delegation of learned men with books to Fatehpur Sikri, as the Emperor wished to be instructed in their faith.

The imperial emissary arrived in Goa few months later, and the letter he was carrying was received with understandable elation: the Purtugesh must have fostered grand illusions about converting the mightiest monarch on earth, and creating a great Firanghi empire in the East.

Hasty preparations were made, and three of the padres sailed to the port of Daman on Gujarat's southern border, from whence they set out to travel overland, via Surat, Sarangpur, Narwar and Gwalior, to Fatehpur Sikri.

As the eldest was taken quite ill with a persistent, severe indisposition of the bowels, the padres were able to make but slow progress. Then at long last, near the end of the of the twenty-fourth year on the 19th of Esfand[273], the first two of them finally arrived at Court, to be followed a few days later by their ailing colleague.

The Emperor, who had been impatiently awaiting their arrival, received them with every possible honor. So eager was he to see them that he had them brought to his presence immediately.

He was much taken with their valuable presents. Of particular value was a beautiful painting representing the blessed Virgin Maryam

---

[272] December, 1578.

[273] February 28, 1580.

(called Mariah by the padres); His Majesty took it in both hands with great respect, bowed and placed it above his head. He ordered to take it immediately to his private quarters, and fix it high on the wall. High, as it would, so he explained, be quite unbecoming for him to look down upon the Blessed Virgin.

The *padres* then presented him with a set of eight voluminous books, bound in white parchment. This, they explained with great pride, was the precious, world-famous *Biblia Polyglotta*[274], containing the entire Holy Scriptures in Hebrew, Aramaic, Syriac, Greek and Latin, a work of exceptional scholarship! His Majesty took each of the volumes in his hands, respectfully kissing them and placing them on his head. He then asked which volume contained the *Injil*[275]. They pointed it out to him, and he again took that book in his hands, kissed it, and placed it on his head. Visibly and understandably impressed and pleased, the padres must have thought it was only a matter of time before the Emperor would convert to their faith.

As is customary with important visitors, the Emperor ordered lavish amounts of gold to be handed to them as a welcome gift. To his surprise, however, they politely but firmly refused to accept it.

'The reverend Padre Rodolfo Aquaviva and I are profoundly touched by Your Majesty's kindness and generosity,' said the oldest one of the two, a squat little man of about forty, who, though he had introduced himself as Padre Francisco Henríquez, didn't look like a Firanghi at all. 'We wouldn't want to appear ungrateful towards Your Majesty; but to accept such valuable gifts would be a breach of the vow of poverty we have taken when we indued these garments, to dedicate our lives to the Lord Jesùs Christ, our Savior. The only things we're allowed to accept for ourselves, is food, shelter and bare sustenance. Your Majesty should rest assured, however, that we're most obliged by his kindness, and that he is in our constant prayers.'

Henríquez went on to explain that he had been born from Persian

---

[274] 1100 copies of the famous Polyglot Bible were printed between 1568 and 1573 on the presses of Christopher Plantin in the city of Antwerp (Antwerpen) in present-day Belgium.

[275] Injīl: the Gospel or New Testament.

parents on the island of Hormuz[276], as Hasan, son of Ali. Orphaned at the age of ten, he had been taken into the care of Isawi priests living in the Firanghi fortress on the island. They had given him his new name, delivered him from the darkness of error, and guided him to the shining light of Truth: the Gospel of Jesùs the Messiah, God's only-begotten Son.

Such was his gratitude, that at the age of eighteen, he expressed the desire to join the holy Society of Jesùs and take the fourfold vow of chastity, poverty, obedience, and unquestioning loyalty to His Holiness the Holy Father, the head of Christianity. His mission had brought him to various Purtugesh settlements in the area, and finally to Goa, where he busied himself with priestly tasks and teaching. Since he was the only Persian-speaking padre, he had been selected to accompany this important mission, and – until such time as they would have acquired sufficient fluency themselves – to act as his brethren's interpreter.

The leader of the mission, he explained, was the young priest standing next to him: Padre Rodolfo Aquaviva, from a very important family of so-called Condes, which are high-ranking Amirs among the Firanghis; and his uncle was a Cardenal, one of only a handful of leading High Priests, from whose ranks the so-called Holy Father or Papa is chosen, Isa's representative on earth.

Aquaviva, who had heard his own name and understood he was being introduced, bowed stiffly, without changing the expression on his face.

Despite the man's young age – he must have been barely thirty – it somehow didn't come as a surprise to me he had been appointed as the head of the mission. His pale, ascetic, unsmiling face had the determined expression of the soldier, or the fanatic; and in his dark, rather deep-sunken eyes smoldered the fire of passion.

His Majesty, much taken with his new visitors and eager to get to know them, entertained them until well after midnight. As is his custom when something catches his interest, he inundated them with questions, skipping constantly from one issue to the other.

'What would you say is the greatest difference between the Isawi and the Muslims?'

'With Your Majesty's permission,' Henríquez answered, 'I'll

[276] Iranian island in the Persian Gulf, occupied by the Portuguese from 1515 tom 1622.

translate Your Majesty's questions, so Padre Aquaviva can participate in this conversation. Not only is he the leader of our mission: despite his youth, there's no one like him when it comes to religious zeal and knowledge!'

They exchanged a few sentences in what I suppose was Purtugesh, a quite incomprehensible language, full of strange nasals and 'sh'-sounds. Again, I observed with disquiet the feverous, hostile expression on the young priest's face, as he set out to enumerate his arguments.

'Your Majesty, the difference between those two couldn't be greater. It's the difference between day and night, light and dark, truth and lie, salvation and perdition!' Henríquez translated.

'Really? Do we not all worship the same Creator?'

'Perhaps, Your Majesty; indeed, there's only one God. But unfortunately, the Moors have been led astray by the lies of an imposter: we worship the Savior of Mankind, Jesùs Christ, the only-begotten Son of God, whereas the Moors worship the liar and imposter Muhammad.'

'You are mistaken, Padre! We do not worship Muhammad: he was mortal, like all of us. We do respect and honor him as the Seal of the Prophets, but we do not worship him – that would be contrary to his own teachings! Nothing and no one should be worshipped, except God Himself, that is what Islam says!'

'That may be so, but the Muslims consider Muhammad as the final messenger of God, and the so-called Qur'an as God's own word, and those tenets are false, entirely false!'

'You claim that Muhammad was a false prophet?'

'We do, Your Majesty, we do. The Scriptures provide ample, irrefutable evidence to that statement!'

'Really? Our ulama claim those very same Scriptures predict the advent of Muhammad!'

'We assure Your Majesty: that's either a blatant lie, or a sad mistake, and we will have no difficulty in proving this!'

'Really? I'd be most interested to hear your arguments! Tell me, do you really think Muhammad was a liar? Do you not think he honestly believed he was God's Messenger?'

'Maybe he did, maybe not. This much is certain: if he really did believe he was a prophet, he was, at the very least, in error! Rather than humbly accepting the true Word of God as he should have, he fell prey to his own vanity!'

'I have to say, I am shocked to hear this, but I will be interested to hear your arguments, Padre. If you allow me to ask you another question: when you say that Jesùs, as you call him, was the Son of God, what exactly do you mean ? You mean to say he was a good, holy man; so close to God, that one could truly call him God's own son – just like I'll call a man my brother, as an expression of my affection for him, even if he's not actually my brother?'

'No, Your Majesty! When we say Jesùs was the Son of God, we mean this in the most literal sense! He truly is God's only-begotten Son, born from the Father before all time, God from God, Light from Light, true God from true God; begotten, not made, one in essence with the Father, and through Whom all things are made!'

'I I'm afraid this isn't very clear to me. You are saying there's two Gods, not one?'

'No, Your Majesty! There's only one God, in three Divine Persons!'

'And those three 'Persons' would be the Father, the Son and the Virgin Maryam?'

'No, Your Majesty! The three Divine Persons are the Father, the Son, and the Holy Ghost. The Holy Virgin is the most blessed of all human beings, because she was sinless, unblemished, and chosen among all women to become the Mother of God incarnate. Indeed: God the Son has come down from Heaven for our salvation! To deliver us from sin, He was incarnate from the Holy Spirit and the Virgin Mary, and became man.'

'I understand your faith states that Isa – or Jesùs – is the Son of God, or God Himself. But could you tell me a bit more about this remarkable concept of one God and three Divine Persons?'

Henríquez and Aquaviva briefly conferred among themselves.

'Well, Your Majesty,' Henríquez answered, translating his colleague's words, 'the Divine Trinity is the most profound, impenetrable Mystery of Faith. In fact, it's impossible for any human to fathom its depths – just like it's impossible for a glass to contain the ocean! However: Divine revelation and reason provide us with valuable insights. In summary: God is one Substance, one omniscient, omnipotent Being, Who eternally exists as three Persons: the Father, the Son (who became flesh as Jesùs the Anointed), and the Holy Ghost. The relationship of these three Divine Persons is one of perichoresis, or mutual indwelling: the Father is in the Son and the Son is in the Father. The Father gives Himself to the Son and the Son gives Himself to the Father; from their unlimited, unending love proceeds the Holy Ghost, the Spirit Who has spoken to us through the Prophets. Father, Son and Holy Ghost are One and of the same Substance, yet three Persons. In the Church's tradition, this Divine Mystery has been symbolized in this drawing, aptly called the *Scutum Fidei* or *Shield of Faith*[277].'

He took a piece of paper with the following drawing:

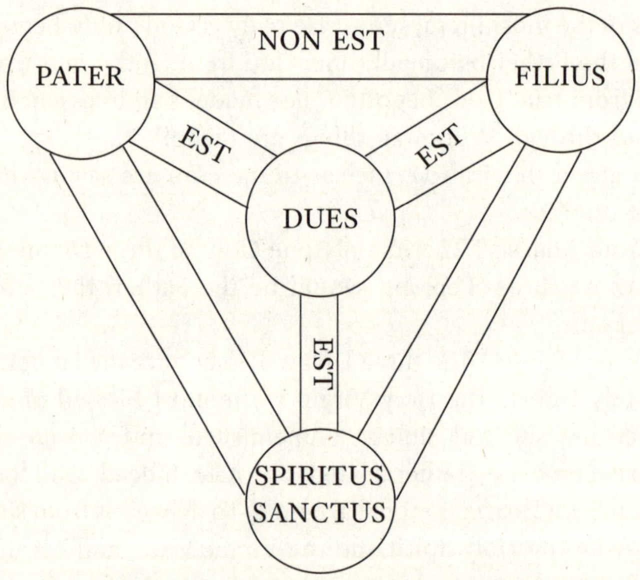

'The word 'Deus' in the middle,' he explained, 'means 'God'.

'*Pater*' is Father (like 'Pedar' in Persian!),

'Filius' is Son, and 'Spiritus Sanctus' means Holy Ghost.

God is Father, Son and Holy Ghost; all three are God; but the Father is not the Son, the Son is not the Holy Ghost, and the Holy Ghost is not the Father. The words 'est' and 'non est', mean 'is' and 'isn't' – like *ast* and *nist* in Persian.'

'If Your Majesty allows me a comment,' Abu'l Fazl said, 'I must confess this is mysterious to me – not to say manifestly incongruous,

277 See, for instance, the entries 'Trinity', and 'Shield of the Trinity' on Wikipedia.

if you don't mind me saying so! If one object is equal to another, and the second object is equal to a third one, then by definition, the first one is equal to the third! Conversely, if an object is unequal to another, then those two – again by definition – cannot both be equal to one and the same third object!'

'Perhaps you'll point out,' Abu-l Fazl continued, before Henríquez was able to react, 'that the three Divine persons are one and the same? Perhaps you mean to say that God is a single Being, that Father, Son and Ghost are but aspects of Him? In that case, dear sir, I have to say I find it rather misleading to speak of three separate Persons! Indeed, one could just as easily say there're a multitude of 'Persons' in God: His Omnipotence, for example, would be a 'Person', just like His Omniscience, His Love, and all the other Divine Attributes.'

'No,' Henríquez protested, 'that's not correct! God is a real Trinity, one God, three Divine Persons. Father, Son and Holy Ghost are real and separate persons, not mere aspects or properties! The three of them are entirely equal to the one and only God! And there's no salvation outside the Divine Savior!'

'Then, honorable Padre, I am I'm afraid I have to insist: the entire concept of the Trinity, the way you've explained it, is logically inconsistent!

'I have to say, this is extremely interesting; and I'd love to continue this conversation for many hours, were it not that it's well past midnight and that we all have important tasks awaiting us in the morning. Besides, I'd be a terrible host indeed, to deprive my guests from their rest, after what must have been exhausting travels. Let's retire, and continue this fascinating debate as soon as possible – preferably in the presence of the ulama!

However, honorable Padres: one last question before we go, if I may. No offence intended, but your last statement, that there is no salvation outside the Divine Savior: I find that quite harsh... and to be honest, very difficult to believe! Consider, for example, the poor and illiterate Hindu peasants, who probably never even heard about the One God, and much less about Isa the Son of Maryam. Surely, you'll not deny there are many good people among them? People who ardently pray and worship, every day, and lead virtuous and industrious lives? Do you really think God will reject them, when they've done their best to honor Him, all their lives?'

'This is a painful and difficult question indeed, and Your Majesty's compassion for our heathen fellow-men is commendable and a sign of the nobility of Your Majesty's character,' replied Henríquez, after having conferred at length with his colleague. 'But I'm afraid these wretched people are in a pitiable state – unless and until they have found their true Savior. Despite their piousness and devotion, they're separated from God, further away from Him than the worst sinners inside the Church. Their offerings, their garlands of flowers, their prayers: all in vain. For – as witnessed by the prophet Isaiah – their idols will not help them[278], whereas the Christian sinners can always obtain forgiveness in the bosom of our Mother the Church.'

'And why would a Hindu sinner not be forgiven, if his remorse is pure and his prayer honest?'

'Because he prays to idols of wood and stone, which are an abomination in the eyes of the Lord. In spite of all their prayers, rituals and sacrifices, the Hindu pagans are really without God: separated from Jesùs, they are without hope, helpless captives of their own delusions. For the Lord God meets us not the way we want, but in His own Way. And that Way is Jesùs of Nazareth, the Christ, our Lord and Savior. I am the Way, and the Truth, and the Life, says the Lord Jesùs. No one comes to the Father, but by me[279]. This is the Gospel's solemn warning: He who has the Son, has life; he who has not the Son has not life[280]. The cross of Christ forever divides mankind in two: light and darkness; believers and unbelievers; the saved and the damned.'

'I still find this extremely hard to believe, Padre! According to you, what happens to a person who is born as a Hindu or a Muslim and has led a virtuous life? Will he be damned for all time and suffer in all eternity, merely because he didn't know Isa, or believed him to be a mere prophet? How could that be called 'just'? Why would God allow the existence of so many different religions and beliefs, if they are an abomination in His eyes?'

'The issue raised by Your Majesty is a thorny one, and we need to

[278] Holy Bible (Douay version), Is. 46:7.

[279] John 14:6.

[280] 1 John 5:12.

tread carefully in answering it. Your Majesty's question is: 'Will all the infidels and all the unbaptized people have to suffer the pains of Hell for all eternity?' The short answer is: 'No, not necessarily, but they will not taste the sweetness of Heaven!'

'How is that?'

'Let's examine this a bit more closely. According to the obvious meaning of the word, an infidel is a person who does not have the right faith, or to put it more explicitly, a person whose intellect does not adhere to the Truths revealed by God. Now, as Your Majesty's question correctly implies, faith may be lacking through the individual's fault, or without his fault. We therefore have to make a distinction between the positive infidel, who refuses his assent to revealed Truth proposed to him with sufficient evidence, and the innocent or negative infidel, who does not have any knowledge of the Divine revelation and therefore cannot exercise an act of faith. The problem is clear, however: without revelation, true faith is impossible, and without faith, salvation is impossible.

There can be no doubt about the fate of hardened infidels, and even less about that of baptized Christians who have fallen into heresy (the denial of some essential truth of faith), or into apostasy (the abandonment of the entire doctrine of faith): these wretches have knowingly and willingly shut themselves off from the path to salvation.

On the other hand, innocent infidels, those who are born in infidelity but are of good will: they will never enter the Kingdom of Heaven, but they may, in exceptional cases, be spared the eternal torments of Hell – albeit with grave difficulty. The word of the Lord in the Gospel of Saint John is very clear about this: no one will enter the Kingdom of Heaven, unless he is born again from water and the Holy Spirit![281] The unbaptized cannot go to Heaven, no matter how virtuous the lives they have lived. Some learned theologians have tried to offer a solution to this problem by suggesting that an infidel who adheres to God and His will, does already in some way belong to the Church: since he has a desire to be united to God, he has an implicit desire of baptism; he therefore belongs to the Church in voto, (which means, by virtue of his wish), and may thus, yet attain sanctification.

[281] Joh. 3, 5.

Other theologians – correctly, in my opinion – believe that the fate of righteous infidels can never be better than that of unbaptized children: they will therefore reside in limbo, in the limbus of Hell. Indeed, the limbus is a place outside of Hell, literally on the fringes of Hell, where the righteous who died in the grace of God before the advent of Christ dwelled before they were liberated by Him, and where the sinless children who die without baptism remain forever. It is, in other words, a place for people who cannot enter Heaven, but who, being without grave personal sin, do not have to share the fate of the damned in Hell. It is believed that the people in limbo do enjoy an existence free from bodily discomfort, but they are afflicted by the wistful sadness of eternal, unfulfilled yearning, as they are forever excluded from the beatific vision of God.

It is thus painfully clear that, while the fate of the infidels is not entirely without hope, the attainment of happiness and salvation is infinitely more difficult for them than for baptized believers. It is for that reason that people like we and many thousands of our brethren, heeding the call of the Lord, dedicate our lives to preaching the Gospel, so that the millions who live in the darkness of error and superstition may see the Light and yet be saved.'

'It would seem to me,' Abu-l Fazl remarked facetiously, 'that many of them would be better off if they had not been exposed to your teachings. If they remain ignorant, they may yet be saved or at least go to that limbo you have spoken to us about. But if they do you preach and do not believe you, they're damned for all time!'

'Go ahead and laugh as much as you want, Sir. But God is not mocked! We ignore His commandments at our peril!'

'Fascinating though this conversation is,' the Emperor interrupted, 'I think we really should allow our honorable guests to retire – indeed, all of us better get some rest! I want to thank you all for your candidness, and I very much look forward to continuing this debate in the presence of the ulama. With the grace of the Almighty, we may yet be united in our pursuit of the Truth!'

Alas and of course, our beloved emperor would be sadly disappointed in his ambitious expectations.

∽

The following day saw the arrival of the third of the Firanghi Padres: one António de Montserrat, a broad-shouldered, red-haired giant of about forty-five years of age, with a wide, rutty face and a broad, fleshy nose, a mouth full of yellow, crumbly teeth, and a bushy red beard. Like his brethren, he was dressed neck to toe in a long, black robe, and on his head, he wore that strange, wide-brimmed black hat of theirs. His illness had left him exhausted and emaciated, but it was obvious that when in good health, this must be a man of considerable bodily strength. In pleasant contrast to his strong build, the expression on his face was one of quiet self-assurance, inner peace, and kindness.

As he is accustomed to do, His Majesty bade his newly arrived guest a cordial welcome. With unfeigned concern, he kept inquiring about his health, urging me and the other court physicians to see to it that the honorable Padre would get the best possible care.

During the further introductions and the usual exchange of civilities, Padre Henríquez happened to mention that Padre António was a *Catalán*, a native of Catalunya, a region in Firanghistan, about a week's traveling north-east of *Purtugal.* To my surprise, His Majesty was highly intrigued by this seemingly trivial information.

'How is it to be explained,' he asked, 'that of the three priests who traveled from Goa to Fatehpur Sikri, not one comes from the country of the Purtugesh?'

'That's merely a coincidence,' Henríquez replied after briefly consulting with Aquaviva. 'You see, Your Majesty: Firanghistan has many kingdoms, but the Holy Church instituted by our Lord Jesùs is One and universal. The priestly order to which we belong, the *Societas Jesu*, includes members from all nations, united by bonds of love and brotherhood, even if the countries where we came from would be at war with each other. Ultimately, we all take our orders from the supreme leader of the Holy Church: the Papa or Holy Father, representative of the Lord Jesùs on earth. In fact, even our kings, at least those who are true believers, all recognize the Holy Father as their supreme leader; in fact, it is from him they receive their crown.'

'Really? How interesting! So the Papa is a sort of High Priest, but also the supreme ruler of all Firanghistan? But if I understood you correctly, not all the Firanghi kings recognize the holy Papa as their superior?'

'There are indeed a few who do not, Your Majesty; but those are nothing but despicable heretics, renegades who have put themselves outside the Church! All the truly faithful recognize the Holy Father as the spiritual leader of Christianity!'

'You say the spiritual leader? Not the actual ruler?'

'The spiritual leader, indeed, Your Majesty. The Holy Father does not have great armies at his disposal, but no true believer could ever ignore his admonitions, for he is Jesùs' appointed representative on earth!'

'I see,' the Emperor mused. His eyes wandered off and he looked absently at the floor in front of him, ostensibly lost in thought.

After a while, he resumed the conversation, now busying himself with the personal comfort of his guests, ordering they be provided with ample and comfortable living quarters, worthy of the highest-ranking ambassadors. Without them even asking for it, he also assigned to them a spacious room which they were free to furnish as a small church, or Capela as they seem to call it.

The weeks came and went, and as was to be expected, the presence of the Firanghi Padres and the growing influence they seemed to have on our Emperor was the subject of almost every conversation at Court.

But the Emperor didn't seem to care. He would seize every occasion to visit the Padres or to invite them to his presence, paying them great respect at every occasion, even though he clearly didn't always agree with what they said. Each time he entered the Capela, he would bare his head, kneel down, and make the sign of the cross as they had taught him, showing great reverence for the crucifixes, pictures, relics and all the other religious objects and ornaments. He could spend an hour or more in silent prayer in front of a portrait of Isa, or in front of what the Padres called the God-lamp, a small oil lamp behind red glass, representing, so they explained, God's immanence, His ever-enduring, wakeful presence.

Sadly, but not unexpectedly, rumors and speculations about His Majesty's imminent conversion to the Isawi cult were spreading like wildfire.

The Emperor's closest confidants and the noble of heart of course understood he was merely attempting to express his respect, his belief in the sacredness of all religions. The Firanghi Padres, however, in their arrogance, eagerly allowed themselves to confuse politeness and respect with agreement, and consideration with conversion; whereas the ulama from their side mistook tolerance for *ilhad*, piety for *bid'ah*, and openness of mind for *kufr*[282].

What neither of the two camps seemed to realize, was that the harder they tried to win the Emperor's favor, the more radical and fanatic their arguments, the less convinced he became. He was looking for the Truth, they wanted to teach him their doctrine. He wanted to unite, conciliate; they only wanted to accuse, condemn and exclude. He wanted to free people's minds, they only wanted to enslave them.

There's little point in trying to recount all those interminable, and I'm afraid, quite pointless disputes.

Every day brought more of the same unsettling spectacle: the padres and the ulama ever more impatient and irritated; the debates between them increasingly acrimonious; the Emperor courteous and respectful, but less and less convinced; and the tension at Court palpably rising.

I find it hard to imagine that His Majesty wasn't aware of this, that he didn't sense the impending danger. If he did, he chose to ignore it – probably assuming he was invulnerable.

It very nearly cost him his throne.

[282] Ilhād: heresy; Bid'ah: forbidden 'innovation' in religious matters; Kufr: infidelity.

Thirty-first Letter

إبادت خانه

Ibadat-Khana (3)

So much knowledge, so much learning; so many hours of deep-delving arguments and intricate, hair-splitting logic; and yet, so little progress... Every argument, every exchange of views only deepened and widened the chasm between the participants. The seeds of respect and understanding I had attempted to sow in people's minds had born me nothing but the acrid, venomous fruits of hatred and fear. I had failed miserably.

And yet, just like even the darkest night is followed by the first glimmer of dawn, it was amidst utter failure that I finally came out victorious. Precisely at the moment where it was painfully evident that no amount of religious debate would ever lead to a conclusion, it became clear to me that it is always possible for people to live in peace and in obedience to God, provided their king correctly understands the task he has before him.

You see, my son: a king cannot erase or reason away the differences between his subjects and their traditions; but he can and must surpass them, rise above them. Like the sun shines down on the world without making any exception or distinction, a king must stand above all distinctions. He must lead and serve his people, while he himself answers to no one but the one God with the many names: Truth, Goodness, Beauty.

Read the following two accounts, my son, and understand it is your duty to rule over all your subjects in fairness and equality, no matter how irreconcilable the differences between them. Read, and see for yourself how brilliantly, compellingly this has been worded by Abu'l Fazl, my faithful friend and helper, whose quicksilver mind and golden tongue are now forever silenced, through your fault. Read, my son, see how much you owe to this man you hated so much. Read, and understand that when you ascend the throne, history will not remember you as a great emperor, unless you take Abu'l Fazl's counsel at heart.

From the Archives of the Imperial Court of Hindustan

Allocution by Shaykh 'Alim[283] Qutb ud Din Jalesari

Your Most August Imperial Majesty,
Shadow of God, King of Kings,
Invincible Commander of World-conquering Armies,
Paragon of Wisdom,
Pious Follower of the Path of God,
Truth-loving Fountain of Justice,
Benevolent Cherisher of the Poor:

It is not without hesitation, and dare I say, apprehension that I've accepted my brethren's plea to present to Your Majesty the opinion of the Muslim ulama, after the vile attacks we've been forced to undergo these past few days. Not because all those Firanghi lies and falsehoods would have caused me to entertain the slightest doubt whatsoever – neither about the truth and excellence of Islam, nor about the blatant error of their creed.

No, if I hesitated to accept this honorable task, it's because I was afraid of being unworthy, of finding myself inadequate, not learned or smart enough to come up with the right arguments to convince Your Majesty and the rest of this assembly. May Allah – the Lord of all worlds, the one to Whom nothing is impossible, the one to Whom belong, among many others, the glorious names of al-Mu'izz, al-Muzill,

283 Ālim: singular of Ulamā – Muslim theologian, Islamic jurist. Qutb ud Dīn of Jalesar was one of the Ulamā present during the religious debates.

and al-Fattah[284] – may He enlighten my spirit, and quicken my tongue!

I have Your Majesty's permission to speak frankly, without any fear of reprisal. And knowing Your Majesty's honesty and most noble disposition, I will not hesitate to do so. Like the Firanghi infidels, I will not mince my words. However, I am proud to reassure this assembly: I will not need to resort to insults and abuse like the Firanghis, for Truth is with us.

I must confess, hardly any sleep has comforted my weary eyes this past week: such was my outrage at the scandalous insults these misguided, perverted infidels have been heaping upon the sacred religion of Islam, and upon Allah's Messenger, Muhammad – eternal peace and blessings be upon him and his household!

'Whose dogs are they,' I kept asking myself, seething with rage, 'to think they can insult God's word and His Messenger in this manner? And why does His Majesty allow all this? Surely, there must be a limit to hospitality and tolerance? Why should we allow these unwashed barbarians who have come here over the waters from the devil knows where, to insult us in our own homes?'

But after a few nights thus spent in impotent rage, I managed to repress my anger, and brought myself to consider, as calmly and methodically as possible, their hollow, baseless arguments. And now, with Allah's help, I do hope to offer a decisive, compelling refutation – based, as much as feasible, on reason only, as this is the only kind of argument Your Majesty is willing to accept in the framework of these debates.

Examining the murky stream of nonsense the Firanghis have been pouring over our heads, it's blatantly clear they hardly ever come up with any argument based on reason. Instead, they call upon what they claim to be divine revelation, quoting a number of incontrollable statements from the Injil, the Tawrat, the Zabur[285] and other writings,

---

[284] Al-Mu'izz: the Honorer – he Who makes one glorious, gives dignity, and treats one with kind respect. Al-Muzill: the Dishonorer, He Who puts the sinners to shame. Al-FattāH: the Opener, He who eliminates all obstacles and brings the solution to all problems.

[285] Injīl: Gospel or New Testament; Tawrāt: the Books of Moses or Pentateuch (Torah); Zabūr: the Psalms of David.

all of which are supposed to prove that the blessed prophet Isa ibn Maryam – upon whom be peace! – was actually a God-man, and that his mission on this earth has been predicted in the books of divine revelation.

When we quote from the Holy Qur'an, they flatly deny Its divine origin, doing their utmost to discredit It and the Messenger to whom It has been revealed. Arrogant or stupid enough to ignore the Holy Qur'an's beauty and matchless perfection, they maintain It is not the word of God, but the malicious invention of a liar, or at the very best, the misguided, delusional ramblings of a devil-obsessed lunatic. They say it's a primitive, tribal creed, favoring divorce, indecency, promiscuity and lasciviousness – even in Paradise. They have the audacity to maintain that the Holy Prophet Muhammad, far from being God's ultimate Messenger and the saint we know he was, was nothing but a lewd, illiterate robber, who invented so-called divine messages to serve his own selfish purposes. The God-man Isa ibn Maryam, in contrast, was the seal of perfection, led a life of holiness, chastity and self-effacement; his divine mission was blessed and endorsed by God through many wonderful miracles – none of which, they hasten to add, ever occurred during Muhammad's life.

Behold, the entire foundation of the Isawi reasoning: a series of blatant lies, outrageous insults, gratuitous allegations, clearly and entirely unfounded and unproven, but supposedly sufficient to reject the final Message of God, and to replace It with a set of blasphemous old wives' tales, about a triune God entering into a piece of bread, and more of that twaddle!

But enough about this pagan nonsense! Merely summarizing it makes me sick to the stomach! The more important question tonight is: how do we get out of this impasse? For alas, an impasse it is: if one party says, 'Black, for my Holy Book says so, and your book is false', and the other one replies, 'White, for my Book holds the Truth, and yours is full of lies', how are we to decide between them?

Fortunately, the Creator has gifted us with reason. And while human reason in itself, I mean reason without revelation, is of course not sufficient to discover the whole truth, it does suffice amply to demonstrate, beyond any reasonable doubt, the truth of Islam and the errors of the Isawis.

Let me start with Isa, peace be upon him. The Firanghis claim the miracles he performed are a clear proof of his divinity. I won't dwell too much on this. It's of course true that Isa, peace be upon him, did perform several miracles with God's help, but so did so many other prophets, and every Muslim knows that Muhammad's life was filled with marvelous wonders and other divine blessings. Besides, I am conscious of the fact that Your Majesty has stated from the beginning of these debates that he does not wish to take a single step on the path of faith, unless it be lit by the torch of reason. I am equally aware that Your Majesty is not easily impressed by miracles – and rightfully so, for as I said: wondrous occurrences are seen in every religion, and moreover, people tend to confuse the unexpected and the unusual with the miraculous.

I won't dwell either on the ridiculous accusations about the alleged moral depravity of Islam. It's plain for everyone to see that quite on the contrary, Islam, more than any other religion, has found the right balance between full engagement in human life, and piousness, restraint, austerity, chastity and self-control. Go wherever Dar-es-Salam[286] has been established: nowhere in the world will you find such civilization; nowhere in the world have science, mathematics and arts made such spectacular progress; nowhere in the world will you find buildings and monuments of such exquisite, matchless perfection; nowhere will you find gardens of such delightful harmony; nowhere do women enjoy this level of protection and respect.

But Your Majesty invited us here to speak about religion. Let me therefore come back a few moments on the person of Isa, peace be upon him. One thing is absolutely clear: he wasn't God, and he never claimed he was. He was without any doubt a saint and a prophet, but also a mortal man, like all of us. Let me, for completeness' sake, briefly remind this honorable assembly of what is said about Isa in the Holy Qur'an, more specifically in Ayat 116 and 117 of the 5th Surah, which reads as follows:

And Behold! Allah will say: 'O Isa the son of Maryam! Did you say unto men, 'Worship me and my mother, as Gods, in derogation of Allah'?'

[286] The House of Peace, i.e. the countries where Islām has been established.

He will answer: 'Glory to You, Lord of Creation! Never could I say what I had no right to say. Had I said such a thing, You would indeed have known it. You know what is in my heart, though I know not what is in Yours. For You know in full all that is hidden. Never said I to them anything, except what You commanded me to say, to wit, 'Worship Allah, my Lord and your Lord'.

And in the 19th Surah, in Ayat 30 to 34, it is stated:

Isa said: I am indeed the servant of Allah. He has given me the Book of Revelation and made me a prophet. And He has blessed me wherever I am, and has enjoined on me prayer and charity as long as I live; has made me kind to my mother, and not overbearing or miserable. So peace is on me, the day I was born, the day that I die, and the Day that I shall be raised up to life. Such was Isa the Son of Maryam: a statement of truth, about which they vainly dispute[287].

The Firanghis will no doubt object that quotes from the Holy Qur'an prove nothing, since they deny Its Divine origin. Very well then, let me remind them of a few statements from their own *Injil.* And let me offer them and the rest of this audience a few simple arguments – plain common sense reasoning, not some kind of far-fetched *falsafah* which ensnares its practitioners in the web they have themselves been weaving! Plain common sense, that's all we need to see the light of Truth!

Let's start with a first example, one out of many: according to the *Injil,* Isa called himself 'Son of Man'. Isn't this clear and direct evidence that he didn't think he was God? How could God be the son of man? How could God be the son of both Himself and of man? And if it is so that Isa and God are one, why did he pray to God, so frequently, so humbly, so devoutly? Surely, God wouldn't pray to Himself?

And if Isa was God Himself, how could the Devil try to tempt him? Why did Isa not just order him to go away? And why did he say to the Devil: 'Go away from me, Shaytan, for I only worship the Lord God? How could God worship Himself?' And on the cross, if Isa really was God, why would he cry out: Into Your hands, I command my spirit, as the Isawi Injil claims he did?

No, clear and undeniable like the sun shines the Truth: Isa, peace

287 Qur'ān, 19, 30–34.

be upon him, was not God, and never claimed he was. But he certainly was one of God's Messengers and most loyal servants, a true Muslim, a saint, who urged people to live good lives, in submission to God. He ordered them to worship God alone, and never made the blasphemous claim that he himself was God!

I therefore want to emphasize once again that if the Isawis had remained faithful to the true message of Isa – upon whom be peace – they would have remained in the true religion. For indeed, the religion of Isa and all the other prophets – peace be upon them all – is the religion of God. His birth was a blessing for all mankind, and it is with good reason that he is mentioned several times in the Holy Qur'an, and that his saintly mother is declared to be above all the women of the world:

O Maryam!
Behold, Allah has chosen you and made you pure,
and raised you above all the women of the world[288].

But over the generations, the Isawis have lost that true religion. Errors were passed down from father to son, and grew worse with every generation. As a consequence, and as a divine punishment for the error of their ways, they now find themselves divided into innumerable divisions, schisms, and sects – much worse, much more violent, I am told, than the divisions in Islam! When Syria was conquered by the Sultan of the Turks, the Isawis supported the Muslim invaders, because they were tired of being persecuted by their fellow Isawis!

I must confess I do not know much about the different Isawi sects, and to be honest, I am not at all interested in them. What I do know: the absurdities they believe in are beyond imagination.

To start with the central tenet of all Isawi creeds: they claim that Isa the Messiah, peace be upon him, died for the sins of mankind – that through his suffering and death, he took upon himself the sins of those who believe in him. Well, isn't it impossible that God could want an innocent person to suffer for the sins of others? And isn't it plain to see that Isawi people continue suffering and committing sins, just like all other human beings? So how can they claim the world is different

[288] Qur'ān, 3:42

before and after Isa, when it's obvious, it's not? They claim no man will enter Paradise, unless he is baptized. What about a saintly man like Ibrahim? And Musa, Danyal, and all those other prophets, peace be upon them?

Everything about this creed is contrary to reason. They admit that God is One, immutable, eternal; so how can they speak of a Trinity, and divide the One God – exalted be He! – in three? And then, they claim one of these three acquired Himself a mother, and was born as Isa? How can they possibly believe the one eternal God to be subject to change, to limitations of place and time, to the needs of the body?

And then they say that Isa, the second Divinity, died the death of a common criminal – temporarily suspending his divinity, I suppose... They say that he was dead and buried for three days, then rose from the grave, went back to his disciples for a short time and promised them he would return to them in the shape of a piece of bread and a draught of wine. Has it ever crossed their mind that no one has ever witnessed any change whatsoever in that bread or wine? Don't they realize that when they worship the bread or the wine they consume in their rituals, they're really no better than the pagans? To adore a bread-God and then eat Him... how is that to be reconciled with the reverence due to God, when one considers that what gets eaten, will leave the body as stinking excrement? How can they think that God would want us to adore Him in such an indecent, odious pagan rite, contrary to nature and rejected by reason? And when we ask them to explain how a body of ten palms high could be contained in a flat piece of bread the size of a coin, they answer that a mirror of the same size can contain the reflection of a mountain, a million times larger than it. In so reasoning, they confound the essence of the mountain with one of its accidents, for that what is shown in the mirror, is not the substance, but an image; they confound the mountain with its reflection. It really is for good reasons that Islam prohibits all these images, lest the people start confusing man-made, limited symbols with the infinite divine reality behind them!

Where does this confusion come from? How is it to be explained that the Isawis have gone so far astray, that they've come to believe this blasphemous nonsense? And what are we to think about the passages in the Injil where it is suggested that Isa was indeed divine? And how is it to be explained that the Yahudis, like us, deny the divinity of Isa and proclaim the Unity of God, but are so hopelessly entangled in a maze of rituals, rules and laws that are redundant at best? And why is it that they believe there is one special people on this earth – themselves? The Yahudis, of course, are relatively harmless, since they do not seek to convert others, and readily admit non-Yahudis can attain salvation. But those Nazariyyas think it's their duty to conquer all other nations and convert them by force – which makes them the most dangerous and warlike creed on earth! How have they gone astray in this manner?

The answer, I am afraid, is as simple as it is sad: both the Isawis and the Yahudis have been given Divine Scriptures, but over the centuries, these scriptures have been adulterated by human omissions and falsifications.

The *Injil* these days consists of four different books; and I've been told they contradict each other. But originally, there was only one *Injil*, not four, and it was God's original Message to Isa. Alas! Out of stupidity, conceitedness, or both, the Isawis have neglected to take the necessary measures to preserve the Injil the way we have kept the Holy Qur'an. Instead, they've corrupted and distorted it.

Because of this, the Creator gave us His ultimate Messenger, Muhammad – may Allah bless and keep him! – to whom He revealed the Fourth and Last Book, as predicted in the prophecy of Danyal – upon whom be peace – when he announced: the religion of the one to whom will be revealed this Fourth Book is the true religion.

The Firanghis will undoubtedly object: 'How do you know that our *Injil* is not the original one?' It is, alas, clear as day that their Injil scriptures are the work of erring human beings, and not of God. Take, for example, the comparison between the Kingdom of Heaven and a grain of mustard seed, where it is said that it is the least of all seeds, but when it is grown up, it is taller than all herbs and becomes a tree, so that the birds of the air come and dwell in its branches[289]. Who is able to believe that Isa the Messiah, peace be upon him, could have said something ridiculous like that? I've seen many mustard plants and asked many people about any such plants they might have seen, here or abroad: nobody ever saw a single one that could sustain a bird! A prophet would never make a mistake like that, much less God himself!

[289] Matthew 13:31–32.

No, as I said: because of the gradual corruption of the original revelation, the need arose for a new and final revelation through the Prophet Muhammad. Isa himself announced it, when he said that he would send the Paraclete[290], who would give testimony of Isa.

And they live in constant violation of their own Holy Book! For example: it is written that Isa said, it will be more difficult for a rich man to enter into the Kingdom of God, than for a camel to pass through the eye of a needle. Yet, that does not seem to bother them one bit – least of all their leaders and priests, who like to live mired in luxury!

I am ashamed, Your Majesty, how much of your precious time I have taken already. I humbly thank Your Majesty and the honorable members of this assembly for their patience and kind attention, and will now proceed to conclude.

In the beginning of this allocution, I have indicated that human reason, as such – human reason without divine revelation, that is – does in itself not suffice to irrefutably prove everything it knows to be true.

In this case, this distinguished assembly is confronted with an argument between two religious traditions. Both claim to be founded on Divine revelation; both deny the validity of the other party's scriptures. One side cannot actually prove the other is wrong. However, when thus confronted with two alternatives, reason and common sense will help us to indicate where the truth lies, and in this case, they will be able do so beyond any reasonable doubt.

Consider, Your Majesty and distinguished members of this honorable assembly: on the one hand, the Isawi summons to believe in a nonsensical story about a triune God with a virgin wife; in delivery of sin, which evidently never took place, and a blasphemous pagan rite where one is invited to eat and drink the flesh and blood of God Himself – as if the Eternal had a human body with blood, and would want us to behave like cannibals!

What a painful contrast with Islam, where there's nothing but clarity, purity, and sacred simplicity. There is only one God; He is One; and there is no other like Him; He begets not, and is not begotten. He is the sovereign Creator of everything and everybody (including

[290] John 15:26.

Isa, peace be with him!); He is the eternal and sovereign Lord of the universe, and blesses those who submit to Him.

Your reason and common sense, I trust, will not find it too difficult to choose between the dark and the light, the blatant error and the manifest truth.

I therefore rest my case.

For my fellow Muslims, I pray that Allah may keep you, and forever be your Guide; and I take my leave from you with the words of the Holy Qur'an:

Say: He is Allah,
The One and Only;
Allah, the Eternal, Absolute;
He begets not, nor is He begotten;
And there is none like unto Him[291].

And for the non-Muslims, and for those whose vision is clouded by needless doubt, I pray that the Compassionate and Merciful may open your hearts and minds, dissipate the clouds that blind you, guide you unto the right path and lead you towards the Truth.

Eternal praise be unto Him, the First and the Last, the eternal Lord of all worlds and of the Day of Reckoning; and uncountable salutations and prayers be upon His Messenger, the Seal of the Prophets, the Lord of Apostles, Muhammad.

Din-e-Illahi

'Well, what do you make of this, my wise and learned friends?,' I asked Birbal and Abu-l Fazl, as we were sitting together after Qutb ud Din Jalesari's remarkable allocution. 'I have to say, I found tonight's plea rather convincing, but I am anxious to hear what the two smartest men in the Empire have to say about it!'

'Your Majesty is too kind,' Abu-l Fazl said, bowing his head and touching his heart. 'If Your Majesty is in agreement, perhaps it would be interesting to hear Raja Birbal's comments first: since he is neither

[291] Qur'ān, 112, 1–4.

an Isawi, nor a Muslim, his opinion will be more unprejudiced than my own.'

'Excellent advice, as always, my friend! Go ahead, Raja Birbal, do tell us what you think!'

'I do not know, Your Majesty,' Birbal answered hesitatingly. 'I should perhaps not speak of other people's religions, or venture to comment upon ways of thinking in which I've never been instructed. Besides, I really wouldn't want to hurt anyone's feelings...'

'Do not be afraid to speak your mind, my friend! We're interested to hear what you think, not what you think we would like to hear!'

'Well, Your Majesty,' Birbal continued, still somewhat ill at ease, 'to be completely honest: these past few weeks, hearing those long and bitter arguments, the thought that most often crossed my mind was: 'Why are all you Westerners so bigoted? Can't you see that God – whatever He, or She, or It may be – must be greater than all your petty differences?'

I am of course no authority on Islam, and even less on the Isawis, but the more I hear them arguing, the more I realize there's hardly any difference between them!'

'What makes you say that? They do not agree on anything!'

'Well, in my mind, they're both right, and wrong, in exactly the same way. Whence this destructive fervor, this urge to condemn and eradicate everything that does not come from their own tradition? Well, I am proud to say, that's not the way Hindus think about these things!

For example, we Hindus have a special devotion towards a certain deity, Lord Śiva for instance, and usually that is because of the caste, the village, the family in which we were born. But that does not stop us from visiting, with equal respect and piety, temples dedicated to Lord Vishnu or any other Deity; nor does it stop us from praying at the shrines of Sufi saints, or baring our heads and feet in an Isawi church! The reason is: we realize that all religions, with all their different deities, saints and rituals, are merely human attempts to get in touch with the same greater, unspeakable, mysterious Reality, which greatly surpasses all comprehension.

Your Majesty and Shaykh Abu-l Fazl may be familiar with a passage from one of our sacred scriptures, the Bradaranyaka Upanishad – an often quoted conversation between the devotee Vidagdha Śakalya and the old sage Yajñavalkya[292]:

'Tell me, Yajñavalkya, how many Gods are there?'

'As many as are mentioned in the ritual invocation within the laud to the All-Gods: three and three hundred, and three and three thousand.'

'Yes, of course, he said, but really, Yajñavalkya, how many Gods are there?'

'Thirty-three.'

'Yes, of course, he said, but really, Yajñavalkya, how many Gods are there?'

'Six.'

'Yes, of course, he said, but really, Yajñavalkya, how many Gods are there?'

'Three.'

'Yes, of course, he said, but really, Yajñavalkya, how many Gods are there?'

'Two.'

'Yes, of course, he said, but really, Yajñavalkya, how many Gods are there?'

'One and a half.'

'Yes, of course, he said, but really, Yajñavalkya, how many Gods are there?'

'One.'

Birbal paused and took a long sip from his beaker of sherbet, closing his eyes as he slowly savored it, as if all the wisdom of the world was contained in that single mouthful of ice and lime.

'As I said, Your Majesty: I am by no means an expert on Islam, and much less on the Isawis, but it seems to me that both are placing an inordinate importance on orthodoxy, on a well-defined, specific set of beliefs. For instance: 'The Holy Qur'an is eternal and uncreated, a part of the eternal Divine Attribute of Speech; It has been revealed to the Prophet Muhammad, the Seal of the Prophets, by the Angel Jibriel'; Isa is God the Son, Who became man to die for our sins'; 'He and the Father and the Holy Ghost are the three Persons inside the one God';

---

292 Bradāranyaka Upanishad, 3.9.1. Based on the Oxford World's Classics edition, translation by Patrick Olivelle.

'Maryam the mother of Isa was a virgin'; and so on, and so forth. The slightest doubt about any of these statements puts one outside the community, subject to persecution in this world and eternal damnation in the next. Why are they so stubbornly unable to accept, as we Hindus do so much more easily, that there are many ways to God, many ways, including Isa, and including Muhammad? We Hindus believe that God is inside everything and everybody. There is, if you will, a spark of God inside all of us; a divine spark, which is destined to return to its Origin, sooner or later. We therefore accept that there are as many paths to God as there are living beings; and that the divergences between the individual beliefs are not that important. For instance, many Hindus will take the countless tales of the great God-heroes and their deeds quite literally; but there's many others, who see these tales as myths or legends, great stories written to convey a deeper meaning. But what difference does that make? Does it really matter that much, if I believe Isa was a saintly prophet, rather than a pre-existing son-God, if I acknowledge that what he taught was a message of wisdom, holiness and love? For us Hindus, the Divine penetrates everybody and everything, and all holiness, wherever it comes from, is part of God!'

He took another sip, closing his eyes as he had done before.

'I am afraid that's all the wisdom I have to offer, Your Majesty... To me, all religions are fundamentally equal: paths towards the same mountain top, rivers flowing to the same ocean, pools of water, reflecting the light of the same moon. That's why the adherents of one religion should never despise the others, but should engage in dialogue, and endeavor to learn from one another, to move nearer to God!

Living at Your Majesty's court, I've come to realize that Islam is probably closer to the truth than most Hindu religions in its rejection of caste differences; Isa's message of forgiveness and brotherly love is an example to all other creeds; and both Muslims and Isawis have much to learn from us Hindus, when it comes to tolerance of diversity. All religions reflect their own facet of the truth, just like a diamond reflects the same sunlight in thousand different colours!

That's where I stand, Your Majesty. If Your Majesty would command me to become a Muslim, I would, without protest, undergo circumcision, and gladly pray five times every day in the direction of Mekkah, in the knowledge that in doing so, I would be serving God. But I could never bring myself to believe that my brethren who continue to worship the Hindu deities have suddenly become unbelievers, destined to burn in Hell! And while I would gladly proclaim that Muhammad is one of the greatest people that ever lived and a true Messenger of God, I could, alas, not bring myself to believe that he was as exceptional as the Muslims claim him to be...'

'Wholesome food for thought have you given us, my friend! Thank you for your wise counsel and truthful observations – if only there were more people like you! Well, Shaykh Abu-l Fazl, how about you? What is your opinion about all this? You've hardly said anything tonight, and that's quite unlike you, if you do not mind me saying so!'

'I do beg Your Majesty's pardon,' said Abu-l Fazl, an amused smile on his face. 'If indeed I did not say too much until now, it was because I've been overwhelmed by so many conflicting thoughts and impressions.'

'Well, we're anxious to hear about them!'

'Let me start by briefly commenting upon Qutb ud Din Jalesari's allocution today. Like Your Majesty, I've been quite impressed! Quite honestly, if I had to write a refutation of the Isawi creed, I couldn't have done it any better! And I have to say, I fully agree with his analysis. These past few weeks, I have been listening with great interest, an open mind and deep respect to the Firanghi padres. Beautiful and moving as their *Injil* may be: my conclusion is that their teachings are, quite simply, not true. I am convinced that Isa was a saint; but all this talk about Trinity, incarnation, atonement, resurrection and so on... it utterly fails to convince me! It's really too far-fetched, too incoherent, too contrary to reason to be believable! No, I could never be an Isawi. In this respect, I am and remain a Muslim!'

'In this respect only?,' I asked, scrutinizing the expression on his face, trying to gauge his thoughts. 'Are there any other respects in which you do not consider yourself a Muslim?'

Abu-l Fazl looked somewhat embarrassed. 'Probably very few people in this world are entitled to consider themselves true servants of the Almighty,' he answered with an evasive smile. He reached for his beaker of wine and took a long, slow draught, in an obvious attempt to gain some time.

'What makes one a good Muslim?,' he resumed, smacking his lips.

'And when does one cease to be one? How much deviation is allowable, before one becomes a *murtadd*[293]? These are important questions, to which not all Muslims will give the same answer...

But if Your Majesty allows me, I would like to come back to this a bit later. Before expounding my own personal religious views – which are anyway neither important, nor orthodox – I would first like to state how wholeheartedly I agree with Raja Birbal!

Like Raja Birbal, I profoundly believe that all Hindustanis – Muslims and Hindus and all the others – should live together in this land like brothers. We should accept and even cherish our differences, we should take every opportunity to learn from each other! If we're all different, it's because we all have something different to offer; if God had wanted us to be the same, He wouldn't have made us what we are! It is clearly His wish that we should live together in peace, competing in wisdom and good deeds. And praise be to the Almighty, that He has blessed us with a King, the wisdom of whom the world has not witnessed since the great and wise King Sulayman ibn Da'ud[294], peace be upon him! Yes, praise be to God, that He wants our steps to be guided by the gentle light of Your Majesty's wisdom; that He allows us to find repose in the cool and soothing shade of Your Majesty's kindness!'

'My dear Abu-l Fazl,' I said, 'much as I enjoy hearing such flowery words of praise – was it not you who once told me that of all lies, flattery is the most effective? – I have to tell you: you are not putting my mind at ease. Yes, like you and Raja Birbal, I am convinced about the value of all religions; like you, I hoped and believed that dialogue between them would bring us all closer to God. In fact, that's exactly why I've ordered the Ibadat-Khana to be built; that's exactly why I've invited representatives from all creeds and denominations to join me in that sacred quest. Yet, if I'm honest with myself – as I would urge you to be as well – I have to admit that so far, these debates have been a bitter disappointment. I often ask myself: have I been able to influence anybody at all? Has anybody changed his mind as a result of

[293] Murtadd: apostate, former Muslim who has abandoned Islām.

[294] Solomon, son of David.

this dialogue? If anything, I have the impression the fanatics have only become more fanatic!'

Abu-l Fazl nodded in agreement and pensively looked down, putting his hand to his forehead.

'Let me first assure Your Majesty,' he answered after a rather long pause, 'that I speak the truth when I express my admiration! There's no doubt in my mind, that Your Majesty's reign is a shining example to mankind, to be studied and followed by the righteous and the wise of all times, for thousands upon thousands of years! Your Majesty's justice, kindness and tolerance is comfort and shade for the wise; soothing balm on the aching souls of the humble and the downtrodden; wholesome food and drink for those who hunger and thirst after peace, justice and truth!

But if we're honest with ourselves, as Your Majesty commands us to be, we have to admit: Your Majesty's example appears to have convinced only those who were honest and prepared to open up their minds in the first place – those who didn't need to be convinced. Sadly, it failed to impress the stubborn and the wicked, those who have hardened their hearts and deafened their ears to the truth.

I've given this matter much thought, and much to my regret, I've come to the sad and distressing conclusion, that it cannot be resolved – at least not entirely, not entirely satisfactorily. This should come as no surprise. By definition, any true faith is intrinsically fanatic: after all, any strongly held conviction or persuasion, religious or other, necessarily implies that in the mind of the believer, only that particular belief is right, and all the others are wrong. Where there is no doubt, there is no tolerance...

It seems we'll have to resign ourselves to the fact that no amount of dialog, no appeal to conscience or reason will ever have the power to bring the fanatics together. On the contrary: any contact between bigots, far from promoting any mutual understanding, only helps to exacerbate feelings of contempt, fear and hatred. In fact, most of them reject the very idea of a dialogue! My father once showed me the writings of one of his own teachers, strongly opposed to any kind of contact with unbelievers. This is what it said:

'The possessor of the truth must not expose himself to the blindness, folly and perversion of those whom it has pleased Allah to leave in error. Idle conversation can never lead to desirable consequences; for Allah knows what He wants, and if it suits Him that the infidel or the *murtadd* find the right path, He needs the help of no one to bring about this miracle. One should therefore hold silence useful, and know that speaking to unbelievers, through exposing the person of the believer, is inappropriate and often even sinful.'

Discouraging, isn't it? I've often wondered: why does it have to be like this? Why are there so many bigots? Why is it so much easier to teach people to despise each other, than to accept and appreciate the differences between them?

Part of the answer is, fanaticism has one major advantage: it makes life reassuringly simple! How comforting, how heartening it is, to be able to say: 'God is almighty, God is all-knowing, I am His faithful servant, the others are not!' No need to think anymore, no need to seek after the truth, no need to form a personal opinion; everything is crystal clear: there's black and white, right and wrong, friend and foe, saved and damned, us and them! How convenient, to find oneself on the right side! And when in doubt or when challenged, the answer is sure to be found in the holy scriptures...

Whether they truly are of divine origin, I do not know, and to be honest, I very much doubt it. One thing I do know: they've never failed to yield an appropriate quote, every time a crime had to be justified!

Reason, alas, is no solution either. Many have tried to prove religion on the basis of reason – a commendable endeavor, no doubt; but alas, doomed to remain fruitless. Reason provokes the very doubts it intends to satisfy! It may amuse the quick-minded and bring tranquility to the wise; but it will, without fail, give grave offence to those who cannot bear to see their certainties undermined.

A king's task is difficult indeed: how should he deal with discord and strife? Is there a way he can convince – or force – people to live together in peace, if friendship isn't feasible?

In my humble opinion, there's only three alternatives: to impose his own religion at the expense of the others; to tolerate other religions next to the official one, or to decree universal tolerance and freedom for all religions.

Most kings will favor their own religion. Driven by religious fervor, political considerations, or both, they'll proclaim their own faith as the religion of the realm – a clear way of ascertaining their authority. The position of the unbelievers varies greatly. In most civilized countries, particularly those under Muslim rulers, other religions are inferior but tolerated, and its adherents protected. But in other kingdoms, particularly in the lands of the Isawis, dissenters are killed, or banished at least!

Sure enough, as the Purtugesh experience shows, it is possible to build a powerful nation on the basis of a single religion, but at what price? Rivers of blood and tears, and the loss of half the population! A kingdom founded on bigotry needs to literally eradicate all dissenters; it's got to cut them out, like a poisonous canker. In doing so, it is bound to lose many of its best and brightest... Failing to do so, sooner or later, it's bound to fall prey to the monster of hatred it has itself created. Compare this sorry state of affairs to the peace and prosperity in a country where, under the guidance of a wise and just king, there is peace for all!'

'Sulh-i-kul, as dear old Mir Abdul-Latif used to say...'

'Sulh-i-kul, indeed, Your Majesty! Not always the easiest way, but certainly the best, and in my opinion, the only one that truly pleases God: *Khuda solh ast*[295]!'

'But as you rightly point out, it's neither simple, nor easy...'

'Indeed, Your Majesty. An empire, ruled by its sovereign, can be compared to a body, ruled by its head. The limbs have to work together, and execute what the head has ordained! That's the God-given task of the king: to be the head of his people, to bring oneness to the multitude!'

'And how should a king accomplish this?'

'By ruling exactly the way Your Majesty does!'

'You always were a shameless flatterer, my friend!'

'May Allah strike me down if I lie! I swear: this is not flattery, this is my honest and well-considered opinion!'

'I am honored, my friend, but I fear you think me wiser than I actually am... Anyway, tell me, how would you describe the way I rule my Empire? What makes it so different from, for instance, the way my grandfather Babur ruled over it, or my father Humayun, or, for that

[295] God is Peace.

matter, his rival Sher Khan Sur and so many others?'

'I would say, it is the difference between the seed and the plant, the mine and the jewel, the unplowed land and the field in crop! It's true that those three rulers endeavored to reign with justice, and were tolerant towards their Hindu subjects. But not one of them had Your Majesty's broadmindedness and vision! Not one of them actually dared to abolish the difference between Hindus and Muslims; not one of them took such drastic measures to rule out arbitrary punishment. Your Majesty is the mightiest king on this earth, but he uses his power to serve: to serve God, and to serve his people. Truly, this is what makes an empire prosperous: when the people submit to their emperor, and their emperor submits to God.'

'I agree, my friend, but this begs the question: how to serve God, when there are many religions? How to bring unity, when dialogue only seems to deepen the rift between the various creeds?'

'This is where I would like to come back to what Raja Birbal said earlier this evening: all religions have a common core, a common core of human decency, and this is sufficient to build a peaceful and harmonious society.'

He reached for his beaker and took a sip of wine.

'Your Majesty asked me a few moments ago, whether I consider myself a Muslim. I do. I certainly am nothing else: I have the highest respect for my Hindu brethren, but I have no use for their deities and rituals; I respect the prophet Isa, but I could never believe what the Firanghi padres urge us to accept as true. Yet, I very much doubt if a man like good old Qutb ud Din Jalesari, Allah bless his soul, would still consider me to be a true Muslim, if he knew my private thoughts on religion!'

'Would he not? And what might those thoughts be?'

'Well, Your Majesty, to be honest, I think that religious people take themselves too seriously. They're much too eager to ascribe to God all kinds of thoughts and intentions that are really their own. They confound the mountain and the mirror in their hands; they confound reality with the constructs of their own minds.'

'You mean to say that religions are mere concoctions, fabrications, figments of the imagination?'

'To a large extent, yes, Your Majesty. However, that does not mean to say they're deliberate lies, nor that there's no value in them – quite the contrary!'

He took another sip.

'Most religions say we're created in God's image; in fact, I think the opposite is true. The image that most people have of God is a reflection of their own hopes and fears, an attempt to make sense of a harsh and unpredictable world. Even if we have every happiness and luxury in life, we realize we're vulnerable: we may lose our loved ones, we may become poor, or ill; and in the end, we're certain to die. Death, in fact, is the only absolute certainty in life... We know we have to die, and yet, we long for eternity. And so, we imagine ourselves a God, one Who will make everything right, even if this life is full of suffering and disappointment – a God Who will reward the good and punish the bad, Who will wipe away all tears, Who will make our lives perfect and eternal.'

'So you actually think that God does not exist?'

'To be honest, I do not know, Your Majesty. I think He does exist, but I do not know what He's like – whether, as Raja Birbal expressed it, He's a He, a She, or an It. I think He coincides with the blind, awesome force of Nature, the Force that creates and destroys, that makes the lion and the lamb, the nightingale and the cobra, all with the same imperturbable indifference...'

'A bit like some people describe Lord Śiva?'

'Indeed, Your Majesty. As I said, I don't know. But I do not think it makes that much difference.'

'Does it not? But if there is no personal God, if God is just a blind force, then there is no good and bad, no morality...'

'With all due respect, Your Majesty, that's what most religious people say, but I do not think that's actually true. The True, the Good, the Beautiful: these are names of God, but above all, they're deeply human values. They're universal principles we all feel we should try to remain faithful to, because they are important in every human life. If I honestly try to serve Truth and Goodness in my life, what practical difference does it make whether I believe these are human realities, or, aspects of an almighty God? Siding with the right honorable Raja Birbal, I would venture to say: there is *no* practical difference. Indeed, we're much indebted to our Hindu brothers for this insight: Hindus have no problem allowing hundreds and hundreds of different concepts of the Deity – even including outright atheism! Their sages have understood, that all our human theories are but imperfect attempts to describe a Reality, which surpasses our understanding.

Does it matter whether I believe the Holy Qur'an is of Divine or of human origin? What practical difference does it make, whether I believe it has been dictated word for word by the angel Jibriel, or whether I think it gradually arose in the mind of a prophet – that is, a human being who was overwhelmed by the True, the Good and the Beautiful? Personally, I am inclined to believe the latter is true, but that does not make my respect for the Holy Qur'an and the Prophet any less! The Holy Qur'an was, is, and will remain, in my mind at least, one of the, if not the, most beautiful and holy scripture that has ever been written. In an unparalleled, sublime way, it expresses Truth, Goodness and Beauty, and in that sense, it is for me, without any doubt, the Word of God.'

'I must admit, my honorable friend,' Birbal said, 'thoughts like these have crossed my own mind as well.'

'And mine,' I agreed.

'I would have been surprised if they had not, Your Majesty. In fact, I think there are very few intelligent people who do not have these doubts. But again, does it really matter? I think – no disrespect intended, Your Majesty – that the debates in the Ibadat-Khana, fascinating as they were, have clearly demonstrated that it's impossible for one believer to convert another. But fortunately, that is not necessary! We do not have to believe exactly the same to be able to live together! One is certain: if God does exist, He's big enough for all of us. The only thing that counts is that we serve Him through goodness and truthfulness. Behold, the common religion that unites us all: *Din-e-Illahi*, submission to that one God, and obedience to the one Emperor, who is God's representative, and whose task it is to serve God through peace and justice!'

'*Din-e-Illahi...* The religion of the One God, the religion that peacefully unites all others, without forcing itself on them ... Truly a wonderful concept, my friends! Let us discuss how we can make this known throughout the Empire!'

Thirty-second Letter

کابل

Kabul

I believe it was Abu-l Fazl who once told me – or was it Shaykh Mubarak? – that all virtue holds the middle between two extremes. Bravery, for instance, holds the middle between cowardice and recklessness; generosity stands in between stinginess and extravagance. The same goes for self-confidence: too little makes you fearful and weak; too much makes you reckless and irresponsible.

Much as I regret to admit it: at the time, the latter was my problem. In my defense, I want to point out it's not easy to remain level-headed when surrounded by lofty buildings and untold wealth; it's difficult not to get overconfident when the world is at your feet ...

Thus, it's inexcusable, but perhaps understandable, that when early in Esfand of the 25th Year[296], Todar Mal informs me a number of zamindars in Bengal refuse to pay their taxes, I am not overly alarmed. Little do I realize, that only a few months later, I will be facing the most dangerous rebellion of my reign, powerful enemies rising up in arms against me in the three corners of the Empire: Bengal and Bihar in the east, the Panjab in the northwest, and Gujarat in the southwest.

As I said, it all begins with what seems to be a simple tax collection issue. Suspecting that the local governor Muzaffar Khan Turbati has possibly been a bit overzealous or heavy-handed, I send Todar Mal

---

296 February 1580.

to appease the parties involved and remove the causes of discontent. I do not give the matter much further attention, until a few weeks later, truly alarming reports come in. Conciliation attempts have been unsuccessful, and every day, the mutiny is growing.

To make matters worse, the newly-appointed qadi of Jaunpur, Mullah Muhammad Yazdi, issues a fatwa, condemning the Emperor's 'religious innovations'!

How convenient, is it not, when Shari'ah law becomes an excuse not to pay taxes? The rebellion, thus, 'legitimized', spreads like wildfire, into Bihar, Odisha, Ghazipur, Varanasi, Allahabad; the outnumbered local garrisons are suddenly confronted with an all-out war.

Alas! The beginning of the campaign is an outright disaster for the imperial army. The Bengali mutineers cross the Ganga at Rajmahal, where they join forces with the rebels from Bihar, and defeat the local imperial forces led by the brave governor Muzaffar Khan, who is captured, and sadly, put to death, after what reportedly were the worst imaginable tortures. May the delights of Paradise be the eternal reward for his loyalty!

Raja Todar Mal, now in peril of death himself, with forces much too small to take on the enemy, is of course unable to avenge him. But despite the grave danger, he staunchly refuses to flee back to the safety of Fatehpur Sikri, and retreats to the fortress of Monghyr, where he and his men are besieged by the rebels.

I am just getting ready to march east and cool my anger with towers of heads, when I receive an even more disturbing dispatch: the rebels are reading the weekly khutbah in the name of my half-brother Muhammad Hakim, a worthless, drunken sot, to be sure; but allegedly and conveniently, an orthodox Muslim...

Gone are my lofty musings, my speculations about God and universe, my grandiose plans for a *Din-e-Illahi* to unite all religions. Gloomy thoughts are racing feverishly through my head: what has started as a trivial dispute over taxes and local autonomy, has assumed the pretense and legitimacy of jihad. Years of toil and labor are at stake, my family's honor, not to mention my own! Seething with impotent rage, I call an urgent meeting with Raja Man Singh and Amir Shahbaz Khan, one of my senior army generals in Fatehpur Sikri.

'I hear those Bengali mutineers, may Allah punish them in this world and the next, are reading the khutbah in Muhammad Hakim's name! Can you believe this? These dogs have the audacity to recognize that worthless idiot, that ridiculous buffoon, that preposterous nincompoop, as Padshah of Hindustan! What do you suggest we do about this?'

'Your Majesty,' says Shahbaz Khan, 'intolerable an insult though this may be, the greatest threat clearly lies in the east. Vast and rich territories are in enemy hands, many of them are experienced army leaders – unlike Muhammad Hakim, who has never led a campaign before. My suggestion is, we quickly march east, and defeat our most powerful enemies first!'

'You may be right, my friend,' says Man Singh, 'but just suppose Muhammad Hakim does invade the Panjab while we're tied up far away in Bengal! If he gets his hands on the treasures of Lahore, Dilli or Agra, all is lost! Even with the fall of Lahore alone, our position would be precarious!'

'And what do you suggest we do about it, honorable raja? That we go to the Panjab to fend off an invasion that may never come? And what if those Bengali rebels attack us in the rear? Have you ever thought of that?'

'With all due respect, honorable Amir: you may be right your solution may win us the battle of Bengal more quickly, but I fear it may actually cost us the war over Hindustan!'

I realize they're both getting angry, and raise my hand: this is no time to be divided.

'Thank you, my good friends, those are exactly the ideas that have been going through my own mind as well. Let's not lose our cool-headedness, for you are both right: Amir Shahbaz Khan correctly points out that the strongest enemy is in the east, but Raja Man Singh is right when he says that the greatest danger to the Throne actually looms across the Khyber Pass. If the treasures of Hindustan fall into Muhammad Hakim's hands, it could, God forbid, be the end of the Empire!

No, we simply have to find a way to deal with both threats at the same time!

Here's what I think: in the east, the most urgent thing is to contain the enemy – making sure we keep fighting in his heartlands, not our own. I therefore suggest, Amir Shahbaz Khan, you immediately march east, with all your troops. I will send an urgent dispatch to my foster brother Mirza Aziz Koka to join you as soon as possible with another strong contingent. He will be a formidable ally: like yourself, he's an experienced soldier who adores a good fight... Try to get a message across to Todar Mal – tell him to hold out at all cost. And once you've relieved the pressure on him, concentrate your efforts on the Teliyagarhi Pass. As I said, the most important thing right now is to contain them. I promise you, we will take care of them later!

Man Singh, my noble brother, I would like you to secure the Panjab. In case Muhammad Hakim does attack, show him and his Afghan rabble what Rajput courage is capable of! Make sure they do not get past Lahore – I promise I will follow you as soon as I can; together, we will crush this vermin, once and for all!'

I won't bore you with the details, my son, but the events soon prove the soundness of my reasoning. Encouraged by the support of the Bengali rebels, Muhammad Hakim indeed prepares for war. Two scouting expeditions led by his generals Nur ud Din and Shadman are repulsed with relative ease by our border garrisons, in the month of Azar of the twenty-fifth year[297]; a few weeks later, however, Muhammad Hakim himself attacks in force, with his entire army.

He crosses the Sindh[298] and heads straight towards Lahore, where fortunately, his advance is brought to an abrupt halt, thanks to Raja Man Singh's staunch resistance. Muhammad Hakim, who clearly counted on a general uprising in his favor, is sadly disappointed to find that nobody in the Panjab is prepared to join him: not the Rajputs, not the Sikhs, not the local Muslims. When he then learns Emperor Akbar himself is not safely occupied in faraway Bengal as he had hoped, but is advancing against him, he beats a hasty retreat. Indeed, such is his panic, that four hundred of his men perish in crossing the Chinab River.

Meanwhile, I've left nothing to chance – absolutely nothing. Personally busying myself with the campaign preparations, day and night, in every possible detail, I have in no time managed to assemble a force of truly overwhelming strength: no less than fifty thousand horse, over five hundred prime war elephants, and a host of foot soldiers

---

[297] December 1580.

[298] Indus.

and cannon. Each soldier has received eight months' pay in advance: never forget, my son, that army loyalty, in the first instance, is based on sound treasury!

On the 29th of Bahman[299], this magnificent army marches northwest, with amazing speed and precision. The Purtugesh padres, traveling with us, are astounded at the perfect organization of the supplies for such an immense host of people and animals. At each stopping place, accommodations are excellent and supplies ample, everything having been prepared in every possible detail by disciplined and courteous purveyors. They've paid in advance and more than in full, for every item – and I mean in freshly minted, unadulterated, pure gold and silver, painstakingly, up to the last stalk of straw. The villagers, of course, are left in peace, their elders and temples respected, their women untouched, just as I learned it from Bairam Khan when I was young.

Soon, this Golden Army's well-deserved reputation precedes its advance. Everywhere on its line of march, villagers gather from far and near, cheering their Emperor.

Near the town of Sirhind, scouts bring me the happy tiding that Muhammad Hakim has taken to flight, head over heels. But that does not change my plan. This time, I'll chase the bastard all the way to Kabul, and make him eat dust.

Advancing via Kalanaur and Rohtas, the army reaches the mighty Sindh, which is crossed with understandable but no less irritating difficulty and loss of time. To make things worse, the Hindu commanders have the greatest trouble persuading their men to cross over to the 'unclean' lands on the other side. I do my best not to lose my temper, but am almost literally bursting with impatience. I've got no time to lose, I need a quick and decisive victory, I can't afford to have my forces tied down in a protracted siege of a big city like Kabul! Much to my relief, Raja Man Singh, who has managed to restore order and discipline among his Rajputs, sees it my way. He volunteers to ride ahead with a fast and powerful vanguard of 20,000 horse, to catch the rebels before they reach the city. Murad, barely eleven years old, but full of fighting spirit, insists on riding with them. He keeps pestering me until I finally let him have his way.

---

[299] February 8, 1581.

On to the Khyber Pass! I hardly allow myself the time to enjoy the majestic landscape, spending my days conferring with the army commanders and devising battle plans, preparing for every conceivable eventuality, good or bad.

I do not need to wait much longer. Ably guided by the scouts, Man Singh catches up with Muhammad Hakim's army and attacks it with neither hesitation nor mercy. With God's help, he inflicts on the enemy a defeat so crushing and bloody that Muhammad Hakim does not have a glimmer of hope of making a stand at Kabul. Scared to death, he flees into mountains further west. My plan has worked perfectly.

Thus, on the 29th of Mordad of the twenty-sixth year[300], the Imperial army of Hindustan proudly marches through the wide-open iron gates of Kabul: the mighty Emperor Akbar the Great makes his triumphant entry into his grandfather's ancient capital. Awe-struck at the sight of my magnificence and power, the inhabitants receive me with humble reverence and every possible honor, but visible dread: what kind of punishment will be meted out on the poor city? How terrible will be the inevitable mass executions, the rape and plunder?

Fear quickly turns to relief, then enthusiasm, when they see for themselves the kindness and clemency a great Emperor is capable of. I leave everything and everybody in peace; I have alms distributed to the poor; and with unfeigned if conspicuous piousness, I render myself to the great Ali Masjid, where I humbly remove my armour, turban and boots, and perform the required ablutions, slowly and thoroughly. Barefoot and in plain white clothes, I enter the *musalla* and prostrate myself in front of the *mihrab*[301], where I remain for a full hour, kneeled on a simple rug, in silent prayer, thanking God for my victory.

Anxious to get back to Fatehpur, closer to the dangerous war in Bengal, I stay in Kabul for only seven days, just the time required to settle the affairs of government. I officially appoint Bakht un-Nissah, Muhammad Hakim's sister and my own half-sister, wife of Khwajah Hasan of Badakshan, as governor over the province, leaving her clear written instructions: that I entrust the government of Kabul and

---

[300] August 10, 1581.

[301] Musalla: prayer hall. Mihrab: niche in the wall, indicating the direction of Mecca.

Badakshan to her personally; that I will take it back, if and when I please; that I do not care if Muhammad Hakim, whose name I never want to hear again, returns to Kabul or not; but that she should warn him, that in the event of any new misbehaving, he should no longer expect the kindness and clemency shown to him.

He will never bother me again. His few remaining years, he confines himself to the only thing he's good at: drinking himself to death. When in the month of Tir of the Thirtieth Year[302], he does indeed die, barely thirty-one years old, I do not have a single rival left. For the rest of my life, I will think, say and do as I please.

Re-crossing the Khyber Pass, the Sindh and the great rivers of the Panjab, I triumphantly make my way back to the capital. On the 20th of Azar[303], I arrive at the gates of Fatehpur Sikri, where grandiose feasts are held to celebrate the victory.

Meanwhile, in the east, the tide has turned. The rebels besieging Todar Mal have taken to flight upon Aziz Koka's arrival; Bihar, Allahabad, Jaunpur have all been recovered by the victorious Imperial armies. The back of the insurrection is broken: slowly but surely and thoroughly, Bengal and the eastern provinces will be pacified.

~

My armies are still mopping up the last pockets of resistance in the east, when a new and equally dangerous revolt breaks out in the opposite corner of the empire: Gujarat. Nothing to do with religion this time, but all the more with taxes. Disgruntled zamindars, eager to throw off the imperial yoke, suddenly find themselves a ringleader, when the former king Muzaffar, who was captured during the conquest of Gujarat but has managed to escape, reappears from his hiding place. He promises them the moon: lucrative jagirs, treasure, freedom of taxes, high offices, glory, honor... and they're foolish enough to believe him. Soon, he assembles a sizeable army, and cleverly takes advantage of the temporary weakness of the imperial garrisons, due to the retirement of governor Sihab ud Din and his replacement by his successor I'timad Khan. Against vastly

[302] July 1585.

[303] December 1, 1581.

superior numbers, Ahmedabad falls to the enemy, and a few weeks later, Qutb ud Din, governor of Baroda, is defeated, and treacherously killed when he surrenders after having been promised a safe-conduct. All of Gujarat, except Pattan, has fallen to the enemy.

I reluctantly start preparations for yet another campaign, when Abdurrahim requests a private audience.

'Your Majesty,' he says with that tone of resolve that so strongly reminds me of his father, 'I would like to request the honor of leading an expedition to punish the Gujarati traitors.'

'Thank you, Abdurrahim, but don't you think I should go myself? The whole of Gujarat is aflame!'

'Your Majesty's wish is my command, of course. However, if I may be so frank, I do believe Your Majesty's presence is required here, in the capital! It's true, our troops in Bengal are doing well, but the war isn't over! If, Allah forbid, there would be a setback, Your Majesty's presence would be needed here! Moreover, with two wars going on in two opposite corners of the Empire, it may be wise to keep a large contingent of troops in the center, to be prepared against any eventualities. With Your Majesty's permission, I will go. I will take only five thousand men, and raise extra troops with Your Majesty's allies in Rajputana. I will ride fast, Your Majesty! The rebellion will be crushed in no time, Your Majesty can count on me!'

'Maybe,' I say, looking at the determined expression on his face with an amused smile. Those cheekbones, that long, bony nose, the fire in those black eyes – how he reminds me of his father!

'Your analysis of our situation is of course quite correct, my young friend. But my question is: can I afford to stay back here, or to allow you to leave with such a small force? You are only twenty-eight, my friend; I do admit you've won your spurs in many battles; You are bright and brave; it is for that reason I have decided to make you Salim's *ataliq*, just like your much regretted father, the great Bairam Khan, may Allah receive him in Paradise, was my own *ataliq*. I like and respect you, Abdurrahim; but do you have what it takes to run such a major campaign, so far away? I mean, do you have the necessary experience? Will you indeed be able to raise all those extra troops you need? Let me tell you what your father taught me: all things remaining equal, God favors the larger army! I hear Muzaffar, that filthy dog, has forty thousand horse at his disposal! Forty thousand horse, do you realize what that means? That's a force to be reckoned with, my young friend! Do you really think you can handle that?'

Abdurrahim looks at me, at loss for words at first, trying to hide his impatience. 'The grave where the bones of my father rest are desecrated by enemy occupation, Your Majesty,' he says softly, bowing his head. 'I humbly request Your Majesty's permission to go and fight for its liberation. If, with Allah's help, I succeed, I will be able to kiss my father's hand in Paradise without shame; and if I fail, I swear Your Majesty will find me amidst the corpses of the fallen!'

I put my hand on his shoulder.

'I am happy to see, my young friend, that the great Bairam Khan lives on in his son. Go with God – may He bless and keep you!'

I was wrong to doubt him. He proves to be as resourceful, bold and brave as his illustrious father. Advancing rapidly through Rajputana, he allies himself with the good Motha Raja [304], may God bless him, and other local Hindu and Muslim zamindars, including Abu-l Qasim Bunyad, Rai Durga, Tulsi Das Jadun, Khizr Aqa, and Mian Bahadur.

Abdurrahim's force – small in numbers, but of excellent quality – crosses the Gujarati border, and comes upon the rebel army at Sakhej, southwest of Ahmedabad, on the sixth of Bahman of the twenty-eight year[305]. The enemy fields an overwhelming force of forty thousand horse and about one hundred thousand foot soldiers, against Abdurrahim's mere ten thousand horse and five hundred elephants. Many officers beg him to retreat, but Abdurrahim refuses to yield and attacks without hesitation. Protecting his right flank against the town walls, he uses the same bold and daring tactic his father once used against Shams-ud-din: a massive elephant charge in the center, combined with a furious cavalry attack on the left, in a deadly pincer. Only here's no rice paddies to slow down the elephants; the enemy is literally crushed between hammer and anvil. Abdurrahim's furious onslaught wreaks havoc on the enemy's center. The elephants, headed by the vicious old bull Shermar, penetrate deep into the enemy ranks, trampling them by the dozen.

---

[304] The 'Fat Rājā': Udai Singh of Jodhpūr, father-in-law of Jahāngīr, grandfather of Shāh Jahān.

[305] January 14, 1584.

At the same time, Rai Durga, with elite Rajput and Turkoman cavalry, slams into their right flank and prevents them from maneuvering. In less than a quarter of an hour, Muzaffar's great army is on the run, leaving behind several thousand dead.

Abdurrahim pursues him to Khambhat[306], and from there, north to Baroda and Nandod, where he inflicts on him a second and final defeat, again with several thousand dead. Muzaffar manages to flee the carnage and goes into hiding – until his capture, a few years later. He slits his own throat, sparing me the trouble of having him executed.

When the good tiding of this great victory is brought to me, I do not hesitate one instant: Abdurrahim ibn Bairam Khan, the brave young officer who once came to my Court as a shy four-year-old orphan, is appointed Khan Khanan, Leader of the Imperial Armies – just like his father before him. Shivers run down my spine when I issue the Firman. High up above in God's sweet Heaven, Bairam Khan, my faithful *ataliq*, is smiling.

[306] Cambay.

Thirty-third Letter

دین الاحی

Din-e-Illahi[307]

From the private notes of Mulazim Hakim Ali Gilani

Something about His Majesty has changed after his return from Kabul. He seems pensive during the celebrations; he spends quite a lot of time on his own: horseback riding, aimlessly strolling around the gardens, meditating on a stone slab in the pale light of dawn. He's brooding on something.

Then, in rapid succession, remarkable things happen.

Mullah Muhammad Yazdi, the qadi of Jaunpur, the pompous windbag, so eager to support the rebels with his ill-considered fatwa, is invited to present himself at the sublime threshold, along with his colleague, the qadi of Bengal. No official reason is mentioned in the firman, but there's little doubt: the Emperor wants them to account for their treachery. But those expecting a sensational trial, are bitterly disappointed: both mullahs perish, when their boat inexplicably founders in the middle of the river.

It's only the first of a series of similar incidents. Leading mullahs expire from mysterious illnesses, meet with fateful accidents, get themselves killed in roadside robberies, or disappear from their homes, for reasons unknown, and under mysterious circumstances.

---

[307] Religion of the One God.

No one doubts, these 'incidents' are nothing less than clandestine executions, ordered by the Emperor, most probably to spare himself the lengthy public trials. In fact, this is what *everybody* believes, but the few who dare to voice their suspicions, do so sparingly, privately and whisperingly.

The Emperor, for his part, seems wholly unperturbed. Not a single comment on the rebellion; not a word about the dead mullahs, neither in public, nor in private. He calmly goes about his duties, as if nothing had happened. The qadis and other dignitaries who have died or disappeared are casually replaced with new incumbents, usually after a brief private audience with the Khan Khanan, or, in some cases, with the Emperor himself.

The outcome is strikingly effective: in a few weeks' time, law and order are restored. Never again will a mullah dare to pass judgement on the Emperor's policies, not even in private. No more doubts, no more arguments, no more criticisms: the Emperor is the undisputed *Imam-i-'Adil*[308], the true *Khalifah*. He is God's vicegerent on this earth, the ultimate authority in all matters temporal and spiritual. No Makhdum ul Mulk, no *Shaykh ul-Islam*: henceforth, the Emperor is the Mujtahid,[309] Emperor Akbar reigns, and reigns alone, in his own way: justly and independently; respectful to all, subservient to none.

With no one left to challenge him, he again indulges in his favorite intellectual pastime: religion. He seems to have lost interest in public debates, of which he convenes but few. Private audiences, however, are granted on a daily basis, day and night if need be. He's insatiable. Sadhus, faqirs, mubids[310]... the more unworldly, the more they evoke his interest. He orders a perpetual fire at Court. To the dismay of some, but with the consent of many, the Hijri lunar calendar falls into disuse: events are henceforth recorded in the Persian solar calendar, starting in the year of His Majesty's accession to the Throne. 'All religions have their own calendars, and there's nothing wrong with that,' explains the

308 *Imām-i-'Adil*: the Just Leader, the Sovereign.

309 *Mujtahid*: highest legal authority, entitled to make original decisions of Islamic law (rather than merely applying precedents already established).

310 Mūbid: Zoroastrian priest.

Emperor, 'but just like there's only one God, and only one sun shining down on all people, there's only one Emperor; it's only becoming there's only one Common Era.'

Every day (at dawn, noon, dusk and midnight) he worships the sun – directly, in the open air, or through the symbols of fire, and light. He kneels down before every sacred fire, wherever it burns, be it the Parsi shrine, the Hindu temple, or the Isawi church. Orders are issued that when the lamps are lit, all courtiers are to rise to their feet and bow their heads: to light a candle is to commemorate the rising of the Sun, and the Sun is the sacred symbol of God's Majesty. One would be inclined to conclude he's become a Parsi fire-worshiper, but that wouldn't be accurate, for the Parsi mubids are clearly not the only people to enjoy his favor.

On the balcony of his private quarters, he listens to the teachings of a feeble old Brahmin priest named Debi. The old man, by his own express request, is hoisted up the wall of the imperial residence in a cot of thick hemp ropes, as it would be impossible for him to set foot in a *mlechcha*[311] home, albeit the palace of a King most high: The rules of Brahmin purity, the old man explains apologetically, are a matter of age-old rituals, and alas, not of human politeness.

The Emperor does not seem to mind the insult. Tears glistening in his eyes, he listens, with baited breath, to the tales of the Mahabharata, and to the old priest's comments on the Thousand Names of Vishnu and Śiva[312]. His scribes take note of every word, so he may hear them whenever he desires.

'Tell me, Shaykh Abu-l Fazl, Raja Birbal,' he inquires one evening, 'when you hear the Names of Vishnu and Śiva, when you compare them to the Beautiful Names of Allah: what is the difference between them, according to you?'

'There's none, really...' says Abu-l Fazl after a brief pause; 'none that matters, anyway!'

'Well said, my brother!' agrees Birbal. 'There really is no real difference between them – or rather: the difference between them

---

[311] Mlechcha: foreign, barbarian, impure, unclean.

[312] The Names of Śiva are found in the Hymn of Thousand Names, Śiva Purāna, Kotirudrasamhitā, chapter 35; those of Vishnu, in the Mahābhārata.

is only apparent. It is of course true that many of the Hindu names, like Candrapida (Having the Moon for Diadem), Trilocana (Three-Eyed); Nilalohita (Blue-blooded), Jatin (of Matted Hair), and so on, are quite different from the Divine Names used in Islam, as they refer to the Hindu imagery. But what to say about the other names, the ones referring to the essence of God, like Puskara (the Nourisher); Dhyanadhara (Object of Meditation); Aparicchedya (the Inexplicable); Paratpara (Greater than the Greatest); Anadimadhyanidhana (With No Beginning, Middle or End), and so on? All those Names are, just like the Muslim ones, mere attempts to describe, in feeble human language, the infinite Reality behind this fleeting world!'

'I think so too,' agrees the Emperor. 'When it comes to outward appearances, no two religions would seem more different. Yet, in essence, they're the same!'

The Brahmin priest is just one of many venerable teachers introducing His Majesty to the many branches of the Hindu tradition. Particular mention should be made of Hiravijaya Suri, Bhanuchandra Upadhyaya, and Vijayasena Suri, three venerable Jain monks residing on the palace grounds, who seem to exert a remarkable attraction on him.

Heeding the summons to come to Court, the three old sages have walked all the way from Gujarat to Fatehpur, politely declining the comfortable transportation provided for them. Upon their arrival, they have of course been received with every possible honor, but once again, they have kindly turned down all the treasures offered to them in recompense for their efforts. The three will accept nothing but a jar of plain, unchilled water, and one frugal meal every day, from which not only meat and fish are strictly banned, but also any carrots, onions, leeks, garlic, and any other kind of vegetable growing under the ground: harvesting plants that grow under the ground, so they explain, might harm some small worm or insect.

The old savants initiate His Majesty in the teachings of the noble Mahavira, the Great Hero, the world-relinquishing Venerable One, twenty-fourth and last of the great Jinas,[313] who achieved ultimate liberation or moksha at the end of a life of veracity, control, penance, goodness, and absence of any kind of violence, in deeds, words, or

[313] Victor, conqueror.

thoughts. Mahavira, who spent the entirety of his blameless life fasting and meditating, naked and possession-less, indifferent alike to the smell of ordure and sandalwood, to straw and jewels, dirt and gold, pleasure and pain, attached neither to this world nor to the one beyond, desiring neither life nor death, until, in his seventy-second year, his soul effortlessly left his mortified body, to rise upward to the very top of the universe. There, it dwells, motionless and absolutely free, for all eternity.

Following the great Mahavira's saintly example, so the teachers explain, is man's true and only road to liberation. And on that road, the most important commandment is ahimsa,[314] the absolute and complete avoidance of any violence, whether of body, speech or mind. The virtuous will never kill nor cause to kill, not even the vilest and lowest of creatures, not even the most vicious of enemies; he will refrain, under all circumstances, from lying, stealing, illicit intercourse, and attachment to worldly possessions; he will avoid negative thoughts of any kind, and maintain equanimity at all times.

Never will he tread on wet soil, lest he might inadvertently kill even the smallest worm or insect; never will he light a lamp or fire of any kind, lest unsuspecting insects be attracted to its deadly glow; he will refrain from any farming requiring soil to be plowed, lest a worm or insect, no matter how despicable or insignificant, be killed or injured in the process.

Touched by these saintly teachings, the Emperor proclaims: 'The duties of the throne will, alas, at times compel a king to leave the path of ahimsa, but nevertheless, for the sake of his own soul and the wellbeing of his subjects, he should endeavor to tread it as much as possible!'

Thenceforth, he refrains from hunting; he abstains from meat, onions, leeks and garlic, and rarely takes more than one meal a day. On more than one hundred days per year, the killing of animals is prohibited throughout the Empire, and the slaughter of cows is banned altogether, as it would be in a Hindu state.

Indeed, his interest in all things Jain or Hindu seems to be growing every day. so that the wisdom of the Hindu Mahabharata may become accessible to all, he orders it to be translated from Sanskrit into Persian,

---

[314] Non-violence.

under the reluctant supervision of Maulana Abdul Qadir Badaoni, an orthodox Muslim scholar. Hindu symbols, customs and rituals become commonplace at court: Holi, Diwali, *Navaratri*, *Durga-Puja* and all the other feasts are celebrated as they would be at the palace of a Hindu king. Sometimes, he actually dresses like one, complete with a bindi on his forehead and a *rakhi*[315] around his wrist. As Abu-l Fazl writes, with his usual discernment and wit: 'the Emperor is Parsi in his rites, Hindu in his food, and Sufi in his heart.'

'True religion is one, as God is one,' the Emperor states. Was it not the great poet Ibn Arabi who once said: 'My heart is a mosque, a church, a synagogue and a temple?' As a human being, I was born in one particular tradition; but as Emperor, as the guardian of sulh-i-kul, I must protect and embrace them all!'

And then, in the month of Bahman towards the beginning of the twenty-seventh year,[316] it becomes official: the Emperor solemnly promulgates *Din-e-Illahi*, the Religion of the One God, the one religion peacefully uniting all others. 'Thus,' the firman states, 'honor will be rendered to God, peace will be given to the peoples, and security to the Empire.'

Or, as Abu-l Fazl observes in the A'In-i-Akbari, with the usual flattery:

'Whenever, from lucky circumstances, the time arrives that a nation learns to understand how to worship truth, the people will naturally look to their king, on account of the high position he occupies, and expect him to be their spiritual leader as well; for a king possesses, independent of men, the ray of divine wisdom, which banishes from the heart everything that is conflicting.'

Up to this day, I do not know – in fact, I would very much doubt that anybody does – what His Majesty's plan was when he decreed this. Was he hoping that the masses of Hindus and Muslims would convert to his mysterious new religion? Or did he merely intend to establish a religious order of his own, a fellowship similar to the Sufi orders, but open to like-minded people of all backgrounds, Muslims and non

---

[315] Hindū protection charm.

[316] Early 1582.

Muslims? Was it a symbolic gesture to show the people of Hindustan that they are all one people, in spite of all their differences, and that their Emperor belongs to all of them? I cannot be sure.

In any case, there never is any pressure on anyone to join the new society; no attempts are made to win converts; no doctrines are issued to disprove or supersede any others. Membership remains limited to a rather small number of devoted courtiers, eager to please their Emperor, proud to belong to his inner circle.

But the common people, illiterate and ignorant though they may be, seem to understand him. From far and wide, Muslims and Hindus alike, they flock to the Court of their great Prophet-King, longing to dwell, if only for a few moments, in the auspicious shadow of his kindness, hoping to obtain a magic token of his blessings: a flask of his washing-water, perhaps; or an earthen drinking-cup that has been taken to his blessed lips; a scrap of paper upon which he has breathed; maybe a shred of cloth that has been worn on his body.

And while he never claims to be the saintly guru the people believe him to be, he visibly enjoys the reverence shown to him. Patiently smiling, he listens to their inept stammering. With great kindness and respect, he touches their foreheads, breathes upon their newborns' little round heads, and accepts their humble, petty gifts as if they were the grandest treasures this world has to offer.

And the people see their king praying, in the direction of the sun, or in front of the Parsi fire; or in the Hindu shrine, kneeling in front of a lingam; or in the mosque, facing the *qibla* on a simple prayer mat; or in church, bareheaded, an Isawi cross on a chain around his neck, kneeling before an image of Isa or the Virgin Maryam. Everywhere, he prays with the same unfeigned devotion and humility, and his message is clear: all your different creeds are equally respectable, and behold: I, your Emperor: I belong to all of them.

'It pains me to hear, honorable Padres, that you wish to leave this Court and return to Goa. Is there anything I can do to make you change your mind? I am in need of your wise teachings, your blessings and prayers!'

'My brethren and I are most grateful for the kind hospitality Your sublime Majesty has been kind enough to bestow upon us,' replies

Padre Rodolfo Aquaviva, in heavily accented but otherwise impeccable, formal Persian – it keeps amazing me, how quickly and thoroughly he has mastered our beautiful language! – 'but regrettably, our task at Your Majesty's lofty Court has come to an end. Our humble services are required elsewhere.'

There is a long pause. The Emperor's countenance remains gentle, calm, and as usual, inscrutable.

'I will not deny,' Aquaviva proceeds, 'that my brethren and I will leave Fatehpur Sikri with great somberness in our hearts, for despite Your Majesty's kindness, we have, alas, failed to guide Him to the light of Truth and Salvation. We can only hope and pray that our preachings will be like seeds of grain, lifeless seemingly, buried for years in dry, barren ground, only to reemerge as healthy green sprouts, when conditions have turned more favorable...'

'So you hope I may yet become a true *Cristião*, as you call it?'

'That is indeed our most ardent prayer, Your Majesty.'

'And you actually think that unless I get baptized, my soul will be lost forever?'

'Alas, Your Majesty, not only do I think so: I know so. Outside Christ our Lord, there is no salvation!'

'But I respect Him, I pray to Him, I allow His churches to be built and His message to be preached in my cities, I keep His effigy in my private quarters...'

'That is of course excellent, Your Majesty. But alas, I am afraid it is not enough.'

'And why not?'

'Your Majesty respects Our Lord as a prophet, not as what He truly is: the Savior of the world, God incarnate Himself. Your Majesty does pray in our church, but with the same zeal, he also prays in Mohammedan mosques and heathen temples. Your Majesty kneels down before the Lord's effigy, but he does the very same before the Mohammedan Koran, or before the most scandalous, pagan idols!'

'So, honorable Padre, if I understand you correctly, the greatest objection you have against my demeanor is not so much my lack of respect towards Isa, God's peace be upon him, but the tolerance and deference I show towards other religions?'

'Not so much Your Majesty's tolerance of other creeds, but Your

Majesty's failure to choose between them! Religion is not a matter of some noncommittal intellectual entertainment, but one of choice, Your Majesty: fundamental choice, between truth and falsehood, light and darkness; the choice to stand with the Lord, or against Him – there is no middle way, no neutral ground! Like all other human beings, Your Majesty must choose! And to put it bluntly: what Your Majesty calls respect for all religions, equals allegiance to none, and rejection by all!'

'You are forgetting your manners, Padre!,' exclaims Abu-l Fazl, losing his usual composure. 'Need I remind you, that you are a guest in His Majesty's palace, that you...'

'Shaykh Abu-l Fazl, let the honorable Padre speak his mind, by all means,' the Emperor interrupts him, friendly but decisive. 'This is precisely why I invited the Padres and all these other wise men to my Court: that I might learn from all creeds, that I might behold the treasures of wisdom they have acquired!'

Silence. For a while, the Emperor just stares at the ceiling, then suddenly looks into Aquaviva's eyes.

'But that is exactly your problem, is it not, honorable Padre? You believe it is unthinkable that true wisdom could be found anywhere outside your own creed, do you not?'

For a few moments, Padre Aquaviva seems to be at loss for an answer, looking at the Emperor with what I would call reluctant admiration. After a while, he regains his composure.

'Alas, Your Majesty,' he says, smiling bitterly, 'that is not my problem, it is yours!'

Abu-l Fazl again wants to say something, but the Emperor gestures him to remain calm.

'Alas, Your Majesty,' Aquaviva proceeds, 'alas, the devil never sleeps... Temptation and evil readily present themselves to the unwary, in the guise of wisdom and profundity...'

'So, according to you, honorable Padre, what I call wisdom is actually the work of the devil? You say that it is inherently wrong to study any religion – other than your own?'

'The word of our Lord Jesùs is clear, Your Majesty: I am the Way, and the Truth, and the Life; no man comes to the Father, but by Me!

When the true believers meet people from other religions, there can, nor should there be, any dialog of equals between them. There is only one God, only one truth, and only one source of religious knowledge: God's Message, brought to us by His only begotten Son, and by the Holy Catholic Church instituted by Him.

As far as the pagans and the heretics are concerned, our duty is to love and pity them, while hating the error of their ways. Our duty is to reprimand them, to teach them the Lord's way, and lead them to the light – not to make common cause with them!'

'And whom do you hate most, Padre? The Hindus or the Muslims?'

'As I told Your Majesty: we do not hate the nonbelievers. They're human beings like us; they're our brothers, and as such, we love them. But with equal firmness and resolution, we have to reject the error of their ways!

And those errors are dangerous and wrong in their own specific way: Mohammedans are heretics, while Hindus are mere pagans. Actually, the Hindus, with their multitude of idols and their barbaric rituals: they're actually less dangerous than the Mohammedans! Mohammedans do believe in the one true God, but, like the Jews, they refuse to accept Jesùs the Messiah and His Divine message. In contrast to the Jews, who are still expecting the advent of the Messiah, the Mohammedans have been led astray by a false prophet, who substituted his own heretical teachings to those of the true Messiah. Their so-called prophet Mohammed is in fact the ultimate schismatic, worse than any heretic the Church has ever seen! It is because of his blasphemous arrogance, that the community of the believers has been split; through his fault, countless hundreds of thousands have been turned away from the light!

Compared to the Mohammedan threat, the Hindus are nothing but ignorant, heathen savages! They are the idolaters of whom St Paul wrote, in his letter to the Romans: professing themselves to be wise, they became fools. And they changed the glory of the incorruptible God into the likeness of the image of a corruptible man, and of birds, and of four-footed beasts and of creeping things[317]!'

'But what about all those timeless words of wisdom, Padre? I have to say, I do not think you are doing the Hindus much justice!'

Aquaviva no longer tries to hide his anger and contempt.

---

[317] Romans 1:22–23.

'Your Majesty may have me killed, he may have me tortured, but I must and I will speak! Let me warn Your Majesty: his soul is in grave, grave danger! Your Majesty takes pride in his interest in the Hindus, the Jains, the Parsis and whatever those misguided fools may be called. Well, he should not! He should run away from them! It is dangerous, foolish, not to say sinful, to study their so-called 'religions'! Nobody can expose himself to the mystic babble and satanic rituals of paganism, without the dark forces behind them trying to take possession of his soul! Beware, Your Majesty, beware, be very afraid: behind those idols stands nothing, nothing but the demonic power of evil! Their true maker is Satan, the fallen angel!'

The Emperor smiles wryly.

'You seem quite eager to attain martyrdom, Padre, but I am afraid I cannot oblige you: You are my guest, you see... Besides: I will never hurt anyone for his beliefs – only for his acts, and only when I have to. But leaving that aside, I have to admit, that what you've been saying here is quite disturbing to me, and let me tell you: I refuse to believe it! Why would God, Who is infinite goodness and mercy, condemn the honest prayers of His own creatures? Why would He deny His blessings to people who are so ardently looking for them?'

'It may be so that in days long gone, before the advent of our Lord, God has allowed the people to find Him – in their ignorance – by trial and error, gropingly, haphazardly. But those days are long gone! God has made it known to the world, unequivocally, that the Lord Jesus is their only salvation. As it is written in the New Testament: God, having winked at the times of this ignorance, now declares unto men that all should everywhere do penance, because He has appointed a day wherein He will judge the world in equity, by the Man whom He has appointed; giving faith to all, by raising Him up from the dead[318]. There is but one God, says Saint Paul, one God, the Father, of Whom are all things, and we unto Him; and one Lord Jesus Christ, by Whom are all things, and we by Him. An idol is nothing, and the many gods worshipped by the pagans are nothing[319]! Your Majesty believes that

318 Acts, 17, 30–31.

319 1 Corinthans 8.

these pagans are still worshipping the one true God, albeit in their own misguided way? No, warns Saint Paul: the things that the heathens sacrifice, they sacrifice to devils, and not to God![320] No, Your Majesty: God has made very clear, what He wants from us: You Shall Not Have Strange Gods Before Me[321]. We should never underestimate or disparage this clear division between light and darkness, good and evil! The Gospel forces us to clearly choose between them. Outside Jesus Christ, there is no salvation!'

'But again, Padre: how can you deny the beauty, the wisdom of the Hindu writings? And what is wrong with seeking wisdom wherever it can be found?'

'Salvation is not the attainment of so-called wisdom, Your Majesty. Salvation is the forgiveness and redemption of sin and its consequences. It cannot be achieved by man on his own, outside the Lord.

'I beseech Your Majesty, before it is too late: turn away from all this error; do not be misled by pagan fallacies! I know: the smartest and best educated among the heathens will try to explain away the errors of their ways. 'Underneath the multitude of Hindu gods, they say, there is the One and only God. All the various religions of the world, they say, are only different paths on the same mountain, leading to the same top. They sometimes even have the blasphemous insolence to suggest there is no real difference between the Lord Jesus, and that fornicating idol Krishna or whatever his name is! We need to keep ourselves far away from all this, and not mingle with the pagans, unless and to the extent necessary to teach and convert them. Saint Paul's warnings are very clear: he who does not live in the doctrine of Christ, does not have God. He who continues in the doctrine, he has both the Father and the Son. If any man comes to you and does not bring this doctrine, receive him not into the house, nor say to him: God speed you. For he that says unto him: God speed you, communicates with his wicked works[322]. The pagan idolaters, says Saint Paul, are dead in their offences and sins, in the desires of their flesh, fulfilling the will of their flesh and their

320 1 Corinthans 10:20

321 Exodus 20:3

322 2 John 9–11.

thoughts – they are Children of Wrath![323] Thus, the Holy Scriptures warn us against all heathens, heretics, and false prophets! We should not even greet them, let alone converse with them, or worse even, study their sinister doctrines of error!

Thus, the Lord God commands, Your Majesty, and we have to obey Him: we accept his offer of salvation through the sacrifice of His Son, or we reject it; there is no middle course. He who despises me and does not hear my words, has someone to judge him. The word that I have spoken, that same word shall judge him in the last day, says the Lord Jesus[324]!'

'Alas, honorable Padre, I can only pray that you are mistaken, for I find it impossible to believe that God is as harsh as you describe Him to be. May God be merciful to both of us, Padre, and may He be your protector and guide on your journey.'

'I will pray for Your Majesty.'

'As I will pray for you, honorable Padre.'

A few months later, the news comes in from Goa. It was to be expected, but still, it comes as a surprise: young Padre Rodolfo Aquaviva has been killed by an angry Hindu mob, for burning down one of their temples.

'What a pity,' says the Emperor with a sigh, slowly shaking his head. 'Such a waste of youth and devotion! Let us pray for him, and for his victims.'

[323] Ephesians 2:1,3.

324 John 12:48.

Thirty-fourth Letter

ظهر

Zọhr[325]

Life is a strange thing, when you think about it. It is either not yet, or no more: we always seem to be craving some unattainable future, or bewailing a bygone past... The gems of life, those rare moments of perfect happiness, with neither wants, nor regrets: they quickly lose their luster, when we realize that they, too, are bound to come to an end? All pleasure lusts for eternity; every moment of human happiness craves the one treasure that cannot be found in this world: permanence...

I am exaggerating, of course: life is a precious gift, to be cherished and enjoyed, an exciting adventure, to be lived to the fullest! Still, it's true what I just wrote: when I was young, I was not yet as powerful as I am right now, not yet the father of a son; but now that I am Emperor and powerful, I no longer have the strength of my youth, I no longer am the center of my son's world; and with wistful dismay, I remember the many good friends of yore who have, alas, passed away for good. Why is it only when we look back, when it's too late, that we fully realize what treasures we had?

Somewhere along this long and winding road of my life, 'it' must have happened; somewhere in between, I was at my highest peak. It was but a fleeting moment, impossible to grasp or hold on to, like the

[325] Noon.

exact time when the sun reaches its highest point: one moment, the shadows are still shortening; the next, slowly but surely, they grow longer again.

Only now, now that the dusk of my life is drawing near at alarming speed, I realize: Din-e-Illahi was my High Noon, the high point of my life.

Din-e-Illahi was everything my reign stands for. It was the living proof that I truly answered to no one – no one but God. All my enemies lay down in the dust; no governor or ulama could even dream of any authority, unless I delegated it to him. Kings of neighbouring regions could only hope, their lavish gifts and letters of abject flattery and pledges of eternal friendship would convince me to let them keep their independence. The common people, of all castes and creeds, loved, admired, not to say worshipped their Emperor, so powerful, so just, so obviously blessed by God.

At the time I decreed Din-e-Illahi, I was thirty-nine years of age, strong as a bull, free of any bodily ailment. My zanana was a haven of merriness and opulence, heaven on earth, where I loved to retire – not only, and not even primarily, to enjoy one or other pretty young dancing girl and her shapely curves. It was the one place where I felt truly at home and at ease, free for a few hours from any commitment, enjoying the always enriching companionship of my strong and wise Salima; of my sweet Ruqqaya and her good-natured gentleness; and of your charming mother, with her quicksilver mind and her thousands of projects.

At the time I decreed Din-e-Illahi, you were thirteen, my son, and what pride and joy it was for me, to see you and your two younger brothers growing up so well! You were growing taller than me, and incredibly strong for your age, and skilled with horses and weapons, and extremely bright, too: fluent in Persian, Turki, Hindustani, and Arabic; good with numbers; a gifted painter and an even better calligrapher, blessed with a steady hand and a keen, observing eye. Never had an empire seen a more promising young prince.

Thirteen you were, my son, exactly my age at the time my father died... The thought confronted me, for the first time, with my own death. What if something were to happen to me? It was without hesitation, that I appointed Abdurrahim as your *ataliq* – just like, twenty-six years before, I had been entrusted to his father. What better teacher and guardian than this skilled warrior, this accomplished scholar, this able governor, this noble and loyal friend? When I saw you in his company, on horseback among the soldiers, or sitting down under the palace arcades, studying battle tactics on a piece of paper, it was as if I saw myself with Bairam Khan, and I was at peace. If, God forbid, I were to die unexpectedly, you would make it. You, protected by Abdurrahim Khan Khanan, with Todar Mal, Birbal, Abu-l Fazl, Bhagwan Das, and Man Singh; you, at the head of this invincible alliance of Rajputs and so-called 'Mughals': who in this world could ever hope to challenge, let alone defeat you?

Once again, I thanked almighty God for putting your revered mother on my life's path. My fortunate alliance with her and her family had more than doubled my power, and it had allowed me to father the best imaginable successor, for in your veins, my son, flows the blood of Genghis Khan and Amir Temür the Iron, harmoniously blended with that of the mighty Hindu kings of yore! I resolved to further strengthen the ties between our two families. And what better way to forge an alliance, than through the bonds of blood? Two more years, and you would be old enough to marry a Rajput princess yourself, just like I had done. God willing, we would soon find ourselves blessed with a new generation of true Hindustani princes, strong, noble and wise, who would, in grateful remembrance of their grandfather, preserve, protect and enhance what I had built.

Yes, the time of Din-e-Illahi was truly the high point of my life and my reign. Ironic, is it not, that the high point of one's life was at the same time an utter failure?

To be sure, thanks to me, Muslims and Hindus are now living together in security, peace, and oftentimes unfeigned friendship – that's an accomplishment I take great pride in. Regrettably, if understandably, I have failed to achieve anything more than that. Disappointingly few people have ever cared to join my so-called 'new religion': a few good friends, plus the inevitable number of sycophants, but it has failed to appeal to the masses. On the contrary: rather than uniting people, it has been a source of much controversy and misunderstandings, and it nearly estranged me from some of my best friends.

It angered Aziz Koka, my faithful but rather bigoted and hot-headed foster brother, to the point that he left and sailed for Mekkah, without asking my permission! I am happy to say, that two years later, upon his return, I found him quite eager to make amends. He even became one of the most fervent Din-e-Illahi disciples: the merchants of Mekkah had fleeced him so thoroughly, that his Islamic ardor had cooled off...

Man Singh wasn't happy either with the new cult. And God bless him, he even had the courage to tell it straight to my face, when I was having a drink with him and Abdurrahim. I brought up the subject of them becoming Din-e-Illahi *murids*[326], upon which he suddenly retorted, with thinly veiled irritation: 'Forgive me, Your Majesty, but I do not know what you mean by becoming your *murid*. If it's my willingness to lay down my life for you, have I not given you more than sufficient proof of that? But if it refers to religious faith, I do not understand what you want to achieve. I am a Hindu, to be sure. If you command me to become a Muslim, I am prepared do so. But I know of no other religion than these two!'

Yes, much as I hate to admit it: Din-e-Illahi was probably a mistake, and it will probably die with me. But what is an Emperor to do, when he's made a mistake, my son? If he can repair it, he should of course do so, but sometimes, trying to fix things only makes them worse. There was no going back: it would only have added to the confusion. And so, I continued to lead the ceremonies and accepted a few disciples, but made no further attempt to convince or convert anyone. And while the cult and its ceremonies will probably die with me, one thing I hope will never die: the thought that all people are brothers; that all their religions, in the eyes of God, are one; and that the emperor, who is the servant of God and the guardian of his people, should stand above all creeds and denominations.

Yes, my son, in spite of its imperfections and ultimate failure, the promulgation of Din-e-Illahi was truly high noon; my sun was at its zenith. From then on, slowly, imperceptibly, but inexorably, the shadows would start lengthening again.

[326] Murīd: *'one who seek'*, disciple, a novice committed to spiritual enlightenment under the guidance of a Murshid (guide, teacher).

Thirty-fifth Letter

سلطنت

Saltanat[327]

It is a muggy afternoon in the height of summer of the Thirtieth Year[328], when a messenger from Kabul brings me the happy tiding of Muhammad Hakim's death. Unexpected news, but hardly surprising: ever since his humiliating defeat two years ago, he has busied himself with little else than drinking himself to death, an endeavor in which, at the age of merely thirty-one, he appears to have finally succeeded. The last of my would-be rivals is rotting in his grave, and I am alive, at the height of my power, strong, invincible. Gone are the whispers and mutters behind my back; the mere mention of my name suffices to turn the stiffest knees into water.

The moment I hear the news, my mind is made up: I am moving up north.

People are surprised, as usual, at the rashness of my decision, but I do have my reasons. For one, I do not want – I can't afford – to take any chances. Reports have come in that the Uzbegs have taken possession of Balkh and Badakshan, the country across the mountains north of Kabul, south of the Amuya River[329]. That in itself is vexing enough, but the situation could quickly become much worse, now that the buffer

---

327 Kingship, Empire.

328 1585.

329 The Amū Dāryā (Oxus) River.

between ourselves and the Uzbegs is gone, and with the dangerous void Muhammad Hakim's death has left in Kabul. If I am not careful to fill it, it won't be long before we'll see Uzbeg bandits marauding our northern mountains. Kabul itself, God forbid, could be in danger one day!

You see, my son, kingship is rather like a game of chess: you should always think a few moves ahead; you should constantly be on your guard for chinks in your armor, for weak spots that a shrewd opponent might use in an attempt to shift the balance of power.

I need to make my countermove, and quickly: that old fox Abdullah Khan Uzbeg Bukhari, may God exterminate his seed through mine, is not be underestimated. Ever since he sits on the throne of Turan, he's been expanding his dominions southward, at the expense of the Shah of Iran. Frankly, I do not care what he does to the Persians – in fact, the more the Uzbegs and the Iranis are fighting each other, the better I like it! But now that the old Uzbeg bastard has gotten himself a foothold across my northern border, things are different. There's no telling what he may be up to next. What if he patches up a peace deal with the Persians, to attack me for a change? No, I simply cannot afford to keep on living hundreds of kos away down south in Fatehpur Sikri, when that wily jackal is loitering about my northern border. I have to go up there myself, in full force, and make it crystal clear to that bastard, any false move from him will have dire and immediate consequences; he needs to understand that if he chooses to challenge me, he has absolutely nothing to gain, but much – if not everything – to lose!

My presence up north, while necessary to keep the Uzbegs at bay, has its distinct advantages, too. I will finally be able to busy myself with the conquest of that exquisite gem I've been longing to add to my crown for so many years: Kashmir. Countless poets have sung the praises of its landscape, the majesty of its snowcapped mountains, the lushness of its green gardens, the breathtaking beauty of its limpid blue lakes, the freshness of its fast-fleeting rivers... Besides, and more importantly, is Kashmir not our natural border? Is it imaginable, is it conceivable I would leave such an important land in the hands of a foreign ruler? Never! Kashmir belongs to Hindustan; it's mine! And besides, I've really had more than enough of its pompous little kinglet Yusuf Khan, a worthless buffoon who has constantly been ignoring my orders, while trying to placate me with vague promises and half-hearted signs of friendship. It is time to put an end to his charade.

Less than a month after the news of Muhammad Hakim's death, the imperial Court is ready to leave Fatehpur Sikri. I take a last stroll around the grounds, pay my respects at Shaykh Salim Chishti's tomb, admire once more the *Panch Mahal's* [330] fiery-red outline against the black monsoon clouds; sit myself down on the stairs of the Buland Darwaza[331] for a while, and watch the bees swarming about their nests, high up in the mighty arch of the gate. Deep in my heart, I realize this is not goodbye, but farewell; Fatehpur Sikri will never again be my capital.

To my own surprise, I feel neither sadness nor nostalgia to leave this city I've built with such zeal, stone per stone, practically with my own two hands. Actually, I am quite eager to leave – I guess I've grown a bit tired of the place; or maybe not tired, but disappointed. The bursting of the dam, two years back, and the interminable difficulties with the water supply have made it painfully clear, that this is, alas, not the place to sustain a large population.

Farewell to Sikri it is. The affairs of state will keep me occupied up north for no less than thirteen years, and by the time I finally return to the area for a hasty visit, I find it as I expected: the imperial residence untouched, like new, beautiful and imposing as ever, but the surrounding area all but deserted, all its shops and houses in pitiful decay. Fatehpur is no longer the lively city of my time; it has become a monument. That is its destiny: to stand, empty, on that lonely hill, for all generations to come, a testimonial to its maker, a symbol of the Hindustan he created. Muslim-style arches and domes, combined, blended, unified with Hindu pillars, terraces, and *chhatris*[332]– sulh-i-kul in stone.

The cortege – several kos long, thousands of elephants, horses, oxcarts, pack camels – sets itself in motion and slowly winds its way northward. As we ride through the gate, I do not look back – not

---

[330] The five-storey open palace at Fatehpūr Sīkrī.

[331] The High (or 'Great') Gate, built by Akbar to commemorate the conquest of Gujarāt. It is reportedly the highest gateway in the world.

[332] Umbrella-shaped cupolas, usually resting on four pillars, used as ornaments on walls, terraces, minarets, etc.

even once. Looking back never makes much sense, my son. We live in the present, and the future is our destination. The past is there to be built – not dwelt – upon!

Barely three months later, we set up camp near Attock, where the Kabul River runs into the mighty Hind. Not a very comfortable place, but an ideal base of operations. From Attock, I oversee the entire north; in a matter of days, my troops can get to Kabul, or Kashmir, or both places at the same time for that matter.

Together with my generals, I take stock of the situation. I am relieved to find it could have been much, much worse. True, the roads around the Khyber Pass and the Sulaiman Hills are infested by unruly Afghan tribesmen (the work of Uzbeg instigators, no doubt), but Kabul itself, thank God, is safe. The new governor appears to have everything under control: no unrest, no sign of any Uzbeg incursions. Kashmir, as expected, begs for peace, while preparing for war. Be it so. I am no longer interested in a negotiated settlement. This time, I won't be fobbed off with a few fair words; this time, they will submit, or die!

It serves little purpose to recount the entire campaign. Besides, is the outcome not known beforehand? Of course, there's a few setbacks: snow and ice hinder our advance; enemy resistance is at times stiffer than anticipated. But the outcome is never in doubt: it may take us one year, two years, three maybe, but in the end, their knees will bend, their necks will bow.

Thus, it happens. A mere eight months after my arrival at Attock, the victorious imperial army under Raja Bhagwan Das marches into Srinagar. The insubordinate Yusuf Khan and his son have but one alternative: unconditional surrender. But this time, no public reconciliation, no appointments to high office, no fat stipends: they are carted off to Bihar, where they remain imprisoned like common criminals for over a year, after which I assign them to humble positions well below their rank, a just retribution for their insolence and a warning to all other would-be rebels. Their proud kingdom is history; it is annexed to the Empire, not as a separate sarkar as everyone expects, but as a mere suba, joined to the sarkar[333] of Kabul. Thus, fare the insolent, the disobedient, the vainglorious...

[333] Sarkar: province. Suba: district.

If the annexation of Kashmir, at first sight a major war, passes off rather smoothly and easier than expected, the campaign against the Yusufzai and Mandar Afghans, supposedly a routine job, turns into an outright disaster, one that could and should have been avoided – and all because of my own stupid mistake.

The start of the operations is successful enough. Simultaneously with the attack on Kashmir, I order a punitive expedition into the mountains under commander Zain Khan. In accordance with his orders, he invades the tribal territories via a two-pronged attack: one via the Bajaur territory to the west, and the second one due north into the Samah plateau, between the Kabul and the Suwat Rivers. After duly chastising any opposing brigands, he crosses the Suwat and occupies the town of Chak-darah, where, entirely in the correct manner, he builds a stronghold from where he can further harass the tribesmen and pacify the country. So far, so good. His forces exhausted from the strenuous marches in difficult country, he sends a messenger back to Attock to ask for reinforcements. Still, so far, so good. But then, I make a stupid and alas, fatal mistake. A number of my courtiers – bored by the tranquil life in the camp, I guess – start quarreling among themselves for the honor of leading the reinforcement troops. I should of course have dismissed them right away: the Afghan mountains are no place for inexperienced courtiers to dabble around in. But because they all keep pestering me, and since the campaign has been going quite well so far, I finally give in and let them have their way. In fact, there are so many candidates that the dispute has to be solved by drawing lots. Fate appoints Raja Birbal, together with Hakim Abu'l Fath. The next day, after a night of celebrations, they ride off, proud as peacocks.

I must have been out of my mind to allow two inexperienced courtiers, a physician and an administrator, to lead an army into an Afghan-infested wilderness! And an even worse, unforgivable blunder was it to send them off without clear instructions.

Where did it go so terribly wrong? I can only rely on the accounts of those who returned...

Barely had Birbal arrived at Chak-darah with his reinforcements, that ignoble disputes broke out between him and Zain Khan – the former, believing himself to be the latter's superior and too proud to acknowledge the better judgement of an experienced soldier.

Zain Khan maintained – quite correctly, of course – that the fortress should be held in strength, while the Afghans were further reduced in a series of punitive raids. Birbal on the other hand insisted, with unusual stubbornness, that it was not at all necessary to occupy the fortress, and that they should make their way back to the base camp in Attock. To make things worse, Birbal – again with highly unusual obstinacy for a man of his intelligence – refused to withdraw through the rather broad and much more easily surveyable Malakhand Pass as Zain Khan recommended, but instead resolved on going back through the Karakar and Malandarai passes. It was a big, big mistake – one that, alas, cost him his life. The retiring army, though grievously harassed by the Afghan tribesmen, had held its own in the narrow Karakar defiles; but when it reached the Malandarai Pass further south and again found itself under attack, the withdrawal degenerated in a humiliating and disastrous rout, a headlong flight where every man tried to save his own skin, without putting up even a semblance of resistance. Zain Khan and Hakim Abu'l Fath survived the disaster, with a little over half of the army; but a full eight thousand men, including poor Birbal himself, were slaughtered like cattle.

The chronicler wrote, truthfully, that I shed bitter tears, and couldn't eat or drink or sleep for days. It's true: I was absolutely devastated. Not only because I grieved the loss of a dear old friend; it was because I felt so terribly guilty and ashamed, ashamed at having been humiliated by a bunch of ragged, unwashed Afghan dogs.

Of course, I made them pay dearly for it. They had shed the blood of a Hindu courtier; Hindu warriors would shed theirs. Todar Mal, later followed by Man Singh in the west, went into the tribal areas and beat the Afghans the only way Afghans can be beaten: by fighting them your way, not theirs. Mountain men are not to be fought in the caves and crevasses where they try to lure you into. Do not waste your time and effort in heroic but pointless and dangerous marches through their treacherous defiles! You have to fight them methodically, determinately; you have to harass them day and night, starting from a number of carefully chosen strong points, near river crossings, road junctions, mountain pass accesses and the like, where you have ample supplies and they cannot dislodge you. Strongholds are the steppingstones of conquest! As Abu'l Fazl phrased it so aptly, they protect the timid, frighten the rebellious, and please the obedient. If you hold enough fortresses, you can do as you deem fit, with impunity: burning and plundering the villages of the rebellious, while showering favors on the obedient. Then, gradually, with the lapse of time, brutal slaughter can be replaced by or complemented with discreet consultation with battle-weary village elders. Confronted with the choice between slaughter and bribery, even the closest alliances are bound to fall apart! Thus, through a judicious mix of wrath and mercy, bravery and stealth, the toughest mountain tribes can be checked, then reduced, and finally, brought to heel.

Anyway, as I said, our valiant Hindu commanders gave the bandits their just deserts. Todar Mal, after availing himself of an appropriate number of well-placed fortresses, harried the eastern mountain tribes so brutally, that they were soon begging for peace; and near the Khyber Pass, Man Singh inflicted on the western tribes a defeat so crushing that it took them years to recover. Our roads were safe again, the mountain passages cleared, and order restored.

Order, or at least a semblance thereof, for who knows what evil broods in the grim darkness of the Afghan soul? Right to this day, the border tribes have never really been conquered, only pacified. Remember that, my son, and beware of the Afghan tribesmen! Never underestimate them, never let down your guard! Know that the Afghan is mean and tough, hardened by icy cold and blazing heat and endless fighting; that he's haughty and proud; and that his mind is a cauldron of bigotry, rancor, spite, deceit, and betrayal. The Afghan is to be controlled carefully: suppressed if necessary, befriended if possible; but never, never to be trusted.

But enough said about that unwashed vermin. It really is not worth the ink I am writing its name with. Let me return to matters weightier: the building of that mighty Empire that you are about to inherit, my son. Let us examine together, if you will, where I succeeded, and where – through your fault, alas – I failed.

The following years of my life – I mean the period roughly between the thirtieth and the forty-third year, between the annexation of Kashmir and my return to Agra – constitute, in hindsight, what one could call the afternoon of my reign. To be sure, vast and rich and crucially important territories were added to the Empire: Sindh, Baluchistan, Qandahar, Berar, Asirghar, Ahmadnagar, they all fell into my hands. But those conquests were like afternoon sunshine: the air keeps getting hotter for a few hours, even though the sun is already sinking lower in the sky; but inexorably, the white heat turns golden, and the golden turns red, and amidst and despite all the simmering heat, the lengthening shadows forebode the darkness of the night.

My dominions were still expanding, I had never been more powerful, but I somehow derived little satisfaction from it. Every new conquest seemed less gratifying, less glorious, more cumbersome than the one before; and for the first time, I felt the true curse of old age – loneliness. I lost many of my most trusted, life-long friends, and with growing despair, I had to witness how my three promising, wonderful sons, rather than making me proud like before, were becoming a cause of grave concern, and disappointment most bitter.

Thirty-sixth Letter

تنہای عصر

Tānhāyi ē 'Aṣr[334]

After the successful campaign in Kashmir and the long-overdue punishment of the Afghan rabble, the northern borderlands were safe again. Safe enough, anyway, for me to retire to the more cultured comfort of Lahore, which was to remain my capital city for the next thirteen years.

From thence, I further built and consolidated the mighty Empire you will now be ruling, my son. Observe carefully, how I got what I wanted: through war and conquest, of course; but equally and at times more importantly, through carefully worded correspondence and elegant conversation, artfully blending courtesy with thinly veiled threats. Take it from me, my son: the sweetest victory is bloodless; when treasure and territory fall into your hands solely because of the power of your name.

I told you that kingship is a bit like a game of chess. Well, in fact, the entire decade was really a gigantic game of chess between me and Abdullah Khan Uzbeg. A game with very high stakes indeed: the entire balance of power in the northwest depended on it. A game that, I am proud to say, I won brilliantly – to the extent that any such game can be won, for history never ends, and what was won by one generation can, alas, be squandered by the next...

[334] Loneliness of the late afternoon.

In hindsight, it wasn't that difficult. I used the Uzbegs to wear down the Persians, and then the Persians to chastise the Uzbegs; and while those two were at each other's throat, I quietly helped myself to the spoils...

Let us take a brief look at the map of Hindustan and its neighbors Iran and Turan, my son. To a certain extent, those three are balancing each other out: one could ever hope to conquer one of the others, unless through an all-out war that would probably take decades, and even more probably ruin the victor as badly as the vanquished. But do not be lulled to sleep: that seemingly unshakable balance is precarious at best!

Cast your mind back at the time when your great-grandfather Babur was still young. Look how things have changed – in the span of barely a single lifetime! At the time your great-grandfather was a young man, there were no three rivals: there was only the mighty Persian empire, stretching from the great Euphrates River to the Hindu Kush Mountains; vast, inexhaustibly wealthy, and powerful. What could that empire possibly have to fear from a handful of petty kingdoms and sultanates in faraway Hindustan, or from the Uzbegs, with their army a hundred times smaller than its own?

And yet, barely a few decades later, that situation looks quite different. Persia's wealthy western provinces – including the eternal city of Baghdad itself! – have been lost to the Turks of Rum (I've been told they call themselves 'Osmaniyye'– Devlet-i Aliye-yi Osmaniyye [335], no less!); and the northwestern borders are under constant threat of invasion by the ever more arrogant Uzbegs.

Learn from this, my son; observe how in just a few decades, a magnificent, invincible empire has been brought to the brink of collapse. All it has taken, is a few shortsighted weaklings on the throne, a few spineless drunks, learned idiots, too preoccupied with feasting and paintings and poetry to recognize how much their armies are antiquated and in need of cannons...

Anyway, in the thirty-first year, I find myself involved in lively correspondence with my two quarreling neighbors: the tremulous, half-blind old Persian king Muhammad Shah Khudabanda, and his ruthless, land-hungry Uzbeg adversary. It's not difficult to see what is behind all

---

[335] Devlet-i Āliye-yi Osmāniyye, i.e. the *Sublime Osmān State*, or Ottoman Empire.

the lavish gifts and pledges of everlasting friendship they both keep sending me: they both want my support, or at least my neutrality, in the longstanding feud that divides them.

If I would follow my heart, I would of course combine forces with the mild-mannered old Shah, and crush the Uzbegs, once and for all. After careful consideration, however, I choose not to. What good would it do to strengthen the Persians? Who's to say the next Shah will not one day turn against me? And why should I be wasting my time on the other side of the Hindu Kush, when there's so much left to do in Hindustan proper? No, I just stay put; and from behind the safety of my borders, I watch them weakening each other, while I am free to do what I want.

Before long, the Uzbegs do invade the Persian northeast and quickly seize Herat, Sistan and Mashhad from the ill-prepared Persians. Humiliated, powerless, the old Shah has no alternative but to abdicate in favor of his sixteen-year-old son Abbas, whose first worry is to stay alive, amidst a wasps' nest of strife and court intrigues.

I have to say, the boy manages admirably. Were it not that he's a potential enemy of ours, it's actually quite enjoyable to see how brilliantly he restores order and rebuilds his empire!

But let me first come back to the situation in Hindustan. As I said, as long as the Persians and the Uzbegs keep each other occupied, I have my hands free for my own projects. It is an opportunity I do not intend to miss.

My first target, of course, is Sindh, the region along the Hind River between Multan and the sea. The local ruler, one Mirza Jani Beg, stubbornly refuses to pay homage to me. What is that fool thinking? Does he really believe I will allow the Hind River, the river to which Hindustan owes its very name, to remain separated from it? Is it at all thinkable that I would leave the Panjab's natural access to the sea, the beautiful cities of Hyderabad and Thatta, the fertile plains around the lower reaches of the river, and my own birthplace Umarkot, in foreign hands? What kind of a wimp does he take me for?

I do not waste my time on futile negotiations. When amicable overtures are of no avail, I send down Abdurrahim with an army, to bring him to reason. Jani Beg attempts to resist, but of course, he's no match for Abdurrahim, who makes quick work of the enemy's army and fleet of warships. Jani Beg has learned his lesson. Meekly surrendering all his cities and fortresses to Abdurrahim, he travels to Lahore to prostrate himself at my feet.

I have half a mind of having him executed, or at least thrown in jail, but when I see his honest, rather pleasurable face, I change my mind, and decide to give him another chance: I let him go back to his native region as its governor. As usual, my instinct does not fail me. For the remainder of his life – which, alas, ends prematurely in a drinking bout a few years later – he serves me faithfully, fighting at my side in the Deccan, and becoming a confirmed Din-e-Illahi adept.

Now that Sindh is mine, I can at last consolidate the other southwestern regions. In the beginning of the fortieth year, my forces invade Baluchistan and quickly capture the fortress of Siwi in the Kirthar Mountains, south-east of Quetta. Barely two months later, the jewel of the crown falls into my lap, when the Persian governor of Qandahar, fearing an imminent invasion by the Uzbegs, delivers the city into my hands. With glee, I hear the reports: no sooner have my troops taken the city and manned the territory's borders, than the Uzbeg hordes withdraw, tail between their legs... Amusing, isn't it? The more power one has, the less one needs to use it! The entire land of Qandahar annexed to the Empire and an Uzbeg invasion repelled, without a single drop of blood, by the mere awe and dread inspired by the name *Akbar-e-Azam*.

With Sindh, Baluchistan and Qandahar firmly in our hands, we can finally rest assured that the north is safe, behind well-nigh impregnable natural borders, and its two entrance gates Kabul and Qandahar well-guarded.

But do keep an eye on that border, my son, for behind it looms our young friend Shah Abbas, and you can be sure he hasn't forgotten Qandahar was once his. Beware of him, my son: he's smart, ruthless, and vengeful. I know, he is preoccupied with Baghdad before anything else, but once he recaptures it – and there is no doubt in my mind that he will, someday – he will be knocking at your door.

Do not underestimate him! Just think about how judiciously, carefully, and ruthlessly he has managed to rebuild his power, in barely ten years' time! Just look at how cleverly he dealt with the Uzbegs! As I said, were it not that he is so dangerous, it would actually have been quite fun to watch...

Swiftly dealing with any would-be rivals – that is to say, having them blinded, poisoned, or strangled – he quickly patches up a peace deal with his powerful adversaries in the west, ceding them some additional territories; and while the Osmaniyye Turks are reveling in their easy victory, he quietly avails himself of Firanghi advisors. With unremitting zeal, he strengthens and reorganizes his armed forces, similar to the model of his Osmaniyye opponents. Cannon foundries are built everywhere, hundreds of thousands of muskets fabricated, ample supplies of gunpowder stockpiled all over the land. Behold, my son, how God favors those who act: barely ten years after his father's humiliating defeat, Abbas' victorious armies wash over the Uzbeg occupants like a tidal wave; only a handful of maimed and blinded survivors are allowed to stumble back to Bukhara, and bring Abdullah Khan Uzbeg the tiding that his grandiose plans have failed. A few years later, the old jackal dies, in the certain knowledge that there is no one of value to succeed him. Gone are the dreams of a great Uzbeg empire...

With Abdullah Khan Uzbeg out of the way, his forces decimated by Abbas, and his successor an impotent weakling, I am strongly tempted to march north, to Samarqand – Samarqand, where the bones of Temür are resting; Samarqand, the priceless jewel that was stolen from my grandfather by the Uzbeg usurpers. But then again, I think to myself: what does this have to do with me? Why would I spend the remaining years of my life in lands where I've never set foot – lands where, reportedly, winters are long and cold, the soil barren, good food scarce, and the women ugly? Growing old is about losing options, my son. When a man is past forty, he shouldn't waste his time on dreams, on things that might have been, on new projects that may take lifetimes to finish. At my age, and very soon, at your age as well, a man needs to be practical. He should make up his mind what he wants in his life, and then finish what he started, not waste his time on pursuits that are not his own. Samarqand can wait, my son; what you and I need to do, is not to waste our strength in faraway regions, but to unite all of Hindustan, from the Himalayas to the southern ocean and the island of Lanka; and then, to make it the mightiest and wealthiest Empire on earth. Let's complete what I started; and if we do that well, the seed of our seed will be able to busy itself with the conquest of foreign lands. By all means, let's be ambitious; let's dream of a Hindustan stretching far north and far across the ocean; but let's first build it, make it strong, and make it one.

Having thus made up my mind, and in the knowledge that the north is safe, I decide to move back to Agra. I am growing old – fifty-six already, how time flies! – and so much remains to be done! The operations in the Deccan are not progressing as fast as they should; I need to move much closer to the action, maybe even get involved myself – it's been too long since I've seen a battlefield.

Alas, little do I realize that my last adversary is not some recalcitrant Deccan ruler, but my own firstborn – you, my son.

⁂

Where did it go wrong? It is difficult, not to say impossible to pinpoint a specific moment, but for a while, I've been tempted to think that all my misfortunes started with Birbal's death at the beginning of the thirty-first year. To be sure, Kabul was safe at the time, the conquest of Kashmir was going well, I was in excellent health, and with three bright sons, my succession was assured; still, no matter how much I tried to console myself, I felt Birbal's death was a bad omen, a very bad omen. Never before had my plans been thwarted so brutally, so unexpectedly; never before had I felt so utterly humiliated; never before had it been even imaginable that a high-ranking official of Akbar the Great's court could be killed by a bunch of Afghan rabble.

Was my lucky star waning? Was the hour of my death drawing near? No matter how well the astrologers did their best to convince me of the contrary, doubt kept lurking in my mind, for quite a few months.

I was wrong, of course: there's no such thing as a 'lucky star'. And even if there were, we should never allow ourselves to be intimidated, much less ruled by it. I know I am repeating myself, my son, but it really cannot be emphasized enough: God only favors those who act! Things never just happen to us: things are what they are, either because we make them so, or because we allow them to be so. True, many events and occurrences around us are of course not under our control; but we decide how we react to them! I would say that only one tenth of our lives is determined by what happens to us; but nine tenths, by how we react to it! Just look at the story of my own life: I could have rested on my laurels, after Sikandar Sur's surrender. Surely, there's more than enough wealth and luxury in the Panjab and central Hindustan; who knows what a cushy, carefree life I could have had! But then again, just suppose I would have chosen that leisurely path: Hindustan would have been exactly like its neighbors – exactly like the petty kingdoms I've subdued and annexed. But I chose not to rest on my laurels, I acted; I didn't take life as it came to me, I changed it. And God has rewarded my resolve: I am more powerful than the Persian Shah or the Uzbeg Khan; I am, most probably, the mightiest ruler on this earth. Not because it was pre-ordained, but because I did something, because I took advantage of the opportunities that offered themselves.

These were the thoughts going through my head, as I traveled back to Agra, and reflected on the thirteen years I had spent up north. I had seen no evidence of lucky or unlucky stars. The years had come and gone, and life had gone its way, as it had before, as it always has, with its ups, and its downs – and more often than not, with lots of hard work to bring about the former, and courage and determination to overcome the latter. Much as the astrologers had toiled and ciphered and done their utmost to sound learned and wise and complicated, they had failed to predict any of the important events, other than the ones that were crystal clear from looking at the earth, rather than at the sky.

Much had happened to me during those thirteen years. Of course, I had my share of challenges and setbacks, but more numerous had been my blessings.

True, my dear old friend Birbal had perished, needlessly – victim, not of God's disfavor, but of his own arrogance, and my error of judgement – but his death had been duly avenged, and vast territories had been added to the Empire, making me the most powerful ruler in the region, if not the world.

True, the loss of Birbal had, alas, not been my only bereavement, as both Todar Mal, my faithful help and stay, and my strong brother in arms Raja Bhagwan Das had both died in the thirty-fourth year, barely one week from each other; and four years later, old Shaykh Mubarak had passed away as well. But thank God, the pain of their loss had been more than alleviated by the birth of three healthy grandsons: Khusrau on the 24th of Mordad of the thirty-second year[336], Parvez on the 19th

[336] August 5, 1587.

of Aban two years later[337], and Khurram[338] on the 25th of Dey of the thirty-seventh year.

Khusrau's birth in particular had been a cause of great rejoicing. Not only was he your firstborn, not only did he ensure the continuity of our dynasty: the fact that he was born to your first-wedded wife, the Princess of Jodhpur, God bless her, again reinforced the bonds of kin and friendship that unites us with the Rajputs. Never forget this, my son: the unity of Amber, Jodhpur and Agra, Muslims and Hindus, that's the basis of our power.

Yet, as I reflected on all this on my way to Agra, my heart was heavy. And it had little to do with Divine blessings or lack thereof, but with time, the inexorable passing of time. Whether I chose to admit it to myself or not, I was a white-haired, aging man; and my sons were grown adults, living their own lives.

At the time I left Fatehpur, I was forty-three, at the top of my strength, and everything and everybody revolved around me. You and your two brothers were merely sixteen, fifteen and thirteen; you were good, promising kids, all three of you – a bit spoilt perhaps, but nevertheless: smart, strong, and always respectful towards their father.

By the time I decided to return to Agra, those three wonderful sons had changed beyond recognition: conceited, quarrelsome, indolent drunks, well on their way, all three of them, to become total failures. And even more worrisome: the brotherly love and friendship that once united them had given way to barely hidden mistrust and resentment. Abu'l Fazl and the other courtiers did their best to spare my feelings, but couldn't hide it from me: the Court was rife with scandalous rumors – rumors that you and Murad were looking for allies in the war of succession that would surely break out the moment I laid down my weary head; that the three of you were living in constant fear of assassins and poisoners.

I of course ignored the rumors, and did my best to talk some sense into the three of you. It truly pained me to see the kind of men you had become: you, secretive, inscrutable, calculating, venomous like a snake;

---

[337] October 31, 1589.

[338] January 5, 1592. Khurram was to succeed Jahāngīr in 1628 under the name of Shāh Jahān, and to achieve worldwide fame as the builder of the Tāj Mahal.

Murad, loud and moody; Danyal, shy and visibly scared. I really tried everything, from fits of rage to friendly encouragement... But whether I kept you in the palace, or entrusted you with important, faraway missions, nothing I said or did seemed to have any effect: all I got was evasive answers and vague promises; all I achieved was that you became even more estranged from me and from each other.

One late afternoon, as I was watching a flock of birds in the pale blue sky, the stark, bitter truth suddenly dawned on me: my years were numbered, there was nothing I could do about it. Another five, ten, twenty years maybe, and I would be dead; and my sons were getting themselves ready for it. I might as well face it: the world no longer revolved around me; and if it did, it was more like a flight of vultures hovering high above some wounded animal, waiting for it to collapse.

Thirty-seventh Letter

مراد، اسیر گڑھ

Murad, Asirgarh

Have you ever seen a cavalry charge bogged down in a marshland, Salim? With every step, the horses lose power and speed; in a few moments, what started as a thundering, overwhelming assault, turns into impotent plodding. Well, that's exactly how I've felt, ever since I left Lahore: bogged down, powerless – not by enemy action, but by my own flesh and blood...

If everything would have gone the way I planned, our borders would now extend at least fifty kos further south than they currently do. The khutbah would now be read in my name in every mosque of Ahmadnagar, Bijapur and Golconda. Who knows, our victorious armies would probably be making their way to the southernmost tip of the continent! Alas, it was not to be...

It really is a crying shame I will have to die before the Deccan has been fully annexed to the Empire. A region of such vital importance, still in the hands of a few petty local kings... the very idea is an insult!

Deccan independence is a thorn in my flesh: Hindustan can never be complete without the Deccan. But with the Deccan, it's only a matter of time before the continent is ours! Think about it: even the arrogant Purtugesh will be brought to heel: once they're our neighbors, they'll have to recognize our sovereignty and pay dearly for our hospitality, or be thrown back into the sea, where they came from.

As early as the Gujarat wars – when, alas, I had other things on my hands – I'd been sending envoys to Khandesh and Ahmadnagar, inviting them to join me. But their submission was temporary, half-hearted at best. On the contrary, one of them (that filthy rat Burhan Shah of Ahmadnagar, not to name him) was insolent enough to call upon my help when he needed it to defeat his enemies, and then ignore me as soon as he got what he wanted! In the summer of the thirty-sixth year[339], I decided to give it one last try.

I dispatched four missions, to Khandesh, Bijapur, Ahmadnagar, and Golconda, under the leadership of Shaykh Abu-l Faizi.

Patiently, I waited, and waited, but the vague reports I received gave me little hope. Two years later, my worst misgivings were confirmed: he came back with a meager fourteen elephants and a handful of jewels as a so-called token of friendship; not only had the bastards refused to submit or pledge allegiance; they hadn't even deigned to treat my emissaries with the respect due to their rank! This time, I really had more than enough.

I sent Abdurrahim with an army, and instructed Murad – at the time governor of Gujarat – to join up with him. The two armies met at Chandur and crossed the border virtually unopposed, laying siege to the fortress of Ahmadnagar on the 15th of Dey of the fortieth year[340]. Things seemed to be going all right, but in fact, they were not – not at all. Disconcerting reports kept coming in, about bad blood between Murad and Abdurrahim, the former reportedly too drunk and arrogant to take advice from a more seasoned warrior, and the latter too proud and stubborn to keep his mouth shut. Murad, so it was reported, went as far as to openly and insultingly question his father's judgement. 'The old man really must be losing it,' he was reported to have said, 'to send a goddamn Shi'a to fight against Shi'a rebels!' I seethed with rage. The nerve! Who did he think he was? Lucky for him he was so far away: I would have personally slapped him in the face!

Anyway, my army leaders seemed to be more preoccupied with their own private feuds than with the war they were supposed to fight. Little wonder, that in the face of Ahmadnagar's stiff resistance – quite

[339] August 1591.

[340] December 26, 1595.

heroic resistance, I am told – they patched up a peace deal with the enemy, whereby the siege was lifted in exchange for the territory of Berar.

I was beside myself with rage when I heard the news. Who were they to conclude a peace agreement I had not authorized? Did they think I was paying for a major military campaign, to be contented with a small border region? But there was little I could do, so far away. Dispatches back and forth took over a week to arrive; all I got was a few polite letters with vague reassurances, while the disturbing rumors about drunken misbehavior and violent rows continued unabated.

The dispatch I received in late Esfand of the forty-second year was the drop that made the cup run over. The rebels had broken the peace treaty, and Abdurrahim – not a word about Murad – had fought them at Ashti, near Supa on the Godavari River. The enemy army had been much stronger than expected, and an indecisive victory had been the result: Abdurrahim had managed to rout them, but his own losses had been so heavy that he had been unable to pursue and annihilate the fleeing rebels.

This time, I had enough of all this bungling. I sent down Abu'l Fazl to assess the situation, and bring Murad back to Court.

Alas, it was too late...

I still see, as if it were yesterday, Abu-l Fazl's messenger presenting himself, a blue handkerchief around his wrist, an ominous blue handkerchief that could only mean one thing: someone very close to the Emperor had died, someone so close, the messenger didn't dare to speak his or her name. I managed to remain outwardly calm and didn't move a muscle, even as I felt the gazes of the entire Court upon me. Inside my head, thoughts were racing feverishly: who had died? Was it Abdurrahim? Abu'l Fazl? God forbid, Murad, my own flesh and blood?

I looked around the crowded diwan-i-am, causing those who had been staring at me to quickly avert their eyes. As I expected, you were prudent enough not to show any emotion. Standing tall, arms crossed, features composed, you confidently looked at the messenger and waited for him to deliver his message. I knew what you were thinking: 'If it's Abdurrahim, that's too bad, but I do not really care; and if it is Abu'l Fazl or Murad: so much for the better!'

'You bring us sad news?,' I asked.

'Alas, Your Majesty, I do,' the man answered timidly.

'Well, tell us what you have to say.'

'I carry with me a letter from the honorable Shaykh Abu'l Fazl, Your Majesty.'

'And?'

'The honorable Shaykh profoundly regrets to inform Your Majesty, that unfortunately, His Imperial Highness the Shahzada Sultan Murad has passed away, after a brief illness.'

I heard myself answering, in a surprisingly calm and steady voice: 'We will discuss this in our private chambers.'

I rose from the Throne and went inside the palace. Few moments later, in the privacy of the Diwan-i-khas, I sat myself down again and resignedly listened to the messenger, my dry eyes staring aimlessly at the floor below the throne platform.

Hesitatingly, almost inaudibly, he proceeded to read out the letter. Behind Abu'l Fazl's usual euphemisms and flowery language, the painful, humiliating truth soon became evident: Murad had drunk himself to death. For months in a row, he had been living like a pig, blind drunk from the morning till the evening, neglecting all his duties except for a few undignified rows with Abdurrahim. In the end, it had become so bad that his friends had to spoon-feed him two full cups of arraq every morning before he was able to do anything, because his hands were shaking so badly! Nothing anyone said tor did seemed to help; in the end, he would drink over thirty cups per day, and hardly eat anything, until he became completely bedridden. The letter remained discreetly silent as to how exactly he died; but it was clear it had been a hell of sweat, filth and vomit.

I dismissed the messenger with an impatient wave of my hand. For what must have been at least an hour, I just sat there, alone in the empty Diwan-i-khas, staring at the floor. Much as I blamed myself for it, I found myself unable to cry, or even to feel anything. My son, dead? It was so unreal, it somehow didn't seem to get through. I tried to picture him in my mind's eye, but all that came to me were a few fragments: the sound of his disturbingly loud voice – which, as Salima cautiously told me one day, sounded exactly like my own; the irritation I felt when time and again, he would show up late when I sent for him; his remarkable prowess with guns and horses; his disturbing laziness and lack of interest in anything other than eating, drinking, treasure, and women.

Then, I thought of him as he had been when he was fifteen, sitting on his horse as if he had been born on it, galloping at breakneck speed, shooting well-aimed arrows at a straw puppet. A hot, burning tear – the first one of many – came running down my face, as I realized my son's life was over. A young life that could have been full of greatness had come to an end; an end so stupid, so shameful, so unnecessary, that I wanted to stamp my feet and shout in impotent rage; but I knew, nothing I could say or do would change anything. There was nothing but the empty hall, and my silent, bitter tears.

Except for the most urgent matters of state, I hardly left my private quarters the following days, spending my time sitting listlessly on my bed or pacing up and down, thinking, brooding. Not that it was of any help or use. It was as if some infernal mill in my head kept churning out the same thoughts, over and over and over. How could Murad do this to himself? How could a strong young man throw away his life like that? Was it my fault? Should I have gone down there myself – talk to him, kick his butt, until he would have come to his senses?

No, why torture myself like that? He brought this on himself! I gave him everything, a life of wealth, power and luxury, and he squandered it all away! Perhaps – God forgive me for even thinking so – it was for the best. Who knows what would have happened if he would have survived me? He was ambitious, an excellent soldier, and far too proud and hot-tempered to live the life of an obedient courtier to his brother. Perhaps God Himself had intervened here, to spare Hindustan the scourge of civil war, a war that would have ruined everything I worked for all my life! No, who was I kidding? Did I really think that God – if He existed – would be bothered with men's thrones and successions? No: what happened, happened. Nothing I said or thought or did would change anything.

After a few days, Hakim Ali Gilani requested a private audience, which I granted reluctantly. With that well-meaning meddlesomeness so typical of men of his profession, he suggested it would be better for my health if I went out more, got some air... I grumpily told him to leave me in peace, but deep down, I knew he was right. The next day, I made up my mind: I would go to the Deccan. Take charge of operations myself. It would be good to hear the roar of cannon, the shouting, the thunder of hooves...

And so, on the twenty-ninth of Tir of the forty-fourth year[341], barely two months after Murad's death, I headed south, to Khandesh and Asirgarh, to pick up where my son had left off.

Asirgarh... merely the name of the wretched place makes me furious! If I could, I would erase it from my memory.

What should have been my last, most glorious conquest, became a most embarrassing, disgraceful spectacle – all because of you, Salim.

As you remember all too well, I left you in charge of Agra during my absence; I ordered you to make yourself useful in the meantime, and lead a campaign into southern Rajastan, to bring the rana of Mewar to heel. Knowing your indolent nature, I kind of suspected that not much would come from the campaign, but how could I expect the kind of treachery you were up to?

While you and your useless sycophants were cooking up evil plans, I headed south, and reached the border of Khandesh near the end of the solar year. Upon my arrival, I found the local ruler Mirhan Bahadur and most of his forces had taken refuge in the fortress of Asirgarh. I quickly seized the opportunity. Bypassing the fortress, Abdurrahim and Danyal were sent ahead further into Ahmadnagar, where they surrounded the capital, and took it by storm on the 7th of Shahrivar[342], imprisoning the local king and his family, and putting to the sword the defending garrison of about fifteen hundred. Meanwhile, I had laid siege to the fortress of Asirgarh. It is there that alas, things started to go seriously wrong.

You have to know that Asirgarh is at least as strong a fortress as Chittor, its ramparts high up on well-nigh inaccessible cliffs, with the added difficulty that the ground around it is solid rock, preventing the construction of *sabats*. It has its own potable water from numerous wells and reservoirs inside its walls, and supplies sufficient to feed the

[341] July 10, 1599.

[342] August 19, 1600.

entire defending garrison for over ten years. As the ramparts could not be stormed, and I did not have enough heavy cannons at my disposal to breach the walls, I found myself stuck. I sent an embassy to Goa, with a message that if the Purtugesh valued my friendship, they would quickly come to my aid with a number of their heavy guns.

As I waited in vain for the Purtugesh – they were apparently not so eager to help me conquer the South and thus, become my neighbors – and was devising alternative plans to either bring in additional artillery from up north, or found extra cannons and mortars on site from locally available bronze and iron, most disturbing dispatches came in from Agra, and alarming letters from Salima and my mother: Shahzada Salim, they wrote, was in open rebellion against his father. He had attempted – in vain, fortunately – to seize the treasuries in Lahore , Dilli and Agra. He had raised an army of over 70,000 horse and taken Allahabad, where he had set up court as an independent king.

My own son, a traitor? I could hardly believe it, but alas, it was true. What was I to do? I couldn't bear the thought of having to run back, tail between my legs, with Khandesh still unconquered, but then again, could I afford to stay away from my capital, with a major rebellion going on? I urgently needed to get back, and talk some sense into you.

I ,thus, hastily proceeded to secure the last but regrettably most inglorious victory of my life. Through the intermediary of a few local nobles, secret negotiations were opened with the leading defenders. As I hoped and expected, gold and silver bribes quickly proved to be more effective than steel and gunpowder. After a few weeks, Asirgarh opened its gates, and without a single drop of blood having been shed, the Imperial standard flew over the ramparts.

I paid a hasty visit to the newly conquered fortress, but found little joy in the sight, however magnificent and impressive. What was supposed to have been my ultimate victory was in fact a smudge on my immaculate armor.

Thus, ended, in disappointment most bitter, my inglorious Deccan campaign. As quickly as honor permitted, I headed back north, to secure my capital from my own son. My firstborn, the one I had so ardently prayed for, was threatening my treasure, my throne, possibly even my life.

PART III

[343] 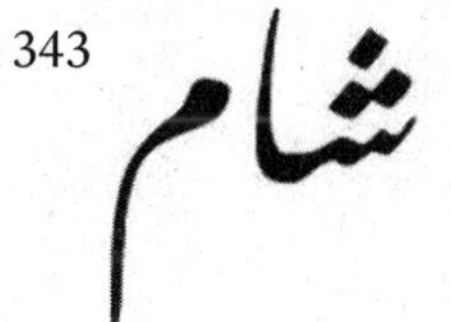

[343] Shām: Evening, Dusk.

Thirty-eighth Letter

الآحاباد

Allahabad (1)

From the Memoirs of Her Imperial Highness
Salima Sultana Begam Chaqaniani,

مخفی [344]

The late afternoon of Yawm as-Sabt, the 9th of Farvardin,
this forty-eighth year of Akbar's reign[345]*;*
on the road to Allahabad, about twenty-five kos east of Agra.

Allah be praised, the messenger has returned, at last – and there's a personal letter from Salim!

The reception was cool, but courteous, the messenger says. Salim was drunk, as usual, and didn't say much; but even so, he did offer him food and refreshments and a place to rest, before sending him back to me, with the letter.

'Tell her Highness, she had better save herself the trouble,' he said, 'but if she persists in her resolve to see me, it will be an honor and a privilege for me to receive her as my guest.'

---

[344] Makhfī, 'The Hidden', artist name used by Salīmā as a poetess.

[345] Saturday, March 19, 1603.

I must say, the tone of the letter is rather encouraging: formal and polite, of course, as can be expected from a king writing to his stepmother, but definitely not unfriendly.

'Most honorable and chaste lady, whom I cherish and revere as I do my own mother,' that's how he addresses me!

He profoundly regrets, he says, that the unfortunate differences between his august father and himself have caused me such distress, that I have thought it necessary to undertake so strenuous a voyage.

Deplorable though the quarrel with his revered father may be, he fears there is very little that I can do about it: I must see, it is his duty to follow the path he has taken – the path he profoundly believes to be in full accordance with Allah's will.

He's concerned about my health and comfort, he says; he wonders whether it would not be wiser for me to return to the safety and convenience of Agra. Not that he does not wish to see me – on the contrary, he has always had the highest respect and deepest affection for me. If I do choose to come, as he suspects I will, for he knows I have the character and perseverance of my glorious ancestors, he will be most honored and pleased to receive me with the highest honor, and he is very much looking forward to this opportunity of seeing me again.

He urges me not to hesitate to call upon him, if there is anything I need during my voyage. He suspects his most noble father will have provided me with ample supplies and a strong enough escort to guarantee my comfort and safety, but again, he would be glad to be of assistance should I so require.

He will for now bid me farewell, and express the wish that Allah may be my guide and protector.

The unfortunate differences between his august father and himself... a deplorable quarrel... Is that all he has to say about the dreadful things he did? Taking possession of the fortress of Allahabad, seizing the imperial treasure there, raising an army, and even striking coin in his own name: what is that, if not open rebellion? And what to say about the cowardly murder of Abu-l Fazl?

I've never seen Akbar so enraged – enraged and devastated at the same time – as when they told him his best friend and most trusted confidant had been butchered by a gang of robbers, led by some petty local warlord, paid and instructed by his own son...

Salim always detested Abu-l Fazl – so much I knew. I knew he was jealous of him, he resented and feared him for the influence he had on Akbar. But who could have imagined he would be capable of such atrocity? What kind of son has his father's best friend murdered in cold blood? How vengeful can one get, to throw the poor man's head in the latrines, leaving it there to rot under the excrements, and making sure your father gets to know about it?

Still, not all is lost. Despite his grief and anger, Akbar has managed to resist the urge to launch his armies against Allahabad. Anyone else, he would have crushed like a bug, but punishing his son is clearly something different altogether... Furious though he may be, he will always put the interests of the Empire first!

And Salim? He yearns to be king, he longs for a court of his own – so much is clear. But so far, he has avoided any direct confrontation, and he does continue to speak about his father with utmost respect. He may call himself King of Allahabad, but hasn't gone so far as to reject or deny his father's overlordship.

No, all is not lost – not yet. With Allah's help, I may still be able to talk some sense into him, show him it's not only his duty to make amends, but also in his own best interest.

Yes, I will put my trust in Allah. With His support, nothing is impossible! I pray to Him, that He may grant me the wisdom to find the right words, and to Salim, the openness of heart to hear them.

Thirty-ninth Letter

الآحاباد

Allahabad (2)

From the Memoirs of Her Imperial Highness
Salima Sultana Begam Chaqaniani

Yekshanbeh the 4th of Khordad, this forty-eighth year of Akbar's reign[346], about two hours before dawn.

Allah be praised a thousandfold, I have succeeded! Salim has agreed to return to Agra with me!

Our conversation has of course been neither pleasant nor easy, but in the end, he did listen to reason. He's a fickle, hot-headed drunk, no doubt, and his mind has obviously been poisoned by that worthless bunch of profiteering flatterers he calls his advisors, but deep down, there's honesty and strength in him, a nobleness of character that, however imperfectly, reminds me of Akbar.

Salim's quite smart, actually – in many respects, smarter and more talented than his father! Unfortunately, he misses Akbar's perseverance and resilience, but then, who does not? And anyway, does he have to be exactly like his father, in order to be a good king? Is it always necessary to be an exact copy of one's predecessor? I would argue, it may be preferable for a country that a conqueror be succeeded by a peacemaker, a wise man by a smart one, a visionary by a pragmatist... No, with Allah's help, Salim can be a good and just Emperor, of that I am quite sure.

---

[346] Sunday, May 15, 1603, Julian Calendar.

It was as I expected: the reception that befell us was lavish beyond imagination – clearly intended to impress, if not intimidate.

At two days traveling from Allahabad, we were met by a powerful, well-equipped cavalry force, much larger than any escort that could be considered necessary under the circumstances. I took care not to show it too conspicuously, but I was truly overjoyed to see that Salim had come in person to greet me. He seemed to be quite eager to please me, calling me his revered mother, and showing me every possible honor, although he did avoid being alone with me. 'We will have ample time to talk when we arrive, revered mother,' he answered evasively, each time I tried to start a private conversation.

We continued our way to Allahabad in great pomp. When the cortege was about one kos from the city gates, Salim rode ahead with his men – to bid me an official welcome upon my arrival, he explained. I followed at the head of my retinue, seated in a beautiful palki, on the towering back of one of Akbar's most impressive elephants.

Upon our arrival at the fortress, an impressive fighting force bade us welcome, with rows upon rows of heavily armored war elephants and beautifully caparisoned horses, rolling kettledrums and blaring trumpets.

I rode through the gates and entered the fortress. Dozens of well-dressed courtiers were awaiting me in the diwan-i-am, bowing deeply as I entered, their right hands touching the ground. I did not deign to wave or nod or otherwise acknowledge their presence: I had nothing to do with the worthless bunch of sycophants Salim called his 'court', despicable liars, profiteers, every single one of them!

The diwan-i-am, though smaller than the one in Agra, was well laid out and quite impressive. Just like at Akbar's court, there was a large shaded area, covered by an elegant roof, its arches artfully sculpted and adorned with beautiful silk curtains, its floor covered with precious Kashmiri silken carpets. In the wall was a balconied platform, supporting an impressive throne, perched above the crowd. On the throne sat Salim, laden with pearls, a bejeweled sword in his hand, broad-shouldered, manly, imposing, and indeed, of eminently royal countenance. I must admit, I did feel somewhat intimidated. This was not a welcome at the residence of some local governor, not even one of royal blood: this was truly the court of a mighty king, receiving a foreign ambassador.

I resolved, however, not to show how impressed I was – definitely not in front of Salim's courtiers! After all, was I not the Emperor's preferred wife and his official Ambassador, invested with an Imperial mission? Was Salim's rank not that of a local governor – lower than mine? Ignoring the servants who had come to help me get down from my mount, I merely opened the curtains of the palki and remained seated on the elephant – higher than Salim's throne. Keeping my face expressionless behind the transparent veil that covered my head, I kept silent, waiting for him to greet me.

'My heart is overjoyed, revered mother!,' Salim said with a slight bow. 'It is a great honor indeed for my Court to receive the visit of such highborn and most noble Begam!'

'I am glad to see you in good health, my son!,' I answered with a brief nod and a faint smile. 'I bring you your noble father's most affectionate greetings! He has instructed me to give you this robe of honor, made of the finest silk and embroidered with gold thread; he has worn it upon his own person for a full day! He also wants you to have this fine Iraqi stallion, faster than the wind, strong and fearless; and this war elephant, which is the pride of the imperial stables; his name, most appropriately, is Fath-i-Lashkar[347].'

'Words fail me, to express my gratitude and joy at these tokens of my noble father's affection and generosity, revered mother,' Salim answered, touching his heart and bowing his head. Was he being facetious? Or did he actually mean what he said? I wasn't sure.

'I bring you his tidings, my son; there are matters of the highest import we need to talk about – in private of course,' I answered. I briefly looked down upon the bunch of sycophants at the foot of the throne, with what I hoped was conspicuous disdain.

Salim seemed to hesitate for a moment, then nodded in approval. 'I look forward to continuing our conversation in private, revered mother. I hope you will find your quarters comfortable – please, do not hesitate to ask if there is anything you require!'

We dismounted. Palace servants guided me and my retinue to the zanana, where I found that an entire wing had been vacated to accommodate us. Food and drink, flowers, exquisite silk, soothing

---

[347] Fath-i-Lashkar: Victory of the Army.

balms, precious perfumes – everything had been provided for in abundance. I took a bath and had something small to eat, then took a brief stroll around the grounds. The zanana was smaller than the one at the Agra Fort, but just as comfortable, and I have to admit, even more refined. The rooms and hallways abounded with beautiful works of art, from all over the world it seemed; the colours and patterns of the carpets and curtains had been combined judiciously and with exquisite taste. This was truly the dwelling of a lover of beauty.

I instructed the servants to inform Prince Salim that I was ready to meet him. He didn't keep me waiting. Servants carried me in a comfortable sedan chair to his private quarters, where he was waiting for me, sitting cross-legged on a cushion in a comfortable, lamp-lit room. Next to him was a precious, gem-encrusted box, a large jewel case so it seemed.

Salim rose to his feet to bid me welcome, embraced me and respectfully bowed down to kiss both my hands. We sat ourselves down, facing each other, a silver tray with fruits and sweets between us. He ordered the servants to bring us some ice-cooled water, sherbet, wine and *some more duatasha arraq*[348] – a yellowish, unsavory-looking liquid, of which from time to time he gulped down a large mouthful – without any obvious enjoyment, judging by the rather painful grimace on his face each time the stuff was making its way to his stomach.

He looked a lot less impressive than back in the diwan-i-am a few hours before. He had been drinking, that much was certain – the room reeked of it. His eyes were reddish, watery, dull; from time to time, however, when something annoyed him, they would narrow to slits and suddenly start glowing, like the eyes of a tiger about to strike.

He did his very best to look relaxed and in control. Each time I mentioned his father's name, though, he would give away his nervousness, inadvertently shuffling on his cushion, belying the confident, disdainful smile around his lips.

'Serve us our drinks and leave us,' Salim ordered the two servant girls who were waiting near the door.

'I think I will just have some lime sherbet,' I said, and the girl standing closest to me made haste to attend to my wish. Salim merely

[348] Twice-distilled spirit.

pointed at his beaker, nearly empty by now. The other servant replaced it with another one, filled it to the rim with some more ice-cooled arraq, and put an entire pitcher of the stuff in a bowl of ice in front of him. Before the girls had left the room, he had taken another swig.

'You have to stop drinking so much of that awful stuff, Salim! Have you forgotten what it has done to your poor brother Murad, may Allah have mercy on him? And still, you and your brother Danyal continue drinking, as if nothing has happened! Why are you both so keen on destroying yourselves that way?'

'I appreciate your concern, most noble Begam and revered mother,' Salim answered stiffly, 'but I can assure you that I am in excellent health!'

'Salim, why won't you listen to me? Hakim Ali has told me all about the dangers of heavy drinking! Do you realize, that...'

He impatiently raised his hand.

'As I said, revered mother, I do appreciate your concern, but you can rest assured, that I have everything under control! Besides, I must assume that you haven't traveled all this way, just to talk about my drinking habits?'

'You are right, I have not. I have come to ask you to come back to Agra with me, Salim! This dreadful feud has to stop!'

'Feud? What feud?'

'Do not play the innocent, Salim! You've been in open rebellion for over two years!'

'Rebellion? As far as I am aware, there is no armed conflict between my father and me!' Again, that cold smile and that dangerous flicker in his eyes.

'What other name is there for your outrageous behavior? Your father leaves Agra to go to war against the Deccan Sultanates, he leaves you in charge of the capital. He orders you to take an army to Rajastan, against the rana of Mewar. And how do you repay his trust? You head back before even reaching Ajmir! You don't listen to Man Singh; you refuse to go and see your grandmother when she asks you to, and you try to steal the treasury, in Lahore and Agra! When that attempt fails, you head east, and take Allahabad!'

'I wanted to be left in peace...'

'To be left in peace? You call this peace? Seizing the local treasury –

thirty lakhs of rupees! – spending it shamelessly on your own comfort and glory, and setting up your own court? Appointing confidants and replacing your father's officers, everywhere from Kalpi to Bijapur?

No apology, no sign of respect, nothing! On the contrary, you have coins minted in your own name – nothing short of a declaration of independence! What do you think your father would have done to you, had you not been his son? He would have crushed you like a bug! But still, out of love for you, he holds his peace. He sends you his best advisor, his most trusted helper, his best friend – hoping that he'll be able to talk some sense into you. And what is your reply? Not only do you refuse your father's hand in friendship: you have the audacity to have his closest friend ambushed and murdered by some dirty roadside robber!'

'I hear indeed that Shaykh Abu-l Fazl was killed in a skirmish with Raja Bir Singh of Orchha. There must have been some kind of enmity between those two...'

'Do you deny it was you who sent that unwashed bandit to kill your father's friend?'

'I wrote him that Shaykh Abu-l Fazl's coming to Allahabad was displeasing to me,' Salim admitted with a phony smile. 'I am sure Bir Singh must have had my best interests at heart, when he attacked the Shaykh's retinue...'

'People say you even had the poor man's head thrown in the latrines!'

'Do they? Well, if I did, I did well, and I had every reason to do so!,' shouted Salim, suddenly seething with rage. 'When I think of all the crap that has come out of that pig's mouth, no place could be more appropriate for it!'

'How can you say this, Salim? And how could you do a terrible thing like that? Your father's most trusted friend!'

Salim did not answer immediately. I could see the muscles around his jaw moving as he struggled to restrain his anger.

'Trusted, most certainly! But my father's friend, he was not!'

'What makes you say that?'

'Abu-l Fazl has never been anyone's friend! Never has he served anybody or anything but his own private interests! Filling his own coffers was the only thing he ever cared for! He was a shameless, ass-kissing opportunist, who cleverly offered my father the jewels of flattery – but at what heavy price!'

'Do you really think your father is a fool who can be taken in by flattery? Well, trust me: he's not! He's an excellent judge of character – you do not get to be as mighty and powerful as he is if you pick the wrong helpers! Of course, he knows that Abu-l Fazl was a shameless flatterer – most courtiers are, by the way, and your own in the first place! But very few people are as competent and hard-working as Abu-l Fazl was – the poor man worked like a dog for your father! And yes, your father did reward him handsomely for it. So what? Do you not think it's normal that a hard-working minister with so many important responsibilities gets rewarded for his faithful service? How about your own helpers: do you not pay them a handsome salary? Of course you do! Well, I bet you they're not half as competent or hardworking than Abu-l Fazl!'

Salim smiled.

'You may rest assured, revered mother: I know my father is no fool. I may have many shortcomings, but blind or dishonest, I am not. And yes, I'll admit to you that Abu-l Fazl was smart and hardworking. But let me tell you: for all his qualities, the Empire is much better without him!'

'But why?'

'I think you know why, revered mother.'

'But I really do not – why don't you tell me?'

'Revered mother, I find that hard to believe! Everybody knows how wise you are, and everybody knows you are my father's preferred wife. I really find it hard to believe that you didn't see how Abu-l Fazl deliberately estranged me from my father and my brothers!'

'I really do not know where you get this from! I've never heard him say anything of the kind!'

'Of course not, he would be more subtle than that! But that has not stopped him from being effective – highly effective!'

'I am sorry – I do not have the faintest idea what you are talking about! You keep speaking in riddles!'

Again, that angry flicker in Salim's eyes. For a few moments, he said nothing, just looking intently at me, trying to read my mind. He must have come to the conclusion that I actually meant what I said, for he resumed, in a much softer tone of voice:

'Revered mother, I trust you are familiar with Abu-l Fazl's chronicle, the *Akbar Nama* [349], aren't you?'

'I am.'

'And you've read it, I suppose?'

'Yes, I have, several times! I agree it abounds with flowery phrases and flattery, but does that not prove his loyalty?'

'Haven't you noticed, revered mother, how often, or rather, how *seldom* he makes mention of me or my brothers? Just think about it: hundreds upon hundreds of pages of chronicles, and hardly a word about the Emperor's own sons! And you know what is even worse? He actually does not need to talk about us, because we hardly ever got to play any role of significance!'

'Aren't you exaggerating a bit, Salim? Has your father not entrusted you – all three of you – with many important missions?'

'Has he, indeed?' Salim sneered. 'Well, we've been sent on a few campaigns, yes – campaigns of little importance, when he had better things to do! But have we ever been involved in any matters of real import? Never!'

He gulped down another swig of his *arraq*, closing his eyes, with that same painful grimace on his face, until the liquid had reached his stomach.

'Revered mother, let me give you another example to prove my point. You are of course familiar with the *Nau Rathan* or *Navaratna*, the Nine Gems of Emperor Akbar's Court, aren't you? As you know, it is the title of honor the people of Hindustan have given to my father's preferred advisors and friends. Most of them are dead now, but they're still quite famous for the high esteem in which they were held and for the influence they had on my father. And who were those famous nine gems? The lists of names vary, but will of course include Abdurrahim Khan Khanan and Raja Man Singh, my father's best army commanders, and Todar Mal, Birbal and Abu-l Fazl, his trusted administrators. The lists will usually include Abu-l Faizi, the poet, Tansen, the famous singer and musician, and one or two religious advisors. The names of those advisors tend to differ, depending on whom you ask, but those

[349] 'History of Akbar', a detailed chronicle of Akbar's reign, written by Abū-l Fazl.

who know my father, will always include old Shaykh Mubarak in the list. Hah! Can you imagine? One of the greatest Empires the world has ever seen, and it has practically been ruled, for decades, by a lowborn, babbling old shaykh and his two fat, conniving sons! Allah be praised they're dead and gone at last, all three of them – at least they will no longer be poisoning my father's ear!'

I wanted to say he was exaggerating, but he impatiently smacked his flat hand on the cushion.

'Do not try to deny it! You know damn well it's true! These three ass-kissing slimeballs have even managed to talk my father into creating that ridiculous new religion of his! The poor man probably does not even realize what a fool he's been making of himself! But these three bastards, rather than advising him correctly, rather than telling him what is really going on in his dominions, actually encouraged him in this nonsense! And you know why? To protect their own privileges and to line their own pockets, that's why!'

'I do not like all this Din-e-Illahi nonsense either,' I admitted. 'But you are wrong to think that Abu-l Fazl was ever unfaithful to your father, or that he tried to estrange him from you! Moreover: can it be denied how exceptionally smart and hardworking he was? He and Mubarak have been absolutely invaluable to him in his disputes with the mullahs!'

He smiled wryly.

'Yes, I'll admit to that. He was smart and hardworking, and yes, my father loved his wit, his freethinking attitude and his contempt for the mullahs; but much more importantly, Abu-l Fazl gave my father exactly the one message he adores to hear: that he, Emperor Akbar the Great, is absolutely unique, indispensable, and irreplaceable! And meanwhile, he cleverly took advantage of my father's vanity to make himself indispensable, and keep *me* out of government affairs! As I said before: he offered him the jewels of flattery, but made him pay dearly for them!'

'Keeping you out?'

'Let me ask you a simple question, revered mother. Has my father ever asked my opinion or advice? Has he ever involved me in any of his decisions? Have I ever been his confidant? Never! All my life, I've been following his orders, as if I were some third-rate officer. And why is that? Because all these years, Abu-l Fazl has subtly but effectively been keeping me out!'

'And how is he supposed to have pulled that off?'

'Oh, he went about it quite subtly! In the first place of course, he would try to keep me away from Court as much as possible – never missing an opportunity of having me sent off on some or other campaign in some or other faraway region!'

He touted his lips and imitated Abu-l Fazl's mannered, servile way of speaking. 'Oh, Your Majesty, this would be an excellent experience for His Highness the Shahzada[350]!'

'And then, with the crown prince safely out of the way, good old Abu-l Fazl has free play! Of course, he knows fine well I hate his guts, and that his game will be finished as soon as I ascend the throne! And so, subtly, cleverly, he's sowing the seeds of doubt in my father's mind, with veiled hints that I am really not fit to succeed him. He rarely misses an occasion to glorify Danyal's wisdom or Murad's soldiery skills, but when it comes to me, he merely mentions my keen eye for the arts, as if I were some stupid harem concubine! Or he points out how wonderful it is that Abdurrahim is just like his father, so courageous, so strong, so wise – while I, of course, am not! Likewise, he never tires of saying that Khusrau, Parvez and Khurram have their grandfather's greatness in them – something he will, of course, never say about me!

And behind my father's back, he's even less subtle: belittling, disparaging, criticizing me in front of everyone who cares to listen! Every Amir, every army leader is given to understand that the Shahzada sadly lacks his father's wisdom and insight, that maybe it would be better if His Majesty would appoint one of his grandsons to succeed Him, and so on, and so forth...'

Salim's face was now twisted with anger. He gulped down what was left in his cup, filled it again, and took another large mouthful.

'Clever little plan, wasn't it?,' he continued. 'You just plant the seeds of doubt and confusion, and quietly let them do their poisonous work in the Emperor's mind... Does Salim really have what it takes? If not, who else does? Murad was probably the best and the strongest of the three, but sadly, he has passed away, and the doctors say Danyal

[350] Shāhzāda: Prince (literally, Son of a Shāh).

is heading the same way if he does not stop drinking... What to do? Shouldn't I appoint my eldest grandson? Khusrau is a fine young man – stronger, healthier, brighter, more disciplined; no drunkard like his father and uncle... And while the Emperor tosses and turns and wonders and worries, Abu-l Fazl, of course, is in high spirits! Salim is far away, and powerless, as long as the Emperor has not appointed him as his successor! And of course, there is nothing to fear from Danyal either, drunk all the time, meek and docile, or from the grandsons, who are still young and perfectly malleable. If one of them gets appointed, no more worries for good old Abu-l Fazl! For the rest of his life, he's got it made! He can be the new young Emperor's *ataliq*, advisor, wakil perhaps...

'Well, I spoiled that neat little plan of his, didn't I? That son of a bitch thought he could just come over, insult me in front of my court, and drag me back to Agra by my ear like a naughty little kid, didn't he? Thought I would never dare to lay a finger on him, didn't he? Well, he was wrong! Yes, I know my father is furious, but I do not care! At least, I gave that conniving bastard what he deserved – at least, he will not be there to reap the rewards of all his slander and intriguing! And so what if my father wants to appoint someone else as his successor? To hell with it! Let him appoint whomever he wants! I am sick and tired of groveling and begging and minding my step and sitting and waiting! I'm thirty-three years old, God damn it! Old and wise enough to start making my own decisions, and I want some respect!'

He grabbed the silver bowl of sweets on the tray in front of him and flung it at the wall. It clanged against the stones with a terrible noise, but not one of the servants dared to show her face and come in to clean up the mess.

For what seemed to me like an eternity, he just sat there, clenching his teeth, breathing heavily, staring at the dented empty bowl and the sweets scattered all over the floor.

Finally, he seemed to calm down. He looked at me, his features surprisingly composed and peaceful again.

'I really appreciate your concern for me, revered mother. I am truly grateful that you traveled all the way over here to see me, and I deeply appreciate your efforts to restore peace between my august father and myself, but as you can see, it's better that he and I go our separate ways. Allow me to express my gratitude, and offer you one of the most valuable treasures of my library – I bought it a few years ago from an Esfahani merchant. I know it will be in excellent hands with you!'

He bent over towards the jewel-encrusted case next to him and handed it to me. I took it in both hands – it was quite heavy, as I expected – and put it on my lap. I opened it; inside was a magnificent book, artfully bound, with hundreds of pages of exquisite calligraphy, illustrated on every single page with beautiful miniatures.

'Jalal-ud-Din Rumi – your favorite poet, is he not? Well, I want you to have this, revered mother, as a sign of my appreciation!'

I wanted to protest, tell him it was too much, but he didn't let me speak.

'I have but one more request, revered mother: when you get back to Agra, please tell my august father that I want no quarrel with him. Tell him, he can appoint whomever he pleases as his successor on the throne of Hindustan. Tell him, I only desire to be left in peace.'

I slowly closed the jewel box. Thoughts were racing frantically through my head. What was I to say?

'Thank you, my son,' I answered, slowly, word for word, trying to buy myself more time to think, 'this is really beautiful, but I cannot possibly accept it!'

'Why not?'

'Books are supposed to be a source of enjoyment, Salim. I could never lay my eyes on this book, beautiful and valuable as it is, without feeling deeply miserable. It would always remind me of the worst failure of my life! No, if you want me to accept it, you'll have to come back to Agra with me!'

He ignored the question, and bent forward to help himself to a few almonds.

'You have to come back with me, Salim! Can't you see you are bringing ruin on yourself, your father, the Empire, and our entire family? Yes, I know what you are going to say: you want no quarrel with your father, you want to be left alone. Can't you see that is impossible? Your father has toiled and labored his entire life to build this Empire; he would rather die a thousand deaths than to see it fall apart! If you want to be on your own, he will give you the governorship of Allahabad or Bengal or whatever, but he will never agree to a partition of the Empire, you have to realize that!

And let me tell you another thing, Salim. Whether you were right or wrong about Abu-l Fazl – I think you were terribly wrong, incidentally, but that's beside the point now – whether or not he was the devious intriguer you say he was, he was still your father's best friend! You broke your father's heart, Salim, you really broke his heart! You should have seen him when they brought him the news – he was devastated! He didn't eat or leave his bedroom for days! In these last few years, he has lost all his closest friends and confidants – Birbal, Todar Mal, Raja Bhagwan Das... and now, you've taken Abu-l Fazl away from him!

But all is not lost, Salim! Think about it: in spite of all the grief and anger you caused him, your father has not renounced or disinherited you – yet! And why do you think that is? Partly, because in spite of everything, he still loves you, he still cannot bear the thought that his long-awaited firstborn son, the one he had such high hopes for, has become his enemy!

But there is another, even more important reason: above all, your father wants to protect his life's work, his Empire! Put yourself in his shoes: what would you do, if you were him? Sure, you could disinherit your unruly firstborn son, have him banished, imprisoned, killed even. You could appoint someone else, but who? Danyal, perhaps? Would you take that risk? Danyal is a fine person, refined, well-educated, but would you entrust the future of your Empire to a hopeless drunk with one foot in the grave? You could appoint your first-born grandson, and sure, Khusrau is a talented young man, but will he be able to keep your Empire together when you are dead and gone? Danyal will feel past over; when they're older, Parvez or Khurram, at least as competent as their brother, may want to try their luck; Salim himself may yet be back to claim his birthright, and all of them will have their ardent supporters. Before you know it, the Empire is plunged in civil war! The winner inherits a weakened, deeply divided country; and when Kashmir, Bengal, Gujarat or other regions try to break away, he's well-nigh powerless to prevent it! Can't you see, Salim? Your father does not want to fight you, but he will, if you force him to! So do yourself a favor: come back to Agra with me, and make amends – you've got nothing to lose, and everything to gain! Do not plunge yourself and the Empire in a disastrous fight, which you will lose, and no one will win!'

'You seem to be quite sure that I would lose that fight, revered mother...'

'I am, and if you're honest with yourself, so are you, Salim! You know your father is a better soldier than you are!'

'Sure, my father is a genius, and I am nothing!'

'You are not worse nor better than your father, Salim. Just different, very different! In some respects, your father is indeed much stronger than you. He is a veteran warrior with an unbroken record of victories that remains unsurpassed; he's disciplined and dedicated, he has an unequaled capacity for hard work. In many respects, however, you are much more talented than he is! You are an outstanding scholar, an accomplished writer, you speak many languages... You do not need to be another Akbar to be a great Emperor, my son: just try to be the best Salim you can be!'

Salim smiled faintly.

'I can see, revered mother, why my father is so fond of you. But are you really sure? Will he be able to forgive me, after all the bad blood between us? Who says he won't throw me in prison, or worse?'

'No, Salim, that won't happen! I told you: in spite of everything, your father loves you very much. You are his firstborn – he would never hurt you! And even more importantly, he would never endanger the Empire for which he has toiled and fought so hard, all his life! Come with me, my son, it will be so much better for everyone!'

'Just suppose, for the sake of the argument, that I do go back to Agra with you. How do you suggest I should go about it? I can't just act as if nothing has happened, can I? Should I apologize for what happened? Should I beg his forgiveness?'

After a few moments' reflection, I answered: 'No. Let the past be the past. Do not ask for his forgiveness, but show him your loyalty and affection, show him you are glad to be back and reunited with him. Impress him. Bring him gifts, lots of gifts. Gifts so lavish they surpass his wildest expectations! And let's go together, as a family. We will stop by your grandmother's residence on our way to Agra, and ask her to accompany us to Court. Don't you see? He would never do anything to displease her – not in a matter of this importance!'

Salim reached for his arraq, then changed his mind. He poured himself a large beaker of lime sherbet and sipped, staring aimlessly at the wall.

After what seemed an eternity, he put the beaker down and looked at me, a faint, amused smile around his lips.

'You are wise and clever, revered mother. And I must say, you do know my father – probably better than he does himself! All right then, I will put my fate in your hands, and follow your advice. Let us head back to Agra.'

Fortieth Letter

الآحاباد

Allahabad (3)

Seven hundred and seventy elephants you offered me, and twelve thousand golden mohurs! I almost lost my composure when the messenger read out Salima's letter. This was not a courtesy gift; this was complete and entire submission; this was your hand, offered in true reconciliation. You truly cannot imagine, my son, how profoundly relieved and happy I felt.

The big day had arrived. You and your retinue would be arriving at noon.

And noon finally came. I could hardly conceal my emotion when you entered through the gate, accompanied by Salima – glowing with pride, and rightfully so – and your noble grandmother. We hadn't seen each other in four and a half years, but you hadn't changed much. A bit thinner perhaps, a bit paler; but you looked strong as before, and noble, and I felt proud of you. I rose from the Throne, came down from the platform and walked in your direction, several steps – an exceptional mark of honor, and the clearest possible sign of my fatherly affection and goodwill. You amply returned the compliment, kneeling down with utmost reverence. I can't begin to tell you how elated I felt when I took your hands in mine, made you stand up, put my arms around you, kissed you on both cheeks, and in front of the entire Court, placed my turban on your head, recognizing you publicly as my heir and successor. Everything would turn out for the best, after all. We would do great deeds together, you and me.

It didn't take more than a few days to make me realize: it was, alas, an illusion. The few private conversations we had were forced and halting, your answers evasive, your eyes furtive. All we had left to offer each other, was a few bland civilities, and long, awkward pauses.

We both knew what was standing between us: not so much the stolen treasury, not your half-hearted rebellion, but the one thing neither one of us spoke about, the murder of Abu'l Fazl, for which you could offer no apology, and I, no forgiveness.

No matter how often I resolved, usually after yet another nighttime conversation with my wise and sweet Salima, to put it all behind me, I could not help milling it over and over in my mind: how I had sent him a letter telling him about your misconduct; how, faithful as always, he had immediately promised he would travel from the Deccan to Allahabad and bring you to reason; and how he had been cowardly murdered, on your orders, by some filthy local hoodlum, one Bir Singh of Orchha.

Poor Abu'l Fazl! He never was a man of the sword, yet – bravely, foolishly – chose to die like one. He had been forewarned by informants. He could have escaped, he could have taken proper precautions, a much stronger escort; but he wouldn't listen to reason. Early in the morning of the thirty-first of Mordad of the forty-seventh year[351], a day that will forever be among the blackest in the history of Hindustan, he and his retinue of barely a handful suddenly found themselves under attack by five hundred heavily armed horsemen. But he didn't flee. On the contrary: he preferred an honorable death over a life in shame, he is supposed to have proclaimed. How naïve, how stupid! What good does it do, to die or nothing? Did he really think God – if He exists – cares about heroes, that He offers them some kind of special protection? What is bravery, against vastly superior numbers?

My poor old friend never stood a chance. Before he could lift a finger, the assassins speared him like a hunted animal.

They robbed him of his possessions, cut off his head, and took it to Allahabad, to collect their blood money. It is said that when you got the severed head – and you've given me no reason to believe otherwise – you ordered it to be tossed in the latrines.

What pained me most: I had been unable to avenge him. The shame

[351] Thursday, August 12, 1602.

of Birbal's death had quickly been erased with piles of Afghan heads; but for the death of Abu'l Fazl, it seemed there was only impotent rage. The troops I sent to Orchha to catch Bir Singh had failed: though wounded, he had managed to escape. Poor consolation, that everything he owned had been confiscated. As soon as I would be gone, the bastard would have no trouble getting into the new Emperor's good graces...

The more I thought about what had happened, the angrier I got. Why this needless, cowardly murder? What had I ever done to deserve this? What kind of a son kills his father's most trusted friend? What kind of a man denies the dead a decent burial?

I thought to myself: was this the kind of man to be ruling Hindustan? But what if I disinherited you? For all your faults, you were too much of a man to accept that. There would be civil war, most probably the breakup of the Empire! Could I risk ruining everything I worked for? Not even poor Abu'l Fazl would have wanted me to do that!

Thus, we went on, you and I. Officially reconciled, but estranged more than ever before. Between us stood a past that neither one of us could forget, and that, as far as I was concerned, tasted more bitter by the day. I resented you for having been such a disappointment; and you, I am sure, resented my living too long. Apart from a few official Court sessions, we saw very little of each other. You spent much time in Fatehpur Sikri; and I avoided you, as much as you did me.

One thing did please me: at least, you were not idling away your days. My informants told me you still drank a lot, but within limits; and that you spent much time meeting with the old Amirs and with the Firanghis. Ostensibly, your conversations with the former were about Shari'a law, and with the latter, about the life of the blessed Virgin Maryam, whose effigies you seemed to hold in particular reverence. Remarkable subjects, for a man who cares so little about religion...

It was all too clear what you were up to. You were of course forging the alliances you would need in the fights to come – against me, against Khusrau, or anybody else. And I have to say, those were smart moves you made: the Amirs would readily believe you were their best guarantee for the protection of Islam; and the Firanghis again had high hopes they would yet be able to convert the 'Great Mughal' to their faith... If I had not been so worried about the future and the obvious rivalry between you and Khusrau, your astuteness really would have amused me. You were made of the right material, after all.

The monsoon went by; weeks of reflection with the soothing rustle of the pouring rains outside finally brought me calm and resolve. I would give you additional responsibilities, involve you more in the affairs of state, give you a chance to prove and redeem yourself. You would go to southern Rajastan and force the arrogant rana of Mewar into submission, like I had ordered you to do before I went to the Deccan.

I should have known better. You of course didn't refuse to execute the order, but it was crystal clear you had little appetence for a war in some faraway hills, where little plunder was to be gained, and more importantly, where you would be unable to keep things under control at Court, should anything happen to me. After weeks of procrastination, delays, extravagant demands for all kinds of completely unnecessary reinforcements, you made your move. You wrote me a letter – elaborate, flowery, flattering, servile, but no less clear. You assured me of your ardent desire to fulfill your august father's wishes, but esteemed it your sacred duty to inform me of your presentiment that the time was inauspicious; you implored the favor of a private audience with me, and permission to return to Allahabad where you felt you would be of better service to me.

I gave up. What would we possibly have to say to each other? What good would it do to have another meeting full of idle talk that would only make me angry? I gave you the desired permission to attend to matters in Allahabad, adding you should feel at liberty to return to Court at any time.

You finally had what you wanted. On the 29th of Aban, you left Fatehpur and went back to Allahabad. Disappointed as I was, it did please me to hear you organized the most brilliant festivities upon your arrival, celebrating our reconciliation. You at least kept up appearances.

My relief was, alas, short-lived. Each new report was more unsettling than the previous one: drunken depravity, vicious cruelty, excesses of all kinds...

I underwent the celebrations for the beginning of the forty-ninth year in the most somber of moods. To what end had been all my hard work? What was to become of my Hindustan?

Forty-first Letter

دانیال

Danyal

Salima's bedroom, late in the afternoon on Shanbeh, the twenty-fifth of Ordibehesht of the forty-ninth year[352].

She's sitting next to me on the bed, her arm around my shoulders; neither of us knows what to say. I am wiping the tears from my burning eyes, but new ones keep welling up, no matter how hard I try to restrain them.

The messenger from the Deccan has left two hours ago, but I keep hearing his halting voice in my head, over and over again: 'I profoundly regret I have to inform Your Majesty...' He didn't need to finish his sentence. There was that dreadful blue handkerchief, that could only mean one thing: His Imperial Highness Shahzada Sultan Danyal had passed away; Danyal, my youngest, my gentlest, my wisest, was dead.

'When did this happen?' I tried to maintain my composure, but my voice was hoarse and barely audible.

'One month ago, Your Majesty.'

'How?'

'His Highness passed away in his sleep, Your Majesty.'

'Why? What was wrong with him?'

'The Hakims say it was his heart, Your Majesty.'

'Leave us alone,' I ordered. All the guards and courtiers instantly left the diwan-i-khas.

---

352 May 5, 1604 of the Julian Calendar (Saturday, May 15, 1604 CE).

'His heart, you say? Just like that?'

'I do not know, Your Majesty.'

'Do not lie to me!'

'The Hakims said it was caused by excessive drinking, Your Majesty,' he admitted hesitatingly.

'Drinking? What do you mean, drinking? I had given explicit orders that my son was not to have any wine or arraq, under any circumstance!'

The man bowed his head and looked down at his boots.

'Speak up, man, or I'll have you hanged!'

'I beseech Your Majesty, have mercy on me! I am innocent! I know nothing! I only know what I overheard other people say!'

'And what did they say?'

'That His Highness felt terribly sick without drink, Your Majesty; that he was sweating, trembling, shaking, unable to eat anything... That he bribed his friends and servants to get him his daily ration of wine and arraq – they smuggled it in, in phials hidden in their turbans and clothes, even in musket barrels! After a few draughts, His Highness would always feel much better, but he still had no appetite for any regular food. They say that the last month of his life, he was completely bedridden and hardly able to eat anything at all. He had gotten dreadfully thin, but his belly was more and more bloated. The white of his eyes was yellow, his face ashen. He grew weaker by the day; in the end, he passed away in his sleep...'

I wanted to yell at him, demand from him the names of those responsible, but couldn't utter a single word. I just sat there, staring, unable to think or even feel anything. Finally, I found the strength to tell the terrified messenger he could go – I even had the composure to award him the customary reward for messengers who have traveled from afar and have dutifully acquitted themselves of their task. When he had left, I rose from the throne and went into the palace gardens. Despite the muggy heat, I kept wandering aimlessly through them, for I do not know how long, numb and dazed in my head. Finally, I went back inside the zanana. When my eye fell on a painted portrait of Murad and Danyal when they were little, my eyes filled with tears at last; my shoulders started shaking uncontrollably, and I heard myself howling like a wounded animal.

For I do not know how long, I just stood there in front of that wretched painting, sobbing like a child. Then, I heard the soft shuffle of women's slippers behind me, and Salima's voice whispering: 'Come with me, azizam[353]!' She put her arm around my shoulders and led me to her quarters, where we sat ourselves down on her bed.

'Danyal,' I whispered, 'Danyal, my youngest, my gentlest... Why? How could this happen? Where has it all gone so wrong, Salima? Where have I gone wrong?'

'Stop torturing yourself, Akbar! This was really nobody's fault – least of all yours!'

'You are very kind, Salima, but...'

'Listen to me, Akbar: this was not your fault! There is nothing you could have done, even if you would have known everything beforehand!'

'What makes you say that?'

'Danyal was sick, Akbar. Very sick, and so was Murad! That's what the hakims say, and that's what I believe. Short of locking him up, and making absolutely sure his guardians could never be bribed, there is nothing you could have done to prevent this. Sooner or later, he was going to drink himself to death.'

'But why? Why did he do this to himself? I must have warned him a thousand times, and so did Hakim Ali, and so many others! Each time, he would promise and swear on the Holy Qur'an he would never drink again, and a few hours later, he would start again!'

'As I said, the hakims say it's a disease, really. Sharab is a very dangerous thing – it is with good reason the Holy Qur'an warns us against it! There may be people who do drink a lot but still manage to keep things under control – just look at yourself, for instance – but many others are not so strong...'

'Tell me, what should I do, Salima? What in God's name can I do? Two of my three sons are dead, and I tremble to think what may happen to the one I have left! Ever since he's gone back to Allahabad, the news I am getting is shocking! Oh, my God! What have I done to deserve this?'

'Is Salim drinking himself to death too?'

'No, not yet, at least I do not think so, but that won't take long, if he goes on like this! I hear he's hardly ever sober – he drinks from the

353 My love.

morning till the evening, not to mention all the opium he takes! As if he actually wants to destroy himself! And everybody's scared stiff of him – all those excesses have made him sick in the head, of course!'

'What do you mean, sick in the head?'

'He's gotten downright insane, Salima! Fickle, moody, unpredictable, cruel beyond belief! Do you know he had one of his men flayed alive in front of him, for some minor, trivial offence? Can you imagine? They say that for more than half an hour, he calmly watched the whole thing, without as much as blinking an eye!'

'What? That's horrible!'

'Yes, it is... Let me tell you, Salima: in the forty-nine years I spent on the Throne, I have pronounced a number of death sentences, but I can honestly say that it was almost always because I had to, because there was no other way! Yes, I'll admit that on a few occasions, I did give the order in furious anger, with vengeful pleasure even; but never, never have I ordered that kind of torture on anyone, not even for the most heinous of crimes!'

'I am still having trouble to believe Salim's capable of a gruesome deed like that! Are you sure this story is actually true?'

'Alas, Salima, I am – I have it from several dependable sources! And to be honest with you, I really do not know what to do anymore! What will become of the Empire, with a man like that?'

'Will you disinherit him?'

'I haven't decided, but yes, I very well may! In fact, I think I would have disinherited him a long time ago, were it not that I am frightened at the thought of what will happen after I am gone... What if civil war breaks out? What if the whole country falls apart?'

'You still have time to decide, Akbar. Do not allow anyone to push you into taking a decision you do not want to take! You are strong and healthy; Allah willing, you may yet have ten, fifteen, maybe twenty more years to live! By that time, your grandsons will be grown men, and you'll know what to do!'

I smiled, in spite of myself. Spoken like a true granddaughter of Babur!

'Yes and no, Salima. You are right I still have time, and yes, I do intend to use it well, but I am afraid I will have to make up my mind much earlier! There's much strife among the Amirs! And they make no secret of it! Aziz and Man Singh, for instance, have given me to understand, more than once, that they would much rather like to see Khusrau on the throne...'

'That's not hard to see why: Khusrau's mother is Man Singh's own sister, and Aziz Koka is Khusrau's father-in-law! If he gets appointed as your successor, their power and influence will be assured!'

'Precisely. But do not underestimate Salim: he has some very powerful supporters too! All the ulama are behind him, and most of the Turkoman Amirs!'

'Why is that?'

'Well, for one, he's supposed to be a much better Muslim than I am, and more importantly, he has all the laws and traditions on his side! The Chagatai Turks of old would never allow a son to be enthroned to the prejudice of his father! And that's not all: there's quite a few Rajputs supporting Salim. Do not forget he is married to a Rajput princess too, and do not underestimate the internal rivalry among the Hindu nobles: many would be glad to supplant Man Singh if they could! So you see, my dear: if it does come to a fight, Salim will be far from powerless! And he's not taking any chances: I hear he's been in correspondence with the Purtugesh of Goa...'

'With the Firanghis? Those unwashed infidels?'

'It's not as strange as it sounds, Salima: they have first-rate guns, and though their numbers are small, they're excellent soldiers; they would be formidable allies in any war!'

'So, you think he would actually take Firanghi soldiers into his army?'

'Of course! Why do you think he's so conspicuously devoted to the Virgin Maryam? Why does he collect dozens of Christian effigies? As far as I know, he has precious little interest in religion! He does love Firanghi paintings, but more importantly, this interest in the Blessed Virgin enables him to spend a lot of time with the Firanghi padres, giving them hope – quite false, I am sure – that he may one day convert! Just think about what would be in it for the Purtugesh, if they could put the next Great Mughal in their debt...'

I took off my turban and slowly rubbed my forehead and the back of my neck, in a vain attempt to ease the throbbing pain in my head.

'You see my problem, Salima? If I appoint Khusrau, or one of my other grandsons, there will be civil war – maybe I will be able to prevent it during my lifetime, but it will certainly break out when I am gone, and that would be an absolute disaster! Not only will kindred blood be spilt – which in itself is terrible enough – but no matter who wins this civil war, he will inherit a weakened and deeply divided land. How long do you think it will take, before the Uzbeg Khan, or the Persian Shah, or some or other ambitious zamindar tries to take advantage of our weakness?

So you see, my dear, there's hardly any options I have left! If I do not appoint an official heir, if I just leave things to run their course as they are today, I am effectively condoning the partition of the Empire, undermining my own authority, and sowing the seeds of lawlessness and war. If I die while Salim is still in Allahabad, Khusrau and his supporters will almost certainly disavow him, saying that he forfeited his right to the throne because of his rebellion. On the other hand, if I do appoint Khusrau, it's almost certain Salim will either go to war, or declare independence and split up the Empire.'

'Is there a solution to this?'

'There's only one: Salim has to come back, and he has to submit to me, unconditionally! Only when we're again reconciled, and only if he shapes up, if he behaves himself, I can appoint him as my successor! Only when he's officially appointed according to the laws and customs of our family, will he have the necessary authority and the support of the Amirs!'

'And if he does not? What if he refuses to come back?'

'Then, I will need to take other measures.'

'Would you fight your own son?'

'Don't you see I have no choice? Either Salim submits to me and I forgive him and I appoint him as my successor, or I have to disinherit him and chase him from the Empire. It's one or the other. I simply can't allow things to go on like they are today – it would ruin everything I worked for!'

'I'll go to Allahabad. I am sure I can talk some sense into him! I've done it before.'

'No, Salima! No more pleading, no more negotiating, no more playing games! There's a limit to my patience! This time, I'll go there myself – and at the head of an army!'

'Surely, Akbar ...'

'I am at the end of my patience, Salima! He will come with me to Agra, or he'll have to fight me!'

And thus, my son, while still mourning the loss of your youngest brother, I once again prepared for war. Not to conquer the Deccan, as I had planned; not to invade Persia or the lands held by the Uzbeg Khans, as I once had hoped; but to fight my own flesh and blood.

There was the usual frantic busyness of soldiers and animals and supplies; but this time, none of the excitement that precedes any great campaign. No prospect of land or booty or glory; only the looming menace of bloodshed and destruction. There was nothing to gain, and everything to lose.

With every gun, every elephant, every horse, every soldier passing by, I felt nothing but anger. Such useless waste of a fine army! All this because of one arrogant, spoilt drunk who called himself my son? Who did the ungrateful bastard think he was? A true son, worthy of that name, would be proud to expand his father's power! But this good-for-nothing was actually squandering it, ruining decades of hard work; disobeying, nay, betraying the father to whom he owned everything, desecrating his ancestors' memory!

With grim determination I continued the preparations, deaf to your mother's and Salima's pleas, ignoring the worried letters your grandmother kept sending me. This time, you would come to heel, if I had to drag you to Agra by your ears!

Alone in my quarters every night, I awaited with dread the moment I would have to go to bed. For I already knew the unbearable, horrifying sight that would come to haunt me in my nightmares: the sight of my victorious army, bringing me your severed head.

Forty-second Letter

سلطنت

Ṣaltanat[354]

From the Memoirs of Her Imperial Highness
Salima Sultana Begam Chaqaniani,

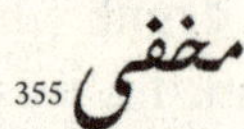 [355]

No matter what I said, no matter how much I begged and prayed, Akbar just wouldn't listen.

'Why do you insist on going there yourself?' I pleaded; 'and why do you need an army to go and see Salim? I know his behavior has been unacceptable, but has he actually rebelled against you? Can't you just tell him to come to Court? You are the Emperor, would he disobey a direct order?'

Akbar – if he deigned to answer at all – would silence me with curt statements like 'enough is enough' or 'do you really think I am going to let him destroy everything I worked for all my life?' Pressing letters from his ailing mother, who feared the ruin of the grandson she had always been so fond of, remained unanswered. Amidst the heavy monsoon rains, Akbar doggedly prepared himself for war.

---

[354] Kingship, Empire.

[355] Makhfī (the Hidden).

After a few weeks, his forces encamped on the other side of the Yamuna, about two kos from Agra, fully equipped, Akbar was ready for battle. But as he was about to march off, he suddenly found himself plagued by all kinds of accidents. His camp was inundated and partly destroyed under a deluge of rain, the barge he wanted to travel on got stuck on a sandbank in the middle of the river... but these setbacks didn't change his resolve. The astrologers, who understandably chose to interpret every incident as an evil omen, were told, in no uncertain terms, to shut up. Akbar's mind was made up. He marched off, at the head of his invincible army.

He had not gone far, when the news reached him that his mother's illness had become critical. At first, he decided to continue his journey, but when the report was reconfirmed, he felt bound to abort the campaign. By the time he arrived at her bedside, he found her barely conscious and unable to speak. Five days later, on the seventeenth of Shahrivar[356], at the age of seventy-seven, the old Empress passed away.

Akbar seemed to be profoundly touched by her demise – more deeply than I expected, to be honest, for he and his mother had never been really close: his policies in religious matters had never met with her approval. But death heals many differences. As a sign of mourning and filial piety, he took off his turban, shaved his head – even his whiskers and eyebrows! – and fasted for several days.

Hamida Banu Begam's body was washed, shrouded, and placed in a bier, which Akbar personally helped carry for a considerable distance. The body was further conveyed to Dilli by a relay of noblemen, to be laid to rest at the side of her husband, whom she had outlived for more than four decades.

Something seemed to have broken inside Akbar after his mother's death; he at least didn't pursue his planned march on Allahabad. After a few listless days, during which he hardly appeared in public and spent his time aimlessly walking in the gardens or brooding in his private quarters, he unexpectedly accorded a private audience to Mir Sadr Jahan, an orthodox mullah and one of Salim's confidants – exactly the reason why the man had never been taken into Akbar's confidence.

The audience lasted for a full two hours. When it was over, the

[356] August 29.

mullah, carrying two sealed firmans with him, hastily packed a few belongings and left for Allahabad. Nobody knows what was written in the firmans, but it's not hard to guess: one of them, most certainly, was an official letter written by the Court scribe, informing Salim of the passing of his grandmother, and inviting him to Court to share in his father's mourning. The second one, most probably, must have been a personal message, warning Salim that if he didn't immediately present himself at Court, Akbar would officially disavow him and appoint Khusrau as his successor.

Whatever was in the letter, it certainly didn't miss its intended effect. Soon after Mir Sadr Jahan's arrival in Allahabad, Salim began his journey to Agra, ostensibly with the intention of offering his condolences for the death of his grandmother. On Jom'eh, the twenty-eighth of Aban[357], he arrived at Court, accompanied only by a small escort, having left his troops at a considerable distance from the city limits, as Akbar had ordered him to do.

The reunion was markedly stiffer, more formal than the previous one, but still, reassuringly warm and friendly. Salim was welcomed with full honors, in the presence of the entire Court, and after a brief but friendly exchange of civilities, invited to join his father in the zanana.

When Salim came in, I rushed towards him to embrace him, but stopped when I saw Akbar's face. He was beside himself with rage; I had never seen him like this. He grabbed Salim by his clothes, dragged him into an empty room, and started slapping him straight in the face, four, five, six times, as hard as he could, with the back and the flat of his hand.

'You goddamn bastard,' he shouted, completely beside himself, his face all red, 'who do you think you are? Is this how you repay me? Is this how you show your gratitude for everything I've done for you? Disobeying my orders, sullying your hands with innocent blood, putting me to shame, wasting my money, drinking yourself to death? What kind of a man are you, anyway? If you hate me so much, why don't you go ahead and fight me? Where are your seventy thousand horsemen? Too much of a coward to use them? Afraid of getting your butt kicked?'

---

[357] Friday, November 9, 1604.

He went on like this for I do not know how long, literally foaming at the mouth with rage, showering Salim with bitter reproaches, mocking him for being a spineless coward, and threatening him that if he dared to disobey him again, he'd kill him with his own bare hands. Nobody dared to say anything. As for Salim, he just stood there, his turban knocked off his head, his eyes downcast, mute; he was sweating profusely and disgracefully reeking of drink.

At long last, Akbar seemed to calm down a bit. His features composed again, he gave orders to call in Hakim Ali Gilani and the physicians.

'My son is ill,' he said in a surprisingly soft voice. 'He needs to be cured.'

Salim was to be locked up in secluded living quarters, under the care of the physicians. He was not to receive any visitors, not to communicate with anybody other than the physicians, in writing or otherwise. Under no circumstances was he to receive any opium, wine or arraq of any kind. 'If anybody dares to give him any wine or opium,' Akbar added, suddenly shouting again, 'I will personally rip his guts out!'

The following days passed by in unbearable tension. Except for the daily darshan, Akbar didn't show himself in public. But he clearly kept busy. In a matter of two days, Salim's army was entirely disbanded, his horses and elephants accommodated in the imperial stables, his main supporters incarcerated. It was eerily silent at court. Except in strictly private conversation, Salim's name was mentioned whisperingly, if at all. The forced abstinence from drink and opium had made him critically ill, it was said. Hakim Ali Gilani and the other physicians didn't move from his side, but official news was sadly lacking.

After ten days – like ten months they seemed – rumors were suddenly buzzing about: the Emperor had paid his son a visit! He had personally brought him some opium, a beaker of opium-laced rosewater on ice! I dismissed the story as just another rumor, but Allah be praised, it proved to be true: soon, Salim reappeared in public at his father's side. The forced abstinence seemed to have done him much good: he seemed in good health, though he had visibly lost weight and looked quite pale.

As if nothing had happened, life at Court retook its normal course.

Father and son are officially reconciled. In accordance with his rank, an entire wing of the palace has been vacated for Salim and his zanana. His supporters have gradually been released from prison. In official ceremonies, he occupies the first place, closest to Akbar's throne. When his father does not require his presence, he busies himself with his favorite pastimes: reading, writing, and collecting paintings. People say he drinks quite a lot and uses opium every day, but he seems to keep himself under control.

Officially reconciled they are, but close to each other, they're not – not at all. They never speak in private; they avoid each other's presence as much as possible; the slumbering enmity between them is almost palpable.

I'm so worried... What is to become of us? No matter how strong and healthy Akbar still is, he is a white-haired old man; how long does he have to live? And what will happen when he's gone? Will he confirm Salim as his successor, will he yet appoint Khusrau? The Court is rife with rumors.

Forty-third Letter

شام

Sham[358]

The Court was rife with rumors, indeed. There was strife, enmity; rivaling factions were forming, alliances were being forged and broken; one could almost smell the putrid stench of civil war. Alas, there was little I could do. The tiger may roar, but the vultures keep hovering above his prey, patiently waiting until he's gone. No one would dare to make a move as long as I was alive, but no man lives forever...

The best thing, the only thing I could do, was to prepare for the future the best I could. And I think I have. Before I leave this earth, I will make sure you are firmly in the saddle, my son.

For I have made up my mind: you, and you alone, will be my successor. Not because of the outcome of the prize fight between your prize bull Giranbar and Khusrau's champion Abrup; I've ceased to believe in silly omens like that a long time ago. No, not because of that stupid elephant fight, and not even because of Khusrau's intolerable misbehavior afterwards. I will appoint you, because it's the law – the God-given law of nature, and the law of our ancestors. It is proper and becoming that a father should be succeeded by his elder son, and it's indispensable that this law be respected and adhered to by everyone, lest the Empire would become ungovernable.

---

[358] Shām: Evening, Dusk.

And thus, we have come to the end of these writings, my son. This is my last letter to you, and it will have to be a brief one, for I am exhausted by the loss of blood, and I desperately long for a bit of opium to numb the burning pain in my entrails. Tonight, the sun will be setting on Akbar the Great; tomorrow, it will rise over Jahangir...

So, you are about to become Emperor, my son. Do not take this lightly, but do not be afraid either. You are smart, my son, and so well learned! If you resolve to take your task at heart, I am confident you can and will be a great Emperor, who will be loved and remembered by his subjects as a just and benevolent ruler.

Just promise me one thing: do not let your laziness get the better of you, do not settle for a life of smallness and self-indulgence. Our task in this short life is to leave the world a better place than we have found it; and from those who have received much, much is expected. To be an Emperor is a great privilege, but for that very same reason, it's also a crushing responsibility: a king's burden is heavy, and his office, full of hard labor.

When I look at this stack of papers, and think of all the work that has gone into it, I wonder: has it been worth all this effort, all those sleepless nights? After all, why would you need to read the story of my life, to lead your own? And who am I to tell you that you have to follow my example in everything? In this world, we walk alone; the book of our life is ours to write.

Fortunately, there are many kinds of good books, and there are many ways to be a good Emperor – you just have to find your own way, my son. Think about it: you can be remembered as Jahangir the Great, the Just, the Wise, the Magnificent – it's up to you to make it happen! My advice to you is very simple: the way you would like posterity to remember you, that is how you should live your life.

What I hope these letters will have shown, is that your father, the loud, overbearing, demanding Emperor you have admired, feared and at times hated, was but a man. A man like you, with his own strengths and weaknesses, hopes and fears; a man, who often succeeded, but also made mistakes; a father who at times may have been too harsh, too distant, too unattainable, but who never stopped wanting the best for his sons. This is my hope, my deepest wish, Salim: that these writings may bring us together, even if it's only after my death.

I've felt a bit better this afternoon, thanks to the opium, but I know, this has been the last flicker. Even if I would stop taking the poison, I am beyond help now. My time has gone by, the hourglass of my life is running empty.

When this letter is finished, I will call in Karim, the old servant, God bless him. I will instruct him to bring all these papers to the archive and put them in their secret hiding place. You can rest assured: never will he mention this to anyone, under any circumstance. He's discrete and devoted; he'd rather die than to disobey me. When he's back and I am sure my instructions have been followed, I will finally treat myself to that opium I've been craving; tomorrow, I'll have you called to my bedside. I will bestow upon you my turban and Humayun's sword, and give you my blessings; all I have to do after that, is to close my weary eyes, and die.

Do not worry, my son. I am ready for it. Sickness and old age have their own way of reconciling a man with his death. Old friends have passed away; eyesight starts to fail, hearing becomes less acute, and in the limbs creeps a leaden heaviness, which makes one yearn to lie down and rest.

Soon, I will return to my Maker. What will it be like? What will He be like? What kind of existence, if any, will await me beyond the grave? I honestly do not know. Makhdum ul Mulk and the likes of him were right to warn me about this kind of thinking: my frantic quest for the truth has made me more confused than I was before. All the effort I've put into *falsafah*, countless hours of debate: they may have made my ignorance more articulate, but I admit, they've failed to bring me any closer to real knowledge or certainty.

May God forgive me if I am mistaken, but I very much doubt that He will be like the Master of the Day of Judgement, of Whom the mullahs speak, or Padre Rodolfo Aquaviva's sweet but stern Jesùs.

I do hope I will behold His countenance as an unspeakably beautiful, gentle, radiant Light, compared to which all earthly majesty pales into insignificance, and in front of which all questions, all worries, and all longings blissfully disappear.

But I must admit: the doubts that dear old Mir Abdul-Latif had before his death are haunting my own mind, too. Sometimes, I wake up in the middle of the night; and in those wretched hours, when one's thoughts tend to be as black as the nightly sky, I tremble with fear. What if I am wrong? What if God punishes me for my misbelief? But then, in the limpid clarity of the morning sky, I know better. How could a God, who is infinitely good, be as limited and narrow-minded as a few self-righteous fanatics would want Him to be?

Be all this as it may, there's only thing I do know with absolute certainty: I am about to die. And when I am dead, what remains of me will become one with the world. Part of my body will remain in a marble tomb, turning first into a loathsome, rotting mass, then into a pitiful heap of dry, brittle bones and dust. But the many other specks of matter that once belonged to my body, that I once inhaled or ingested, will continue to pass in and outside other things. They will become flower petals, desert dust, ants and God knows how many hundreds of thousands of other things and creatures, large and small, beautiful and ugly. For countless millions of years, they will be part of the Great Dance of the all-encompassing, unknowable Lord Śiva Nataraj...

Most probably, that's all there is to it. My soul will simply perish with my body, and be gone forever; it will be lost in an endless, dreamless sleep, unaware it ever was alive. Some of my thoughts, some of the words I've spoken, will live on in your mind, my son, and in the minds of your own sons, and later, unbeknownst to them, in the sons of your sons and so many other people. Most probably, that's the only immortality I can hope for. But that does not make my life unimportant. If I've made the world a bit more enlightened, I've served Truth and Goodness, which is nothing less than God Himself.

Farewell then, my son. Praise be to God, you'll help me close my eyes in peace tomorrow. Light a lamp on my grave from time to time, pray a few *Fatihas*[359] for the peace of your father's soul; and take good care of Hindustan for me – she deserves a wise ruler!

May God be your guide and protector. And many years from now, after you've led a wonderful and fulfilling life, may it please Him to reunite us in Paradise.

[359] The Sūrah al-Fātiha is the opening chapter of the Holy Qur'ān.

Epilogue (I)

From the Memoirs of Mulazim Hakim Ali Gilani

On Doshanbeh, the 21st of Mehr of the fiftieth year[360], the day after the elephant fight, His Majesty was suddenly taken ill with severe stomach cramps.

I wasn't overly alarmed. Loose stools are a way for the intestines to cleanse themselves of harmful elements; and knowing his Majesty's strong constitution, I felt rather confident he would soon recover. The first few days, therefore, I didn't give him any medicines; I merely made sure he got enough of the right liquids and nourishment. I advised him to abstain from fatty and spicy foods, from raw fruits and vegetables, and sharp-tasting condiments other than salt. I told him to eat small amounts of plain boiled rice and curds and to drink plenty of strengthening fluids, including broth made from lean meats and vegetables; plain Ganga water without ice; and tea with moderate amounts of mint leaves, cinnamon, cloves, saffron, and if necessary a tiny bit of opium, to ease the bowel pains.

But his condition failed to improve. As mild herbs seemed to have little effect, I administered astringents, which stopped the diarrhea, but alas, badly worsened his condition: within a few hours, he got high fever, severe belly cramps, stabbing flank pains, and – perhaps the most alarming symptom of all – he couldn't pass water.

I stopped the astringents and gave him herbal infusions, which relieved the kidneys and brought down the fever, but soon, the diarrhea returned. The next day, it worsened to acute dysentery, with quite alarming and increasing amounts of blood in the stools.

---

[360] Monday, September 23, 1605 (Julian Calendar).

Truly a strange illness it was. His condition would sometimes improve without any apparent reason, then worsen dramatically. More than one courtier has suggested – whisperingly, of course – that he was poisoned. I would have sworn too that poison was involved, but that was completely impossible! I solemnly swear I took every possible precaution to protect him: not a single grain of rice, not a crumb of bread, not the tiniest drop of water was offered to him, unless in my presence, and after it had been tasted by three different people, the last one always being myself. Moreover, if poison would have been involved, how was it to be explained that the course of the illness was so strangely irregular? Why would any would-be assassin have bothered to administer poison in varying, non-lethal doses? A few people have suggested that the Emperor might have accidentally poisoned himself – that he had mistakenly eaten poisoned food which he had destined for someone else. That's of course entirely preposterous: if he wanted to eliminate someone, he wouldn't have needed to resort to poison! Moreover, if he would have accidentally poisoned himself, he would have died in a matter of hours or days, not weeks. I at least know of no poison that would produce symptoms like that. No, any way I look at it, I am convinced he died of natural causes.

Desperate to find a treatment, I worked tirelessly, consulting all the books I could lay my hands on: at-Tabari's *Paradise of Wisdom*; al-Kindi's *Manual of Medicines*, ibn al-Baitar's *Study of Medicinal Herbs in the East*; Hunain ibn Ishaq's *Greek and Roman Medicine*; Ishaq al-Israili's treatise on fever; Musa ibn Maimun's *Kitab al-Fusul*; Ibn Rushd's *Kitab al-Kullijat*; Ibn Sina's *al-Qanun fi al-Tibb*; Ibn Zuhr's *at-Taisir*; the *Kitab al-Hawi* and *Kitab al-Mansuri* of ar-Razi, and the insightful discussion of intestinal diseases in Ali ibn al-Abbas' *Kitab al-Malaki*.

Entire nights I spent sleepless, studying and praying. Setting aside all unwarranted pride, I consulted the Hindu physicians Mahadev, Bhima, Narayin, and Sijav: possibly, their Ayurvedic knowledge could be of help? In my despair, I granted permission to try their narayana powder, and fruits bitten by a furious cobra.

But it was to no avail. Every herb, every potion, every remedy only seemed to make his condition worse. There we were, the most learned and experienced physicians in the Empire, utterly powerless against what had seemed a simple case of indisposed bowels.

'Stop worrying, Hakim Ali', said His Majesty, noticing the somber preoccupation on my face, in spite of the care I took to keep it hidden from him. 'Aren't we in the hands of God? I want you to know you've served me well, and you've given me the best possible care!'

He was obviously in a lot of pain at times; yet he seemed strangely cheerful and patient – as if he actually welcomed his predicament! The only thing I could do was to stand by and watch, trying to alleviate the pain and ease the cramps with moderate amounts of opium. Day after day, in impotent despair, I watched him growing weaker and weaker.

As his condition worsened, the Court became rife with gossip and speculation about the succession. Such, alas, is life...

The supporters of Prince Khusrau, headed by Mirza Aziz Koka and Raja Man Singh, were in favor of placing the young prince on the throne. Prince Khusrau, they argued, was a pious young man, his body youthful and strong, his character noble, his conduct exemplary, his record unblemished. His father, in contrast, was a capricious weakling, an opium addict, a hopeless drunk! Besides, was he not thirty-six years old already, and had his two younger brothers not died from exactly the same vice? How much longer could he hope to have left?

It was a heated argument, but in the end, the majority, supported by the legal scholars, rejected the proposal.

'On what ground could we allow the son to take precedence over his father?' they argued. 'How to prevent war between Khusrau's supporters and those of his father, or, for that matter, those of one of his brothers? It would mean the ruin of the Empire!'

Their arguments convinced the assembly. Anxious to prevent civil war, they all pledged to support Prince Salim, provided he would swear two solemn oaths: first, that he wouldn't punish or injure any of Khusrau's supporters, nor hold any grudge against them; and second, that he would protect Islam.

So he did; and, it must be said: he honored both promises.

Adequate security measures were taken in agreement between the Amirs and army leaders. A strong Rajput force was sent to guard the imperial treasure, and the Prince's personal guard was strengthened with a contingent of elite soldiers.

Meanwhile, the battle for the Emperor's soul continued. On

Shanbeh, the 30th of Mehr[361], the Firanghi Padres presented themselves at his quarters and demanded to be admitted to his presence. Having heard he was critically ill, they again tried to persuade him to embrace their ridiculous faith.

'It's my Christian duty,' Padre Machado began, 'to solemnly warn Your Imperial Majesty that His immortal soul is in the gravest danger! I beseech Your Majesty, now that there's still time, to renounce evil and accept the Lord Jesùs, Who is the light, the way, the truth and the life, mankind's only Savior. Failure to do so exposes Your Majesty to the eternal torments of hell!'

The Emperor, while remaining courteous in spite of his ailments, indicated he was in no mood for religious debate. He thanked the Padres for their concern, and granted them leave to retire.

Unusually relaxed and cheerful he was that day; he seemed to be in slightly better health than the days before, and spent the remainder of the afternoon and evening in pleasant conversation, in the company of Abdurrahim Khan Khanan, Raja Man Singh and other trusted friends.

But the following morning, his condition had worsened dramatically. He was hardly able to speak, his breathing alarmingly shallow, his eyes sunken deep inside his skull. Again, I would have sworn that poison was at work, were it not that His Majesty, on his own request, had spent the night alone, and that Raja Man Singh, Abdurrahim Khan Khanan and the other attendants who had kept him company the day before were clearly above any suspicion.

The next day, the Padres made another attempt to visit the Emperor; but this time, he flatly refused to see them. Instead, he sent for his son, together with Abdurrahim Khan Khanan, Raja Man Singh and the other leading Amirs.

The prince, who had up to that moment not found the courage to visit his father, presented himself immediately. Mumbling a respectful greeting, he prostrated himself, his forehead touching the floor.

The Emperor smiled weakly and moved his lips, trying to speak, but no sound came from his mouth. Signaling his son to come nearer, he looked at him for a while, faintly nodding his head in approval,

[361] Saturday, October 12 of the Julian Calendar.

smiling, his eyes moist with tears. He put his hand on his turban beside him, and gestured the prince should put it on his own head. He then pointed at Jannat - Ashyani's[362] sword hanging near the bed, and had his son gird himself with it.

Looking at the Amirs in the room, he slowly turned the palm of his right hand upward, and pointed in the direction of the prince. All bowed deeply to show their respect and loyalty to their new Emperor.

Emperor Akbar gave his son a last look, and made a weak gesture for him to leave the room and let him rest. The prince took his father's hand, kissed it and placed it on his own heart and forehead, then slowly went out of the room, walking backwards, bowing deeply all the way, tears streaming down his cheeks. The Emperor watched as his son left the room, reclined on the pillows, and closed his eyes. He had completed his last deed as Emperor of Hindustan.

Outside the imperial apartments, the Amirs and other courtiers took turns kissing the ringed hands of Prince Salim, who received the honors in silence, smiling faintly, his eyes glistening with tears.

It became eerily silent at Court. The rumors about the succession had died down and given way to whispered speculations about the dying Emperor's condition. Contrary to everybody's expectations, Prince Salim was rarely to be seen. I saw him very briefly from afar, the same night he had received the imperial sword and turban, outside the imperial archives, carrying a stack of documents. It must have been a confidential matter that preoccupied him, for normally the prince would take along a servant to carry his books for him. Anyway, I saw he pretended not to have noticed me, and thought it wise to do likewise. The following days, he spent most of the time in his private apartments, alone.

Meanwhile, the Emperor's condition further worsened. From the moment he had appointed his son as his successor, he refused all food and drink, apart from a few drops of water to comfort the dryness of his mouth. It was as if, after the example of the Jain monks he so admired, he had now decided to hasten his death through fasting. He

---

362 *Who is Nested in the Garden of Paradise*, posthumous title of Emperor Akbar's father Humāyūn.

grew weaker by the hour, and though obviously in a lot of pain at times, a weak, peaceful smile hardly ever left his lips.

As is customary, the faithful Amirs and mullahs present at his bedside constantly repeated the Shahada, inviting His Majesty to demonstrate his agreement with it, for the Prophet – peace and blessings of Allah be upon him and his household! – has affirmed that he who dies with the sacred Shahada on his lips, will surely enter Paradise. It vaguely seemed the Emperor did try to pronounce the first sentence, 'Ashadu an la ilaha illa-Llah', 'I declare that there is no God but God', but I am not sure. After a while, his lips stopped moving altogether and he seemed to lose all interest in his surroundings. His eyes glazed over, and stared into the flames of the candles.

Towards the later afternoon of Shanbeh, the 7th of Aban[363], it seemed he had lost consciousness.

His deep-sunken eyes were still open and kept on gazing at the candles, but I do not think there was any light left in them. They just remained wide open, moving nor blinking, staring from the darkness of their sockets into the void of death. Only a few irregular intervals of deep, rattling breathing, with long, long pauses in between them, indicated there was still a spark of life left in his emaciated body.

Towards the middle of the night, in the early hours of Yeksanbeh the eighth of Aban[364], his breathing became ever shallower, and the pauses in between grew longer and longer, until, without any apparent transition between life and death, he breathed no more. I put my ear to his chest, and found that his brave heart had finally stopped beating.

I closed his eyes, and we all prayed, as is customary on such sad occasions, the last verses of the Surah As-Saffat[365]:

Glory to You, my Lord
The Lord of Honor and Power!
Free is He from what they ascribe to Him!
And peace on the Messengers

---

363 Saturday, October 19.

364 Sunday, October 20

365 Qur'ān 37: pp. 180–182.

And Praise to Allah
The Lord and Cherisher of the Worlds.

On an impulse, I took his right hand in mine, kissed it, held it to my face and wetted it with my tears. My voice broken and shaking, I sobbed:

'Farewell, Your Majesty, farewell! May Allah keep and protect you, and may it please Him to reunite us in Paradise!'

We bathed and washed the dead body twice with clear, cold water, then rubbed it over with lime, salt, and camphor. Even I was surprised to see the pitiful state of his martyred body. The disease had literally wasted him away. His strong arms and legs, his broad shoulders: the muscles were gone, nothing seemed to be left but pale, wrinkled skin over bones and sinews. With his fallen-in cheeks and the black-blue rings around his deep-sunken eyeballs, his face hardly bore any resemblance to the imposing countenance of the strong bull of a man we had known before.

As is customary, we bound the feet together, placed the arms alongside the body, put a stone slab on the stomach to prevent any bloating, and clothed the body in simple white linen.

The next morning, in accordance with time-honored Sunni custom and the teachings of the Prophet, the mortal remains were taken to their last resting place.

A gap was broken in the sandstone wall of the fort, and the charpai[366] was carried out; Prince Salim and his sons took it upon their own shoulders and carried it as far as the diwan-i-am. From thence, the Amirs and courtiers, anxious to receive the honor of carrying His Majesty's mortal remains, followed each other in quick succession, taking the body out of the fortress. The entire Court, heads and feet bare, followed the body to the tomb at Sikandra, two kos to the north, where our Emperor's body was placed in the beautiful mazar[367], still under construction at that time, which he had designed himself.

The building is exactly like the great king whose mortal remains it houses: open to light and air from all directions, bringing together

[366] Bier.

[367] Tomb, mausoleum.

many different styles; aspiring to belong to all traditions, yet, belonging to none in particular.

Belonging to all traditions, and thus, to none... Was our beloved Emperor still a Muslim when he died? Had he become a Parsi as people say, or a Hindu? Was he guilty of ilhad, had he become a *murtadd*[368]?

I've given this matter much thought, and have come to the conclusion, that he lived and died as a true believer – albeit admittedly a highly unorthodox one – and that whether or not one can still call him a Muslim, depends more on the outlook of the beholder, than on the piety of our Emperor.

What gives me the right to say he was a true believer? First of all, because he believed in God's unity and worshipped Him, all his life, with all his heart and soul. Second, because he never converted to another religion. He highly respected the Hindus and the Jains, to the point of rejecting the slaughter of animals and believing that there might be some truth in the idea of transmigration of souls, but he had no use for any of their gods and statues and rituals; he liked the Parsi fire symbols, but didn't find much use in their concept of God; he revered the Prophet Isa and his saintly mother – upon both of whom be peace! –, but found it impossible to accept the obvious nonsense of a triune divinity, the virgin birth of a God-man, and all those other errors and superstitions.

What made him unorthodox, to the point of incurring, not entirely undeservedly, the reproach of being a heretic and an unbeliever? I think his worst heresy from the point of view of Islam was the rather low esteem in which he held the Prophet Muhammad and the Holy Qur'an: in his eyes, they were merely a prophet and a holy book among many others. The constant quarrels between the ulama had convinced him that the Muslim law and religion were far from indubitable, since there were so many differences between the scholars themselves. In the Ibadat-Khana, he had been looking for unity and insight, but had found nothing but confusion and disagreement.

In the end, his concept of religion was a rather simple one. There is but one God, and all must worship and honor Him, and allow other

---

368 Ilhād: heresy; Murtadd: apostate, person who has renounced Islam.

people to do so in the way they prefer. All must subdue evil passions and practice virtue. All must be led by reason, and not merely bow to the authority of any one man or tradition. Differences in creed or ritual are of little importance: the people of the land should be united under their king, whom God has placed above them, and whose duty it is to serve God through bringing justice and prosperity to the people entrusted to his care.

Was Emperor Akbar a Muslim, or a kafir? Birbal – or was it Abu-l Fazl? – once said: 'Our Emperor is a Hindu in his food habits, a Parsi in his rites, and a Sufi in his heart.' As far as I am concerned, he was like the Sikh Guru Nanak, or the great poet Kabir: both men denied they were either Muslims or Hindus, for such names seemed useless to them. As Kabir sang so eloquently:

Hindus call Him Ram, Muslims Khuda
Kabir says: whoever lives, should not bother about this:
Ka'bah becomes Kashi, Ram becomes Rahim

Abdul Haqq, the great scholar, wrote that his father, when still a child, had asked his own father whether Kabir had been a Muslim or a Hindu. The grandfather replied that Kabir had been a Muwahhid, a believer in the Unity of God. His father then asked whether a Muwahhid was a Kafir, or a Muslim. Upon which the old man replied: 'To understand this is difficult: you will understand when you grow up.'

Allah willing, one day, when it grows up, the world will understand.

On the southern entrance of Emperor Akbar's tomb, there's an elegant inscription, written by the famous calligrapher Abd al-Haqq, son of Qasim as-Shirazi:

'These are the Gardens of Eden. Enter them, to live forever.'

And there's no doubt in my mind: the gardens of Paradise will forever be the abode of our beloved Emperor. Allah, the omnipotent Ruler of all worlds, the supreme Lord of the past, the present and the future, He who is greater than anything conceivable or imaginable, He who defies any description or limitation, He who is merciful, compassionate and all-forgiving, He will smile upon our good Emperor. He will mercifully forgive him all his sins, doubts, errors and shortcomings; He will make his grave wide and pleasant, illuminate it with the splendor of His soft-shining light, and fill it with the sweet companionship and gentle conversation of His angels.

And on the day of the Resurrection, He will call him forward, among the best of His faithful servants, to share in the eternal, unspeakable bliss of Paradise.

Epilogue (2)

From the Memoirs of Father António Machado S.J.,
Superior of the Jesuit Order in Agra,
Member of the third Jesuit mission to the Court of Akbar the Great
(...)

Thus, ended the mighty emperor Akbar... His funeral was astoundingly, disgracefully simple and austere. No pomp, no circumstance of any kind, no ceremonies, no chants, no hymns, no eulogies. Back in Castilla, or any other Christian country, even a simple peasant would have gotten a more dignified funeral than this! Akbar's corpse, placed on a plain wooden bier, was carried off to the mausoleum with indecorous haste, and as soon as it had been placed in the tomb, everybody immediately left the grounds. It seemed they all wanted to get away as quickly as possible from the burial place of a man they knew was damned forever.

In spite of everything, I pity the old emperor, for I do believe there was much nobility in his soul. Unfortunately, his vainglorious pride and arrogance prevented him from dying in the State of Grace. Stubbornly refusing to accept our Lord and Savior Jesus Christ, in spite of all the evidence, in spite of all the prophecies, in spite of the countless many hours of patient instruction he received, in spite even of a personal letter from His Holiness the pope of Rome himself, he rejected the one true religion, and in doing so, damned his immortal soul, and brought irreparable ruin upon countless others. He was guilty of Adam and Eve's original sin – which is not, as many people believe, the sin of lust and lasciviousness, but the much more dangerous evil of Superbia, ὕβρις[369]:

[369] Greek *Hubris,* Latin *Superbia*: Pride, one of the cardinal sins.

arrogant, conceited, sinful pride, the delusion that man himself is the ultimate judge of right and wrong. It was pride, that same damnable pride that made Adam and Eve yield to the Serpent's temptation and eat from the Forbidden Fruit.

It saddens and angers me to think about what might have been, and what has been lost by the stubbornness of that one man. Blinded and misguided by his own worldly power, Akbar thought that he could find 'true religion', all by himself. In the end, it brought him nothing, nothing but confusion, error, and sin; it made him a skeptic and a misguided muddlehead, who, in his eagerness to show respect to all religions, put himself outside every single one of them. With that, he not only endangered and finally damned his own immortal soul, but also that of so many millions of his poor, misguided subjects, who might have found the light of our Lord Jesus Christ, if only their emperor had shown them the way. Their error remains on his head, and there can – alas! – be no doubt about it: it has earned him the eternal flames of hell.

One week after Akbar's death, on Sunday, the 6th of November of the year of our Lord 1605[370], shortly after sunrise, Prince Selim ascended the throne in the Hall of Public Audience in the Red Fort.

The imperial crown, which had been crafted in the days of Akbar after the crown worn by the great kings of Persia, was brought to him. He put it on his head, and as an omen auspicious to the stability and happiness of his future reign, kept it there for a full hour. The so-called khutbah was read in his name for the first time.

As a formal sign of his accession, he assumed the title of Jahangir, which in Persian means 'Seizer of the World'. To seize the entire world, his courtiers said, was his destiny.

May almighty God preserve us from such disaster!

(...)

---

[370] Father Machado uses the Gregorian Calendar (the current Common Era), which was proclaimed by Pope Gregory XIII and took effect in most Catholic states in 1582, in which October 4 of the traditional Julian calendar was followed by October 15 in the new one. Britain and her colonies only adopted the Gregorian Calendar in the year 1752, when Wednesday the 2nd of September was followed by Thursday the 14th.

Epilogue (3)

جهانگیر

Jahangir

From the Memoirs of
Shaykh Bishotan ibn Abdurrahman ibn Abu'l Fazl Allami,

Mansabdar of Seven Thousand Zat and Three Thousand Suwar[371]
In the service of
His Majesty Shihab ud Din Muhammad Shah Jahan[372] Padshah,
May Allah perpetuate his reign and expand his dominions;

Son of Shaykh Abdurrahman Afzal Khan[373],
Grandson of Shaykh Abu'l Fazl Allami,
Great-grandson of Shaykh Mubarak Allami,
May Allah receive them and all their ancestors in His infinite Mercy,

(...)

---

[371] Mansabdār: Commander in the imperial army. The words *Zat* and *Suwar* indicate the rank, and refer to the (theoretical) number of cavalry and auxiliary cavalry under the incumbent's command.

[372] Shihāb ud Dīn: Flame of Faith; Shāh Jahān: King of the World. Shāh Jahān, grandson of Akbar, third son and successor of Jahāngīr, became famous as the Mughal emperor who commissioned the universally admired Tāj Mahal.

[373] Abdurrahmān, son of Abū-l Fazl, was born in the Hijrī year 979 (1571 CE).

It was in the late hours of the night, on one of those occasions when too much wine and loud conversation makes men careless, and their questions impertinent.

I must have been twenty or twenty-one years old at the time. The breeze was pleasant, the moonlight soft. We were sitting together in the inner courtyard of my father's home – me, my father Abdurrahman and my mother's brother Ahmad, may Allah be well pleased with them, and a few other army officers, all good friends of my father. A man of means, he had invited them to a feast in his home, for no particular reason – just to share a few 'raisins of life', as he used to call such moments of leisure and laughter among friends. We were enjoying the most succulent dishes of lamb and fowl, and many – too many – pitchers of cool wine; it all tasted wonderful on a calm and balmy evening after a hot and strenuous day. The conversation had taken us from lamb and the best ways to cook it, to cloves, pepper and other condiments, to tiger hunting, elephants and horses, life in the army, and Emperor Jahangir's successful campaigns in Mewar. I said little, listening to the elder men's conversation and busying myself with drinking, something to which I was at that time not at all accustomed.

Late in the night, when all the guests had left, and my father rose to retire to his bedchamber, I heard myself saying: 'Father, there's something that I've been wanting to ask you for a long time.' My speech sounded more slurred than I had hoped, and I instantly regretted my impertinence.

My father's face registered surprise. 'This must be very important, that you want to bring it up at this late hour,' he said softly, 'but go ahead.'

It was too late to go back now. 'I've been meaning to ask you,' I said, trying to sound as articulate as possible, 'You are a wealthy and powerful man, father; the Emperor has promoted you several times, he entrusts you with tasks of high import...'

'And?' There was irritation in his voice.

'And yet, people say – to be honest, everybody says – that my revered grandfather Abu'l Fazl, may Allah be well pleased with him, was assassinated on orders of that same Emperor Jahangir!'

'That is, alas, correct.'

'But why?'

'Jahangir – Shahzada Salim at the time – was estranged from his father. I should rather say, he was in open rebellion against him, for he was holding his own court in Allahabad, against his father's wishes. Why he had your grandfather killed, I do not know for sure. For some reason, he suspected him of setting Emperor Akbar against him, of trying to persuade the Emperor to appoint Shahzada Khusrau as his successor.'

'And was that true?'

'No, I refuse to believe that. It's true that your grandfather didn't think much of Prince Salim, but I am convinced he never tried to harm him.

But he was extremely close to Emperor Akbar and had his ear, and that's why Salim resented and feared him.'

'But when he became Emperor, he left our family alone?'

'He did... To be honest, I was l very afraid when he became Emperor. I thought he would have me and my entire family assassinated or at least banned, if only to prevent us from taking revenge, or to get his hands on your grandfather's considerable wealth! But for some reason, he chose not to; he left us in peace. He also forgave Khusrau and his supporters, as he had promised he would.'

'And have you never...' I did not dare to finish my sentence.

'I know what you are going to ask. Have I never considered avenging my father? Yes, I have, and more than once! In fact, when people told me in what a terrible way my poor father had met his end, I could think of little else than revenge. But what could I do? Salim was closely guarded all the time; I could not even come anywhere near him. Besides, had I not my family to think about? You were only twelve at the time!

Still, the thought of revenge never left me, and I promised myself that one day, I would kill Salim. Three and a half years later, when Emperor Akbar had passed away and Salim – Jahangir – had succeeded him to the throne, I suddenly saw my opportunity. He was inspecting his troops outside the Agra fort, early in the morning, and contrary to his usual routine, he was casually walking among the ranks, all alone... He also passed me by, very slowly; he stopped briefly and looked at me, then turned his back and continued his way. I only had to draw my dagger and plunge it in his back! Of course, I would be killed myself as well, probably after unspeakable torture, but at least the honor of our family would be avenged! Then again, I didn't mind dying myself, but what about my family? I was still hesitating, when Jahangir suddenly turned around, and looked me in the eye. Instantly I knew, I just knew, with absolute certainty, that he sensed what I was thinking.

'Shaykh Abdurrahman,' he said, in a soft, surprisingly friendly tone of voice, 'we would like to have a word with you, in private. Kindly present yourself at the Diwan-i-Khas, one hour from now.'

When I arrived at the hall, the guards let me pass without a word; they clearly had received their instructions. Surprisingly, they didn't ask me to hand over my sword and dagger as they always do. I went into the hall and found Emperor Jahangir sitting cross-legged on a cushioned platform. In front of him lay his sword, and a bit further, a beautifully bound copy of the Holy Qur'an on a small, jewel-encrusted bookstand. I bowed, touching the floor with my right hand, and he signaled me to approach the platform.

'You and I need to talk, Shaykh Abdurrahman,' Jahangir said slowly, a tired smile on his face, as I was approaching the platform.

'You know, Shaykh Abdurrahman,' he proceeded, 'that I've just succeeded my revered father, may Allah receive him in His mercy, to the Throne of Hindustan, and much is expected from me. It is my God-given task to perpetuate and augment what my revered father, and may I add, your father, too, have worked for all their lives. I want to know, Shaykh Abdurrahman, I want to know, with absolute certainty, that I can rely on you, just like my revered father has been able to rely on yours.'

Before I could answer, Jahangir proceeded, 'I know, Shaykh Abdurrahman, you probably dislike me – no, you probably hate me. You feel that I've wronged your father. Well, I confess. Although I didn't think so at the time, I must admit, with the wisdom of hindsight, that I probably have wronged him. You know, my father and I were estranged at the time, and I was convinced, mistakenly no doubt, that your father was bent on my ruin. I also was convinced that, the shameless flatterer that he was – he really was, you know! – he had nothing but his own private interests at heart.

I confess: maybe, probably, I have judged him too harshly. Despite the fact that I distrusted him and resented the influence he had on my father, I have to admit he was a clever, hardworking and highly competent man, and he served Hindustan well.

One thing is certain: what has happened cannot be undone. And tell me, Shaykh Abdurrahman: if your father could talk to you now, what do you think his advice to you would be? Would he advise you to try and take your vengeance, bring ruin to yourself and your family, and go to your grave as the traitor who endangered the Empire, or would he tell you to go on living honorably in the service of the Empire that that he has helped my father to build?

I am ready to forget the past, if you are too, Shaykh Abdurrahman; but I want your answer, and I want it now. As a man of honor, put your right hand on the Holy Qur'an and pledge your loyalty to me and the Empire; if you cannot, go in peace and take your family and your belongings to another country: I will not try to stop you, and I even will provide you with a strong escort, so that you may travel safely. Or,' – his voice flattened out until it was barely a whisper – 'or, if you must, reach for your dagger or your sword or both, and fight me.'

He caressed the jade, horse-shaped hilt of his own dagger, and casually took out a golden coin from his belt. 'I do believe I am stronger than you,' he said, casually bending the coin in two between his thumb and forefinger – it's a well-known fact he's blessed with great bodily strength, which he likes to show off in public – 'but who knows? Perhaps you are quicker or more agile than I am...'

The Emperor took the Holy Qur'an from the bookstand and held it out towards me, with both hands. If I was to draw my sword, he would be at a disadvantage. I looked at the Qur'an, at the hilt of my sword, only a palm's breath away from my hand... Then, I bowed my head, laid my right hand on the Holy Book, and in a calm, surprisingly firm voice, swore to Emperor Jahangir that I would serve him and Hindustan with my life.

There was kindness, and I think honest gratitude in Jahangir's eyes, as he nodded and said: 'Thank you, Shaykh Abdurrahman. I knew you are a true son of your father, may Allah be pleased with him. Go in peace; may God protect you and your loved ones.'

My father stared at the candles, many of which had already died out. He helped himself to another beaker of wine, and poured me one as well.

'I've often thought back to that morning, my son. Time and again, I've searched my soul and challenged myself, but each time, I've come to the conclusion that I made the right choice, and that my father, had he been in my stead, would have done the same. I know what he would have said to me: 'My son, there are things in life that are more important than our own wants and needs. You may hate Shahzada Salim for what he did, but it is your duty, before God, to honor and obey Jahangir Padshah. To betray him, is to betray everything I've worked for, all my life.'

He took a sip of his wine; then a second, larger draught.

'I know,' he continued, as if he guessed what I was thinking, 'I know, Jahangir does not have the genius, nor the stamina of Akbar. I know, some speak of him as a fickle-minded tyrant, a pleasure-seeking weakling, slave of leisure, wine, women, and opium. Well, there's much truth in it, but that reproach is not entirely fair. On the whole, he is a noble man who sincerely tries to rule with justice, and to treat all his subjects equally, irrespective of religion, rank or birth. Such is his respect for justice, that he has a long silver chain with a bell suspended from his balcony; whosoever of his subjects rings the bell and thus, appeals to the Emperor's justice, can be ensured that Jahangir Padshah will personally hear his case.

It is true that in fits of rage, he can be extremely cruel, but following the example of his father, he has issued instructions that when he condemns someone to capital punishment, the order is not to be executed before sundown.

He is deservedly popular with the common people for the peace and prosperity he has brought to the land. There is no hunger in Hindustan, no unjust taxation; people live in safety, commerce flourishes.

He's respectful to his mother and the members of his family. Although he did rebel against his father, I believe he did so under the influence of evil people. In any case, now that he sits on the Throne and his father is no longer a rival to him, he has really changed. He cherishes his father's memory, and holds him in great reverence.

Whenever he resides in Agra, he often visits his father's mausoleum. He dismounts at the gate, and walks on foot to the tomb; at the entrance, he gets down on both knees, and rubs his forehead on the marble doorstep.'

Annex 1

Historical Documents

Akbar's first letter to the Jesuits of Goa[374]

In the Name of God,

Letter of Jalal ud Din Muhammad Akbar, King placed in the Seat of God.

To the Chief Priests of the Order of Saint Paul:

Be it known to them that I am a great friend of theirs.

I have sent thither Abdullah my Ambassador, and the translator Domenico Perez, in order to invite you to send back to me two of your learned men, who should bring books of the Law, and above all the Gospels, because I truly and earnestly desire to understand their perfection; and with great urgency, I again demand that they should come with my Ambassador aforesaid, and bring their books. For from their coming I shall obtain the utmost consolation; they will be dear to me, and I shall receive them with every possible honor.

As soon as I shall have become well instructed in the Law, and shall have comprehended its perfection, they will be able, if willing, to return at their pleasure, and I shall send them back with great honors, and appropriate rewards. Let them not fear me in the least, for I receive them under my pledge of good faith and assure them concerning myself. (...)

[374] Smith, pp. 120–121.

Letter of Pope Gregory XIII to Akbar – Rome, February 18, 1582 [375]

Gregorius Episcopa
Servant of the Servants of God
to Akbar
Illustrious King of Mogor

May the Merciful God, Who deigned to inspire you to listen to the teaching of the evangelical doctrine, transfer you as soon as possible from darkness to light. This We expect from the interest which, as it reached Our ears, you have shown in the Christian religion. First of all, you summoned to your court Our dear sons, priests of the Society of Jesus and ministers of the true faith. You received them graciously and heard them discussing on the Kingdom of God. All these are clear indications of your zeal and useful steps to receive the truth, but in such an important matter no delay should be admitted, lest this movement of your spirit, which undoubtedly comes from God, be frustrated by tardiness in deliberation. Your Majesty should place, so to say, in one plate of the scales your kingdom, power, sons, the countless subjects, all riches and goods of this world; and in the other the dignity of your soul and the salvation promised by Christ to those who believe in Him. If you weigh it aright, you will find in comparison with the latter that those are worth nothing; an everlasting Kingdom compared with one of short duration, perishable and subject to many contingencies; transform your mortal power into undying bliss; prepare for yourself a new family and treasures in Heaven. God will perhaps grant you that, if it be expedient for your salvation, you enjoy also this earthly kingdom. Life is short and human condition uncertain. See that you do not neglect your own salvation or appear to fail to the grace of God that calls you. Meanwhile do not brush aside this thought, and continue listening as you did before, to the aforesaid priests (by the help of whose prayers and labors both in the past and in the future you will be greatly helped in a matter of such moment), whom I recommend to you. Your personal interest and concern for them shall not go unrewarded by Him, Who invites you to acknowledge the truth, the Lord God Almighty.

Given in Rome at Saint Peter's, in the year 1581 of the Lord's

---

[375] *Letters from the Mughal Court*, pp. 119–120.

Incarnation, the 18th day of February, the 10th year of Our Pontificate.

Jahangir's account of the murder of Abu'l Fazl[376]

Toward the end of my exalted father's reign, Shaykh Abu'l Fazl, one of the Shaikhzadas of Hindustan who was outstanding in his learning and wisdom, had ostensibly adorned himself with loyalty and sold it to my father for an exorbitant price.

He was summoned [by my father] from the Deccan, and since he was suspicious of me, he was always making snide remarks. At that time, because of the corruption of mischief-makers, my exalted father's mind was quite turned against me, and it was certain that if Abu'l Fazl succeeded in reaching him, he would create more discord and prevent me from rejoining my father. It was therefore absolutely necessary that he be prevented from reaching him. Since Bir Singh Deo's territory lay in his path, and at that time Bir Singh was in the circle of insurgents, I sent him a message that he should waylay the miscreant and dispatch him to nonexistence, in return for which he could expect great rewards from me. Success smiled on the endeavor, and as Abu'l Fazl was passing through Bir Singh Deo's territory, Bir Singh blocked his path, scattered his men in a skirmish, and killed him, sending his head to me at Allahabad. Although this caused great distress to His Majesty Arsh-Ashyani [Akbar], in the end it resulted in my being able to proceed to kiss the threshold of my exalted father's court without fear, and little by little the bad blood between us subsided.

Jahangir's account of his own drinking habits

I myself did not drink until the age of eighteen ( ). After that, I started drinking wine, increasing it day by day until grape wine had no longer an effect on me, and I started drinking liquor. Little by little, over nine years, it increased to twenty phials of double-distilled spirits, fourteen

376 Jahāngīrnāmā, pp. 32–33.

during the day and the rest at night. ( ) Things got so bad that in my hangovers my hands shook and trembled so badly I could not drink myself, but had to have others help me. Finally I summoned Hakim Humam, Hakim Abu'l Fath's brother and one of my exalted father's confidants, and informed him of my condition. In perfect sincerity and compassion he said, with no beating around the bush: 'Highness, the way you are drinking, in another six months – God forbid – things will be so bad it will be beyond remedy.' Since his words were spoken in benevolence, and life is precious, it made a great impression on me.

From that date I began to decrease the amount ( ). Over a period of seven years, I got it down to six phials, the weight of a phial being seventeen and three-quarters mithcals. I have now been drinking like this for fifteen years without increase or decrease.[377] ( )

Jahangir on his father

My exalted father's good characteristics were too many to be described. If books were to be composed of his good qualities, without exaggeration and disregarding our father-son relationship, not even a small portion could be contained therein. Despite his rulership and such treasuries and treasures beyond enumeration, despite his war elephants and Arabian horses, never did he place his foot one iota above the level of humility before the divine court, and he considered himself the least of all creatures. Not for an instant was he unaware of God. ( )

Followers of various religions had a place in the broad scope of his peerless empire – unlike other countries of the world, like Iran, where there is room for only Shiites, and Rum, Turan, and Hindustan, where there is room for only Sunnis. Just as all groups and the practitioners of all religions have a place within the spacious circle of God's mercy, in accordance with the saying that a shadow must follow its source, in my father's realm, which ended at the salty sea, there was room for practitioners of various sects and beliefs, both true and imperfect, and strife and altercation were not allowed. Sunni and Shiite worshiped

[377] Jahangirnama, page 21.

in one mosque, and Frank and Jew in one congregation. Utter peaceableness was his established way. He conversed with the good of every group, every religion, and every sect, and gave his attentions to each in accordance with their station and ability to understand.

His nights were spent in wakefulness and he slept so little during the day that in a twenty-four-hour period he slept no more than a watch and a half, and he considered vigilance at night to be a renewal of life.

His courage and bravery were so great that he could ride uncontrollable, enraged elephants, and subdue into obedience elephants so murderous they wouldn't allow their mates near them. Usually, no matter how bad-tempered an elephant may be, it does not harm its mate or its keeper. Nonetheless, when an elephant so frenzied that it might have killed its keeper and wouldn't allow its mate near, or an elephant that had killed its mahaut and gone berserk passed by a wall or tree, my father, relying on divine grace, would throw himself on the elephant's back, and as soon as he sat down, he would bring the elephant under control and calm it down. Such a scene has been witnessed more than once.[378]

[378] Jahangirnama, page 26, and pp. 184–185.

Annex 2

Historical Notes & Acknowledgements

While I've tried to paint an historically accurate picture of Akbar's life and reign, Akbar's Farewell is and remains a novel: it is a romanced attempt, by a 21st century Western European, to read into the mind of a 16th century Indian monarch.

To avoid any misunderstandings about what is fact and what is fiction, I've thought it appropriate to add a few comments. Generally speaking: the letters and dialogues are fictional, but the events described in them are historical facts, with two notable exceptions: Akbar's writing skills, and his suicide.

Akbar's Persona

Abu'l Muzaffar Jalal-ud-Din Muhammad Akbar (1542-1605), Padshah of Hindustan, was a truly remarkable human being. Conqueror of a vast empire, aptly called *Akbar-e-Azam* (Akbar the Great) by his own contemporaries, and still deservedly popular in present-day India, he was the true founder of the Mughal Empire and the greatest of the so-called Great Mughals. Not only was he among the most powerful and wealthiest sovereigns of his time, but without any doubt, one of the most enlightened ones. Educated as a Sunni Muslim, Akbar quickly revealed himself a highly unorthodox eclectic, and a firm proponent of universal tolerance and freedom of worship.

His practical, political views on religious diversity can be summarized in two simple lines:

- people are free to worship the Divine in whatever way they please, provided they do not hurt other people in the process; and
- the duty of any sovereign is to put himself above all religious differences, and to treat all his subjects justly and equally.

Akbar eagerly welcomed to his court representatives of all religions and factions known to him[379]: Sunni and Shiite Muslims, Hindus, Jains, Parsis, Jews, and even Jesuit priests from the Portuguese settlements in Goa.

In a splendid – if vain – attempt to resolve all differences between the various creeds, he even attempted to establish a completely new, ecumenical cult, the *Din-e-Illahi* (which means the Religion of the One God), which he hoped would peacefully unite all people.

Akbar's Farewell has been written from Akbar's personal perspective and that of his most ardent supporters. It should therefore come as no surprise that the portrait painted of him in this book is biased, and arguably, perhaps too flattering.

Does Akbar deserve to be called 'The Great'? In reality, if he has had many admirers, there have been quite a few harsh critics; some have argued that his reign and persona have been grossly over-idealized in popular tradition. Admittedly, Akbar's critics do have a point: in today's terms, he was an unashamed, ruthless imperialist, who didn't hesitate to act with merciless brutality whenever it suited him.

Quoting the eminent historian Vincent A. Smith in his authoritative biography (1917): '(Akbar's) ruling passion was ambition. His whole reign was dedicated to conquest. His aggressions, made without the slightest regard to moral considerations, were not determined in any instance by a desire to better the condition of the people in the kingdom attacked.'

Smith's judgement is harsh, but not entirely unjustified: Akbar was an absolutist if there ever was one. Neighbouring states were attacked without provocation, and many people, whose only crime was they wanted to stay independent, were ruined, imprisoned, or killed.

But despite the reservations one may and should have about imperialism, it is impossible to deny: Akbar really was one of the most enlightened monarchs of his time. He sincerely desired the welfare

[379] Buddhists were a notable exception.

of his subjects, and attempted to treat all of them justly and equally. His character a remarkable combination of mysticism, rationalism and melancholy, he honestly aspired to know God's will and lead his life in submission to Him. He actively protected religious freedom, forbidding only those practices which he considered to be unjust or inhuman (including, for instance, child marriage and the forcible burning of widows). Whatever criticism one may want to express about his maladroit and vainglorious attempt to create a new creed (Smith, for instance, states[380] that the Divine Faith was a monument of Akbar's folly, not of his wisdom), it cannot be denied that Din-e-Illahi was one of the very first conscious attempts to create a 'secular' state, where the sovereign obligates himself to remain neutral and impartial, and to treat all his subjects equally. His tolerance in religious matters, which he pushed through in spite of stiff opposition and at great personal risk, was truly exceptional, and that alone merits him a place among the greatest rulers in history.

Measured by the standards of his own time, he was exceptionally broad-minded, forgiving and tolerant. In an age where 'cruel and unusual punishment' was the rule rather than the exception, he was altogether rather moderate. It is well documented he issued orders that the death penalty could never be executed, unless he had personally reconfirmed it three times.

From a personal point of view, he appears to have been a captivating personality: imposing, majestic and daunting, yet at the same time, congenial, kind and charming. One imagines he must have been an excellent judge of character, and gifted with a manipulative, 'Godfather-like' personal style, a mixture of awe and personal charm found in many great leaders, good and bad, from Caesar to Hitler.

Whether we choose to like him or not, Akbar's story deserves to be remembered and reflected upon, as it remains highly relevant to this day.

Dyslexia?

It's a well-documented historical fact that Akbar was, as Eraly phrased

---

[380] *Akbar the Great Mogul*, page 160.

it, an illiterate savant. Other than signing his own name, he's not known to have written anything, and Jahangir in his memoirs confirms that his 'Illustrious Father'was indeed illiterate.

Nevertheless, he was a great lover of knowledge. Whenever he had a moment's leisure, he had books of all kinds read out to him, and in his conversations, he amazed everyone with the breadth of his knowledge and the quickness of his wit. People who didn't know him could hardly believe that such an educated man was illiterate.

It has been speculated that Akbar may have had at least some knowledge of reading and writing, despite his dyslexia. Be that as it may, it's a historical fact that no one ever saw him reading or writing anything.

Suicide?

Akbar died of dysentery, on Thursday, October 27, 1605, or October 17 of the Julian calendar (which was still in use by the British at that time). His illness had started three weeks before, the day after a fight between Salim's prize elephant and that of his eldest son Khusrau. The open animosity between the supporters of both princes during and after the fight had greatly upset him. The next morning, he was taken ill with the intestinal disease that would eventually kill him.

The illness showed a rather erratic course, with brief intervals of improvement, alternating with acute attacks. Despite the desperate efforts of his personal physician Hakim Ali Gilani, the symptoms gradually worsened. When his condition had become critical, Akbar sent for his son, and gestured him to put the imperial turban on his head and gird himself with Humayun's sword, thus, confirming him as his legitimate successor.

There's no evidence that Akbar's death was due to anything other than natural causes. As usual, there have been widespread speculations (all of them unproven) that he had been the victim of poisoning, probably by Salim's or Khusrau's supporters. It even has been suggested that his death was accidental, that he mistakenly took poison which was, in fact, intended to kill someone else[381]. I have used the latter

[381] Smith, pp. 234–235.

hypothesis (for which, it should be repeated, there is no historical evidence whatsoever) as the storyline of this book, hypothesizing that Akbar might have killed himself, not by accident, but deliberately, in order to prevent civil war and ensure an orderly succession.

Bairam Khan

The importance of Akbar's faithful *ataliq* cannot be overestimated. Without Bairam Khan, the Mughal Empire would never have come into existence. Whatever Akbar's shortcomings, he was not dishonest, and he has always acknowledged the debt of gratitude he owed to his guardian. The story of their estrangement and reconciliation is not known in full detail, but did develop along the lines of the narrative in the book. Bairam Khan's second (and victorious) battle against Akbar's vanguard under Sultan Husayn Jalair is only mentioned by a limited number of sources, but the story of their reconciliation, including the fact that Akbar took his own scarf to wipe off Bairam Khan's tears, is historical, as is the account of Akbar taking Bairam Khan's family under his care after his old friend had been assassinated.

Hamida Banu Begam

Akbar undoubtedly loved and greatly respected his mother, but it seems the two did not get along too well. It is well documented that Hamida Banu resented her son's liberal attitude towards *Firanghis* and other infidels, and that she preferred to live on her own, rather than taking up residence in the imperial zanana.

Maham Anaga, Adham Khan

The pernicious influence of Akbar's foster mother Maham Anaga and her overly ambitious, unruly son Adham Khan is historically accurate, as is the account of their downfall.

Salima Sultana Begam, 'Makhfi'

Unlike other Great Mughals (including Jahangir and Shah Jahan), it seems Akbar was not a very romantic man. While he did sleep with countless many women, particularly when he was still young, it seems he had no real 'love of his life'. It is however well documented that his cousin Salima Sultana, whom he married after Bairam Khan's death, was clearly his favorite, in spite of the fact that she didn't bear him any children. She was highly influential, probably much more than Akbar's mother was, and Akbar greatly valued her opinion. She appears to have been an intelligent, exceptionally well-read woman and an accomplished poetess, but to my knowledge, her writings have been lost to posterity.

The story of her escape from Gujarat after Bairam Khan's assassination is authentic, as is the fact that she personally traveled to Allahabad and brought about the initial reconciliation between Salim and his father. The detailed story of her betrothal to Akbar and their joint hunting trip are fictional.

Maryam uz-Zamani, Jahangir's mother

Surprising though it may be, there's much confusion around Jahangir's mother's name (Akbar's first Rajput wife), apart from the title of honor (*Maryam uz-Zamani*, 'Mary of the Age'), which she received when she gave birth to Salim. In Abu'l Fazl's *Akbar Nama* (translated by H. Beveridge), she is identified as the eldest daughter of Raja Bihari Mal of Amber, but her maiden name is not mentioned.

The consensus among historians is that Maryam uz-Zamani's maiden name was Rajkumari Hira Kunwari, alias Harkha Bai. Popular tradition in India calls her by the name Jodha Bai or Jodh Bai , which means 'Lady of Jodh(pur)', but Akbar never married a princess from the Jodhpur area, and he certainly never had a wife called Jodha Bai: that nickname belongs to Jahangir's wife Manmati, daughter of the so-called 'Mota Raja (fat Raja)' Udai Singh of Jodhpur.

Mir Abdul-Latif

The influence of Akbar's old teacher cannot be overestimated. It is indeed Mir Abdul-Latif who imparted on his pupil the concept of *Sulh-i-kul*, or Peace for All. The old man's memoirs quoted in the book are, of course, fictitious.

Shaykh Salim Chishti

Akbar's reverence for the old Shaykh who predicted the birth of his three sons has been recorded extensively. His decision to build his capital city near the old Shaykh's dwelling is historical, as is the fact that he abandoned the city fourteen years later.

Hakim Ali Gilani

Hakim Ali Gilani was Akbar's treating physician during his terminal illness. However, Hakim Ali's close personal relationship with the emperor and with Mir Abdul-Latif remains a matter of speculation: he was undoubtedly an important courtier, but probably not as close to Akbar as is intimated in this book.

Birbal, Todar Mal, Abu'l Fazl and the others

'Birbal-and-Akbar stories' are immensely popular in India. In reality, Birbal was probably much less influential. Akbar did enjoy his company and wit, but as administrators and army leaders, Todar Mal, Raja Man Singh, and Abdurrahim Khan Khanan played more important roles.

From a political point of view, Akbar has been deeply influenced by the views of his teacher Mir Abdul-Latif, later further developed and reinforced by Abu'l Fazl and his father Shaykh Mubarak. The so-called Infallibility Decree[382] has been written by Mubarak, most probably assisted by Abu'l Fazl.

Contemporary sources describe Abu'l Fazl as an exceptionally erudite, highly intelligent man, with an almost prodigal capacity for hard work. His manner appears to have been perfectly courteous and amiable – his only obvious weakness (well known to his contemporaries) being an extraordinarily voracious appetite. A shameless flatterer and quick-witted freethinker, Abu'l Fazl had Akbar's ear and sympathy; no courtier has been more influential. Abu'l Fazl was the architect behind the infamous *Din-e-Illahi* cult, as well as its main proponent. His enemies – of whom he had many among the ulama – claimed he was

---

[382] The all-important formal declaration giving Akbar precedence over the Ulamā (mentioned towards the end of the *29th Letter*).

an atheist. This may or may not be true; but he was firmly convinced of the fundamental equality of all faiths and denominations. His views are probably best summarized in the following verses he wrote towards the end of his life[383]:

> O God, in every temple I see people that are seeking You,
> and in every language I hear, people are praising You!
> Polytheism and Islam feel after You,
> each religion says, 'You are One, without equal!'
> If it be a mosque,
> people murmur the holy prayer,
> and if it be a Christian church,
> people ring the bell
> out of love to You.
> Sometimes I frequent the Christian cloister, and sometimes the mosque,
> but it is You whom I search, from temple to temple.

Bishotan, grandson of Abu'l Fazl

There's no evidence (and it is, admittedly, highly unlikely) that a conversation like the one related in Epilogue 3 ever took place between Jahangir and Abu'l Fazl's orphaned son Abdurrahman.

It is, however, historically correct that Jahangir, upon his accession, took no vindictive action whatsoever against Khusrau's supporters or anyone else who had opposed him. He was magnanimous enough to appoint Abu'l Fazl's son Abdurrahman as a high-ranking cavalry officer. Also Bishotan, Abdurrahman's son and Abu'l Fazl's grandson, was an officer in the army.

Ibadat-Khana, Din-e-Illahi

The religious debates have actually taken place: among Muslims at first, and later between Muslims and representatives of other faiths. The discussions were probably less erudite or systematic than is suggested

383 Fragment of an inscription on a temple in Kashmīr, quoted in the introduction to the *Ā'Īn-ī-Akbarī* cited below, pp. liv–lv.

in the novel, but it is beyond any doubt that they've influenced Akbar's thinking tremendously.

Critics of Akbar will never fail to point out that it was his all-consuming lust for power that was the real motive behind his religious tolerance and the ill-advised establishment of a cult of his own. This is only partially correct: it is true that Akbar didn't want religion to interfere with his subjects' loyalty; on the other hand, it can't be denied that his policy of universal tolerance – which he pushed through at great personal risk – also reflected his strong personal convictions on the matter.

Did Akbar renounce Islam?

Hundreds, if not thousands of pages have been written about Akbar's religious beliefs and practices.

From a dogmatic point of view, Akbar's beliefs appear to have been the result of two competing tendencies in his mind. On the one hand, he had an inquisitive, fundamentally rationalist intellect: beliefs were to be based solely on evidence and reason. Had he been a European monarch, he would have been called a typical Renaissance man. On the other hand, he was also a melancholy mystic, with a deep and unfeigned reverence for the Creator and an almost obsessive interest in religious truth.

Did he renounce Islam? As I have Hakim Ali Gilani state in Epilogue 1, the answer is probably dependent on one's definition of Islam. If a Muslim is defined as a person who holds the profound belief that there is only one God, Lord of the universe, to Whom every human being should humbly submit, then Akbar was a devout Muslim. However, when one considers the other central tenets of Islam – in particular, the unique position held by the Holy Qur'an and the Prophet Muhammad – Akbar was no longer a Muslim, or at best a highly unorthodox one, for in his mind, the Prophet Muhammad and the Holy Qur'an occupied a much less prominent place than they do in orthodox Islam.

It has frequently been pointed out that if Akbar was tolerant towards other religions, he was much less so towards Islam. More than one chronicler has claimed that he actually persecuted the religion of his ancestors, or was at least prejudiced against it. While the evidence for that is less clear than some sources suggest, it is definitely true that Akbar was extremely critical of the Muslim clerics of his time – partly for religious, but mostly for political reasons. Akbar was an absolutist, with very little tolerance for any real power next to him. Both the so-called Infallibility Decree and the Din-e-Illahi cult were deliberate attempts to neutralize the power of the Muslim jurists and strengthen his own position as Padshah and ultimate religious authority. However, it's equally important to emphasize that Akbar never formally renounced Islam, and never converted to any other religion, publicly or privately. He had an unfeigned and profound respect for Jesus of Nazareth, but clearly rejected the fundamental tenets of Christianity, i.e. the divinity of Christ and the concept of the Holy Trinity. It's equally clear he never became a Hindu or a Jain or a Parsi, impressed and heavily influenced though he was by their philosophy, practices and symbols.

Akbar fundamentally was an eclectic, a rationalist as well as a mystic, who came to regard all religions as merely human attempts to honor and serve an ineffable, unattainable Reality.

In his own words: *Each person, according to his personal condition, gives the Supreme Being a Name, but in reality, to name the Unknowable is vain.*

Transcription and Spelling

Transcription of Perso-Arabic words into Roman alphabet is notoriously challenging. In the end, the writer inevitably needs to select one of many possibilities and variants between two extremes, i.e., on the one hand, a 'scientific' transcription – with a well-nigh illegible set of confusing apostrophes, accents and diacritical marks, utterly meaningless except to a few specialists; and on the other hand, an easily legible but hardly accurate westernized approximation (e.g., Koran instead of Qur'an).

For a number of reasons, esthetic as well as practical, I have opted for a kind of middle ground. In this edition, no diacritical marks have been used in the main text of the novel (e.g., Jahangir instead of Jahāngīr). In the footnotes, diacritical marks have been used, taking into account that the testimonials in the novel supposedly have been written in Persian, by native or at least habitual speakers of that language. Akbar himself, for instance, had had a bilingual education; and though he fluently spoke the Chagatai Turkish of his ancestors (he must have spoken it, occasionally at least, with other Turks like Bairam Khan, his aunt Gulbadan and his wives Ruqayya and Salima), he usually spoke Persian, the official lingua Franca at his court. His knowledge of Arabic (which he never actually spoke, except when reciting the Qur'an) and of the local Hindustani dialects must have been less than perfect, and it can readily be assumed that his pronunciation of other languages was strongly influenced by the Persian language.

The following principles have been applied in the footnotes:

- A clear distinction has been made between long and short vowels (an essential distinction in both Hindi and Persian), and also between the Arabic letters K and Q[384], (a distinction that educated Muslims will not fail to make). I have followed (in that order) the spelling used in Beveridge's translation of Abu'l Fazl's works, Irfan Habib's *Atlas of the Mughal Empire*, and R.C. Majumdar's *History of India*.
- Typically Arabic glottal stops have only been indicated occasionally, and no attempt has been made to distinguish between the letters Alif, Hamza and 'Ayn[385].
- The distinction between so-called retroflex and non-retroflex consonants (highly important in the pronunciation of Hindi and most other languages on the subcontinent) has not been indicated either, as it does not occur in Persian[386].
- Generally speaking, an attempt has been made to remain as close as possible to both the original Perso-Arabic spelling and at the same time to the pronunciation, although this is not always possible without at least some kind of compromise. I have, for instance,

---

[384] ك and ق

[385] ا, ء, and ع.

[386] For example: the sounds त (dental) and ट (retroflex) have both been transcribed as **T**; and the sounds थ (dental) and ठ (retroflex), as **TH**.

opted not to use unaesthetic transliterations like *Mueen od Deen, Mooeen-oddeen,* etc., although they arguably are closer to the pronunciation in English; nor have I opted for *Muīn Al Dīn,* which would the literal transcription of the actual Perso-Arabic letters, but *Muīn ud Dīn,* which does respect the original spelling, while at the same time taking into account the different pronunciation of so-called 'Sun' and 'Moon' letters in Arabic. The distinction between 'Sun' and 'Moon' letters is also the reason why I have preferred to write, for instance, Abdurrahim, Abdurrahman, and Shams-ud-din, and not 'Abd-Al-Rahim, 'Abd-Al-Rahman and Shams-Al-Din.

- In all scientific transcriptions of Hindi, the long 'o' sound (somewhat like the 'o' in the French word 'corps') is transcribed as 'au'. As this could be confusing for most Western readers, I have elected to write *Kalanor* instead of Kalanaur, *Chittor* instead of Chittaur, etc.

Bibliography

It will be clear that any historical novel with some pretense to authenticity cannot be written without extensive reference to, and indeed, borrowing from, various sources. In the bibliography below, I've added the references to the books I am most indebted to – the most important ones have been highlighted in bold. May these references be an encouragement for interested readers to find out for themselves what scholarly history has to say about Akbar and his reign.

The free **Calendar Convertor**, which can be found on the highly interesting website **www.fourmilab.ch,** under the section Astronomy and Space, has been invaluable to me for the conversion of Muslim and Persian dates into Julian and Gregorian (Common Era) calendar dates and vice versa. I've also used it to check the position of Venus and the other planets at the time of Humayun's death.

Historical Documents

Abu'l Fazl Allami, *The Ā'Īn-i-Akbari (Institutions of Akbar)*, **three Volumes, the First Volume translated from the Persian by H. Blochmann (1873), revised by D.C. Phillott (1927), Second and Third Volume by H.S. Jarrett (1893-96), revised by Jadunath Sarkar (1949),** *Bibliotheca Indica No 61,* **reprinted Delhi, 1988.**

Abu'l Fazl Allami, *The Akbar Nama*, **translated from the Persian by H. Beveridge, Delhi, 1902-39, reprinted 1998 (ISBN 81-7536-139-5).**

Ibn al-'Arabi, *El secreto de los Nombres de Dios*, Introducción, edición, traducción y notas de Pablo Beneito, Murcia, 1996 (ISBN 84-7564-197-0).

Ibn al-'Arabi, *El tratado de la unidad y otros textos sufíes*, Madrid, 1987 (ISBN 84-7651-462-X).

Babur, Emperor of Hindustan, *The Baburnama: Memoirs of Babur, Prince and Emperor*; Translated, edited, and annotated by Wheeler M. Thackston, introduction by Salman Rushdie, New York, 1996-2006 (ISBN 0-375-76137-3).

BADAUNI (MULLA 'ABDUL-KADIR MULUK SHAH OF BADAUN), *Tarikh-i Badauni (Muntakhabu-t Tawarikh)*, in *The History of India: As Told By Its Own Historians, The Muhammadan Period, The Posthumous Papers of the Late Sir* H.M. ELLIOT, Edited by Prof. JOHN DOWSON, Calcutta, 1875, third reprint 1961.

AL FARABI, *El camino de la felicidad (Kitab al-tanbih 'ala sabil al-sa'ada)*, Traducción, introducción y notas de Rafael Ramon Guerrero, Madrid, 2002 (ISBN 84-8164-540-0).

AL-GHAZÂLÎ, *Les dix règles du Soufisme (Al Qawâ 'id-l-'ashra)*, Traduction, notes et commentaire de MUHAMMAD DIAKHO, Paris, 1999 (ISBN 2-84161-044-6).

AL-GHAZALI, *O Disciple*, translated by George H. Scherer, Beirut, 1951.

Father PIERRE DU JARRIC, S.J., *Akbar and the Jesuits: An Account of the Jesuit Missions to the Court of Akbar*, **Translated with Introduction and Notes by C.H. PAYNE, London, 1926 – New Delhi, 1999 (ISBN 81-7536-162-X).**

Father FERNÃO GUERREIRO, S.J., *Jahangir and the Jesuits, With an Account of the Travels of Benedict Goes and the Mission to Pegu*, **Translated by C.H. PAYNE, London, 1930 – Edition New Delhi, 1997 (ISBN 81-215-0769-3).**

JAHANGIR, EMPEROR OF HINDUSTAN, *The Jahangirnama: Memoirs of Jahangir, Emperor of India*; **Translated, edited, and annotated by WHEELER M. THACKSTON, New York, 1999 (ISBN 0-19-512718-8).**

Letters from the Mughal Court, The First Jesuit Mission to Akbar (1580-1583), **Edited with an Introduction by JOHN CORREIA-AFONSO and a Foreword by S. NURUL HASAN, Published for the Heras Institute of Indian History and Culture, Bombay, by Gujarat Sahitya Prakash, Anand, 1980.**

MUHAMMAD BAQIR NAJM-I-SANI, *Advice on the Art of Governance (Mauizah-i-Jahangiri), an Indo-Islamic Mirror for Princes*, Persian Text with Introduction, Translation, and Notes by SAJIDA SULTANA ALVI, New York, 1989 (ISBN 0-88706-918-5).

Śiva Purana, Translated and annotated by a Board of Scholars, Edited by Professor J.L. SHASTRI, Four Volumes, Delhi, 1970 (ISBN 81-208-0269-1).

R.NATH, *India as seen by Babur (AD 1504-1530)*, Delhi, 1996 (ISBN 81-7533-000-7).

FAKHR AD-DIN AR-RAZI, *Traité sur les Noms Divins, Lawami' al-baniyyat fi al-asmawa al-sifat (Le Livre des Preuves Éclatantes sur les Noms et les Qualités*, Introduction, traduction et annotations par MAURICE GLOTON, 2 Volumes, Paris, 1986-1988 (ISSN 0397-3069).

ABU'L WALID IBN RUSD (AVERROES), *El Libro de las Generalidades de la Medicina, [Kitab al-Kulliyyat fil-tibb]*, Traducción de MARÍA DE LA CONCEPCIÓN VÁZQUEZ DE BENITO y CAMILO ÁLVAREZ MORALES, Madrid, 2003 (ISBN 84-8164-602-4).

JOSEPH A. KECHICHIAN and R. HRAIR DEKMIJIAN, *The Just Prince: A Manual of Leadership, Including Sulwan al-Muta' Fi 'Udwan al-Atba' (Consolation for the Ruler During the Hostility of Subjects), by* MUHAMMAD IBN ZAFAR AL-SIQILLI, Singapore – Kuala Lumpur, 2003 (ISBN 981-05-1948-6).

Upanisads, Translated from the Original Sanskrit with an Introduction and Notes by PATRICK OLIVELLE, Oxford University Press, New York, 1996 (ISBN 0-19-283576-9).

Religion & Philosophy

KHALED ABOU EL FADL, *The Place of Tolerance in Islam, with TARIQ ALI, MILTON VIORST, JOHN ESPOSITO, and others,* edited by JOSHUA COHEN and IAN LAGUE for Boston Review; Boston, 2002 (ISBN 0-8070-0229-1).

MONTSERRAT ABUMALHAM (Ed.), *Textos fundamentales de la tradición musulmana,* Barcelona-Madrid, 2005, ISBN 84-8164-749-7.

PETER ADAMSON and RICHARD C. TAYLOR (Ed.), *The Cambridge Companion to Arabic Philosophy,* Cambridge, 2005 (ISBN 0-521-52069-X).

KHWAJA JAMIL AHMAD, *Hundred Great Muslims,* Chicago, 1987 (ISBN 0-933511-16-7).

SALAHUDDIN AHMED, *A Dictionary of Muslim Names,* New York, 1999 (ISBN 0-8147-0674-6).

SHABBIR AKHTAR, *The possibility of a philosophy of Islam,* **in** *History of Islamic* **Philosophy, by SEYYED HOSSEIN NASR and OLIVER LEAMAN (Ed.);** *Routledge Histories of World Philosophies, Volume I,* **London and New York, 1996; 2003 edition (ISBN 0-415-25934-7).**

Self Building: An Islamic Guide for Spiritual Migration towards God, writings of AYTULLAH IBRAHIM AMINI, translated from Persian by SAYYID HUSSEIN 'ALAMDAR, Qum, Iran, 1997 (ISBN 964-438-000-2).

(THOMAS AQUINAS, *Summa Totius Theologiae*) SAINT THOMAS D'AQUIN, *Somme théologique: La Trinité; traduction Française par H.-F. DONDAINE, O.P.,* 2 Volumes, Paris-Tournai-Rome, 1942.

ULFAT AZIZ-US-SAMAD, *A Comparative Study of Christianity & Islam,* New Delhi, 2007 (ISBN 81-7435-294-5).

WAHID BAKHSH RABBANI, *Islamic Sufism: the science of flight in God, with God, by God, and union and communion with God, also showing the tremendous Sufi influence on Christian and Hindu mystics and mysticism,* first edition Lahoree, 1984 – Fifth revised edition, Aligarh (India), 2001.

HANS BAKKER & MARTIN GOSMAN (red.), *De Oriënt: Droom of Dreiging?, Het Oosten in Westers perspectief,* Kampen (NL), 1988 (ISBN 90-242-7607-1).

BERNHARD BARTMANN, *Katholieke Dogmatiek, vertaald uit het Duitsch (2de uitgave) door J. Lammertse Lz., met een voorwoord van Dr. A. Terstappen,* Roermond, 1935 (Dutch translation of *Grundriss der Dogmatik,* Freiburg im Breisgau, 1931).

Bâtonnier A. Benzakour, & Maître T. Bouab, *L'Islam et la liberté de culte,* Casablanca, 1992.

Thomas Bokenkotter, *Dynamic Catholicism: a Historical Catechism,* New York, 1985 (ISBN 0-385-23243-8).

D. Bont and C.F. Pauwels O.P., *De Katholieke Kerk, Godsdienstleer en Apologie,* 3 Volumes, Utrecht-Brussel, 1946.

Jan Bor en Karel van der Leeuw (red.), *25 eeuwen Oosterse filosofie: teksten, toelichtingen,* Amsterdam, 2003 (ISBN 90-5352-822-9).

H. Brink O.P. e.a., *Theologisch Woordenboek,* drie delen, Roermond, 1952.

Titus Burckhardt, *Introduction aux doctrines ésotériques de l'Islam,* Paris, 1969.

Brian Carr and Indira Mahalingam (Ed.), *Companion Encyclopedia of Asian Philosophy,* London and New York, 1997 (ISBN 0-415-24038-7).

P.N. Chopra (ed.), *Religions and Communities of India,* London, 1982 (ISBN 0-85692-081-9).

Henry Corbin, *Histoire de la philosophie islamique,* Paris, 1964-1974-1986 (ISBN 2-07-032353-6).

Diané Collinson, Kathryn Plant and Robert Wilkinson, *Fifty Eastern Thinkers,* London-New York, 2000 (ISBN 0-415-20284-1).

Edward Craig e.a. (General Editor), *Routledge Encyclopedia of Philosophy,* 10 Volumes, London and New York, 1998 (ISBN 0415-07310-3).

Ali Daddy, *Le Coran contre l'intégrisme,* Paris, 2000 (ISBN 2-912587-33-6).

Mawil Izzi Dien, *Islamic Law, From Historical Foundations to Contemporary Practice,* Edinburgh and Notre Dame, Indiana, 2004 (ISBN 0-268-03174-6).

E. van Donzel, *Islamic Desk Reference, Compiled from The Encyclopaedia of Islam by E. van Donzel,* Leiden - New York - Köln, 1994 (ISBN 90-04-09738-4).

John Dowson, *A Classical Dictionary of Hindu Mythology & Religion: Geography, History, Literature,* New Delhi, 1982.

Eknath Easwaran, *Thousand Names of Vishnu, A Selection with Commentary,* Mumbai, 1997 (ISBN 81-7224-581-5).

Carl. W. Ernst, *The Shambhala Guide to Sufism: An essential introduction to the philosophy and practice of the mystical tradition of Islam,* Boston and London, 1997 (ISBN 1-57062-180 2).

John L. Esposito, *The Oxford Dictionary of Islam,* Oxford, 2003 (ISBN 978-0-19-512559-7).

Michael Frassetto and David R. Blanks, *Western Views of Islam in*

Medieval and early modern Europe: Perception of Other, New York, 1999 (ISBN 0-312-21891-5).

Shems Friedlander with al-Hajj Shaikh Muzaffereddin, *Ninety-nine Names of Allah, The Beautiful Names*, San Francisco, 1993 (ISBN 0-06-063034-5).

Marc Gaborieau, *Un autre Islam: Inde, Pakistan, Bangladesh*, Paris, 2007.

Maneka Gandhi, *The Penguin Book of Hindu Names*, New Delhi, 1989, 1992 (ISBN 0-14-012841-7).

Maneka Gandhi and Ozair Husain, *The Complete Book of Muslim and Parsi Names*, Delhi, 1994-2004 (ISBN 0-14-303184-8).

Narayani Ganesh (Ed.), *The Best of Speaking Tree*, Volumes I-IV, 2004-2007, (ISBN 81-903995-2-7; -3-5; -4-3; and 978-81-89906-02-3).

Norman L. Geisler and Abdul Saleeb, *Answering Islam: The Crescent in Light of the Cross*, Grand Rapids, Michigan, 1993-2002 (ISBN 978 -0-8010-6430-2).

Cyril Glassé, *The Concise Encyclopaedia of Islam*, **London, 1989 (ISBN 0-905743-65-2).**

Paul J. Griffiths (Ed.), *Christianity Through Non-Christian Eyes*, New York, 1990 (ISBN 0-88344-661-8).

Ludwig Hagemann, *Christentum contra Islam: Eine Geschichte gescheiterter Beziehungen*, Darmstadt, 1999.

Peter Heehs, *Indian Religions, The Spiritual Traditions of South Asia, an Anthology*, New Delhi, 2002 (ISBN 81-7824-038-6).

A.M. Heidt, *Catholica, Geïllustreerd encyclopedisch vademecum voor het katholieke leven*, 's-Gravenhage / Antwerpen, 1955.

A.G. Hogg, *The Christian Message to the Hindu: being the Duff Missonary Lectures for nineteen forty five on the challenge of the Gospel in India, London, 1947.*

Richard Holloway, *Godless Morality: Keeping Religion out of Ethics*, Edinburgh, 1999 (ISBN 0-86241-909-3).

Thomas Patrick Hughes, *Dictionary of Islam, Being a Cyclopaedia of the Doctrines, Rites, Ceremonies, and Customs, together with the Technical and Theological Terms of the Muslim Religion*, **1886; edition Kazi Publications, Chicago, 1994.**

Enrique Gallud Jardiel, *Diccionario de Hinduismo*, Madrid, 1999 (ISBN 84 886 7677-8).

Abd al-Rahman Ibn al-Jawzi, *The Attributes of God*, Translation, Notes and Appendices by 'Abdullah bin Hamid 'Ali, Introduction by Khalid Yahya Blankinship, Bristol, 2006 (ISBN 0-9552359-0-1).

V.P. (Hemant) Kanitkar and W. Owen Cole, *Teach Yourself Hinduism*, London, 1995-2003 (ISBN 0-340-85967-9).

Subodh Kapoor, *A Short Introduction to Vaisnavism*, New Delhi, 2002 (ISBN 81-291-0004-5).

Katechismus van de katholieke kerk, Vaticaanstad, Baarn, Brussel (ISBN 90 -6858-034-5).

Tarif Khalidi (Editor and Translator), *The Muslim Jesus: Sayings and Stories in Islamic Literature*, Cambridge, Massachusetts, 2001 (ISBN 0-674-01115-5).

Hazrat Inayat Khan, *The Wisdom of Sufism: Sacred Readings from the Gathas*, Shaftesbury / Boston , 2000 (ISBN 1-862204-700-6).

Muhammad Zafrulla Khan (Transl.), *Gardens of the Righteous (Riyadh as-Salihin) of Imam Nawawi*, with a Foreword by *C.E. Bosworth*, London, 1975 (ISBN 0-7007-0073-0).

Farida Khanam, *A Simple Guide to Sufism*, New Delhi, 2006 (ISBN 81-7898-482-2).

Al-Kindi, *Apología del cristianesimo*, translation from Arabic and introduction by Laura Bottini, Milano, 1997 (ISBN 88-16-40457-4).

Anton Koch S.J., *Praedica Verbum, Homiletisch Handboek, Bronnen, thema's, schetsen en plannen, voorbeelden en gelijkenissen ten dienste van de geloofsverkondiging der christelijke heilsleer en heilsmysteries*, 15 delen, Hasselt, 1956-1966 (vertaald uit het Duits, Freiburg im Breisgau / Würzburg, 1937).

Stella Kramrisch, *The Presence of Śiva*, Varanasi, 1988 (ISBN 81-208-0491-0).

James Kritzeck (Ed.), *Anthology of Islamic Literature: From the rise of Islam to modern times*, New York, 1964.

Bharatan Kumarappa, *The Hindu Conception of the Deity, as culminating in Ramanuja*, London, 1934.

Henri Laoust, *Gli scismi nell'Islam, Un percorso nella pluralità del mondo musulmano*, (translation from French, Paris, 1990) Genova, 2002.

Oliver Leaman, *An Introduction to Classical Islamic Philosophy*, **Cambridge, 1985, 2002 (ISBN 0-521-79757-8).**

Michiel Leezenburg, *Islamitische filosofie: Een geschiedenis*, **Amsterdam, 2001 (ISBN 90-5460-046-2).**

Donald S. Lopez, Jr., *Religions of Asia in Practice: an Anthology*, Princeton-Oxford, 2002 (ISBN 0-691-09061-0).

Pierre Lory, *La science des lettres en Islam*, Paris, 2004 (ISBN 2-84454-321-9).

Gabriele Mandel, *I novantanove Nomi di Dio nel Corano*, Milano, 1995.

Axel Michaels, *Hinduism: Past and Present*, Princeton-Oxford, 2004 (ISBN 0-691-08953-1); translated from German, Munich, 1998.

Maulana Muhammad 'Ali, *The Religion of Islam: a comprehensive discussion of the sources, principles and practices of Islam*, **Lahoree, 1936 – Columbus, Ohio, 1990 (ISBN 0-913321-32-X).**

From the same author:

- *A Manual of Hadith*, **first edition 1941; edition 2001 (ISBN 0-913321-15-X).**
- *Introduction to the study of the Holy Qur'an*, **Lahoree, 1936; Dublin, Ohio, 1992 (ISBN 0-913321-06-0).**
- *The Living Thoughts of the Prophet Muhammad*, **Lahoree, 1947; Dublin, Ohio 1992 (ISBN 0-913321-19-2).**
- *Muhammad and Christ*, **Lahoree, 1921; Dublin, Ohio, 1993 (ISBN 0-913321-20-6).**
- *The Muslim Prayer-Book*, **Lahoree, 1939 – reprint Vancouver, 1998 (ISBN 0-913321-13-3).**

SEYYED HOSSEIN NASR, *The Garden of Truth: The Vision and Promise of Sufism, Islam's Mystical Tradition*, New York, 2007 (ISBN 978-0-06-079722-5).

SEYYED HOSSEIN NASR and OLIVER LEAMAN, *History of Islamic Philosophy*, **in** *Routledge Histories of World Philosophies, Volume I*, **London and New York, 1996; 2003 edition (ISBN 0-415-25934-7); (See, in particular, pages 1162-1172: SHABBIR AKHTAR,** *The possibility of a philosophy of Islam*).

SEYYED HOSSEIN NASR, *Islam and the Plight of Modern Man*, Chicago, 2001 (ISBN 1-930637-13-6).

REYNOLD A. NICHOLSON, *The Mystics of Islam*, London, 1914-1989 (ISBN 0-14-019168-2).

CONSTANCE E. PADWICK, *Muslim Devotions: A Study of Prayer-Manuals in Common Use*, Oxford, 1961, 1996 (ISBN 1-85168-115-9).

PIETRO PARENTE, ANTONIO PIOLANTI, and SALVATORE GAROFALO, *Dictionary of Dogmatic Theology*, Milwaukee, 1951; translated from the second Italian edition, Rome, 1945.

The Parsis, Classic Collection (set of MARTIN HAUG, *The Parsis, Essays on their Sacred Language, Writings and Religion*; JOHN WILSON, *The Parsi Religion*; and RUSTAM MASANI, *Zoroastrianism: The Religion of the Good Life*); New Delhi, 2003 (ISBN 81-292-0044-9).

BANSI PANDIT, *The Hindu Mind: Fundamentals of Hindu religion and Philosophy for All Ages*, Delhi, 2001 (ISBN 81-7822-007-5).

I.P. PETRUSHEVSKY, *Islam in Iran*, (translated from the Russian by Hubert Evans), London, 1985 (ISBN 0-485-11257-4).

EMILIO PLATTI, *Wat gelooft een goede moslim?*, Amsterdam, 1996 (ISBN 90-417-0326-8).

DR UTZ PODZEIT, *Duisternis uit het Oosten, Goeroes, sekten en valse hoop als voorlopers van de Antichrist*, Translated from German by Mrs Drs. R.C. Vink, Introduction by Dr W.J. Ouweneel, Vaassen, 1982 (ISBN 90-6353-123-0).

MGR. P. POTTERS, *Verklaring van den Katechismus der Nederlandsche Bisdommen*, 7 delen, 's-Hertogenbosch, 1940.

Holy Qur'an comments and translations:

- *The Holy Qur'an, Transliteration in Roman script, by M.A. Haleem Eliasii, with original 'Arabic Text, English Translation by Abdullah Yusuf Ali,* Lahoree, 1934; Eliasii Family Book Service, Charminar, Hyderabad-India, 2000.
- *The Holy Qur'an, with English Translation and Commentary,* **by Maulana Muhammad 'Ali, first edition, 1917; 2002 edition Dublin, Ohio (ISBN 0-913321-01-X).**
- *The Message of the Qur'an, The Full Account of the Revealed Arabic Text Accompanied by Parallel Transliteration, Translated and Explained by Muhammad Asad,* **The Book Foundation, Bristol, 1980; 2003 Edition, printed in Dubai (ISBN 1-904510-00-0).**
- *Concordance of the Qur'an, Extracted from the M.H. Shakir translation of The Qur'an,* New York, 2005 (ISBN 1-879402-72-9).
- Ahmad ibn Naqib al-Misri, *Reliance of the Traveller: A Classic Manual of Islamic Sacred Law,* translated by Nuh Ha Mim Keller, Beltsville, Maryland, 1991-1994 (ISBN 0-915957-72-8).
- Sayyid Abul A'la Maududi, *Towards Understanding Qur'an,* Abridged Version of *Tafhim al-Qur'an,* Translated and Edited by Zafar Ishaq Ansari, Delhi, 2006 (ISBN 0-86037-545-5).
- Mawlana Abul Kalam Azad, *The Opening Chapter of the Qur'an (Surah al-Fatihah),* Edited and rendered into English by Syed Abdul Latif, Kuala Lumpur, 2001 (ISBN 983-9154-28-1).
- Farid Esack, *The Qur'an, A User's Guide,* A guide to Its Key Themes, History and Interpretation, Oxford, 2005 (ISBN 1-85168-354-2).
- *Interpretation of the Meanings of the Noble Qur'an in the English Language: A Summarized Version of At-Tabari, Al-Qurtubi and Ibn Kathir with Comments from Sahih Al-Bukhari; Summarized in One Volume, by Dr Muhammad Taqi-ud-Din Al-Hilali, and Dr Muhammad Muhsin Khan,* Ryadh, 1996 (ISBN 9960-740-79-X).
- *An Interpretation of the Qur'an, English Translation of the Meanings, A Bilingual Edition, Translated by Majid Fakhry,* New York, 2000-2004 (ISBN 0-8147-2724-7).
- *De Koran Arabisch-Nederlands; De Heilige Qur'uan, met Nederlandse vertaling, onder auspiciën van Hazrat Mirza Bashir-ud-Din Mahmud Ahmad, hoofd van de Ahmadiyya Beweging,* Rahwah, Pakistan - Soest, Holland, 1953-1994 (ISBN 90-72540-52-2).

Sarvepalli Radhakrishnan and Charles A. Moore, *A Source Book in Indian Philosophy,* Princeton, 1957.

Al Razi, *La conducta virtuosa del filósofo*, Traducción, introducción y notas de Emilio Tornero, Madrid, 2004 (ISBN 84-8164-659-8).

John Renard, *Responses to 101 Questions on Hinduism*, **New York, 1999 (ISBN 0-8091-3845-X).**

Abdullah Saeed, *Islamic Thought: An Introduction*, London and New York, 2006 (ISBN 0-415-36409-4).

Omid Safi (ed.), *Progressive Muslims on Justice, Gender and Pluralism*, Oxford, 2003 (ISBN 1-85168-316-X).

Leo Schaya, *La doctrina sufí de la unidad*, Traducción de Francesc Gutiérrez, (Paris, 1962-1985), Barcelona, 1985-2001 (ISBN 84-7651-000-4).

Stephan Schuhmacher and Gert Woerner (ed.), *The Rider Encyclopaedia of Eastern Philosophy and Religion: Buddhism, Taoism, Zen, Hinduism*, London, 1989 (ISBN 0-7126-7097-1); translated from German, Bern-Munich, 1986.

Theodor Schneider e.a. (Red.), *Manual de teología dogmática*, Barcelona, 1996 (ISBN 84-254-1913-1); translation from the German edition (Düsseldorf, 1992).

Michael A. Sells (Ed.), *Early Islamic Mysticism: Sufi, Qur'an, Mi'Raj, Poetic and Theological Writings, Translated, Edited and with an Introduction by Michael A. Sells, preface by Carl W. Ernst*, New York, 1996 (ISBN 0-8091-3619-8).

Shah Ismail Shaheed, *Taqwiyat ul-Iman (Strengthening of the Faith)*, Riyadh, 1995.

M. Saeed Shaikh, *A Dictionary of Muslim Philosophy*, **New Delhi, 2006 (ISBN 81-7435-477-8).**

Arun Shourie, *The World of Fatwas; or the Shariah in Action*, **New Delhi, 1995-2002 (ISBN 81-7167-641-3).**

Janine Sourdel et Dominique Sourdel, *Dictionnaire historique de l'islam*, Paris, 1996 (ISBN 2-13-054-536-X).

Mazheruddin Siddiqi, *Modern Reformist Thought in the Muslim World*, New Delhi, 2007 (ISBN 81-7435-085-3).

Fauozi Skali, *Jésus dans la tradition soufie*, Paris, 2004 (ISBN 2-226-15437-X).

Mokhtar Stork, *A-Z Guide to the Ahadith: a must-have reference to understanding the Traditions of the Noble Prophet Muhammad*, **Singapore, 2004 (ISBN 981-232-238-8).**

Mokhtar Stork, *A-Z Guide to the Qur'an: a must-have reference to understanding the contents of the Islamic Holy Book*, Singapore, 1999, 2002 edition (ISBN 981-204-739-5).

Wolf-Dieter Storl, *Shiva, The wild God of Power and Ecstasy*, Rochester, Vermont, 2004 (ISBN 1-59477-014-X).

Satguru Sivaya Subramuniyaswami, *Dancing with Śiva, Hinduism's*

Contemporary Catechism, **Himalayan Academy India-USA, Hawaii, 1997 (ISBN 0-945497-97-0).**

YEMBAL P.V. THAJAMUL MOHAMMAD, *Religious Harmony: An Islamic Doctrine*, **Newlight Book Corner, Pudukkottai, India, 2000.**

MEL THOMPSON, *Teach Yourself Eastern Philosophy*, London, 1999 (ISBN 0-340-72126-X).

AYATULLAH AL-'UZMA HAJJ and SHAYKH LUTFULLAH SAFI GULPAYGANI, *Discussions Concerning al-Mahdi (May Allah hasten his return)*, Translated by SAYYID SULAYMAN 'ALI HASAN, Qum, 2001 (ISBN 964-438- -).

RIANNE VAN DER SMITTE and JAN VAN DER HOEVEN, *Als het licht duisternis is..., een aangrijpend getuigenis en onthullende feiten over new-age en occultisme*, Hoornaar, 1989 (ISBN 90-6067-490-1).

ED. VISWANATHAN, *Am I a Hindu? – The Hinduism Primer*, **San Francisco, 1992 (ISBN 1-879904-06-3)**

BENJAMIN WALKER, *Hindu World: An Encyclopedic Survey of Hinduism*, **1968-2005, New Delhi (ISBN 81-291-0670-1).**

A.J. WENSINCK und J.H. KRAMERS, *Handwörterbuch des Islam*, **Leiden, 1941.**

TIM WINTER (Ed.), *The Cambridge Companion to Classical Islamic Theology*, Cambridge, 2008 (ISBN 978-0-521-78549-5).

INTEGRAL YOGA INSTITUTE, *Dictionary of Sanskrit Names*, Buckingham, Virginia, 1989 (ISBN 0-932040-35-7).

R.C. ZAEHNER, *Hindi & Muslim Mysticism*, Oxford, 1960, 1994 (ISBN 1-85168-046-2).

Imam A'LI IBNUL-HUSAYN ZAYNUL-A'ABIDEEN AS-SAJJAD, *The Psalms of Islam (As'-S'ah'eefatul-KaamilatusSajjaadeetah)*, Translated by WILLIAM C. CHITTICK, With a Foreword by S.H.M. JAFRI, Qom, Iran, 2001 (ISBN 964-438-242-0).

Cultural, Political and Military History

FRANCO ADRAVANTI, *Tamerlano, La stirpe del Gran Mogol*, Milano, 2003 (ISBN 88-452-9221-5).

MUZAFFAR ALAM and SANJAY SUBRAHMANYAM (Ed.), *The Mughal State 1526-170*, (in *Oxford in India Readings, Themes in Indian History*), New Delhi, 1998 (ISBN 019-565-225-8).

S. ALEXANDRE, *Judeus, Cristãos-novos e a Inquisição*, Lisboa, 2002 (ISBN 972-8563-71-X).

M. ATHAR ALI, *Mughal India: Studies in Polity, Ideas, Society, and Culture*, with a Preface by IRFAN HABIB, New Delhi, 2006 (ISBN 0-19-564860-7).

MEHDI AMINRAZAVI, *The Wine of Wisdom: The life, Poetry and Philosophy of Omar Khayyam*, Oxford, 2005 (ISBN 978 1-85168-504-2).

Catherine B. Asher, *The Cambridge History of India I.4: Architecture of Mughal India*, Cambridge, 1992 (ISBN 0-521-26728-5).

António Baião, *A Inquisição de Goa: Tentativa de Historia da sua Origem, Estabelecimento, Evolução e Extinção (Introdução á Correspondência dos Inquisidores da India 1569-1630)*, Vol. I, Academia das Ciências, Lisboa, 1945; and Vol. II, Coimbra, Imprensa da Universidade, 1930 (Volume II was published before Volume I).

S.R. Bakshi, and S.K. Sharma (Ed.), *Akbar the Great Moghul*, New Delhi, 2000 (ISBN 81-7629-163-3).

S .R. Bakshi, and S.K. Sharma (Ed.), *Humayun the Great Moghul*, New Delhi, 2000 (ISBN 81-7629-162-5).

S.R. Bakshi, and S.K. Sharma (Ed.), *Jahangir the Great Moghul*, New Delhi, 2000 (ISBN 81-7629-164-1).

A.L. Basham (Ed.), *A Cultural History of India*, edited by Oxford, 1975 (ISBN 019-563921-9).

Valérie Berinstain, *Mughal India, Splendours of the Peacock Throne*, London, 1998 (ISBN 0-500-30083-6), translated from French (1997); also published under the title *India and the Mughal Dynasty*, New York, 2001 (ISBN 0-8109-2856-6).

Michele Bernardini, *Il mondo iranico e turco*, in *Storia del mondo islamico (VII-XVI secolo)*, Volume secondo, Torino, 2003 (ISBN 88-06-16833-9).

Dirk Collier, *The Great Mughals and Their India*, Delhi, 2016 (ISBN 978-93-81431-88-7).

Stephan Conermann, *Das Mogulreich, Geschichte und Kultur des muslimischen Indien*, München, 2006 (ISBN 3-406-53603-4).

Frederick Charles Danvers, *The Portuguese in India, Being a History of the Rise and Decline of their Eastern Empire*, in two volumes, New Delhi-Madras, 1992 (ISBN 81-206-0391-5).

Leo de Hartog, *Genghis Khan, Conqueror of the World*, London / New York, 1989-2004 (ISBN 1-86064-972-6).

S.M. Edwardes, and H.L.O. Garrett, *Mughal Rule in India*, Delhi, 1956.

Abraham Eraly, *The Mughal Throne: The Saga of India's Great Emperors*, **New Delhi – London, 1997-2000 (ISBN 1-84212-723-3).**

Abraham Eraly, *The Mughal World: India's Tainted Paradise*, (originally published under the title *The Last Spring: The Lives and Times of the Great Mughals*, New Delhi, 1997), London, 2007 (ISBN 978-0-297-85209-4).

Jorge Flores and Nuno Vassallo e Silva (Ed.), *Goa and the Great Mughal*, Lisbon-London, 2004 (ISBN 972-8848-05-6).

Bamber Gascoigne, *A Brief History of the Great Moguls*, **London – New York, 1971, 1988, 2002 (ISBN 0-7867-1040-3).**

R.C. Gaur, *Excavations at Fatehpur Sikri (A National Project)*, New Delhi, 2000 (ISBN 81-7305-178-X).

Rumer Godden, *Gulbadan, Portrait of a Rose Princess at the Mughal Court*, New York, 1980 (ISBN 0-670-35756-1).

Jos Gommans, *Mughal Warfare: Indian Frontiers and High Roads to Empire, 1500-1700*, **London-New York, 2002 (ISBN 0-415-23989-3).**

Professor Dr. Olivinho J.F. Gomes, *The Religious Orders in Goa (XVIth–XVIIth Centuries)*, Chandor, 2003.

Gul-Badan Begam, *Humayun Nama: The History of Humayun*, translated by Annette S. Beveridge, New Delhi, 1902-2001 (ISBN 81-87570-99-7).

Irfan Habib, *An Atlas of the Mughal Empire: Political and Economic Maps with Detailed Notes, Bibliography and Index*, **Delhi, 1982-1986 (ISBN 19-560379-6).**

Irfan Habib (Ed.), *Akbar and his India*, **New Delhi, 1997 (ISBN 019-564-6320-0).**

Gavin Hambly, *Asia Central*, in *Historia Universal Siglo Veintiuno, Volumen 16*, Madrid, 1972 (ISBN 84-323-0068-3).

J.C. Harle, *The Art and Architecture of the Indian Subcontinent*, in *The Pelican History of Art*, London, 1986-1987 (ISBN 0-14-0561.49-8).

Ibn Hasan, *The Central Structure of the Mughal Empire, and Its Practical Working up to the Year 1657*, London, 1933; reprint Karachi, 1967.

J. Hellings S.J., *De Geestelijke Oefeningen van de Heilige Ignatius van Loyola, Tekst, uitleg, overwegingen*, Voorhout (NL), 1953.

Dilip Hiro, *History of India, Rough Guide Chronicle,* **London, 2002 (ISBN 1-85828-842-8).**

H. Hosten S.J., *List of Jesuit Missionaries in 'Mogor' (1580-1803)*, **Journal of the Asiatic Society of Bengal, Vol VI, Number 10, 1910, pages 527-541.**

Takeo Kamiya, *The Guide to the Architecture of the Indian Subcontinent*, translated by Geetha Parameswaran, edited by Annabel Lopez & Bevinda Collaco, Tokyo, 1996 – Bardes, Goa, 2003–2004.

John Keay, *India: a History*, London – New Delhi, 2000 (ISBN 0 00-638784-5).

A. Khoshkish, *Fársi Robáiyáte Omar Xayyám; Omar Khayyam, in English by Edward J. Fitzgerald, en Français par J.B. Nicolas ou C. Grolleau*, Los Angeles, 1997 (ISBN 1-883819-15-6).

Ebba Koch, *Mughal Architecture: An Outline of Its History and Development (1526-1858)*, Munich, 1991 (ISBN 3-7913-1070-4).

Ruby Lal, *Domesticity and Power in the Early Mughal World*, New York, 2005 (ISBN 0-521-61534-8).

A.K.S. Lambton, *Persian Vocabulary*, **Cambridge, 1954 (ISBN 521-09154-3).**

Ira M. Lapidus, *A History of Islamic Societies*, Cambridge, 1988 (ISBN 0-521-29549-1).

Elias Lipiner, *Os baptizados em pé, Estudos acerca da origem e da luta dos Cristãos-Novos em Portugal*, Lisboa, 1998 (ISBN 972-699-592-2).

R.C. Majumdar (Ed.), *The Mughul Empire, Bharatiya Vidya Bhavan's History and Culture of the Indian People, Volume VII*, **Bombay, 1974.**

E.D. Maclagan, *Jesuit Missions to the Emperor Akbar*, **Journal of the Asiatic Society of Bengal, Vol. LXV, 1896, pages 38-113.**

G.B. Malleson, *Akbar and the Rise of the Mughal Empire*, edited by William Wilson Hunter, New Delhi, 2005 (ISBN 81-291-0697-3).

Justin Marozzi, *Tamerlane, Sword of Islam, Conqueror of the World*, London, 2004 (ISBN 0-00-711612-8).

K.S. Mathew, Teotonio R. de Souza, and Pius Malekandathil, *The Portuguese and the socio-cultural changes in India, 1500-1800*, Meshar, Telicherry, 2001 (ISBN 81-900166-6-0).

Antoni de Montserrat, and Josep Lluís Alay, *Embajador en la corte del Gran Mogol, Viajes de un Jesuita Catalán del siglo XVI por la India, Paquistán, Afganistán y el Himalaya*, **Lleida, 2006 (ISBN 84-9743-175-8), translated from Catalan (Barcelona, 2002).**

Harbans Mukhia, *The Mughals of India*, Oxford, 2004 (ISBN 1-4051-3318-X).

R. Nath, *Private Life of the Mughals of India (1526-1803 A.D.)*, Jaipur, 1994 (ISBN 81-85105-20-0).

David Nicolle and Angus McBride, *Mughul India 1504-1761*, **Men-at-Arms Series 263 (Lee Johnson, editor), Oxford, 1993 (ISBN 1-85532-344-3).**

Konstantin S. Nossov and Brian Delf, *Indian Castles 1206-1526: The Rise and Fall of the Delhi Sultanate*, Osprey Publishing, Oxford, 2006 (ISBN 1-84603-065-X).

Ahsan Jan Qaisar, *Building Construction in Mughal India: The Evidence from Painting*, Delhi, 1988 (ISBN 19-562260-X).

Muhammad Qamaruddin, *A Politico-Cultural Study of The Great Mughuls (1526-1707)*, New Delhi, 2004 (ISBN 81-7435-386-0).

Religion at Akbar's Court, www.columbia.edu/itc/mealac/pritchett/00islamlinks/ikram/part2_12.html

Francis Robinson, *The Mughal Emperors and the Islamic Dynasties of India, Iran and Central Asia, 1206-1925I*, London, 2007 (ISBN 978-0-500-25134-8).

Isaías Rosa Pereira, *A inquisição em Portugal, Séculos XVI-XVII-Período Filipino*, Lisboa, 1993 (ISBN 972-699-384-9).

J.J. Saunders, *The History of the Mongol Conquests*, London – Philadelphia, 1971-2001 (ISBN 0-8122-1766-7).

Annemarie Schimmel, *As Through a Veil: Mystical Poetry in Islam*, Oxford, 1982-2001 (ISBN 1-85168-274-0).

Annemarie Schimmel, *The Empire of the Great Mughals: History, Art and Culture*, **with a Foreword by Francis Robinson, London – New Delhi, 2004-2005 (ISBN 019-567334-4), translated from German (München, 2000).**

Annemarie Schimmel, *Mystische Dimensionen des Islam, Die Geschichte des Sufismus*, München, 1992 (ISBN 3-424-1116-9).

Annemarie Schimmel, *Islamic Names*, Edinburgh, 1989 (ISBN 0-85224-563-7).

Robert Sigaléa, *La Médecine traditionnelle de l'Inde: Doctrines prévédique, védique, âyurvédique, yogique et tantrique; Les Empereurs Mogols, leurs maladies et leurs médecins*, **Genève, 1995 (ISBN 2-88086-179-9).**

Chob Singh Verma, *Mughal Romance*, New Delhi, 2004 (ISBN 81-7234-080-X).

Som Prakash Verma, *Art and material Culture in the Paintings of Akbar's Court*, New Delhi, 1978 (ISBN 0-7069-0595-4).

Vincent A. Smith, *Akbar the Great Mogul 1542-1605*, **Delhi, 1917; Second (Revised) Edition; Third Indian Reprint, 1966.**

Vincent A. Smith, *The Oxford History of India*, Oxford, 1919, Fourth Edition, Chennai, 1958, 19th impression 2001 (ISBN 0-19-561297-3).

G.H.R. Tillotson, *Architectural Guides for travelers: Mughal India*, London, 1990 (ISBN 0-670-82642-1).

S.A.I. Tirmizi, *Mughal Documents (1526-1627)*, New Delhi, 1989 (ISBN 81-85054-71-3).

Roberto Tottoli, *Vita di Gesù secondo le tradizioni islamiche*, Palermo, 2000 (ISBN 88-389-1587-3).

Carter Vaughn Findley, *The Turks in World History*, Oxford, 2005 (ISBN 0-19-517726-6).

Joseph Velinkar, S.J., *India and the West: The First Encounters, A historical study of the early Indo-Portuguese cultural encounters in Goa*, Heras Institute of Indian History and Culture, St. Xavier's College, Mumbai, 1998.

Richard von Garbe, *Akbar, Emperor of India: A Picture Of Life And Customs From The Sixteenth Century*, translated from the German by Lydia G. Robinson, Chicago, 1909 (reprint ISBN 1-43251927-1).

Andrew Wheatcroft, *Infidels: A History of the Conflict between Christendom and Islam*, New York, 2005 (ISBN 0-8129-7239-2).

Zeenut Ziad (Ed.), *The Magnificent Mughals*, Oxford – Karachi, 2002 (ISBN 0-19-579444-3).

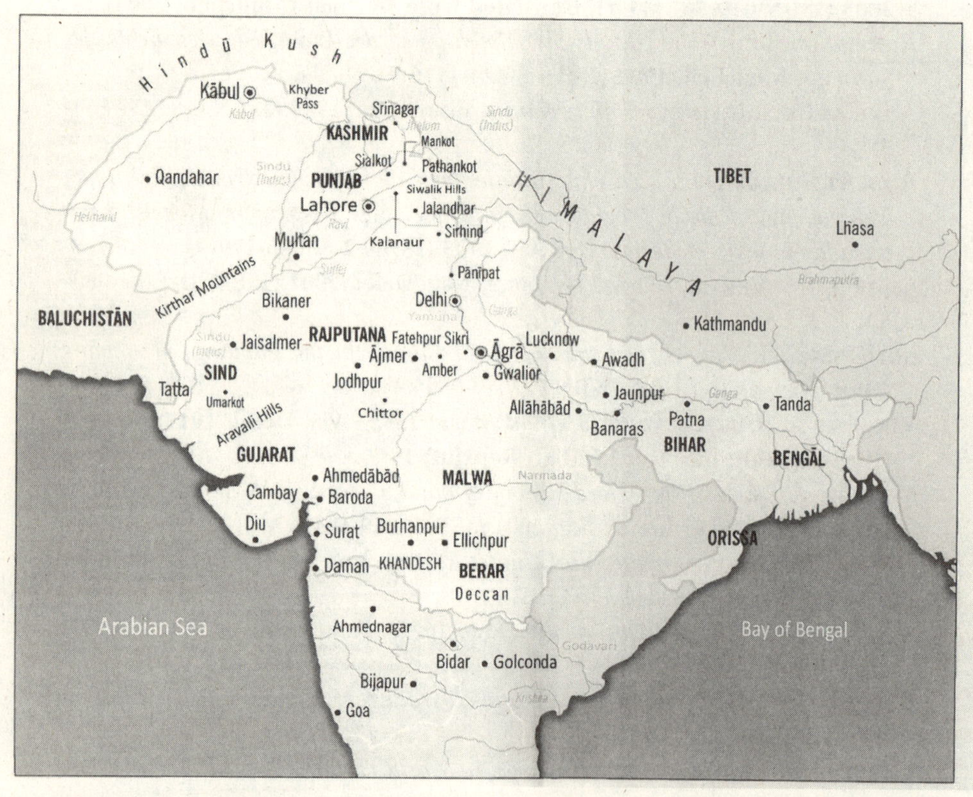

The Mughal Empire in 1605 (the year of Akbar's death).

Courtesy: Lannoo Publishers (*Afscheid van de keizer* (2011), Dutch translation of Dirk Collier's *The Emperor's Writings*).

Note: The contents of this map (especially the international borders) are neither accurate nor drawn to scale. This map only shows the geographical areas and places.